More heat than light

Historical Perspectives on Modern Economics

*General Editor: Professor Craufurd D. Goodwin,
Duke University*

This series contains original works that challenge and en-
lighten historians of economics. For the profession as a
whole it promotes a better understanding of the origin
and content of modern economics.

More heat than light

**Economics as social physics:
Physics as nature's economics**

Philip Mirowski
Tufts University

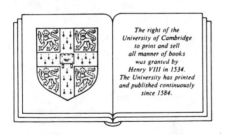

The right of the
University of Cambridge
to print and sell
all manner of books
was granted by
Henry VIII in 1534.
The University has printed
and published continuously
since 1584.

CAMBRIDGE UNIVERSITY PRESS

Cambridge
New York   Port Chester
Melbourne   Sydney

Published by the Press Syndicate of the University of Cambridge
The Pitt Building, Trumpington Street, Cambridge CB2 1RP
40 West 20th Street, New York, NY 10011, USA
10 Stamford Road, Oakleigh, Melbourne 3166, Australia

First published 1989

Printed in the United States of America

Library of Congress Cataloging-in-Publication Data
Mirowski, Philip, 1951–

    More heat than light: economics as social physics:
    physics as nature's economics/Philip Mirowski.

      p.   cm. – (Historical perspectives on modern economics)

    ISBN 0-521-35042-5

    1. Economics. 2. Physics. I. Title. II. Series.
HB74.P49M57 1990
330–dc20

                                          89-9728
                                            CIP

British Library Cataloging in Publication Data
Mirowski, Philip

    More heat than light: economics as social physics:
    physics as nature's economics.

    (Historical perspectives in modern economics)

    1. Economics. Theories
    I. Title II. Series
    330.1

    ISBN 0-521-35042-5 hard covers

To the most profound economic philosophers of the 20th century:
Thorstein Veblen
Nicholas Georgescu-Roegen

As late as a week ago, such a phrase as "hopefully awaiting the gradual convergence of the physical sciences and the social sciences" would have provoked no more than an ironic tingle or two at the back of my neck. Now it howls through the Ponchitoula Swamp, the very sound and soul of despair.

–Walker Percy, *The Moviegoer*

Contents

Figures

Acknowledgments

Every author needs an implied reader, and I have been extremely fortunate to have known some people who have been willing to give me page-by-page and even line-by-line comments. Mere academic acknowledgments cannot begin to express my gratitude to Avi Cohen, Ann Hendricks, Edward Norton, Martin O'Connor, and Robert Fisher.

The following colleagues have made comments upon the manuscript over its six-year gestation period, and I am deeply in their debt: Randall Bausor, Bruce Caldwell, Bob Coats, William Darity, Neil de Marchi, David Ellerman, Craufurd Goodwin, Christopher Grandy, Carol Heim, Samuel Hollander, Albert Jolink, Arjo Klamer, Martin Klein, Donald McCloskey, Joseph Marsh, Perry Mehrling, Ted Porter, Salim Rashid, Larry Samuelson, Margaret Schabas, Martin Shubik, David Weiman, Roy Weintraub, Norton Wise, and Robert Paul Wolff. The students of Economics 785b at Yale University, in particular Michael Hobbs and Kori Udovici, tried not to let me get away with too many unfounded assertions; I am grateful for what must have seemed to them an endless task. I particularly acknowledge the kindness and hospitality extended to me by Joe Marsh of UMIST in the summer of 1983, when no other British historian of science felt inclined to encourage an economist who was asking silly questions about the economic influences upon famous physicists. I also thank Pam Cook for invaluable help with all sorts of translation problems.

I thank too the archivists at the following repositories for their patience and help: the Columbia University Library manuscripts room for access to the papers of Henry Ludwell Moore, Wesley Clair Mitchell, Harold Hotelling, and Edwin Seligman; the Sterling Library Manuscripts Archive at Yale University for access to the papers of Irving Fisher and Tjalling Koopmans; the library of the Royal Society of London; the archivists at Harvard University for the papers of Edwin Bidwell Wilson; and the University of Manchester Library for access to the James Joule collection.

Given that in the United States the National Science Foundation has been one of the premier sources of support for much of the scientific work in economics described in Chaptes 6 and 7, I am proud to gratefully acknowledge the support of the National Endowment for the Humanities during the final stages of the composition of this volume. It couldn't have come at a more critical juncture.

Portions of this book have appeared in much earlier versions in the *Cambridge Journal of Economics* and *Studies in the History and Philosophy of Science*. I thank Henry Steffens for permission to reproduce Figure 2.2, Academic Press for permission to quote from Szegö 1982, and Ilya Prigogine and Isabelle Stengers to quote from their *Order out of Chaos* (1984).

Somerville, Massachusetts   Philip Mirowski
September 1989

CHAPTER 1

The fearful spheres of Pascal and Parmenides

One of the greatest writers of the twentieth century, the Argentinian Jorge Luis Borges, once penned an essay titled "The Fearful Sphere of Pascal" (Borges 1962, pp. 189–92). It begins, in Borges's exquisite parody of the academic authorial voice: "It may be that universal history is the history of a handful of metaphors. The purpose of this note will be to sketch a chapter of that history."

The essay then commences with Xenophanes, who was revulsed by the poets of his time who sung the praises of anthropomorphic gods, and so offered in their place a single god, one who was an eternal and perfect sphere. Next Borges traces the metaphor of the Divine Sphere through its various vicissitudes from classical Greece to medieval Europe and thence to Bruno and Pascal. Although the metaphor of the sphere is the common denominator throughout, it glacially sheds some connotations and gathers others. Through time, the gods become God, and God becomes conflated with Nature; the universe grows from a closed bounded sphere to an infinite one; and throughout, man shrinks and shrinks to a puny insignificance. By the time Pascal took up the metaphor, he started to write, "Nature is a fearful sphere, whose center is everywhere and whose circumference is nowhere." Borges points out in his mock pedantic tone that Pascal later crossed out the word "fearful." The essay then concludes with the deadpan sentence, "It may be that universal history is the history of different intonations given a handful of metaphors."

The book that lies open before you may best be explained as a gloss upon Borges's little essay, although one that lacks his virtues of cunning imagination and stunning economy of expression. It, too, tracks the thread of a metaphor, one entwined with some of our most basic cultural self-images. It, too, is concerned with irony, with oblivion to humanity's own self-generated conundrums. And ultimately, it, too, is concerned with "universal history," although that is not what the author thought he was doing when he set about this task. Indeed, one does not become an economist in order to dabble in universal history; nor does one, once an economist, dabble in the history of physics without risking one's reputation in the community of economists. Among historians of physics, he has no prospects at all.

1

Since the contents of this volume will at first appear odd to anyone concerned with economics *or* the history of physics, something in the way of a justification might be in order. The origins of this work can be traced to an innocent comment made in passing in an economics seminar at Stanford University sometime in 1979 or 1980. The speaker tossed off an observation to the effect that "value had to be conserved" in his model if some mathematical assumption in the model were to hold; the tone of his voice suggested that no one in his or her right mind would find that a problem. Like so many other assertions in economics, this one was passed over without further comment, in the interests of getting on to the main topics of the seminar. For some reason, the comment haunted me afterward. I didn't care much about the model per se, but the very notion that such an assertion would go unchallenged seemed to me of profound import. Having had some background in physics, I knew how important conservation principles were in that arena; in physics great efforts were made to render them explicit. In economics, no one to my knowledge had systematically confronted the issue, at least in the textbooks. Yet this reference had passed without comment. Also, there was the concomitant issue of the importance of "value theory" in economics: It was my impression that in the modern period discussions of value theory had either descended into banalities or withered away. What did the demise of value theory have to do with the curious behavior at the seminar?

Such a vague and diffuse question has no instruction manual on how to approach it, so I thought; Why not start from the vantage point of intellectual history and see how the physicists arrived at their conservation principles? My initial inclination was to pick up at leisure some good basic history of conservation principles in physics—the concept was so important, surely there would be many tomes to choose from. To my dismay, I discovered not only was there no surfeit to chose from, but that there was no comprehensive or synoptic survey to be found. Even worse, with some minor caveats, none still exists.[1] Further, the otherwise superb *Dictionary of the History of Science* (Bynum, Browne, and Porter 1981) contained no entry for "conservation laws" or "conservation principles"; and the listing for "conservation of energy" has no text, merely directing the student to the entries for "energy" and "heat and thermodynamics."

At this stage, most people would have come to the conclusion that knowledge was simply not divided up according to such categories; prudence, if not exactly wisdom, would dictate the cultivation of other, more readily accessible fields. The alternative would be to end up like the madman in the Borges story "Tlön, Uqbar, Orbis Tertius" who feverishly searches encyclopedias for an entry that is never there. Yet the madman's logic in that story was strangely prophetic:

> It is useless to answer that reality is also orderly. Perhaps it is, but in accordance with divine laws – I translate: inhuman laws – which we never quite grasp. Tlön is surely a labyrinth, but it is a labyrinth devised by men, a labyrinth destined to be deciphered by men. (Borges 1962, pp. 17–18)

So for a time my interest in the history of science was a secret indulgence and a surreptitious pleasure, one that stole moments away from my legitimate research work in economic history and economic theory. Thoroughly unexpectedly, during one of those stolen moments, I suddenly realized that my hobby and my vocation were not as separate as they had seemed. Indeed, at that moment I saw that the history of physics and the history of economics are so intimately connected that it might be considered scandalous.

I should briefly explain, although the salacious details of the *liaison dangereuse* can be found in Chapter 5. The dominant school of economic theory in the West, which we shall call "neoclassical economics," has in the past often been praised and damned by being held up to the standards of physics. However, in my little epiphany, I realized that no one had ever seriously examined the historical parallels. Once one starts down that road, one rapidly discovers that the resemblances of the theories are uncanny, and one reason they are uncanny is because the progenitors of neoclassical economic theory boldly copied the reigning physical theories in the 1870s. The further one digs, the greater the realization that those neoclassicals did not imitate physics in a desultory or superficial manner; no, they copied their models mostly term for term and symbol for symbol, and said so.

It may not show in the subsequent chapters of this volume, but at the time I was staggered by the enormity of it. What did it mean to say that the economic theory used in the West to discuss all manner of events and issues was essentially a simulacrum of the physics of the mid-nineteenth century? Was the evidence of the metaphorical inspiration of neoclassical economics just a harmless artifact of the context of discovery, effortlessly shed as the research program gained confidence? Or, on the contrary, did it have more insistent implications for the subsequent development of economics? What was the significance of the fact that its origins had been forgotten, buried under the avalanche of "influences" that impinge upon any intellectual project?

I do make a stab at answering these questions in this volume. Nevertheless, even those questions do not do justice to the *telos* of this work. As I pushed the inquiry on to periods both later and earlier than 1870, I began to suspect that the fundamental issue was not simply the wholesale piracy of some physics by a doughty band of economists, but rather something akin to what Borges called "universal history." Perhaps what I had been doing was excavating a primal metaphor of Western thought, a vein winding through both physical theory and social theory, changing from gangue to fool's gold over time, with chutes passing back and forth between physics and economics. Although it was ultimately called "energy" in physics and "utility" in economics, it was fundamentally the same metaphor, performing many of the same explanatory functions in the respective contexts, evoking many of the same images and emotional responses, not to mention many of the same mathematical formalisms.

I must confess that for a while I toyed with the notion that I had uncovered something very like what Michel Foucault had termed an *episteme* in his *Les Mots et les Choses*. Our questions certainly bore close resemblances:

> On what "table," according to what grid of identities, similitudes and analogies, have we become accustomed to sort out so many different and similar things? What is the coherence – which, as is immediately apparent, is neither determined by an *a priori* and necessary concatenation, nor imposed on us by any immediately perceptible contents? (Foucault 1973, p. xix)

However sympathetic his project initially appeared, I eventually concluded that it would be pointless to try to pack my concerns into Foucault's restrictive and ultimately unpersuasive scheme of *episteme*s; nor could I accept his assertion that "The analysis of wealth is to political economy what general grammar is to philology and what natural history is to biology" (Foucault 1973, p. 168). I could appreciate Foucault's insistence that "man" as we perceive him did not always exist, as well as his demonstration that the significance of knowledge is inseparable from the uses to which it is put; however, I shall try to argue in this book that the structural resemblances of thought across disciplines are simultaneously more subtle and more crude than he makes out, and that the role of mathematics and metaphor looms much larger than he allows. It always did seem odd that Foucault never extended his inquiry to the physical sciences. The problem turned out to be, strangely enough, that Foucault had not sufficiently tapped into the resonances by which Western social theory and the sciences of the "natural" world resound their triumphs. If I were to summarize the overall theme of this volume, it is that the *Geisteswiss-enschaften* and the *Naturwissenschaften* are much closer than anyone has previously suspected; but this is surely no occasion for dancing in the streets.

It may help to signpost the inquiry that follows if I cite two bodies of literature that I have found extremely useful in systematizing this thesis. The first was the writings of the early twentieth-century French school of philosophers of science, encompassing such figures as Pierre Duhem, Gaston Bachelard, Henri Poincaré, and Alexandre Koyré, but more important, the undeservedly lesser-known Emile Meyerson. The single most characteristic feature of this school was its allegiance to the comprehensive integration of the history of science and the philosophy of science. This is a conviction that is now much more commonplace, but still not realized with the panache of these earlier writers. The second source has been the revival of the sociology and anthropology of science in the modern period, most notably associated with such thinkers as David Bloor, Bruno Latour, and Mary Douglas. This latter movement has revived the long-moribund aspiration to fashion of social theory that is something better than a pale reflection of the natural sciences.[2]

However, books that command some modicum of authority are not written by committees, and parades of citations do not substitute for the ideas themselves. In an introductory chapter, the reader should merely be introduced to the principles of inquiry that motivate the subsequent chapters. To that end, it will prove profitable to briefly summarize Emile Meyerson's now-dated book *Identity and Reality* (Meyerson 1962 [1908]), the work whose influence is most felt in the intersticies of our impending narrative.

In a nutshell, Meyerson managed to update the age-old philosophical conflict between the sphere of Parmenides and the Hericlitian flux by demonstrating that the same tension inhabits the historical development of physics (Kelly 1937, p. 41). Physics is torn between a search for identity and invariance on the one hand and the acknowledgment of diversity and change on the other; and this tension is most obvious in the history of physical conservation principles. Meyerson indicated that the status of conservation principles within science has never seemed on a par with other "laws," with questions continually raised about their empirical or a priori nature, as well as the related issue of their importance in the mathematization of discourse. In Meyerson's view, conservation laws were just a special case of the more sweeping postulate of the identity of things in time, a postulate he insisted was central to all human thought:

> The external world appears to us as infinitely changing, becoming
> incessantly modified in time. Yet the principle of causality postulates
> the contrary: we must needs understand, and yet we cannot do so
> except by supposing identity in time . . . The possibility of this
> conciliation depends evidently upon the particular nature of our
> concept of displacement. Displacement is and is not a change . . .
> [Meyerson 1962, pp. 92–3]

Hence it came to pass that motion became the symbol of the
mollification of change by invariance, as well as the avatar of
quantification and rigor. One merit of Meyerson's historical work was
to reveal how susceptible scientists have been to belief in conservation
principles, even in the absence of any compelling evidence; and
conversely, how loath scientists have been to relinquish a conservation
principle once accepted. The reason for this susceptibility is not
inborn gullibility, nor a brainwashed passivity, nor the intransigence
of a stubborn conservatism. I suspect that there are strong cultural
reasons for it (mooted in Chapter 3); whereas Meyerson saw it as the
bedrock of the causal structure of the process of explanation, and the
fundamental intuition of the relation of equivalence:

> the postulate of the identity of things in time intervene[es] powerful-
> ly in science . . . (1) It is powerful enough to create in us illusions that
> are contrary to evidence; it makes us accept as substance what in the
> beginning is but a relation between two limited terms, such as veloc-
> ity, or a concept impossible to clearly define in its entirety, such as
> energy. (2) It is this strange prestige of the principles of conservation
> which explains why we are inclined to exaggerate immoderately
> their importance to the extent of making their formulation coincide
> with the causal postulate itself: Nothing is created, nothing is lost . . .
>
> [We observe] the tendency to transform a relation into a thing in
> order to see conserved, not only the law, but also the object, and this,
> we know, is the true sense of the causal tendency. It is because we
> obey this tendency that we prefer to give our laws such a form that
> the change does not appear to depend directly on the flow of time –
> in other words, we seek to eliminate time from our formulae [Meyer-
> son 1962, pp. 215, 222].

More than one commentator has noted that Meyerson's thesis dis-
pels the Platonic mysticism that marvels at the "unreasonable
effectiveness of mathematics in the natural sciences" (Zahar 1980).
The reason mathematics "works" so well in science is that it is the
result of a long and arduous process of adjustment of the formalism
to our contingent experience. Meyerson's story goes roughly as follows: Someone proposes some hypothesis, and then a mathematical

savant constructs an "equivalent" statement $H^*(x)$ of the hypothesis, highlighting some mathematical entity x. The Meyersonian tendency then exerts its sway, and x begins to be treated analogously to the general philosophical category of substance: Namely, it is thought to obey some conservation laws. These conservation laws, in turn, provide the accounting framework that enables quantitative manipulation. Somewhere along the line, entity x gets conflated with object $\hat{x}$, which becomes associated with all sorts of metaphorical overtones, such as the permanence of natural law, the bedrock of phenomenological reality, the identity of mind and body, and so forth. Then as is frequently the case, some troublesome class of phenomena violates those laws. The repertoire of responses includes the usual range of methods of neutralization of empirical results, generally summarized under the rubric of the Duhem/Quine thesis, but also a more fruitful tactic, which is to modify the mathematical formalisms expressing the hypothesis, say to $H'(x)$, which preserves the conservation law while subtly redefining the entity x and perhaps even the object $\hat{x}$, but concurrently presenting a new set of formalisms to recast existing theoretical statements. Thus, mathematics does not come to us written indelibly on Nature's Tablets, but rather is the product of a controlled search governed by metaphorical considerations, the premier instance being the heuristics of the conservation principles.

What has all this to do with economics? A tremendous amount: so much that one wonders why these issues have only been present at a subterranean level in the history of economic thought. Meyerson himself saw that there might be implications: "The expression [of equivalence] is borrowed from the language of economics. When I affirm that such a thing is worth such a price, that means that I can buy or sell it at that price . . ." (Meyerson 1962, p. 283). In the interim, the hint that "value" and "energy" might be performing essentially the same explanatory functions in the respective disciplines of economics and physics fell upon barren ground; the view that there might be economic influences upon the structure of physics was regarded as akin to blasphemy. Perhaps the time is now propitious to revive Meyerson's inquiry.

The puzzle is how best to conduct the inquiry. Things are not made easier by the necessity of having to deal in the formidable languages of modern economics and modern physics. It is difficult to say which of the two is more forbidding, although it seems there are no two other domains of human inquiry equally impenetrable to the average literate layperson. Some choices had to be made, and for better or for worse, mine have been to presume that my reader thinks more like an

economist than a physicist. This means that, among other things, I am
going to take a certain level of mathematical sophistication for granted –
not because I am going to fill pages with mathematical symbols, but
rather because I want to talk about what the mathematics means without
having first to teach it. It also means that I shall dwell on some things that
are calculated to make an economist squirm, although they may seem a
tempest in a teapot to those more imperturbable souls with a different
education. Finally, it means that I shall take it upon myself to teach just
enough physics background in Chapter 2 for someone relatively innocent of it to be capable of understanding what follows. Rest assured,
however, that my tutorial will not resemble a conventional "Intro to
College Physics": That would be much too authoritarian, too stereotypi-
cally calculated to weed out the tender-minded humanists, especially
given the philosophical positions I wish to espouse. The alternative was
to take a cue from Meyerson: The best way to talk about science is to
examine how people have done it. This has resulted in a Chapter 2
tutorial structured around the history of the concept of energy conservation; we shall see it is no accident that a discussion of so much of
physics can be organized with that single principle. All this is not to say
that I harbor no hopes that the interested historian of science, or philosopher, or physicist might find some things here and there to pique their
curiosity.

From the history of physics, we shall open out our horizons in
Chapter 3 to entertain the notion that the energy concept is not really
indigenous or specific to physics, but may be found elsewhere, sometimes under different guises and sporting different names. The pattern is the same as the one Meyerson identified in physics: To quantify something we reify what started as a mere relationship into an
anthropomorphic character and a conserved substance, conflating
this formulation with the causal postulate that *ex nihil nihilo fit* (from
nothing comes nothing). From there the nature of the conservation
principle becomes more baroque, violating the substance conception
in certain ways, but depending upon "external" metaphorical resonances to preserve the research heuristic. In both economics and
physics, the three metaphors of body, motion, and value mutually
reinforce the validity of conservation principles, even in the face of
disconfirming evidence. This heuristic encapsulates the Western
mode of reconciling the flux and diversity of experience to "natural
law," and also provides the avenue along which the economy influences Western science. However, every avenue which lives up to its
name is a two-way street, and that brings us to the balance of the book,
which is concerned with the history of economic thought.

Chapter 4 documents in some detail how the early history of political economy resembles the early history of physics. Metaphors of motion and of the physical world were a primary rhetorical resource of even the earliest political economists, one that in many respects set the tone of the discourse. But more significantly, the early disputes over value reveal that the protagonists were looking for a value substance, something that could reify an invariant in social life, and could then subsequently provide the basis for quantification and formalization. The fact that late classical economics settles upon the labor theory of value merely reiterates the metaphoric triad of body, motion, and value that was already present in rational mechanics and Cartesian and Leibnizian natural philosophy. Yet the program faltered in the mid-nineteenth century, for reasons not heretofore discussed.

Chapter 5 chronicles the escalation in the physics/economics synergy dating from the 1870s. We retell the tale of the "Marginalist Revolution," but now without the usual hymns of praise. Neoclassical economics made savvy use of the resonances between body, motion, and value by engaging in a brazen daylight robbery: The Marginalists appropriated the mathematical formalisms of mid-nineteenth-century energy physics, which for convenience we shall refer to as "proto-energetics," made them their own by changing the labels on the variables, and then trumpeted the triumph of a truly "scientific economics." Utility became the analogue of potential energy; the budget constraint became the slightly altered analogue of kinetic energy; and the Marginalist Revolutionaries marched off to do battle with classical, Historicist, and Marxian economists. Unfortunately, there had been one little oversight: The neoclassicals had neglected to appropriate the most important part of the formalism, not to mention the very heart of the metaphor, namely, the conservation of energy [3] This little blunder rendered the neoclassical heuristic essentially incoherent; but heedless of that fact, the Marginalists triumphed under their banner of Science.

Chapters 6 and 7 tour the landscape after the Long March of Neoclassicism, surveying the victory and the wreckage. In Chapter 6, we argue that the notion of "production," so fundamental to economics, is a direct corollary of the classical "substance" conception of value, one inherently incompatible with the neoclassical "field" theory of value. Instead of directly confronting this inconsistency, neoclassical economists contrived to graft classical substance notions onto their physics field equations, with the predictable dire consequences. In Chapter 7, we take up the chronicle of diplomatic relations between modern neoclassical economics and modern physics. Earlier, in Chapter 2, we had observed that modern physics has revised its approach to conservation principles and their significance, essentially leaving behind the nineteenth-century conception of energy. But then, what does it now mean to be a science? The modern neoclassical economists, never having really understood the conservation principles in the first place, are left in the dark, clutching tight to their original proto-energetics metaphor.

Chapter 8 is an attempt to insist that this book should be regarded both as a preliminary exercise in the history of social thought and as a prolegomenon to a social theory of value. Perhaps too frequently this book appears to sport a combative stance and a negative cast, to the extent of portraying most economists as stumbling blindly in a labyrinth of their own making. Let me make clear at the outset that I think there is much that is wise, perceptive, and important to be found in the history of economic thought, and even in the texts of authors herein criticized. Moreover, the modern evolution of economic thought has shown some distinctly hopeful turns, especially from the vantage point of an alternative social theory of value. For instance, there are recent developments in game theory that portend a realization that those techniques need not be wedded to the neoclassical theory of value, and indeed, are central to the description of economic institutions[4]; there is a profound reconceptualization of the very notion of private property[5]; there are deep discussions of the notion of "dimension" and "formalization" in economics.[6] The importance of stochastic concepts in economics is approaching a profound reevaluation[7]; and the importance of the work of Nicholas Georgescu-Roegen permeates this text. There is a wealth of important work to be discussed and assimilated into economic theory; however, each of these innovations has been obstructed by the dominant conception of economic value rooted in the imitation of physics. Hence, prudently restricting ourselves to one argument at a time, the present book focuses solely upon a critical survey of the determinants of the theory of value.

But, when all is said and done, the mutual symbiosis of natural and social concepts is just *messier* than anyone has heretofore anticipated, mostly because of the absence of any Archemedian point to get outside of it all. In lieu of solutions, we take the cowardly academic way out, and tender a promissory note for further work on the prevalence of metaphor in all thought, mathematical or vernacular, plodding or poetic, grandiose or mundane, sacred or profane. "It may be that universal history is the history of a handful of metaphors. The purpose of this book will be to sketch a chapter of that history."

Everything an economist needs to know about physics but was probably afraid to ask: The history of the energy concept

> The "invariance" character of the theory of the conservation of energy is responsible for the frequent feeling that the theory is incomprehensible, even after it has been explained. We naturally expect an explanation in terms of a substance and its modifications. If we have instead an invariance law and don't realize it, then we keep looking for the substance and do not find it. [Berkson 1974, p. 136]

> One who sees the essence of historical development solely in the discovery of fixed scientific truths is badly misled. [Georg Helm, quoted in Deltete 1983, p. 189]

The denizen of the late twentieth century who fills his automobile with gasoline, covers himself with suntan lotion to block out the ultraviolet, turns on his VCR by means of a remote control device and worries about the nuclear power plant just down the river probably feels himself to be quite at home with the concept of energy. Depending upon his education, he may or may not be aware that there are some cryptic mathematical equations behind it all, but on the whole he is content to turn the switches on and off and let someone else worry about the details. I daresay the reader, even if he or she is an economist, more or less falls into this category. Perhaps somewhere in the murky past they were drilled to memorize that momentum equals mass × velocity, and that force equals mass × acceleration, and that energy has something to do with the integral of forces × displacements, but it was all deadly dull, and in any event, now water safely under the bridge.

My first task is to convince the reader otherwise: that there is no way of understanding economics and social theory in the twentieth century without first understanding "energy" in some detail; and further, that the knowledge of energy will still prove inadequate unless it is embedded within a familiarity with the historical development of the energy concept. It will subsequently prove useful to see that the energy concept traced a trajectory from being thought of as a substance to being regarded as a mathematical artifact of a field to being just another way to express a symmetry. Similarly, the timing of various changes in the way scientists thought about force and the conservation of energy will later be critical in explaining certain developments in economic thought with respect to the theory of value. But most important, it will prove instrumental in clearing away a lot of rubbish that litters the history of social theory. Let me just give one example why the reader should put up with a long and arduous tutorial in the history of physics.

Probably the most-consulted reference work in the history of economic thought is Joseph Schumpeter's *History of Economic Analysis.* In the beginning of that work, Schumpeter asserts that his only interest lies in "scientific economics," which without further ado is equated with the methods of physics. But this raises an unsavory thought: Did the economists who have achieved the label of "scientific" do so simply by slavish imitation of the physicists? No, says Schumpeter, it is pure accident that the mathematics eventually used by the school of economists he favors was also used by the physicists (Schumpeter 1954, pp. 17–18). But then how about the physicists? Was their evolution explainable by some other influences, which would dictate that a valid intellectual history must cast its net more widely in the cause of understanding? No, says Schumpeter, for however much it appears at the time that "external" influences reinforce the conceptions of key players at critical junctures, the historian of science knows that any and all "philosophical garb" is easily divested from the true science underneath. Then, to button down his case, he refers to the discovery of the conservation of energy by Joule and the development of variational principles by Euler (Schumpeter 1954, p. 30).

This is a breathtakingly audacious misrepresentation of both the history of physics and the history of economics; but unless the audience has some prior background in the relevant histories, Schumpeter is free to pronounce such ex cathedra statements as a justification for restructuring the entire history of economic thought. The reason that there is altogether too much loose talk about "science" among social theorists is that there has been too little history of science in their diets. If so much revolves around the question of scientific legitimacy, then let us grit our teeth and learn a little about what it meant to participate in the project of attempting to render the physical world intelligible. I guarantee that afterward nothing will ever seem the same.

Energy before "energy"

To state, as does for instance Stallo (1960, p. 97), that the conservation of energy is coeval with the dawn of human intelligence is to severely confuse a number of issues at the outset. The word "energy" is derived from the Greek word *energia,* but we should not assume from this that the respective concepts were the same, or even similar. Aristotle uses the word in several senses: in his *Ethics,* in the sense of "activity" as opposed to mere disposition; in his *Rhetoric,* for a vigorous style. It is also employed to distinguish activity from potentiality, and to imply the ceaseless transformation of the potential into the actual. One important way *energia* does not translate into modern usage is that it seems there is no adequate Greek synonym for our word "work." In Greek thought, each thing is a product of its own specific virtue in its motion from the potential to the actual; words with more direct overtones of economic life only refer to narrowly specific activities, such as agricultural or financial endeavor (Lindsay 1974, chap. 1).

More to the point, Stallo's claim conflates the conservation of energy with the larger concept of conservation principles in general. The concept of a conservation principle is practically inseparable from the meaning of "energy," so much so that much of the history that follows will end up being an exegesis of conservation principles. The abstract notion of a conservation principle is not easy to define in any concise manner. Richard Feynman's (1965, p. 59) notion of "a number that does not change" is a quick and dirty definition, but is too restrictive. He also uses the analogy of a game of chess, where once we understand the rules, we know that a bishop will always be perched on the same color square: "This is in the nature of a conservation law. We do not need to watch the insides to know at least something about the game" (Feynman 1965, p. 60). This does give some flavor of how conservation principles are used in physics, but at the expense of pushing all the problems off onto an unstated distinction between "insides" and "outsides." Perhaps our best provisional definition of a "conservation principle" is the rule that some particular aspect of a phenomenon remains invariant or unaltered while the greater phenomenon undergoes certain specified transformations.

As an example, consider the circle with its center at point *A* in Figure 2.1. A number of conservation principles coule be pressed into service for the purposes of describing this circle. One, which one might call "the law of the conservation of identity in the plane," says that if the circle were lifted off the page, turned over (i.e., rotated back to front 180 degrees), and set back on the page so that its center was again at point *A,* we would not be able to distinguish this latter situation from the previous situation. Another principle might state that any rotation of the circle around point *A* in the plane of the page

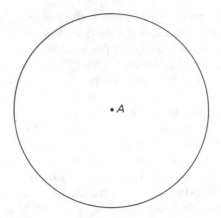

FIGURE 2.1   A circle.

would be indistinguishable from any other similar rotation. Finally (although this claim might be somewhat more controversial), we could postulate "the law of the conservation of the circle through time." That is, if you looked at this page tomorrow or next week, it would appear that the circle remained the same – it didn't become a square overnight while the book was closed.

It is practically impossible to trace all of what could be interpreted as prototypical conservation principles in Western thought. In Greek thought, the qualities of hot and cold, and of "heavy" and "light," were thought to be balanced in the totality, and there is some discussion of the indestructible eternity of the universe as a whole. Some of the same words are also used to describe the balance of political power. Historians of conservation principles have not been much concerned with this plethora of possibilities, but instead have generally restricted themselves to searching texts for anticipations of various aspects of the conservation of *energy*. For the purposes of this chapter, we shall follow their lead.

A tension is present in many histories of physical science, engendered by the following two questions: How far back can one really find a notion of the conservation of energy? and If the answer is anything prior to the 1840s, why does one then find a sense of "simultaneous discovery" of the principle in the 1840s? Historians such as Mach (1911), who dated the principle much earlier than 1840, tended to play down the questions of simultaneous discovery—or indeed, any questions of discovery in most senses. For Mach, "All ideas of conservation, like the idea of substance, have a solid foundation in the economy of thought. A mere unrelated change, without fixed point of support or reference, is not comprehensible, is not mentally reconstructable" (quoted in Deltete 1983, p. 44). Conversely, those such as Elkhana (1974) and Harman (1982a), who see distinct transformation in the middle of the nineteenth century, are more concerned to explain the discontinuity. Much of this diversity of interpretation springs from the greater dichotomy of world views, one of which sees science as incrementalist and as a unified discipline from the earliest times to the present, the other of which sees a proliferation of competing schools and rival methodologies, punctuated by shifts in allegiances.

For Ernst Mach, energy was more or less defined as the ability to do work. Although "work" could mean many things to many people, Mach felt it was merely an historical accident that the term was defined mechanically in early physics: that is, lifting a known weight through a certain distance. Although there was nothing intrinsically necessary about this conceptualization of work, once it had become widespread, Mach thought that the statement of the law of the conservation of energy would follow directly, in the format of an assertion that perpetual motion was impossible.

One respected text (White 1962, pp. 130–4) claims that the idea of a perpetual motion machine was introduced into Europe from India in the tweltfth century, and that great interest was elicited in the West in making the perpetuum mobile do something useful. By the sixteenth century, various thinkers had criticized particular manifestations of perpetual motion devices as faulty. For example, Leonardo da Vinci examined two kinds of overbalance wheels, where weights on strings or on movable internal ranges would supposedly cause a wheel, once set in motion, to rotate forever (or very nearly so). Leonardo explained that the center of gravity of the weights at rest would always be below the center of the wheel, and therefore the wheel must soon come to a halt (Lindsay 1975, pp. 72–3).

Mach nevertheless settled not upon Leonardo but upon Simon Stevin (1548–1620) as the man to win the laurels for the first complete statement of the impossibility of perpetual motion in general, in his *Beghinselen Der Weegkunst,* published in Leiden in 1586. Stevin, a polymath who also wrote works on bookkeeping and military engineering, discussed the equilibrium of a number of balls strung together and resting on an inclined plane. In actual fact, Stevin only assumed the impossibility of perpetual motion, and then used it to geometrically prove the configuration in static equilibrium of the string of balls (Stevin 1955).

Mach's praise of Stevin, however well-intentioned, was excessive on two grounds; (1) he did not give any explicit reasons why perpetual motion is impossible in a pre-Newtonian context (Gabbey 1985, p. 74); (2) in any event the assertion of its impossibility is not *identical* to the idea of the conservation of energy. Perpetual motion machines may be impossible because God directly intervenes to banish any activity displeasing to Him; or they may stop because imperfect construction does not approximate a frictionless state; or they may grind to a halt when unseen and ill-understood external forces act upon the machine. Galileo, among others, explicitly argued that craftsmen could not "cheat nature" (Drake 1960, pp. 147–8); but this argument lacked plausibility until a clearer idea had evolved of what it was that entered into the prosecution of motion, and what it was that came out the other end. This "illegitimate transaction" would not be banished simply because it was abhorrent to certain theorists' sense of the just order, as evidenced by the stream of tramontane engineers and tinkerers claiming to have discovered the secret of perpetual motion well into the nineteenth century.

The conviction of the impossibility of perpetual motion was a necessary, but not sufficient, condition for the full development of the concept of the conservation of energy. In an impressionistic way, the history of Western physics can be portrayed as a search for the right conservation principle with which to explain motion, and after 1850, to explain all physical phenomena.

Live force and dead force

This search for the "thing" to be conserved is often dated from 1644, the year of the publication of Descartes's *Principles of Philosophy*. (See Scott 1970; Westfall 1971; Stallo 1960; Hiebert 1962, pp. 65–6). It is well known that Descartes propounded the rationalist program of the reduction of all phenomena to matter in geometrical motion. To understand the structure of Cartesian explanation, one must keep in mind that Descartes scorned any idea of action at a distance, and hence endeavored to give a systematic treatment of motion and impact. The Cartesian world was composed of various-sized grains of matter, swirling in huge vortexes at high speeds, transmitting pressure instantaneously to grosser bodies. As the finest matter, the "ether," coursed about in a vortical motion around the earth, it moved faster than terrestrial matter, pushing bodies towards the center of the earth. All bodies possessed a "force," which was proportional to mass × velocity, or in modern notation, $m \times |v|$. Upon impact, the force lost by any one body was gained by the other; this motion was communicated (or perhaps "traded" is a better word) between bodies, and therefore was conserved.

In his *Le Monde*, Descartes gave three principles the status of laws of nature: (1) the conservation of modes of bodies, including motion and rest, in the absence of disturbing factors; (2) conservation of the total quantity of "force of motion" in collisions between bodies; and (3) the determination of this force of motion to act in a straight line tangent to the path of the body (Schuster 1977, p. 632). The character of these laws was derivative of the attributes of the Divine Lawgiver in defining what was immutable and what could change in the world.

For Descartes, this quantity as well as other quantities began to assume the attributes of a substance in a predominantly metaphorical sense, as can be observed from his statement that philosophers "should not find it strange if I assume that the quantity of matter which I described does not differ any more from its substance than number differs from numbered things, and if I conceive of its extension, or its property of occupying space, not as an accident but as its true form or essence" (quoted in Clarke 1982, p. 90). The advantage of this conception was that it rendered motion an abstract category that could itself be subject to further regularities and laws. One of those regularities was an embryonic idea of an economy of this new abstract stuff–that "when two bodies with incompatible modes collide, some change in these modes must truly occur to make them compatible, but that this change is always the least possible" (quoted in Clarke 1982, p. 225). By means of these and other statements, Descartes constructed the first comprehensive mechanical physics.

Here at the very birth of our deterministic physics, there was also an incipient clash between "law" and the program of reduction of all the world to substance in motion. Gabbey (1985, pp. 19–21) reports that Descartes was aware that there was an objection to his portraying the mind as subject to his laws of nature. If the will is free, and the mind can add any speed at all to any body it influences, then the total quantity of motion in the universe is not conserved. Descartes tried to circumvent this objection by insisting that the mind can only change the direction, and not the speed of bodies; but this auxiliary hypothesis was clearly weak, and it prompted Leibnitz, among others, to doubt the status of Descartes's law of conservation.

Descartes's suggestions bore fruit in the continental school of natural philosophy.[1] Some, like the philosopher Nicholas Malebranche, linked the conservation of Cartesian motion to a general notion of "the Economy of Nature." Others, such as Christian Huygens, sought to clarify the Cartesian conception of the conservation of mechanical properties in a closed mechanical system (Elzinga 1972, pp. 87–8). More important, Gottfried Wilhelm Leibniz, in reaction to the Cartesian system, was prompted to create a philosophical system, invent the calculus in order to discuss that system, and in the process, give the first extended consideration to physical conservation principles. In all instances, Leibniz stringently applied the precept that simplicity prevailed in the world.

It was Leibniz's doctrine that this was the best of all possible worlds, exhibiting the greatest simplicity in its premises and the greatest wealth in its phenomena, that Voltaire satirized so ruthlessly in his *Candide*. Leibniz's conviction was exemplified by his description of the phenomena of motion, leading him to state that "the perfectly acting being . . . can be compared to a clever engineer who obtains his effect in the simplest manner one can choose" (quoted in Yourgrau and Mandelstam 1955, p. 9). Simplicity was time and time again comprehended as mathematical in nature. For example, Leibniz championed a "law of continuity," that *natura non operatur per saltum,* or nature does not manifest itself in large and abrupt changes. That belief found its expression in the technique of summing sequences of infinitely small quantities – that is, in the calculus (Bos in Grattan-Guinness 1980).

Another example is his insistence that "each entire effect is equivalent to the cause." This requirement was made operational in his mechanics as the requirement that something be conserved in the motion of bodies through space. Leibniz's keen analytical sense could not accept Descartes' dictum that the quantity of motion was itself conserved, and he attacked the Cartesians in an article in 1686, which had repercussions all out of proportion to its length (Leibniz 1686; translated in Lindsay 1975, pp. 119–21). In this article, he distinguished between motive power *(potentia)* and moving force *(vis motrix),* and claimed that the Cartesians had confounded the two. He examined the two cases of a weight of one pound falling through four feet, and a weight of four pounds falling a distance of one foot. The Cartesians, measuring motion by mass times velocity, would say that the quantity of motion in the two cases was identical $(1 \times 4 = 4 \times 1)$. Leibniz objected that the force involved should be measured by the effect it can produce, and in that case Galileo had shown that (abstracting from friction, resistance, and other disturbances) all bodies fall at the same accelerated rate. In the above example, the 1-pound body would achieve twice the velocity of the 4-pound weight just before impact, and it would take half the "work" to restore the 1-pound weight to its original position than to restore the 4-pound weight ($m \times v$ equals 2 for the former, and 4 for the latter). As Leibniz had written elsewhere: "That a definite law persists which comprehends in itself all future states of the subject which we regard as identical – it is precisely this that constitutes the identity of substance" (in Cassirer 1956, p. 14). Leibniz was beginning to call into question the presumption that Cartesian "motion" was some kind of undifferentiated stuff.

Simplicity demands that some quantity remain fixed, if motion itself is portrayed as continuously varying; Descartes just had settled on the wrong conserved entity. Leibniz's revision of this requirement came in 1695. After a review of various writers' notions of force, he proposed his own distinction: Force is dual in character; there is dead force (vis mortua) and living force (vis viva). The former was dubbed "dead" because phenomenal motion does not yet exist, but has only a potential existence, like a stone in a cocked slingshot; at any moment it would be measured by the mass of the body times its virtual or potential velocity. Vis viva was dubbed "living" because it was actualized force in motion; it was measured by its effect, conceptualized as a body falling in space, as mass times velocity squared (mv^2). Holding that cause must be equated with effect, Leibniz asserted that vis viva was conserved in the process of phenomenal motion. He believed that by means of this discovery he had founded a new science of "dynamics" concerned with the finite and determinate velocities of bodies acquired by infinitely small degrees or "impressments" – in other words, vis viva was the summation (integral) of the infinitely small increments of vis mortua. Leibniz accused the Cartesians of being concerned only with statics, and thus mistakenly having taken vis mortua as the measure of force.

Although it may seem dry and technical to the modern reader, the dispute between the followers of Leibniz and of Descartes became a cause célèbre well into the eighteenth century, drafting recruits from literary and philosophical brigades as well as those of the always-contentious natural philosophers. (Indeed, the vis viva controversy also seems to have become one of the all-time favorite topics in the modern history of science. See, for citations, Papineau [1977] and Iltis [1973].) Everyone, it appears, was extremely anxious to decide what it was that got passed around between moving bodies. Leibniz's approach did seem to produce many striking results, as witnessed by the prolific inventiveness of Johann Bernoulli, Leonhard Euler, Daniel Bernoulli, and others; but it also gave rise to many doubts and problems. The most troublesome was the conception of motion after inelastic collision (Scott 1970). What happened to the conservation of *vis viva* or force when two apples of equal mass and velocity hit each other straight on? If they both stop "dead," where did the force go? Leibniz himself responded to the objections of the theologian (and Newtonian mouthpiece) Samuel Clarke in 1717:

> The Author objects that two soft or un-elastic bodies meeting together, lose some of their force. I answer: No. 'Tis true, their wholes lost it with respect to their total motion; but the parts receive it being shaken by the force of the concourse. And therefore that loss of force, is only in appearance. The forces are not destroyed but scattered among the small parts. The bodies do not lose their forces; but the case here is the same as when men change great money into small [quoted in Hiebert 1962, p. 89].

Elsewhere, Leibniz compared this apparent disappearance of force to the result of hitting a bag of billiard balls: The contents of the bag shift, but the bag itself does not move. Contemporaries were quick to notice that this just transported the problem to the microscopic level (what if the billiard balls were themselves inelastic?), and this led to further controversies about the characteristics of atoms (Scott 1970).

A second objection to the conservation of *vis viva* was the observation that many physical changes appeared to be irreversible. Contemporaries asked what happened, for instance, to all the *vis viva* used in grinding grains. Was there as much mv^2 in the resulting flour as was expended in the grinding? While the followers of Leibniz could give no satisfactory answer, they were spurred to further research, and to discuss an ever-widening circle of phenomena by their espousal of the conservation of *vis viva*, in a way that the early followers of Newton were not. The Newtonians had produced their greatest triumphs in the field of astronomy: regular, continuous, repeated motions of celestial (and therefore very distant) bodies that never collided. The Leibnizians were tempted to look at their more immediate environment with a mathematical armory and format better suited for discussing motions through time as well as through space. Being closer to their objects of study, they were forced to consider deformations, pressure, heat, and so forth on a much more familiar basis than were the Newtonians.

Leibniz bequeathed another fruitful intellectual innovation to later mechanics, one as important as his calculus, his mathematical notations, and his conservation of *vis viva*. The continental tradition took his suggestions about a clever engineer working in the simplest manner and transformed them into mathematical statements of what are today known as variational principles. A variational principle starts with some quantity or conserved function of a quantity and asks:

Where does the first variation (often, but not always, the first derivative) equal zero? The result identifies where the quantity or function is stationary. For instance, one might ask where the rise and fall of a mountain is stationary – more simply: Where are the flat parts of the mountain? This question is the application of a variational principle. An extremum principle is a special case of a variational principle that also inquires after the second variation of the quantity or function. Asking whether the flat part really is the top of the mountain or not would be an example of an extremum principle.

Many historians date the introduction of general extremal principles into mechanics at 1744, with the publication of Maupertuis's principle of least action.[2] Maupertuis defined a quantity called "action" as mass times velocity times distance; he then maintained that Nature acted so as to make this quantity a minimum. Many of his mathematical techniques were vague and unsuccessful, and the fact that he failed to specify a time interval for his definition of action played havoc with a consistent application of his principles (Brunet 1938). Nevertheless, Maupertuis's principle of least action created quite a stir, not the least because Maupertuis claimed that it was a proof of the existence, wisdom, and efficacy of God. Wisdom, at least in this context, was clearly conflated with economic calculation: "The quantity of action varies directly as the velocity and the length of the path described; it is proportional to the sum of the spaces, each being multiplied by the velocity with which the body describes it. It is this quantity of action which is here the true expense (dépense) of nature, and which she economizes as much as possible . . ." (in Cohen 1981, p. 5).

In order to build bridges to the followers of Leibniz, Maupertuis suggested that the conservation of vis viva was a special case of his principle of least action, since mv^2 was conserved only in the case of the collision of elastic bodies. In the ensuing controversies, the principle of least action and the conservation of vis viva were much confused (Scott 1978, p. 78). The difficulty lay in the fact that the necessity of the relationship between conservation principles and variational principles was not evident to any of the participants in the controversy: Maupertuis's definition of action did not specify with precision what quantity or entity remained fixed with each application of the minimization procedure, or the explicit conditions for an etremum. It took more than one hundred years to untangle the significance of the coupling of conservation principles to variational principles.

The writings of Leonhard Euler, although characteristically less metaphysical than those of Maupertuis, were an important bridge to the development of the mathematical techniques that linked variational principles to conservation principles. Euler connected force to *vis viva* in what we would now consider a modern manner, through the artifice of writing that the force times an infinitesimal increment of time is equal to the mass of the body moved times its incremental change in velocity, or $F[dt] = m[dv]$. Dividing both sides by dt, we arrive at the modern definition of force, $F = m(dv/dt)$. Integrating both sides of this equation, Euler demonstrated that the sum of the forces impressed upon the body will be equal to one half mv^2; this provided the analytical foundation for *vis viva* (Euler 1752, translated in Lindsay 1975, pp. 139–42). Euler also provided a more sturdy foundation for the use of variational principles in mechanics (as well as founding the mathematical technique of the calculus of variations) by asserting that when a particle travels between two fixed points, it follows the path in which the sum of $v\delta s$ (the instantaneous velocity times a small variation in the path traveled) is generally a minimum (see Yourgrau and Mandelstam 1955, chap. 4). In contrast to Maupertuis, Euler desisted from endowing either the minimization procedure or the thing minimized with any metaphysical interpretation, insisting that forces were something acting from the outside of bodies, and not inherent in the bodies themselves:

> Since all the effects of Nature follow a certain law of maxima or minima, there is no doubt that, on the curved paths, which the bodies describe under the action of certain forces, some maximum or minimum property ought to obtain. What this property is, nevertheless, does not appear easy to define *a priori* by proceeding from the principles of metaphysics . . . [quoted in Goldstein 1980, p. 106].

Euler was very circumspect in his enthusiasms over variational principles, to the extent of expressing reservations about their applicability in cases of moving particles in a resisting medium; questions of the putative disappearance of *vis viva* were no closer to being settled.

Variational principles in mechanics were clarified immensely by Joseph Louis Lagrange, in his *Mécanique Analytique* of 1788 (Lagrange 1965). Lagrange is often credited with the first modern treatment of motion because he demonstrated the great generality of the description of mechanical systems by means of variational principles, especially in instances where the analyst is free to choose a convenient set of coordinates. Lagrange recast d'Alembert's principle of virtual velocities into a method for solving (as he claimed) any mechanical problem purely as a paper-and-pencil exercise; it later became clear that this could only be claimed of situations where the sum of *vis viva* and an unnamed quantity could be written in analytical form. Nonetheless, in the *Mécanique Analytique* Lagrange explicitly rejected the principle of least action because it was "metaphysical" and could be derived from more basic laws of motion. As a consequence, as the mathematics grew in importance the significance of the conservation rules and extremum principles remained obscure.

Although the appropriate mathematics were in place by the turn of the nineteenth century, it appears that the conceptualization of analysis as extremal principles coupled to conservation principles was not much farther along than it had been during the storm over Maupertuis's principle of least action. This conceptual stasis was rooted in the fact that a science of dynamics, predicated upon the specification of maximization or minimization, was struggling to describe a system undergoing change, yet simultaneously founded upon some unchanging natural phenomenon that would serve as a benchmark; it had yet to suggest a legitimate quantitative conserved unit. Some natural philosophers focused their attention upon the calculation of extrema; others were strictly concerned with the mathematics of variational principles; while others searched for some metaphysically conserved quantity in nature. No group recognized that the labors of any of the others were a necessary complement to their own. The result of this oblivion was the relegation of Lagrange's equations, as well as the principle of least action, to an inconsequential role in rational mechanics, at least until the middle of the nineteenth century. Lagrangian multipliers were not generally used to derive new results in mechanics of this period; nor were they taught in courses on engineering or rational mechanics.[3] As late as 1837, Poisson, described the principle of least action as "only a useless rule" (quoted in Yourgrau and Mandelstam 1955, p. 32).

The motive force of fire

When we reach the first decade of the nineteenth century, we can no longer consider the development of conservation principles as a simple elaboration of the internal logic of improvements in mechanics. The conviction that each of the myriad of phenomena could be fully reduced to special cases of matter in motion grew increasingly forlorn. All the while there was a proliferation of separate ethers, imponderable fluids, and attractive and/or repulsive forces proposed to explain these phenomena (Agassi 1971, pp. 4–7). Doctrines thought to have been definitively settled, such as the impossibility of perpetual motion, once again became open issues. For example, Volta claimed that his electric pile was a perpetual motion machine, which only stopped because it had become "clogged" in the process of operation (Berkson 1974, p. 63). Mathematical theorists were also willing to entertain the possibility of perpetual motion; George Airy, for instance, attempted to model certain mechanical vibrations that were not strictly time-independent, and therefore would violate the conservation principles understood in that era (Airy 1830, pp. 369–72). It was by no means obvious that mechanics, such as it was at the beginning of the century, would provide a sufficient paradigm for the understanding of the physical world in general.

The next formidable advance in the understanding of conservation principles was an outgrowth of the evolution of engineering, in the attempt to formalize the value of work, and more particularly of that subset of engineering occupied by the harnessing of steam power and the study of heat. This major tradition of engineering was located in the *grands écoles* of Napoleonic France and the Bourbon Restoration (Grattan-Guinness 1984). The first concern of these schools was military engineering. In that area Lazare Carnot extended considerations of the physics of impact to the more inclusive category of work. He stated that, in order to obtain maximum work output from a machine, it would be necessary to reduce as much as possible the occurrence of impact in the translation of motion; in other words, maximum efficiency would be obtained whenever the conservation of *vis viva* held. The practical motivation behind such inquiries was to codify the principles of efficient construction of large civil projects, such as fortifications, turbines, and water wheels.

In effect, the avatars of pure abstraction cleansed of all metaphysics, such as Euler and Lagrange, were incapable of synthsizing the sought-after conservation principles because they had lost touch with the metaphorical ground of rational mechanics. It was Carnot and the engineering tradition who never lost sight of the importance of machine theory for mechanics. For instance, in contrast to Euler and Lagrange, Carnot avoided assuming that expressions for work assumed a potential and instead gave analytical prominence to conservation principles. This tradition, slighted in the history of physics literature because it was too "applied," ran from Carnot through Hachette, Navier, Montgolfier, Coriolis, and Poncelet; most of the principals were either associated with the *Ecole Polytechnique* or the *Ecole des Ponts et Chaussées*. Navier made it quite clear that practical considerations motivated the mathematical definition of work as uniting concepts of path and force: "The comparison of diverse machines, for the merchant and the *capitaliste*, comes naturally after the quantity of work which they execute, and the price of the work" (quoted in Grattan-Guinness 1984, p. 11).

This engineering tradition could not long remain confined to rational mechanics, especially given the increasing importance of steam engines in the comparison of the cost effectiveness of various machines. Lazare's son, Sadi Carnot, applied his father's ideas to the steam engine, and as a result reconceptualized the nature of heat. Although his writings did not receive much attention in his lifetime, Sadi Carnot is now credited with being the founder of thermodynamics.

At that time in France, heat was thought to be caused by an imponderable fluid called "caloric," which surrounded the grosser particles of matter. In Carnot *fils's* published treatise, he denied that the motive power generated from steam engines was the result of the consumption or destruction of caloric; rather, it was due to the migration of caloric from a warmer to a colder body, in direct analogy with the fall of water on a water wheel from a higher to a lower elevation. This model led to a startling conclusion: *Only* the existence of a difference of temperatures allows the production of "moving power," and the ideal efficiency of a machine employing heat to produce power depends solely upon the temperature differential between source and sink, and not upon the nature of the working substance heated and cooled. His "proof" of this assertion was equally striking, because it depended solely upon the *assumption* of the impossibility of a perpetual motion machine. Carnot argued that if two working substances differed in their maximum efficiencies, we could link in sequence a heat engine using one of the substances to a refrigeration device using the other substance, and because their efficiencies differed, each could reverse the operation of the other with power to spare. Since perpetual motion is assumed impossible, then motive force must be a function of temperature differentials alone. The fact that the impossibility of perpetual motion in 1824 was still a controversial thesis, and hence his "proof" might not convince everyone, was revealed by Carnot in a footnote:

> The objection may perhaps be raised here, that perpetual motion, demonstrated to be impossible by mechanical action alone, may possibly not be so if the power either of heat or electricity be exerted; but is it possible to conceive the phenomenon of heat and electricity as due to anything else than some kind of motion of the body, and as such should they not be subjected to the general laws of mechanics? Do we not know besides, *a posteriori*, that all the attempts made to

produce perpetual motion by any means whatever have been fruitless? . . . The general and philosophic acceptance of the words
perpetual motion should include not only a motion susceptible of
indefinitely continuing itself after a first impulse received, but the
action of an apparatus, of any construction whatever, capable of
creating motive power in unlimited quantity . . ." (Carnot 1960,
p. 12).

Perhaps it is only hindsight, but this does appear in embryo to be
the doctrine of the conservation of energy. Particularly notable is the
appeal to the reduction of all energetic phenomena to their mechanical equivalents, all the while assuming the retention of the existing
theory of rational mechanics. On the basis of some unpublished
manuscripts discovered after his death, Sadi Carnot is sometimes
credited to be one of the discoverers of the idea of conservation of
energy.

It is worthwhile stressing that a requirement of the quantification of
the theory of heat was a prior assumption that something specific was
conserved in temperature fluctuations. For Carnot, the conserved
quantum was the subtle fluid caloric. Unfortunately, conservation of
caloric inevitably raised obstacles to the conceptualization of conversions of heat into mechanical work because, notwithstanding Carnot's hostility to perpetual motion, it was not at all clear where the
work came from in a heat engine. If caloric was conserved, then what
did the heat engine "lose" in order to create the work? The most
significant debate that preceded the establishment of thermodynamics in the nineteenth century was the controversy over whether caloric
could be portrayed as a conserved entity (Kuhn 1958; Caldwell 1971,
p. 65). Getting the relevant conservation principles straight was an
important part of the drive to quantify and formalize the new areas of
physical theory. This lesson was not lost on the next generation of
physical theorists.

The Laplacian Dream

By the 1820s it was hard not to notice that the character of physical
science was changing its attitudes toward fundamental issues of ontology and epistemology, and that it was these changes in deep structure
that acted to bring variational principles to the fore. C. G. Gillispie
(1965, p. 118) has suggested that once the Encyclopedists boasted of
liberating science from metaphysics, the French Revolution completed the task by liberating science from ontology. The ramparts
were not stormed all at once, nor did they necessarily fall in every

engagement, but each subsequent skirmishh pointed to a substantially novel style of doing science. Some examples of the altered temperament were: assertions that it did not matter what the actual process underlying a theory really was; the demotion of intuitive plausibility as a criterion of theory choice; increasing denial of direct sensory access to the workings of phenomena; that formalization and quantification came to be embraced for their own sake; and that technical utility became more admissible as a positive criterion for theory choice (Heidelberger 1981). For the sharp-eyed, the writing was on the wall: In contrast to some mechanical image, the mathematical format of a theory was to be more and more bound up with the theory's meaning, as well as with its success.

This liberation of science from ontology found its champion in Joseph Fourier and his equations of heat flow, and was taken up by the positivist program, which believed that it could renounce all specification of the underlying structure of reality and confine description to phenomenological mathematical equations (as if that were not an oxymoron). This trend subsequently established a beachhead in Cambridge, England (Cross, in Harman 1985, p. 138). Those outside physics frequently confused this movement with a contemporary parallel school of mathematical physics that was predicated upon a rigid doctrine of determinism founded upon a presumption of the atomic structure of matter.

For lack of a more appropriate name, we shall refer to this second ontological stance as the Laplacian Dream. Pierre-Simon Laplace founded a school of physics, at the fledgling Ecole Polytechnique in the first decade of the nineteenth century, which was based upon applying the calculus of potentials to forces among particles of various descriptions. In designating Laplace to represent a particular era in physics, we do not intend to signify his specific contributions, or even those of his narrowly defined school (Fox 1974), but rather what Capek has called "the corpuscular-kinetic view of reality," which was coextensive with the first precise formulation of a relentless and thoroughgoing determinism. The Laplacian Dream signifies a challenge to physics, a goal best expressed in Laplace's own words:

> An intellect which at a given instant knew all the forces acting in nature, and the position of all things of which the world consists – supposing the said intellect were vast enough to subject these data to analysis – would embrace *in the same formula* [my italics] the motions of the greatest bodies in the universe and those of the slightest atoms; nothing would be uncertain for it, and the future, like the past, would be present to its eyes" (quoted in Capek 1961, p. 122).

In the Laplacian Dream, science aspired to discover the single mathematical formula that described the entire world (or the universe, depending on the extent of the hubris). The only real difficulty with the use of such a formula would be the required collection of the staggering number of facts that characterize the system at a given point in time. It is of profound importance to note that the world, the subject of prediction, is assumed to be fully captured by the equation at any point in time, and therefore must be indifferent to the passage of historical time. The world retains its physical identity in any epoch, so transitions in time do not alter its the essential properties. The Dream was inclined to expect that this super-equation would be rooted in the formalism of the differential calculus: hence there was every expectation that the super-equation would itself be subject to a variational principle. The Laplacian Dream gathered together a formidable collection of components present individually in the eighteenth century, but integrated and elaborated only in the nineteenth: the independent reality of an external, timeless physical world; the mathematical expression of the Platonic ideal; a rigid determinism, spare and ascetic; variational principles; and the later metaphor of the force field. Further, in Laplace's own philosophical essay on probability, one finds the suggestion that human psychology should be regarded as merely a continuation of the same set of natural laws; for instance, he posited a seat of all thought which he called a *sensorium*, to be modeled upon a system of mechanical resonators equally subject to the identical laws of dynamics. Contemplation of this program certainly suggests that one motive of the Laplacian Dream was the barely disguised usurpation of God's place in the universe.

The Laplacian Dream heralded a new type of physics, one that (despite its avowed atomism) began to shift the location of fundamental theoretical status from matter and its ontological characteristics of persistence, impenetrability, and inertia, and nudged it closer to the fundamental concept of force. Early intimations of this shift were to be found in Kant's critique of Newton's conceptualization of substance in his *Metaphysical Foundations of Natural Science* (cf. Harman 1982, pp. 57–63). Kant claimed therein that the motion of entities in space, described in terms of forces, was a fundamental a priori structure of all empirical science. Nonetheless, the shift was so subtle that one must consciously look for it to find it. In England, its lineage can be traced from Descartes through to Boyle, Newton, Priestley, and thence to Faraday, as the primacy of inert extension gave way to the proliferation of active forces (Heimann and McGuire 1971; Gooding 1980). One reason that the transition was not patently apparent was that it often assumed the framework of the postulation of "subtle fluids," intangible ethers that permeated tangible solids, fluids, and gases (Cantor and Hodge 1981). The function of these ethers was to act as the bearers or mediators of the forces that traversed vast distances, seemingly independent of intervening tangible matter. The more the emphasis that was placed upon the action in the intervening space, the less important became the character of the corpuscular matter that occupied the poles of the particular physical interaction.

The eventual terminus of this movement away from concern with "substance" was the concept of the field. The English word "field" was not incorporated into the vocabulary of physics until the 1850s and 1860s (Cantor and Hodge 1981, p. 38). However, this should not disguise the fact that much of the mathematical formalisms of fields were worked out well before the discovery of the conservation of energy. The military metaphor of a field of action was undoubtedly a vernacular influence, providing a visualization of what is otherwise an extremely unintuitive mathematical notion. In military parlance, the field of action is a space that an army would move to defend, were it to be entered by the enemy. In physics, a field is a configuration of potentials in space, the potential at a point being defined as the amount of work required to bring a test body to that point from an infinite distance away. The archetypal image of a field is still the curves assumed by iron filings strewn on a sheet of paper placed above a magnet, revealing the lines of force that were previously invisible.

Even this definition evokes a highly idealized picture, itself conditional upon nineteenth-century innovations in the energy concept. Fields existed in physics before they were recognized as such, but they were present at first only in their mathematical incarnations. Early field theories were defined over a region in which each geometrical point was associated with some quantity or quantities (i.e., a scalar field or a vector field), which were themselves only functions of the spatial coordinates and time. The properties of the field were described by partial differential equations in which the field quantities were dependent variables, and the spatial coordinates and time were the independent variables.

The earliest example of the mathematics of a field theory can be found in 1743, in Euler's work on fluid dynamics (Hesse 1965, pp. 189–95). Euler associated each geometrical point of a fluid in a pipe with a particular velocity at a point in time. These velocities were then related mathematically to the density of the fluid, the pressure at that point, and any external force on the liquid. This formalization of hydrodynamics later served as a paradigm for any number of ethers whose purpose was to transmit heat flow, electrical current, magnetic flux, light, and so on. It was the seemingly endless applications of the hydrodynamics/field formalism that played an important role in the change in the style of theory construction from the 1820s to the 1850s (Cantor and Hodge 1981, p. 46). The Laplacian Dream was both cause and consequence of the heightened degree of formalism as well as the transmutation from substance to field paradigms in nineteenth-century physics. The positivist renunciation of ontology helped render the field paradigm more palatable. This complex interplay was the catalytic prerequisite for the concept of energy.

Some mathematics of conservation principles

Up to this point in our narrative we have managed to avoid the mathematics; yet the message of the previous section has been that by the nineteenth century the theory *is* the mathematics for all practical purposes. There is no escaping a quick but nasty brush with the calculus in order to see what has happened to motion by the 1840s. The faint of heart may skip this section, but should at least be forewarned: There can be no understanding of the meaning of the field, and, what amounts to the same thing, *there can be no understanding of modern neoclassical economics* without some familiarity with the formalisms of Lagrangian and Hamiltonian mechanics in their historical context. A brief formal outline of Lagrangians and Hamiltonians may be found in the Appendix. On the other hand, those for whom Hamiltonians are second nature can also skip this section and consult Goldstein (1950) for the intricacies of the problems of classical mechanics.

To provide the necessary background, attention will be centered upon the conservation principles in the mathematical formalisms of Lagrange and Sir William Rowan Hamilton, as well as the early-nineteenth-century understanding of a potential field. In this summary exposition, we shall not adhere rigidly to early-nineteenth-century notation and format.[4]

Suppose a mass point is moved by some force from point A to point B. It was well known and widely accepted by the beginning of the nineteenth century that force was defined as the product of the mass of the particle times its acceleration, or

$$F = ma = m[d^2s/dt^2]$$

As we had occasion to observe in our commentary upon the Descartes/Leibniz controversy, acceleration may vary over the path from

A to B, so any process that claims to account for the total force involved in a motion must add up the impressed forces along infinitesimal displacements all along the path; that is, it requires the evaluation of the integral:

$$\int_A^B F\,ds = \int_A^B m\,\frac{d^2 s}{dt^2}\,ds = \frac{1}{2}\,m\int_{v_A}^{v_B} d(v^2)$$

$$= \frac{1}{2}\,mv_B{}^2 - \frac{1}{2}\,mv_A{}^2$$

Here was recognized the mathematical relationship between the quantum of the force of motion and the change in the *vis viva* (mv^2) of the particle. The achievement of the Lagrangian tradition of rational mechanics was to show that, in the case of the constrained motion of a number of particles, equilibrium could be characterized by the sum of mv^2's attaining either a maximum or a minimum.

Now, suppose that both the force and the displacement of the particle could be resolved into their three-dimensional orthogonal components. Hence $\mathbf{F} = \mathbf{i}F_x + \mathbf{j}F_y + \mathbf{k}F_z$ and the displacement $ds = \mathbf{i}dx + \mathbf{j}dy + \mathbf{k}dz$, where the boldface $\mathbf{i}$, $\mathbf{j}$, and $\mathbf{k}$ are unit vectors along each axis and the boldface $\mathbf{F}$ stands for the force vector. In this instance, one could then define a new quantity T, where

(2.1) $\quad T = \int_A^B \{F_x dx + F_y dy + F_z dz\}$

If the expression ($F_x dx + F_y dy + F_z dz$) in (2.1) is a perfect (or "exact") differential, then it is possible to define a scalar potential function $U = U(x, y, z)$, where in equilibrium $F_x = -\delta U/\delta x$, $F_y = -\delta U/\delta y$, and $F_z = -\delta U/\delta z$.

Lagrange interpreted the function $U(x, y, z)$ merely as an artifact of the positional coordinates, and did not invest much importance in it. It was only much later, in the 1850s and 1860s, that the scalars T and U were endowed with greater significance by redefining them as, respectively, kinetic and potential energy. But until that time, in the Lagrangian tradition, there was confusion as to what precisely was conserved in this description of motion. Here, *vis viva* is not conserved, contrary to some claims at the time. The assumption of the exact differential does imply that the sum $T + U$ is conserved in certain circumstances: in a closed system $T + U = k$, a constant. Prior to the 1840s this sum had little significance, not least because it looked like the addition of chalk and cheese.

The general statement of the Lagrangian and its solution can be found in the Appendix. To see how the Lagrangian technique works, let us derive one of the simpler laws in physics, the equilibrium of two masses A and B perched upon the two arms of a lever. The *vis viva* of the two masses would be, respectively, one half $m_A v_A{}^2$ and one half $m_B v_B{}^2$, whereas the gravitational potential would be $m_A g x_A$ and $m_B g x_B$ respectively, where g is the gravitational constant and the x's are the vertical displacements. The motion of each of the masses is constrained to remain on each arm of the lever, and so $x_B = -(b/a)x_A$, where a is the distance of mass A from the fulcrum and b is the distance for mass B. Writing out the Lagrangian for total energy = *vis viva* + potential (remembering that no such concept yet existed), we would get:

$$E = (1/2) \dot{x}_A{}^2 \{(m_A a^2 + m_B b^2)/a^2\} + g x_A (m_A a - m_B b)$$

Now we apply the principle of least action, the variational principle, to discover where the energy of the system is minimized, by finding where:

$$\frac{\partial E}{\partial x_A} = m_A a - m_B b = 0$$

Solving this condition by substituting in the constraint gets us the law of the lever, namely $m_A/m_B = b/a = -x_B/x_A$. To the natural philosophers of the late eighteenth century this must have seemed an exceptionally roundabout and baroque way of arriving at a very simple static result.

Perhaps this fact goes part of the way toward explaining the less-than-enthusiastic textbook reception of the Lagrangian conception of mechanics. Nonetheless, one can observe how the Lagrangian formalism would resonate with the new philosophical currents, for it did not commit itself to any ontological model of the process of motion, made little appeal to intuition, was stylized in the extreme, and was much more sophisticated in mathematical technique than the standards of the day. In fact, it was hard to give it much of a mechanical interpretation at all, with its undefined terms and its obscure variational principle, neither consistently a maximum or a minimum of a mysterious quantity.

The mathematics of potentials was honed to a sharp instrument in the second quarter of the nineteenth century, especially by George Green, George Stokes, and William Thomson (Cross, in Harman 1985, pp. 129–45). These authors' endeavors considerably clarified the meaning of a conservative field of force. In particular, they explored cases where line integrals around a closed curve c would conform to the condition:

$$\oint_c \mathbf{A} \cdot ds = 0$$

If this condition were fulfilled everywhere in a vector field $\mathbf{A}(s,t)$, then the field would be called "irrotational" and $\{\mathbf{A} \cdot ds\}$ would be a perfect differential equation. As a consequence, the vector field could be expressed as the gradient of a scalar field (i.e., a "potential function").

Now, let us bring this mathematics into the realm of rational mechanics. We begin with the vector field of forces $\mathbf{F}$. If the work accomplished between any two points in space, s_1, and s_2, written as

$$T = \int_{s_1}^{s_2} \mathbf{F} \cdot ds$$

occurred in such a manner as to be path-independent, then the vector field would be a gradient of some scalar potential function $U(s)$. Now, irrotational fields are evaluated at an instant, which allows for the possibility that they may be time-dependent. However, work takes time, so for a field of kinetic forces to conform to an irrotational vector field, it is necessary that the field also be time-independent; hence, these mechanical fields must be *conservative*. A force field is conservative if and only if it can be expressed as the gradient of a time-independent scalar field; here, $\mathbf{F} = \text{grad } U(s)$.

The next step was to work backward, demonstrating how to decide whether any given field under consideration would qualify as a conservative force field. Define the gradient of the suspected potential function as:

$$(2.2) \qquad \text{grad } U = \left[\frac{\partial U}{\partial x}, \frac{\partial U}{\partial y}, \frac{\partial U}{\partial z}\right] = \{X, Y, Z\}$$

and the curl of the field $\mathbf{F}$ as

$$(2.3) \qquad \text{curl } \mathbf{F} = \left[\frac{\partial Z}{\partial y} - \frac{\partial Y}{\partial z}, \frac{\partial X}{\partial z} - \frac{\partial Z}{\partial x}, \frac{\partial Y}{\partial x} - \frac{\partial X}{\partial y}\right]$$

Then the test for an "integrable" or conservative field of force is to check whether (Kellogg 1929, pp. 71–3)

$$(2.4) \qquad \text{curl } \mathbf{F} = 0$$

After the clarification of the nature of conservative fields of force, the next step in promoting variational principles from the status of a supernumerary to an organizing principle in physical thought came in the 1830s; it was the handiwork of Sir William Rowan Hamilton, an Irishman. Hamilton was well situated to make this next intuitive leap, because of his familiarity with French analytical mechanics, German metaphysical idealism, and the British tradition of the invocation of analogies between existing analytical processes and novel phenomena. He was quite explicit about the philosophy that guided his mathematical endeavors:

> Power, acting by law in Space and Time is the ideal base of an ideal world, into which it is the problem of physical science to refine the phenomenal world, that so we may behold as one and under the forms of our understanding, what had seemed to be manifold and foreign [quoted in Hankins 1980, p. 62].

Hamilton did not strive for practical results, but rather for a unified abstract mechanics, ruled by an organizing principle both esthetic and evocative, and imposed by mankind upon an unruly world. While he fervently believed that mathematical formalization was the most effective vehicle for achieving this goal, he was appreciably more sophisticated in his justifications than later proponents of the efficacy of mathematics in physical theory:

> [I]n the application of mathematics themselves there must (if I may venture upon the word) be something metamathematical. Though the senses may make known the phenomena, and the mathematical methods may arrange them, yet the craving of our nature is not satisfied till we trace in them the projection of ourselves, of that which is divine within us; till we perceive an analogy between the laws of outward appearance and our inward laws and forms of thought . . . Do you think we *see* the attraction of the planets? We barely see their orbits . . . [in Hankins 1980, pp. 176–7].

The fruits of this realization appeared in Hamilton's classic articles "Essays in a General Method in Dynamics" of 1834 and 1835. In these papers, Hamilton argued that the principle of least action was a special case of a much more general principle, which he dubbed "the principle of varying action." To implement this general principle, he assumed that there was a conservation of a particular sum – the sum of *vis viva* "T" and an undefined "U" (his notation, by the way: this will come in handy in Chapter 5) – throughout the process of motion. He avoided explicit discussion of the U by writing down the conservation principle without much ado as

(2.5) $T = U + H$

Bowing in the direction of Lagrange, he justified this assumption as "the celebrated law of *vis viva*" (Hamilton 1834, p. 250). In modern terminology, the U would be the negative of potential energy, while H would be interpreted as total energy.

The reader should not be misled by the absolute inability of modern writers (present company included) to discuss Hamilton's achievement without resorting to anachronistic appeals to modern notions of

energy. Hamilton, following the time-honored convention of his contemporaries, called the quantity H the "action," and simply referred
to U as a "force function" (Hamilton 1835, p. 96). These vague
referents probably did not encourage immediate comprehension of
Hamilton's reconceptualization of the problem of dynamics. Further,
Hamilton's actual method is much more tedious and messy in practical applications than the corresponding Lagrangian formalism that
it encompasses, and so it did not filter down to the level of British
textbooks of mechanics until Thomson and Tait's *Treatise on Natural
Philosophy* in 1867. Hamilton's variational principle was only one side
of a two-sided formalism; until the conservation principles were
accorded equal status, it just was not clear what the Hamiltonian
meant for physical theory. The importance of Hamilton's work in the
1830s was that it implicitly conjured its alter ego, the energy principle.
Only after the two principles were jointly developed in the hundred
years following Hamilton's papers, and their applications spread to
every corner of physics, would a Nobel-prize winner state in 1926 that
"The central conception in all modern theory in physics is 'the
Hamiltonian'" (Erwin Schrödinger, quoted in Hankins 1980, p. 64).

The "discovery" of the conservation of energy

The closer we come to the decade of the 1840s, the more appropriate
grows the terminology of energy, because it is in that period that most
historians of science locate the "simultaneous discovery" of the conservation of energy. This doctrine is something more than the genesis
of a locally significant physical theory; rather, it is the event that
eventually recast the entire content of nineteenth-century physics.
Energy became the novel organizing principle of physical research,
linking the previously disjunct and disparate studies of motion, light,
heat, electricity, and magnetism. After this "discovery," the very science of physics was redefined to be the reduction of all phenomena to
their energetic foundations, and hence implicitly the reduction of all
phenomena to mechanics (Harman 1982a, p. 158). Only after 1850
did physics become the king of the sciences, usurping the throne from
physical astronomy (Cannon 1978, p. 2). Energy was the reason.

So thoroughgoing a revision and so momentuous a change would
be bound to attract many candidates for the laurels of discovery;
there are a surfeit of them in this instance. Thomas Kuhn (in Clagett
1959, p. 343) collects *sixteen* possible names. As a prelude to awarding
laurels, Kuhn divided the aspirants into three categories of descend-
ing order of legitimacy. The first group, whose work "combined

generality of formulation with concrete quantitative application" and therefore, according to Kuhn, deserve the most credit, is comprised of J. R. Mayer, James Joule, Hermann von Helmholtz, and Ludwig Colding. The second group possesses a more diminished claim to fame, because they only discussed the interconvertability of heat and mechanical work: there are four of these. The final residual group gets short shrift from Kuhn because their only achievement was to claim in sundry ways that all natural phenomena are manifestations of a single "force," without implementing this notion in a quantitative format. Once the legitimate claimants are thus neatly packaged, Kuhn then takes it upon himself to explain the influences shared by the first group of "winners." The last step was to assert that these shared influences conditioned and determined the simultaneous or near-simultaneous discovery.

The snag in the running of this particular (Hambletonian?) horse race is that it assumes that there was just one thing – energy – to be discovered, and that all the supposed rivals were headed for the same finishing line. Was energy really "in" Nature, waiting to be discovered? And did the premier favored four really discover the same thing? This objection has troubled some historians (Boyer, in Clagett 1959, p. 385; Cannon 1978, p. 117; Elkhana 1974, p. 178); Kuhn himself skittishly notes that "the early exponents of energy conservation could occasionally read each other's works without quite recognizing that they were talking about the same thing" (Kuhn, in Clagett 1959, p. 334, fn).

Just as the horses approach the finish line, the finish line dissolves into the mist? This is exceedingly strange, not at all what one expects from the history of a science. Or is it? Let us delve further into this curious turn of events.

Mayer

Julius Robert Mayer is frequently credited with making the first coherent statement of the principle of the conservation of energy, although usually grudgingly so. The credit is awarded for the earliest publication of a quantitative estimate of the mechanical equivalent of heat and a sketchy discussion of some of its consequences. The credit is grudging because Mayer was an outsider – not a physicist, not recognized by other natural scientists – and because he did not pursue his thesis by means of the then-sanctioned procedures of scientific research. If this were a romantic narrative, the temptation would be to portray him as the plucky rebel or underdog, ahead of his time and facing discouraging odds. If it were true it would be a good moral tale; but the ratification of a scientific discovery rarely assumes the format of such uplifting parables because it is, of necessity, a complex social phenomenon (Brannigan 1981). Certainly in Mayer's case the final curtain was not brought down upon cheering crowds and a cathartic vindication.

Mayer was trained as a physician at Tubingen in the 1830s. Characteristically, he eschewed a conventional career and signed on as a ship's doctor aboard a Dutch vessel trading with the East Indies. According to his own account, his discovery was prompted by an observation in East Java in July 1840 that upon letting the blood of a few of the sailors, he noticed that it was of a much brighter hue than he would have expected. He eventually decided that the explanation must be that the tropical environment was less taxing upon the maintenance of the internal heat of the body; therefore, less of the food intake was oxidized, and the blood returning from the limbs was a brighter red (Lindsay 1973, pp. 125–7). Next Mayer made the inductive leap that there should be a constant relationship between heat and work. His first expression of that conviction, in a paper of 1841, was extremely inept and innocent of existing physical theory; it was rejected out of hand by one of the leading journals of the day, *Poggendorf's Annalen.*

With a little help from his friend Carl Baur, Mayer drafted another article in September 1841, and was able to get it published in Liebig's *Annalen der Chemie und Pharmacie* in 1842. This is the paper that is Mayer's claim to fame and as such, it is a curious performance. He began it by asserting that forces (or *Kraft* in the original German) are causes, and since causes must equal effects, forces must be quantitatively indestructable, although they may undergo qualitative transformation. He then wrote, "No account can be given of the disappearance of motion without the recognition of a causal connection between motion and heat . . . Water when shaken violently experiences a rise in temperature as the author found" (in Lindsay 1973, p. 71). The experiment there indicated was not taken seriously enough to warrant any further description. From considerations such as, "the steam engine serves to transform heat into motion and the raising of weights," Mayer deduces that he must relate a fixed quantum of heat to the distance a fixed weight could be lifted above the earth. Very abruptly, and with little further in the way of explanation, Mayer concludes the paper thus:

> We find the decrease in the height of a mercury column compressing a gas equivalent to the quantity of heat associated with the

> compression. If we put the ratio of the specific heat capacities of the gas at constant pressure and constant volume respectively equal to 1.421, it turns out that the fall of a weight from a height of about 365 meters corresponds to the heating of an equal mass of water from 0° to 1°C. Comparing this result to the efficiency of our best steam engines, we see what a small part of the heat transferred to the boiler is really transformed into motion [in Lindsay 1973, pp. 73–4]

Not only was this paper buried in a pharmacology journal, but even the sympathetic reader would have a hard time deciphering where Mayer got his numbers from, since he does not report how the calculation was made. In retrospect, we can more or less reconstruct the procedure. The work done is the compression of the gas in the column. In modern notation, it is $P\Delta V$, where P is the pressure and V is the volume of the gas. For an ideal gas, these terms must conform to the relationship $PV = RT$, where R is a constant parameter (the gas constant) and T is the temperature. Now, the reason that the specific heat of a gas at constant pressure (s_p) is greater than the specific heat of the same gas at constant volume (s_v) is because work (i.e., expansion) occurs in the former case, but not in the latter, because $\Delta V = 0$. Mayer decided that this meant that the difference between the specific heats was fully converted into work. Therefore, the mechanical equivalent of heat would be given by

$$\frac{PV/T}{s_p - s_v} = \frac{R}{s_p - s_v}$$

If this calculation had been made explicit, its readers might have noticed a particularly strong assumption hidden in the algebra, namely, that the internal state of the gas is not altered by these changes (Hutchison 1976). In essence, Mayer's hypothesis was restricted to situations where heat changes are only expressed as external mechanical work. Hence, the claim that this paper discussed the conservation of *energy* is somewhat misleading. At a minimum, experimental support for a mechanical equivalent of heat energy should have included some auxiliary argument that other effects could be isolated, or that they could be abstracted away. Nevertheless, most of these objections are beside the point, since it is clear that Mayer's paper was never intended to be the painstaking chronicle of a deliberate empirical research program.

In 1845, Mayer published a long pamphlet at his own expense extending these considerations to electricity, chemical reactions, and organic metabolic phenomena. This pamphlet was more explicit on the source of the above calculations, but contained little else that was novel. In the meantime, Mayer assumed a medical practice in Heil-bronn, and was thoroughly ignored by the scientific community. In the interim, James Joule had published his first estimates of the mechanical equivalent of heat in 1843 in Britain. Some jockeying for claim to priority of discovery of the mechanical equivalent began to develop in the late 1840s, and as a result Mayer was subjected to some vilification by the British scientific community. For reasons that are still not entirely clear, Mayer entered a mental sanitorium in 1851, where he stayed until 1853. There is a story that Liebig announced in a lecture of 1858 that Mayer had died ignominiously in a mental asylum due to the vilification, and when Mayer protested to Liebig that such eulogies were premature he was ignored.

It is hard not to portray Mayer as a pitiable underdog, given that he had to suffer slights from Joule and Helmholtz, as well as from lesser mortals. However, such an opinion could only be justified if it is taken for granted that there was a single idea, which is to be credited to the deserving party. It is true that one can find an estimate of the me-chanical equivalent of heat in Mayer's papers, but his true proclivities are better characterized by statements like: "According to current estimates the power production of a strong working man is one-seventh that of a horse" (Lindsay 1973, p. 104); or, "Muscles which through whatever circumstances remain for some long period incap-able of service degenerate into a bloodless mass. With wise economy Nature follows the fundamental principle: whoever does not work shall not eat" (Lindsay 1973, p. 132). Mayer was not discriminating in his employment of the term *Kraft;* the use of this term rapidly became one of the flashpoints in the dispute over what it was precisely that had been discovered. Mayer did not commit himself to a particular theory of heat; nor did he perceive the potential mathematical or empirical research that his conception made possible. He was a man with a single idea, and that idea was the qualitative reduction of organic phenomena to inanimate physics, in order to dispel the "in-scrutable" and "hypothetical" character of vital forces. He could not express his reductionist program mathematically, and this was his fatal flaw. In a very real sense, it was the mathematics that lay waiting to be discovered. Yet, on the other hand, it was not solely the mathematics that eventually constituted the energy concept. Mayer's equation of the vital force of the body with natural force and his insistence that causes must equal effects were both important com-ponents of what eventually emerged as "energy."

Joule

The second member of the favored four, James Prescott Joule, is remembered much more favorably, at least in Anglo-Saxon quarters. Joule was the son of a wealthy brewer in Manchester, and an example of that particularly nineteenth-century English phenomenon, the gentleman amateur scientist. His experiments, carried out after his day working at the brewery, began as a search for the appropriate principles of the construction of an electromagnetic engine that would rival steam engines with respect to commercial efficiency. By 1841, he realized that the inherent limitations of the motor would not allow it to outperform the steam engine; this prompted him to consider the interrelationships between heat and electricity. His inquiry was also guided by a hostility to the then-popular caloric theory of heat. Since he was convinced that there was a fundamental connection between quantities of electricity and the mechanical lifting of weights, and likewise a stable relationship between electricity and heat, it may have seemed a likely step to impose transitivity and postulate a mechanical equivalent of heat.

His first paper on this question was read to the meeting of the British Association for the Advancement of Science in August 1843 (Steffens 1979, p. 40). In what was to become a trademark of Joule's work, much of the paper was a lovingly detailed description of a baroque experimental apparatus, adjusted to accommodate a great number of contingent objections. The main objective of the paper was to take a highly unpopular stand against the conservation of caloric: "We have therefore, in magneto-electricity an agent capable by simple mechanical means of destroying or generating heat." For someone so keen to take the measure of Nature, it is to Joule's credit that he realized: If caloric is not conserved, then something else must be fixed theoretically for the purposes of measurement. His choice was to opt for a mechanical equivalent of heat, whose magnitude he then attempted to determine in sixty-five separate trials. His results varied between the raising of a weight of 587 English pounds and a weight of 1040 English pounds one perpendicular foot (Steffens 1979, p. 43). These were hardly a range of "equivalents" destined to inspire confidence, but Joule, being the sort of fellow he was, interpreted the wide differences as due to flaws and imperfections in his apparatus. The scientific community, with some justification, ignored his paper.

In 1844 and 1845, Joule set himself the task of developing more novel and precise ways of measuring the mechanical equivalent, the most renouned of which is his famous paddle-wheel experiment. In retrospect, the paddle-wheel device was the complex realization of

Mayer's rather cavalier assertion that the agitation of water would raise its temperature. Joule's device was designed to foil water from adopting a smooth path of translational rotation, as can be observed from its schematic drawing in Figure 2.2.

Weights attached to the pulleys rotated the axis through a fixed distance, and a thermometer of great precision was immersed in the water. Joule himself stood behind a wooden screen to prevent his own body heat from influencing the apparatus. In his report of this brace of experiments, Joule expressed the opinion that the new result – a

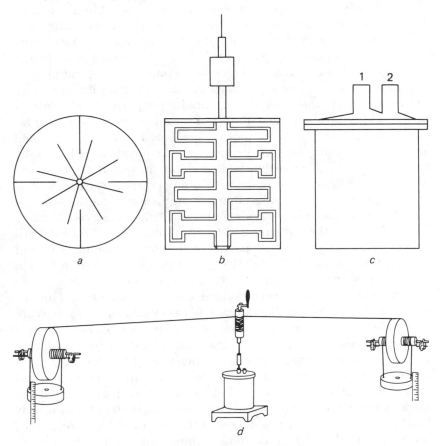

FIGURE 2.2   (a) Top view diagram of the arms and vanes of Joule's paddle wheel apparatus. (b) Side view diagram of the apparatus. (c) Container for paddle wheel apparatus: Hole (1) is for axis of rotation; hole (2) is for the thermometer. (d) General illustration of Joule's paddle wheel apparatus. (Reproduced with the permission of Henry Steffens)

weight of 890 pounds through one foot – was still too high for his tastes, so he decided to average this report with an assortment of estimates from other experiments (Steffens 1979, p. 93).

The indeterminacy that plagued Joule's estimates of the mechanical equivalent of heat throughout the 1840s is worth highlighting for three reasons. First, it goes a long way to explain why a rational member of the natural-science community of the 1840s might feel justified in ignoring Joule's work. Second, it should serve to undermine the conventional wisdom that Joule's genius was the possession of homely yet acute powers of observation that led him to empirically discover the conservation of energy. Third, it should raise some doubts about the very meaning of the term "discovery" in the context of the conservation of energy, not to mention the ontological identity of the quest. Joule, this most ingenious wizard of the experimental apparatus, could not produce a set of numerical results that were clustered in such a manner that it would seem reasonable to infer a stable coefficient of conversion of heat into mechanical work. By his own account, there were a plethora of auxiliary hypotheses that could impugn his measurement of the mechanical equivalent. If his single-minded theoretical conviction had been absent, would not his quest for finer and finer measurements of temperature, pressure, and so on have seemed monomaniacal and monumentally misguided?

Conservation principles are devilishly difficult to discover. Nothing bears witness to this fact more eloquently than Joule's own experiences in the course of his purported "discovery." Some historians of science, for example Elkhana (1974, p. 184), take pains to insist that Joule does not deserve credit for the discovery of the conservation of energy, since all that he ever claimed was that some vague "forces" were able to be converted into heat. He never said that all forces are essentially differing manifestations of the same ontological "thing"; nor did he claim that the sum of suitably converted forces was equal to a constant in any system, closed or otherwise. The modern reader naturally finds this hard to swallow: How could Joule not understand the necessity of a closed system when he went to such great lengths to shield his apparatus from all outside influences, such as his own body heat? How could he not postulate that the energy in his system was a constant, for otherwise would not the thing that was the object of his persistent measurement attempts fluctuate wildly between experimental situations? The answer seems to be that Joule harbored a cacodemon that chanted "heat is motion;" and the rest is explained by Joule's single-minded devotion to the measurement of a simple fixed equivalent, irrespective of the fact that his wildly differing estimates could have been explained within the ambit of the existing caloric theory. As late as 1847, it seemed that no one else was convinced by Joule's demon. It is conceivable that he could have met the same ignoble fate as Mayer (Steffens 1979, pp. 100–1). Joule's scientific reputation was rescued, however, by a fortuitous encounter with William Thomson (later Lord Kelvin) at the 1847 meetings of the British Association.

At those meetings, Joule gave a brief presentation on a (further!) "improved" version of the paddle-wheel experiments, because he was denied an opportunity to read an entire paper to the section. Thomson was disturbed by Joule's report precisely because the claim that heat was generated by mechanical processes clashed directly with the doctrine Thomson had imbibed from Carnot that "heat is a *substance*, invariable in quantity, not convertible into any other element, and incapable of being *generated* by any physical agency" (quoted in Steffens 1979, p. 108). Thomson had already published mathematical studies of heat based upon Carnot's principle, and perhaps because Joule's results contradicted their premises, Thomson initiated a correspondence with Joule. It was Thomson's at first qualified and later strongly favorable citations of Joule's work in his own mathematical reinterpretations that led to Joule's vindication after 1850; but it was also through the instrumentality of these mathematical renditions that larger issues of loss, gain, and constancy were broached. The culmination of these developments was the eventual statement of the first *two* laws of thermodynamics, a topic to which we shall shortly return.

Helmholtz

The third "discoverer" in the favored four is the most significant claimant to the title, and yet, strangely enough, is the least well understood of the four. Hermann von Helmholtz is the towering nineteenth-century figure of physical theory, physiology, optics, acoustics, and the philosophy of mathematics. His eminence is ill served by the fact that he has only one serious biography, now rather dated (Koenigsberger 1965). It is to Helmholtz more than to any of the others that we owe the modern conception of the conservation of energy, although the reader should be forewarned that even in this instance Helmholtz's conception is not fully identical with the modern notion. Helmholtz's preeminence is due to the fact that he, more than any other scientist, pointed the way to a unified science of physics that was larger than rational mechanics, celestial mechanics, and the study of the phenomena of heat and electricity and light, and yet managed ultimately to encompass all of them under a single principle.

The imposition of a unifying principle for all of physics sounds much more like a conceptual or a priori innovation than a discovery, and there is much to be said in support of this view in the case of Helmholtz. By his own admission (Helmholtz 1971, p. 49), he was very much under the influence of the Kantian a priori when he wrote the 1847 memoir "Uber die Erhaltung der Kraft." Many are familiar with the project of Kantian philosophy as the elaboration of the transcendental or a priori categories that provide the cognitive framework within which we structure our experience and knowledge; but it is less well known that Kant explicitly tried to reconstitute the foundations of the physical theory of his day by building bridges between Newtonian and Leibnizian theories of substance and force (Harman 1982b). A good short summary is found in Heimann (1974, p. 220, fn):

> Kant argues that phenomenal changes were manifested as actions:"action signifies the relation of the subject of causality to its effect," and the succession of appearance is manifested as forces, for "causality leads to the concept of action, [and] this in turn to the concept of force." Kant thereupon claims that this presupposes the performance of substance, stating that "whenever there is action – and therefore activity and force – there is substance, and it is in substance alone that the seat of this fruitful source of appearance must be sought." The manifestation of forces, that is, the phenomenal appearance of changes, presupposes an "ultimate subject which is the substratum of everything that changes," and this is "the *permanent*, that is, substance," for actions themselves cannot be found in a subject which itself changes.

The problem of the conceptual necessity of constancy for the comprehension of change certainly did not originate with Kant.[5] Nonetheless, it was under the influence of Kant that explicit consideration of the interaction of substance and force as epistemological categories entered the physical theory of conservation principles. Nowhere can this be observed more strikingly than in the introductory remarks to the *Erhaltung der Kraft:*

> We are compelled to and justified in this undertaking by the fundamental principle that every change in nature must have a sufficient cause. The proximate causes, to which we refer natural phenomena, are themselves either variable or invariable; in the latter case, the same fundamental principle compels us to seek further for the causes of variation and so on, until we arrive finally at the causes which operate according to invariable law and which consequently

produce under the same external conditions the same effect every time. Thus the final goal of the theoretical natural sciences is to discover the ultimate invariable causes of natural phenomena. Whether all processes may actually be traced back to such causes, in which case nature is completely comprehensible, or whether on the contrary there are changes which lie outside the law of necessary causality and thus fall within the regions of spontaneity or freedom, will not be considered here" [Helmholtz 1971, p. 4].

Helmholtz then asserted that all science is premised upon two abstractions: that of *matter,* which is "inert and without effect; the only qualities we distinguish in it are spatial distinctions and quantity (mass)," and *forces,* which are "the qualitative differences of the effects of matter." Since matter itself can purportedly undergo no change other than spatial movement, "natural phenomena should be traced back to the movements of material objects which possess unalterable motive forces that are dependent only on spatial relations" (Helmholtz 1971, p. 5). On a superficial reading, it would appear we are no further along with this than with Descartes's reduction of all phenomena to matter in motion. However, the key differentiation here was the slow transmutation of the concept of *Kraft,* or force, from a general and quite vague synonym for "activity" into a Kantian substance; a process that was only completed a decade later with the meiosis of the concept into a more substancelike "energy" and a more characteristically active "force."

If this were the sum total of Helmholtz's accomplishment, it would not have sufficient to differentiate him from many of the nature philosophers of the mid-nineteenth century. Although few of the *Naturphilosophen* would have found the reduction of all qualities to matter in motion congenial, the search for an *Urkraft* or proto-force was quite common, especially in Germany (Gower 1973). Helmholtz's innovation was to start with the constancy of *Kraft* in a mathematical sense (Harman 1982b, p. 125, fn 15), to combine it with the Lagrangian tradition of rational mechanics, and then to formally extend the mathematics of the variational principle to heat and electromagnetism. Experimental natural scientists initially regarded Helmholtz's method as just another ploy of speculative metaphysics, strongly redolent of the a priori (Koenigsberger 1965, p. 43). It was due as much to this skepticism as to its curious novelty that Helmholtz's memoir was rejected at Poggendorf's *Annalen,* and he had finally to publish the essay at his own expense.

The structure of the main text of *Der Erhaltung der Kraft* is built up from a base of familiar mechanical concepts toward more tenuous ideas concerning heat, electricity, and magnetism. The first section on

The Principle of the Conservation of Vis Viva begins without apology "with the assumption that it is impossible by any combination whatsoever of natural bodies, to create force continually out of nothing" (Helmholtz 1971, p. 6). He proceeds to assert that the impossibility of a perpetuum mobile is expressed mathematically as the conservation of *vis viva,* and then associates this with the Newtonian central force laws. Next follows the actual principle of the *Erhaltung der Kraft,* which is phrased as, "Whenever bodies act upon one another by forces of attraction and repulsion which are independent of time and velocity, the sum of their vires vivae and tensional forces *(Spannkrafte)* must be constant. The maximum quantity of work which can be obtained from them is therefore fixed and finite" (Helmholtz 1971, p. 15). The mathematics, minus the vector formalism, are essentially identical to the example developed above in the section on variational principles.

Helmholtz correctly identified *vis viva* with the quantity one half mv^2, and defined "tensional forces" as those which "tend to move the point m before the motion has actually taken place"; this more or less corresponds to what is now called the potential. Curiously enough, there is no explicit citation of the Lagrangian/Hamiltonian variational principles, or any constrained extrema, in the original 1847 memoir. In the early stage of his career, it seems that Helmholtz believed that the constancy of the Kantian substance contained the essence of the principle of causality; it was only later in his life that conservation principles became subordinate to variational principles.

Helmholtz's mathematical acuity did lead him to make the further observation, which is not found in the work of any of the other progenitors of the conservation of energy, that this principle can be expressed in seemingly different yet fundamentally isomorphic ways: the impossibility of perpetual motion is the "same" as the conservation of *vis viva;* the postulate of the independence of the force laws from time and velocity is the "same" as the postulate that the sum of *vis viva* and tensional forces is equal to a constant. This habit of spying the "real" unity hidden in phenomenal diversity is a preternatural trait of the mathematical mind. Helmholtz elevated this inclination to a heuristic principle for all natural science by revealing how form (i.e., the mathematical contrivance) mirrored content (*Kraft* as protean substance). This invocation of isomorphism as the fundamental structure of the world (or at least of our thought about the world— Helmholtz straddled the fence on this issue) became the font from which fruitful suggestions for further research flowed, much more so than from the limited achievements of Mayer, Joule, or Colding. To a

mathematically inclined mind, the assertion that *Kraft* was reducable
to mechanics suggested mathematical analogies among a whole range
of physical phenomena.

Take, for instance, the work integral, the summation of force
components times the infinitesimal displacements of a mass point,
$\int F\ ds$. If all energetic phenomena are now pronounced to be seemingly different manifestations of the same fundamental forces, should it
not follow that all phenomena should be amenable to mathematical
description in the same format? For instance, would it not be possible
to express the work done by the expansion of gases as the integral of
the pressure times the infinitesimal displacements of volume, $\int P\ dV$?
Or, analogously, to express the work done in an electric circuit by the
integral of the force (in volts) to move a charge (in coulombs) from a
point of lower to higher potential, $\int v\ dc$? Or, to broach an analogy
constructed after the implications of the 1847 memoir were sufficiently digested, to portray the work done by heat in a reversible
cycle as the integral of temperature times the infinitesimal change in
thermal efficiency (measured as entropy), $\int T\ dS$? These were the sorts
of analogies suggested by Helmholtz's memoir. The Kantian moral of
the principle of energy conservation is the reduction of all diversity to
homogeneity.

With hindsight we see this all clearly, but it was hardly transparent
in the 1840s. Helmholtz and most everyone else in that period failed
to conceptually quarantine the capacity factor and the quantity of
work (say, the F from the $\int F\ ds$); hence the terms *Kraft* and "force"
were used to refer to diverse and sometimes contradictory notions
(Elkhana 1970). But far from being a handicap, this laxity probably
encouraged the "simultaneous discovery" of the energy concept. The
myriad uses of the term "force" in Western European languages
combined a formidable set of connotations and concerns under one
umbrella word.

Helmholtz's own background, like that of Mayer, was as a physician
with a hostility to the school of vitalism in physiology. Maintaining
that living organic processes could not be adequately explained by the
ordinary laws of physics and chemisty, vitalists sought to develop an
explanation of animal heat. Ironically, the "vital force" of the vitalists
and the *Kraft* of Helmholtz were similar enough that the former
undoubtedly provoked the latter. Force in Newtonian mechanics had
one meaning; Helmholtz believed he could reconcile the Newtonian
and Leibnizian/Lagrangian traditions with his new principle. Force
meant something else in Kantian philosophy; this, too, provided some
of the charm of the new principle. Finally, there was the connotation

of force as efficaciousness of soul or spirit; we shall discover this plays an important role later in our narrative. Everywhere one turned in the later nineteenth century, one encountered "forces" and was swept up in their fervor. Helmholtz himself provides a description of the atmosphere:

> "[T]here happened what so often happens when a fertile new discovery is made, making possible a whole group of previously impossible things. People's enthusiasm led them overboard. They hoped that everything which had been impossible before would now be possible [Helmholtz 1887, p. 288].

As Helmholtz aged and observed the further development of the energy concept, he came to reevaluate the meaning and significance of the conservation of energy. These second thoughts were prompted by developments in abstract algebra (cf. Helmholtz 1977, pp. 90–1), as well as the new theories of thermodynamics and electrodynamics, which did employ the energy concept but simultaneously appeared to be undermining the program of the reduction of those phenomena to mechanics. In the 1880s he increasingly adopted the attitude that the unifying principle of physics was not the conservation of energy, but rather the principle of least action. Under the banner of variational principles, first one, and then another subset of physical phenomena were encompassed with mathematical formalization. But concomitant with the successes, the meaning and significance of the energy concept grew more obscure and abstruse. Helmholtz's longevity allowed him to be both progenitor and transitional figure in the history of energy conservation, in reaction to this trend. His lectures in the 1880s on the history of the principle of least action (which, incidentally, are not included in the German edition of his collected scientific papers) reveal him in cautious retreat from the conception of energy as a mechanistic substance (Helmholtz 1887, p. 287):

> The condition is of great importance for the fundamental questions of knowledge, of actual and legitimate natural philosophy (as the physics of the English is still called), that with regard to the two most universal laws – those of the *constancy* of energy and the principle of least action – it is more a question of energy *states* than of quantitative magnitudes which determine the evolution of natural processes; it is no longer simply a question of the reduction of a force to its mechanical components, which now appear only as calculated derivative values. All that occurs is described by the ebb and flow of the eternally indestructable and unaugmentable energy supply of the world, and the laws of this ebb and flow are completely comprehended through the principle of least action.[6]

Thus, over the course of his scientific career, Helmholtz changed his estimation of his own greatest achievement, a fact that has not received much attention from historians of physics. Conservation principles first arose apart from variational principles, yet later variational principles appeared to subsume (or at least imply) conservation principles, raising the question whether the two are not really differing sides of the same coin. Energy, first intended to reduce all life to mechanism, later seemed to undermine the existence of an independent inert matter (Wise, in Cantor and Hodge 1981, p. 298). These and other aspects of the shifting character of the energy concept within his own lifetime should provoke doubt as to whether Helmholtz really discovered any one "thing."

Colding

The fourth and final member of the favored four will not detain us long, because he had the unfortunate fate to be a little too late, a little too prosaic, a little to idiosyncratic, and the extreme bad luck to write in Danish. Ludwig August Colding was a student of the physicist and nature philosopher Oersted, who later became civil engineer of the city of Copenhagen. Colding conceived of a "principle of the perpetuity of force" in 1840, but was persuaded to postpone an enunciation of the principle until he had produced some empirical support. His experiments concerning the heat generated by the friction of the rails of a brass sled upon variously constituted tracks were reported to the Royal Danish Society of Sciences in late 1843, but the paper was refused publication in the Society's *Transactions*.

Unlike Joule, Colding was not an experimentalist by temperament, and so most of his subsequent papers attempt to justify his principle by insisting that the forces of nature must be immaterial, and therefore spiritual. As he later wrote, "it was the religious perception of life which led me to the idea . . . In this way I became convinced that as it is true that the human intellect is immortal, so it must be a general law of nature that the forces of nature must be imperishable" (quoted in Dahl 1963, p. 183). Still, the closest similarity was to Joule, with an experimental determination of the mechanical equivalent of heat to his credit. Colding's subsequent acquaintance with the more widely disseminated results of Mayer, Joule, and Helmholtz appears to have stifled rather than encouraged further inquiry on his part. Thus Colding is relegated to the footnotes of the history of physics.

What was discovered?

In the best traditions of classical drama, one should now expect that two millennia of anticipations of "energy" finally culminated in a joyous chorus of discovery of the true entity and we, the grateful audience, can relax and thoroughly enjoy the catharsis of the full fruition of physical theory. Life rarely imitates successful art, however; our constructions of events never completely succeed in pinning reality down like dead butterflies in a glass case. Our favored four themselves stumbled upon this difficulty. No sooner had they written their works than they began falling upon one another and upon subsequent challengers in a feud over priority as to the discovery of the novel entity, not to mention a rearguard action to maintain their own constructions of what had been discovered. These two problems, that of the phenomenon of simultaneous discovery and of the purported continuity of tradition within an intellectual discipline, will occupy our attention in the later context of the history of economics, and so it may be worthwhile to linger a bit longer in bringing things into focus.

The assertion of the "discovery" of the conservation of energy actually conflates four distinct ideas: (1) the formation of a concept of energy; (2) an ontological claim that there was an energy "out there" and "in here" waiting to be found; (3) the mathematical statement that this energy is neither created nor destroyed; and (4) some procedure of justification for ideas (2) and (3). The incongruity of claiming a simultaneous discovery of energy conservation in the 1840s is that each individual so far identified only achieved a subset of the above conditions, and *no individual succeeded in implementing them all.* Colding and Joule really only managed to suggest (3) and make a very inadequate stab at (4). It seems somewhat groundless to maintain that force is conserved when one really has no clear idea what force consists of; and yet, that is what Joule and Colding (and scores of others who were influenced by nineteenth-century philosophical currents) did. The thing that set Joule and Colding apart was their experimental program to measure the mechanical equivalent of heat, but the mechanical equivalent of heat is not isomorphic to the conservation of energy: The latter is independent of any particular theory of the nature of heat. This fact is tellingly illustrated by the anomaly that Mayer denied that the kinetic theory of heat was necessary for his thesis. Probably the major reason Joule gets any credit for the conservation of energy is that William Thomson's later mathematical elaborations of Joule's work provided some of the missing conceptual components.

Mayer and Helmholtz are the more interesting cases. Mayer thought of force as a substancelike but nonmaterial entity that was conserved in a manner analogous to the conservation of matter. Essentially this achieved points (2) and (3). Mayer did also provide an estimate of the mechanical equivalent, but did not prosecute this research program as a justification of (2) and (3). Instead, he argued that the quantitative equality of causes and effects implied the ontological necessity of something that persisted and endured. In other words, his only contribution to concept (4) was this broad metaphysical pronouncement. His lack of facility with mathematics prevented any further elaboration of this doctrine.

Helmholtz qualifies as the greatest integrator of the various components of the conservation of energy. He clearly provided the rudiments of theses (2), (3), and (4). It should be stressed, however, that his justification procedure was not experimental by any stretch of the imagination; it was instead the provision of *mathematical analogies* between various physical phenomena and the abstract *vis viva* and "tensional forces." (Parenthetically, this was also the forte of William Thomson. See Wise [1979].) These mathematical analogies were coupled with Kantian ontological considerations which dominated those argued by Mayer. Yet, even in acknowledgment of this tour de force, his was not really a sufficiently comprehensive characterization of the conservation of energy.

First, as has been observed by many historians of physics (Elkhana 1970; 1974), the concept of energy itself was still in a confused state: force had to be differentiated from energy, substance notions differentiated from those of action. Even more significantly, as we shall shortly argue, there were three further clarifications of the energy concept that nearly immediately thrust physics into disarray: the problem of irreversibility, the problem of mechanical reductionism, and the rise of the concept of the field. In a very fundamental sense, Helmholtz never clarified the concept of energy itself, thus rendering any claim that he was responsible for its discovery dubious.

Second, one should note the inherent contradiction between points (2) and (4) in Helmholtz's research program. He truly believed that energy was "in here," waiting to be discovered; but as one of the premier German experimental physicists and physiologists of the nineteenth century (Jungnickel and McCormmach 1986, I, pp. 304–10), he never provided any experimental evidence for that claim. (Recall that Joule's results were neither satisfactory nor sufficient.) Perhaps this was prescient on his part, because if we seek the empirical discoverer of our modern conception of the conservation of ener-

gy in the nineteenth century, we shall never find him. We now believe
that there are many more energetic phenomena than were known in
the mid-nineteenth century; hence, in that era there were just too
many ways energy could get lost. To put it bluntly: If physics is now
right, then the energy accounts should not have summed to equality
back then.

Some of those who do not now get credit for the "discovery"
understood this principle quite early on . W. R. Grove, in a lecture in
1842, had already claimed that:

> each force is definitely and equivalently convertible into any other,
> and that where experiment does not give the full equivalent, it is
> because the initial force has been dissipated, not lost, by conversion
> into other [N.B.] unrecognized forces. The equivalent is the limit
> never practically reached [in Youmans 1868, p. 189].

What a curious phenomenon is this "conservation of energy"!
There seem to be a slew of discoverers, but no single actual discovery.
There were endemic battles for priority over a concept that was as
elastic and protean as the onotological object that it was intended to
signify. Perhaps it was not a matter of discovery in the conventional
sense at all. Instead, there are signs that the energy concept was closer
to a heuristic principle of organization rather than an entity per se,
which goes a long way in explaining why Helmholtz is considered the
most respected "discoverer." One might suggest that Helmholtz pre-
sided over the wedding ceremony of the variational principle and the
conservation principle, which marks the beginning of the energy
revolution in physics.

We might view the a posteriori reification of the "discovery" as
primarily a social process, where the award of priority is part and
parcel of the construction and institutionalization of the theoretical
object, a process of negotiation and assimilation of novelty (Brannigan 1981). In this particular case, there were literally dozens of
people in the nineteenth century who insisted in one form or another
that the world was really One, that there was no free lunch, that life
and force were identical, and that protean interchangeable and in-
terconvertable natural forces governed the world. There were even
quite a few who insisted that heat was mechanical work, hardly an
earthshaking notion when one recalls that railways and steamships
were becoming commonplace. "Energy" progressively came to signify
a diverse set of concepts, and that precisely was the point: As the
diverse bundle was consolidated, it had to be reified into a single
"thing." Alas, historically there was no single architect or discoverer of
this protean concept.

The energetics movement

The problem faced by physics after Helmholtz was to stabilize the interpretation of the ontology of energy, as well as its terminology. The fixation of the terminology was achieved in the 1850s, being principally the handiwork of the Scot William Macquorn Rankine; ironically, he was also the first to seriously destabilize the ontology. Rankine differentiated the primal concept into its now-familiar sub-components of potential, force, and state, and was as well the first to correctly use the terminology of energy from the modern point of view:

> In this investigation the term *energy* is used to comprehend every affection of substances which constitutes or is commensurable with a power of producing change in opposition to resistance, and includes ordinary motion and mechanical power, chemical action, heat, light, electricity, magnetism and all other powers, known or unknown, which are convertable or commensurable with these. All conceivable forms of energy may be distinguished into two kinds; actual or sensible, and potential or latent. *Actual energy* is a measurable, transferable and transformable affection of a substance, the presence of which causes the substance to change its state in one or more respects; by the occurence of which changes, actual energy disappears, and is replaced by *potential energy* . . . The law of the conservation of energy is already known, viz., that the sum of the actual and potential energies in the universe is unchangeable [Rankine 1853, in Lindsay 1976, p. 96].

Rankine did not rest content with cleaning up the terminological confusions left by Helmholtz and others. He too had high hopes for "energy" as an all-encompassing principle to reform the method and the content of science. To that end, in 1855 he proposed to found a new science of "energetics." His paper began with a philosophical preface that divided physics into those theories that had direct connection with sense data and those that dealt in terms of hypothetical conjectures, either because the conjectures had a high probability of being linked to sense data or else merely because the conjectures were convenient. Mechanics, said Rankine, was clearly a theory in the former category. But the success of mechanics had seduced those impressed with its efficacy, enticing them to import mechanical hypotheses into other branches of physics; this assumed the format of inventing conjectural "motions" in the explanations of heat, light, and so on – motions (he implied) that would never be accessible to sense confirmation. "Instead of supposing the various classes of physical phenomena to be constituted, in an occult way, of modifications of motion and force, let us distinguish the properties which those classes possess in common with each other, and so define more extensive classes denoted by suitable terms" (Rankine 1881, p. 213).

The body of the paper developed taxonomies for the variable and invariant properties of a generalized transformation based upon energetic considerations, without any commitment to the branch of physics being discussed. The modern reader of the paper is struck by the similarities between Rankine's general schema and the fundamental priniciples of abstract algebra, which also discuss regularities of operations without any commitment to the nature of the objects discussed. One is also struck by Rankine's unusual flirtation with what would later have been called "instrumentalist" attitudes:

> One of the chief objects of mathematical physics is to ascertain, by the help of experiment and observations, what physical quantities or functions are "conserved" . . . In defining such physical quantities as those, it is almost, if not quite, impossible to avoid making the definition imply the property of conservation, so that when the fact of conservation is stated, it has the sound of a truism" (in Moyer 1977, p. 254).

Nineteenth-century readers, on the contrary, caught a whiff of the corruption of the ideal of the reduction of all the rest of natural philosophy to mechanics. Rankine was personally noncommittal, stating merely that mechanistic hypotheses were useful in the early stages of a science. Others were not so circumspect. Even during his lifetime, there was a push to revise Helmholtz's program of reductionism, to reduce a dualistic world consisting of matter and energy to a unified world consisting only of energy.

The involution of mechanical reductionism did not happen all at once. Rankine's conception was largely introduced into the textbook literature with Thomson and Tait's *Treatise on Natural Philosophy* of 1867 (Moyer 1977), and was given its biggest boost on the continent in 1887, when a schoolteacher named Georg Helm published a book reiterating Rankine's claim to have reduced all of physics to a single pattern of energetics, and linking that program to Ernst Mach's positivism and to hostility toward atomism in physical explanations (Helm 1887). Helm's credentials and rhetorical style probably would not have attracted the attention of the German scientific community, had he not been adopted and championed by Friedrich Wilhelm Ostwald, the premier physical chemist of fin de siècle Germany. Ostwald was later to win the Nobel prize for his work in chemistry, but he was not of the sort of temperament to remain confined within any narrowly defined disciplinary boundaries.

In the early 1890s, Ostwald joined forces with Helm to argue that the only concepts that found application in all areas of the physical sciences were space, time, and energy. In Ostwald's view (certainly idiosyncratic for a nineteenth-century *chemist*), matter was "nothing but a spatially distinguishable composite sum of energy quantities," and therefore a derivative and superfluous notion. He proposed to found a new science of energetics upon the above three primitive concepts and two fundamental principles: the first, "a perpetual motion of the first kind is impossible"; and the second, "a perpetual motion of the second kind is impossible" (Ostwald 1892, translated in Lindsay 1976, pp. 339–41). The first principle was a restatement of the notion that energy may be neither created nor destroyed, and as such was only a rephrasing of the by-then uncontroversial law of the conservation of energy. The second principle stated that even where the sum total of energy was fixed, energy could not flow endlessly among its various configurations and manifestations. Armed with these parsimonious principles, as well as with Rankine and Helm's distinction between capacity factors and intensity factors, Ostwald believed one would eventually be able to deduce the whole of physical theory.

By the early 1890s, it appeared as if the energetics program might just hold the key to the unification of all science. Ostwald championed the work of physicists such as J. Willard Gibbs, whose phenomenological approach to thermodynamics was said to exemplify the future of mathematical energetics. In Germany, at least a dozen authors had published treatises dealing with various aspects of physics from an energetics standpoint. The work of Le Châtelier and Pierre Duhem were regarded as indications of a nascent French branch of energetics (Deltete 1983, p. 408). More significantly, energetics began to be applied in fields external to physics. There was Ostwald's work in physical chemistry; there were applications to physiological and botanical research; there were Helm's extensions of energetics to political economy; and there were Ostwald's bold attempts to extrapolate energetics into epistemology and even a solution to the problem of free will.[7] In some countries, an effusion of enthusiasm over the fruitfulness of the energy concept shaded over imperceptibly into something like energetics, the most notable example being England and Scotland in the era circa 1860–1890 (Deltete 1983, p. 165).

Because of the subsequent precipitous decline of the program in physics, it is important to keep in mind that energeticists at no time spoke in a single voice. Some, such as Gibbs, never publicly allowed themselves to be associated with the movement. Others, such as Max

Planck, were regarded as energeticists by outsiders until they publicly rebuked the program in the mid-1890s. And then, the two putative leaders of the program in Germany had very dissimilar stances on almost every aspect of energy. Ostwald, while enjoying the greatest fame and visibility, was unquestionably the least able of all of the expositors of energetics. His mathematical abilities were severely limited (Deltete 1983, pp. 386–7); he wrote as though all irreversible physical phenomena (explained in the next section below) could be analytically interpreted as if they were composed of reversible phenomena; and he misunderstood the most basic attributes of the energy concept, namely, that energy must be a variable of state. Max Planck tried to explain this to him in their correspondence over and over again, without success:

> [A]n energy is a quantity which depends only on the instantaneous state of the system, not on the manner in which the system reached this state or on the manner in which it later changes its state. The whole importance of the concept of energy rests on this property; without it the principle of the conservation of energy would be illusory [Planck, quoted in Deltete 1983, p. 526].

Ostwald's greatest error was to persistently conceptualize energy as if it were a literal substance, precisely when energy was being stripped of its substantial character by new developments in physics. Helm, on the other hand, was certainly less famous, but also more mathematically sophisticated, and hence less inclined to regard energy as an ontological substance:

> But the idea that a body's intrinsic energy is divided into special funds cannot, in general, be maintained . . . Our knowledge of the energy of a body is thus always represented only by differentials. About energy in general we know only that all of the energy changes, dE, of all the bodies entering into a reaction must vanish, a proposition already contained . . . only in the case of reversibility. Any integration of the differential equations which exists for reversible processes is correct only under certain conditions . . . According to this conception of energy transformation, energy exists in one of its forms only at the moment of its *transfer* from one internal energy to another [quoted in Deltete 1983, p. 620].

In 1895 the issue of whether energetics was capable of displacing the atomist perspective and restructuring physics came to a head in Germany. The central issue, admitted as such by both sides, was the question of whether formal analogies between various classes of energetic transformations were significant or superficial (Deltete 1983, pp. 52, 569). The turning point of the energetics movement is

usually dated from the Lübeck meeting of the German Society of
Scientists and Physicians in September of 1895 (Jungnickel and
McCormmach 1986, II, pp. 218–27; Hiebert 1971; Deltete 1983). In a
special symposium on the new energetics, Ostwald was violently
attacked by Ludwig Boltzmann and raked over the coals by Klein and
Nernst. After the meeting, the prestigious *Annalen der Physik* published an extended critique by Boltzmann, and more significantly, by
Max Planck. Both physicists derided errors in Ostwald's mathematics,
of which there were indeed many to choose from. In what Planck
considered to be the coup de grâce, he complained, "energetics
achieves the apparent and surprising simplicity of its proofs by the
simple process of pushing the content of the laws to be demonstrated
(which must always be known in advance) backward to their definitions" (Planck 1896, translated in Lindsay 1976, p. 361). We shall have
frequent occasion in the remainder of this book to meditate upon the
potential validity or invalidity of this complaint concerning energetics,
wherever it may be found.

Some modern historians of science appear to regard the phenomenon of energetics as an aberration on the part of an otherwise
eminent scientist, extinguished soon after it was ignited by the empirical demonstration of the reality of atoms (and hence matter) by Jean
Perrin, Ernest Rutherford, Frederick Soddy and J. J. Thomson in the
period 1902 to 1906 (Hiebert 1971; Pais 1982, pp. 82–6). It is true
that in 1909, the preface to the fourth edition of his textbook of
physical science, the *Grundriss der allgemeinen Chemie*, Ostwald did
recant on his denial of the existence of atoms. However, contrary to
the impression given by some historians, he never recanted his belief
in energetics, and in fact extended its purview in his later years to
encompass economics and social theory. To assert that energetics was
"falsified" by some *experimentum crucis* and then promptly withered
away is much too simple a caricature of the actual historical record. A
more sensitive reading of that record (McCormmach 1970; Jungnickel and McCormmach 1986, II, chap. 24) suggests that energetics was
rapidly displaced as an alternative foundation of physics by the
electromagnetic world view, that is, one that sought to derive the laws
of mechanics from those of electromagnetic theory. Since energetics
had not made much headway in electromagnetism, it was frozen out
of the frontier research area in physics at the turn of the century.

Nevertheless, however close to the mark were Planck's jabs at the
weaknesses of energetics, they did not pierce to the heart of the
matter. The energetics movement, far from being the inexplicable
aberration of the modern portrayal, was instead just one phase of the

active construction of and negotiation over the ill-formed and amorphous energy concept of the later nineteenth century. Was energy in fact a substance, or was it a relation, or perhaps merely only a bookkeeping mechanism? How extensive was its ability to unite all the sciences? Was it really a "simplification"? One of its original sources of inspiration lay in the push toward mechanical reduction in the vital and biological sciences: Could this mean that it would also encompass the study of man's behavior? The irony was that the greater the enthusiasm for energy as an explanatory principle, the more the very definition of energy appeared to erode. For instance, if psychic energies existed, or even if the various manifestations of energy that composed the vital activity of man entered into his observation of physical processes, then the very conservation of energy would appear to be compromised by the neglect of these previously unaccounted-for energy flows. (The reader may notice that this is merely a rehash of Descartes's dilemma of the duality of mind and body.)

Conversely, suppose that this prospect prompted scientists to restrict the concept of energy to its already elaborated forms: mechanics, heat, electromagnetism and chemical relations. Such a restricted definition would not suffice to erase all doubts about the energy concept in the late nineteenth century, as witnessed by the existence of a number of respectable skeptics, now ignored by orthodox historiography. For example, Croll (1876) suggested that gravitation itself could be construed as violating the energy conservation law. Along the same lines, O'Toole (1877) pointed out that the "potentiality" of energy is an incoherent concept if energy as portrayed as a substance, whereas if it referred instead to a relation of position, then the materiality of mass dissolves, and conservation is reduced to geometrical relationships. The conservation of energy kept undergoing the figure–ground reversal central to Gestalt psychology: depending upon how you looked at it, it was either the most obvious and most important principle in science, or simultaneously the most metaphysical, convoluted, and implausible doctrine to have come down the pike in a long time. Either conviction could be held while also admitting that the energy concept had proven extremely useful in many fields of research. Thus, forty years after its supposed discovery, the mathematical expression of the energy concept had achieved some stability, but its ontological significance and epistemological interpretation had not.

Indeed, these observations suggest a third explanation of the demise of the energetics movement within physics after 1900. The energetics movement was a logical extrapolation of some major themes surrounding the original construction of the energy concept: the promise of the unification of all science; the reification of the fundamental substratum underlying the diversity of phenomena; the expression of the belief in causal continuity and the determinism of the Laplacian Dream; and the prosecution of research by analogy. Yet, as the energy concept was being elaborated outside of rational mechanics, it was precisely these connotations that were being eroded away by new findings. A program dedicated to their preservation tended to be regarded as reactionary and obscurantist, because, in a sense, the energy concept had already begun a process of fragmentation within physics. (That Ostwald *was* obscurantist only cemented the impression.) However, energetics was only so regarded from within the physics community after 1900; as we shall see in later chapters, it managed to live on and on in other disciplines.

Entropy: More heat than light

By the 1870s, the concept of energy became coextensive with the entire range of physics. For this reason, all narrative histories of the conservation of energy tend to stop in the later nineteenth century, probably because from that time forward the history of energy would of necessity be the history of the whole of physics. This problem in narrative strategy creates the false impression that the energy concept lapses into a solid and self-satisfied stasis in the twentieth century. In more popular expositions, one often finds assertions that the law of the conservation of energy is "among the most well-tested physical laws" (Pagels 1982, p. 72). Capek (1961, p. 327) notes in passing that although one often hears of the crisis of determinism in physics, one never hears of the crisis of conservation laws, although the two would seem to be necessarily linked.

The function and status of the conservation of energy (and, indeed, conservation principles in general) has profoundly changed in the last century. This transformation will be crucial for our discussion of economic laws, and therefore the reader must become familiar with its broad outlines. The impediment to making this case in preparation for the rest of our discourse is that a complete understanding of the transformation would require a familiarity with most of the various branches of twentieth-century physics, as well as a fair grasp of some advanced mathematics, such as tensors and the theory of groups. Rather than address such a small, suitably prepared audience (who, as a result of their training, would probably not find the question of economic laws very compelling) the author has instead chosen to present a few highlights from the history of recent physics, in order to impressionistically illustrate key aspects of the transformation of conservation laws. The drawback of this mode of presentation is that explanation of the theories in which these conservation laws are embedded is beyond the scope of our narrative.[8]

Energy, as Planck had reminded Ostwald, is a variable of state. This means that if a physical system begins in a particular state and then returns to it, by whatever means and after however long, the system will possess the identical energy. In this notion reside the ideas of persistence, of invariance, and of independence from the passage of time. Equivalence of this strong type is a two-way street: energy type A gets transformed into energy type B at a fixed rate, and this process can also be reversed at the same rate of transformation. The great vulnerability of this portrait of a fully reversible world is that it is patently counterfactual. Most physical processes, especially those that involve heat, cannot be simply reversed. People do not get younger. Burnt logs do not reconstitute themselves out of smoke and ash. Heat engines do not even approach 100 percent efficiency with respect to their fuels. Freely moving objects on earth grind to a halt because of friction. One plausible interpretation of these phenomena is that energy is "lost" in these processes. This interpretation is prohibited by the law of the conservation of energy, which states that in a closed system all energy must be accounted for. The conflict between the existence of irreversible processes and the assertion of a mechanical equivalent of heat was one of the reasons that Joule's claim to have discovered the mechanical equivalent was initially greeted with such derisive scepticism.

The problem in the mid-nineteenth century was to reconcile existing theories of heat with the new notion of energy. We have already mentioned that Sadi Carnot asserted that the motive force of a heat engine must be solely a function of temperature differentials, basing this assertion upon the conservation of the substance "caloric." The genesis of the energy principle and its conservation was associated with the mechanical theory of heat, which denied the existence of caloric. But, more urgent, how could energy conservation be reconciled with the peculiar proposition that *only* temperature differentials mattered? William Thomson was the first to realize that the reconciliation required two independent principles: (1) the conservation of energy, and (2) the law that heat can only flow from a warmer to a colder body. Thomson's genius was to see that these two principles might not be contradictory. The first states that the best that any sequence of energetic transformations can do is to get you back to where you started, whereas the second says that there is a further subset of transformations that are permanently blocked, such that you cannot go home again. Thomson chose to interpret this prohibition as a statement that the universe was headed toward a final state of thermal equilibrium, where there were no more temperature differentials that could result in mechanical effect: hence the gloomy nineteenth-century prognosis of "the heat death."[9]

In 1865, Rudolph Clausius reformulated these two principles and introduced the new concept of *entropy*. In reading Clausius, it becomes apparent that he was guided by the heuristic principle that if Thomson's two axiomatic principles were to be formalized, they would both have to be expressed as equivalence relations (Clausius 1867). To achieve that goal, Clausius constructed an ingenious but intuitively opaque quantity called "entropy," which had the desired property that it was a variable of state in a reversible system (just like energy).[10] With this formulation, Clausius managed to found the science of thermodynamics on two laws: the first, that the energy of the universe is a constant, and the second, that the entropy of the universe increases to a maximum.

Clausius's formalization of the laws of classical thermodynamics was rapidly embraced by the nineteenth-century physicists because of its close resemblance to the already existing formalism of mechanics; but, indeed, the resemblance was and is deceptive. There is the familiar conservation principle, and there is also the extremal principle of the maximization of entropy in equilibrium. The conjunction of conservation principle and variational principle looks roughly similar to the Lagrangian/Hamiltonian formalism in mechanics, but the two could not be more dissimilar. The Hamiltonian framework describes the evolution of a deterministic system over time, using energy conservation to track its identity. Classical thermodynamics, on the other hand, says that within the confines of an isolated system, all nonequilibrium situations evolve toward the same quantitative equilibrium state. In other words, by the time equilibrium has been reached, the system has forgotten its initial conditions (Prigogine and Stengers 1984, p. 121). You cannot get back there from here, because you cannot remember where "there" was.

As if that were not bad enough, classical thermodynamics also cannot tell you how quickly you will get where you are going. The reason for this is that entropy is not really a conserved quantity like energy. It conforms instead to an "as-if" conservation when all systems are reversible. Only in the fully reversible case can entropy be portrayed as a "substance" that is maximized. In the real world of functions and irreversibility, all Clausius could say was that in a closed system entropy would increase (i.e. $dS/dt > 0$). The *rate* of increase is not specified, as it is the result of a very large number of specific considerations. Hence the classical notion of entropy boils down to a "distinction between 'useful' exchanges of energy in the Carnot cycle and 'dissipated' energy that is irreversibly wasted" (Prigogine and Stengers 1984, p. 117).

At this point the reader who thinks there is something funny going on here should not feel alone. Recently Thomas Pynchon has written:

> Since I wrote this story ["Entropy"] I have kept trying to understand entropy, but my grasp becomes less the more I read. I've been able to follow the OED definitions, and the way Isaac Asimov explains it, and even some of the math. But the qualities and quantities will not come together to form a unified notion in my head. It is cold comfort to find out that Gibbs himself described entropy in its written form as "far-fetched . . . obscure and difficult of comprehension" [Pynchon 1984, p. 14].

A good deal of this cognitive anxiety derives from the improbity of asserting that energy and entropy are jointly coherent and congruent terms. This was a premier example of a situation that would recur time and again in the twentieth century: the mathematics made sense, but the physical interpretation seemed off-kilter. The conservation of energy traced its lineage from the principle of quantitative causality that *ex nihil nihilo fit* and its obverse, nothing disappeared into nothing. The second law of thermodynamics pretended also to descend from the same tradition, except it postulated that some energy was "wasted" rather than "lost," and moreover, that one could not specify the exact rate of "wastage." As Scott (1970, pp. xi–xii) has admirably put it:

> [I]t was agreed by all that any energy apparently lost was always converted into equivalent amounts of work, electricity, heat, etc. All was then well except for the disadvantage that according to the second law of thermodynamics, "available energy" is constantly decreasing in the universe as a result of heat wasted during energy conversions. Thus the law of the conservation of energy was restricted to conservation of "unavailable energy." One may wonder whether there is any real distinction between what is called *unavailable* energy and lost energy?

Given that every freshman physics student is told that energy is the ability to do work, the notion of energy that cannot do work does seem a contradiction in terms (Meyerson 1962, p. 280). While repeated acquaintance eventually can cause one to make peace with the idea

– after all, it only means that some configurations of energy just will not go anywhere else – the point we should focus upon is that the rise of thermodynamics drastically revised the meaning of energy and its conservation; and all the while various physicists were trying their hardest to deny that anything fundamental had changed. (One indication of this problem was the great difficulty that the energetics movement encountered in attempting to subsume the entropy concept within their unified framework.)

From now on I shall need a term that will serve to identify a type of physical theory that includes the law of the conservation of energy and the bulk of rational mechanics, but excludes the entropy concept and most post-1860 developments in physics. This collection of analytical artifices is more an historical than a systematic subset of physics: It includes the formalisms of vector fields, but excludes Maxwell's equations, or even Kelvin's mechanical models for light. Since this resembles the content of the energetics movement, I trust it will not do the phenomena too much violence to call it "proto-energetics." Classical thermodynamics diverges from proto-energetics in one very critical respect: Thermodynamic processes only change in one direction. In proto-energetics, time is isotropic, which means that no physical laws would be violated if the system ran backward or forward in time. (Indeed, we shall see in the next section that this is the hallmark of proto-energetics.) The second law of thermodynamics states that a system can only be oriented in one direction in time precisely because it cannot go back the way it came, if its path involved the dissipation of heat. The use of the energy concept in classical thermodynamics most certainly exacerbated the cognitive dissonance of claiming that all other physical laws were indifferent to the reversal of the flow of time. If heat really was nothing other than motion at the molecular level, then it should be subject to the orthodox laws of motion, which were themselves time-reversible. The attitude of many physicists in the century from 1850 to 1950 was that this must be the case, and that they would reduce entropy to mechanics. Starting with Maxwell's famous demon, the second law was reinterpreted to mean that things go in one direction in time, not because they *cannot* go back the reverse way, but rather because it is just *extremely unlikely* that they go backward in time. Hence, because of an incoherence at the heart of the energy concept, notions of probability and random behavior were introduced into physical theory.

The penetration of probability theory and randomness into the bastion of determinism is a fascinating story in its own right (Brush 1976, 1983; Porter 1981a; Prigogine 1980; Forman 1971). Initially, indeterminacy was introduced apologetically, not as an attribute of nature per se, but rather as an artifact of the level of our ignorance of the exact positions and velocities of all of the constituent components of a fundamentally deterministic phenomenon (Jevons 1905a, p. 198). However, once Pandora's box was opened, there seemed to be no stopping the spread of probabilistic concepts in physics. Probabilistic gas theory led to statistical mechanics, which begat quantum mechanics, which begat probability waves, which begat nonergodic and weakly stable systems, all of which begat (as we anticipate the end of this chapter) a seemingly accidental universe. Once randomness was introduced into the theory of the external world, it spread like wildfire, or a cancer, or the crystallization of a supercooled liquid, the choice of metaphor prudently contingent upon the attitude of the audience toward its seemingly inexorable advance.

It has not been fully realized that the proliferation of probabilistic concepts in physics is the first of many manifestations of the self-contradiction of the global energy concept; energy is very nearly dialectical. The energy concept was intended to embody the rational, lawlike, determinate behavior of nature, in that it was the reification of the independence of natural law from all temporal or spatial accident, as well as from the accident of human observation. As the energy concept was thrust upon a world that appeared to abound in such accidents, and as "external" cultural considerations sometimes encouraged scientists to elevate the accidental in nature (Forman 1971), ideas of probability and randomness were absorbed into physics. First the accidents were attributed to the frailty of the human observer, but later it was allowed that accident might be intrinsic to nature itself. After this process of conceptual evolution, there was still something called "energy" in the mathematics, and in the introductory textbooks, but it was less and less an embodiment of the original ideal of natural law.

The energetics movement was in many respects a product of the controversy over the incompatibility of the second law of thermodynamics and conventional energy mechanics. The energeticists proposed to resolve the controversy by downplaying the mechanics, and (unwittingly) neutralizing the entropy law. The contrary, and ultimately more popular position, of which Ludwig Boltzmann was the chief advocate, was that it was possible to reconcile mechanics and entropy. The method proposed was to circumvent the super-Hamiltonian with its hopeless calculations of the velocities and positions of billions and billions of gas molecules, and to replace it with the description of the evolution of a statistical distribution whose arguments were the velocities of the particles in some bounded region of space. After making some assumptions about the average velocity of particles after collisions, Boltzmann derived an expression that resembled the entropy function. Botlzmann's claim to have derived irreversible movements through time from mechanical dynamics drew fire as soon as it was published in 1872.

From the 1870s through the 1890s, Josef Loschmidt, Ernst Zermelo, E. P. Culverwell, and a host of others raised objections in various formats that it was inconsistent to derive irreversible consequences from reversible premises (Brush 1976). From the present perspective, the most significant challenge came from Henri Poincaré. Poincaré concluded that classical thermodynamics and Hamiltonian dynamics were incompatible, because no function of coordinates and momenta could have the properties of the Boltzmann entropy function. This result has been shown recently to retain its validity, even within the context of modern formulations of statistical mechanics (Prigogine 1980, pp. 156–73). Botlzmann's response was to suggest that there might be "fluctuations" in the evolution of entropy – that is, sometimes time did run in reverse – but that such fluctuations were small and highly unlikely. Just before his suicide in 1906, Boltzmann had essentially capitulated to the onslaught of Poincaré and Zermelo, reducing the law of entropy to a tautology. He claimed that the direction of time was itself purely a convention that observers introduce into the world; still he insisted there was no fundamental distinction between the past and the future. His adherence to the original interpretation of the energy concept was stronger than his respect for the fundamental irreversibility of time, perhaps to the very point of losing a hold on the fundamental distinction between death and life.

The faith in the Laplacian Dream of a determinate universe dies hard, much harder than the death of any human being. Most textbooks of thermodynamics today still give no indication that there might be an inconsistency between classical dynamics and classical thermodynamics, that a controversy over this issue raged at the turn of the century, or that it might be considered to be still unresolved. One finds instead that the issue is kept alive by those largely outside of the discipline of physics: by philosophers and historians of science, by the Brussels school of thermodynamic chemistry, and in a particularly notable case from our present vantage point, by an economist (Georgescu-Roegen 1971, chap. 6). One also discovers upon further inquiry that the triumph of statistical mechanics has been somewhat overstated. For instance, if the proof of the pudding is supposed to be in its eating, it comes as a shock to learn that it has been estimated that 90 percent of all engineering systems cannot be treated by currently available methods of statistical mechanics, and are instead resolved by resort to classical thermodynamics or phenomenological procedures (Cartwright 1983, p. 63). This is not intended to suggest that statistical mechanics has not been fruitful in the suggestion of further hypotheses in the development of physical science; quantum mechanics is only the premier example of the fruits of its elaboration. It is instead intended to suggest that the citation of statistical mechanics as the justification of the success of the program of mechanical reductionism is premature and unwarranted.

The awakening from the Laplacian Dream

The ontology of the energy concept came into its own in the second half of the nineteenth century when it congealed into the theory of the field. The idea of a field of potentials, first broached in gravitational mechanics and in fluid dynamics and then tentatively extended to electricity and heat, became one of the characteristic modes of discourse of the physical scientist. Rapidly the tendency spread to regard any phenomenon as suitable for description by field formalisms if the propagation of the phenomenon was affected by material changes in the intervening space, if it took time, if a mechanical model could be imagined for the action of a medium in producing the observed effect, and if energy could be said to be located in the space between bodies (Hesse 1965, p. 197). The requirement that a mechanical model of the medium be imagined allowed those so inclined to interpret the field formalism as if it were a variant of the older and more familiar substance theories; this explains the fascination of the nineteenth century with various ethers. Nevertheless, these mechanical models were little more than wistful nostalgia for a tangible and intuitively satisfying world, a world that was rapidly fading away. In hindsight, we now realize that the function of field theories was to liberate energy from all dependence upon matter (Theobald 1966, p. 98; Nersessian 1984).

The most concise definition of a physical field is "a spatial distribution of energy that varies with time" (ignoring as irrelevant some fields in physics not defined explicitly in terms of energy). The novelty (as well as the aura of implausibility) of a field derives from the fact that the energy is portrayed as being in the space and not necessarily in the material bodies that occupy the space. The distribution of energy is generally not uniquely defined for a given field, although the total energy associated with the field has a definite value. The incongruity of this statement might be compared to the trick of the rhetorical stylists who write as if war or anxiety were in the air, rather than being localized in human beings. Nineteenth-century physicists were prepared to entertain fields as a rhetorical flourish, but were uneasy about admitting them as "real" without their being accompanied by some matter in some form, however contrived.

The problem mainly resided in the mathematics. The format of a field is a set of differential equations describing forces, joined to some variational principle. The Lagrangian (or the Hamiltonian) formalism had been developed with reference to classical mechanics, and as such seemed firmly grounded in corpuscular reality. Once imported into field theory, however, it appeared to assume a life of its own. Nowhere did this tension result in more agonizing reappraisals than in the work of James Clerk Maxwell, one of the men most responsible for the development of field theory in the nineteenth century. The story is often told of Maxwell's curious wheels-and-vortexes model of electromagnetism (Harman 1982a; Nersessian 1984), as well as his interest in ether theories. Ultimately, prudence forced Maxwell to admit it was the mathematics and not the physical model that called the tune:

> The substance here treated must not be assumed to possess any of the properties of ordinary fluids except those of freedom of motion and resistance to compression. It is not even a hypothetical fluid which is introduced to explain actual phenomena. It is merely a collection of imaginary properties which may be employed for establishing certain theorems in pure mathematics in a way more intelligible for many minds . . . I wish merely to direct the mind of the reader to mechanical phenomena which will assist him in understanding the electrical ones. All such phrases in the present paper are to be considered as illustrative, not explanatory. In speaking of the Energy of the field, however, I wish to be understood literally (quoted in Hesse 1965, pp. 208–10).

As we can observe, the world was turned upside down, because it was now the material substance concept that was hedged round with doubts and excused as a rhetorical device, whereas the energy of the field was treated as a palpable literal entity. This reversal was due, at least in part, to the form of the mathematics. Lagrangian techniques were used to effectively eliminate forces of an as-yet-undefined nature, so as to bypass corpuscular considerations, as well as to provide a synthetic account of the effects of the field (Harman 1982b, p. 127). The Lagrangian techniques therefore elevated energy to a position of prime theoretical importance. But Maxwell's equations went even further, although this was not evident until well into the twentieth century. Once the mathematics of the field freed energy from matter, it also implied a reversal within the original definition. Instead of a physical field being necessarily a spatial distribution of energy that varied in time, physicists found they could also read the mathematics in such a way that any well-behaved scalar function with a vanishing time derivative could be identified with energy (Theobald 1966, p. 97). Once energy became incorporeal, there really was no stopping it from becoming an eidolon.

The philosopher Emile Meyerson was the first to describe the tension between the imperative of the mathematics and the physical portrayal. He wrote in 1908, well before the significance of the theory of relativity became apparent, that

> Energy is really only an integral; now, what we want to have is a *substantial* definition, like that of Leibniz, and this demand is justifiable to a certain degree, since our very conviction of the conservation of energy rests in great part on this foundation . . . And so the manuals of physics contain really two discordant definitions of energy, the first which is verbal, intelligible, capable of establishing our conviction, but false; and the second which is mathematical, exact, but lacking verbal expression [Meyerson 1962, p. 280].

Just as energy was captivating the public imagination through the intermediary of literary popularizers, the mathematical content of the energy concept was to further elude popular intuitive understanding. Since there is no adequate conceptualization of the energy concept of the twentieth century without a passing acquaintance with its mathematics, we shall beg the reader's indulgence as we very briefly tour some of the highlights of the latter's development. Again, we have no intention to actually teach the mathematics.

The fact that energy became more a mathematical concept and less an intuitive one cannot be divined solely from the terse expression of energy as an integral of forces multiplied through displacements. Rather, the joint development of variational principles and conservation principles erected a scaffolding of intricate complexity around the initial energy concept. The primary example of this process occurred in rational mechanics, deriving from the tradition of Lagrange and Hamilton already discussed. The later nineteenth century witnessed the closest approach to the equation of the Laplacian Dream, the equation that would predict the entire past and the entire future. Increasingly in the later nineteenth century, it appeared that this equation would be the Hamiltonian, suitably altered and augmented to encompass subsequent developments in energy physics.

As we have already seen, for a mechanical conservative system the general form of Hamilton's principle is:

$$(2.6) \quad \delta H = \delta \int_{t_1}^{t_2} (T - U)\,dt = 0$$

where T represents the kinetic energy and U represents the potential energy, t is the time variable, and δ represents a small variation in the path traversed. In principle, there is no need to restrict the mechanical system in isolation to be conservative, since in general we expect there to be other forms of energetic interaction with the mechanical system. In that case, Hamilton's principle can be written:

$$\delta H = \delta \int_{t_1}^{t_2} (T + W)\,dt = 0$$

where δW is the work done on the system from outside. However, it is critical to distinguish between this case and the case of a violation of the law of the conservation of energy. In the former, we can take external forces into account because energy is assumed to be conserved in its transference into the mechanical system, whereas in the latter, any such calculation would be rendered impossible. Nonconservative systems do not imply the violation of the conservation of energy, so the terminology is somewhat misleading.

While the above integrals express the general principle of the Hamiltonian, they are frequently of a form that defies practical solution. The most common practice in solving mechanical problems (Goldstein 1950, p. 217) is to first rewrite the coordinates of the system in "canonical form," which incorporates any constraints of the system into the new coordinates. These new coordinates q_i are generally not of the dimensions of Cartesian coordinates, thus initiating a process of abstraction from intuitive concepts. Next, a Lagrangian equation is written as a function of the q_i's, the time derivatives, and time itself. Then, a set of variables called the "generalized momenta" are defined as:

$$(2.7) \quad p_i = \frac{\partial L(q_j, dq_j/dt, t)}{\partial \dot{q}_i}$$

Finally, the Hamiltonian equation is defined by:

$$(2.8) \quad H = E_{\mathrm{kin}}[p_1, \ldots, p_s] + V_{\mathrm{pot}}[q_1, \ldots, q_s]$$

By this procedure, we have managed to write the Hamiltonian equation as the sum of the kinetic energy of the system, expressed as a function of the generalized momenta, and the potential energy of the system, expressed as a function of the generalized canonical coordinates. The solution for the system at any point in time can then be expressed by the Hamiltonian equations:

(2.9) $\dfrac{dq_i}{dt} = \dfrac{\partial H}{\partial p_i}$

$\dfrac{dp_i}{dt} = -\dfrac{\partial H}{\partial q_i}$

$-\dfrac{\partial L}{\partial t} = \dfrac{\partial H}{\partial t}$

These were the Laplacian Dream equations. Combined with suitable initial conditions, the solution of these differential equations, derived from a single energy equation, promised to describe the evolution of any physical system. With a few strokes of pencil on paper, the past and the future would collapse to the present, all within the ambit of comprehension of the mathematician. Time, as it were, could be brought to a stop through knowledge of the Hamiltonian. The formalism of the Poisson bracket even allowed one to search for the true invariants of a system, the fundamental relations that were eternal. If one were interested in an arbitrary function $f(q_1, \ldots, q_s, p_1, \ldots, p_s)$, and wished to discover how it evolved over time, one would define its Poisson bracket as (Goldstein 1950, pp. 250–5):

(2.10) $\dfrac{df}{dt} = \sum_{i=1}^{s} \dfrac{\partial f}{\partial q_i} \cdot \dfrac{\partial H}{\partial p_i} - \dfrac{\partial f}{\partial p_i} \cdot \dfrac{\partial H}{\partial q_i}$

$\equiv [f, H]$

If $[f,H] = 0$, then it would follow that $f(q, \ldots, p)$ was an invariant of the Hamiltonian. But the Poisson bracket pointed the way to a deeper insight.

As physicists accumulated experience with their Hamiltonians, they came to see that much of the trick of solving Hamiltonians lay in choosing appropriate generalized momenta and coordinates so that the Hamiltonian could be rewritten in such a way that the potential function is eliminated (Prigogine 1980, pp. 30–1). As Lanczos (1949, p. xxi) wrote, "The mathematical and philosophical value of the variational method is firmly anchored . . . in the freedom of arbitrary coordinate transformations." The coordinate transformations that are preferred are those that, in a loose manner of speaking, get rid of all the potentials between bodies and portray the entire energy of the system as allocated among the bodies, as if they were in isolation; or better yet, as if energy really were a substance. If a physical system is susceptible to being expressed in this manner, it is called an *integrable system*. Hence, integrable systems are those for which a solution of the

Hamiltonian may be readily found, because all the energy of interaction may be transformed away through a suitable choice of coordinate transformations, called "canonical transformations."

The formalism of the Poisson bracket entered into consideration at this point, because it was found that the set of coordinate transformations that possessed this desirable property of being canonical transformations were those that left the Poisson bracket invariant (Lanczos 1949, p. 215). Within the class of the canonical coordinate transformations, the application of the Poisson bracket had a particularly transparent form, which resembled simple algebraic operations (Goldstein 1950, p. 255). This perception led in the twentieth century to the application of group theory to integrable systems.

The application of abstract algebra to mechanics would take us particularly far afield; however, it is possible to suggest a certain intuitive interpretation of this development. The Poisson bracket of the Hamiltonian with itself (i.e., $[H,H] = 0$) raised the possibility that the time invariance of the Hamiltonian *implied* the conservation of energy, rather than vice versa (ter Haar 1961, p. 49). We have already noted that in practice it had become common to identify any well-defined scalar function displaying a vanishing time derivative with energy. In effect, the formalism of the Poisson bracket suggested that it was the *symmetry* of certain coordinate transformations that really mattered in integrable physical systems. Hence the conservation of energy was really just another way of saying that the Hamiltonian was symmetric in time. Other Poisson brackets that left the Hamiltonian invariant were expressions of other symmetries of the system – for instance, the symmetry of space would imply the conservation of angular momentum.

Such insights fostered a new way to think of conservation principles, and the general solution of mechanical systems, one that prescribed that the analyst should look for all the symmetries in any given Hamiltonian problem, and should use those symmetries to transform away as many interactions in the system as possible, as well as to discover the constraints of motion. This practice was given an analytical basis with the publication of the famous Noether Theorem in 1918 (Brewer and Smith 1981, p. 16; Sarlet and Cantrijn 1981). Using group theory, Noether showed that in physics, to every invariance or symmetry property of a physical law there corresponds a conservation principle, and vice versa.

The importance of this development for twentieth-century physics (and, patient reader, for economics) cannot be overstated. Noether's theorem has not only found application in classical mechanics, it has also prompted seminal results in general relativity, quantum mechanics, modern particle physics, and cosmology. However, it has not often been appreciated that Noether's theorem heralded the next phase of the transmutation of the energy concept as well. In demonstrating the isomorphism between invariance, symmetry, and conservation laws, she drove another nail into the coffin of energy as a substance. The mathematics shifted attention away from energy per se, and toward the role of invariants in physical theory. Energy was downgraded to merely one among many possible invariant properties of physical systems. In fact, in the later twentieth-century theories, the presence of energy as an actual scalar quantity sometimes was unattainable or was dispensed with for reasons of convenience or pragmatism. This caused no alarm, however, so long as time symmetry was maintained, since Noether's theorem reassured all and sundry that the two situations were really the same.

Nevertheless, there was a definite tarnish upon the sheen of the *law* of the conservation of energy. Noether's theorem was a general theory of many conservation principles, each of equal systemic status. Any given conservation principle might be present or absent due to the presence or absence of a symmetry in a particular physical problem. Conservation principles were not so much laws as they were convenient calculation devices or heuristics for recasting a mathematical problem. Better yet, they were the gesso, the coat of whitewash on the canvas that provided the featureless contrast against which regularities could be discerned.

It should be kept in mind that all these developments in the understanding of symmetric solutions applied to integrable systems. In the later nineteenth century, many physicists and most engineers happily believed that Laplace's dream was coming true, and therefore it was just a matter of time and mathematical ingenuity until all physical problems could be written as Hamiltonian equations with suitable canonical coordinates that would facilitate their solution. Much effort was expended to recast such critical problems, such as the three-body problem, in integrable form. Hence it was an abrupt awakening from the Laplacian Dream when Henri Poincaré demonstrated in 1889 that many of the most interesting problems in classical dynamics would never be converted into integrable systems (Poincaré 1889). In simplistic terms, certain well-defined problems, such as the generalized three-body problem, have no general Hamiltonian invariants that would facilitate their solution. As Prigogine (1980, p. 32) has written, "this was in a sense the point at which the development of classical dynamics ended."

How could something so abstract as a mathematical proof promote the dissolution of the Laplacian Dream? I know of no better way of explaining it than to quote the pellucid prose of Ilya Prigogine and Isabelle Stengers (1984, pp. 74–6):

> [I]ntegrable systems have been the model par excellence of dynamic systems, and physicists have attempted to extend the properties of what is actually a very special class of Hamiltonian equations to cover all natural processes . . . there is the fascination always associated with a closed system capable of posing all problems, provided it does not define them as meaningless. Dynamics is such a language; being complete, it is by definition coextensive with the world it is describing. It assumes that all problems, whether simple or complex, resemble one another since it can always pose them in the same general form. Thus the temptation to conclude that all problems resemble one another from the point of view of their solutions as well, and that nothing new can appear as the result of the greater or lesser complexity of the integration procedure. It is this intrinsic homogeneity that we now know to be false . . .
>
> To the extent to which dynamics has become and still is the model of science . . . [it] is still the prophetic announcement of a description of the world seen from a divine or demonic point of view. It is the science of Newton, the new Moses to whom the truth of the world is unveiled; it is a *revealed* science that seems alien to any social or historical context identifying it as the result of the activity of human society.

Nonetheless, the reader should not get the impression that it was curtains for the Hamiltonians, or classical dynamics, or Western physics, or anything else equally melodramatic, by 1890. Nearly one hundred years later, it is not even apparent that the intervening generations of physicists have discerned this particular brand of writing on the wall. Modern textbooks of classical mechanics such as those by Goldstein (1950), Percival and Richards (1982), or Lanczos (1949) do not even mention the Poincaré result; and it is still true that for many scientists, Hamiltonian dynamics remains the ideal of scientific explanation. Thus, if the Poincaré theorem was the rude awakening from the Laplacian Dream, most of the dreamers merely rolled over and fell back asleep.

However, by the 1980s, the development and popularization of nonlinear dynamics under the rubric of "chaos theory" had finally brought home to the Laplacian dreamers the elusive nature of their dream. To quote the mathematician James Yorke, "If you could write down the solution to a differential equation, then necessarily it is not chaotic, because to write it down, you must find regular invariants, things that are conserved, like angular momentum. You find enough of these things, and that lets you write down a solution" (quoted in Gleick 1987, pp. 67–8). Imposing linearities on a system was like imposing energy conservation; but mathematicians were revealing that, in nonlinear systems, the boundaries between deterministic and random behavior dissolved. Indeed, the simplest nonlinear deterministic recursive difference equations could give rise to patterns of the most exquisite complexity, and even outputs nearly indistinguishable from random noise. Confronted with such "deterministic chaos," some physicists decided that the best strategy was to relinquish the Hamiltonian formalism altogether – and that includes the energy concept – and instead search for a different kind of phenomenological symmetry, one defined as symmetry at different scales of the phenomenon (Gleick 1987, pp. 185, 210, 263). Whether this was the final break from determinism remains to be seen, but it is not irrelevant to this narrative that a best-seller in 1987 was promoting the idea that "chaos was the end of the reductionist program in science" (Gleick 1987, p. 304).

The spread of field formalisms, the elaboration of Hamiltonians, the rise of statistical mechanics, Noether's theorem, Poincaré's result, and chaos theory were tearing the energy concept in three or four different directions, and nobody felt inclined to pick up the shreds and knit them together again. The formalism of fields increasingly endowed energy with an independent existence, but one much conditional upon the conservation of energy, since it was this condition that guaranteed the identity and integrity of the field. However, this conception of conservation was increasingly global rather than local, since the energy could not be located within the field. The elaboration of Hamiltonian dynamics very much depended upon energy as a tractable integral, but examination of what characteristics rendered the integral tractable led investigators to comprehend that it was symmetry in time that lay at the crux of the representation of energy. Noether's theorem further dematerialized energy by reconceptualizing it as an algebraic property in a system of operators, one invariance condition among many. Poincaré's result sealed the demise of Laplacian energy by revealing that, as a paradigm of scientific explanation, it was impotent to explain a vast range of physical phenomena precisely because its conservation excluded the emergent novelty that grows out of complex interactions. Chaos theory intoned the funeral rites by summoning the "fractal geometry of nature" to explain the futility of Hamiltonian dynamics.

At this juncture, energy as the avatar of invariance and determinism collided head on with energy as protean Ur-stuff, the purpose of which was to make the world of change and diversity intelligible. Poincaré, master both of mathematical formalism and philosophical hermeneutics, understood better than anyone else that energy conservation was a dialectical concept:

> If, in fact, the system were completely isolated from all external action, the values of our own n parameters at a given moment would suffice to determine the state of the system at any ulterior moment whatsoever, provided that we still clung to the determinist hypothesis. We should therefore fall back on the same difficulty as before. If the future state of the system is not entirely determined by its present state, it is because it further depends on the state of bodies external to the system. But then, is it likely that there exist among the parameters x which define the state of the system of equations independent of this state of external bodies? And if, in certain cases, we think we can find them, is it not only because of our own ignorance and because the influence of these bodies is too weak for our experiment to be able to detect it? If the system is not regarded as completely isolated, it is probable that the rigorously exact expression of internal energy will depend upon the state of the external bodies . . .
>
> To formulate Mayer's principle by giving it an absolute meaning, we must extend it to the whole universe, and then we find ourselves face to face with the very difficulty we have endeavoured to avoid. To sum up, and to use ordinary language, the law of the conservation of energy can have only one significance, because there is in it a property common to all possible properties; but in the determinist hypothesis there is only one possible, and then the law has no meaning. In the indeterminist hypothesis, on the other hand, it would have a meaning even if we wished to regard it in an absolute sense. It would appear as a limitation imposed upon freedom (Poincaré, 1952, pp. 133–4).

As Poincaré understood, the energy concept was not at all a descriptive entity, but rather an assertion of the very ideal of natural law: the mathematical expression of invariance through time, the reification of a stable external world independent of our activity or inquiry. This ideal, at first so very plausible and reassuring in its form and appearance, was turning out to be a ticket to Bedlam if followed to its logical consequences. The search for a comprehensive integral that reified the independent and self-sufficient existence of a physical system certainly had had some successes, but it was increasingly apparent that expectations that the Laplacian Dream equation would simply grow and grow until it encompassed the universe were incoherent and self-contradictory.

There was, of course, the one horn of the dilemma, the nagging worry that physicists had not yet gotten energy right, because of some phenomena or interconnection that had been overlooked. That would imply that all existing physics would require reevaluation. But even more drastically, suppose physicists had ultimately gotten the true megalithic Hamiltonian equation right, and it did describe all physical reality. The other horn of the dilemma would imply that there could be no such thing as an approach to equilibrium, because everything always had been in equilibrium and always would be in equilibrium, the solution to the ultimate Hamiltonian. But that would mean that the energy concept would be superfluous in a practical sense, because such a world would never experience physical change. Natural law would then be reduced to a statement that the physical world was immutable and eternal: Who needs an exorbitantly complicated integral to insist that all change is illusory?

Poincaré's answer was that change is not illusory, and that the only coherent interpretation of energy was that something is invariant over some subsets of physical reality. Poincaré's conventionalism permitted him to entertain the notion that the invariant aspect might itself be different, depending on the context and the problem under consideration. It also opened a second breach in the walls of the bastion of determinism. Thermodynamics had already been the site of the first intrusion of probability and stochastic processes into physics. Poincaré showed why stochastic processes must be introduced into the heart of determinism itself, classical mechanics. Motion itself had to be treated as stochastic, if only to provide the backdrop of "freedom" against which the convergence to conventional mechanical equilibrium could be defined. If mechanical problems were not integrable, a much less restrictive invariance condition could be defined within a stochastic framework, namely ergodicity (Prigogine 1980, pp. 33–8). Modern research has indicated that, in many instances, even this specification is too restrictive, which has led to the development of weakly stable systems (Prigogine 1980, pp. 38–45). The ultimate in this tradition has been the development of chaos theory, which tells us that determinate differential equations may exhibit indeterminate and seemingly stochastic evolution of dependent variables.

The saga of how the most fervent acolytes of determinism were eventually driven to see chaos everywhere is one of the most fascinating stories in Western intellectual history, one to which justice has been done by Gleick (1987) and Porter (1981a). For our more modest purposes, it remains only to ask what has happened to the talisman of determinism, the law of the conservation of energy? The answer is that the twentieth century has transmuted it beyond all recognition and coherence. First in the theory of relativity, then in quantum mechanics, and finally in modern cosmology and particle physics, energy was turned on its head. Each new innovation served to qualify and transform the conservation law further and further, until no one is willing to state definitively and specifically what has been preserved. The issues involved are very complicated, so we can afford only the most cursory glance at the topsy-turvy world of twentieth-century physics.

The theory of relativity

Einstein and the theory of relativity are names to conjure with in modern culture. This is undoubtedly due more to Einstein's role as a media celebrity than to a general cognizance of the significance of the theory, since quantum mechanics and cosmology have done much more to upset the nineteenth-century notion of natural law than the theory of relativity. In many ways, the research program of relativity theory is a direct extrapolation of the program of Hamiltonian dynamics; its guiding heuristic principle is to search for symmetries and invariances in the laws of nature. Variational principles retain their significance as well as their deterministic role in identifying equilibria. Contrary to the untutored perception that asserts "everything is relative," the theory of relativity is built upon the precept that true laws of nature should be invariant as between different inertial frames of reference.

As it is explained in any competent exposition of the theory of relativity (cf. Angel 1980, pp. 46–59), Newtonian mechanics regarded space as an absolute substance, in that it was always identical, was not subject to modification, and yet acted causally upon everything else; it regarded time as entirely absolute, in that the temporal coordinates of a phenomenon would be the same whatever the frame of a reference chosen. Absolute space did not, however, imply that spatial frames of reference made no difference to the phenomenon; only that there is absolute motion as well as relative motion. In Newtonian mechanics, velocities produce no dynamic effects, but accelerations do. The classical relativity of motion is based on the notion that choosing a uniformly moving reference frame will "transform away" a particular uniform velocity, but that certain accelerations must be absolute because their effects cannot be traced to their reference frame.

It was the elaboration of field theory, and in particular electromagnetic field theory, that placed Newtonian mechanics in jeopardy. Maxwell's equations suggested that all electromagnetic phenomena, including light, are propagated in a vacuum with a uniform velocity of approximately 186,000 miles per second. Classical relativity demanded that this uniform velocity should be susceptible to being transformed away by a moving reference frame; but various empirical tests were unable to detect this effect. Given the perennial tendency to assert the unity of all physics, it is perhaps understandable that physicists at the turn of the century regarded this conflict as a crisis; whereas, with hindsight, we might interpret it as the inevitable collision of the earlier physics based on the substance concept with later physics, which owed most of its innovations to the development of the concept of the field. Once space was permeated with fields, any residual substance characteristics were eventually rendered redundant. For the sake of consistency, all vestiges of the substance concept had to be winnowed out of mechanics. In fact, once energy had become the central unifying concept in physics, mechanics itself had to undergo a process of de-materialization. It was the genius of Einstein to recognize this fact, and to reveal how mechanics had to be revised in order to subordinate it to the field concept.

In 1905, Einstein proposed the theory of special relativity. The theory was "special" in the sense that it was confined to the consideration of uniform rectilinear motion – those motions that do not involve accelerations, and therefore dynamic effects. It was based on two assumptions: the first, that all fundamental laws of nature (primarily those of mechanics and electrodynamics) should be unaffected by uniform rectilinear motion, or in other words, the reference frame should not 'matter' to them; and the second, that the velocity of light identified in Maxwell's equations is a universal constant, independent of the velocity of the source. The only way to simultaneously preserve such seemingly contradictory propositions was to alter the primitive concepts of mechanics: space, time, velocity, and mass. These alterations show up in popular expositions as "contracting" rods, "slowing" clocks, paradoxical twins, and so forth. We must pass this all by, however much we might be bewildered and tittillated by it all, because there is no such thing as a legitimate brief introduction to relativity. Our modest purpose is merely to point out one particular subset of implications of the theory of relativity, and indicate how they relate to the larger story of the conservation of energy.

In special relativity, time is no longer treated as an absolute, independent of space or of reference frame. Because mass, time, and length are now considered as interactive and dependent, any analytical term that is constructed from these primitives must itself be revised. Recall that the energy concept began as an extension of rational mechanics to other physical phenomena, and that its organon was exemplified by kinetic energy, one half mv^2. If the motion of the particle is now taken to influence mass and the components of velocity (space and time), it must follow that the conservation of momentum, and indeed, the conservation of energy itself must be compromised. In Einstein's theory, the compromise involved a revision of the law of the conservation of energy, resulting in the famous equation $E = mc^2$.

In special relativity, this equation performs the function of the conservation principle, informing us that mass may be converted into energy, and that energy must possess inertia. There has been a lot of ink spilled over the decades in trying to decide whether mass and energy are really the same ontological thing in special relativity (Angel 1980, p. 95; Zahar 1980, p. 40; Theobald 1966, p. 103). While this issue cannot be settled here, it is important to note that, in classical mechanics, matter was the underlying substrate of the world, and energy was a mode of existence of matter. The turn-of-the-century energetics movement claimed that these two principles were contradictory, and that matter must ultimately be reduced to energy. If the claim of energetics is interpreted as an extrapolation of the logic of the energy concept, we can now observe that it was fundamentally correct.

The independent existence of substance is inexplicable within the context of proto-energetics. When field theories began to generate conflicts with classical mechanics, classical mechanics which bore the brunt of revision, and the substantial independence of mass was relinquished. Nevertheless, the energy concept did not pass unscathed through the wholesale redefinition of the world so that it would conform to the ideal of uniform law. Energy was increasingly characterized by its conservation, but this conservation principle itself was revised, if not relinquished, in the conservation of matter and energy. After all, what can the conservation of energy now mean, if time itself is no longer path-independent? The answer in special relativity was to construct a more complicated invariance principle, one where the divergence of a tensor that represents the density of energy and momentum vanishes when all relevant types of energy are accounted for (Trautman 1962, p. 170). In this representation, energy was itself divested of substance connotations, which has led many commentators to suspect that mathematical abstraction had smothered physical intuition in science. This complaint is not strictly legitimate in the theory of special relativity, because the zero divergence of a field could still be interpreted to mean that the field had no source or sink, preserving some of the fundamental intuition behind the conservation of energy that *ex nihil nihilo fit*. Unfortunately, even this vestige of the energy concept is lost once one moves on to the general theory of relativity.

For the sake of simplicity, the theory of special relativity was confined to inertial reference frames. Einstein realized that his theory of motion had to be extended to accelerating reference frames, and that this would require a reconsideration of the theory of gravity. This extension of the theory of relativity was founded upon the principle of equivalence, the claim that inertial fields and gravitational fields, together with their effects, are indistinguishable from the vantage point of natural law. In a loose sense, general relativity treats gravity as if it were a deformation of the geometry of space-time, reducing gravity to a Riemannian geometry. In general relativity, Einstein completed the principle of least action introduced by Maupertuis with the geodesic hypothesis (that the path of any free particle is a geodesic in spacetime). Gravitation is no longer a force in the conventional sense because it is the same as inertia; it is what a body does when there are no external disturbances. But while the variational principle in general relativity has almost attained the status of the Laplacian Dream equation, the conservation of mass/energy, and conservation principles in general, have not fared nearly so well.

The notion of energy loses most of its physical content in the theory of general relativity. Intuitively, the conservation of mass/energy in special relativity is linked to the presumed symmetry properties of space-time. Once we add the proposition that space-time is irregular due to gravitational fields, few overall symmetries are left to justify general conservation principles; and indeed, there is no general conservation principle that has any claim to "preserve" the conservation of mass/energy in general relativity. One can begin to understand the mathematical evolution of the theory following the discussion of Trautman (1962). Familiarity with tensors is not absolutely necessary in order to understand the point of this example.

In special relativity, the conservation of mass/energy is expressed by the divergence of the tensor field.

$$T^{\beta}{}_{\alpha,\beta} = 0$$

Total energy and momentum can be obtained from this tensor by a suitable integration over the relevant three-dimensional space. In general relativity, in the presence of gravitation, energy and momentum are no longer conserved. There has been much effort to augment the tensor in order to describe the distribution of gravitational energy and momentum, that is, to discover a pseudotensor $t_{\alpha}{}^{\beta}$ such that

$$(T_\alpha{}^\beta + t_\alpha{}^\beta), {}_\beta = 0$$

The problem is not that no such pseudotensors have been found; rather, it is that a very great variety have been discovered. Unfortunately, these varieties either have no tensorial transformation properties, or else they depend on arbitrary vector fields, and therefore lack the generality of conservation principles. This in turn has led to a proliferation of categories of conservation rules in general relativity, distinctions being made between local and global conservations, as well as weak and strong conservation laws. Whereas mathematical proofs are available for the local and weak cases, these are special cases indeed because, in effect, they define away the gravitational field and ignore the fact that energy is an incoherent notion unless extended to the global field, as discussed in previous sections. Moreover, in the case of local laws, relativistic effects are negligible anyway, so that it would seem that the whole exercise of saving the conservation laws this way is rather like saving the whales with taxidermy (Will 1981, p. 106).

The perplexity is that the format of the theory of general relativity differs in a crucial way from previous physical theories. The algebraic transformation group that characterizes general relativity was the first to require that the simplest invariant law no longer be linear or homogeneous in the field variables and their differential quotients – in other words, the whole field does not equal the sum of its parts (Graves 1971, pp. 215–16). Another way of thinking about the same situation is that, for the first time since the reification of the conservation of energy, a model of field interactions was proposed where the field itself could be considered to be self-generating, since it acts upon its own source. By 1915 the last bastion of the energy concept fell: Something *could* come from nothing.

Only those who have followed the development of the energy concept from its *inception* will realize just how drastic a departure this was from every justification that has been offered to rationalize the conservation of energy. It was not quite the rediscovery of perpetual motion – at least, not yet. Physicists have hesitated to set themselves up as wizards and magi, conjuring lots of somethings from nothing.[11] In practice, at least until the 1980s, they prudently kept the implications of the terribly involved mathematics of general relativity to themselves.

If pressed on the issue, they tendered three distinct defenses. In the first, any queasiness about the status of energy in general relativity was suppressed with the assertion that, with greater expenditures of mathematical ingenuity and a little bit of luck, the appropriate invariant would be discovered in the near future. The second defense, which incidentally was Einstein's personal choice, was to interpret the pseudotensor as an adequate expression of gravitational energy, irrespective of the fact that it was frame-dependent and therefore should represent no physically significant entity in relativity theory (Zahar 1980, p. 37). The third (and in this author's opinion, the most honest) response has been to admit that "the general energy concept should not be considered a single concept at all in general relativity. From this viewpoint there are really a host of distinct and useful notions, each of which can be embodied in its own conservation law" (Graves 1971, p. 224). Of course, none of these limited, provisional, yet useful conservation principles partake of the broad scope or sweeping consequences of the law of the conservation of mass/energy. In fact, none of these conservation principles remotely correspond to the conventional notion of natural law as a covering law independent of contingent circumstance. Absence of global symmetries implies no profound invariants, and that means no real conservation law. And no real conservation law means no "real" energy.

Something exceedingly odd has happened in physics, and its repercussions still reverberate throughout our culture. Energy begat field theory, and field theory begat Maxwell's field equations. The field equations begat the constant velocity of light, and this begat Einstein, who undermined classical mechanics. Einstein begat special relativity, which begat $E = mc^2$. But, as Zahar (1980, p. 22) has argued, "It was precisely the law concerning the interchangeability of mass and energy, one main result of Special Relativity, which brought about the downfall of the latter." So $E = mc^2$ begat general relativity, which undermined the energy concept at its most fundamental level. Cheerfully using the language of "inner contradictions," and reveling in their Hegelian overtones (as does Zahar), the energy concept certainly does appear to have given birth to its own antithesis. Does this mean that we anticipate some resultant higher synthesis?

The story of twentieth-century physical theory is somewhat more complicated and somewhat less cathartic than all that.

Quantum mechanics

There was a time when most nonscientists had at least heard of Einstein and his theory of relativity, but would have greeted quantum mechanics with dazed incomprehension. But no more: the popular science literature is now bubbling over with dancing wu-li masters, taoist and zen-buddhist gurus, and many-worlds enthusiasts. Even the cat lovers are enticed into the realm of the quantum with cute pictures of Schrödinger's doomed cat. Once inside, the novice is dazzled with a world of mirrors much more elaborate than that found in any Fun House. On any given joyride, perhaps the universe is slumbering in a state of schizophrenia until the intrusion of an observer "collapses" the wave packet into prosaic reality; or perhaps the universe is a fortuitous (at least from our own point of view) bubble, a random fluctuation for which our own act of observation was a necessary prerequisite, irrespective of the minor complication that said observation took place long after the fact. It is all very heady stuff, and its extravagance of *bizarrerie* has provoked much philosophical wailing and gnashing of teeth. We cannot (and would not even find it amusing to) summarize the luxuriant strangeness of quantum mechanics here.[12] In lieu of all that, we merely want to briefly indicate the impact of quantum mechanics upon the concept of the conservation of energy.

The wellsprings of quantum mechanics, just as with the theory of relativity, can be traced backwards to imperatives of the later-nineteenth-century program of energy physics. The father of quantum mechanics was Max Planck, a physicist we have encountered previously in this narrative, both as debunker of the energetics movement and as historian of the conservation of energy. Planck was very concerned to reconcile the entropy law and the apparent temporal irreversibility of our experience with the conservation of energy (Mehra and Rechenberg 1982, I, p. 34). As part of his quest to explain the radiation spectra emitted from a black body, Planck was led in 1900 to posit that energy was distributed among the cavity resonators only in integral multiples of finite energy elements (Mehra and Rechenberg 1982, I, p. 51). Planck regarded this assumption of discrete quanta of energy as a measure of desperation, and even in his Nobel Prize lecture of 1918 he cautiously allowed it might only be a "fictitious magnitude, and the whole deduction of the law of radiation more or less an illusion, little more than a game played with formulae" (quoted in Cohen 1985, p. 421).

Most physicists were hostile to the quantum hypothesis in the first decade of this century, and no wonder, because until that time energy had been an expression of the intrinsic continuity of physical phenomena. But quanta then began to show up in other important physical theories: the photon theory of light-quanta; the Bohr model of the atom; the structure of spectroscopy; and then, in 1925/6, the full-fledged quantum mechanics of Heisenberg and Schrödinger. By the 1930s it had become clear that the quantum hypothesis was indispensable in the theory of physics at the atomic scale. Nevertheless, the successes of the quantum hypothesis were a mixed blessing, because the quantum hypothesis could not be understood as a simple extrapolation and elaboration of energy physics.

Quantum mechanics, as developed by Schrödinger, was based upon an analogy between wave phenomena and mechanical phenomena, the same analogy that had given rise to the original formulation of the Hamiltonian. The fundamental abstraction in Schrödinger equations was a wave function Ψ, whose arguments consisted of position variables and time. Unlike previous physical entities expressed in mathematics, the values of Ψ could be complex numbers, thus rendering simple physical interpretation difficult. The kinetic and potential energies of the electrons in an atom were expressed as mathematical operators on the wave function Ψ; in an appeal to the analogy with conventional Hamiltonians, these were dubbed the Hamiltonian operator H. The Schrödinger equation is an eigenvalue problem, expressed as $H\Psi = E\Psi$, which is solved for the unknown wave function Ψ and the unknown energy E. A major difference between the Schrödinger equation and the conventional Hamiltonian in mechanics is that there are several possible solutions for Ψ and the corresponding E; these are now interpreted as the allowable discrete configurations of electrons and energy states in the system.

It was the interpretation of the mysterious wave functions as probabilities by Max Born that really opened Pandora's Box in quantum mechanics. First, it was denied that the resort to probability was due to the fact of our provisional inadequacies in measuring the velocity, position, and energies of electrons without error. Later, the equations were interpreted to state that the positions and velocities are inherently random, and as such cannot be said to have definite values prior to measurement. This was more familiarly expressed as Heisenberg's principle of indeterminacy (or uncertainty, although this terminology is misleading).

Heisenberg argued that there are certain pairs of physical properties of a particle that cannot be simultaneously measured to a particular degree of accuracy. The conventional expression of the indeterminacy principle is that the position x and the momentum p of an electron cannot be simultaneously determined within a range of

$$\Delta x \cdot \Delta p \geq h/2\pi$$

where h is Planck's constant. Since the value of Planck's constant is very small – 6.625×10^{-27} erg-seconds – this scale of indeterminacy really only resides at the subatomic level. However, recalling that energy itself can be defined by components of velocity and position, the indeterminacy principle also implies that

$$\Delta E \cdot \Delta t \geq h/2\pi$$

In other words, in quantum theory an electron cannot be said to have an exact energy at a precise point in time. Again, this is not due to flaws in the measurement apparatus, but is inherent in the phenomenon.

Much of this can be rendered more comprehensible, if not actually more plausible, by the realization that quantum mechanics uses terms like "position," "velocity," "energy," and so on as analogies with like phenomena in macro-scale Hamiltonian physics, but that the concepts are not identical. If probabilities are conserved, than the operators H in quantum mechanics look very similar to Hamiltonians, except that they are solved for a set of states rather than for an equilibrium path of an electron (Theobald 1966, p. 129). Position and momentum are solved for average values. The term "path" is inappropriate in quantum mechanics, because the very notion of continuity has been relinquished. Energy levels can themselves only be expressed in terms of probabilities. The persistent use of identical linguistic terms cannot disguise the fact that some violence has been perpetrated upon the energy concept.

Nowhere are the scars of this violence more apparent than in the notorious "tunnel effect" (Landshoff and Metherell 1979, pp. 24–6). The tunnel effect can be visualized by a representation such as the one in Figure 2.3.

Figure 2.3 portrays the energy of repulsion of an alpha particle as a function of distance from the nucleus of an atom at the origin. The positive charge of the nucleus repels the alpha particle, and the repulsion increases as the particle approaches the nucleus until, at very close range, the strong attractive force overcomes the charge repulsion. This pattern of repulsion and attraction forms a "well" in three dimensions (shown as the ravine near the origin in Figure 2.3).

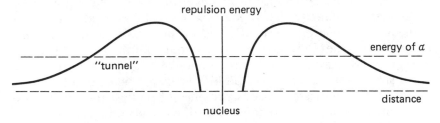

FIGURE 2.3   Electric repulsion near nucleus of alpha particles.

Also plotted on the figure is the energy of the alpha particle. As one can observe, the alpha particle in the well is not sufficiently energetic enough (in the classical sense) to climb out of the well and escape the nucleus. But in quantum mechanics, energy is only a stochastic quantity; no particle actually possesses a well-defined energy within the bounds of the Heisenberg indeterminacy limit. Using a metaphor found in most physics texts (Theobald 1966, p. 131; t'Hooft 1980, p. 109; Davies 1980, pp. 76–9), it is possible for the alpha particle to "borrow" enough energy (ΔE) for just long enough (Δt) to make it over the hump of the potential and then be ejected from the nucleus. It is just as if there were a small probability of the alpha particle tunneling through the energy barrier and then making its great escape. This tunnel effect is not some rare anomaly; rather it is vital in the explanation of one of the most significant phenomena of the twentieth century – radioactivity.

From a practical point of view, the tunnel effect is the repeal of the law of the conservation of energy, albeit in the small and only in a stochastic sense. The particle may be said to have borrowed the energy, but after it has repaid its debt the world is surely different as a result. The *fons et origo* of the energy concept, that nothing can spring from nothing, is surely on its way to being rendered meaningless. This tendency was taken to its ultimate consequences in twentieth-century cosmology, where the claim is made that literally everything came from nothing.

We have yet to exhaust the revisions of the energy concept wrought by quantum mechanics. In the late 1920s and early 1930s, Paul Dirac was attempting to apply the theory of relativity to quantum mechanics in order to improve the description of the energy of a free electron. He was stunned to find that the equation he had derived admitted of two solutions: one, the conventional positive solution; the other, a *negative* solution for kinetic energy. As Davies (1980, p. 83) has written, "Energy, like money, was formerly regarded as a purely positive quantity." But Dirac entertained the notion that the negative solution might have physical significance: negative energy states might be possible states of matter. He then proposed that the world was packed with unobservable electrons in energy states less than $-mc^2$. In this construction, these invisible electrons could jump up into positive energy levels, leaving behind an absence of negative energy, or, as Dirac suggested, a presence of positive energy. The mathematics was interpreted to indicate that this presence of an absence would have the properties of a particle; and indeed, particles fitting the description of these "positrons" were discovered by Carl Anderson in 1932

(Hanson 1963). The floodgates of particle production were thenceforth opened, and to this day, the whole motley menagerie of subatomic particles has yet to be definitively taxonomized and catalogued, much less caged.

As an explanation of a statement from Feynman (1965), it now becomes clear that the combination of two twentieth-century subfields of physics, such as relativity and quantum mechanics, can lead to counterintuitive and sometimes contradictory "laws." If only for the sake of completeness, we should also note that attempts to combine thermodynamics and quantum mechanics also impugn the "law" of the conservation of energy, in the sense that it can only be expressed as an approximation (Park and Simmons 1983, p. 306). The crux of the matter is that all of the original functions and connotations of the energy concept have either been undermined by internal developments within the subfields of physics, or else are undermined in the process of attempting the unification of physics by combining subfields. This quandary is very much a turnabout from the nineteenth-century promise that the energy concept would unify the entire discipline of physics.

The ideal role of the energy concept is displayed with the greatest clarity in the prinnacle of classical rational mechanics, the classical Hamiltonian. Energy was the touchstone by which we were enabled to *identify* what it was we wished to *analyze*. In this respect, there is no improvement upon the lucid paragraph by Theobald (1966, p. 49):

> Energy does not characterize particles, but processes; this becomes obvious from Hamilton's work onwards. But compensating advantages are gained by being able to describe motion in terms of scalars such as energy, instead of vectors such as momentum. In any physical system it is of the utmost importance to ascertain what it is that is being conserved absolutely during physical processes, for something conserved there must be. If nothing whatever is conserved absolutely in a physical system during change, then we have no means of re-identifying the system as the one with which we are concerned.

The trick to understanding the rise and fall of the energy concept is to observe that the Laplacian dream of the unification of all physics was actually quite short-lived, in that "the same system" is not at all the same when viewed from the vantage point of any of the branches of twentieth-century physics. Even in classical Hamiltonians, the energy concept embodied quite a collection of subsidiary concepts. As Emmy Noether showed, the conservation of energy served to express the purported symmetry of physical laws in time. This postulate of invariance in time served the dual purpose of tagging the identity of the system, and enabling the application of a variational principle. As if that were not enough, it also reified a particular construction of causality, the one most often expressed in the eighteenth and nineteenth centuries as "a cause must equal its effect," or "something cannot come from nothing." Finally, energy acted to constrain the notion of process by tethering it to the notion of continuity, or to revert to Leibniz, *natura non operatur per saltum*. All this (and more, as we shall discover in the next chapter) from one little integral.

Now, if the world managed to exhibit this rigid continuity, this absence of emergent novelty, this indifference to temporal location, this undifferentiated unity, then energy physics would have attained its completed perfection in the guise of something like proto-energetics by roughly 1870. The spanner in the works was that this picture does not correspond to the world as we know it. I do not mean to imply that the undermining of energy physics was a simple matter of empirical falsification: as we have noted, empiricism always had to be drugged when enticed to lie down with the law of the conservation of energy. Instead, as Poincaré understood, the fully determinate world of the classical conservation of energy would be a world that could do quite well without any physicists, thank you, since there would not exist anything even remotely resembling change. The simple fact was: As it was poised upon the very brink of the unification of all physical knowledge, physics had to diversify and fissure precisely so that it could comprehend change.

The hallmark of the fragmentation of physics was that the energy concept in each of the twentieth-century subfields of physics had to shed one or more of its connotations in the context of classical Hamiltonian dynamics. The first of these diverstitures was Poincaré's draconian demonstration that many of the most significant problems in mechanics were not integrable. This pointed to the introduction of stochastic concepts into mechanics, which in turn began to compromise the rigid identity of mechanical systems, even though earlier ideas of causality and continuity might retrench through positing the conservation of probability density functions and suchlike. But then thermodynamics denied that all physical processes were perfectly symmetrical in time, which had to compromise the full invariance character of the energy concept. The general theory of relativity dictated the generalization of the very notion of a metric, and as a consequence relinquished certain symmetries associated with the energy concept. Finally, reaping the whirlwind, quantum mechanics attacked the last bastion of the energy concept, the assertion of continuity, and discovered to its horror that strained and tenuous analogies with classical Hamiltonians could not prevent the realization that all commonsense notions of causality, persistence, and identity were lost for good.

The philosophical aftershocks of quantum mechanics are still being absorbed half a century later. In the short space remaining in this chapter, we merely wish to rehearse those aspects of debate that are germane to our survey of energy conservation, or to put it in more robust terms, germane to the dismantling of the energy concept. In quantum mechanics, as in the general theory of relativity, energy has a very problematic status, and it is hard to see how classical notions of conservation could apply to such an entity. One glaring symptom of the poverty and unintelligibility of the principle is that conventional constructions of causality do not apply. As Capek (1961, p. 323) has written:

> If we continue to use the term "energy," then the indeterminacy principle forces us to speak about "fluctuations of energy." Then we face the following dilemma: either these fluctuations are *caused,* and then we are back in classical determinism, or . . . energetic quantities spontaneously, that is, *causelessly,* fluctuate around certain mean values.

Another symptom of the lack of intelligibility of the energy concept in quantum mechanics is that, in the absence of continuity, it becomes very difficult to accurately conceptualize *process* (Theobald 1966, p. 124). Obviously, things do happen with quantifiable regularities at the macro level of phenomena, but explanation can no longer strike a pose of unmasking of the ultimate determinants of nature. Instead, within the ranges of experience specified by quantum mechanics, we must apparently rest satisfied with a very loose phenomenological description. The third symptom of the incoherency of the classical energy concept in quantum mechanics is the stipulation that every act of measurement or intervention in the world is, at some level, fundamentally irreversible (Prigogine 1980, p. 48). If this is the case, then the dissolution of the energy concept was inevitable, because energy was the reification of a world metric independent of our endeavors to know it. The energetic specification of time symmetry had deep, perhaps archetypal content. It said the world was not like us: we were born, grew old and decrepit, and died; the world persisted with an immortality that we could only dream about. That dream was the

Laplacian dream, and we could taste immortality as knowledge of that other immortality, that natural law.

But we are sons of Sisyphus, and must rebel against every god that we create.

Who's afraid of the nonconservation of energy?

Our narrative of the history of the law of the conservation of energy is nearly complete. We have surveyed the precursors, marveled at claims that energy was "simultaneously discovered," watched as energy begat the concept of the field, observed as variational principles and the correlative conservation of energy become ensconced as the pinnacle of nineteenth-century deterministic physics, and then wondered as twentieth-century developments undermined the content of the energy concept. The historian's favorite curve, the rise and fall of X, is almost irresistible, except for one nagging fact: the dissolution of the energy concept is not acknowledged or discussed in modern physics. As one can observe from Feynman's 1965 lectures, if the conservation of energy is discussed at all, it is touted as an immutable law of nature, and even more than that, a law of nature of profound privileged status. It is not uncommon to find modern physicists referring to this "law" (with intended or unintended irony) as "sacred" (Pagels 1982, p. 245); to find assertions that the law was only briefly in doubt only a very long time ago (von Laue in Koslow 1967, p. 264); and to find assertions that this doughty law has withstood unremitting vigorous and sustained testing in the domain of particle physics (Feinberg and Goldhaber 1963, p. 36). But even outside the monastic cloisters of the physics lab, "energy" is a word on every layman's tongue. There have been energy crises, energy shocks, energy conservation measures, and scare scenarios, that we are on the brink of exhausting our energy resources, which date back to William Stanley Jevons's *Coal Question* in the 1860s. Bookstores have entire sections devoted to energy, but one would search them in vain to find any inkling that the energy concept has no unique theoretical referent. How can this be? Is the conservation of energy a law of nature or is it not?

One potential explanation of this anomaly could be that here is where the actual intellectual history and the pedagogical version packaged for mass consumption diverge.[13] Much of the pedagogical rhetoric of physics depends heavily upon the energy concept, and the intuitive plausibility of that concept and the mathematics that accompanies it are themselves premised upon the conservation of energy. On a practical level, the conservation of energy remains indispensable in many branches of physics, especially in the classical mechanics of Hamiltonians. To admit all of this is one thing, but to then claim that the conservation of energy has not been subject to doubt throughout the twentieth century is quite another. This doubt has been endemic in two particular areas of physics: the physics of the very very small and the physics of the very very large. The legacy of this doubt has obviously not been the out-and-out repudiation of the classical energy concept; what has borne the brunt of revisionism has been the status of natural law.

It is a bit of an embarrassment to the Polyannas of upbeat confidence that surround the law of the conservation of energy that, in the past, it has been the object of skepticism by some rather famous physicists. One of the first to entertain the possibility of the nonconservation of energy as an alternative to the awkward quantum structure of radiation was Albert Einstein. Ultimately, however, he did repudiate this alternative, writing in 1911 to a friend, "Who would have the courage to make a decision of this kind?" (quoted in Pais 1982, p. 418). In 1916, Walter Nernst proposed the efficacy of a statistical version of the conservation of energy. In 1919, Charles Galton Darwin wrote, "No one can doubt that energy is approximately conserved, but ordinary dynamical and electrical experiments only establish it statistically, and so really only put it on the same footing as the second law of thermodynamics" (quoted in Mehra and Rechenberg 1982, I, p. 538). Paul Forman (1971) has demonstrated that a Spenglerian hostility to science and causality had a direct impact upon the Weimar physics community, and hence certain prominent members of that community began to make disparaging comments about the law of the conservation of energy.

The most famous attack in the annals of the twentieth-century vicissitudes of energy conservation was the paper that marks the dying gasp of the old quantum theory, the Bohr–Kramers–Slater (BKS) paper of 1924 (Mehra and Rechenberg 1982, I, pp. 536–53; Stuewer 1975). This paper explicitly proposed a stochastic version of the law of energy conservation in order to explain the interactions of radiation and matter. The paper raised quite a *frisson* of excitement in the physics community, with Einstein and Pauli vehemently opposed to its program, but with Schrödinger strongly in favor of it. Among Einstein's objections was the dark warning that "Abandonment of causality as a matter of principle should be permitted only in the most extreme emergency" (Pais 1982, p. 420). Schrödinger's defense consisted mainly of the development of some of the mathematical implications of the BKS theory, but also to appeal to an analogy with the rampant German hyperinflation of 1924:

> a certain stability in the world order *sub specie aeternitatis* can only exist through the interrelationship of each individual system with the rest of the world. The disconnected individual system would be, from the viewpoint of unity, chaos. The interrelationship is necessary as a continuous regulative factor, without which, with respect to energy considerations, the system would aimlessly wander about – Is it idle speculation if one is reminded of this by a similarity in social, ethical and cultural phenomena?" (quoted in Stuewer 1975, p. 299).

One of the curious aspects of this episode is how it is treated in the modern history of science literature: time and again the demise of the BKS theory is cited as a definitive vindication of the law of the conservation of energy (Koslow 1967, p. 264; Pais 1982, p. 421; Mehra and Rechenberg 1982, I, p. 537). The BKS theory was impugned by the Bothe–Geiger and Compton–Simon experiments on the scattering of radiation, which were reported close on the heels of the BKS paper and were widely interpreted at the time as support for the conservation of energy and momentum (Mehra and Rechenberg 1982, I, p. 612). Bohr, with his characteristic generosity, rapidly capitulated to this interpretation, promising to "give our revolutionary efforts as honorable a funeral as possible." His capitulation was widely viewed as a victory for Einstein and Pauli, as well as for the heuristic rule that "the energy concept should not be modified" (quoted in Stuewer 1975, pp. 303–4). Nevertheless, the entire controversy was superseded by the advent of Heisenberg and Schrödinger's new quantum mechanics, which we have described in the previous section. The rub is that the new quantum mechanics does not conform to the Einstein–Pauli heuristic in content, although perhaps the point might be argued on grounds of form. While it is certainly true that the Bothe–Geiger and Compton–Simon experiments killed the BKS theory, it is a particularly shortsighted interpretation to also claim that those experiments proved the conservation of energy.

A further embarrassment to the conventional wisdom that claims that energy conservation was conclusively tested by 1925 is that certain eminent physicists persisted in their skepticism about the principle well after this date. Schrödinger, for one, continued to moot the incoherence of the energy concept well into the 1930s (Capek 1961, p. 301). At the urging of Bohr, Heisenberg contrived to distance himself from a commitment to energy conservation in his work on the neutron in 1932, after having written to Bohr in 1930 that he doubted that energy conservation held within the dimensions of the Compton wavelength (Bromberg 1971, pp. 325–35). Paul Dirac (1936) wrote a short note in *Nature* proposing that energy conservation should be relinquished in the case of relativistic quantum mechanics, especially in the case of beta decay.

It is an interesting pastime to speculate why more has not been made of these doubts in the interim. One suspects that the controversies that gave voice to this skepticism are now considered satisfactorily resolved; but the nature of the resolution is indicative of the role of the energy concept in rebuffing potentially contradictory evidence. In subatomic physics many of the problems of energy conservation were rendered nugatory by the proliferation of novel subatomic particles, beginning with the positron, the neutron, and the neutrino. The existence of these particles was originally justified as accounting for any troublesome energy deficits (Brown and Hoddeson 1983, p. 6). In the 1950s the sequential discovery of each new particle was repeatedly touted as a vindication of the conservation of energy (Feinberg and Goldhaber 1963). But the game of conjuring new particles was not simply a matter of adding up all the relevant energies and attributing any deficit to, *voilà*, a new particle. At best this procedure would work only a few times, and not for the over 400 particles known to date. Moreover, as energy itself is a stochastic quantity, only the moments of the relevant distributions could be aggregated under certain strict conditions. In actual practice, energy conservation has been compromised numerous times in the postwar period, but these calculations have ceased being interpreted as disconfirmations of the conservation law. Instead, they have been read as heuristic imperatives to either reshuffle the cages or admit new members to the particle zoo.

Perhaps we are too close to the rush of events in modern physics to accurately assess significant trends, but it seems safe to say that recent physics has undergone a profound change in attitude with respect to the conservation of energy, a change perhaps as profound as the original revolution of the 1840s and 1850s. Past a certain point in the postwar period, it appears that the previous agony and angst over the possible or potential failure of the conservation of energy tends to just fade away. This is not due to any critical experiments; but rather to a fundamental shift in the *role* of the energy concept in modern physics. Energy, it seems, has finally become a purely instrumental and mathematical entity, transformed along its history from a substance to an entity to a relation to, finally, a gestalt.

After World War II, the research program that began with Noether's theorem and continued through Eugene Wigner's work on symmetry recieved a new infusion of mathematical talent familiar with the vagaries of general relativity, quantum mechanics, and so forth. This new generation invested much significance in the fact that conservation principles were isomorphic to the symmetries built in at the most fundamental levels of physics: for example, the assumption of spatial homogeneity under displacement is isomorphic to the conservation of linear momentum; invariance under spatial rotation is isomorphic to the conservation of angular momentum; and, of course, invariance under time translation is isomorphic to energy conservation. While these symmetries of classical mechanics had been tacit knowledge since the time of Noether's theorem, general relativity and quantum mechanics brought the instrumental significance of invariance principles to the foreground of attention (Sklar 1974, p. 360). In special relativity, symmetry under translation in space-time implies the conservation of mass and energy (or, strictly, momentum-energy); however, one could not help but notice that older and more prosaic notions of invariance were compromised by this revision. The resultant of these trends was to encourage exploration of a more subtle appreciation of symmetry principles.

Following Sklar (1974, p. 362), we can distinguish at least two different interpretations of invariance principles. The first, or active, interpretation deems that symmetry is exhibited when "same states of differing systems evolve into same states." In quantum mechanics, for instance, invariance under spatial translation means that the transition probabilities of System X will be identical to System Y. The concept of two entities being the same has been considerably slackened here, as we have already observed that energy states are not deterministic in quantum mechanics. Nevertheless, *as a mathematical expression*, its symmetry is a straightforward elaboration of the previous classical symmetry.

The second, or passive, interpretation of invariance deems that if the same system is described by different observers, they may possibly describe it differently from their respective points of view, but all lawlike connections between their descriptions will be symmetrical. This passive interpretation is exemplified by relativistic scenarios about observers in differing reference frames. As one might expect, these two interpretations of invariance do not always coexist: for example, under a regime of noncontinuous transformations, generally only the active interpretation retains its relevance. As Sklar says, a right-handed glove cannot be made to look like a left-handed glove by changing my orientation; but a right-handed world can duplicate a left-handed world. The cumulative force of such distinctions is that, from a theoretical perspective, it is not energy itself that really matters, but rather the forms of the symmetries that it has encapsulated or expressed. Adherence to the original prosaic conception of energy might serve to obscure the importance of the set of deeper symmetries implicitly imposed in order to characterize a given physical situation. As we have observed, we might (for instance) relinquish the aspect of energy that reified continuity in quantum mechanics, but retain an active appreciation of the symmetries (perhaps such as spatial invariance) that serve to anchor the theory in some residual deterministic notions. Or, as in chaos theory, we might relinquish the Hamiltonian approach altogether in order to concentrate upon the symmetries of scale present in the fractal geometries of phase spaces. In a sense, an appreciation of symmetry allows a blending of relativist and determinist theorizing.

The adoption of the new mindset has proved particularly fruitful in subatomic physics, fostering an open-minded attitude toward the presence or absence of a particular symmetry at alternative levels of a given analysis. For instance, symmetries under spatial reflection do not have important conservation-rule implications in classical mechanics, but were used extensively in subatomic physics under the rubric of "conservation of parity" to categorize the products of particle collisions. In 1956, when it was shown that parity conservation was violated in the presence of weak interactions, the world did not fall apart: instead, it was then asserted that parity was only a good quantum number for the strong and electromagnetic interactions (Pickering 1984, p. 54). The usefulness of the conservation of electric charge at the subatomic level provoked a reinterpretation as the postulate of symmetry under charge reversal.

These examples might naturally provoke the objection: Aren't we just restating the various conservation laws in different words? Actually the process is a little more involved than that, since it has engendered innovations at the level of mathematical technique and innovations at the level of notions of scientific behavior. The symmetry approach suggested the formalisms of group theory, and in particle physics these by themselves provided theoretical guidance as to classification, predicted some decay patterns by ruling out others, and even predicted the existence of some new subatomic particles (Pickering 1984, p. 60). In general, the mathematics of symmetry imposes a lot of structure on a problem, even if it is incapable of explicitly describing dynamics of interaction. At a deeper level, the symmetry approach freed up the activity of theoretical speculation vis-à-vis the dictates of natural law. It allowed scientists to shrug off the ironclad rule of conservation laws without appearing to repudiate the precursor theories predicated upon their existence. This new-found freedom encouraged theorists to consider the possibility that previous conservation laws might be special cases of a larger law, but also that they might be broken under specific circumstances. A premier instance of this freedom was the 1956 enunciation of parity violation. As one physicist said in reaction to this announcement, "The old prejudice in favor of symmetry is dying out. You used to have to explain why when it fails. Now you have to explain why it is respected" (*Science,* 7 Nov. 1980, p. 619; Franklin 1979).

It did not take long before the new conventional wisdom in physics was that the expression of symmetries was the most general way to summarize the content of physical theories; and it took even less time to turn that insight around and to use phenomenological symmetries to construct new physical theories. As it turned out, a very effective method of instilling discipline in the expanding population of the high-energy-particle zoo was to *invent* conservation principles as taxonomic devices (Pickering 1984, pp. 50–ff.). Principles such as the conservation of baryon number and lepton number were postulated in direct analogy with the conservation of electric charge to summarize the allowable states of the evolution of particle interactions. The successes of this gambit led to further conservation principles of strangeness and parity. Soon came a proliferation of conservation laws, which were needed to describe why a certain subset of subatomic particles did or did not decay into some other subset of particles; but because conservation principles are isomorphic to symmetries, the next step was to array the particles along the various axes of attributes in a manner reminiscent of the periodic table of chemical elements. Symmetries in such multidimensional tables would then correspond to the known conservation rules; and further, holes in the tables could be interpreted as predicting the existence of unknown particles (Llewellyn Smith, in Mulvey 1981, pp. 62–4). The resulting quark model hence owes its structure to the newly liberated attitudes concerning symmetry principles.

Another reason the enthusiasm for the symmetries framework has prevailed in the postwar period is that it has come to represent the latest incarnation of that holy grail of physics, the grand unification of all physical theory. In the 1960s the concept of gauge symmetry – the idea that one can make local transformations of certain classes of quantum field from one space-time point to another without affecting the predictions of the theory – came to attract a lot of attention (Weinberg 1977). It had been discovered that the simplest field that exhibited gauge symmetry in the quantum theory of electrons was the one described by Maxwell's equations. This opened up the possibility that the laws of electrodynamics could be said to have been derived from the condition of gauge symmetry. The implication of this statement was that the long-sought-after grand unification theory (GUT) of the four nuclear forces – strong, weak, electromagnetic, and gravity – should assume the format of a general gauge symmetry. One effect of the general excitement surrounding the quest for GUTs has been the subsequent reconceptualization of the entire history of physics as a slow progressive recognition of the symmetries that characterize physical phenomena: from Galilean symmetries to Lorentzian and global-gauge ones, and from local Abelian-gauge to local non-Abelian-gauge symmetries (Galison 1983, p. 49). While it would be foolhardy to pronounce upon the meaning and significance of this contemporary research program, it may be interesting to note that this invocation of the culmination and closure of all physics resembles that which accompanied the first flush of energy physics in the mid-nineteenth century. Could it be that the push to see all theoretical knowledge as a unified, complete, and coherent whole is merely the emotional side of any program to reconceptualize a research program's conservation principles, as first suggested by Meyerson (1962)?

Whatever the future might bring, it is safe to say that the nonconservation of energy will no longer be regarded as it was by Einstein – namely, as the abdication of all that is causal and rational. In quantum electrodynamics, infinite energies generated "out of nowhere" by self-interaction are routinely subtracted away in the process of "renormalization." In cosmology, negative energies are routinely added to positive energies such that the energy of the universe sums to zero (Guth 1983, p. 201). In theories that would have made the hair of a Helmholtz or a Kelvin stand on end it has now been seriously proposed that the entire universe began as a vacuum fluctuation: by a process of quantum tunneling the great blooming buzzing confusion that we call everything originally came from nothing (Tryon 1973; Akatz and Pagels 1982). To quote Guth (1983, pp. 201, 215):

> If the universe is described by a Robertson–Walker metric, as is generally assumed in simple models, then there is no globally con-

served energy . . . Probably the most striking recent development in the study of cosmogeny is the realization that the universe may be completely devoid of all conserved quantum numbers. If so, then even if we do not understand the precise scenario, it becomes very plausible that our observed universe emerged from nothing or from almost nothing. I have often heard it said that there is no such thing as a free lunch. It now appears possible that the universe is a free lunch.

No doubt about it; this has got to be bad news for an economist.

CHAPTER 3

Body, motion, and value

Energy, someone may say, is a mere abstraction, a mere term, not a real thing. As you will. In this, as in many another respects, it is like an abstraction no one would deny reality to, and that abstraction is wealth. Wealth is the power of purchasing, as energy is the power of working. I cannot show you energy, only its effects . . . Abstraction or not, energy is as real as wealth – I am not sure that they are not two aspects of the same thing [Soddy 1920, pp. 27–8].

Why is it that people in this way never ask what is the nature of gold, or what is the nature of velocity? Is the nature of gold better known to us than that of force? [Hertz 1956, p. 8]

Historians of science often take for granted an efficient market theory of their own . . . But the history of ideas is not always so neat [Gleick 1987, p. 181].

It is said that in Poland of the 1980s, when a director wants to stage a realist drama, he chooses *Waiting For Godot*. Let us say I have just subjected you to a similar sort of experience. I anticipate that you, especially if you are an economist, just want to understand the way things really are. You don't want art; you want *information*. You are not all that thrilled about physics, especially the arcane theoretical bits; yet considering yourself open-minded (after all, you are still with me) and tolerant, you have put up with a dreadfully laborious slog through the history of physics, only to be left with the outrageous suggestion that energy doesn't exist. Now, what is the point? Where is the plot?

Rest assured that the author does not subscribe to the fashionable avant-garde contempt for plot. The narrative latticework will soon come into view, although I fear that, as with *Waiting for Godot*, we are not headed for a happy ending. The story so far: The discipline of physics owes its coherence and unity to the rise of the energy concept in the middle of the nineteenth century. However, as soon as the discipline was consolidated, further elaboration and scrutiny of the energy concept began to undermine its original content and intent. Early anticipations of the energy concept treated it as though it were a substance, but various imperatives led the concept to be recast into the format of a field, which really can only be understood in its mathematical incarnation. Energy seemed to embody reversibility, but an irreversibility proviso in the form of the second law of thermodynamics had to be appended almost immediately. Energy formalized the principles of continuity and determinism, but these were soon compromised when it was decided that energy came in little quantum packets. The more one looked into it, the more these progressive reformulations suggested that energy was not really any one thing, but rather a flexible means of expressing symmetry principles. Yet even that was too dessicated and technocratic a perspective on the phenomenon. Energy served a lot of functions: It tagged the identity of natural phenomena; it defined "process" by counterposing it to continuity; it was impregnated with all the language used in Western theological discussions; it was part and parcel of the application of extremal principles; it was in the vanguard of classical determinism; it was the One in the Many; it was conflated with causality itself; and most important, it decreed "something cannot arise from nothing."

It is this last theme, the conviction that nature is *economical,* that ushers us into the world familiar to the economist. It is the world of debit and credit, of profit and loss, of productive citizens and beggars and thieves. It has been no accident that metaphors of money and trade cropped up periodically in the narrative history in the previous chapter. True, it was I who salted the narrative with those particular quotes, but they did exist, and they do raise the possibility that certain economic themes insinuate themselves throughout the history of physics.

Now, in raising the specter of Mammon, there are some rather tired and worn themes that I am *not* aiming to invoke. One is the prosaic fact that tehcnological innovations may have provided inspiration for certain physical theories. Another path not here taken is the old Weberian chestnut about capitalist rationality writ large. Nor, for that matter, am I referring to the perennial whipping boy of the history of science literature, the Marxist-inspired Hessen thesis.[1] Instead, I intend in this chapter to explore the ways in which one might suggest that there is an economic core to Western physical theory, one encased in metaphor and analogy, specific to a particular configuration of economic relationships, molded firmly within the energy concept.

As we extract the energy metaphor from out of its narrowly orthodox disciplinary context, it will inevitably become even more slippery and elusive and protean. Now we shall need to pin it down against an economic backdrop in order to discern its chrematistic character.

The discovery of energy conservation *Réchauffé*

Energy has been such a useful concept that if it did not exist, we would have had to invent it. But of course, there is a sense in which we did invent it: Its earliest usage (according to the *Oxford English Dictionary*) connoted a species of metaphor that evoked a mental picture of something acting or moving; this usage significantly predated any specific physical reference. While our present concern is with the physical definition, it will shortly become apparent that there is no understanding of energy without a broader purview. Nowhere is this more evident than in the literature that grapples with the purported "simultaneous discovery" of energy conservation in the mid-nineteenth century.

In the last chapter, we acknowledged the existence of a large exegetical literature on the history of the physical energy concept; we also allowed that it did not add up to any coherent or comprehensive picture. The overall superior text, though now growing a bit dated, is the paper Thomas Kuhn delivered to the Institute of the History of Science in 1957 (Kuhn 1959). In that paper Kuhn noted that there was something incongruous about the fact that the history of what was indisputably the most important concept in physics should remain in such obscurity, particularly when one realized that anywhere from twelve to sixteen people had some claim to be considered discoverers, and further, that they operated in an environment in which we now see anticipations of the concept "so close to the surface of scientific consciousness" over such a great duration of time. Kuhn felt that the answers must be located in a set of prior factors, which conditioned and suggested the energy concept to all concerned. As he put it, "We know why they are there: Energy *is* conserved; nature behaves that way. But we do not know why these elements suddenly became accessible and recognizable" (Kuhn 1959, p. 323).

In answer to his own question, he proceeded to propose three such factors. The first, which he called "availability of conversion processes," consisted of the fascination with electrical phenomena following Volta's invention of the battery at the turn of the century, as well as the spreading implementation of steam engines in the same period. Although piston-fired engines such as the Savery pump and the Newcomen atmospheric engine dated from the beginning of the eighteenth century, it was only upon the heels of James Watt and his investigations that steam as a generalized power source became practical, and it was not until the 1820s that the prospects of turning heat into motion were made patently manifest by the steam railways (Cardwell 1971). In this text, Kuhn (1959, p. 324) maintains that it was only by the 1830s that all these activities began to be regarded as processes of *conversion;* yet in a footnote Kuhn admits that it was fairly frequent in the eighteenth century to use the metaphor of conversion for steam devices. He sums up this first factor in the discovery of energy conservation by asserting that the individual conversion processes were all discovered in the laboratory, and it was the sheer prolifera- tion of controlled conversions that acted to suggest a global conserva- tion principle. "This is the concept of the universal convertability of natural powers, and it is not, let us be clear, the same as the notion of conservation. But the remaining steps proved to be small and rather obvious" (Kuhn 1959, p. 328).

Kuhn's second factor was dubbed a "concern with engines," a "well-known by-product of the Industrial Revolution." He points out that, of his nine certified candidates for discovery – that is, those who actually succeeded in quantifying a conversion process – all but Mayer and Helmholtz were either trained as engineers or were working directly on engines at the time of their research. As engineers, they were concerned to compare the amount of work with the amount of fuel, and this, Kuhn claimed, was tantamount to asking for a coeffi- cient of conversion between energetic phenomena. Yet this seems so only in retrospect: If one believed that the conversions varied under differing conditions, as many did, then it is not at all clear that a law of nature was just around the corner.

These two factors would probably statisfy positivist philosophers of science. In their perspective, these natural conversions just kept hit- ting the engineers in the face until they woke up and acknowledged the conservation of energy. But here Kuhn showed his true colors: skeptical of positivism, wary of simple empirical claims, and sensitive to the ambiguities surrounding the historical actors.

> This study of simultaneous discovery might well end here. But a last look at the papers of the pioneers generates an uncomfortable feeling that something is still missing, something that is not perhaps a substantive element at all. This feeling would not exist if all the pioneers had, like Carnot and Joule, begun with a straightforward technical problem and proceeded by stages to the concept of energy conservation. But in the cases of Colding, Helmholtz, Liebig, Mayer, Mohr and Séguin, the notions of an underlying imperishable metaphysical force seems prior to research and *almost unrelated to it* [my italics]. Put bluntly, these pioneers seem to have held an idea capable of becoming conservation of energy for some time before they found evidence of it" [1959, p. 336].

Prodded by this nagging doubt, Kuhn therefore suggested a third factor, which he identified as the *Naturphilosophie* movement of Schelling, Coleridge, and Hebart. This was an early-nineteenth-century school of philosophy that posited the existence of a single force that suffused throughout all of nature. Of course, Kuhn had to link all his candidates to this school somehow; and as he began to attempt to do so this, he found himself stretching the definition of a *Naturphilosoph* to encompass Kant. This after-the-fact enlargement of the club was dubious; one can't help but feel that Kuhn knew he was clutching at straws, especially when he was driven to such expedients as smoothing over Helmholtz's obvious lifelong commitment to a reductionist version of mechanism (1959, p. 339). That Helmholtz was heavily influenced by Kant is indisputable (Heimann 1974; Galaty 1974); but the influence of the *Naturphilosophs* is quite another matter.

Following Kuhn's lead, there have been a number of forays to gauge the impact of *Naturphilosophie* upon the evolution of physics (Snelders 1971; Gower 1973). The results, particularly with respect to the genesis of the energy concept, have been disappointing. This literature demonstrated that the key tenets of *Naturphilosophie* were: a hostility to experimental methods; an exaltation of intuitive speculation ratified by the purported *organic* unity of nature; a mode of analogical reasoning in terms of polar antinomies such as mind and matter, irritability and sensibility, oxygen and hydrogen, acid and base, and so forth; and an advocacy of numerology as a legitimate research technique. In the middle of his survey, Gower raises the question of the philosophical cogency of this school, and concludes:

> As a contribution to philosophical debate it has been, and can be, safely ignored. Certainly, it would be a mistake to think that philosophers who credit science with metaphysical foundations, in one sense or another, have anything so insubstantial as Schelling's speculative physics in mind [Gower 1973, p. 320].

As for the mere assertion of the unity of nature, it was hardly a doctrine original with this school, nor was it plausibly reprocessed in a format attractive to any of the discoverer of the energy concept.

Hence, we are left with Kuhn's qualms, and little else. The conversion processes and the steam engines were not like Samuel Johnson's stones, lying about here and there, needing only to be kicked to squeal "energy!" Either we should be convinced that these pioneers saw in their engines and Volta piles what we see, and that the empirical phenomena summoned forth the obvious inference of the conservation of energy, or else there was some other factor, some as-yet-unidentified something that explains why so many individuals in such disparate environments and cultural backgrounds harbored the conviction that something was conserved as an a priori precept of nature.

Kuhn touched on such qualms lightly, and with good reason, because if scrutinized with a more intense gaze, the qualms degenerate into trepidation and worse. The distinguished commentators at the 1957 conference were quick to sense the disquiet. Professor Carl Boyer took exception to Kuhn's remark that energy conservation was transparently "in" nature; instead, he suggested, perhaps energy was merely a concept that we had contrived in order to describe nature. Further, just because we opt to view some phenomenon as a conversion process does not mean it actually is one, much less that earlier physical researchers saw it that way. Here he cited Rumford's cannon-boring experiment: "Did the motion *become* heat or did it merely act as a catalytic agent to release the heat?" (Boyer, in Clagett 1959, p. 385).

Such doubts strike at the very core of the conviction that energy conservation could be discovered in nature. To prepare the reader, I broached many of these objections in Chapter 2. At the most fundamental level of objection, Joule, who conventionally gets the lion's share of the credit for *empirical* discovery, did not in fact produce a plausibly narrowed band of estimates for the mechanical equivalent of heat; Mayer essentially calculated his estimate from a priori considerations; whereas Helmholtz really only deserves credit for the mathematical linkage to *vis viva*. Yet, when all is said and done, what does it matter who did what when? We know that energy is really conserved in nature, don't we? Isn't energy conservation just a matter of common knowledge?

The latter part of Chapter 2 was calculated to call those convictions into question, but let us not stop there. Some fascinating experiments at Johns Hopkins University in what we might call philosophical anthropology can also shed some light on these supposedly commonsense notions.

The basic research design of the Hopkins group was to confront high school and college students with various scenarios about simple problems in motion, such as the description of the path of an object dropped while walking, or the path of an orbiting ball cut free from its central restraint. Their stunning finding was that 87 percent of the students who had had no training in physics gave answers considered incorrect according to modern physics, but consonant with Aristotelian notions to of motion and impetus. A further result, which gave even greater pause, was that 27 percent of those who *had* studied physics gave Aristotelian answers (McCloskey 1984). The relevance of these results for our present concerns is that Aristotelian impetus theory explicitly violates all the modern conservation principles regarding motion. Thus, more than a century after the so-called discovery of energy conservation, the quotidian muscular familiarity with motion does little to convince the average educated person of the transparent truth of rational mechanics.

We may press this point even further. One of the most notable things about the history of the energy concept is the frequency with which innovators find it necessary to refer to the impossibility of the perpetual motion machine, as if this were an axiom or a self-evident truth. There are two reasons such appeals are noteworthy: the first, that for every natural philosopher or physicist prior to 1850 who condemned the quest for perpetual motion, there was another natural philosopher or mechanic who claimed to have mastered it (Dircks 1870, chap. 9); and the second, that the great preponderance of denials of perpetual motion never rose above the format of bald assertions, with their "proofs" mostly consisting either of metaphors or direct appeals to metaphysics.[2] The very few detractors who felt it incumbent upon themselves to offer a mathematical demonstration of the impossibility of perpetual motion tended to restrict their disquisitions strictly to rational mechanics, primarily because there were no widely held principles that insured that some baroque sequence of energetic phenomena (including some transformations that were not yet understood) might not result in a net gain of work. But, of course, it is the prohibition of any such *sequence* that sets apart the principle of the conservation of energy from a principle of the conservation of momentum, or *vis viva,* or what-have-you. Hence the assertion that the obvious impossibility of perpetual motion implied the conservation of energy was a *petitio principii,* at least in the early nineteenth century context (Meyerson 1962, p. 204). The general prohibition of perpetual motion machines was deduced from the conservation of energy, and not the reverse.

With a small modicum of imagination and sympathy, one can readily come to realize that the idea of perpetual motion is not a patently absurd and ridiculous notion, an ignis fatuus dreamt up by cretins and charlatans. For the denizens of Europe in the Middle Ages, a windmill situated in a windy area, or a water mill on a stream that never runs dry were effectively perpetual motion machines (White 1962, p. 131). Even later, the model of the revolutions of the planets or the ebb and flow of the tides could easily be regarded as instances of perpetual motion (Ord-Hume 1977, p. 22). Clocks driven by changes in barometric pressure would have seemed to have brought perpetual motion within reach of human artifice. The crux of the issue of perpetual motion is to learn to *see* what would legitimately count as a net gain of work or power or force; which indeed is tantamount to embedding a definition of work within a larger system of accounts capable of taxonomizing all contingencies. After all, as Meyerson (1962, p. 208) observed, when we calculate kinetic energy today, we blithely ignore the contributions to mv^2 of the velocity of the earth, the velocity of our solar system, and so on.

Thus the supposed commonsense character of the conservation of energy is spurious, nothing but specious dogmatism. What is required is an historically grounded understanding of how physicists came to settle upon the construction of events, the prohibitions and the enthusiasms, the pluses and the minuses that they finally reified in the conservation of energy. The other distinguished commentator upon Kuhn's 1957 paper, Erwin Hiebert, made essentially the same point:

> What was needed more than, and in addition to, the collection of new facts unknown in the eighteenth century, was a workable agreement on a conceptual level of what may be referred to as a general notion of "completed action," over and against the then already-clear notion of "force" [Hiebert, in Clagett 1959, p. 392].

In other words, there had to be a common context of *evaluation,* or, if we may be venal about it, a *system of accounts* for keeping track of completed or useful action. Where did the gaggle of far-flung natural philosophers get their common set of accounts from? Not to indulge in too much periphrasis, they all got it from something shared in their social context; more specifically, they all derived it from their economic milieu.

This statement is bound to raise the hackles of a wide range of scholars. Many will think they detect in that statement some version of a Marxist historical materialism, wherein the economic base determines the superstructure, containing not only legal and social relationships but also science itself. Among historians of physics, it conjures the specter of the Hessen thesis, which caused a commotion in the 1930s by claiming that much of Newton's *Principia* was derived from artisanal craft knowledge of that era (Hessen 1931). However, it should be clear from the totality of the rest of this volume that this chapter is not inspired by those Marxist themes. Indeed, modern commentators such as Gouldner (1980) have explained with great perspicacity how Marxist attempts to incorporate science within the ambit of the base/superstructure framework of historical materialism have resulted in profound contradictions, which, among other effects, may account for the bifurcation of modern Marxism into warring camps.[3]

In the last quarter of the twentieth century discussions of the interplay of science and society have outgrown the crude dictums of historical materialism, as well as transcending the incoherent dichotomy of internalist and externalist intellectual histories. To cite just a sampling, the writings on the history of science of Brush (1978), Barnes and Shapin (1979), Mackenzie (1981), Freudenthal (1986), Elster (1975), Breger (1982) Sohn-Rethel (1978), Latour (1987), Pickering (1984), Collins (1985), Markus (1987), Forman (1971), and Porter (1981a, 1985, 1986) are evidence of a great flowering of efforts all concerned with a reconsideration of the interplay of science and social forces. Much of this literature has been inspirational for what follows, and yet, there is a sense in which the subsequent text aspires to go a bit further than these predecessors. For it is the intention of this chapter to transcend the simple notion of intellectual influence and aim for a higher plane of synthesis, one that uncovers the unity of discourse behind the quotidian barriers of fields or disciplines, or indeed, between the social and the natural.[4]

This is a tall order; it will not be achieved without treading upon some disciplinary prerogatives. The remainder of this chapter will subject the energy concept to scrutiny from what might be construed as the three corners of a pyramid that supports its meaning, similar to that in Figure 3.1.

Just as the pyramid itself is a metaphor, in this instance it is constructed from metaphors: of motion (physics), of the body (anthropomorphics), and of value (economics). These three metaphors constituted the a priori content as well as the common context that made the energy concept possible, if not necessary. However, as the pyramid metaphor implies, these constituent metaphors are misconstrued if they are regarded as independent and self-sufficient intellectual influences. In their historical manifestations, each was an inseparable part of the energy metaphor and of each other, with boundaries shading off imperceptibly one into another. Of course, this is not to say that differing aspects of the pyramid may not look dissimilar. It would be fair to observe that the motion/value face of the pyramid was the most responsible for the quantification and mathematization of the energy concept, while the body/motion face

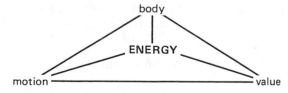

Figure 3.1 The architectonic of the energy concept.

was more responsible for the symmetry character of the energy concept. The body/value face will prove in many respects the most controversial aspect, because it is responsible for the less-acknowledged anthropomorphic and social character of the energy concept, the religious overtones and the cultural influences so often spurned as the opposite of scientific argument. Precisely for that reason the body/value axis will receive the lion's share of attention in this chapter.

Thus, instead of discrete influences, imagine, if you will, the energy concept as an ever-expanding pyramid with the three metaphors of body, motion, and value at the base vertexes. As the vertexes grow further and further apart, the metaphorical distance between physics and economics also widens, until it becomes commonplace to assert that they are indeed separate and distinct systems of explanation. Nevertheless, they operate in the same cultural milieu, partake of much the same language and formalisms, and most important, maintain a reciprocal metaphorical legitimation and support: They remain a pyramid.

I promised at the beginning of this chapter to tell all and openly reveal the subsequent plot; and yet, perhaps the economists in the audience still are dissatisfied and disgruntled. I can imagine them impatiently wondering: "What does this all *mean* for economics?" Therein lies the rub, because the implications of this thesis are much more profound and disturbing for economics than they are for physics. No one who examines the historical record could maintain that physicists have been lax or unimaginative in their expansions and elaborations of all the vertexes of the pyramid – and yes, they have not just confined themselves to motion. Physicists have in the past displayed a dynamism and flexibility with regard to the meaning of their metaphors for which they can rightfully be proud. But with economics it is another story. Economists have consistently lagged behind physicits in developing and elaborating metaphors; they have freeloaded off of physicits for their inspiration, and appropriated it in a shoddy and slipshod manner. In effect, the pyramid has one weak strut, particularly in the twentieth century. Perhaps this indictment sounds harsh, but then, that can be adequately judged only after our stressometers are in place. So, first the promised plot synopsis.

Measurement, mammon, momentum, and man

An authentic genetic account of the development of the energy concept must expand to encompass social and economic history. While this may appear a prescription for mental fatigue, the task is made easier by the fact that most of the groundwork has already been laid (albeit unwittingly) by the eminent Polish historian Witold Kula. In his formidable book *Measures and Men* (Kula 1986), he excavates an entire dimension of the problem of discourse concerning nature which is often hidden from modern eyes. Kula formulates the history of what he terms "metrology," which turns out to be nothing other than an archaeology of the metaphors that preceded our own seemingly timeless systems of measurement. As it so happens, his discussion neatly dovetails with our own pyramidal construction above. To simplify the exposition for our own purposes, we shall portray metrology as consisting of three consecutive stages: the anthropometric, the lineamentric, and the syndetic.

Suppose we start with the pyramid in Figure 3.1, only now we imagine it shrunk to a point so that all four vertexes coincide. Here energy does not exist as a separate entity; body, motion, and value coincide because they have not been articulated as separate realms of discourse. Let us call this situation the first stage of metrology, a situation Kula dubs an "anthropometric" stage, corresponding to the earliest Western development of metaphors of measurement. In this stage, the world is not comprehensively differentiated from the body, and this is made manifest in the units of measurement: the ell (elbow), the foot, the arm, the hand, the pace, the finger, and so forth. While this may strike the modern reader as an exceptionally capricious and unreliable system, based as it was on obviously varying biological characteristics and the intentions of the person performing the measurement, it did not bother the historical actors. It is only an observer situated in a later stage, say, an Adam Smith, who would find this situation unnatural:

> But as a measure of quantity, such as the natural foot, fathom, or handful, which is constantly varying in its own quantity, can never be an accurate measure of the quantity of other things; so a commodity which is itself continually varying in its own value, can never be an accurate measure of the value of other commodities [Smith 1976, I, p. 37].

The contemporaries of the anthropometric stage understood that human caprice and intention were inseparable from their measures. In this metrological stage honesty was no ideal calibrated to abstract or transcendental standards; it was inseparable from fair or just measurements, as a reflection of the personality of the individual involved. One might think of it as a freedom to signify any set of qualities, be they obligation, or friendship, dominance, or what have you. The right and ability to measure was an integral part of political power – for instance, the lord of the demesne was responsible for providing the volumetric measures of grain that was due to him from his serfs, a situation that strikes us today as intolerably abusive and cynical. And yet, we preserve as one of our iconic symbols of justice a set of scales.

It is of paramount significance that the measures found in the anthropometric stage lack the most basic attributes of *number*. It is one of our modern vices to confuse and conflate measure with number (Katzner 1983). Kula (1986, p. 25) points out that anthropometric measures were *not* related by any set of fixed conversion factors. For instance, the pace could not be reliably divided into a whole number of ells; further, single anthropomorphic measures resisted expression in simple multiples. From the perspective of modern abstract algebra, one could infer from the absence of certain abstract operations that, in general, anthropometric measures did not conform to the structure of an abstract group or field, and therefore were not isomorphic to the system of natural numbers (Durbin 1985, chaps. 2–4).

In most respects, these same observations apply equally to conceptions of body, value, and motion in the anthropometric stage. The conflation of measure, value, and the body were reflected in medieval notions of the just price. Justice was not abstract or quantifiable in these early formulations, but rather was the outcome of a myriad of imponderable considerations tethered to the individual case and the specific context. A just price was intended to be imbedded in and a reflection of social relations, and not the reverse. One observes this attitude in Aristotle's scattered discussions of price, as well as in the practices of certain precapitalist market formations (Polanyi 1968). In parallel with the anthropometric system of measures, prices in these situations are not fully quantitative, since they also lack the algebraic structures of the system of natural numbers.[5]

As for the metaphor of motion, one might point to Aristotelian physics as yet another instance of the same conceptual structure. According to Aristotle, motion was a process of the realization of the specific nature of a specific body, with natural motion defined as the tendency of a body to seek its natural place (Koyré 1978, chap. 1). The teleological implications of this natural order and its connections to a conception of a static social order in Aristotelian physics have been the subject of much commentary; the parallels are obvious. More relevant to our present concerns is the fact that Aristotelian impetus theory – while intuitively plausible even today, as mentioned above – implies the nonadditivity of forces in a vector sense. Here forces and motions do not display the algebraic structure of the real number system. Motion displays no persistence, no "identity," because for Aristotle rest is a state of privation that needs no explanation, but motion, as continuous actualization, requires a continuous impetus, if only to explain why not everything is yet in its natural place. The conceptualization of motion is reduced to the sheer animal experience of muscular exertion. One of the best examples of the collapse of the metaphors of body, motion, and value into a single point in the anthropometric stage of metrology is the fact that the two most common measures of the area of cultivable land in early European history were derived either from the labor time required to plow it, or else from the amount of seed required to plant it (Kula 1986, p. 29).

In the second stage of metrological development, the lineamentric, the vertexes of our pyramid grow and separate to a certain extent. Body, motion, and value become distinct but overlapping metaphors of existence, and the formalism of natural numbers comes to be instituted within each sphere of discourse. In dubbing this the lineamentric stage, we make use of the multiple referents of the word "lineament" as: a line, an element, a characteristic position of the body, and the most common connotation of a given distinctive feature. Kula tends to differentiate this stage by acknowledging that quantitative metrics now exist, but observing that they are fragmented by their dependence upon context, purpose, and interpretation. While individual quantitative indicies do exist, they are not united by any global quantitative synthesis. To quote Kula (1986, pp. 70, 87):

> It was the norm that the apothecary's pound was miniscule, the spice merchant's pound somewhat larger, the butcher's pound somewhat larger still, and so on. The *wan* of barren soil in Poland was larger than the *wan* of fertile soil; the bushel for measuring oats was larger than that used for selling wheat. The unit of measure, albeit bearing the same name, varies immensely in size with the value of the substance measured . . . The perfect divisibility and cumulativeness of the metric system enables us to "compare" very great magnitudes, such as the length of the terrestrial meridian, with very small ones, such as the thickness of a piece of paper. It took 1000 years to form this abstract-quantitative relation of certain properties of objects . . . It would appear that the primitive mind conceived of objects in a synthetic-quantitative manner. Conceived of thus, since there is nothing in common between a piece of linear cloth and a stretch of road . . . different measures have to be applied to such objects.

The hallmark of the lineamentric stage is the principle that systems of grouping and division are of overwhelming concern, while considerations of absolute magnitude are of secondary importance. Individual measures do now display the properties of abstract algebraic groups, and quantification procedes apace. Yet there remains the issue of incommensurate domains, continually posing the problem of the One and the Many. While the identity of specific domains of body, motion, and value are now susceptible to algebraic manipulation, there is as yet no structure of abstract identity between domains. The problem in the lineamentric stage is to construct similarity and identity *within* the individual metaphor of body, of motion, or of value. Let us briefly examine each metaphor in turn.

With respect to the metaphor of the body, the lineamentric stage of metrology subsumes the period of macrotaxonomy in the history of biology (Mayr 1982, chap. 4) – that is, the long struggle to decide how to taxonomize living things prior to our modern notion of classification by common ancestry. There are a myriad of ways to see resemblances and differences amongst animals, and the macrotaxonomists from von Megenberg to Schelling proposed a corresponding myriad of types of "identity." Some categorized by behavior of animals; others by the presence or absence of (relatively) arbitrary body parts; others by internal anatomy; some by the great chain of being; and still others by some anthropomorphic suggestion of families or kingdoms. Bodies were conceived as having a separate existence; but what metric quantity rendered them all alive was beyond the ken of researchers.

In this stage, human qualities are metricized according to the sensuous capacities of the body, but in the process, the body as an entity is threatened with fragmentation and dissolution. Because the reified qualities were perceived as incommensurate, the body could now be at war with itself, as in the mind-body problem or in the realm of sexuality (Foucault 1980). This fragmentation also was evident in the marketplace, with commodity metrics dictated by arbitrary sensuous aspects, such as butter sold by the round, wool by the fleece, honey by the hand, and so on. Comparisons across metrics were only rendered possible by the putative integrity of the body, an integrity always in danger of dissolution. Practical measures of area were not related in a fixed manner to practical measures of volume, and neither were calibrated in any stable way to measures of length.

The metaphor of motion also grew estranged from its fellow metaphors in the lineamentric stage, fragmenting into different alternative identities. The rise of rational mechanics was necessarily premised upon the separation of the inorganic "mass point" from the organic intuition of exertion, as well as the artificial separation of primary from secondary qualities. Rational mechanics renounced all quotidian metrics and instituted the system of Cartesian coordinates to express motion on any scale. These coordinates imposed the commensurability of volume and length, but not, say, length and warmth, or area and value. Abstract motion, confined to such spaces, became subject to addition and subtraction, irrespective of the fact no one had actually seen a mass point under the influence of a large number of infinitely small and separate impressments.

Given that rational motion had been sundered from physical reality, the problem of taxonomy arose in relation to the rest of sensuous experience. All sorts of pneuma, ethers, subtle fluids, humours and imponderable airs were postulated to account for such secondary qualities such as light, heat, nervous activity, electricity, and so forth. When motion was identical and when it was fundamentally diverse became a central question of the lineamentric stage, but no causal principles could settle the matter.

As for the economic sphere, value was slowly dismembered from the body and from motion. A primary characteristic of the lineamentric stage in the economic sphere is a profound suspicion of the commodity as being able to express its value in its own metric, followed by a skepticism over the fitness of money to adequately signify the value metric. Value could no longer be associated with the commodity in itself, as stated in the earlier quote from Smith (1976, I, p. 37). What was required was an abstract coordinate system that would serve to separate the primary quality of value from such secondary characteristics as fluctuations in monetary conditions or the accidents of particular conjunctures of events. The preferred mode of the reification of a separate value metaphor was to posit an invariance of some sort. The clearest example of this reification comes not from theory, but from a now-defunct practice. In some of the earliest market formations, it was decreed by fiat that value was constant. The way that this happened was that market pressures were not expressed by changes in money price, but rather by changes in the physical magnitude of the commodity to which the price referred (Kula 1986, pp. 72–78; Polanyi 1968). In the exact reversal of our present market practices, prices were held constant by fiat, and altered sizes of the unit of allotment were used to allocate allotments. As value grew distinct from the sensuous aspects of the body, that tenuous and abstract notion had to be maintained by an enforced invariance, one that violated the newly instituted metrics of motion. Both value and the measuring rod were directly subject to political and geographical ukase. The pound of the marketplace was not the pound of the natural philosopher, and neither rated the pound of flesh, which early on became the synonym of human effort.

That brings us finally to the third metrological stage, the one we will call the syndetic stage. This stage is marked by the unification of the metaphors at each vertex of the base of the pyramid in Figure 3.1 by means of a fourth metaphor rising up above the foundations. In more technical terms, each individual measure is now seen to be a subset of a larger algebraic set, a subgroup of an algebraic group. The major difference between the anthropometric and syndetic stages is that in the anthropometric stage the metaphors of body, motion, and value are not regarded as distinct because they are undifferentiated, whereas in the syndetic stage, the metaphors maintain their differentiation while subjected to a larger synthetic structure which is purely conventional.

The historical incident that typifies this third stage is the institution of the metric system by the French Revolution, a tale related in detail by Kula. The irony of that situation, savored by Kula, is that "The Protagorean maxim that 'man is the measure of all things' has had to yield in our quest for the objective and the immutable. How difficult, though, it is to find immutable elements where nothing stays unchanging!" (Kula 1986, p. 120). The French Revolutionaries, among whose ranks were numbered some of the engineers and philosophers encountered in Chapter 2, wanted to sweep away all of the "confusion" of the previous metrological stages by means of a single consistent system of measures based upon nature rather than upon man. To achieve this, they fashioned the cornerstone of their new system, the meter, upon the supposedly supranational and suprasomatic criterion, namely 1/40,000,000 part of the earth's meridian.

Now, the true significance of such an act was not its actual dependence upon nature. It had occurred to many at the time that contemporary standards of precision were not commensurate with the desired standards of precision that would relate the terrestrial globe to the span of a man's reach; although it must be admitted that the hubris of asserting that it was possible was important for the scheme's acceptance. Rather, the overwhelming significance lay in the consolidation of all of the various units of measure under one fixed invariant set of transformations. Now, lest the reader think this a trivial or insignificant feat, let us note that the destruction of lineamentric systems and the imposition of the syndetic metric system is a comparatively recent event over much of the face of the globe. In Germany it dates from 1868; in Austria from 1871; Poland 1919; Russia 1918; Japan 1921; and China from 1959 (Kula 1986, p. 279). The coincidence of many of these dates with political upheaval is no coincidence. It reveals that, more than anything else, the syndetic stage is an act of will, not a fact of nature.

In the syndetic stage, may becomes the measure of all things by subterfuge. After the metaphors of body, motion, and value have become disassociated during the era of the quantification of qualities, the ideal of unification is restored by means of a purely abstract, conventional standard. The reader has by now undoubtedly realized that this was accomplished in physics with the invention of the metaphor of energy. In biology, we shall suggest it happened with the stabilization of the metaphor of the gene. With respect to the metaphor of value, this was practically accomplished by the economic actors when the institution of money was cut adrift from any specific ties to any particular commodity, and was instead left to merely serve as the eidolon of pure abstract value. Nevertheless, this does not imply that the syndetic stage has been attained within the discipline of *economics*. (The behavior of the economic actors is not necessarily reflected in the prognostications of economists.)

It is of paramount importance that, in the syndetic stage, these consolidations hinge crucially upon the postulation of invariance or conservation principles; but it is precisely the integrity of those invariants that has no external warrant, cannot be guaranteed, and therefore must be maintained by convention (Meyerson 1962). This is the sense in which man remains the measure of all things. Each of the intellectual disciplines constructed around the central metaphors of body, motion, and value will thus exhibit strong structural homeomorphisms, not because of the intrinsic subject matter, but rather because they all grow generically out of the same process of understanding.

Take, for instance, Darwinian evolutionary theory, our own culture's theory of the body. What had in the lineamentric stage seemed the fractured congeries of sensual chaos was transformed into a biological unity. The dual concepts of the organism and of natural selection bind together the set of fragmented biological functions and link the entity both backward and forward in time and to other organisms, while subjecting it to a formalism amenable to calculation. There are variational principles and conservation principles. For the theory to be viable, it is of the essence that the organism exhibit greater stability than the environment so that the process of selection can operate, but it is precisely this stability that cannot be definitively demonstrated in the relevant circumstances (Kitcher 1985; Dupré 1987). Or instead, consider the behavior of modern economic actors:

This implicitly insists that money can only serve as a standard and measure of value if its own self-relation is stable, but it is precisely the ubiquity of inflation (or deflation) that calls the whole structure of accounts into question. Or indeed, the entire structure of physical theory would be unified and consistent if the conservation of energy could be demonstrated to hold identically in each theoretical subfield, but we have seen that it does not. Nevertheless, the researchers situated at each vertex of the pyramid persist undaunted. How can that be?

One answer is to notice that the metaphor that synthesizes the research program at each vertex is *essentially the same metaphor*. Here is the sense in which we are no longer dealing with prosaic notions of intellectual cross-disciplinary influences, *Zeitgeist,* or epistemes. *The research program situated at each vertex derives legitimacy for its radically unjustifiable conservation principles from the homeomorphisms with the structures of explanation at the other vertexes.* This legitimation function is central to the success of each research program, because the central syndetic principle at the heart of each is purely conventional, and thus, from a disinterested and detatched point of view, simply false.

It is this thesis that, if you will, constitutes the real plot of this book. I should like to convince the reader that the energy concept derives much of its cogency from its structural resemblance to our understandings of the body and of economic value, just as our theories of economic value derive whatever legitimacy they may claim from structural resemblances with our theories of motion and energy and the body. In this work I am much less concerned to elaborate the other face of the pyramid, although for the sake of completeness we shall presently devote a very brief passage to considering how our theories of economic value and energy and motion tend to buttress our present theory of the body, the theory of Darwinian evolution. In any event, the overall effect is reminiscent of an archetypal Escher print, one where every pillar of an imposing edifice directly or indirectly supports every other pillar, but no pillar touches the ground.

In the last two centuries explanation, the explanation of the pragmatic scientist and not the epistemologist, has actually assumed a very standardized format in the modern West. Explanation is deemed to be cogent when a primal metaphor of our culture is tamed to conform to the format of a conservation principle and a variational principle. However, because the Achilles heel of any such explanation is always located at the validity of the conservation principle, there is always an endemic problem of justifying what is at best a dubious procedure. To put it bluntly, the world does not itself point to its own invariants, or wear them on its forehead like the mark of Cain. The fundamental justification of a conservation principle in any research program then always comes to rest in the evocation of other conservation principles in other similarly structured disciplines. Conservation principles in natural philosophy referred to body and value; conservation principles in biology refer to energy and motion and value; finally, as we shall demonstrate, conservation principles in economics have made reference to body and energy and motion. As the metaphors constitute a pyramid, the buck may continue to be passed ad infinitum: It stops nowhere.

The reader should be forewarned that the evidence that we shall muster for this thesis will be distributed in a markedly unequal manner when we come to each of the various struts of the pyramid. This should not be taken to represent the relative importance of each. In truth, were I an advocate of the principle of maximum entropy in all things, I would endeavor to distribute the evidence evenly at all the vertexes. Yet there is no denying the role of interests in research; and mine clearly lie nearer the value–motion–energy face of the pyramid. Accordingly, for the sake of completeness I shall insert a page or two sketching out the barest inadequate outlines of the implications of this pyramidic paradigm for the theory of Darwinian evolution. Then we shall conclude this chapter with some evidence for the importance of the value and body metaphors to the history of the energy concept. Economists may readily skip the rest of this chapter with little or no qualms about losing the thread of the argument, as it narrowly impinges upon their own discipline. (I know from experience that economists don't like long books.) For those impatient readers, the vitals of the argument that economics has been governed by the constituent metaphors of energy will commence with Chapter 4.

Darwinian evolution as metaphor

The thesis that the genesis of the Darwinian theory of evolution hinged on a few crucial metaphors has been argued with great force and verve by Robert Young (1985). The historiography of Darwin is so extensive that we cannot even begin to do it justice here. However, it is well known that his theory of evolution posits a relatively stable (non-Lamarkian) organism whose analytical features are delimited by some definition of fitness. This is the crux of the essential Darwinian conception of the body as the unification of an acervation of otherwise disparate biological attributes. Of course, there has been persistent controversy among evolutionary theorists as to precisely where to inscribe the boundaries of the organism, ranging anywhere from the selfish gene through the individual to the kinship group and the population (Mayr 1982, p. 588). From our pyramidal perspective, we would interpret this as the problem of the conceptualization of the conservation principle in the sphere of the body metaphor; more explicitly, it is the problem of the relative stability of the organism vis-à-vis the environment.

Once this is appreciated, it takes only a little further effort to see the survival of the fittest as the requisite complementary extremal principle. Natural selection is the maximum formalism attatched to the structural identity provided by the conservation of the organism, serving to explain some equilibrium configuration. Consequently, change has been reduced to stasis. Explanation is deemed cogent when it is demonstrated that some biological attribute or "mean fitness" (Dupré 1987; Kitcher 1985, p. 218) is optimal within a given environmental context. It is no accident that the overall framework resembles the principle of least action in physics, or indeed, the principle of the maximization of utility in neoclassical economics (Shoemaker 1984; Hirshleifer 1977).

The role of the external framework in tying together the metaphors of motion and value, even to the extent of explicit appeals to the energy metaphor, has been explained by the biologist Richard Lewontin:

> The whole purpose of optimality as a heuristic is to avoid the problem of measuring the Darwinian fitness of different types and of treating the full dynamical problem of changes in the population composition by selection. Optimality arguments use proxies for fitness, such as energy expenditure, growth rate, territory size and feed efficiency, precisely because these are thought to be measurable and to be in some simple relationship with the unmeasurable, fitness [in Dupré 1987, pp. 153–4].

Given that the root problem is to justify (in a self-consciously awkward oxymoron) the conservation of the organism, evolutionary theorists have had recourse time and again to metaphors of value, motion, and energy. One notes the metaphor of motion making its appearance primarily in mathematical formalizations of evolutionary theory, such as in stationary-state growth models of expanding populations (Charlesworth 1980, chap. 3), in variations upon the "substance" connotations of "biomass," and in portrayals of the migration of genes in population genetics. Resorts to metaphors of economic value are equally rife. They begin with Darwin's own admission that his reading of Thomas Malthus's *Essay on Population* prompted his synthesis (Young 1985, pp. 40–4). They continue down to the present in the appropriation of game-theory models by population geneticists, and even more explicitly in the new field of sociobiology, where constrained optimization models are openly appropriated from neoclassical economic theory (Dupré 1987 p. 204; Wilson 1975; Oster and Wilson 1978, pp. 297–9; Kitcher 1985, chap. 7).

Lineamentrics from Stevin to Whewell

It is possible to regard the concept of energy as no different from the metric system. Neither was given to us by nature; neither arrived overnight; both historically started out from anthropomorphic practices, evolved through a stage of fragmentation, and then were finally synthesized in a dramatic manner with implications for all other areas of human endeavor. In Chapter 4, the same argument will be made for the value concept.

In each case, it is only in the onset of the lineamentric stage that we begin to note some metaphoric differentiation, and hence our quest in the present section for some evidence of economic influences on the conceptualization of motion and energy. In the history of physics, the lineamentric stage stretches from perhaps the sixteenth and seventeenth centuries through to the mid-nineteenth. Its most apparent artifacts are theories of rational mechanics and the theories of fluids and ethers in the discussions of heat, light, magnetism, electricity, and so forth. The syndetic stage begins with the "discovery" of energy conservation in the middle decades of the 1800s. I think it is not insignificant that these two stages roughly coincide with, respectively, the rise of the world mercantile economy and the institution of the world industrial economy. This is not for some metaphysical reason such as "the base controls the superstructure," but rather because experience with evolving economic structures altered the perceptions of the metaphor of value, and that in turn set off resonances with the attendant metaphor of motion.

A serious inquiry into all the ways in which this happened would demand an entire volume, and would be an immense undertaking in the history of science. In lieu of that, I would like to offer some sketchy suggestions as to just how and why the metaphoric resonances between value and motion were heard and felt.

Although it does not seem to have been the object of much scholarly interest, it is striking how the major innovations in the theory of motion follow the changing center of gravity of the major trading axis of early modern Europe, stretching from northern Italy through the

low countries and terminating in southeastern Britain. This is significant because that same traverse along the diagonal axis describes the
earliest diffusion of modern accounting techniques. In the early
seventeenth century all of these vectors pointed toward Holland, the
merchant clearinghouse of Europe, the land of Simon Stevin and the
adopted home of René Descartes. As Descartes wrote in a letter of
1631, "And thus in the city where I now am, since I seem to be
practically the only one here who is not a merchant or in trade"
(quoted in Levi 1974, p. 185); and it could hardly have been otherwise, since in that era it was the Dutch who were busily occupied with
the innovation of the first entirely mercantile culture in Europe
(Barbour 1963). It is true that neither Stevin nor Descartes explicitly
dealt in the sorts of direct metaphorical connections between motion
and money that crop up with some regularity later in the century;
nonetheless, there are some telling circumstances that point to the
laying of the foundations of the value/motion axis by the progenitors
of the earliest conservation principles in physics.

It is interesting that the earliest attempts to conceptualize the
quantification of motion in this period often were cast in terms of
actien in archaic Dutch ("action" in both French and English), which
was the mass of a body multiplied through its velocity, with the
definition later augmented to be mass × velocity × time. In the same
period, the other major connotation of *actien* was something dear to
the hearts of the Dutch burghers, namely, the shares (or their prices)
of the newly chartered joint-stock trading companies. The Dutch
were the innovators of this novel and eminently abstract form of
value, which involved owning a company without directly owning any
of its physical goods, a situation that raised subtle issues of how one
could gain merely from trading pieces of paper, especially in the
outrageous situation where ownership itself was only virtual, a phenomenon personified in that other new urban phenomenon, the
financial speculator. As a contemporary wrote, "The seller, so to
speak, sells nothing but wind and the buyer receives only wind"
(quoted in Barbour 1963, p. 79). There may have been some connection between the early attempts to understand motion abstracted
from all secondary qualities, reduced to mere number, and the problem of value abstracted from all tangible trade and reduced to mere
number.

A more palpable influence shared by Stevin and Descartes was a
common concern to generate a set of accounts for motion, a concern
that prompted Descartes to consult Stevin's unpublished manuscripts
after his death (Stevin 1955, I, p. 8). Simon Stevin, as we stated in the

previous chapter, was a polymath, writing treatises on military fortifications, geometry, arithmetic, the theory of statics, the Dutch language, engineering, and last but not least, tables of interest and
manuals of bookkeeping. In fact, Stevin is remembered in the history
of accounting for introducing the Italian method of double-entry
bookkeeping into Northern Europe, and for placing emphasis upon
an early precursor to the income statement over and above the more
conventional balance sheet (Chatfield 1977, pp. 69–70). His method
of argument in his famous work on physical statics appears to have
been influenced by his bookkeeping studies, since his description of
the equilibrium of a string of balls hinges most critically upon his
assertion of the impossibility of perpetual motion (Stevin 1955, I, pp.
111–81). Since this was not a widely shared empirical conviction at
that time, Stevin can be understood as insisting that the accounts (i.e.,
motion upward and motion downward) must balance, and in that
eventuality equilibrium is attained.

It is Descartes who takes the accounts a step further. Grossmann
(1987, p. 160) argues that as early as the *Discours* of 1637, Descartes
justifies the mathematical abstraction which he advocates as leading to
the quantification of mechanical work, or as he puts it, "pour l'invention d'une infinité d'artifices qui feroient qu'on jouiroit sans aucune
peine des fruits de la terre et de toutes les commodités qui s'y trou-
vent" ("for the invention of an infinity of artifacts which would mean
the unconditional enjoyment of the fruits of the earth and all its
commodities"). His principle of the conservation of motion can thus
be understood as a means of accounting for what machines can be
expected to do to augment pleasure and value. Yet Descartes also
went beyond Stevin in elaborating upon the metaphorical triad of
body/motion/value. As is well known, Descartes was an early champion of the full reduction of the human body to the phenomenon of
matter in motion, especially in his *Treatise on Man* (Descartes 1972).
Here the work of machines is conflated with the labor of men so that
both would be subject to the same natural regulative principles.
Nevertheless, certain inauspicious aspects of the metaphor are overlooked: for instance, human beings reproduce, but machines do not.
(Descartes sidesteps the issue by never once considering the genitalia.)
Even this silence has its counterpart in the contemporaneous theory
of value, however. As Chapter 4 will demonstrate, if trade was to be
comprehended as the exchange of equivalents (and thus value conserved in exchange), then it was unclear just how nations might
experience an expansion of value.

It was precisely the broad scope of the Cartesian conception of science that immediately gave rise to what were perceived as inconsistencies in his system of accounts. Leibniz's critique isolated one inconsistency; another, broached during Descartes's lifetime, juxtaposed the strict conservation of motion with the accomodation of the "soul" or the "mind" into the broad scheme of things. From various unpublished manuscripts it is clear that Descartes worried the eventuality of mind initiating motion would jeopardize his conservation principle and his entire mathematical account of motion (Gabbey 1985). How could the mind influence a fixed sum of motion? How could work increase value? Descartes himself was extremely reticent about these issues, but they became the staple of argument for later generations of Cartesians, such as Malebranche, who did explicitly resort to metaphors of the "Economy of Nature" (Elster 1975, p. 25).

The issue of the relevant and consistent conservation principles requisite for the apprehension of motion was raised to a higher plane by Leibniz, and it is in his writings that one first encounters extensive metaphorical connections forged between the theory of motion and the theory of economic value. Not only did Leibniz frequently express an intention to apply the mathematical method to "matières oeconomico-politiques" (Elster 1975, p. 144) and concoct a system of accounts for purposes of mine surveillance (p. 108), but Elster (chap. 3) goes on to explain how Leibniz's early experience as a mining engineer in the Harz mountains prompted his later concerns with *vis viva*. The problem he faced in supervising the mining operations was to discover a way to convert the irregular and undependable wind power used to pump out the mines into some more dependable power source. Leibniz's solution involved reversing the original situation by pumping water up into a reservoir, and then using the water power as a smoother, more continuous, and more reliable power source. Not only did this situation bear a close structural resemblance to the later discussion of the conservation of *vis viva* described in Chapter 2, it further involved an explicit metaphorical connection made with a system of accounts:

> On peut économiser la force du vent et pour ainsi dire l'emmagasiner. Cela revient à dire que, grâce à cette méthode, on amène l'eau dans le réservoir, où elle est emmagasinée. On peut ensuite l'utiliser au profit commune des mines en la déversant dans les machines hydrauliques, les carrières, etc. Ainsi cesse aussi d'être valuable l'objection principale selon laquelle on est hors d'état d'être maître du vent et d'en avoir quant on en veut. Toute eau qu'on amènerait ainsi dans le réservoir vaudrait son pesant d'or. Et quand on en aurait tant, on pourrait très bien l'utiliser. [The force of the wind can be accumulated and stored. Water is by these means conducted into

the reservoir where it is stored. It can then be used with benefit for the mines by being poured into hydraulic machinery, quarries, etc. Thus there is no validity to the objection that it is impossible to master and dispose of the wind at will. The water in the reservoir is worth its weight in gold and may be put to good use when enough has been collected.] [Quoted in Elster 1975, p. 93.]

It would seem plausible to argue, and indeed it has been argued by Elster and others, that it was because of the commingling of metaphors of motion and economic value that Leibniz, and not, say, Newton, became the progenitor of the program of recasting rational mechanics in the format of conservation principles and variational principles. Although Leibniz never explicitly wrote out the mathematics of variational principles, he certainly did stress their importance in metaphorical terms, asserting, for instance, that God was like an architect who has to worry about his funds (Elster 1975, p. 198). His insistence upon the metaphysical aspects of variational principles paved the way for the later mathematical explication of principles of least action by Maupertuis, the Bernoullis, Euler, and others.

Leibniz also advocated an analogy that later became a leitmotiv in classical political economy, the analytic isomorphism between measures of extension and those of economic value (Elster 1975, p. 147). Consequently, he was one of the first to forge explicit links between money, the abstraction of economic value, and force, the abstraction of phenomenal motion. In various contexts, he maintained that, "Krafte sind frucht barkeit, volk und geld" (Elster 1975, p. 115). However fruitful this analogy, it did also give rise to some cognitive dissonance, particularly with regard to the conceptualization of the passage of time within the framework of the set of accounts:

> When there are two bodies perfectly equal and resembling each other, and which have the same speed, but which speed has been gained by one in a sudden collision, and by the other in descent over a certain length of time, shall we say therefore that their forces are different? That would be as if we were to say a man is richer because he spent more time earning the money [quoted in Elster 1975, p. 164].

The error in analogy does appear doubly egregious, since Leibniz was much concerned about the reasons behind conservation principles, and also because he had written elsewhere in support of the calculation of compound interest. The problem, as always, lay in the relationship of the accounts to the passage of time. The error was to compare what was putatively a variable of state – the net equity of the balance sheet, and not, by the way, *money per se* – with force, which when defined as $m(dv/dt)$ must necessarily be variable for identical masses in differing time frames. Metaphorical confusions such as these bedeviled the *vis viva* controversy well into the eighteenth century.

It is to be noted that the heirs to the Leibnizian tradition, the eighteenth-century systematizers of rational mechanics such as Euler and Lagrange, did not make any explicit reference to economic metaphors in their writings. In truth, the vernacular metaphorical content of their writings drops nearly to nil, a phenomenon bound up with the rise of an assertive, decontextualized, and seemingly nononsense style of discourse innovated in the eighteenth-century physical sciences (Markus 1987). The metaphorical component of reasoning retreated almost entirely into the mathematics itself. There analogies abounded: force fields were compared to the formalisms of hydrodynamics; hanging chains were compared to the paths of comets; vibrating strings were compared to water waves, but these comparisons were only elaborated in the mathematics, and not in the vernacular. However, the value/motion metaphor was not entirely left behind, but rather emerged in contexts where austere formalism had not made the same degree of headway, and was not so enamored of the distant charms of celestial mechanics. In the eighteenth century the most significant location of the economic metaphor was to be found in the Grandes Ecoles of Paris, with their concerns over engineering and the nascent theory of heat.

The full articulation of the physical concept of work in rational mechanics happened at a surprisingly late stage, by all accounts culminating in the 1820s. The critical issue (at least in retrospect) seemed to be a delineation of the precise circumstances in which the integral of forces times displacements would be conservative, thus providing a suitable index of the expenditure of effort. Grattan-Guinness (1984, pp. 5–6) traces this inquiry from the writings of Daniel Bernoulli, one of the more eminent followers of Leibniz. In 1753 Bernoulli wrote an essay on the powering of ships that contained "a new theory of the economy of forces and their effects." It was explicitly cast in terms of the metaphors of body and value by means of beginning with a survey of the work capacities of animals and men, defining this quantity by the expression force × velocity × time. This essay gave birth to a French tradition of comparing the efficiency of various machines to men and animals as benchmarks, indeed searching for ways in which one might formalize a stable and reliable equivalence with economic terms. This tradition extends from Lazare Carnot to Montgolfier, Hachette, Navier, Dupin, Coriolis, and Poncelet.

As an example, in 1808 Montgolfier suggested explicitly that each species of force had a price, such that the cost of any task should be subject to strict economic calculation. A decade later, Navier insisted upon the "need to establish a kind of *mechanical exchange,* if one can express it thus, with which one may estimate the quantities of work employed in order to effect all kinds of manufacture" (Grattan-Guinness 1984, pp. 8–13). This quest for a natural ground for value reached a peak in French physics and in English political economy at essentially the same time, as we shall observe in Chapter 4. There was also the subsidiary phenomenon of the concentration of many of the earliest French writers on mathematical political economy at the *Ecole des Ponts et Chaussées,* who were working on the same kind of engineering problems (Ekelund and Hebert 1978; Etner 1986).

One attempt to consolidate the disjoint metaphors of motion and value in the early-nineteenth-century French context were the writings of Charles, later Baron, Dupin. Dupin (1827) proposes that the entire productive and commercial activities of a nation be reduced to a single index, force. He further distinguished inanimate and animate varieties of force: The former were derived from his contemporaries' engineering definitions of work, while the latter were subdivided into animal, human physical, and human intellectual activities. All varieties of force were ultimately reduced to an adult male equivalent – this included water power, wind power, and steam power. Dupin then calculated the total force available in France and compared it to the force to be found in Great Britain. To France's shame, Britain's superiority in inanimate forces gave it a surplus of productive forces, a finding that Dupin claimed accounted for British political and economic superiority.

The most illustrious resident at the *carrefour* of French engineering and economics was Sadi Carnot, the founder of thermodynamics. As argued in Chapter 2, Carnot's proof of his famous principle, that the work output of a heat engine is solely a function of temperature differentials, was fundamentally predicated upon the prohibition of perpetual motion, the getting of something for nothing. The fact that the first law of thermodynamics is derived from what was essentially an economic metaphor was conditioned by the dual influences of the French quest for a quantification of work, and the fact that Carnot himself had been a student of early-nineteenth-century French economics (Centre National de la Récherche Scientifique 1976, pp. 383–85).

Carnot's economic interests are illustrated by various essays concerning economic topics that were left among his unpublished papers (CNRS 1976, pp. 389–95; Carnot 1978, pp. 273–312). Even more to the point, it has been recently noted that Carnot's conceptualization of the output of the heat engine resembles quite closely the *Tableau Economique* of the eighteenth century French physiocrat François Quesnay.[6] In the Tableau, a single value substance is followed in its motion between the three classes of French society, with economic equilibrium defined as the exact reconstitution of the initial advances in all sectors, implying the exact conservation of the value substance, excluding both loss and gain. Similarly, the Carnot cycle traces the transfer of a single substance, "caloric," between reservoirs of differing temperatures, with equilibrium defined as the exact reconstitution of the caloric, with the influence of the working substance ruled irrelevant by a prohibition of pure gain.

By the early nineteenth century, the steam engine was finding application in many areas of industry; as a result, it became more urgent to bring the various conversions of human labor to motion and steam power to motion together and to subject them to a single calculus of economic efficiency. As the most developed tradition to take this as their concern, the French engineering literature was imported into other countries. In England, the polymath William Whewell introduced Hachette and Poncelet into Cambridge textbooks (Becher 1971, p. 16; Cardwell 1971, p. 237). Whewell, interestingly enough, also wrote on political economy, and was in the vanguard of the application of mathematical models to theoretical discussions in the fledgling discipline (Whewell 1830; 1833). For Whewell and his contemporaries, while the overall imperative of relating the "duty" of engines to the "labour" of workers was fairly well understood, the set of accounts implied by such an imperative was not at all transparent. This shows up in a number of instances as an uncertainty as to which aspects of the metaphor of motion and value should predominate. For instance, in the following letter of Whewell to the economist Richard Jones, dated 14 February 1843, there is a confusion of the relative status of the balance sheet *cum* asset account and the income statement *cum* depreciation account, leading to a vague conception of "work" (Todhunter 1876, II, pp. 312–13):

> In every machine, or rather in every mechanical work, you have these three things to consider – moving *power*, trains of *mechanism* connecting power with the work, *work* done. Willis begins his book with the example of a knife-grinder – moving power = muscular power of the knife-grinder; mechanism = grinder's wheel; work = knife-grinding. It is plain that *quoad* knife-grinding, the power is much increased by the mechanism, for the man could get on very ill without it. Now your question seems to be how much the value of the work done exceeds the value of the moving power. I reply, it exceeds

it by the value of the mechanism, at least; otherwise people would not acquire the mechanism. The value of all the knife-grinding done in Britain must exceed the mere wages of the knife-grinders by at least the value of the grinder's wheels.

Now this appears to me to be general – the value of the work done must be the value of the moving power *plus* the value of the machinery. In the case you mention, a cotton mill, the value of its produce must equal the value of the moving power (coals and engine) *plus* the value of the mechanism (wheels, spindles, etc.) And the productive powers of nations must be compared by comparing the moving forces *plus* the whole quantity of the working mechanism; for the latter would not exist if it did not add its own value to that of the moving force.[7]

With Whewell's (and his contemporaries') confusion we arrive on the threshold of the syndetic stage of the energy metaphor. Phenomena such as the lifting of weights, the motive force of fire, and the force of electricity had been isolated, broken out of the body and the larger confederation of natural powers. They had been subjected to individual quantitative indexes; and had been found to be useful in the social scheme of economic values. Their metaphorical structures had clear structural similarities: They were each individually subject to the prohibition of perpetual motion; they were all worth something in the sense that they had to be paid for; they were all expressions of aspects of the activities of the laborer's body. It is this metaphorical unity, this commonwealth of concepts, that accounts for the a priori convictions that Kuhn felt were missing from his narrative of the "discovery" of the conservation of energy.

Energy as metaphoric synthesis

One advantage of our pyramidic perspective is that it now becomes apparent why the original favored four did not discover the same thing, and why there can be sixteen or more aspirants to the enunciation of the energy concept. Because the energy concept has three metaphorical planes, a scientist situated on any one of them can be regarded in retrospect as an anticipator of "energy" while his ideas are arrayed on an acute angle vis-à-vis some other anticipator. The historian of science, perhaps more enamoured of mathematical expression to the exclusion of other metaphorical expressions, has tended to award laurels on the basis of the mathematical inscription of an estimate of the mechanical equivalent of heat, slighting the placement of any given "discoverer" on the entire pyramid. To redress this situation, we shall briefly reconsider the achievements of Joule and Helmholtz, with a few side-glances at Mayer.

The writings of James Joule would initially appear the very epideictic dream of the positivist philosopher of science, since they consist almost exclusively of meticulous descriptions of experiments overshadowed by a neurotic vigilance against any metaphysical or metaphoric speculations. For precisely that reason, however, Joule does not bear much of the credit for the elaboration of the energy concept, yet he provides the important construction of one face of the pyramid, the one that is bounded by energy, motion, and economic value. From his earliest experiments, which were intended to prove that the electromagnetic motor would provide an "economical source of power" (Joule 1884, p. 48), Joule clearly held as his goal the tabulation of fixed rates of exchange between various power sources. Now, the surviving biographical materials on Joule are sparse indeed, but it may just be possible to reconstruct Joule's problem-situation in order to understand the importance of the economic metaphor of value.

Joule supported himself during his early experimental activities by managing and keeping the books of the Salford Brewery. The accounts of the brewery have not survived, but three facts about the economic structure of British breweries in the nineteenth century are relevant. First, prior to the full-scale arrival of the railroads, the most highly advanced and articulated systems of British accounting were to be found in the English breweries. Among other reasons, this was due to the fact that brewers' transactions were very numerous but of relatively small magnitudes, in conjunction with the fact that inventory spoilage and delinquent publicans were the bane of the industry. Records of timing and of magnitudes were indispensable for survival, much less success, and these were made manifest in elaborate and detailed accounting systems (Mathias 1959, p. 28). Second, the control of temperature was absolutely critical in the fermentation process, and by the 1820s, very finely graded thermometers had come into use throughout the brewing industry (chap. 3). Joule's access to the most sensitive thermometers of the day and his familiarity with their use was no accident, given that one of his biggest headaches was the day-to-day control of temperature in huge vats of liquid. Third, the arrival of steam power had virtually mechanized the entire brewing process by 1800, the first industry in which labor was displaced on such a scale (p. 106). No one to my knowledge has yet noticed that Joule's famous paddle-wheel experiment is just a minor variation on the mashing machine that was standard equipment in large breweries in Britain after the turn of the century (p. 94).

These aspects of the nineteenth-century brewing industry were not merely "influences" upon Joule's thought. Rather, they mark out the boundaries of the economic problem that Joule was anxious to resolve. Because brewing was already largely mechanized, Joule was not absorbed with the problem of animal heat or the mechanical equivalent of human labor, and thus there are few traces of the metaphor of the body in his work. Instead, Joule wanted to cost out the amount of heat held within vats of liquid, in order to compare it to the cost of the power required to control it. With the methodical attitudes and predispositions of the accountant, he endeavored to debit each cost to a separate account, for the most part bypassing Whewell's confusions between the stocks of capital and the rates of conversion of income and outgo. Joule never possessed a flair for a theoretical narrative of the underlying processes – his descriptions of the mechanical nature of heat are perfunctory at best – but was untiring when it came to evaluation. Accountants, by their very training, have little curiosity about the real activities that their ledgers describe; and indeed, the prevalence of accounting conventions breeds a certain disrespect for such questions. Joule behaved just like an accountant; moreover, when the final balances did not match, he determinedly "cooked the books" in order to absorb the discrepancy.

In contrast, it was Helmholtz and, to a lesser extent, Mayer who were busy putting the other faces of the pyramid in place. Both, significantly enough, did not come from engineering backgrounds, a fact that perplexes those who insist that the "discovery" of energy conservation came from workaday experience with conversion processes. On the contrary, both Helmholtz and Mayer were physicians, and had little experience with heat engines and so forth. Instead, it was their organicist milieu, combined with their adherence to a mechanical reductionist perspective and a sensitivity to the nuances of the concept of labor that which rendered them capable of uniting the metaphors of body, motion, and value in an ultimately successful synthesis.

A sampling of the statements of Mayer concerning the economy of Nature and the equestrian equivalents of a man's labor were quoted in Chapter 2, so there is no need to recapitulate them here. The case of Helmholtz, who in any event conventionally gets the lion's share of the credit for "discovering" the conservation of energy, is much more complicated, and deserves a bit more scrutiny. Prior to 1847, Helmholtz was a member of a circle of physiologists including du Bois-Reymond, Brücke, and Müller, all of whom were concerned to purge the vitalist tendencies in contemporary physiology and medicine. As early as 1845, Helmholtz was scrutinizing the contention of Liebig that animal heat could be entirely accounted for by the combustion of food, pointing out that there was no rigorous theoretical justification for such a claim. Hence, in the 1847 memoir Helmholtz proceeds to forge links between the metaphor of the body and the metaphor of motion. In the first few pages he equates causality with the principle that "natural phenomena should be traced back to the movements of material objects which possess inalterable motive forces that are dependent only on spatial relations." He then immediately cites the writings of Carnot and Clapeyron on heat as illustrations of the sorts of causal explanations of which he approves, and notes that they are premised upon the prohibition of perpetual motion. Asserting that he, Helmholtz, should be permitted to extend the analogy, there follows a demonstration that the principle of the conservation of *vis viva* is merely a special case of the very same paradigm of causal explanation. This nicely ties together the French tradition of the quantification of work with a loftier goal of causal explanation *tout court*. After extending the same consideration to heat, electricity, and magnetism, he closes with a modest but significant reference to his original physiological concerns:

> Animals take in oxygen and complicated oxidizable compounds which are generated in plants, and give them back partly burned as carbonic acid and water, partly reduced to simple compounds. Thus they use up a certain quantity of chemical tensional forces and, in their place, generate heat and mechanical force. Since the latter only represents a small amount of work compared with the quantity of heat, the question of the conservation of force [*Kraft*] reduces to the question whether the combustion and transformation of the substances which serve as food generate a quantity of heat equal to that given out by animals (Helmholtz 1971, p. 48).

It will prove profitable to pay close attention to what this pivotal memoir *Die Erhaltung der Kraft* does and does not do. It does *not* demonstrate that animal heat can be fully accounted for by the burning of food. It does not provide any stable equivalent between heat and motion or electricity and motion. It does not even "prove" that perpetual motion is impossible. What, then, are its central contributions?

First, it suggests that the mathematical formalization of all the disparate motley of forces should be patterned along the lines of existing French rational mechanics, dividing theoretical terms into what would later be called their potential and kinetic components, and actually gives some mathematical pointers as to how this might be done. Second, in a concise manner, it synthesizes the three com-

ponent metaphors of body, motion, and value. The explanation of
animal heat is the main link between motion and body; the evocation
of the French tradition under the rubric of causal explanation links
body to value; and the stress upon the impossibility of perpetual
motion and its conflation with mathematical formalization links motion and value. Helmholtz's lasting achievement was to cement the
fundamental triad of metaphors together in a stylobate that would
resist the perturbations of a few contrary facts. This becomes even
more apparent in his series of popular lectures in subsequent years.

From this perspective, the richest metaphorical gold mind is his
1854 lecture on the "Interaction of Natural Forces," a text rapidly
translated into the other major European languages (Youmans 1865,
pp. 211–47). In that lecture he cites various stories of machines that
are simulcra of animals and humans, and then, ever so subtly, insinuates the third metaphor of economic value:

> From these efforts to imitate living creatures, another idea, also by
> a misunderstanding, seems to have developed . . . It was now the
> endeavor to construct a perpetual motion . . . Beasts and human
> beings seemed to correspond to the idea of such an apparatus, for
> they moved themselves energetically and incessantly as long as they
> lived, were never wound up, and nobody set them in motion . . . The
> perpetual motion was to produce work inexhaustibly without the
> corresponding consumption, that is to say, out of nothing. Work,
> however, is money. Here, therefore, the practical problem which the
> cunning heads of all centuries have followed in the most diverse
> ways, namely, to fabricate money out of nothing, invited solution [in
> Youmans 1865, p. 213].

Here, in a nutshell, is the preeminent problem of the nineteenth
century: How can labor, or indeed Nature, bring about the expansion
of value? Helmholtz's answer was flatly that it could not: Nature was
also subject to capitalist calculation. In a masterful tethering of the
economic metaphor to the metaphor of the body in motion, he hinted
that it would be nothing less than immoral, fraudulent, and venal to
question the law of energy conservation. Nevertheless, Helmholtz's
justification of the energy concept bore only a tenuous relation to the
physical theories of his time. Indeed, as Breger (1982, pp. 244 ff.)
indicates, Helmholtz elided the distinction between the physics definition of work and its colloquial economic usage numerous times.

For Helmholtz, the world is a machine; man is a machine. Men
work for men; the world works for man; you can't swindle Nature; in
the Natural state no one is swindled. Even his fascination in later life
with the significance of variational principles only served to amplify
the metaphorical resonances. Nature works in the most efficient man-

ner; the natural state of man is to minimize effort and maximize profit.

Innumerable writers took their cue from Helmholtz, and the latter half of the nineteenth century was awash with further elaborations of this metaphoric triad. The mathematician De Morgan wrote, "The purse of Fortunatus, which could always drop a penny out, though never a penny was put in, is a problem of the same kind" (quoted in Dircks 1870, p. 148). Across the Channel, Bernard Brunhes waxed eloquent: "In nature, the course of the exchange is uniform and invariable . . . Nature never pretends to realize a profit on the transformations of energy which she permits . . . The role of [modern] industry is precisely to produce artificial transformations of energy" (Brunhes 1908, pp. 24–5, 198; my translation). But the most explicit popularizer was one Balfour Stewart:[8]

> It is, in fact, the fate of all kinds of energy of position to be ultimately converted into energy of motion. The former may be compared to money in a bank, or capital, the latter to money which we are in the act of spending . . . If we pursue the analogy a step further, we shall see that the great capitalist is respected because he has the disposal of a great quantity of energy; and that whether he be nobleman or sovereign, or a general in command, he is powerful only from having something which enables him to make use of the services of others. When a man of wealth pays a labouring man to work for him, he is in truth converting so much of his energy of position into actual energy . . .
>
> The world of mechanism is not a manufactory, in which energy is created, but rather a mart, into which we may bring energy of one kind and change or barter it for an equivalent of another kind, that suits us better – but if we come with nothing in hand, with nothing we will most assuredly return [Stewart 1883, pp. 26–7; 34].

Economists, please take note of the period – Stewart's book was in its sixth edition by 1883 – and of the profound shift of metaphor from production to circulation. Nature, before the bestower of bounteous gifts, had now become our niggardly paymaster.

Physics off the gold standard

The enthusiasm for the energy megalith built to a fever pitch at the end of the nineteenth century; heat and motion swept up together to ever greater heights. In truth, the energetics movement of Helm and Ostwald was just the tip of the pyramid, the seemingly natural extrapolation of the metaphors of body and value. From this perspective, perhaps Ostwald did not seem such a ridiculous figure with his assertions that the conversion factors for various forms of energy were their "exchange rates," and that these were the fundamental facts upon which to found a unified social and political theory. Helm wrote in 1887 that "In the law of energy a *world formula* is developing such as Laplace had in mind, but which extends far beyond the domain of Newtonian knowledge" (in Deltete 1983, p. 210). And yet, after all was said and done, the energetics conception of the world formula had expired by the second quarter of the twentieth century – or, at least, Helm and Ostwald's version was dead. (However, steel thyself, dear reader, for Chapter 5.) What happened to it?

There are, to be sure, the standard reasons tendered in the history of science literature. Helm and Ostwald made mathematical mistakes and numerous conceptual errors (Deltete 1983, pp. 386 ff., 798, 808; Hiebert 1971). Moreover, they tended to misrepresent the entropy concept. Ostwald had the unfortunate habit of thinking of all the forms of energy as individual substances, rendering him incapable of understanding the field concept. Nonetheless, these are all quibbles, symptoms rather than causes of the decline of energetics. After all, we have before us the subsequent dissolution of the energy concept in orthodox physics. For the energetics, the law of the conservation of energy was the very paragon of physical law, the epitome of what science could aspire to truly know about the world. Yet it has been the conservation of energy that has come unraveled – without fanfare, to be sure, but come undone nonetheless.

Just as with Kuhn's reservations over the conventional stories of the discovery of energy conservation, we might also harbor reservations about narrowly conceived stories of the demise of energetics and the dissolution of the energy concept. Since the world never pointed to the energy concept in the first place, it seems a little tendentious to assert that the world pointed to its demise. One might instead suggest that the pyramid was never rock-solid, but shifted because of seismic movements in the base metaphors at the three vertexes. Energy was (and I suppose still is) the expression of a specific world view, one bound up with Laplacean determinism, temporal symmetry, a reductionist conception of the body, and the exchange of equivalents. Yet the perturbations emanated from the fact that these structural underpinnings were starting to go out of fashion almost as soon as energy had come off the rack. *Fin-de siècle* Western European culture was contriving to glimpse more change in the world than the energy concept would permit, and while the raiments were not actually discarded, they came out of the wardrobe with noticably less frequency.

By the twentieth century, particularly the metaphors of body and value were becoming further fragmented, creating cracks in the energy pyramid. Developments in evolutionary biology and Freudian psychology were beginning to feed back into the metaphor of the body: The history of the organism was assuming greater significance, and the organic was coming to be synonymous with continuous change and mutation, the opposite pole of mechanism. But more important, the energetics vision of the body left out an aspect of organic life that could not suppressed: Organisms embodied a teleology because they grew old and died. There was a fundamental asymmetry to life that could not be easily reconciled with the energy concept. These increasingly insistent aspects of the metaphor of the body began to make their presence felt in such areas of physics as classical thermodynamics and quantum mechanics.

More significant, transformations at the value vertex of the pyramid eventually weakened the energy metaphor. Money and value in the nineteenth century had seemed so uncomplicated, so substantial, so *physical*. Money was gold, or in the worst case, some troublesome amalgam of gold and silver; because it was essentially indistinguishable from a commodity, it could safely be taken as possessing all of the substantial characteristics of commodities. Trade was ultimately barter, equals putatively given for equals. Paper money did exist, but merely as a sign of the underlying physicalist determinants of value. Yet the evolution of the economy appeared to belie this construction of value. By the end of the nineteenth century, it was becoming evident that Britain was being surpassed as a manufacturing power and moving towards an economy based on finance and trade. Indeed, the expansion of the Western economies implicitly broached the objection that if trade really were trade of equivalents, then whence came profits?[9] Then another sequence of events exploded the doctrine of money as commodity: countries found they could go off the gold standard; their currencies backed by "nothing." By the 1920s financial wizards were defeating captains of industry left and right with little more than smoke and mirrors, accumulating huge fortunes seemingly out of nothing. By the 1930s, all the pious verities of sound finance and stable value rang hollow.

The dematerialization of the value concept boded ill for the tangible world of stable time and concrete motion (Kern 1983). Again, the writer Jorge Luis Borges (1962, p. 159) captured the mood of the metaphor:

> I reflected there is nothing less material than money, since any coin whatsoever (let us say a coin worth twenty centavos) is, strictly

speaking, a repertory of possible futures. Money is abstract, I repeated; money is the future tense. It can be an evening in the suburbs, or
music by Brahms; it can be maps, or chess, or coffee; it can be the
words of Epictetus teaching us to despise gold; it is a Proteus more
versatile than the one on the isle of Pharos. It is unforeseeable time,
Bergsonian time . . .

It was not solely in art that the reconceptualization of value gripped
the imagination. Because the energy concept depended upon the
value metaphor in part for its credibility, physics was prodded to
reinterpret the meaning of its conservation principles. In an earlier,
simpler era Clerk Maxwell could say that conservation principles gave
the physical molecules "the stamp of the manufactured article" (Barrow and Tipler 1986, p. 88), but as manufacture gave way to finance,
seeing conservation principles in nature gave way to seeing them
more as contingencies, imposed by our accountants in order to keep
confusion at bay. Nowhere is this more evident than in the popular
writings of the physicist Arthur Eddington, the Stephen Jay Gould of
early twentieth century physics:

> The famous laws of conservation and energy . . . *are mathematical
> identities*. Violation of them is unthinkable. Perhaps I can best indi-
> cate their nature by an analogy.
>   An aged college Bursar once dwelt secluded in his rooms devoting
> himself entirely to accounts. He realised the intellectual and other
> activities of the college only as they presented themselves in the bills.
> He vaguely conjectured an objective reality at the back of it all –
> some sort of parallel to the real college – though he could only
> picture it in terms of the pounds, shillings and pence which made up
> what he would call "the commonsense college of everyday experi-
> ence." The method of account-keeping had become inveterate habit
> handed down from generations of hermit-like bursars; he accepted
> the form of the accounts as being part of the nature of things. But he
> was of a scientific turn and he wanted to learn more about the
> college. One day in looking over the books he discovered a remark-
> able law. For every item on the credit side an equal item appeared
> somewhere else on the debit side. "Ha!" said the Bursar, "I have
> discovered one of the great laws controlling the college. It is a
> perfect and exact law of the real world. Credit must be called plus
> and debit minus; and so we have the law of conservation of £. s. d.
> This is the true way to find out things, and there is no limit to what
> may ultimately be discovered by this scientific method . . ."
>   I have no quarrel with the Bursar for believing that scientific
> investigation of the accounts is a road to exact (though necessarily
> partial) knowledge of the reality behind them . . . But I would point
> out to him that a discovery of the overlapping of the different
> aspects in which the realities of the college present themselves in the

world of accounts, is not a discovery of the laws controlling the college; that he has not even begun to find the controlling laws. The college may totter but the Bursar's accounts still balance . . .
Perhaps a better way of expressing this selective influence of the mind on the laws of Nature is to say that *values* are created by the mind [Eddington 1930, pp. 237–8, 243].

Once physicists had become inured to entertaining the idea that *value is not natural,* then it was a foregone conclusion that the stable Laplacean dreamworld of a fixed and conserved energy and a single super-variational principle was doomed. Again, Eddington stated it better than I could hope to:

[Classical determinism] was the gold standard in the vaults; [statistical laws were] the paper currency actually used. But everyone still adhered to the traditional view that paper currency needs to be backed by gold. As physics progressed the occasions when the gold was actually produced became career until they ceased altogether. Then it occurred to some of us to question whether there still was a hoard of gold in the vaults or whether its existence was a mythical tradition. The dramatic ending of the story would be that the vaults were opened and found to be empty. The actual ending is not quite so simple. It turns out that the key has been lost, and no one can say for certain whether there is any gold in the vaults or not. But I think it is clear that, with either termination, present-day physics is *off the gold standard* [Eddington 1935, p. 81].

The denaturalization of value presaged the dissolution of the energy concept into a mere set of accounts, which, like national currencies, were not convertable at any naturally fixed rates of exchange. Quantum mechanical energy was not exactly the same thing as relativistic energy or thermodynamic energy. Yet this did not mean that physics had regressed to a state of fragmented autarkies. Trade was still conducted between nations; mathematical structure could bridge subdisciplines of physics. It was just that everyone was coming to acknowledge that money was provisional, and that symmetries expressed by conservation principles were contingent upon the purposes of the theory in which they were embedded.

Increasingly, this contingent status was expressed by recourse to economic metaphors. The variability of metrics of space-time in general relativity were compared to the habit of describing inflation in such torturous language as: "The pound is now only worth seven and sixpence" (Eddington 1930, p. 26). The fundamentally stochastic character of the energy quantum was said to allow nuclear particles to "borrow" sufficient energy so that they could "tunnel" their way out of the nucleus. And, inevitably, if we live with a banking system wherein money is created by means of loans granted on the basis of near-zero fractional reserves, then this process of borrowing energy could cascade, building upon itself until the entire universe is conceptualized as a "free lunch." The nineteenth century would have recoiled in horror from this idea, they who believed that banks merely ratified the underlying real transactions with their loans.

Even more recently, this value/instrumentalist attitude has even begun to erode the concept of the field. "In the Wheeler-Feynman picture, the electromagnetic field is not a real physical entity, but a book-keeping device constructed to avoid having to talk about particles teleologically" (Barrow and Tipler 1986, p. 151). Equally devastating is the realization that the entire contraption of a variational principle tied to a conservation principle is just an artifact of our language, something we project onto nature. Indeed, Yourgrau and Mandelstam (1960) have argued that, given any set of evolutionary equations, some kind of action could be contrived that assumes an extremum for the observed path. One might infer that variational principles therefore have no physical content; but then, why are they found everywhere in physics? The answer to that question could only be entertained late in the twentieth century: Variational principles are ubiquitous because that is how we, the relevant language community, make sense of our economy and hence our social life. It is, quite deliberately, second nature.

Atavism and a nostalgia for a supposedly simpler past may make it difficult to apprehend that the breakdown of the energy concept is not tantamount to the Decline of the West. If it is indicative of anything, it is rather the further consolidation of the syndetic metrological stage of discourse. Metaphors of the body, of motion, and of value are more perfectly reconciled by means of the realization that each is a fiction, but the *same* fiction, a fiction necessary for the organization of human discourse. In many ways this trend is exemplified by a recent controversial book entitled *The Anthropic Cosmological Principle* (Barrow and Tipler 1986). The book argues that the lesson of twentieth-century physics is that mankind's existence should be a relevant consideration in picking and choosing our theories of physical phenomena. The authors point to such twentieth-century ideas as the act of observation having a nonnegligible influence on the phenomena observed; the Bell inequality experiments, which suggest that observer/observed interactions in quantum mechanics have nonlocal effects; that the so-called dimensionless numbers of nature assume the values they do because they are the only values consistent with the existence of our life-forms. They quote John Wheeler to the effect that: "Time is defined so that motion looks simple."

In effect, these physicists are bringing the metaphor of the body back into the physics in a more profound manner, reconceptualizing the universe as a reflection of our social and somatic selves. For those who view this prospect with some alarm, perhaps it becomes less disturbing in light of this chapter's argument that physicists have been doing just that for centuries. The broad outlines of these authors' metrological project becomes most apparent when they discuss their own specialty:

> Instead of assuming that Nature is described by gauge symmetries whose particular form then dictates which elementary particles can exist and how they interact, one might imagine that there are no symmetries at high energies at all: in effect, that there are no laws of physics. Human beings have a habit of perceiving in Nature more laws and symmetries than truly exist there . . . during the last 20 years we have seen a gradual erosion of principles and conserved quantities as Nature has revealed a deep, and previously un-suspected flexibility . . . even gauge invariance may be an "illusion": a selection effect of the low energy world which we necessarily inhabit (Barrow and Tipler 1986, pp. 255–6).

If these authors are correct, Meyerson's prescient philosophical writings have been vindicated. Invariants are not to be seriously found "out there"; in a real sense they are "in here". Our understanding of the world is structurally inseparable from our understanding of our somatic selves and our social selves. Our very livelihoods, in the broadest possible sense, are predicated upon invariants whose existence cannot be proven but whose instrumentality renders our actions coherent.

CHAPTER 4

Science and substance theories of value in political economy to 1870

The economic laws aimed at and formulated under the guidance of this preconception are laws of what takes place "naturally" or "normally," and it is of the essence of things so conceived that in the natural or normal course there is no wasted or misdirected effort . . . the resulting economic theory is formulated as an analysis of the "natural" course of the life of the community, the ultimate theoretical postulate of which might, not unfairly, be stated as some sort of law of the conservation of economic energy . . . there prevails an equivalence of expenditure and returns, an equilibrium of flux and reflux, which is not broken over in the normal course of things. So it is, by implication, assumed that the product which results from any given industrial process or operation is, in some sense or unspecified aspect, the equivalent of the expenditure of forces, or the effort, or what not, that has gone into the process out of which the product emerges [Veblen 1969, pp. 280–1].

But, since a strict uniformity is nowhere to be observed at first hand in the phenomena with which the investigator is occupied, it has to be found by a laborious interpretation of the phenomena and a diligent abstraction and allowance for disturbing circumstances, whatever may be the meaning of a disturbing circumstance where causal continuity is denied. In this work of interpretation and expurgation the investigator proceeds on a conviction of the orderliness of natural sequence [Veblen 1969, p. 162].

The entire exchange abstraction is founded upon social postulate and not upon fact. It is a postulate that the use of commodities must remain suspended until the exchange has taken place; it is a postulate that no physical change should occur in the commodities and this still applies even if the facts belie it; it is a postulate that the commodities in the exchange relation should count as equal despite their factual difference; it is a postulate that the alienation and acquisition of things between commodity owners is tied to the condition of exchangeability; it is a postulate that the commodities change owners by a translation from one locality to another without being materially affected. They are all norms commodity exchange has to obey to be possible and to enable anarchical society to survive by the rules of reification [Sohn-Rethel 1978, p. 68].

There is no denying that late-twentieth-century physics is a frightening and demoralizing place: a universe sprung full-blown from nothing; no real natural laws; chaos wherever one turns; the physical world a speculum serving us back our own gaze. It is not enough that we owe to this physics the ability to destroy our world in a space of minutes; it also corrodes and debases every little piety we may happen to cherish. No doubt many will bid adieu to the physics portion of this book with ill-concealed relief. How much more civil and staid a prospect, then, to turn to the pastoral greens and blacks and reds of that eminently practical intellectual endeavor, known in the eighteenth and nineteenth centuries as political economy and thereafter as economics . . .

Of course, I am being a little bit facetious here. I'll wager that prior to this moment, the reader harbored the conviction that it was *physics* that constituted a tranquil and reassuring body of commonsense wisdom, whereas economics was nothing more than a cacophony of groundless claims, wishful thinking, smoke and mirrors and vanity. But after the last chapter, the dollar, the accelerometer, and the mirror are all starting to look the same.

Once one enteres the House of Mirrors, images tend to double back upon themselves, to reflect, to refract. In this chapter we turn to economics, only to find our images again, the same yet distorted. Here the mirror of society has been confronted with the mirror of nature so that social life could be portrayed as the reflection of natural relationships, and the resulting images cascade off into infinity. To keep from getting lost in the funhouse, we have to avert our gaze from the mad proliferation, to search for the focal point of the mirrors. The confocal points of both economics and physics are, not surprisingly, the same: They reside at the conservation principles of the respective disciplines. The reason so many have been stranded in the funhouse prior to the present is that, while the language of conservation principles is well ensconced in physics, it is a comparative stranger to economics, with the possible exception of some perceptive but underdeveloped remarks by Thorstein Veblen, such as those that head this chapter. Since it may seem ungracious to indict an entire discipline with astigmatism, it may be prudent to approach the House of Mirrors slowly, deliberately, and from a distance. Let us then commence with the crucial metaphor of *value*.

The metaphor of value

Value, it has already been argued, is part of the metaphoric triad motion/body/value that undergirds the energy concept. The definition of that term was purposely left vague in the previous chapters, emphasizing the fact that metaphoric license allows one to slide effortlessly from economic connotations to those of quantitative measurement to those of general worth or virtue. In economics proper, however, the concept has come to be tethered to somewhat more narrow concerns.

Value theory in economics will be defined as the combined responses to the following three questions:

1. What is it that renders commodities commensurable in a market system, hence justifying their value?
2. What are the conservation principles that formalize the responses to (1), permitting quantitative and causal analysis in a Meyersonian sense?
3. How are the conservation principles in (2) united with the larger metaphorical simplex of body/motion/value described in the previous chapter, which provides the principles with their justification?

It will be apparent that the answers to all of these questions are intimately bound up with the postulation of conservation principles in economics; and yet, we did begin Chapter 1 by noting that the language of conservation principles has not made much headway into economic discourse. Both observations can be reconciled by a third, namely, that value theory itself has not flourished in the orthodox economic schools of the last hundred years. I would venture to think that the majority of economists, upon hearing the topic "the theory of value," would regard it as the province of endless nattering metaphysical speculations upon the ultimate nature of the economy. These economists, out of frustration, or perhaps a disdain for philosophy, have sought to pass over these issues as rapidly as possible, in order to get down to the "real work" of economics. This attitude has been nowhere as prevalent as in the United States, where in the postwar period an important book could be titled *The Theory of Value* (Debreu 1959) and yet be devoid of any explicit discussion of the above three questions.

After Debreu, citations of value theory tend to use it as a synonym for price theory. Value theory is indeed concerned with prices and the mathematical expression of chrematistical relationships, but it is a mistake to regard that as exhausting the purview of value theory. Of course, value theory also evokes overtones of morality and social norms, but that doesn't get to the heart of the matter, either. The only way to fully comprehend value theory in economics is to situate it within the pyramid of Figure 3.1, the metaphorical simplex of energy, motion, body, and value, and to regard it as part and parcel of the same structures that undergird Western physics. The payoff to this reconceptualization of value theory is a clarification of the entire history of economic thought. In the realm of value theory, the concepts of the discipline called economics have persistently been dominated by somewhat prior developments with regard to concepts of motion in physics.

The primary reason that the structural developments of physics and economics so resemble one another is that the elementary problem in both spheres was the same: how to successfully reify a notion of causality in the Meyersonian sense? The imperative to reconcile phenomenological change with causal invariance dictated a search for conservation principles indigenous to an external Nature. Needless to say, the early political economists did not start on Day One with this imperative clearly fixed in their minds; it developed gradually, passing through the metrological stages identified in Chapter 3. In the earliest, anthropometric, stage, the absence of differentiation among body, motion, and value was reflected in an absence of a conception of economic value separate from animal needs and natural teleology. In the subsequent lineamentric stage, the conviction grew that the economic sphere requires a separate mode of discourse. This happened because the triadic metaphors had become separate and subject to individual elaboration; and thus if value was to maintain its status, it had to be subject to laws of its own. The quantification of specific aspects of social life proceeded apace, with the primal metaphors of motion and body providing the raw material as well as the ultimate rationalization for a number of chrematistic value theories. A marked characteristic of this stage was that, no matter what permutation of underlying metaphors prompted the individual theory, all value theories conformed to the same explanatory pattern: Value was reified as a conserved *substance*, conserved in the activity of trade to provide structural stability to prices, and differentially specified in the process of production. Almost all of the theories conforming to this pattern are now remembered under the rubric of Classical Political Economy.

While it is an occupational hazard of historians of economic thought to effectively homogenize and pasteurize every writer from roughly 1758 to 1870 as just another classical economist (if not worse, to write them all off as mere anticipators of something called neoclassical economics), I would suggest that those texts can withstand the fomentation here proposed without cauterizing their individuality or curdling their originality. The task of this chapter is to demonstrate that it is possible to regard the variegated theories of Quesnay, Smith, Ricardo, and Marx as manifestations of a single class of value theory, associated with the lineametric stage of metrology, rendered coherent by a particular conception of science.

This is not at all meant to echo recent statements by respected economists that "Marx was a minor post-Ricardian," or that "it was all in Smith." What these authors all shared was a particular approach to value theory, the accounting systems that supported their ultimately divergent and diverse architectonics. This "classical" conception roughly divided the social world up into three exhaustive categories: production, circulation, and consumption. Production became associated with any activity or locus where the purported value substance was created or augmented according to fixed natural principles. Circulation identified the function of trade, which was to shift the location of the value substance between sectors, classes, or other functional categories subject to the condition that the trade of equivalents would guarantee the conservation of the value substance in that process. Consumption was associated with any activity or locus where the value substance was destroyed or diminished. One should notice that the three questions of value theory are directly addressed in this schema: objects naturally embody a generic value; the reified invariance of this value substance is the predominant conservation principle; the system of accounts is structured by the imperatives of the lineametric stage of metrology, in particular those characteristic of pre-energy physics.

It may help to preface our narrative of this era of economic thought by noting that the classical schema displayed much of the vulnerability with regard to fragmentation that is so characteristic of the lineametric stage. Just as in pre-energy physics, the metaphors of motion of the value substance often collided with the metaphors of the integrity of the body. For instance, there was the uneasy doctrine that consumption was the ultimate *telos* of the economic process; this did not resonate harmoniously with the fixation of analysis upon the motion and growth of the value substance, nor was it well integrated with the sensuous aspects of the vernacular usages of "consumption." An ever-present tension in classical political economy was the tendency to elevate production above consumption and circulation as the true arbiter of the wealth of nations, even though the doctrines of free trade and respect for the self-determination of the economic actors seemed to suggest it was of subordinate importance. Such struggles to articulate the metaphorical simplex of body, motion, and value constitutes the theme of this chapter.

Anticipating the remainder of the story, one might then think that economics also experienced a straightforward evolution of value theory into the last, syndetic, metrological stage, following in the footsteps of physics. Alas, our story takes an unexpected turn around 1870. For those who don't like suspense, all we can offer at this stage is a preview: Economics does indeed attain a synthesis of sorts with the rise of neoclassical economics, and the synthesis does have something to do with the changes in physics, and it did involve a move away from value conceived as a substance; yet it can hardly be regarded as a metaphorical synthesis on a par with what happened in physics. But, as they used to say in eighteenth-century novels, we get ahead of ourselves. First, let us attend to the embryonic beginnings of value theory in Western social thought.

Aristotle discovers the economy

Whatever else he may represent in the history of Western thought, Aristotle was patently a precapitalist thinker, and hence will serve as an uncontroversial paradigm of a writer operating in the anthropometric stage of value theory. His observations on value are particularly poignant because he wrote at a time when markets had gained a tenacious foothold in Greek society, a phenomenon he found disturbing. This tension in his writings on politics lends his thought a modicum of modernity not to be found in other Greek writers. Because of the reams of subsequent commentary spawned by the *Politics* and the *Nichomachean Ethics,* the Aristotelian corpus could be regarded as the starting point of the Western elaboration of the metaphor of value.

In the *Politics,* Aristotle divides the provisioning aspects of social life into separate spheres of household management and trade; then, in phrases discordant to modern readers, he proceeds to demean trade as an unnatural pursuit, contrasting it with the natural provisioning of the household. The natural wealth of the household is bounded, we are told, whereas the generation of wealth in external exchange, mediated by money, is unlimited. External trade incurs suspicion and reproach because it may threaten to upset the polity, the collectivity of individually self-sufficient households, itself based upon the naturally fixed and immutable statuses of men. Within the confines of the household, social roles are fixed and well understood. In retail trade, however, men of differing estates are brought together, and this raises the problem of their equalization. As Aristotle puts it in the *Ethics:* "[In trade] . . . association is formed, not by two doctors, but by a doctor and a husbandman, and generally by people who are differ-

ent, and not equal, *and who need to be equalized*. [My italics] It follows
that such things as are the subjects of exchange must in some sense be
comparable" (in Monroe 1924, p. 27).

In a society where retail activity was increasingly the province of
slaves, the equalization brought about by trading activity must have
provoked disquiet. If this equalization were of dynamic consequence,
then it would indeed disrupt the polity, but Aristotle instead takes the
position that the equalization is of a static character. Market intercourse, because of its arbitrary and external character relative to
the self-sufficient household, does not disrupt the natural order of
status, rather it oddly reproduces that status in the objects of trade.
For Aristotle, the artificial equalization of the objects in trade reflects
the illegitimate equalization of the traders in the act of exchange. This
equalization of unlike objects as commodities, in turn, requires an
arbitrary and conventional means of equalization: in other words, a
notion of *value*.

> This is the reason for the invention of money. Money is a sort of
> medium or mean; for it measures everything and consequently
> measures among other things excess or defect, for example, the
> number of shoes which are equivalent to a house or a meal. As a
> builder is to a cobbler, so must so many shoes be to a house or a meal:
> for otherwise there would be no exchange or association . . . the
> reason why it is called money is because it has not a natural but a
> conventional existence, and because it is in our power to change it,
> and make it useless" (Monroe 1924, pp. 27–8).

Herein lies the embryo of the Western value concept, but also,
remarkably, the reason why Aristotle himself declines to discuss what
we would now identify as the sphere of the economic in any further
detail. Money, as the Greeks were aware, could easily be devalued or
debased. This eventuality did not trouble Aristotle, because for him
the value of money was just a signifier of an inauthentic equalization,
an artifice of the polity that could be altered at will. Alterations of
value were not disruptive of social intercourse because they only
impinged upon external trade, which was itself artificial and arbitrary. In this sense, the market was little more than an excrescence
upon the body politic (Polanyi 1968).

The anthropometric character of Aristotle's reasoning is represented by his sequence of determinations standing in exactly the
reverse order of later stages of value theory. In Aristotle, the polis,
the collection of independent households, is the obvious starting
point of social theory. The social constitution of the households is
fixed, only to be perturbed from time to time by interhousehold

trade. This trade is not to be deduced from the bodily needs of the household, which are autonomous. Trade instead resembles Aristotelian motion, the resultant of violent displacements from the natural rest point of the body. Both Aristotelian value and Aristotelian motion are not quantitative concepts, and more important, there is no conserved entity that reifies either notion. Value is represented by money, something intrinsically unstable because the function that it performs is likewise unstable, unnatural. Only after we leave the anthropomorphic stage does it become conceivable that value is a law-governed phenomenon, a reified natural entity, and that social status and trading ratios are governed by it. That, in turn, only happens when social theorists conceive of a separate economic sphere and renounce money as an adequate value principle.

In this sense, body and motion have not yet become so dissociated from value as to warrant a separate metaphor. Nevertheless, Aristotle had set the pattern for subsequent reasoning. All economic theory after Aristotle endeavored to reduce the complex of social interactions to the relationship of the traded objects, and thence to reduce the myriad of commodities (through an abstract equalization) to a single value index. Although Aristotle did not elaborate upon them, the notion of equalization was rich in connotations. From a quantitative perspective, equalization suggested that a market operated so as to effect a valid equalization of the commodities traded. From a juridic perspective, it suggested that a healthy market would be one in which symmetrical transactors met on grounds of parity: "Money is therefore like a measure that equates things, by making them commensurable; for association would be impossible without exchange, exchange without equality, and equality without commensurability" (in Monroe 1924, p. 28).

As long as the market was a subsidiary support of the organization of livlihood, it was the more qualitative connotations of value that predominated in Western thought. For example, Thomas Aquinas, following Aristotle, does proclaim that "a contract ought to be based on the equality of things" (in Monroe 1924, p. 54). However, as already mooted in Chapter 3, the just price in fact draws upon all sorts of considerations beyond the object vended, in effect resisting the dictum that the social relations of the traders can be reduced to the interrelations of commodities. This resonated with the conviction that trade for purposes of gain was dishonorable because it also rendered the notion of gain incoherent. There was effectively no need for a reified value index.

Two kinds of mercantilism

Against the backdrop of centuries of scholastic texts, the contrast of the sixteenth- and seventeenth-century proto-economic literature is all the more stark. Modern writers, perceiving their own doctrines first presaged there, have been tempted to suggest that these writers, under the sway of Baconian empirical doctrines, merely commenced describing what had been there all along under their noses:

> Being the action of a human being, every economic act is also a social act deriving its utility and meaning from the economic organization and the intellectual traditions of a particular society. Yet despite these obstacles to economics being treated in a scientific mode, early in the seventeenth century writers chose to ignore what was fortuitous, capricious or socially conditioned about commercial transactions and to fix instead upon the regularities in the buying and selling patterns they observed [Appleby 1978, p. 242; see also Pribram 1983, p. 37; and Letwin 1963].

While it is certainly true that the increasing pressures of market organization in social intercourse were in some sense responsible for the rise of political economy (if only because these early pamphleteers were hired propagandists for various mercantile interests), it is profoundly implausible that the rise of value theory could ever be adequately portrayed as a discovery or an empirical generalization. (Shades of Chapter 2!) I should think the most compelling counterargument would be that today value theory remains in a highly unsettled state – as later chapters will document – and hence, few could specify what was "there" to be discovered. Returning to the seventeenth century, this pamphlet literature, now called mercantilist, was in fact the confluence of a number of late Rennaissance influences: the increasingly respected "natural philosophy" tradition, Aristotelian notions of equalization and equality, the Galilean and Cartesian emphasis on a universal mathematics, an the incipient meiosis of the body–motion–value metaphor described in Chapter 3. As one of these new theorists, Edward Misselden, wrote in 1623, "Wee felt it before in sense; but now wee know it by science" (in Braudel 1982, p. 204).

Attempts to summarize these early tracts are made difficult by the fact that they were not written with an eye toward system; hence the essence of mercantilism is extremely elusive, reconstructed after the fact by detractors such as Adam Smith and supporters such as J. M. Keynes. Nevertheless, it does not overly distort the pamphlet record to divide the literature into two subsets: the first, which can be called the balance-of-trade school, found in the early to mid-seventeenth century, then eclipsed for half a century, then revived in the first half of the eighteenth century; and the second, the free-trade school, filling in the hiatus from 1660 to 1700.

The hallmark of the balance-of-trade mercantilism was an attempted translation of Aristotelian (and later, Carteisan) notions of equalization into quantitative and substantial terms, beginning with a realization that the first implication of a closed and bounded system of equivalent exchange is that, as Francis Bacon argued, "whatever is somewhere gotten is somewhere lost." Subsequently, this was interpreted in the pamphlet literature to suggest that: "Increase and Wealth of all States is ever more made upon the foreigner for whatsoever is gained by one Nation from another in one part of this Kingdom must necessarily be lost in another part, and so the public stock nothing thereby Augmented" (in Appleby 1978, p. 161; see also Pribram 1983, p. 35). In more modern terms, equivalence in exchange implies that trade is a zero-sum game.[1]

Although not terribly explicit, this is the first appearance of a conservation principle in Western economic thought. Here the aggregate of value is thought to be conserved in the sphere of commodity exchange conducted entirely with the national currency. It should be noted, however, that a more restrictive conservation principle – one where value is conserved *for every individual* in exchange – was generally avoided, even though it could be a legitimate inference from the doctrine that equivalence governed all transactions. The problem of full equivalence had been raised by a number of Schoolmen in the Middle Ages (Pribram 1983, p. 15). Some had puzzled over the inference that full equalization of trade would dictate no advantage for any of the parties involved. In parallel with the contemporaneous theory of motion, these theorists were groping toward a reconceptualization of the conservation principle that might reconcile it with preexisting theoretical concepts.

The balance-of-trade mercantilists, following Aristotle, settled upon money as the appropriate value index, and identified the state as their unit of analysis. Since the state itself defined the monetary unit, by definition no value surplus could be generated by internal domestic trade. As the nation-state depended upon a fixed quantity of specie to serve as the monetary unit, then value itself could only be increased or decreased by means of external sources or sinks of gold and silver. In this way, one can come to comprehend the paramount importance of a positive trade balance for these writers, and their identification of a positive balance with the augmentation of value.

While later commentators, from Smith (1976, II, p. 65) onward,

have feigned incredulity at the naiveté of this identification of money
with value, a more sympathetic reading of these pamphlets would
reveal a landmark transition into the lineamentric stage of value
theory. What these mercantilists achieved was a rejection of the global, all-encompassing (and therefore analytically ineffectual) "equivalence" of the Schoolmen, and the first reification of a physicalist
notion of value conservation. In their view, the norm of international
commodity trade would be exchange of equivalents; if it were violated, the balance would be tipped and monetary metals would flow
between nations. The metaphors of weight and scales were absolutely
critical to the genesis of this concept (Price 1905, p. 167; Mayr 1986,
p. 146; Pribram 1983, p. 48), and in this respect we observe a typical
characteristic of the lineamentric phase, where trade is conceptualized as the motion of an undifferentiated and conserved value
substance, with the cessation of motion as equilibrium. The secondary
qualities of actual commodity flows both within and between countries could be analytically abstracted away, because all relevant information was signified by flows of specie as long as the system was closed.
The economy was treated as a separate law-governed sphere, rooted
in a metaphor of motion, and to boot, the entire conception could be
reconciled with Artistotle's strictures on the role of money as bringing
about equivalence.

One can discern in this structure the first outlines of the Meyersonian pattern of causal explanation in the newly distinct economic
sphere. First, the reification of a value index is mooted. Next, the
index is asserted to be subject to conservation principles, which inscribe the analytical identity of the phenomenon. In this case, as long
as the community of trading nations were considered as a closed set,
the sum total of specie was fixed as a physical principle – barring, of
course, complications of wear and tear, and of newly mined metal.
Finally, because these first two principles were not simply a matter of
straightforward empiricism – for instance, the complication of mines
and external sources of metal – the legitimacy of the entire vision was
predicated upon explicit appeal to an imitation of the discourse of
natural philosophy and to metaphors of motion and body.

At the nexus of the body/motion/value triad were the writings of
Harvey, Hobbes, and Descartes. Harvey's discovery of the circulation
of the blood in the third decade of the seventeenth century was itself a
major triumph of the body/machine, with Harvey comparing the
body to a kind of mini–solar system, justifying his thesis by an assertion of the conservation of the blood (Barrow and Tipler 1986, p. 53;
Brown 1981). Hobbes was very taken with Harvey's discovery and
further buttressed the metaphor by reducing the biological aspect of

life to nothing more than the motion of the blood (Spragens 1973, p. 69). Descartes, as already noted, aimed to reduce all phenomena to matter in motion, including his own *homme-machine;* yet in some respects it was Hobbes who pointed the way more clearly for social theory, writing that "Substance and Body signifie the same thing" and that "Quantity is nothing else but the Determination of Matter; that is to say of Body" (in Spragens 1973, pp. 77, 95). With Harvey, the newly distinct concept of motion was reflected back onto the body; with Hobbes, both were reflected onto the polity. The balance-of-trade mercantilists drew their sustenance from this nexus, comparing value with substance, gold with the lifeblood of the polity, economic prosperity with bodily health, and trade with motion. In this sense, the balance-of-trade mercantilists were the pioneers of what would later become the standard format of explanation in political economy, lasting for at least two centuries.[2]

Remarkably, the other branch of mercantilism, the free-trade school, also claimed descent from natural-philosophy metaphors: It is this which allows the subsumption of these two very different schools under the larger rubric of mercantilism. The impetus for free-trade mercantilism was located in the admission by the East India Company that roughly half of the goods imported from India were consumed domestically and hence not reexported in order to recoup the gold initially exported to India to purchase the goods. The balance-of-trade camp clearly viewed such practices with opprobium; what was needed (from the merchants' vantage point) was a new argument that domestic markets were not a zero-sum game and that gold was not the natural value substance, and thus a different definition of the wealth of nations.

The response was to be found in the pamphlets of those such as Nicholas Barbon, John Houghton, Dudley North, and William Petty – all of whom decried the doctrine that money was value and denied that wealth must be pried from the foreigner by suppression of domestic consumption and the hothouse forcing of exports. In place of that, they maintained that the domestic market was natural, channeling interests for the benefit of all. The creation of new domestic wants, such as the British penchant for Indian calicos, only served to spur the nation onward to greater achievements, harder work, greater power, and augmented wealth.

Although this literature is pockmarked with the language of the natural virtues of the market, it was not so very compelling for many contemporaries, primarily because it lacked the recourse to perceived methods of natural philosophy and the connected metaphors of body/

motion/value. For instance, when the free-trade mercantilists denied that money was a central value substance, they went so far as to deny the need for any value principle at all. Barbon, for one, wrote "there is no fixt price or value of anything"; "things are just worth so much, as they can be sold for"; and "Things have no value in themselves, it is opinion and fashion brings them into use and gives them value" (in Appleby 1978, pp. 179, 229). Such self-denying ordinances belied any attempt to reduce value to a unique index, rendered quantification practically hopeless, and undermined any conception of the unilineal progress of a nation. The free-trade mercantilists, in their repudiation of the zero-sum game, did not comprehend that the game must then be replaced by some other conservation principle if they were to refer to natural forces and scientific explanation. Hence their program was a dead end. If value displayed no permanence or integrity, then how could the free-trade school recognize improvement or the accumulation of wealth? Given their hostility to nominal and monetary signs and their aversion to the doctrine of the trade of equivalents, how could they ever hope to pronounce any trade "fair" or "legitimate"?

All of these conundrums of the free-trade mercantilists converge in the writings of William Petty, many of which languished unpublished until long after his death. One could, in retrospect, regard his entire sprawling corpus as a search for an alternative value principle rooted in natural relations, a potential rival substance to gold that would transparently reveal the natural operation of a market. Petty was located at the core of the fledgling British scientific community in his roles as a physician, a scholar, and a founding member of the Royal Society. Very early on, he had conceived of his quest as a search for the connective natural principles that lay behind appearance. In a revealing set of notes to himself, he listed what he thought were the "Fundamentall Questions" of all inquiry (Petty 1967, II, p. 39):

> 1. What is a Common Measure of Time, Space, Weight and Motion?
> 2. What is the greatest & least Body in Things & Number? . . .
> 8. How to give names to names, and how to adde and subtract sensata & to ballance the weight and power of words; which is Logick and reason.

Petty, as is obvious, was deeply concerned with metrology, the attribute for which he is most commonly lauded by historians of economics, who ritually reproduce his most famous methodological utterance, viz., "to express my self in Terms of *Number, Weight,* or *Measure;* to use only Arguments of Sense, and to consider only such Causes, as have visible Foundations in Nature" (Petty 1899, I, p. 244).

The ironic aspect of this praise is that it is by and large unwarranted, because it was the balance-of-trade school, and not Petty and his comrades, who possessed the clearer understanding of how to construct a theoretical system of accounts that would imitate the causal explanations of the natural philosophers.

Petty clearly believed in the existence of a market mechanism that operated independent of the inclinations or wills of its participants (1899, I, p. 48) and rejected the notion that money could ever be a valid representation or embodiment of value (pp. 89–90, 183). His stumbling block was the precise specification of value. In numerous instances (I, pp. 49–50; II, pp. 625 ff.) he constructed taxonomies of all the physical attributes that might enter into the determination of what he called the "intrinsec" value of a commodity. Yet these Baconian exercises came to nought, because these were no guiding principles as to the ordering and significance of the relevant influences, much less criteria for inclusion or exclusion. Petty never managed to confront this weakness directly; the only place he approaches the problem of Substance is in another oft-quoted passage:

> All things ought to be valued by two natural Denominations, which is Land and Labour . . . This being true, we should be glad to find out a natural Par between Land and Labour, so as we might express the value of either of them alone as well as or better than by both, and reduce one into the other as easily and certainly as we reduce pence into pounds [I, pp. 44–5].

The phrasing is inadvertently revealing: Petty here admits that what is required is a natural value substance with fixed ratios of transformation, which would perform all of the functions of money. That the object of the exercise is the usurpation of the balance-of-trade mercantilist value principle is patent. Yet Petty could not carry this program forward. His failure came precisely in the inability to identify the natural Par, but also because he cast his net of Political Arithmetick far too widely. This becomes most evident in his *Political Anatomy of Ireland:*

> By the same way [as we equate Land and Labour] we make our Equation between Art and Opinion. For if a picture maker, suppose, makes pictures at 5£ each; but then, finds that more Persons would employ him at that rate than his time would extend to serve them in, it will certainly come to pass that this Artist will consider whether as many of those who apply to him at 5£ each Picture, will give 6£ as will take up his whole time to accomodate; and upon his Computation will pitcheth the rate of his work. By the same way also an Equation may be made between drudging labour; and Favour, Acquaintance, Interest, Friends, Eloquence, Reputation, Authority, etc. All which I

thought not amiss to intimate as the same kind with finding an Equation between Land and Labour" (in Monroe 1924, p. 219).

In this burst of Enthusiasm (for which he is even inclined to intimate some Embarrassment), Petty discloses the incoherence of his conception of science. If everything – the whole of social existence – may be indifferently bought and sold as commodities, where is the Archimedean point from which one might posit a value index other than money? A more natural value index might provide a more dependable value expression, except for the admission that the two putatively natural determinants of Land and Labour display no stable par; what hope, then, could there be for a par between Eloquence and Authority?

Petty saw the need for something like a conservation principle, but could not bring himself to commit to any specific entity. This was decisive, since no conservation principle meant no quantification and therefore no valid physical analogy. For this reason, it is misleading for Petty to be heralded as some sort of early prophet of quantification and a scientific economics. An Enthusiasm for counting everything in sight can be as ineffectual as an elaborate but pointless literary conceit. Petty and the free-trade mercantilists were torn between a desire to portray the economy as naturally dynamic and vital, stronger than any attempt to subject it to conscious direction, and the competing desire to root their doctrines in natural philosophy, which were cast in terms of static equilibrium and the reduction of all change to quantitative motion.

All of these various tensions and conflicts for both species of mercantilist came to a head in the treatment of the question of equalization in trade. The protagonists of the pamphlet debates could not definitively decide (sometimes even within the confines of a single screed) whether or not trade was intrinsically the exchange of equivalents. Everyone who championed the Aristotelian doctrine eventually became mired in conundrums of the expression of equivalence and the origins of profit. On the other hand, many of the free traders abjured equalization: "Trade is nothing else but a Commutation of Superfluities: for instance: I give of mine, what I can spare, for somewhat of yours, which I want, and you can spare" (North 1846, p. 2). For this group economic surplus was conceivable, but vulnerable to the objection that what you can spare might be offset by my own gain. Further, the denial of equivalence raised the specter of indeterminate trading ratios, pushing the determination of surplus back into vague needs and desires that were not subject to further analysis. And finally, the free-trade school could not face up to the implication of their position that the sale of labor itself would also have to be portrayed as a sale of a Superfluity, especially in the face of the literature of the time, which bemoaned the difficulties of constituting a dependable labor force. How could profit, predicated upon accumulation above needs, be reconciled with the shedding of Superfluities?

Rather than basing their analysis exclusively upon either equivalence or nonequivalence, most economic writers of the eighteenth century chose to encapsulate the contradiction by a proliferation of concepts. Starting with Petty and Richard Cantillon, it became common to postulate a distinction between intrinsic value, naturally determined and fundamentally stable, and market price, an epiphenomenon of the myriad conjunctures of the historically specific market. In effect, equivalence was thought to hold sway for intrinsic values, whereas market price was relegated the subordinate function of clearing the market, with reference to the ephemeral psychologies favored by nonequivalence theorists. Some not very strenuous attempts to reconcile these disparate conceptions of the operation of a market revolved around desultory appeals to the supposed physical metaphor of gravitation, where market price was held to gravitate toward natural price. Appeals to this metaphor were baseless because the two sets of determinants were thoroughly nonintersecting, with no conservation principles to connect them, a forced melding of natural and unnatural determinants lacking any common denominator (Levine 1980).

Physiocracy: More wheat than *Zeit*

The economic analogue of the rise of the Cartesian school of rational mechanics with its resulting reification of motion into a conserved quantity was the rise of the physiocratic school of political economy in France. These followers of François Quesnay, the first self-styled *économistes*, accomplished what the mercantilists could not: They combined advocacy of free trade and the natural basis of the market economy with a reification of a natural value substance in motion – *blé*, best translated as "corn" or "wheat" – and a hostility to money as an adequate value principle. The similarities between Cartesians and physiocrats, of course, were no accident. Quesnay was an avid admirer of Descartes and Malebranche (Pribram 1983, p. 103; Foley 1973, p. 143; 1976, p. 129; Mourant 1940, p. 5). The physiocrats imported the full Cartesian conception of science into political economy as only Frenchmen could; it is not often understood that this is one important reason why many conventional histories of modern economic thought feel impelled to start with Quesnay.

In many respects, the *Tableau Economique* of François Quesnay is the purest instance of the classical substance theory of value, and therefore it is worthwhile to examine his motivations and influences. Quesnay's accomplishments were unusual: He managed to rise from humble beginnings to become a famous spokesman for the profession of surgeons in the 1730s, and from there to become court physician; only then, at age 60, did he take up economic topics (Meek 1962; Foley 1976, chap. 7). His early medical fame derived from a controversy where he was pitted against one Jean Baptiste Silva, who had argued that due to the "fact" that blood would rush away from a wound faster than it would flow toward it when a vein was opened, the blood tended to concentrate in the parts of the body furthest removed from the site of the wound. The significance of this claim was that it had profound implications for the widespread practice of bloodletting in that era, suggesting that the surgeon should locate incisions conditional upon the specific malady being treated. Quesnay's attack on Silva, first published in 1730, asserted that experiments with tubes of tin and water pumps had revealed that this purported phenomenon was false; the prognosis was thus that incisions could be administered anywhere that was convenient for the surgeon and the patient. This refutation altered the delicate balance between the professions of surgeon and physician in France, and earned Quesnay great renown.

The Cartesian influence on this work is pervasive. The human body is treated as interchangeable with a machine, and more to the point, the coronary system is reduced to a pump and some tubes. The vital process is equated with the motion of the blood, which, notably, had to conform to both conservation of volume and conservation of motion for Quesnay's results to be intelligible. Quesnay, in going to great lengths to configure the tubes in parallel to his understanding of the circulation system of the body, with two major circuits emulating the two major arteries leaving the heart (Foley 1976, chap. 7), reveals an appreciation of metaphor as model. While the connections between Cartesian science and medicine appear fairly straightforward in this instance, we owe it to the research of Vernard Foley to have demonstrated that the same set of influences governed the creation of the *Tableau Economique* in 1758.

In Figure 4.1 we reproduce the "Third Edition" of the *Tableau*.

The Tableau is best comprehended as a schematic that traces the circulation of a generic value substance originating in agriculture and

TABLEAU ÉCONOMIQUE.

Objets à considérer, 1.º Trois sortes de dépenses ; 2.º leur source ; 3.º leur avances ; 4.º leur distribution ; 5.º leurs effets ; 6.º leur reproduction ; 7.º leurs rapports entr'elles ; 8.º leurs rapports avec la population ; 9.º avec l'Agriculture ; 10.º avec l'industrie ; 11.º avec le commerce ; 12.º avec la masse des richesses d'une Nation.

DÉPENSES PRODUCTIVES *relatives à l'agriculture, &c*	DÉPENSES DU REVENU, *l'Impôt prélevé, se partage aux Dépenses productives et aux Dépenses stériles.*	DÉPENSES STÉRILES *relatives à l'industrie, &c*

Avances annuelles pour produire un revenu de 600.ᵗᵗ sont 600.ᵗᵗ

Revenu annuel de

Avances annuelles pour les Ouvrages des Dépenses stériles, sont 300.ᵗᵗ

600. produisent net 600.ᵗᵗ

Productions .... *moitié passe ici* .... *Ouvrages, &c.*

300.ᵗᵗ reproduisent net .... 300.ᵗᵗ 300.ᵗᵗ

150. reproduisent net .... 150. .... 150.

75. reproduisent net .... 75. .... 75.

37.10.ˢ reproduisent net .... 37..10. .... 37..10

18..15. reproduisent net .... 18..15. .... 18..15

9..7..6. reproduisent net .... 9..7..6. .... 9..7..6.

4..13.. reproduisent net .... 4..13..9. .... 4..13...9

2..6..10. reproduisent net .... 2..6..10. .... 2..6..10

1...3 5 reproduisent net .... 1..3..5. .... 1..3..5

0..11...8 reproduisent net .... 0..11..8. .... 0..11...8

0..5..10 reproduisent net .... 0..5..10. .... 0..5..10

0...2..11 reproduisent net .... 0...2..11. .... 0..2..11

0....1..5 reproduisent net .... 0....1..5 .... 0....1....5

&c.

REPRODUIT TOTAL .... 600.ᵗᵗ de revenu ; de plus, les frais annuels de 600.ᵗᵗ et les intérêts des avances primitives du Laboureur, de 300.ᵗᵗ que la terre restitue. Ainsi la réproduction est de 1500.ᵗᵗ compris le revenu de 600.ᵗᵗ qui est la base du calcul, abstraction faite de l'impôt prélevé, et des avances qu'exige sa reproduction annuelle, &c. Voyez l'Explication à la page suivante.

FIGURE 4.1 *Tableau Economique* of François Quesnay.

transported among three classes of economic actors within a fixed accounting period. As the period begins, the Tableau portrays all value in the hands of a small landlord class situated in the center of the schematic. At the top of the Tableau, the landlords advance half the value to the tenant farmer class on the left, and use the other half to purchase manufactures and luxury goods (the two were conflated in Quesnay's France) from the artisan or "sterile" class on the right. Now, imagine the circulation of value as the flow of a substance: It emerges from a single font, and is immediately subdivided into two flows – and this is none other than Quesnay's earlier tubes of tin. Back in the Tableau, the subdivided flows now criss-cross in a clutter of "zig-zags" (the term used by Quesnay's acolytes when complaining of the headaches that resulted from its contemplation). The farmer class takes its portion, plants half of that, and receives back from the bounteous earth twice that magnitude of value, of which half is paid back to the landlord class. The residual of the original endowment is paid to the sterile class to purchase manufactures.

The sterile class likewise spends what it gets, but as its name implies, it is impotent to increase the magnitude of the value substance by any of its activities; hence, it can only act as a conduit. These sequence of transactions then repeat themselves down the length of the Tableau, with subdivision following upon subdivision in a geometrically declining series, until all amounts asymptotically approach zero. Arriving at the bottom line, one learns that in a healthy Tableau, the original advances have been just exactly reproduced, equal to the sums of each column of flows within the accounting period. The major moral thus drawn from the Tableau is that, if for any reason, there are unbalanced expenditures on "luxuries" produced by the sterile class, or else if trade between classes is hindered or clogged, then the advances will not be reproduced, and the whole economy will succumb to the serious malady (consumption?) of a downward spiral towards zero.

The parallels between Quesnay's medical theories and his political economy are extensive. Quesnay's understanding of the configuration of the cardiovascular and economic systems are identical; health in both instances means the unobstructed flow of a conserved substance through the system. More profoundly, just as the major vital processes had been supposedly reduced to the motion of a single substance, so, too, were the motley of economic activities reduced to the motion of a unique value substance across some class boundaries. Although the quantities of the Tableau might sometimes be denominated in *livres*, it is clear that money did not constitute value: "A nation's wealth is not regulated by the amount of monetary wealth" (in Meek 1962, p. 77).

Far from merely operating on the plane of broad analogy, Quesnay's Tableau reflects his physical theories down to small details. For instance, the Tableau reproduces the tubes of tin, with all flows eventually returning to the pump/landlords. As the aim of bloodletting was to free up circulation in order to restore health, the physiocratic advocacy of freer trade was to free up the circulation of value to restore national wealth. Indeed, the physiocratic doctrine of a single tax was a projection of Quesnay's surgical doctrine that a single incision during bloodletting was the most efficient and efficacious regimen (Foley 1973).

With the identification of the unique value substance as *blé*, a natural physical entity independent of trade, all of the major themes of the classical theory of value fell into place. The natural law of society was reduced to physical law in form and in content, or as Quesnay put it, "Les lois naturelles de l'ordre des sociétés sont les lois physiques mêmes de la reproduction perpetuelle des biens nécessaire à la subsistence, à la conservation et al commodité des hommes" [The natural laws of social order are the very same physical laws of the reproduction of goods necessary for subsistance, for conservation and the comfort of men.] (in Mourant 1940, p. 55). In a theme to be repeated ad nauseam over the next two centuries, his disciple Mirabeau insisted, "la science économique est approfondie et développée par la raisonnement; mais sans les calcules, elle serait toujours une science indéterminée, confuse et livrée partout à l'erreur et au préjugé" [economic science is deepened and developed by reason; but without calculation, it would always be an indeterminate science, confused and confounded everywhere by error and prejudice] (in Weulersse 1910, p. 46). In retrospect, Quesnay did not manage to remain untainted by all confusion, but he certainly did manage to fuse the metaphors of body, motion, and value into a coherent economic system – no mean achievement.

Nature as synonymous with agriculture was fused with Nature as experienced in the body, conjoined to Nature as mathematical motion, and the result was indisputably *science,* or as Quesnay put it, agriculture "gives rise to settled laws, weights, measures, and everything which is concerned with determining and guaranteeing possessions" (in Meek 1962, p. 60). Thus the conviction grew that the economy was a law-governed sphere unto itself, separate from but resembling the worlds of rational mechanics and "animal oeconomy." This breakthrough prompted the first comprehensive set of national economic accounts, as well as the first coherent theoretical account of equivalence in trade.

The physiocratic tenet that only agriculture was productive of value has subsequently been subject to ridicule by commentators from Smith (1976, II, p. 195) to Boss (1982); this has been unfortunate, since these writers have misunderstood the significance and importance of the distinction between productive and unproductive in the physiocratic system, or in the metaphorical interplay of the entire history of economic thought.[3] The distinction between productive and unproductive sectors of the economy, although obviously freighted with overtones of moral opprobrium and political ostracization, from an analytical point of view is isomorphic to the statement of a conservation principle in the theory of value. If one is intent on portraying trade as motion, it is of paramount importance that the value substance in motion be identified by constants that are themselves not influenced by said motion; the parallels to the history of physics are evident. One method of expressing those constants is to construct a system of value accounts that distinguish between sectors of the economy where the magnitude of value is altered and those where it is conserved. If one chooses, as did the physiocrats, to locate the augmentation of value in a single sector, then it follows that trade between sectors can readily be defined as the trade of equivalents: this is the real meaning of the *Tableau Economique*.

In this schema, production is well defined as the locus of the increase of the value substance; trade or circulation as where the value substance is conserved, and finally, consumption as the locus of value destruction. Such accounts make it possible to attribute quantitative cause and effect to any particular economic event, as well as to link the actions of any sector to the experiences of another. Quesnay went even beyond this, postulating a second conservation principle: The conservation of the advances is defined as the health of the national economy. This second conservation principle is fully detachable from the first, in that there is nothing to prevent the reconciliation of the trade of equivalents with the phenomenon of the progressive growth of the value substance, although Quesnay did not entertain this possibility. Indeed, this amendment to the physiocratic value accounts concisely describes the subsequent evolution of classical political economy. The expansion of the annual advances would bring the reduction of economic change to the motion of a value substance to its fruition: The aggregate of value was not fixed, as in some versions of mercantilism, but instead would vary conditionally upon the behavior of the economic actors.

The physiocrats were the first to make the postulation of unproductive sectors a hallmark of their analysis; perhaps a better way of stating it is that it became the hallmark of a substance theory of value. This analytical option has been regarded by subsequent neo-classical theorists as an egregious error; in particular, Boss (1982, p. 44) thinks it a fallacy to indict any economic activity as simultaneously necessary-but-intermediate and yet unproductive. This criticism reveals a serious misunderstanding of the role of value theory, a misunderstanding also found in the later neoclassical theory of production (see Chapter 6). Although it cannot be denied that the use of the epithet "unproductive" more often than not reveals who or what a particular economic theorist thinks the world would be better off without, this should not obscure the fact that the imposition of conservation principles in the context of a substance theory of value essentially dictates the existence of such categories.

One of the great fallacies of economic reasoning is to confuse requisite with productive. It is perfectly possible (and indeed it is the curse of all social theory) to regard the entire history of the human race as necessary-but-intermediate for the value of, say, a bottle of Coca-Cola, to be analytically intelligible, but that is not rational. Our own mortal limits dictate that some subset of human experience is sufficient to explain the value of the Coke; this insight is given precise expression by means of a conservation principle. If it is believed that the exact circumstances of the sale of this bottle of Coke are not critical for an analytical understanding of its value, then a conservation principle that posits that value is conserved in exchange will operationalize that insight. To instead posit that merchants and retailers are unproductive and do not augment the value of the Coke is just another way of asserting a similar analytical option. Most assuredly, if the local Safeway had not existed, then I would not have had this particular bottle of Coke, at least not at the present price; but my conservation principle merely asserts that, given the present configuration of society, such considerations may safely be ignored.

It should be apparent that conservation principles reify certain analytical prejudices, all the while platting the social boundaries of a law-governed economy. Another example along the same lines would be an analytical predisposition to believe that the apparatus of the state can be effectively ignored in the explanation of value: This analytical option can be restated in a conservation principle that property rights are conserved in trade (or in production), or, alternatively, that government activity is unproductive. One may or may not subscribe to such principles, but there is no such thing as causal analysis without them.

The conventional objection to the physiocratic doctrine that the farmers could not exist without the products of the artisans – whether or not that was the actual conviction of Quesnay – misses the point. As numerous writers have never tired of reminding us, there would be no economy without the air; but from that one should not necessarily infer that the air should enter economic analysis in a fundamental manner. The sterility of the artisans was merely the obverse side of the productivity of the farmers, just as black is the obverse of white. A thoroughly black tableau is featureless; any theory that purports to assert that everything is productive is meaningless. The use of terms like "productive" and "unproductive" by classical political economy platted the boundaries of economic explanation, the drawing up of a system of accounts, and the deployal of conservation principles by other (albeit political) means.

Be that as it may, it was the unequivocal statement of the physiocratic conservation principles that went a long distance in precipitating their demise. Adam Smith, Jean-Baptiste Say, and a host of lesser lights each took their turn ridiculing the idea that agriculture was the sole productive sector, and in this they merely echoed the opinions of their readers, the rising class of mercantile and manufacturing interests. Doubtless the integrity of perishable and organic grain as a natural value unit also exacerbated the vulnerability of the *Tableau*. (Lest we become too abstract and blinkered, the French Revolution also helped.) But what was not well understood at the time was the heuristic principle that when you relinquish a conservation principle, you give up the gyroscope of a research program. The writings of A. R. J. Turgot, a man often indescriminately and erroneously categorized as a physiocrat, provide an illustration of how the internal coherence of Quesnay's theory crumbled when the conservation principle was removed.

Turgot begins his paper of 1769 on "Value and Money" (in Groenewegen 1977, pp. 133 ff.) by comparing money to language: There seems to be a profusion of versions of both, and yet this diversity is conventional and arbitrary. As an Enlightenment figure, Turgot could not accept that this diversity was completely arbitrary; it had to have some common denominator or natural ground. In contrast to Quesnay, Turgot thought that in both cases, money and language, the common denominator was psychological. The currencies of various nations can be related by the value of the objects which they can purchase and that value is independent of the money that completed the purchase, just as a thought or idea is purportedly independent of the language in which it is expressed. He then notes that the term "value" is often used in contradictory senses, both as some quality intrinsic to the object traded and as an estimation of usefulness relative to the observer. At precisely this point, the lifeline of the physical metaphor slips out of his grasp:

> Where we assume that our two men are each provided more than abundantly with the thing they possess, and are accustomed to attach no price to the surplus, their discussion on the conditions of exchange will not be animated; each would let the other take . . . which he himself does not need. But let us vary the assumptions a little: let us give each of these two men an interest in keeping the surplus, a motive to attach some value to it. Let us suppose [a commodity endowment] which may be preserved a very long time . . . [In that case, price] is evidently none other than the *average* of the esteem values which the two contracting parties attach to each object [in Groenewegen 1977, pp. 142–3].

Turgot clearly wanted to escape grounding value in a natural external entity, but did he succeed? In trying to locate value in the superfluousness of a commodity, he finds himself driven to the expedients of recourse to physical durability (obviously to evade the imperative of immediate market-clearing) and the incongruous condition that although the traders feel their stocks are superfluous, they still doggedly attach some value to them. Then what does value have to do with psychology? But that is just the tip of the iceberg. If the commodities in question are easily stored, then why would anyone every be forced to accept any market-clearing price subject to the imponderables and fleeting circumstances of psychological whim? Further, in specifying price as an average of (incommensurable) values, there is no sense in which equivalents are traded, and hence no compelling reason for the traders to choose the average. In effect, once the value substance is repudiated, nothing is conserved, nothing is stable, and analysis stumbles in a labyrinth of incoherence. This is most apparent in Turgot's discussion of money:

> Why then do we use these terms [price and value] for one another? . . . The reason is the impossibility of expressing value in terms of itself . . . all that human language can express in this regard is that the value of one thing equals the value of another. The benefit evaluated, or rather, felt by the two men, establishes this equation in each particular case, without anyone ever thinking of summing of resources of man in order to compare its total to each needed object. Value, like size, has no measure other than itself, and if values are measured by comparison with other values, as length is measured by comparison with other lengths, then, in both means of comparison, there is no *fundamental unit* given by nature, this is only an *arbitrary*

unit given by convention. Since in all exchange there are two equal values, and since the measure of one can be given in terms of the other, there must be agreement about the arbitrary unit [in Groenewegen 1977, p. 145].

As Turgot twisted and turned, he found himself advocating a relatively unpopular doctrine in the history of economic thought: the denial of value. (Another champion of this position is Samuel Bailey, discussed in the final section of this chapter.) If indeed each exchange were a particular case with no implications for any other exchange, then there would be no such thing as value. And yet, caught in blatant contradiction, Turgot maintains that equivalents are exchanged, after earlier denying it. The comparison of value to length is indeed already implicit in substance theories of value: it is Turgot who cannot comprehend what this implies for the existence of a stable value unit. And finally, to deny a unit given by nature was to jettison the entire metaphorical simplex attached to value, leading it inexorably into a cul-de-sac. As Turgot states, his nonquantitative psychological values were never meant to be aggregated, but that banished any coherent concept of wealth from political economy. Without a coherent concept of wealth, there was no reason to believe in determinate price.

Smith and Say: Cartesian crossroads

After physiocracy, European approaches to the problem of value tended to diverge along national lines. Prior to the end of the eighteenth century, the Germans seem to have been immune to bites from the Cartesian bug, and I have yet to discover any explicit Leibnizian influences upon what would later be called economic theory. The cameralist tradition appeared to harbor an entirely antiphysical conception of natural law and natural order, one predicated upon a ceaseless intervention and monitoring of *Statistik,* rooted in Aristotelian metaphors of the household and the family. The French and Italians tended to make repeated attempts to rescue the psychological approach to value reminiscent of Turgot. Because this conception of value had no stable notion of causal explanation and no metaphorical resources to consolidate a research program, French political economy fragmented into a thousand disjoint polemics in the later eighteenth and early nineteenth centuries. The English, oddly enough, were the ones to adopt the Cartesian conception of value as a physical substance from the physiocrats, nurture it, and extend it to its logical conclusions. For this reason they are given the lion's share of attention in any Western history of economic thought as the architects of classical political economy. The decisive influence (contrary to the assertion in Hayek 1979, p. 19) was the willingness of the English to deal in natural science metaphors.

Although Adam Smith is often cited as the father of modern economics (Mirowski 1982), he has not been given adequate credit as the prime suspect in the smuggling of Cartesian economics into the backyard of Newton.[4] Unusual for a classical economist, he had a strong interest in the history of science and epistemology, and wrote in his early "Essay on the History of Ancient Physics":

> To render, therefore, this lower part of the great theatre of nature a coherent spectacle to the imagination, it became necessary to suppose, first that all the strange objects of which it consisted were made up out of a few, with which the mind was extremely familiar: and secondly, that all their qualities, operations and rules of succession, were no more than different diversifications of those to which it had been long accustomed, in these primary and elementary objects [Smith 1869, p. 386].

While this description of causal reification could serve as a credible summary of Emile Meyerson's philosophy, it is doubly significant that Smith saw it best exemplified by Cartesian physics:

> The supposition of a chain of intermediate, though invisible, events which succeed each other in a train similar to that in which the imagination has been accustomed to move, and which link together these two disjointed appearances, is the only means by which the imagination can fill up this interval, is the only bridge which, one may say so, can smooth its passage from the one object to the other. Thus, when we observe the motion of the iron, in consequence of that of the lodestone, we gaze and hesitate, and feel a want of connection betwixt two events which follow one another in so unusual a train. But when, with Des Cartes, we imagine certain invisible effluvia to circulate round one of them, and by their repeated impulses to impel the other, both to move towards it, and to follow its motion, we fill up the interval betwixt them, we join them together by a sort of bridge, and thus take off that hesitation and difficulty which the imagination felt in passing from one to the other . . . Motion after impulse is an order of succession with which of all things we are most familiar. Two objects which are so connected seem no longer to be disjointed, and the imagination flows smoothly and easily along them [Smith 1967, pp. 40–1].

While we are busy enjoying the filling up of the interval, our attention is diverted away from Newtonian action-at-a-distance, which presumably the imagination would regard with disquiet and revulsion.

Given these early programmatic statements, one might have expected Smith to embrace physiocracy when his attention turned to political economy, or at least to lay down an explicit set of value accounts to bridge the gap of trade. Actual events were a bit more complicated than that. Smith's conception of political economy was undeniably shaped by his acquaintance with Quesnay; and at one place in *The Wealth of Nations* he goes so far as to assert that physiocracy was "the nearest approximation to the truth that has yet been published upon the subject of political oeconomy" (Smith 1976, II, p. 199). But it is equally clear that he could not countenance their primal value precept that only the agricultural sector was productive of value. Smith's situation was further complicated by the fact that his partiality to Cartesian theories of motion was decidedly unfashionable by the time he was writing. Cartesian physics was considered by most eighteenth-century Europeans to have been superseded by the Newtonian account of motion, as well as the famous *hypotheses non fingo*. (This was not the last time an epoch-making economic theorist became enamoured of an outmoded or repudiated physical theory, as we shall observe in the next three chapters.) Smith, in a word, was in a pickle. How to reduce the confusion of economic life to a few principles of motion to which the imagination was accustomed?

The answer, in brief, is that Smith cooked up a weakened form of physiocracy, simmered it in a watered-down Cartesianism, molded it into a cosmology adapted from early Epicurean physics, and served it up in a great bed of digressions consisting of everything from a paragraph on why dogs don't talk to an appendix on the herring bounty. We shall bypass the whole question of Greek cosmology here, since it has been admirably explicated in Foley (1976, chap. 8). The connections between the theory of value and the Cartesian substance tradition will, on the other hand, warrant closer attention.

Smith's theory of value is a weakened version of physiocracy because it retains a substance theory of value, but without the straightforward accounting system and quantitative pretensions of Quesnay. It is difficult to speculate why Smith recoiled from precisely those aspects of physiocracy that were firmly rooted in the triad of body/motion/value, but it may have had something to do with his intentions to paint a rosy picture of the natural development of market structures. Smith's disdain for the country peasant and the agricultural economy probably led him to attenuate much of the body component of the triad, leaving only the most tenuous links between labor and value. This Scots wariness of the body also began to wreak havoc with the classical system of accounts, since he clearly wanted to posit consumption as the ultimate *telos* of the national economy; but used the substance theory of value to laud parsimony and production as the true causes of the wealth of nations.

Smith, following his own epistemic formula, opted to reduce wealth to a phenomenon with which "the mind was extremely familiar," even if it was only the mind of the merchant or manufacturer. He defined wealth as stock, and resolved it into goods destined for immediate consumption and goods destined to yield a revenue, which he called capital. Now, stock is a collection of items of an extraordinarily heterogeneous nature, and Smith only compounds the problem by suggesting that stock is comprised of physical goods and education, talents, and abilities. Without hesitation over the enormity of the task of reduction, he then proceeded to treat this agglomeration as a coherent and homogeneous aggregate for the individual, much as an early merchant would lump together all of his assets (including even his household silverware) in a single stock book. The next step was to assert what was true for the individual was true for the nation, or, "The general stock of any country or society is the same as with that of all its inhabitants." Wealth, then, is the collection of everything – although later in the book it gets restricted to physically tangible commodities – that is indifferent between consumption or investment, treated as though it were a single homogeneous substance. "The increase of revenue and stock is the increase of national wealth" (1976, I, p. 78).

Endless disputations over Smith's doctrine of value are to be found in the historical literature, many of which can be attributed to Smith's ambivalence regarding physiocracy. For instance, the quarrel over whether Smith confused labor-embodied and labor-commanded values (Dobb 1973) is, for our purposes, beside the point, when value theory is construed in the larger sense explained above. If Smith's "wealth" were to aspire to the same characteristics as the physiocratic *blé*, then it also should exhibit "substantial" properties and possess a "natural" unit of measurement. Yet Smith's arbiter, the merchant, generally aggregated the stocks in his account according to their money prices, usually at historical cost. This left Smith with a quandry: One could not go behind the veil of money looking for the real substance of value using what was indisputably a monetary measure. Smith, as in so many other instances, stared the problem briefly in the face and then waited a few hundred pages for the reader to get distracted, only to press onward without further ado. Smith proposed a number of potential value principles early on in Book 1 of *The Wealth of Nations*, but by the time we reach Book 2, we discover value is stock, and that stock will be analyzed independent of relative price changes, a formless incompressable jelly, effortlessly rendered suitable for either consumption of investment. In a manner of speaking, Smith avoided the value conundrum that had so engrossed his predecessors by essentially bypassing it save for some early comments on labor, which are dropped in the subsequent analysis. The primary function of those comments were to keep open a few tenuous lines to the metaphor of body, which only later in classical political economy grows in significance.

If one accepts stock as a primitive value substance, then much of the latter two-thirds of *The Wealth of Nations* becomes intelligible. The Cartesian influence is retained by means of subjecting stock to a number of conservation principles in the course of its motion. This explains, among other curiosa, why it appears to the modern reader that Smith is always confusing flows and reservoirs; the problem is that Smithian stock consists both of stocks and flows. Stock consists of both capital and revenue (Smith 1976, I, p. 294), an analytical awkwardness which causes Smith to trip up now and then and double-count value (1976, II, p. 196). Nevertheless, stock is held to obey certain accounting identities in the Smithian system, as schematized in Figure 4.2.

The resemblances to Quesnay's *Tableau* are striking, although one must persevere through to Book IV, Chapter 9 of *The Wealth of Nations,* the chapter criticizing the physiocratic system, in order to observe the final parts of this accounting system fall into place. The fact of the substance theory of value comes into clear perspective in the discussion of the productive/unproductive distinction. For Smith, unproductive work "consists in services, which perish generally in the very instant of their performance, and does not fix or realize itself in any vendable commodity which can replace the value of their wages

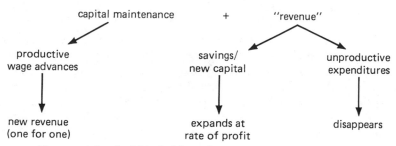

Figure 4.2   Smith's "tableau."

and maintainance" (1976, II, p. 196); in other words, they leave no evidence of substance. The conflation of value with a tangible, physical, substantial entity is reminiscent of the physiocratic "corn"; yet, as with much in Smith, it is Janus-faced, because it is much less solid and identifiable with nature; worse, it could easily be confused with Turgot's reliance on durability as a means to circumvent the whole question of superfluity and equivalence.

The left axis of Figure 4.2 is essentially identical to Quesnay's treatment of the sterile class, an analogy broached by Smith himself:

> But if [the physiocrats] had expressed themselves more accurately, and only asserted that the revenue of this class was equal to the value of what they produced, it might readily have occurred to the reader, that what would naturally be saved out of this revenue, must necessarily increase more or less the real wealth of the society . . . The increase in the quantity of useful labour actually employed in any society, must depend upon the increase of capital which employs it; and the increase of capital again must be *exactly equal* [my italics] to the amount of savings from revenue [1976, II, p. 197].

Capital maintenance is equated to advances to productive labor, who then generate an equivalent revenue; they are merely conduits, passing along existing value.

It is a little-noticed fact that Smith never once locates the increase of stock in the activities of labor per se. Instead, the increase of stock is always attributed to parsimony. Everything that is saved from revenue is equivalently turned into new capital. This new capital creates an expansion of stock, and hence of value, at the rate of profit. Thus the middle axis of Figure 4.2 plays the same role as the agricultural class in Quesnay's *Tableau;* it is the location of the natural expansion of the value substance. "Like the unknown principle of animal life, it frequently restores health and vigor to the constitution, in spite, not only of the disease, but of the absurd prescriptions of the doctor" (Smith 1976, I, p. 364). However, the actual rate of the expansion of value is left to float freely, with Smith offering a number of conflicting determinants of the profit rate (Mirowski 1982).

Smith's novel contribution to the classical system of value accounts in his attempt to reconcile the conception of the trade of equivalents with some more sharply drawn possibilities for the creation and the destruction of the value substance. The physiocratic system had been poised on the very brink of a discussion of the growth of corn, but drew back at the last minute, unable to reconcile it with their imperative of "health." Smith breached the barrier by asserting that, along the central axis of Figure 4.2, capital is transformed one-for-one into new stock, poised, as it were, on the brink of growth. This prohibition of the diminution of value in the act of saving is the first statement of that law, which John Maynard Keynes later erroneously attributed to Jean-Baptiste Say (Baumol 1977, p. 158). It is also the first appearance of yet another conservation law, one that decoupled the trading activities of the parsimonious merchant from the expansion or contraction of the value substance. In fact, the only place in Smith's system where one finds the possibility of value diminution is along the rightmost axis in Figure 4.2, in the category of unproductive expenditure out of revenue. In Smithian political economy, this is the only possible cause of economic contraction. In order that this avenue of disruption not severely compromise the "simple system of natural liberty," Smith associates unproductive expenditures with the famous litany that includes menial servants, ballet dancers, and others of that ilk. In effect, Smith shades the meaning of "unproductive" over into "insubstantial," and from there into "frivolous," essentially exiling this category from the realms of the natural and the economic.

Thus, the entire operation of the economy has been reduced to the motion of a value substance through three possible channels of trade (a metaphor Smith found congenial). In positing that everything that is saved is successfully metamorphosed into investment, preserving the value intact in transit such that "the quantity of every commodity brought to market naturally suits itself to the effectual demand," the way was foreclosed for anything – not trade, not pricing, not finance – to alter the magnitude of invested stock. It should begin to be evident that this "Smith's Law" is but one of a class of conservation principles found throughout the history of economic theory whose function is to decouple the production side of the economy from considerations of monetary circulation, fragmenting the economy into independent subsets. Such fragmentation is itself characteristic of the lineamentric stage of value theory.

This class of conservation principles need not always assume the format of "Smith's Law"; a comparison with the version found in Say reveals they need not even be stated in the same manner. This was inevitable, since J.-B. Say was not a proponent of Smith's substance theory of value. Following the inclinations of Turgot, he maintained that "the utility of things is the ground-work of their value, and their value constitutes wealth" (Say 1821, p. 4). Interestingly enough, even given the different value orientation, Say also derives his conservation rule from Descartes: "Objects, however, cannot be created by human means; nor is the mass of matter . . . capable of increase or diminution. All that man can do is to reproduce existing materials under another form, which may give them a utility they did not before possess" (1821, pp. 4–5). Hence, Say decouples production from exchange by evoking the authority of natural philosophy and the conservation of matter.

The spectacle of both Say and Smith appealing to essentially the same structural physical metaphors and arriving at such disparate theories demonstrates the free play inherent in metaphorical reasoning. Say also compares the laws of the social body to those of the human body (1828, I, pp. 28–34), but cannot find a good word to say about physiocracy (pp. 92–93). For Say, substance is eminently a literal term, and since the natural philosophers have decreed that matter cannot increase, then there can be no natural expansion of a value substance in the guise of physical commodities (p. 170). Presumably, then, the expansion of value is confined to the act of exchange. Yet here Say perceptively notices that if equivalents were exchanged in trade, there would "be to the community no production of value whatsoever." In yet another variant of the Cartesian reduction of all phenomena to matter in motion, he then asserts that increase in value is brought about solely by transport and recombination, favorably quoting Verri to the effect that "Commerce is in fact nothing more than the transport of goods from one place to another" (Say 1821, p. 16). If physiocracy was the world according to the larger farmer, then this was the world according to the merchant shopkeeper.

The conservation of matter plus the absence of the conservation of value in exchange results in the version of "Say's Law" actually found in Say. It is logically impossible to overproduce the aggregate of commodities, because the magnitude of aggregate demand is brought into equality with the value of existing commodities by means of the unhindered operation of the market: Goods transported from Paris to Lyon serve to adjust the two respective magnitudes, just as does the "transport" of goods from shoemaking to wineskin production. Only in this sense is the aggregate of commodity values independent of the magnitude of the values offered in exchange, that is, after the market has shifted them to their appropriate "spatial" locations. However, since Say was apparently ill equipped to actually understand the rational mechanics of his time, he had no inkling of what was involved to render this metaphor determinate; therefore, he initiated a tradition in nineteenth-century France of mere polemical assertion of the market's efficacy based on little more than bravado. Even the simplest extrapolations of the metaphor of motion – for instance, that the value of goods should also be altered by their "acceleration" – was entirely lost on Say, given that it is not even considered in his chapter on the supposed benefits arising from the quickened circulation of money and commodities.

Ricardian vices

With Ricardo we encounter for the first time (but not the last) a new phenomenon in political economy: a zealot intent on raising the scientific status of political economy who himself possessed little or no familiarity with either the contemporary practices of scientists or the history of the sciences. Some modern authors have strained mightily to render Ricardo a "Newtonian" (Pribram 1983, pp. 144–5; Holland-er 1987), but it is characteristic of Ricardo that the only reference to Newton, directly or indirectly, in the entire collected *Works and Corres-pondence* is a passing trivial mention of Newton's late involvement with recoinage (Ricardo 1952, III, p. 203). Thus it is no wonder that Ricardo is the darling of the internalist historian of economic thought; it seems fairly evident that he was possessed to take up political economy solely by reading a few previous economic writers, taking it upon himself to tidy up their loose ends. Yet, acknowledging all of this, it is not correct to maintain that contemporary scientific trends had no influence upon Ricardian political economy. The major influences were two: the Millian penchant for an associationist/mechanist psychology (Halévy 1972); and the already cited Cartesian tradition of the physiocrat/Smith provenance.

Ricardo was a fellow-traveler of the school of Benthamite Philosophical Radicalism, deriving encouragement at critical junctures throughout his career from the preeminent publicist of that school, James Mill. One of the tenets of Philosophical Radicalism was an attempt to pattern human psychology upon the physical sciences, a conception given voice in Mill's manifesto in the *Westminster Review:*

> Man is compounded of a fixed and a flowing quantity; the princi-ples of his constitution are eternal as the heavens, and the modes of their development not less diversified than the appearances of cloud and sunshine. Nature always makes him the same, and events always make him different. . . . The sameness is in all cases much greater than the diversity; the essentials of humanity are mightier than climate, education, habit, society, government, and events [Mill 1824, p. 1].

Homing in on the exact nature of the "fixed quantity" was a leitmotiv of all the members of this school, and it was probably here that

Ricardo derived many of his implicit notions of science. On the other hand, the Cartesian motif is most apparent in Ricardo's repeated attempts to extract the natural-law component out of *The Wealth of Nations*, streamlining the substance theory of value by shedding all of Smith's other motley concerns. His first attempt was the infamous corn model (Sraffa, in Ricardo 1952, I; Dobb 1973). From a certain stylized point of view, this was nothing other than a rediscovery of Smith's physiocratic roots, conflating the single good "corn" with the natural value substance.

Ricardo, as a stickler for consistency, soon realized that he could not legitimately argue for his purported tendency for the rate of profit to fall without recourse to at least a two-good economy; this prompted a move in his *Principles* to an embodied-labor theory of value. There natural price was identified as the magnitude of an embodied value substance, consisting of the hours of labor required to produce the good in question plus the labor required to produce the nonlabor inputs, and so on backwards ad infinitum. This portrayal of the passing along of a stable value substance in the sphere of production marked the reappearance of a conservation principle, one that suggested that value was "reincarnated" in the physical output pursuant on the "death" of the physical input. However, things got sticky when Ricardo also endeavored to preserve the trade of equivalents: Value was implicitly conserved in exchange, because the approach of market price to natural price was held not to affect natural price. Marx was the first to point out that these two conservation principles were one too many, since there was no room left for the increase of the value substance, and hence, for profit.

Effectively, Ricardo's *Principles* was a profound but flawed attempt to reconcile the Smithian concept of stock and its attendant metaphor of Cartesian substance in motion with the metaphor of the body, in its guise of human effort or labor. The two metaphors proved to be immiscible when poured together in Ricardo's mold because, as most textbooks delight in explaining, the stock or capital concept dictates an equalized rate of profit, whereas a true labor-embodied theory of value does not (Blaug 1985; Dobb 1973). The time patterns of "reincarnation" of the capital substance diverged drastically from those of the application of labor, as the interminable discussions of the value of wine stored in a cellar tried to articulate (Ricardo 1962, IV, pp. 375–6; Halevy 1972, pp. 343–56). Followers of Ricardo did not acquit themselves with dignity in the subsequent rows over value, in that there was a tendency to cover up these sorts of problems by restricting theoretical statements exclusively to a world of circulating capital (Blaug 1985, p. 95), thereby obscuring the question of what it was precisely that was conserved through time; or as Ricardo (1962, IV, pp. 386–7) put it, "the commodity valued must be reduced to circumstances precisely similar (with respect to the time of production) to those of the commodity in which the valuation is made."

The problem was not so much in "the abuse of language" (a favorite charge hurled by both Ricardians and their foes) as it was in the confriction of simultaneously but unwittingly held conservation principles. The lack of linearity of the various calculations of the embodied labor substance should have revealed that it was not being used consistently in the manner appropriate to a conserved value substance (Ricardo 1962, IV, p. 382). This problem was encountered time and again by Ricardian critics, and in particular by the indefatigable Colonel Torrens (quoted in John Henderson 1984, p. 96):

> Manufacturing industry would cease, if the value produced did not exceed the value expended. But it is the excess of value . . . that constitutes the master's profit; and therefore, we cannot assert that the profit of stock is included in the cost of production . . . we cannot maintain that the amount of profit is included in the amount of expenditure, or the cost of production, without urging the contradiction, that 300 £ are equal to 360 £.

We owe a great debt to the Sraffa edition of Ricardo's *Works and Correspondence* for its demonstration that this barrage of criticism over value theory was hounding Ricardo into retreat from the labor theory of value, just before his untimely death. The *Works* contains two fascinating drafts of an unfinished and unpublished paper titled "Absolute Value and Exchangeable Value," dated 1823, which expose the drawbacks of a substance theory of value in sharp relief (Ricardo 1962, IV, pp. 361–412). The most notable aspect of these drafts is that they reveal Ricardo as congenitally unable of recognizing the problem as that of the appropriateness of various conservation principles. Instead, he persistently phrases the problem as one of *measurement* – in his opinion a secondary issue, one he insists is subordinate to his larger theoretical concerns. He admits that he would prefer that value be given by nature:

> All measures of length are measures of absolute as well as relative length. Suppose linen and cloth to be liable to contract and expand, by measuring them at different times with a foot rule, which was itself neither liable to expand or contract, we should be able to determine what alteration had taken place in their length . . . There can be no unerring measure either of length, of weight, of time or of value unless there be some object *in nature* [my italics] to which the

standard itself can be referred and by which we are enabled to ascertain whether it preserves the character of invariability [1962, IV, pp. 399, 401].

This is a succinct précis of the structure of a substance theory of value; but if in nature no objective correlatives for value exist that correspond to those thought to exist for physical motion (length, time, etc.), then it is the metaphor of a value substance in motion that is in jeopardy. However much Ricardo wished it so, the problem was not yet put on the same footing as the institution of the metric system (1962, IV, p. 380), because the metric system had only just reified the conservation principles that had been only just coming to be fully articulated in mid-nineteenth-century physics. Ricardo's problem was distinctly different: The entire program of a "scientific" political economy was flagging.

Ricardo's tragedy was that he was at the mercy of an image of science derived from his predecessors, an image glimpsed through a glass darkly because of his own remote familiarity with "science": this was the real "Ricardian vice." The inexorable Ricardian logic and the dogged Ricardian commitment to the truth were not up to the task; ultimately, the project also demanded an empathy with the mutually reinforced metaphors of body, motion, and value, which did not yet exist even in physics. Persistently he wrote as though the conserved value entity was something subject to empirical discovery – indeed, incarnated as a particular physical commodity (1962, IV, p. 361). And yet, out of an instinctive skepticism (or else a theorist's disdain for empirical activities), he never once himself actively tried to find such a commodity. His last writings counseled a return to gold as an imperfect but pragmatic stopgap value substance. This was tantamount to a repudiation of the entire project of classical political economy, because as we have already observed, the classical tradition began as a program to denounce the arbitrary and contrived character of money, exhorting all to dig beneath the surface to find the true natural determinants of value, and consequently the real conservation principles that governed economic science. No wonder that those contemporaries most familiar with science and most inclined to mathematize political economy – William Whewell, T. Perronet Thompson, Antoine Cournot, Dupuit and the *Ponts et Chaussées* school – all were skeptical of the Ricardian system.

Karl Marx and the swan song of substance theories of value

The writings of Karl Marx have been the subject of such a surfeit of exegesis that it must surely seem quixotic to try to gain a new perspective upon them. And surely enough, the effort in this section to untangle the place of conservation principles and substance theories of value in Marx discovers a precursor in the work of Lippi (1979). Nevertheless, what has apparently been missing in the Marxian litera-ture is a willingness to situate Marx within the larger cultural pre-occupations that we have summarized in our simplex of body, motion, and value. The ways in which the tensions between those metaphors play themselves out in the three volumes of *Capital* are extremely subtle and indicative of the vicissitudes of the substance theory of value in an era when the physical sciences were moving rapidly towards the alternative formalism of the field.

While the significance of the Hegelian heritage in the Marxian *oeuvre* remains a topic of endless controversy among Marxists, it will be useful to note that one portion of Hegel's bequest to Marx was a skeptical posture toward a slavish imitation of the natural sciences, a trait absent in every other political economist considered in this chap-ter. Hegel's *Phenomenology of Mind* is chockablock with sneers at "the so-called proofs of propositions like that concerning the equilibrium of the lever," disparaging comments that "mathematics . . . gets its material from lifeless space, and the equally lifeless numerical unit" (Hegel 1967, p. 107), and puffed-up snarls such as: "Formalism in the case of *Naturphilosophie* takes the shape of teaching that understand-ing is electricity, animals are nitrogen, or equivalent to North or South and so on" (p. 109). And yet, the Hegelian heritage is not wholly unambiguous, since the concept of *Kraft* or Force also occupies a central place in Hegel's Phenomenology. As he explained it, un-derstanding consists of a kind of motion where "elements set up as independent pass directly over into their unity, and their unity di-rectly into its explicit diversity, and the latter back once again into the reduction to unity. This process is what is called *Force [Kraft]*" (p. 183). Such suggestions must have proved provocative once Marx encoun-tered similar metaphors in French and English political economy in the 1840s.

It is well known that Marx's texts are studded with warnings con-cerning the misleading character of physical analogies in political economy:

> The folly of identifying a specific social relationship of production with the thing-like qualities of certain articles is what strikes us most forcibly whenever we open any textbook on economics . . . this is a very convenient method by which to demonstrate the eternal validity of the capitalist mode of production and to regard capital as an immutable natural element in human production as such [Marx 1976, I, pp. 996, 998].

Or, there is the infamous passage where he decries:

> "the bewitched, distorted and upside-down world haunted by Monsieur le Capital and Madam la Terre, who are at the same time social characters and mere things. It is the great merit of classical economics to have dissolved this false appearance and deception . . . this personification of things and reification of the relations of production . . . by presenting the circulation process simply as a metamorphosis of forms, and finally in the immediate process of production reducing the value and surplus-value of commodities to labour [1981, III, p. 969].

But here we are brought up short. As we have taken pains to demonstrate in this chapter, the most basic practice of reification in classical political economy was the postulation of a metaphor of value as a discrete substance in motion, created in production, conserved in the exchange of equivalents (Marx's metamorphosis of forms), and destroyed in unproductive consumption. This constituted a reification of the economy as a naturally law-governed entity no less fictitious than those great stick figures le Monsieur/la Madame. Hence, if it were in fact the case that:

> [T]he commodity form, and the value relation of the products of labour within which it appears have absolutely no connection with the physical nature of the commodity and the material relations arising out of this. It is nothing but the definite social relations between men themselves which assumes here, for them, the fantastic form of a relation between things [Marx 1976, v.I, p. 165],

then Marx's own advocacy of the labor embodied theory of value ran the risk of failing by his own criteria.

Ultimately, Marx's ambivalence and his tergiversations over the meaning and status of science were, if anything, more extreme than those of Hegel. He coyly admitted in his "postface to the second edition" of Volume I of *Capital* that he had "coquetted with the mode of expression peculiar to [Hegel]," but never was equally self-reflexive about his flirtation with physical metaphors. His project to wed the Hegelian dialectic to a species of materialism is well known and needs no comment here. Less often considered is his rhetorical practice of veering between organic and physical analogies. It would seem that many of the organic analogies are used predominantly for dramatic effect: "Capital . . . vampire-like, lives only by sucking living labor" (1976, I, p. 342), or the so-called organic composition of capital. In contrast, the physical metaphors are central in understanding the Marxian conception of value.

There are, for instance, the comparisons of the law of value to the law of gravity (p. 168), which reveal the profound importance of the metaphor of motion for the inner workings of the value concept. Not only is it clear that value metamorphoses in production and travels in exchange, but to my knowledge Marx is the only economic theorist to expend concerted effort to explore the relative significance of the velocity and the acceleration of the value substance, especially in the sections of Volume II of *Capital* devoted to turnover and circulation. Market prices are asserted to gravitate to their natural values in a now-familiar attempt to reconcile the labor theory of value to the accidents of supply and demand; in one place Marx even toys with an analogy between the motion of capital and D'Alembert's principle of virtual velocities (1978, II, p. 158, fn.).

Notwithstanding all that, it was the physical metaphor of motion that gave Marx the greatest amount of grief. After all, his ultimate objective was to prove that social relations could not be understood as assuming "the fantastic form of a relation between things," but how could his own stable of physical metaphors avoid such a fate? And then there was a further problem: Marx unwittingly had the great misfortune to be situated on the cusp of the evolution of natural philosophy into physics, which occurred from the 1840s to the 1870s. It would have been too much to expect Marx to have forseen that the very ontology of the physical world was also experiencing metamorphosis in his lifetime, and yet, it can be argued that the scientific community's transition from substance to field had some influence on his understanding of the labor theory of value, in that there ended up being not one but *two* Marxian labor theories of value: the first rooted in the older substance tradition, the other sporting resemblances to nascent field theories in physics. These two versions of the labor theory of value will be illustrated in the rest of this section.

The tension between the alternative images of science was not only evident in Marxian value theory, it made its way into the philosophical aspects of the Marxian system. For instance, the desire to demonstrate that modes of production were transient and unstable clashed in places with the doctrine of historical materialism in ways now regularly debated in the Marxian literature. The no-nonsense attitude that our primary constraints were those real objects "out there" led Marx to maintain that the single most important motor of history was the incremental progress of natural science. To find such strong reductionist tendencies in the one social theorist most engrossed with the physicalist presuppositions of economic thought has induced vertigo in certain observers, and suggested to others that there are actually two or more Marxisms (Gouldner 1980; Sahlins 1976).

Here we shall only concern ourselves with the theory of value. Marx started as an inheritor of the classical traditions of equivalence and of substance. From there, he endeavored to incorporate the concerns of the traditions of nonequivalence by confronting the seeming superfluity of commodities offered in trade: He asserted it derived from the social activity of traders regarding each other's needs and wants as independent from their own, and therefore seemingly of no consequence (Marx 1976, I, p. 182). His intention was to sweep aside these appearances in order to insist that regular capitalist trades are normally trades of equivalent values (Mirowski 1986, pp. 222–32).

The next question is, What is it that all commodities possess in common, that they may be judged equivalent? Of course, here he has recourse to the language of substance, but substance reified by social interaction:

> The secret expression of value, namely the equality and equiva-
> lence of all kinds of labor because and insofar as they are human
> labor in general, could not be deciphered until the concept of hu-
> man equality had already acquired the permanence of fixed popular
> opinion. This, however, becomes possible only in a society where the
> commodity form is the universal form of the product of labor, hence
> the dominant social relation is the relation between men as posses-
> sors of commodities [Marx 1976, I, p. 152].

In the general classical tradition, Marx then sharply differentiated this substance from money, which is only a veil and which could be dispensed with in future modes of production (1978, II, pp. 390, 434).

Marx represents the culmination of the substance theory of value tradition because of his burning preoccupation with the question of the origins and implications of surplus value (1976, I, p. 651). He was one of the very few theorists to ask seriously how one could maintain that surplus value arose solely within the process of exchange; his predisposition for physical metaphors precluded any final appeal to psychological explanations. It is significant from the vantage point of conservation principles that his arguments against the generation of value in exchange explicitly appeal to symmetries: a buyer is also a seller, a producer also a consumer, and so on. Any advantage of seller over buyer, and so on, would then necessarily be wiped out in the aggregate, if not at the individual level. In retrospect, this is the first rigorous argument that the trade of commodities must be a zero-sum game: "The capitalist class of a given country, taken as a whole, cannot defraud itself . . . Circulation, or the exchange of commodities, creates no value" (1976, I, pp. 263–6; 1978, II, p. 408). Yet the dialectical contradiction, as Marx wanted to phrase it, was that the entire capitalist system was predicated upon the persistent expansion of value in the aggregate. How could these facts be reconciled?

The increase of value, he maintained, must be restricted to the sphere of production. This did not mean that production was exempt from the prohibition of widespread fraud, for workers were also maintained to receive their equivalent value in the form of wages. The divergence, and the source of profit, came in the distinction between labor power and labor actually performed. Labor power is the virtual ability to do work, its value rated at the reproduction cost of the relevant abilities and talents; wages in abstract equilibrium reflect the value of labor power. The labor performed, on the other hand, is the hours of labor embodied in the output of a production process; for Marx, this had no fixed relationship to the wages paid. If the employer, both by diligent coercion and by dint of the larger macro operation of the market, managed to ensure that the value of labor performed was greater in magnitude than the value of the labor power, then a surplus value was generated in the process of production. It is a nice touch that the location of surplus generation and the justification of the value substance are one and the same, namely, the labor process.

Marx is an epoch-making economist because he combined the metaphor of a value substance in motion with the metaphor of the body in motion in the concept of labor, fusing them both with historical and sociological elaborations of power and hierarchy in the workplace. But the Hegelian dialectic and quantification had never been cozy bedfellows – as Hegel said, "Number is just that entirely inactive, inert and indifferent characteristic in which every movement and relational process is extinguished" – (Hegel 1967, p. 317) and it was precisely in rectifying the metaphors with a quantitative set of accounts that Marx ran afoul of the imperatives of a substance theory of value.

Ricardo had stumbled upon the incompatibility of asserting the trade of equivalent labor values with the dictum of an equalized positive profit rate. Marx was wary of this pitfall, as we can observe from numerous comments in *Theories of Surplus Value*. It is now fairly well understood that Marx wrote the three volumes of *Capital* in reverse order, first working out his own solution to this problem in the draft of the third volume, only to abstract it away in Volume I. This first volume of *Capital*, the only one to be published during his lifetime, essentially argues the plausibility of a labor-embodied theory of value without spelling out the quantitative accounts or the resulting implications for prices. One consequence of this rhetorical stance is the inattention to strict application of the physical substance metaphor in Volume I; this ambivalence blossoms in Volume III into clashing sets of value accounts. Marxian economists have dubbed this failed quantification of the labor theory of value the "transformation problem" (Steedman 1977).

In effect, and apparently unwittingly, Marx simultaneously argued for two contradictory versions of the labor theory of value: the first of which we shall call the crystalized-labor or substance approach; the second is called the real-cost or virtual approach. The first is, of course, the culmination of the substance-theory tradition chronicled in this chapter. Labor time, extracted in the process of production, is reincarnated (or perhaps "buried" is a better term, since Marx calls it "dead labor") in the commodity, to subsist thereafter independent of any market activity. This version of value is used to assert that trade and circulation can create no value, because, by definition, crystalized labor is impervious to market fluctuations; this independence from market phenomena circumvents the ineffectual tautology of all previous cost-of-production theories, which stated that prices of outputs were determined by prices of inputs. But, in a further innovation, crystalized-labor values do not evaporate or disappear when the physical commodity is consumed by use; rather, the labor crystals are passed along to the next commodity (if use were located in the sphere of production) or incarnated in a human being if the commodity is consumed to support labor power. Marx, when dealing with this version, discourses explicitly in the language of the conservation of substance:

> As regards the means of production, what is really consumed is their use value, and the consumption of use value by labor results in the product. There is in fact no consumption of their [labor] value and *it would be inaccurate to say it is reproduced. It is rather preserved* [my italics] [Marx, 1976, I, p. 315]. A quantity of labor has no value, is not a commodity, but is that which transforms commodities into value, it is their *common substance* [1971, III, p. 135].

This entire scheme can be concisely summarized in a conservation principle, one that states that value is conserved in the entire economy with the single exception of the labor process, and that there surplus labor "substance" is generated. This is essentially the same analytic manuever as the physiocratic postulate that value is only generated in agriculture.

The second, antagonistic conception of labor values as real-cost values is also present cheek-by-jowl with the first in Volume I of

Capital, and grows more in importance as the transformation problem looms on the horizon in Volume III. In this real-cost approach, in direct contradiction to the crystalized approach, value as substantial entity is renounced; it is instead postulated that value is a contingent state. In this view, a commodity can only be said to possess a labor value in relation to the contemporary configuration of production. Although its physical complexion or its past history might persist unaltered, its real-cost labor value would be subjected to change by technological alterations anywhere in the economy, or even by *market phenomena* such as market-clearing adjustments, including those that did not directly impinge upon the commodity in question.

An instance of this real-cost definition in Volume I would be: "It is the quantity of labor required to produce it [under present circumstances], and not the objectified form of that labor, which determines the amount of the value of a commodity" (Marx 1976, I, p. 677). A clear example of the real-cost labor theory is provided by Marx's discussion of the effects of a harvest failure upon the existing stocks of cotton harvested in the previous year (p. 318). In this passage he insists that a harvest failure would instantaneously revalue the embodied labor value of the cotton inventories in an upward direction, under the reasoning that the "socially necessary" amount of labor time to produce a bale had risen. This discussion stands in stark contrast to what would happen in a regime of crystalized values: There the cotton inventories would undergo no revaluation, even though the newly harvested cotton would.

In the real-cost version of the labor theory of value, even identical terminology assumes wholly different meanings, something that doesn't render the project of Marxian exegesis any easier. For example, the language of "living" and "dead" labor assumes an entirely different set of interpretations in the real-cost version: The appropriate analogy, especially given Marx's citation of D'Alembert, is now to *vis viva* and *vis mortua*. "Dead labor," just like "dead force," has only a virtual or potential existence, conditional upon the entire configuration of forces which constitute its context. "Living labor," like *vis viva*, exists only in its actualization/exploitation, and is not susceptible to quantification outside of that situation. In this real-cost theory, *all history is defined away as irrelevant;* in this, the theory parallels the fledgling developments of the field concept in physics in the same period. The evaluation of the labor value of any particular commodity in this instance depends solely upon the best-practice techniques available in conjunction with the effective demand conditions expressed at that moment, and is entirely independent of the past production history of the commodity.[5]

Perhaps a little linear algebra can sharpen the distinctions between the crytalized-labor and real-cost approaches to the labor theory of value. Most mathematical accounts of Marxian economics such as Morishima (1973) or Steedman (1977) begin with a technology represented by a static input/output matrix **A**. If the number of inputs m is constrained to equal the number of outputs (Mirowski 1988, chap. 10), it follows that **A** is of dimensions ($m \times m$); a vector of outputs **y** is produced by means of a vector of inputs **x** and a vector of live labor exertions **h**:

$$\mathbf{y} = \mathbf{Ax} + \mathbf{h}$$

These texts instruct us that the appropriate method to calculate embodied labor values **l** is to solve:

$$\mathbf{l} = \mathbf{Al} + \mathbf{h}$$

or

$$\mathbf{l} = (\mathbf{I} - \mathbf{A})^{-1}\mathbf{h}$$

which can be rewritten in a Taylor expansion:

(4.1) $\mathbf{l} = (\mathbf{I} + \mathbf{A} + \mathbf{A}^2 + \mathbf{A}^3 + \cdots)\mathbf{h}$

In the Marxian literature, Expression 4.1 is misleadingly called "the reduction to dated labor." In fact, the only coherent interpretation of 4.1 is that *if the present technology had been with us back to Adam*, then the amount of labor embodied in each good would be equal to the live labor presently expended in production plus the labor values of the inputs used in production plus the labor that went into the making of the tools and instruments of production plus . . . ad infinitum.

This, of course, is nothing other than the real-cost version of the labor theory of value: Present conditions alone determine present embodied-labor values of all commodities jointly and simultaneously. Contrary to many modern Marxist writers, this is definitely not the crystalized-labor approach, except under the most counterfactual of circumstances that there has been no change in the entire history of capitalism with regards to the means of production. Because a Marxist, more than any other theorist, is committed to asserting the dynamism of the capitalist mode of production, Expression 4.1 is simply false, unless one hews exclusively to the real-cost doctrine. But in real-cost doctrine there is no such thing as "dated labor"; you can't date something that has no persistence. Worse, it is generally an impossible task to write down an analytical expression for crystalized-labor values, because we would need to know (at the very least) every different $A(t)$ and $h(t)$ back to Adam.

Hence, Marx was trapped between Scylla and Charybdis: The classical substance conception of value, even though it had "metaphorically" served to conjure the determinacy of science, was in fact so analytically riven with indeterminacy that it was quantitatively intractable. Conversely, the real-cost doctrine was apparently analytically tractable, but violated almost every precept that Marx wished to champion concerning the importance of history, the primacy of production, the continuity of classical economics, the exchange of equivalents, and the inevitability of the fall of the capitalist rate of profit. Rather than confront such a Hobson's choice, Marx instead indescriminately mixed both versions of the labor theory of value throughout *Capital,* using one or the other as it suited the problem at hand, as if they were effectively interchangeable.

The crippling problem, as will be endemic in value theory in economics, was a disregard for the significance of the relevant conservation principles. In the crystalized-labor approach, the value substance is necessarily conserved in exchange, with Marx adding the further stricture that value is conserved in the transition between productive input and the output. The value accounts are clear and straightforward, not the least because they conform to the previous pattern of classical political economy. When it comes to the real-cost approach, all of the above principles are violated in one or another transtemporal phenomenon; and Marx was not at all forthcoming about what he intended to put in their place. If we let the mathematical formalism dictate what is conserved, then Expression 4.1 dictates that it should be the technology that is conserved, for that plays the role of the field in the formalism; but as Marxian economics, this is nonsense.

The crystalized-labor/real-cost dichotomy is the key to deciphering much that is confusing or otiose in *Capital.* Since the real-cost principle is in many respects the inverse of the crystalized-labor theory of value, the unwitting attempt to apply both simultaneously sets the theory down the short slippery road to perdition. Some examples: (1) The extensive discussions of turnover time in Volume II of *Capital* possess an exemplary logic in the crystalized-labor version of value, because the persistence of the value substance dictates a careful accounting of the rate of depreciation at which it is "poured" from inputs to outputs. However, in the real-cost labor theory, turnover is meaningless, because depreciation and hence turnover are simultaneously determined along with the magnitudes of the labor values:

the sequential reevaluation takes care of the problem of value transfer not, as in Volume II, by regulating a flow through time, but by revaluing all stocks at every point in time (Pasinetti 1980). (2) Statements to the effect that capital goods cannot themselves account for the increased value of the output make perfect sense in the crystalized approach – by construction you can't get something for nothing – but in the real-cost approach, windfalls are ubiquitous. (3) The crystalized-labor method can construct a viable dynamics based upon an invariant unit because "an hour is an hour is an hour"; the real-cost method, devoid of explicit invariants, can only calculate a sequence of static equilibria in which the labor-value unit is not comparable from one calculation to the next (unless, of course, we retrogress to Ricardo's search for an invariant standard of value).

More importantly, the crystalized-labor approach is entirely consistent with the classical distinction between productive and unproductive labor, precisely because the locus of surplus generation is fairly well defined. Conversely, in the real-cost doctrine, the magnitude and distribution of the surplus is contingent upon the simultaneous reevaluation of all labor values, so that all processes are "productive." Here the only means by which to judge productivity is with reference to value at a point in time, which is now rendered contingent. (Then there is a further problem of whether the real-cost values should be average or marginal labor values, but that just further muddies the issue.) Far from being an arcane technical point, this dichotomy threatened to undermine Marx's overarching theoretical project, which was to discover the origins of exploitation and surplus value. This tension within his system came to a head in the transformation problem.

Once we grasp their implications, we can perhaps understand why Marx vacillated between two mutually exclusive labor theories of value, and understand also the incoherence of his attempt to solve the transformation problem. Crystalized labor highlights exploitation and fixes the locus of surplus generation in production; real-cost labor values obscure the generation of surplus and open up the possibility that the global magnitude of profit is altered (and hence generated) in exchange. Crystalized labor continues the hallowed tradition of natural-substance theories, which were intended to imitate the structure of explanation in the Cartesian natural sciences; real-cost labor values were the first imitation of an incipient format of explanation by variables of state in the new physics of the nineteenth century. Crystalized labor said that history mattered in a fundamental way, and yet could not quantitatively operationalize that insight; real cost was quantifiable (ideally), but threw history out the window.

Apparently Marx thought the only way out was to attempt to enforce the synthesis between these two profoundly incompatible doctrines. This solution was found in Volume III of *Capital,* published after his death, the answer to all those skeptical economists clamoring for a Marxian price theory. There are many aspects of Marx's solution about which one might legitimately complain (Howard and King 1974, pp. 107 ff.; Steedman 1977), but the aspect of his analysis most relevant to our present concerns is Marx's choice of method to close his price and value system. Marx's procedure involved two externally imposed assumptions: that the sum of all goods aggregated at their prices was set equal to the sum of all goods evaluated at their labor values; and that the sum of all profits denominated in prices was set equal to the sum of all surplus value denominated in labor hours. These joint assumptions constituted a serious mathematical error because, in general, there is only one degree of freedom to impose such an assumption, not two. In Marxian economics, this is known as the choice of the invariance condition in the transformation problem (Laibman 1973). For someone attuned to the necessity of clearly stated conservation principles, the language is more than suggestive.

Why did Marx commit this blunder? A generous interpretation would suggest that this was his attempted reconciliation of the two contradictory labor theories of value. In the crystalized-labor approach, both assumptions would seem to have been true by definition: You can't get something for nothing. However, this would also dictate that rates of profit in price terms could not be equalized, except in the highly unlikely case of equal organic compositions of capital in all industries throughout all history. Conversely, in the real-cost approach, one can easily enforce equalized rates of profit, on pain of giving up the invariance of the labor unit itself. Hence, you can't have both the global invariant magnitude of value and the invariant magnitude of surplus. However, this destroys the preeminent claim of the Marxian system that surplus is only generated in production and is passed around among industries in the pricing process. In order to impose one conservation principle too many, Marx resorted to cooking the figures so his numerical example seemed to come out all right. No wonder he never published it while he was alive.

The watershed

From the mercantilists to the mid-nineteenth century, from Maylnes to Marx, Western economic thought was dominated by an effort to reduce economic value to a conserved substance in motion, and thus consequently to elevate moral philosophy and political economy to the status of a natural science. It was not simply a case of envy or misplaced obeisance (although one can't rule that out *tout court*) — after all, was there a better paradigm of effective causal explanation close to hand? And then there was the ever-expanding simplex of metaphors discussed in Chapter 3, the bootstrapping justification of reified invariance of which political economy was an integral component, an unavoidable port of call on the cultural chart. In this sense theoretical questions of conservation principles had to arise; and as they experienced revisions in the natural sciences, the reverberations were bound to be felt in political economy. Was value like length, or was it not? Was commodity exchange a species of motion? Was the economy like the body, with its circulation of the lifeblood? If so, what precisely constituted health? If only political economy could attain the certainty of the natural philosophers . . .

But maybe natural philosophy was not all that self-assured, or at least not as imperturbable as the outsiders had thought. Some of the first warning signals emanated from the mathematicians. As long as every schoolboy was taught that Euclidean geometry was self-evidently true, then there was a single appropriate portrait of a stable natural world, and science had discovered it. To political economists, much of the appeal of the analogy of value with distance was derivative of this faith in the ineffable truth of the Euclidean construct. The abstract notion of invariance was embedded in the Euclidean construct, and as such could be taken for granted as a corollary of the "obvious" empirical correspondence of a yardstick to the underlying geometric intuition. Invariance was not an analytical option; it was the surd of the world.

Historians of mathematics date the first signs of breakdown of this Euclidean self-assurance around the first part of the nineteenth century (Kline 1972, chap. 36). Johann Lambert, a colleague of Euler and Lagrange at the Berlin Academy, published a book in 1786 that considered a quadrilateral with three right angles and speculated upon the possibility of the fourth angle being right, or obtuse, or acute (i.e., equal to, greater than or less than 90°). Following through the implications, he noted the obtuse-angle version gave rise to theorems resembling those for the geometry of the surface of a sphere. This later broached the possibility, elaborated upon by Gauss, Lobatchevsky, and Bolyai, that such a thing as a non-Euclidean geometry could exist, and could describe the properties of physical space just as accurately as could Euclidean geometry. It was inevitable that this would provoke a certain uneasiness concerning ideas of absolute space with absolute coordinates, as well as the palpable truth of rigid rods that maintained their length and orientation when trasported through space.[6] In 1828 Gauss demonstrated that various geometries could be constructed upon curved surfaces and could be distinguished by means of a measure we now call Gaussian curvature. He further demonstrated that only if this Gaussian curvature were constant, would it be the case that any geometric figure could be freely transported and rotated without in any way influencing the inner configurations of the geometric object. (Such a space is now called isentropic.)

Now, this was the problem of the rubber ruler with a vengeance. Political economists from Turgot to Ricardo had been using the metaphor of a ruler that stretched and shrank in a rather bemused fashion, as if it were something outlandish, a mere figure of speech. But here were respected mathematicians taking the metaphor seriously; and worse, if you understood the implications of what they were saying, they were raising the issue of whether not only the ruler but also the wielder of the ruler stretched and shrank in the course of measurement, and who could be certain whether he would be able to know it or not? This was heady stuff, guaranteed to shake up those smugly complacent about their natural Euclidean world with its natural rulers (Edgeworth 1877, p. 13). Metaphors relying on rulers were at risk in political economy, as well as in the physical world, and it was only a matter of time until the theory of value would experience sympathetic perturbations. The earliest shocks were low on the Richter scale, but we can detect the fault line running through the attack of Samuel Bailey upon Ricardian political economy in 1825. Bailey's first complaint was about:

> analogies, which had a merely imaginary existence, [that] have been assumed as incontrovertible premises or universally conceded postulates . . . The analogies suggested by the word measure seem to have bewildered almost every author who has touched upon the subject. It has been taken for granted that we measure value as we measure extension, or ascertain weight; and it has been consequently imagined, that to perform the operation we must possess an object of invariable value [Bailey 1967, pp. vi, 94].

The first significance of Bailey's complaint is that he is one of the few figures in the classical period to subject the analogy of value and length to any sustained scrutiny. In a series of comments reminiscent of the *Sturm und Drang* precipitated by the rise of non-Euclidean geometries, he takes as a fact not in need of further justification that

"The very term absolute value, implies the same sort of absurdity as absolute distance" (p. 24). Nothing could be further from obvious to Ricardian political economists, whose most heartfelt wish was to ground value in the absolute invariants they thought were provided by physical reality. Nevertheless, the Ricardians felt they could ignore Bailey's critique because the conclusions he drew from this novel ontological position were so outrageous and so idiosyncratic that no one could take them seriously. And, indeed, no one did.

Samuel Bailey is one of the very few representatives of the position that value does not exist, or rather, that the question is of no analytical consequence for economic science. Because Bailey is persistently folded, spindled, and mutilated by the orthodox history of economic thought literature as a precursor of neoclassical theory, it may repay the effort to carefully summarize his entire argument.[7] In effect, Bailey believed that he could absolve political economy of all dependence upon our metaphorical pyramid, ridding it of all analogies. He maintained that value cannot be an intrinsic property of commodities; at best, it is pure relation. From this he deduced that value was nothing more and nothing less than a ratio:

> What then is it possible to do in the way of measuring value? . . . All that is practicable appears to be simply this: if I know the value of A in relation to B, and the value of B in relation to C, I can tell the value of A and C in relation to each other and consequently their comparative power of purchasing all other commodities. This is an operation obviously bearing no resemblance at all to the measuring of length [Bailey 1967, p. 96].

One would like to know precisely how this differs from the process of casting off lengths, and Bailey's answer sets him apart from both the classical and neoclassical traditions. He asserted that when length is conventionally measured, it is predicated upon an assumption that the instrument used is invariant. In the economy, Bailey avers, there is absolutely no presumption of invariance of our standard (in the above quotation, commodity B), because we can choose any commodity to be the standard interposed between the two commodities to be compared (pp. 106–10). In other words, there are no economic invariants through time:

> It is impossible for a direct relation of value to exist between A in [A.D.] 100 and A in [A.D.] 1800, just as it is impossible for the relation of distance to exist between the sun at the former period and the sun at the latter . . . When we accumulate, we add one thing to another, but it is essential to the process, that both should remain in existence.

> But labour, consisting in the mere exertion of muscular power, or the equally evanescent notions of the brain, continually perishes in detail, and therefore admits no accumulation [pp. 73, 220].

Since one often hears superficially similar statements from neoclassical economists, it is of paramount importance to delineate Bailey's position and to understand its flaws. In sum, he claimed that since there was no such thing as an economic invariant, *there is no such thing as value*. All that exist are fleeting and transitory ratios between commodities; however, and here is the rub, these ratios are *transitive* at a point in time. Since any third commodity may be interposed between any other two in order to express their relation as ratios, money is just as good or as bad as anything else; hence, it is the best measure of value to which we can aspire. It is important to notice that all references to body and motion as the natural grounds of value are spurned, and this extends even to references to psychology.

Bailey's assertions are thoroughly self-contradictory, as is to be expected from one who claims to renounce all metaphorical reasoning. First, the assumption of transitivity of price ratios implicitly posits path independence of trading ratios at a point in time, a condition isomorphic to the postulation of an identity element and hence virtual invariance of the value relation.[8] One might be concerned to differentiate between the conservation of value in virtual exchange and the conservation of value through time, but it is clear that Bailey persistently confused and conflated these two conservation principles; this would explain his fallacious assertion that the mere existence of any economic invariant would imply that all economic change would be analytically prohibited (Bailey 1967, p. 60). Bailey's great weakness was his obliviousness to the fact that he was incapable of any conceptualization of price as a ratio without surreptitiously and unwittingly reintroducing the conservation of value in exchange.

Second, Bailey took it for granted that his trading ratios were constructed from the natural exogenous primitives of the physical units of the commodities involved, not realizing the extent to which this simply pushed the dependence upon "natural" value units just one step back in the analysis (Mirowski 1986). To put it bluntly, it is not any more convincing that two apples should be added and subtracted than it is that value should be subject to the same operations. Indeed, why does anyone ever find it necessary to interpose a third commodity between any arbitrary pair in order to express price? If the choice of that third commodity really is arbitrary, then why is it required at all? If there really is no function for money to perform (Bailey 1967, p. 118), then why does it exist? Bailey ends up advocating a species of nihilism, repudiating the value concept by the Pyrrhic gambit of denial of all calculation of consequences of all economic activity.

Third, Bailey could not understand that the substance metaphor was by and large the only metaphorical resource available to his contemporaries to use in their visualizations of the interconnectedness of market transactions, both at a point in time and through time. Nowhere is this more apparent than in the reactions of Karl Marx to Bailey's broadside. Bailey had gotten under Marx's skin, to judge by the number of pages alloted to this one essay in Marx's own history of economic doctrines, his *Theories of Surplus Value*. There his primary objection to Bailey is that the denial of the very idea of value renders all theorizing about the economy ineffectual and impotent. Of course, this would never have ruffled Bailey, but it does serve to clarify Marx's theoretical project, concerned as it was with

> the proportion in which one thing exchanges for an infinite mass of other things which have nothing in common with it . . . for the proportion to be a fixed proportion, all those various heterogeneous things must be considered as proportionate representations of the *same common unity*, an element quite different from their natural existence or appearance . . . If we speak of distance as a relation between two things, we presuppose something "intrinsic," some "property" of the things themselves, which enables them to be distant from one another. What is the distance between the syllable A and a table? The question would be nonsensical . . . we equalize [things in space] as being both existences of space, and only after having them equalized *sub specie spatii*, we distinguish them as different points of space. To belong to space is their unity [Marx 1971 III, pp. 128, 143].

Here Marx is much clearer than he is in all of *Capital*. There is something which permits our comparison of commodities and induces an order upon them; one way to think about this is a resort to the metaphor of motion of bodies in space. Stones and birds and puffballs really have little in common; but we must impose some accounts in order to deduce what it is that makes all of their motions "the same." These accounts tended to be phrased either in terms of descriptions of symmetries of "space" or in terms of conservation principles. (Recall from Chapter 2 that conservation principles and symmetry principles are really isomorphic statements.) Now, a garden-variety skeptic may come along and maintain that there really is nothing called motion, which after all is nothing more than a metaphor, and that all there really is in the world are stones and birds and puffballs, but as Marx would probably retort, this skeptic will never be a physicist. Or, to return to political economy, a single case of true barter isolated from money and markets has no analytical implications for price or for anything else.

Marx does manage to make one other telling criticism of Bailey, although it is one that cuts two ways, since it also threatens the integrity of *Capital*. Marx observes that the theorist cannot absolve himself from comparing values over time, because one major activity of the capitalist is to compare values between temporal locations (Marx 1971, III, p. 162). The simple phenomenon of merchant profit is prima facie evidence of such a comparison. In effect, Bailey treats the entire capitalist system as fortuitous and adventitious, a jumble of random encounters with no antecedent determinations and no future consequences of any intelligibility. If the capitalist acted like Bailey's political economist, asserts Marx, neither would be long for this world. Marx is right; the actors behave as if they had a theory of value.

Unfortunately, this also has implications for Marx's own writings, although he does not evince an awareness of that fact. Insofar as the real-cost version of the labor theory of value deals in a value unit that has no stability over time, by Marx's own strictures, it must be an incoherent economic theory. Only in such a topsy-turvy world is it even possible for such a question to arise as: Which comes first, the labor values or the prices? (Steedman 1977, p. 65)

Bailey's broadside against the Ricardian program, while by no stretch of the imagination a "masterpiece" or a "complete success" (Schumpeter 1954, p. 486), was an omen of things to come.[9] The winds of change were blowing in the physical sciences and in mathematics, and it did not auger well for substance theories of value. Theories of ethers, subtle fluids and other such pervasive substances were in retreat by the beginning of the nineteenth century (Cantor and Hodge 1981, p. 173). The cozy Euclidean world was being eyed speculatively by certain mathematicians. Alternative explanations in terms of forces and fields were gaining adherents (Hesse 1965). Perhaps it is no accident that no really novel work on substance theories of value appears in economics for almost a century after Marx's *Capital*. (This thread will be picked up again in Chapter 6.)

Entr'acte

Classical political economy was not a self-contained discipline, propelled throughout the eighteenth and nineteenth centuries under its own momentum and following its own trajectory. Instead, it was one component of a metaphoric simplex, one instance of a particular pattern of explanation in Western culture. Conceptions of the world largely borrowed from the physical sciences channeled the evolution of economic theory far more profoundly than the idiosyncratic whims of any individual or of any school could possibly explain. This structure of explanation was situated within a number of themes, which, at first blush, may have seemed unrelated: The search for an independent natural ground for economic value; the reification of the economy as a distinct law-governed structure; the relegation of money to epiphenomenal status; the problem of equivalence in exchange; the distinction between productive and unproductive pursuits; the search for an invariant standard of value. All of these concerns were rendered coherent by situating them in the larger framework of substance theories of value. The name of the substance changed from the seventeenth to the nineteenth centuries, but the general structure of explanation was the same. The reason it was the same was that it was invariably suggested by the structures of the physical sciences in the same era.

Classical political economy displayed a relatively fixed pattern in response to our three questions in the theory of value broached at the beginning of this chapter. Commodities were commensurable precisely because they were conceived to embody a homogeneous value substance. This substance was conserved in exchange, augmented in production, and diminished in consumption. This pattern of conservation rules as justified by direct reference to natural metaphors of motion and of the body. These appeals were critical to the success of classical political economy, because there simply was no other method of "proving" that the rules were valid.

The conservation of value in trade; the conservation of value with respect to property rights; Say's (or Smith's) Law; the conservation of "dead labor" in production – these were the mirror images of natural philosophy. But the permanent and stable and substantial world, the existence of which had been assured to one and all by the natural sciences, was being eroded, chipped away, and dematerialized by, irony of ironies, those pesky natural scientists. The solid earth was being spirited away out from under the feet of the classical political economists, and they, trusting souls, were not the least bit aware of it.

Neoclassical economic theory: An irresistable field of force meets an immovable object

> I believe that I have succeeded in discovering the force (*Kraft*), also the law of the effect of this force, that makes possible the coexistence of the human race and that governs inexorably the progress of mankind. And just as the discoveries of Copernicus have made it possible to determine the paths of the planets for any future time, I believe that my discoveries enable me to point out to any man with unfailing certainty the path he must follow in order to accomplish the purpose of his life. [Hermann Gossen [1853] 1983, p. cxlvii].

> The truth is, most persons, not excepting professional economists, are satisfied with very hazy notions. How few scholars of the literary and historical type retain from their study of mechanics an adequate notion of force!" [Irving Fisher [1892] 1926, p. v].

Most people with some academic training in economics are aware that the rise of the theory that commands the greatest allegiance in the United States (which we shall call neoclassical economics) was located in the 1870s in several European countries. A little more familiarity with the conventional histories of economic thought will foster the impression that neoclassical theory was "simultaneously discovered" by an Englishman (William Stanley Jevons), a Frenchman (Leon Walras), and an Austrian (Carl Menger), and that after its improvement by a host of others, it eventually displaced all other competing schools of thought in those countries. Some familiarity with post–World War II trends in economics in Europe, Japan, and elsewhere would also reveal that American-style neoclassical economic theory has rapidly become the scholarly standard in postgraduate education and research. Yet, oddly enough, those convictions often reside cheek-by-jowl with another common impression, that twentieth-century economics is but a continuation and an extrapolation of basic concepts and themes enunciated in Adam Smith's *Wealth of Nations*. Does this imply that the change was continuous or discontinuous?

The stress on the purported discovery of neoclassical economics would suggest a strong discontinuity, perhaps to the extent of near incommensurability, between the world views of classical and neoclassical theory. The word "discovery" also suggests a palpable existence independent of our supposition of a neoclassical economic system, which would inevitably have been discovered by any number of persons with the adequate preparation, education, powers of perception, and so forth. This, for instance, was the view of Jevons, who wrote: "The theory in question has in fact been independently discovered three or four times over and must be true" (Jevons 1972, IV, p. 278).

Modern historians of economic thought (and some protagonists in the Marginalist Revolution, such as Alfred Marshall) have been much more reticent in sharing Jevons's enthusiasm. Instead they stress the continuity of neoclassical theory with the laissez-faire traditions of the physiocrats and Adam Smith, the implicit marginalist analysis of Ricardo, and the utilitarianism of Bentham. A representative textbook asserts that "to try to explain the origin of the marginal utility revolution in the 1870s is doomed to failure: it was not a marginal utility revolution; it was not an abrupt change, but only a gradual transformation in which the old ideas were never definitely rejected; and it did not happen in the 1870s" (Blaug 1978, p. 322). So which one was it, drastic change or nothing really new? A common response would be to throw up one's hands and say that both sides have some plausible points, and that the truth must lie somewhere in between.

In most instances, the dispute between continuity and change ends up in a hung jury. Readers of the previous chapters will have noted a marked tendency not to accept orthodox assertions of either continuity or change in the context of the history of science. In the case of economics, however, to rest satisfied with some vague intermediate position is to thoroughly misrepresent the historical phenomenon and, more important, to thoroughly misunderstand the fundamental content of neoclassical economic theory. Starting at the level of the historical record, the thesis that innovations in economic theory in the 1870s and 1880s were unexceptional and merely a logical extrapolation of the unbroken threads of economic discourse in the preceding half-century meets a number of difficulties. The first impediment is that all of the major protagonists would not have agreed with such an assessment. One cannot read the letters and published works of Hermann Gossen, William Stanley Jevons, Leon Walras, Francis Edgeworth, Irving Fisher, Vilfredo Pareto and others without repeatedly encountering assertions that their work constituted a fundamental break with the economics of their time. Much of their professional lives were spent promoting the works of this small self-identified coterie. Given that they were such a contentious bunch to begin with, how did they recognize each other as prosecuting the same research program? The second impediment to the gradualist view is the fact that the most discontinuous aspect of the Marginalist Revolution was not the postulation of a utilitarian theory of value, but rather something no historian of economic thought has ever discussed in any detail: the successful penetration of mathematical discourse into economic theory. Both in their correspondence and in their published work, the early neoclassical economists recognized each other as *mathematical theorists* first and foremost, and when they proseletyzed for their works, it took the format of defending the mathematical method in the context of economic theory. It should have been obvious, however, that *mathematics alone* dictates the acceptance of no specific economic theory. The third impediment to the gradualist view is the fact that all of the major protagonists were concerned to differentiate their handiwork from previous political economy on the explicit grounds that it was of a scientific character. While we have observed that the claim that one's theory is scientific (and therefore deserves some respect) echoes throughout the last three centuries of social theory, in the case of Jevons and the rest, this claim assumes a very specific and narrow format, shared by all the principals. An understanding of these three points will lead inexorably to a reevaluation of the significance of the rise of neoclassical economic theory.

The time has come to redraft the map of continuity and discontinuity in economic theory. Henceforth we shall call into question Marshall's dictum (actually appropriated from Leibnitz by way of Darwin) that *Natura non facit saltum*. We shall argue that neoclassical economic theory is best understood as a sharp and severe break with the doctrines characteristic of the classical theory of value, which subsequently implied extensive revisions in most other areas of economic theory. And yet, there is one very important way in which neoclassical theory is merely a logical extrapolation of the prior development of classical political economy. The metaphorical simplex of body/motion/value was not repudiated or relinquished by neoclassical economics, quite the contrary. We shall argue that the attractions of the neoclassical portrayal of the market were traceable to revisions in the metaphors of motion and of the body.

As we discussed in our earlier chapters, Emile Meyerson taught that change cannot be comprehended unless it is juxtaposed to invariance; here we must apply this lesson to our own narrative. If we are to assert a discontinuity in economic thought, what were the invariants against which we could discern such a sea-change? Some continuity is provided by our three questions in the theory of value, first broached in Chapter 4:

1. What is it about a market system that renders commodities commensurate, and hence valuable?
2. What are the conservation principles that formalize the response to Question 1?
3. How are those conservation principles linked to the larger simplex of body/motion/value (in order to provide them with justification)?

The new neoclassical school of economic theory changed the answers to all three questions vis-à-vis classical political economy. It displaced the weight of commensurability from external substances to the mind, but the mind portrayed as a field of force in an independently constituted commodity space. Yet it was not enough that the economic actor merely testify that she felt capable of the comparison of relative values; some conservation principles had to be posited in order to proceed with formal analytical models. Here the neoclassical stance toward value grows opaque, because for at least the first sixty years of its existence, partisans of the neoclassical research program did not consciously adhere to any single conservation principle – although, it must be immediately added, this was more out of ignorance than out of analytic timidity. Nonetheless, they did attain an analytic statement of their concept of trade by means of direct references to the metaphors of body and motion. They achieved this roundabout feat by identifying the field of force with energy, both literally and figuratively. In effect, the neoclassical theory of exchange was an offshoot of the metaphor of energy, buttressed by the mathematics of rudimentary rational mechanics; such humble beginnings eventually set neoclassicals down the path of reconstructing for themselves the meaning of a conservative vector field.

We shall also argue that the term "discovery" is singularly inappropriate for describing this break, just as it was inappropriate in the description of the enunciation of the energy concept in the middle of the nineteenth century. It was not changes in the objective economic structure that elicited the discontinuity, nor was it some naggingly insistent bit of empirical data; rather, neoclassical theory was made inevitable by the discontinuity in physics that we described in Chapters 2 and 3. To put it bluntly, economics finally attained its objective to become a science through a wholesale appropriation of the mid-nineteenth-century physics of energy, or, as we dubbed it in Chapter 2, proto-energetics. The seemingly simultaneous discovery was the direct result of the preceding watershed in nineteenth-century physical theory, and the fact that all of the progenitors of neoclassicism were trained in engineering-level physics and subject to particular philosophical trends of the time.

Thus we shall argue that the fundamental continuity in economic thought between classical and neoclassical economics derives not from laissez-faire or utilitarian traditions (which were not necessary corollaries of either classical or neoclassical economics), but rather from the expansion of the body/motion/value simplex and the attendant drive to imitate physical theory. The irony of classical and Marxian economics is that just as those theorists thought they had discovered the natural foundations of social exchange, the physicists swept it out from beneath their feet.

The location of neoclassical economics on this recalibrated map is not merely a matter of antiquarian interest. The innovations in physics and their subsequent absorption into economics embodied a revision in the way social change itself was to be conceptualized, as well as a radical transformation in the very ideal of social theory. The change in label from political economy to economics (Jevons 1970, p. 48) was not only a public-relations ploy; natural philosophy had, after all, become physics, and henceforth both the economist and the object of analysis, that stick-figure Economic Man, were never to be the same again. Although the tyro neoclassicals had just adopted a model of a perfectly reversible world, their own choice was irreversible. Adopting proto-energetics set those economists off on a course of inquiry that they themselves little understood, one that continues to constrain their activities down to the present day. And the worst part of it was that their own physics envy effectively prevented them from seeing over the walls of their own self-constructed labyrinth.

If the history of physics could be taught to neophytes as if it were a single unbroken thread from Newton to the present (although the cognoscente would know this as merely a fairy tale), then the history of economic thought would be woven on the same loom. The myth of the stasis of theoretical content of the physical sciences was to be clutched at neurotically in the history of economic thought.

Classical political economy: Paradoxes of motion

Motion, as the Greek philosophers understood, only appears to be easily comprehensible on the most superficial of levels, and they produced some of the pithiest paradoxes of all time to prove their point. Classical economics, as we have seen, was very much predicated upon the intelligibility of the metaphor of motion for its discussions of value, but the metaphor of motion did not stand still, and this metamotion gave rise to some paradoxes for classical political economy by the middle of the nineteenth century. While one paradox, or a budget of paradoxes, is not sufficient to bring down a research program, it certainly can go a long way in demonstrating just how the classical program grew increasingly vulnerable to its challengers, accounting in part for its final demise.

The first of these paradoxes has already been identified in the previous chapter. Starting with Adam Smith's history of astronomy, the main theorists of classical economics sought to capture the essence of the scientific method in order to employ it in the sphere of economic research. As the natural sciences rose in general esteem, the claims for the efficacy of the methods of science became increasingly strident. For Smith, the essence of science was the evocation of order, wonder, and intellectual delight; it was primarily an esthetic response (see Mirowski 1982). For Ricardo, it was an assertion of rigid adherence to the canons of a proto-mathematical logic, the dictates of which overruled any casual empiricism or sentimentality. For Marx, science was the main motor of economic advance as well as the only instrument capable of piercing the veil of ideology. The escalation of the dependence upon science and its purported methods as a source of legitimacy for economic research had reached such a plateau by the mid-nineteenth century that John Stuart Mill, the paragon of late classical economics, could maintain in his System of Logic that the methods of research deployed in economics should be identical to those already in use in astronomy (Mill 1973, 8, VI, Chap. IX). Another representative of late classical political economy could write well into the 1870s: "Political Economy is as well entitled to be considered a 'positive science' as any of those physical sciences to which this name is commonly applied . . . This character, as I have endeavored to establish, is identical with that of the physical principles which are deduced from the laws of gravitation and motion" (Cairnes 1875, p. 69).

Far from being mere rhetoric to be doffed as one would remove a mask or a scarf, this increased dependence upon science had a number of perverse side effects. The first was that the more fervent the invocation of science by political economists, the correspondingly lesser were their efforts in delineating precisely in what those methods consisted, or in finding out what it was that contemporary scientists actually did. One might aver that this was not the case with Mill; but as one recent scholar put it: "[Mill's] understanding of the physical sciences was mostly acquired second-hand . . . Far less than most philosophers of science, Mill cannot be taken as a sound observer of contemporaneous research" (Schabas 1987, p. 49).

Second, as a consequence, there was little if any discussion of the reasons for the appropriateness of natural-science methodology in economic research; consensus on this point was simply taken for granted. Third, this was the period of the institution of the first chairs of political economy at major universities (Checkland 1951b; Henderson 1984). As political economy became an actual profession, as opposed to an avocation of clergymen and polemicists for hire, its pretensions to impartial and definitive knowledge rested more and more upon its supposed alliance with science. The resultant of all these trends was that the increased dependence of classical political economy upon science left it vulnerable to criticisms that the resemblance was at best vague, as well as leaving it liable to be caught in a compromising position when science itself underwent profound transformation.

The second paradox of motion was an outgrowth of the neo-Kantian revival of the mid-nineteenth century. We have already discussed in Chapter 2 the influence of Kant on some of the major physicists of the era, such as Helmholtz and Hamilton. The conundrum of Kantian influences on classical political economy lay in the elaboration of the notion of the a priori and its application to basic physical concepts (Harman 1982). For Kant, nature is only a unity in the mind of the observer. This conflation of the mind and the world did much to undermine the hierarchy of explanation in classical economics, which began with the purportedly certain structures of the external world, and only secondarily invoked the more treacherous psychology of man. In a more narrow and specific sense, the neo-Kantian movement of the nineteenth century sought to emphasize the reductionist and mechanistic aspects of Kant's thought, mainly found in his *Prolegomena and Metaphysical Foundations of Natural Science* (Kant 1953). Partisans of this movement believed that Hegelian philosophy had gone too far in the direction of idealism and that this had resulted in travesties of the method of science. In his later writings, Kant had insisted that, in any field, as much true science as was to be found would be found to be the amount present in mathematics. This was re-interpreted by the neo-Kantians to state that the true science in any discipline was to be found in its mathematical component. This was further buttressed by citing Kant's argument that any change in perception must involve movement in space, and therefore motion must be the basis of all phenomena. Kant defined the cause of motion as a "moving force" (employing the terminology of *Kraft);* hence all explanation of change could be reduced to the scientific explanation of forces. There was also the passage that was to prove suggestive: "the understanding can anticipate sensations . . . by means of the principle that all sensations without exceptions have degrees. This is the second application of mathematics to natural science" (Kant 1953, p. 67). This had little or no resemblance to the existing practices of classical political economy.

The third paradox for classical economics was the reevaluation of the relationship between mathematics and the physical world. As surveyed in Chapter 4, the classical economists were heavily dependent upon the metaphor of value as length and a measure of value as a yardstick. The moral lurking within this analogy was that there was a natural geometry and a natural algebra that provided the basis for quantification and mathematical analysis if only scientists were perspicacious enough and lucky enough to find it. However, unbeknownst to the classical economists, the conception of mathematics as a straightforward reflection of physical relations became a world turned upside down in the nineteenth century (Kline 1980). By the 1860s, how one would know which of the possible geometries was true was a widespread topic of speculation (Kline 1980, p. 88; Richards, in Barnes and Shapin 1979; Edgeworth 1877, p. 13). At the beginning of the century Ricardo could envy the physical scientists because their rulers did not stretch or shrink. How much of a shock it must have been when Hermann von Helmholtz, one of the most respected physicists of the century, ventured to suggest:

> But we should not forget here, that all geometrical measurements rest upon the presupposition that the measuring instruments which we take to be fixed, actually are bodies of unchanging form, or that they at least undergo no kinds of distortion *other than those we know* [my italics], such as those due to temperature change, or the small extensions which ensue from the different effect of gravity in a changed location. [Helmholtz 1977, pp. 18–19].

The fourth paradox of motion that confronted classical economics was the alteration in the standards of acceptable theory formation in the natural sciences in the nineteenth century (Cantor and Hodge 1981, p. 46; Heidelberger, in Jahnke and Otte 1981). Earlier theories, especially of light, heat, and electricity, were cast largely in terms of fairly prosaic substance analogies and were closely tethered to intuitive concepts. As explained in Chapter 2, after circa 1840, the analogies give way to more general theories expressed more self-consciously in terms of models in the mathematical sense. There was a noticeable withdrawal from a commitment to specify which of the underlying phenomena were the subject of mathematical description; fewer concessions were made to intuitive plausibility; there were more strident imperatives for quantitative measurement in conjunction with a noticeable lack of precision with regard to what was being measured; and there was a predisposition to accept the usefulness of a model for certain limited practical purposes as an acceptable argument in its favor. In sum, the Laplacian dream came to capture the imaginations of those longing for certainty in explanation.

It is of paramount importance to observe that political economists were getting mixed signals in the middle of the nineteenth century as to the fundamental essence of science. For instance, there was a shift from astronomy (or rational mechanics) as the king of the sciences to physics, as the latter seemed to hold out the promise of the unification of all science. The style of physics associated with Fourier claimed a pure search for the phenomenological equations of systems without specifying any underlying ontology. The contrasting style of physics associated with Laplace was wedded to an ontology of atomism, and posited the paradigm of all science to be the variational principles. According to this latter view, science was indifferent to history, because it posited its goal as deterministic and hence fully reversible equations. Then, to top it off, ontological preferences gradually shifted from inert matter to active force. It is clear that partisans of each position could claim that their approach had been vindicated by the assertion of the conservation of energy and energy physics in the 1840s. If it is possible to speak here in terms of style, the earlier mode of argument that had been adopted by classical economics was passé by the 1860s.

These paradoxes of motion were combined and compounded by the gradual supersession of field theories over substance theories in physics over the course of the nineteenth century. The rise of field theories was the most decisive influence because it finally provided the definitive epistemic break between classical and neoclassical economics, the rupture setting free the tensions built up in the above paradoxes. In short, classical economics had become inextricably identified with the paradigm of substance theories in physics, and therefore its days were numbered. As physics progressively moved toward field theories and models of motion, and energetics seemed to hold out the promise of the unification of all the sciences, economists (with some lag) adopted their own field theory of value, which we now call neoclassical theory.

The metaphor of motion had grown radically estranged from the metaphor of value harbored within classical political economy: It no longer had any recognizable relation to the simplex of body/motion/ value that was expanding and bounding modern culture. Something had to give, but it was not at all obvious a priori what the resolution of the tension would look like. With hindsight it might appear obvious: Reconceptualize value as a relation rather than as an intrinsic embodied substance; portray commodities as moving through "potentials" in commodity space; redefine the impossibility of perpetual motion as the natural state of scarcity. However, just as no one individual was actually responsible for the energy concept, no one individual can be credited with the full reconceptualization of value as a field. Indeed, what is most striking about the actual course of events is the halting and groping character of what ended up as a rather bald imitation of proto-energetics.

Precursors without energy: Canard, Bentham, Cournot

The business of searching for precursors of neoclassical economic theory does seem to be one of the few precarious niches that most historians of economic thought have carved out for themselves in the modern economics profession. Hence, what little of intellectual history can be gleaned from modern journals of economics consists of assiduous efforts to ferret out the remining obscure writers who perhaps once said something favorable concerning utility as a determinant of prices, or perhaps wrote down a Lagrange multiplier, or complained loudly about the absurdity of the labor theory of value, all and sundry lifted totally out of context. One can't help but feel less than enthusiastic about such exercises, primarily because they are carried out with such blithe disregard for their significance and meaning for the understanding of economics as an intellectual activity. After all, what is the message of such antiquarian pursuits other than the implicit parable that neoclassical economics lay somewhere waiting to be discovered, and therefore anyone who said anything resembling current dogma should be lauded as stumbling upon some external truth?

An alternative to this rather drab procedure is to start from an understanding of what it was and is that makes neoclassical economics a (relatively) coherent research program, and then to engage in a rather different sort of historiography. Hence, here we begin with the metaphorical simplex of body/motion/value; and then turn to reevaluate the plethora of precursors claimed for neoclassical economics. This new perspective immediately explains one fact: The reason one can find so many candidates for precursor in so many disparate cultural contexts is that they all were imitators of science *as they understood it.* One corollary of this thesis is that it now becomes possible not only to explain the sense of déjà vu enjoyed by partisans of neoclassical theory when confronting these texts, but more important, to explain the divergences of these precursors from standard orthodoxy. What one finds is that much of what at first appears idiosyncratic and perhaps even bizarre becomes, upon reconsideration, merely a reflection of the state of physics in their time frame. This, then, is intellectual history with a difference: The map of continuity is redrawn, some are elevated while others are deflated, and mistakes and gaffes grow as significant as insights and successes.

Alas, there simply are too many of these precursors to encompass within an brief survey. In lieu of all that, we shall here consider a sample of three writers: one who is conventionally excluded from orthodox hagiographies (Nicholas-Francois Canard) and two who are often celebrated as illustrious precursors (Jeremy Bentham and Antoine-Augustin Cournot). The purpose of this selection is to illustrate how different the history looks when the map of continuity and rupture is redrawn according to the principles just enunciated. For starters, the rejected and despised Canard, grows in esteem, whereas Bentham is marginalized and discounted, and in the case of Cournot, the explicitly nonneoclassical themes loom larger in importance.

Canard has not been treated well by subsequent generations of economists. Cournot, for one, acknowledged Canard's book *Principle D'Economie Politique* (Canard 1969) as his own point of departure, as well as the only book of mathematical economics he had read prior to composing his own treatise, and yet, for all that, was so scornful of it that he felt impelled to write: "These pretended principles are so radically at fault, and the application of them is so erroneous, that the approval of a distinguished body of men was unable to preserve this work from oblivion. It is easy to see why essays of this nature should not incline such economists as Say and Ricardo to algebra" (Cournot 1897, p. 2). Schumpeter (1954, p. 499) characteristically slammed Canard's book without giving any reasons or justification. More recently, Baumol and Goldfeld 1968, p. 156) have written:

> It is not easy to take very seriously the use of symbols to represent such indefinable concepts as "need" and "competition" of buyers and sellers, or Canard's willingness to multiply the symbol for "need" by the symbol representing "competition" to yield a product which he describes as the buyer's or seller's "power" (*force*).

Resisting mightily the temptation to rehearse the old saw about people in glass houses, let us instead briefly recapitulate what Canard actually was trying to do.

Canard begins his text by dismissing embodied labor time as an adequate measure of value, and purposes to embark upon a model of equilibrium price as the resultant of the opposing forces of buyers and sellers. He invents the concept of a range or latitude L of the price of a good, which extends from the highest price named by the sellers to the lowest price offered by the potential buyers, then combines this with a decision variable x, representing the magnitude that buyers are ultimately willing to subtract from the upper bound of the latitude. Defining N as the number of buyers and B as an index of their need, as well as n as the number of sellers and b as the index of their willingness to acquiesce in the offered price (Canard 1969, p. 29), he then posits that the decision variable is proportional to the *force* exerted by either side of the market: Namely, x is proportional to BN and $(L - x)$ is proportional to bn. By analogy with the principle of virtual displacements, the equilibrium price is located where the sum of forces equals zero – that is, where $bnx = BN(L - x)$ (Canard 1969, p. 29). Just in case we don't recognize the analogy with rational mechanics, Canard explicitly states that this equation "exprime l'égalité *des moments de deux forces opposées*" (p. 30), and in a comparison that will come to haunt neoclassical economics, likens it to "the principle of the equilibrium of the lever, which underlies all of statics" (p. 31).

For the remainder of the volume, Canard proceeded to enumerate a list of external determinants that, serve to further delimit the extent of the latitude – including the extent of the market, the existence of monopoly, the subsistence floor to wages, the instability of tastes, and so on – yet we need not follow him further into his somewhat tedious algebra in order to gauge his significance in the nineteenth-century context. By those standards, he does not deserve the calumny that has since been heaped upon his work. However awkward his algebra, Canard is clearly the earliest precursor of the neoclassical research program. The reasons are numerous: He is the first to employ the new ontology of force and the new conceptions of motion in a mathematical model of price determination (one that metaphorically linked force to psychological predispositions, to boot). His language of moments reveals that he was consciously imitating d'Alembert's principle (Lanczos 1949, chap. 4), which was the centerpiece in Lagrange's coupling of dynamics to statics. It is true that any discussion of conservation principles is absent; but then, Canard obviously was not straining too hard to concoct some economic analogue of *vis viva*. Later on in the volume, Canard also managed to bring in the metaphor of the body with an extensive discussion of the analogy with the circulation of the blood (apparently de rigueur in France at that time). He even had recourse to the metaphor of *énergie,* although one must keep in mind that this was referring to a more archaic connotation of the word, since it preceded the energy concept in physics by half a century. All in all, one may or may not find the entire attempt salutary, but compared with what came afterwards, Canard's model was not extremely far-fetched; in any event, he clearly was an occupant of the main line of development of the simplex of body/motion/value.

By contrast, Jeremy Bentham was an entirely different kettle of fish. Those who portray Bentham as a precursor of neoclassical theory tend to alight on Jevons's endorsement (1970, p. 94) and a few suggestive quotes, rather than to evaluate his work as a whole. While Bentham did belabor the claim that he was instituting a science of morals and justice, his was an earlier, and by the time he wrote, already antiquated notion of science.

Bentham was a lifelong student of chemistry (Halévy 1972, p. 23), which in the version with which he was familiar was not integrated with physics, and was largely a taxonomic and classificatory affair (Hufbauer 1982).[1] One observes his tedious and fruitless penchant for taxonomy in his numerous "Tables," be they of the "springs of action" (McReynolds 1968, p. 359) or his more prolix and grandiose attempt to taxonomize the sciences themselves (Bentham 1952, I, pp. 88–9).

This conception was carried over into Bentham's project of a social science: "Arithmetic and medicine – these are the branches of art and science to which, in so far as the maximum of happiness is the object of his endeavours, the legislator must look for his means of operation: – the pains or losses of pleasure produced by a maleficent act correspond to the symptoms produced by a disease" (quoted in Halévy 1972, p. 29). Bentham's relatively few discussions (all unpublished until well after his death) of the actual manipulation of the arithmetic of utility reveal this predisposition to see science as taxonomic, as well as his total ineptitude when it came to mathematics. His analysis of the value of a pleasure or pain posits seven dimensions: intensity, duration, certainty or uncertainty, propinquity or remoteness, fecundity (the chance of being followed by sensations of the same kind), purity (the chance of not being followed by sensations of the opposite kind) and extent (the number of persons affected) (Bentham 1954, pp. 435–7). If one were feeling charitable, one might explain that Bentham conceived of utility not as a scalar, but rather as a vector of these seven dimensions. One drawback of this interpretation is that vector formalisms were developed much later, in the second half of the nineteenth century. Another is that Bentham revealed his lack of quantitative comprehension by flirting with the idea that utility should equal the product of intensity × duration × proximity × certainty (in Baumgardt 1952, p. 564), another speculation that he wisely left unpublished. The true flavor of the eccentricity of such Benthamite texts can be savored in yet another assertion – that the pulse rate might serve as an independent measure of affection (McReynolds 1968, p. 353).

However, even to overlook these little enthusiasms would be too charitable, since there is appreciable evidence that Bentham never intended to take the formal mathematical aspects seriously, and neither did he aspire to imitation of the formal sciences in the construction of a serious theory of value. In one place he admits that intensity is not susceptible to measurement (McReynolds, 1968, p. 353); in another he proliferates his original categories by postulating fourteen different kinds of simple pleasures and twelve different kinds of simple pains (Halévy 1972, p. 31); in yet a third he warns against stretching the imagination with mechanical or biological analogies (Bentham 1952, I, p. 96) – something to which he was immune, since he never understood physics or biology in the first place. More significant, he persistently stated that money was the best measure of pleasure or pain (in Baumgardt 1952, pp. 561–2). This more than any of his other infelicities reveals his ultimate lack of ambition in the construction of a true theory of value. Chapter 4 has demonstrated that the drive to fashion a theory of value grew out of a conviction that money was merely a veil and a singularly inadequate value index. If money really was the same thing as pleasure, wasn't it a waste of time to develop all of those baroque taxonomies?

How, then, could Bentham persistently assert that he was the inventor and exponent of a *calculus* of the greatest happiness of the greatest number? The answer is to be found in an unpublished manuscript of his titled, "Dimension of Happiness" (quoted in Halévy 1972, p. 495):

> 'Tis in vain to talk of adding quantities which after the addition will continue distinct as they were before, one man's happiness will never be another man's happiness: a gain to one man is no gain to another: you might as well pretend to add twenty apples to twenty pears, which after you had done that could not be forty of any one thing but twenty of each just as there was before . . . This addibility of the happiness of different subjects, however, when considered rigorously, it may appear fictitious, is a postulation without the allowance of which all political reasoning is at a stand: nor is it more

fictitious than that of the equality of chances to reality, on which the whole branch of the Mathematics which is called the doctrine of chances is established.

It was convenient that this defense of a moral arithmetic was left unpublished, because it reveals the great extent to which Bentham's appeals to science were baseless. First, he admitted the simplest rules of algebra cannot hold for utility. Next, he allowed that his whole system would fail if this fact were admitted, and he equated the fall of his system with the fall of all political theory. Finally, he misleadingly suggested that the theory of probability also violated the rules of algebra, which was simply false. The equiprobability assumption might prove to be empirically false, but the problem with Benthamite utility was that it had no algebraic regularities at all.

For Bentham, a moral arithmetic was merely a convenient fiction and a didactic artifice and nothing more. It was the application of a monetary metaphor to nonmonetized phenomena with neither concern nor care to justify commensurability. Putting it another way, it was not intended as a theory of value. His writings in political economy bear no resemblance to such classical texts by Say or Ricardo, precisely because he cared so little for physical science and for abstract theory (Halévy 1972, p. 271). Indeed, whatever connection there was between classical political economy and Benthamite utilitarianism was manufactured out of whole cloth by James Mill, as Halévy was argued (Halévy 1972, pp. 281, 309).

A more interesting and challenging case is Antoine Augustin Cournot's *Recherches sur les Principles Mathématiques de la Théorie des Richesses*, published in 1838. Cournot was a mathematically sophisticated philosopher who wanted to implement a physical metaphor in economic theory, but was convinced that Canard's attempt was flawed because of its links to an underlying ontology of individual psychology. He explicitly compared exchange to the motion of particles (Cournot 1897, pp. 19–20), and even wrote, "In the act of exchange, as in the transmission of power by machinery, there is friction to be overcome, losses which must be borne, and limits which cannot be exceeded" (Cournot 1897, p. 9; see also Menard 1980, p. 533).

The language of power, loss, and limits was very evocative to his contemporaries, as was the insistence upon the necessity of mathematical models. The year of publication is critical, however, in understanding the metaphor of *puissance*. Savants of the French school of rational mechanics would be familiar with the notion of mechanical duty of Lazare Carnot and the French engineering tradition with its formalization of the work concept in the 1830s, but would not yet be aware of the (as yet undiscovered) energy concept and its implications, and would have little or no acquaintance with the field concept. They would likewise have been impressed with Fourier's theory of heat, with its insistence that mathematical equations describing phenomenological entities were viable without any ontological commitments concerning the underlying phenomena. Cournot, student at the Ecole Normale Supérieure, obtaining his doctorate in physics with a thesis on the motion of rigid bodies, protégé of Poisson, and close friend of Hachette (Menard 1978, pp. 100, 307–9), was located at the center of these developments.

This is directly reflected in Cournot's development of his understanding of the mechanical analogy. He did believe that the economy is naturally quantitative, but not in the manner of Canard, and most emphatically not in the neoclassical manner:

> The abstract idea of wealth or value in exchange, a definite idea, and consequently susceptible to rigorous treatment in combinations, must be carefully distinguished from accessory ideas of utility, scarcity and suitability to the needs and enjoyment of mankind . . . These ideas are variable, and by nature indeterminate and consequently ill-suited for the foundation of a scientific theory . . . there is no fixed standard for the utility of things [Cournot 1897, pp. 10–11].

He even suggested that commerce may be a cause of the destruction of values, which is consonant with Carnot's concern over the destruction of *puissance* with resistance and friction, but is inconsistent with the conservation of energy and the later neoclassical insistence that trade always leads to Pareto improvement. In what sense is Cournot's economy naturally quantitative?

This is where it becomes apparent that Cournot's economics is closer to classical than neoclassical economic theory. The basis for his mathematicization of economic theory rests on the fervent conviction (and little more) that relative values are self-evidently quantitative, and that mathematical science may proceed along purely phenomenologically descriptive lines. The similarity to Ricardo's search for the invariable standard of value is striking:

> There are no absolute values, but there are movements of absolute rise and fall of values . . . If theory should indicate one article incapable of absolute variation in value, and should refer to it all others, it would be possible to immediately deduce their absolute variations from their relative variations; but very slight attention is sufficient to prove that such a fixed term does not exist, although certain articles approach much more nearly than others to the necessary conditions for the existence of such a term. The monetary

metals are among the things which, under ordinary circumstances and provided that too long a period is not considered, only experience slight absolute variations in their value . . . But in no article exists having the necessary conditions for perfect fixity, we can and ought to imagine one, which, to be sure, will only have an abstract existence. It will only appear as an auxiliary term of comparison to facilitate conception of the theory, and will disappear in the final applications. In like manner, astronomers imagine a mean sun endowed with uniform motion, and to this imaginary star they refer [Cournot 1897, pp. 24, 25, 26].

Here, in a nutshell, we have the classical quest for the natural invariant substance of value; the insistence that money cannot be that natural substance; then the begrudging resignation in the fact that the actors persist in treating money as if it were the substance of value, condoning their intransigence by the Ricardian excuse that monetary metals vary in value less than other commodities; and the belief that an analyst could mathematically construct an artificial invariant value substance.

Also in resemblance to classical theory, Cournot's analogy with motion is poorly developed. Newtonian celestial mechanics did appeal to an absolute frame of reference in order to explain intertia; however, in practice the celestial mechanics of the eighteenth century could choose an arbitrary reference frame for the solar system because it also imposed all of the conservation principles of mass, angular momentum, *vis viva* and so on, so that relative motion could be considered translationally invariant (although this was not understood until later in the century). Cournot gives no indication of grasping that such principles would be equally required in the context of economic value, or that his physical analogies clashed with his economic models.[2] In effect, all that Cournot's discussion of physical analogies achieved was to create an impression that the quantification of value was legitimate; he did not employ the analogy for the purposes of suggesting the conditions under which quantitative values would possess legitimacy.

This is nowhere more evident than in his theory of price. He openly admitted that since price must depend on an incredibly large set of phenomena, some quantitative, and some not, it would be unlikely that an algebraic law could encompass the behavior of prices (Cournot 1897, p. 47). Undaunted, Cournot then asserted that it is empirically true that price is related inversely to the virtual quantity sold of a commodity, and that this relation has the stability and continuity of a mathematical function. One can speculate that Cournot thought he was doing for prices what Fourier had done for heat – postulating a mathematical phenomenological description with no underlying ontological justification (Menard 1978, p. 205).

Nevertheless, Cournot's work lacks any *raison d'être* for the mathematical formalization of political economy, which may explain to a certain extent its fall into oblivion for half a century. With an unsatisfying notion of value, part substance and part convention, and the postulation of a price function without plausible motivation or stability, Cournot then did proceed to apply the one element of the physical analogy that was destined to become the linchpin of the future neoclassical system: He used calculus to find an extremum, although in his instance it was the maximum of total revenue $pF(p)$, the area under the phenomenological curve relating virtual purchases to price, $D = F(p)$. However, it is an extreme misrepresentation to call this a demand curve, since there was no opposed supply curve, no derivation of the $F(p)$ curve from any underlying utility or force determinants, and a deficient definition of equilibrium price that merely set the derivative of total revenue with respect to price equal to zero, or $p^* = -F(p)/F'(p)$. A more faithful rendering of Cournot's *loi de debit* would be "law of sales."

Again, Cournot's conceptualization reflects the situation of physics in his period. Variational principles were well known in French rational mechanics in the early nineteenth century, but it was not yet understood that these analytical techniques were necessarily linked to the corresponding conservation principles, or to each other. That realization would only become widespread well after the genesis of the doctrine of the conservation of energy in the 1840s. Later neoclassical economists could discern with hindsight their own techniques in Cournot's maximization hypothesis, just as later physicists could recognize their energy concepts in Lagrange's rational mechanics. Nevertheless, in the 1830s neither energy nor utility were coherent analytical constructs, as is made manifest in the arbitrary character of the respective mathematical formalisms.

Hermann Gossen and the transition to neoclassical economics

The consolidation of physical theory under the aegis of energy was not an instantaneous event, but rather a process whereby earlier substance theories were gradually reinterpreted in terms of the mathematical abstractions of fields. The key transitional figure in this process was Hermann von Helmholtz, who resisted the further abstraction away from his substance connotations by other physicists such as James Clerk Maxwell:

> But I confess I should really be at a loss to explain, without the use of
> mathematical formulas, what he [James Clerk Maxwell] considers a
> quantity of electricity and why such a quantity is constant, like that of
> a substance. The original, old notion of substance is not at all identi-
> cal with that of matter. It signifies, indeed, that which behind the
> changing phenomena lasts as invariable, which can be neither gener-
> ated nor destroyed, and in this oldest sense of the word we may
> really call the two electricities substances. [Helmholtz 1887, p. 292]

Likewise, the consolidation of economic theory of value under the
aegis of utility was not an instantaneous event, but also a process
whereby substance theories grounded in concepts of force and energy
gradually gave way to fields. Early confusions over whether force or
energy were substances in Helmholtz were mirrored in confusions
over whether utility could be treated as a substance, creating an
impression of greater continuity between classical political economy
and the later neoclassical theory than actually existed. The parallel
transition figure in economics was Hermann Gossen, whose *Laws of
Human Relations* was privately published in Cologne in 1853.

The similarities between the two men's works are extraordinary.
Both were brought up in a German environment in which their
respective disciplines were dominated by vitalist and spiritual (*Geist*)
conceptions, and both viewed the reassertion of scientific rigor as
their primary aim. For both men this reassertion took the format of a
strict reductionist program based upon the postulate of identity,
which provided the justification for the importation of an elevated
level of mathematical formalism. As if these similiarities were not
enough, the central concept and term in each of their respective
vocabularies was *Kraft* or "force."

Helmholtz's views have been summarized in chapters 2 and 3.
Here, we merely cite the parallels in Gossen. Both believed that the
structure of causality must be tethered securely to the postulate of
identity. As early as 1843–4, Gossen wrote in an essay for his civil
service exam: "The possibility of acquiring knowledge rests on the
postulate that under identical conditions the imprints of anything
upon us and on the surrounding world must always be the same, that
is, on the postulate that a complete regularity rules in reality" (Gossen
1983, p. xxxv). Helmholtz, of course, linked the postulate of identity
directly to energy conservation; Gossen's argument is not so clearly
structured. For the latter, the key is still the concept of *Kraft,* but the
stages of the reduction to identity are more elaborate. As we should
now expect, however, the metaphors of body and motion held pride
of place. In his *Laws,* Gossen insists:

> If we assume that the laws of nature are actually known, then our action consists merely of the motions by which we bring the various materials available in nature into such an initial combination that the inherent forces of nature produce by themselves determined effects . . . Even when something is brought about by a chemical process, however, our intervention is limited simply to movement [Gossen 1983, p. 40].

Although his grasp of the underlying physical principles was unsteady, Gossen shared Helmholtz's desire to see all physical processes as manifestations of matter in motion. Also like Helmholtz, Gossen did assert that all actions of biological man upon the external world are ultimately mechanical, or as he put it: "the generation of motion by our muscular power." Whereas Helmholtz completed this reduction by defining force as the mathematical expression of *vis viva*, Gossen tried to carry the reduction to a different destination. The ultimate ground of explanation for Gossen is in life-pleasure, which appears to have many of the same substance-attributes that Helmholtz attributed to energy. The bridging assumption for Gossen is that human labor can be reduced to force (*Kraft*), and human labor is directly (and even proportionally!) related to *negative* pleasure, so that by direct translation, force or power can be reduced to pleasure (Gossen 1983, p. 41). He then applied his mathematical formalism directly to pleasure (or utility), with the implied presupposition that the laws of mechanical force could be later reconciled with his laws of human behavior to provide a truly unified science.

Very little is known about Gossen's life and intellectual influences (Cf. Georgescu-Roegen, in Gossen 1983). The timing of his civil service exams does suggest that at least part of his system was conceived of prior to the publication of Helmholtz's 1847 memoir, and there is no evidence of any direct influence of Helmholtz on Gossen. In the absence of such direct influence, the similarities between their respective works might be understood as both arising out of the German revival of Kantian thought in response to the writings of Hegel and the *Naturphilosophs*, as well as the pan-European elevation of force to pride of place in the explanation of social and physical phenomena. The absence of more explicit links to mid-nineteenth-century physics probably worked to Gossen's disadvantage. As it was, the manuscript of a self-taught minor Prussian bureaucrat with no academic credentials or reputation was not destined to be taken seriously by the German academic establishment. Further, as Germany in the second half of the nineteenth century was the primary center of resistance of the importation of the natural-science models and metaphors into social theory, Gossen's reductionist program did not meet the welcome in political economy that greeted Helmholtz's program in physics and physiology. Thus the fates of the two men could not have been more dissimilar: Helmholtz became the doyen of German physics, while Gossen was frustrated in his attempt to get a university teaching post and died in 1858, a dilettante and an unknown.

Gossen's theory of value appears to us a curious hybrid, as it was patterned on the transition in physical theory, which itself was based upon a transition between substance and field concepts; it ended up as not quite a labor theory of value, and yet not quite a theory of subjective psychological value. His mode of presentation was primarily geometrical, and only in a supplementary and incomplete manner did he construct algebraic models. His fundamental tool of analysis was a functional relationship between what he called the pleasure experiences and the time duration during which the pleasure was experienced, which he graphed as in Figure 5.1 (Gossen 1983, p. 9):

The first fact to be noted (contrary to Schumpeter 1954, pp. 910–11) is that this is *not* identical to the later neoclassical notion of diminishing marginal utility. That framework depends critically upon a marginal decrease in the rate of augmentation of total utility with a virtual increase of an infinitesimal unit of a single generic commodity at a point in time, whereas Gossen: (a) confused marginal increments with total amounts[3]; (b) posited a function whose dependent variable was the time spent in enjoyment and *not* of commodity units, which rules a field formalism out of court; (c) was forced to assume a linear decrease over time, due not just to exigencies of computational convenience (as he claimed), but also because in many contexts he still was treating utility as a substance and, therefore, (d) had no concept of utility as a variable of state. The widespread notion that Gossen anticipated modern neoclassical price theory is thus fallacious, if what is meant is the actual analytical structure of neoclassicism. What he did manage to anticipate was the linking of value theory with energy physics, his only mistake being that he jumped the gun.

Gossen's position on the theory of value was as close to that of a

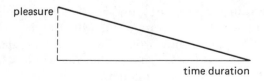

FIGURE 5.1 Gossen's "Kraft" function.

transitional figure such as Samuel Bailey or Cournot as it was to that of a Walras or a Fisher. For instance, Gossen makes much of the dictum that there exists no absolute value (Gossen 1983, p. 54). He, too, appealed to the metaphor of the yardstick, but had great difficulty in extricating himself from the labor theory of value. Most notably, he did not deal in terms of the "natural" commodity units, but felt he must reduce all commodities to a homogeneous measure *prior* to their translation into pleasure units:

> In the preceding example, reference was made repeatedly to equally large quantities. This did not refer to pounds or feet, but rather to such quantities of each good as can be produced by the same amount of labor effort. The required expenditure of effort serves as a yardstick, *and only with reference to it can there bay any discussion of equality or inequality* [my italics] [p. 101].

Although Gossen proposed to find the constrained extremum of life pleasure, he was very vague about what was conserved during the maximization calculation, although this was ultimately dictated by his supposedly harmless assumption of the linearity of the decline of pleasure over time. Gossen was quite insistent upon the primacy of exchange over production and the claim that the act of exchange can actually create or augment value (p. 96). He perceptively realized that:

> The reason for not seeing the importance of exchange is obviously the fiction of an absolute value whose scale is conceived in terms of physical properties. With such a concept of values, exchange obviously can have no effect on value since physical properties do not undergo any change through barter [p. 102].

In our own terminology, the function of a conserved embodied value substance is precisely to argue that value is conserved in exchange. It might seem plausible to respond that, if the conserved quantity does not reside in the object, then perhaps it resides in the beholder. Here Gossen wavers, neither willing nor unwilling to relinquish the substance concept. He cannot posit a fixed structure of preferences toward an array of commodities, because they have no independent existence in his system; they have all been reduced to a single substance of the dimension of time. One analytical drawback of this reduction is that, outside of a one-good world, the very temporal order and sequence of consumption will influence the final outcome – in other words, equilibrium would be path-dependent. Nicholas Georgescu-Roegen has further noted that the whole scheme is compromised by the fact that choice generally precedes the temporal act of enjoyment, thus creating further problems with regard to the meaning of a temporal sequence of temporal units which cannot be made congruent with one another (in Gossen 1983, p. lxxxi). Gossen's solution was to neutralize these sorts of objections by treating all pleasures as if they were independent, additive (p. 32), and a linear function of time. These conditions are isomorphic to the postulation of pleasure as a substance that is itself conserved in exchange, with the only control variable being the absolute total duration of time spent in consumption and production. Given a set of preferences and a technology (the shapes of the relevant triangles) and a time constraint (i.e., a fixed lifetime), a constrained optimization problem became feasible.

We say feasible, but not implemented, because outside the simplest one-person, two-commodity model, thorny issues still arose. Pleasure may be treated as a substance for a single person, but does it make sense to portray it as comparable between minds, and hence possessing an independent existence and integrity? Gossen at first evaded the issue by treating everyone as identical and later sketched a model with differing preferences that can only be determined if prices are already fixed – that is, we revert back to a substance embodied in the goods instead of the actors (pp. cviii–cx). Hesitant about such artifacts, he then proposed a third solution: that his theory does not really depend upon subjective judgments at all, but instead refers to an average economic man, whose preferences are formed by the culture of the particular society (p. 151). This, in turn, raised insuperable problems of knowledge and learning (p. 106). These did not perturb Gossen, for the simple reason that he was never really interested in psychology, but only in the construction of a physical metaphor.

In a system so enamoured of emulating the "objective" world of science, it is ironic that a major corollary of this choice was to downgrade the role of production vis-à-vis its central function in classical economics. In Gossen, production was reduced to the exercise of effort or *Kraft,* which was in turn reduced to pleasure and displeasure. Since trade increased pleasure, production itself seemed a fifth wheel: The only sort of production that would have repercussions significantly different from trade would require the creation of novel goods, or at least an increase of goods that was not offset by some correspondingly equal consumption of their equivalent in trade. Gossen did not opt to discuss this physical aspect of production, but instead imposed another analytically gratuitous though ideologically salubrious conservation principle in the realm of production:

> Upon removal of all obstacles that interfere with not only each person's most purposive use of money but also his choice of productive activity that, under the circumstances, is most advantageous to him, each person will receive a portion of the means of employment that corresponds exactly to the burden assumed by him in the productive process. Thus what socialists and communists conceive to be the highest and ultimate aim of their efforts is accomplished here by the cooperation of the forces of nature [p. 114].

Here the seductive influence of the Laplacean dream is evident in the conflation of a natural system with a timeless, just, and immutable world. In such a system, where goods turn into pleasure/*Kraft* and then back again at identical reversible ratios into the same quantity of goods, there is no analytical room for aggregate growth and transformation. This is the reason that even this earliest attempt at neoclassical theory is conjoined with a strong version of a form of Say's Law that denies the possibility of any general glut (pp. 115, 173). (This connection is explored in more detail in Chapter 6.)

This demotion of production is also made manifest by the shift in the very concept of equilibrium. The classical substance theories of value were all predicated upon the condition of an equalized rate of increase of the substance in the sphere of production, or more familiarly, an equalized rate of profit. Obviously, this has no meaning in a world of the constant reincarnation of identical goods and identical consumers. The physics of *Kraft* dictated a different notion of equilibrium in the economic sphere, and here it took the form of market-clearing: "The price for each commodity settles exactly at the point that allows the exchange of the entire quantity produced" (p. 110). This prescient innovation was only nascent in Gossen's work, in part due to the extreme complications of a many-good world which we have discussed above, and in part, as Walras (1965, p. 205) noted, because Gossen did not restrict every generic good to trade at the same fixed price. This was due to the fact that goods lost their identities at an extremely early stage in his analysis, being dissolved into the Ursubstance of *Kraft*.

We have expended a goodly sum of our own effort on Gossen's relatively neglected work because it illustrates the fact that the importation of a physical metaphor into economics is highly contingent upon the particular vintage of the physics imported, and that certain elements of the canonical neoclassical model are more contingent than others upon the fuller development of energy physics. By the 1840s, the analogy of an all-pervasive force was already present, as was the elevation of exchange over production and the imposition of a market-clearing condition as an obvious corollary of constrained maximization. Nevertheless, the full system had to await the consolidation of energy physics.

The marginalist revolution of the 1870s

It may be difficult for the modern reader to imagine the gulf between the physical theory of the 1840s, with its proliferation of fluids and ethers and forces and unconnected mathematical models of specific phenomena as celestial motion and heat flow and electrical conduction, and the consolidated discipline of the 1860s, unified around variational principles and the conservation of energy. Lagrangian methods were extended to all energetic phenomena, and the exigencies of reconciling the conservation of energy with electromagnetic action at a distance gave rise to an even more abstract entity: the field. Initially, this new entity retained the language of substance, but that did not last long. As Maxwell wrote in his seminal paper of 1856, "On Faraday's Lines of Force":

> The substance here treated must not be assumed to possess any of the properties of ordinary fluids except those of freedom of motion and resistance to compression. It is not even a hypothetical fluid which is introduced to explain actual phenomena. It is merely a collection of imaginary properties for establishing certain theorems in pure mathematics [quoted in Hesse 1965, pp. 209–10].

Maxwell's construct spread to the Francophone world in the 1860s and 1870s and was disseminated in England by Thomson and Tait's popular 1867 textbook *Treatise on Natural Philosophy*. Only in Germany, curiously enough, did a residual hostility to *Naturphilosophie* retard the acceptance of force fields until the 1880s (Wise, in Cantor and Hodge 1981, p. 275).

Knowledge of this chronology is critical in understanding the so-called simultaneous discovery of neoclassical economics (sometimes known as the Marginalist Revolution) in the 1870s and 1880s. The supposed mystery is dispelled when it is realized that energy physics had filtered down to some textbooks by the 1860s, and was rapidly becoming the primary metaphor for the discussion of the physical world. It is no accident that, however otherwise diverse the cultural and social influences upon the various European progenitors of neoclassical theory, they all received training in the natural sciences. The impact of this training upon their economic writings was not at all subtle, or difficult to detect.

In many ways, the episode of the supposed simultaneous discovery of neoclassical value theory in the 1870s resembles nothing so much as that other putative instance of simultaneous discovery, the so-called discovery of energy conservation in the 1840s. This, of course, is no accident, because they were both instances of the elaboration of the same metaphorical simplex, as argued in Chapter 3. Changes in the metaphor of motion dictated changes in the metaphor of value and vice versa. What was hailed as simultaneous discovery in retrospect was not at all regarded as such by the participants, and historical research reveals that the protagonists did not all discover the same thing. First energy and then value were conceptualized as substances, only to be later reinterpreted in field formalisms. This, indeed, explains the curious habit of early neoclassical theorists of writing their utility functions as separable functions of the individual commodities, namely $U = U_1(x) + U_2(y) + U_3(z) + \cdots$. Both energy and utility were based on large-scale prohibitions of "something for nothing": perpetual motion was banished in physics; natural scarcity was reified in economics (Brown 1987). Both elevated extremal principles to teleological research heuristics. And both proclaimed the dawn of a new era of unified science.

All the major protagonists of the Marginalist Revolution explicitly stated in their *published* works from whence they had derived the inspiration for their novel economic theories. (Jevons 1970, pp. 144–7) in his *Theory of Political Economy* wrote that his equation of exchange does "not differ in general character from those which are really treated in many branches of physical science." He then proceeded to compare the equality of the ratios of marginal utility of two goods and their inverted trading ratio to the law of the lever, where in equilibrium the point masses at each end are inversely proportional to the ratio of their respective distances from the fulcrum. For someone with Jevons's training, it was common to have some familiarity with the equilibrium conditions of rational mechanics without any grasp of the kinematic conditions requisite for a conservative vector field – such as those described in equation (2.4) – much less the Lagrangian or Hamiltonian formalisms of dynamics. It was enough to be captivated by the image of mental energy suffusing a commodity space in order to "discover" that prices were proportional to marginal utilities. Indeed, whether (for instance) Jevons actually ever fully understood the concept of a field is open to serious doubt.

Far from being an isolated and insignificant metaphor, this invocation of the physical realm is always present in Jevons's writings on price theory. In his posthumous *Principles of Economics* (Jevons 1905b,

p. 50), he wrote quite explicitly: "The notion of value is to our science what that of energy is to mechanics." In his defense of the mathematical method before the Manchester Statistical Society, he insisted:

> Utility only exists when there is on the one side the person wanting, and on the other the thing wanted . . . Just as the gravitating force of a material body depends not alone on the mass of that body, but upon the masses and relative positions and distances of the surrounding material bodies, so utility is an attraction between a wanting being and what is wanted. [Jevons 1981, VIII, p. 80].

When one observes that more than half of Jevons's published work concerns the logic and philosophy of science, one begins to see that the metaphor of physical science was the unifying principle and not merely the rhetorical flourish. In his major book, *The Principles of Science* (Jevons 1905a, pp. 759–60), he suggests that the notion of the hierarchy of the sciences justifies "a calculus of moral effects, a kind of physical astronomy investigating the mutual perturbations of individuals." The reduction of social processes to simple processes to simple utilitarian considerations is compared to the reduction of meteorology to chemistry and thence to physics, implying that there is only one scientific methodology and one recourse of explanation (i.e., physics) in all of human experience.

Schabas (1987) has suggested that Jevons was motivated to write on the philosophy of science in order to justify his program of methodological monism, with the hidden agenda of forging a different (non-Millian) science of political economy. With a modicum of hindsight it is not difficult to read between the lines of his summary chapter of *The Principles of Science* (Jevons 1905a, pp. 735–6):

> Life seems to be nothing but a special form of energy which is manifested in heat and electricity and mechanical force. The time may come, it almost seems, when the tender mechanism of the brain will be traced out, and every thought reduced to the expenditure of a determinate weight of nitrogen and phosphorus. No apparent limit exists to the success of the scientific method in weighing and measuring, and reducing beneath the sway of law, the phenomena both of matter and of mind . . . Must not the same inexorable reign of law which is apparent in the motions of brute matter be extended to the subtle feelings of the human heart?

Leon Walras was equally explicit concerning the motivation behind his published work. In his *Elements of Pure Economics* (Walras 1969, p. 71), he wrote that "the pure theory of economics is a science which resembles the physico-mathematical sciences in every respect." As we shall discover, this was no idle boast. The reason why Walras was preoccupied with "pure economics" is explained in great detail in Lessons 1 through 4 of the *Elements*. In his opinion, a pure science is only concerned with the relationships among things, the "play of the blind and ineluctable forces of nature," which are independent of all human will. Walras insists that there exists a limited subset of economic phenomena that are capable of passing muster as the objects of a pure scientific inquiry: They were the configurations of prices in a regime of perfect competition. (For further elaboration see Mirowski [1981].) It is the existence of these pure relationships that justifies, and indeed, for Walras demands, the application of the *same* mathematical techniques as those deployed in mid-nineteenth-century physics. In Walras's scheme of things, other social phenomena tainted by the influence of human will would be relegated to studies employing nonscientific literary techniques.

The proposed unity of technique in physics and economics is fully revealed in Walras's article of 1909, "Economique et Mécanique," reprinted in Mirowski and Cook (1990). In this article the two favorite physical metaphors of the early neoclassical economists (the rational mechanics of the equilibrium of the lever and the mathematical relations between celestial bodies) were developed, and the assertion was made that the physico-mathematical science of the *Elements* uses *precisely* the identical mathematical formulas. Walras then proceeded to scold physicists who had expressed scepticism about the application of mathematics to utilitarian social theories on the ground that utility is not a measurable quantum; Walras retorted that the physicists themselves have been vague in their quantification of such basic terms as mass and force. The proposed connections between the terms of the sciences could not have been made more manifest: "Aussi a-t-on déjà signalé celle des *forces* et des *raretés* comme *vecteurs,* d'une part, et celles des *énergies* et des *utilités* comme *quantités scalaires,* d'autre part." (Walras 1909, p. 318). Of course, as in the case of Jevons, a desire to imitate physicists need not be backed up by a competent or comprehensive grounding in physics. Indeed, this last quote was added to the article in the proof stage under prompting from Irving Fisher, who, as we shall shortly observe, did possess a more thorough grounding in physics.

Francis Ysidro Edgeworth was a third partisan of "mathematical psychics" who was quite explicit about the wellsprings of the neoclassical movement. If only because of his extravagant and florid style, he is worth quoting directly (Edgeworth 1881, pp. 9, 12):

> The application of mathematics to the world of the soul is countenanced by the hypothesis (agreeable to the general hypothesis that every psychical phenomenon is the concomitant, and in some sense

the other side of a physical phenomenon), the particular hypothesis adopted in these pages, that Pleasure is the concomitant of Energy. *Energy* may be regarded as the central idea of Mathematical Psychics; *maximum energy* the object of the principle investigations in that science . . . "Mécanique Sociale" may one day take her place along with "Mécanique Celeste," throned each upon the double-sided height of one maximum principle, the supreme pinnacle of moral as of physical science. As the movements of each particle, constrained or loose, in a material cosmos are continually subordinated to one maximum sub-total of accumulated energy, so the movements of each soul whether selfishly isolated or linked sympathetically, may continually be realising the maximum pleasure . . .

Edgeworth was quite clear about the subordinate role played by Benthamite utilitarianism in his path to a scientific economics, writing in one place that: "Morality might be no more injured by physical science than music by acoustics" (Edgeworth 1877, p. 22) – a not-so-oblique reference to the later work of Helmholtz – as well as accusing the progenitor of Utilitarianism with metaphoric confusion: "Bentham says 'greatest quantity of motion of the greatest mass!' " (p. 39).

Vilfredo Pareto, a fourth confederate of the marginalist cadre, adopted a much more pugnacious, but essentially identical position:

> Strange disputes about predestination, about the efficacy of grace, etc., and in our day incoherent ramblings on solidarity show that men have not freed themselves from these daydreams which people have gotten rid of in the physical sciences, but which still burden the social sciences . . . Thanks to the use of mathematics, this entire theory, as we develop it in the Appendix, rests on no more than a fact of experience, that is on the determination of the quantities of goods which constitute combinations between which the individual is indifferent. The theory of economic science thus acquires the rigor of rational mechanics [Pareto 1971b, pp. 36, 113].

In some ways, Pareto was the most ruthless proponent of the physical metaphor. In place of the flowery language and Victorian prolixity of Edgeworth, the technocratic obscurity of Walras, or the coy indirect invocation of the philosophy of science by Jevons, Pareto openly admitted from the start from whence the marginalists derived their inspiration, practically daring the reader to express any demurrer:

> Let us go back to the equations which determine equilibrium. In seeing them somebody – and it might be the writer – made an observation . . . "These equations do not seem new to me, I know them well, they are old friends. They are the equations of rational mechanics." That is why pure economics is a sort of mechanics or akin to mechanics . . . mechanics can be studied leaving aside the concept of forces. In reality this does not all matter much. If there is

anyone who does not care to have mechanics mentioned, very well, let us disregard the similarity and let us talk directly about our equations" [Pareto 1953, p. 185].

Pareto could not curb his sharp pen, even when addressing his marginalist comrades. In a letter of 1897 to Irving Fisher, he wrote:[4]

> People who know neither mathematics or rational mechanics cannot understand the principal conception of my book . . . The discussions concerning the terms ophelimity, entrepreneurs, capital, etc., are of exactly the same type as found in the last century surrounding the term *force vive* in mechanics. Eh! Call what you will the quantity one half mv^2, won't the results always be the same?

Once one begins these passages for the manifestos that they are, one sees that they are ubiquitous in the writings of early neoclassical economists. They can also be found in Fisher (1926), Antonelli (1971), and Laundhardt (1885). In fact, the explicit appropriation of this specific physical metaphor is present in every major innovator of the Marginalist Revolution, with the single exception of the Austrian school of Carl Menger. (This exception is discussed below.) The adoption of the proto-energetics metaphor and framework of mid-nineteenth-century physics is the birthmark of neoclassical economics, the Ariadne's thread that binds the protagonists, and that can lead us to the fundamental meaning of the neoclassical research program.

However, let us make one thing as clear as possible. Wanting to copy the proto-energetics formalism and understanding the proto-energetics formalism are two entirely different things. Indeed, none of the conventional triumverate of Jevons, Walras, and Menger understood the energy concept with any degree of subtlety or depth, but this need not have stopped them from the appropriation of some part of physics, only to later discover that its implications stretched far beyond anything they might have imagined. We can only understand the differences of the so-called discoverers if we first have a clear idea of what an analogy of energy and utility implies. Hence, we shall not begin with the original protagonists' texts, but rather with the text of the one early neoclassical who displayed the most sophisticated (although hardly comprehensive) understanding of the energy formalism: the American, Irving Fisher.

The canonical neoclassical model

The economist Paul Samuelson once called Irving Fisher's 1892 doctoral thesis "the best of all doctoral dissertations in economics"

(Samuelson 1950, p. 254). One advantage of centering attention on this version of the neoclassical model is that it was the first to implement a vector characterization of an economy, and therefore is more easily compared to the development of the history of physical theory outlined in Chapter 2. A second advantage is that Fisher's thesis was the first (and last) published work to explore the physical metaphor in great detail. Both attributes can be traced to the influence of Josiah Willard Gibbs, the great American thermodynamicist, who was one of Fisher's thesis advisers. Fisher's version is best suited to begin a presentation of the canonical neoclassical model because he remained more scrupulously faithful to the proto-energetics model than did his predecessors; his version has persisted as the teaching model long after the versions of Jevons and Walras were repudiated or altered beyond recognition.

We begin with the description of the motion of a mass point through a field of force already discussed in Chapter 2, namely equation (2.1). The integral of the forces times the displacements represents the work accomplished, or the change in kinetic energy:

$$\int_A^B (F_x dx + F_y dy + F_z dz) = \frac{1}{2} m v^2 \Big|_A^B = T_B - T_A$$

In all of rational mechanics the concept of force is *primitive*, in the sense that forces are simply the posited causes of changes in motion. The central question in the construction of a mechanical explanation is: How should one introduce the force concept? Generally this is done through the postulation of force fields. Recall from Chapter 2 that, for the work function in the system to be path-independent, the vector force field must be irrotational and conservative. These conditions are that given a vector field **F** there is a scalar potential field U such that:

$$\oint \mathbf{F} \cdot ds = 0$$

or, {**F** · ds} is an exact or perfect differential equation; also

$$\mathbf{F} = \text{grad } U = \left[\frac{\partial U}{\partial x} \quad \frac{\partial U}{\partial y} \quad \frac{\partial U}{\partial z} \right]$$

and curl **F** = 0.

The key to understanding neoclassical economics is to realize that prices constitute a conservative vector field – here **F** – such that, given a scalar field of utility $U(x, y, z)$, the price vector field may be deduced from it. Price vectors represent the direction of maximum virtual desire; each dimension of space corresponds to a specific commodity; and in equilibrium prices are proportional to marginal utilities.

So far, this language of fields and forces is simply a metaphor for the functions performed by a market. What is next required is an extended bout of metaphorical reasoning, attempting to discern what implications this metaphor may hold for the economic phenomena of interest, searching out dissonances as well as resonances. Let us begin with Fisher's own comparison of the relevant analogies (Fisher 1926, pp. 85–6). We reproduce Fisher's concordance in Table 5.1. (The asterisks indicate aspects of the analogy that we shall shortly call into question.)

Table 5.1 Fisher's Translations

Mechanics	Economics
*a particle	*an individual
space	commodity
force	marginal utility or disutility
*work	*disutility
energy	utility
*work or energy = force × space	*utility = marginal utility × commodity
force is a vector	marginal utility is a vector
forces are added by vector addition	marginal utilities are added by vector addition
work and energy are scalars	disutility and utility are scalars
The total energy may be defined as the integral with respect to impelling forces.	The total utility enjoyed by the individual is the like integral with respect to marginal utilities.
Equilibrium will be where net energy (energy minus work) is maximum; or equilibrium will be where impelling and resisting forces along each axis will be equal.	Equilibrium will be where gain (utility minus disutility) is maximum; or equilibrium will be where marginal utility and marginal disutility along each axis will be equal.
If total energy is subtracted from total work instead of vice versa the difference is "potential" and is a minimum.	If total utility is subtracted from total disutility instead of vice versa the difference may be called "loss" and is minimum.

There are a few curious omissions from Fisher's table that, when added, will further illuminate the analogy.

component force along an axis in equilibrium	price of a commodity in equilibrium
kinetic energy	total expenditure
displacement	incremental unit of commodity
conservation of energy	conservation of utility plus expenditure

The analogy is rendered more tangible by expressing the relationships graphically, as Fisher himself did (1926, pp. 72–81). In Figure 5.2, we see the force vector at point $A(x_0, y_0)$ reinterpreted as the relative amounts of x and y that an individual would purchase given an infinitesimal relaxation of constraint (that is, an increase of income) when the individual already possesses amounts (x_0, y_0) of the commodities.

The primary feature of a field theory of value is the assertion that the person in question knows his or her vector of virtual choices not just at point A, but at every point on the graph. Thus the graph of commodity space is filled with a gradient that at every point describes the direction and magnitude of greatest desire. In a conservative vector field every gradient is directly related to a scalar potential function. In Figure 5.3, the potential is represented by the locus of points where the particular combination of commodities X and Y in the possession of the individual results in the *same quantitative utility*. This point deserves some emphasis because of the conventional habit of referring to the curves of potential as indifference curves. Fisher pioneered this terminological innovation (Fisher 1926, p. 70) because,

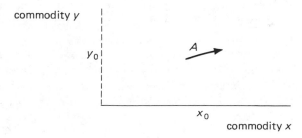

FIGURE 5.2   The utility gradient.

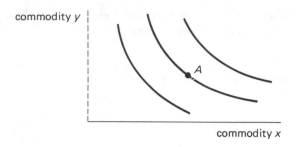

commodity y

A

commodity x

FIGURE 5.3   The utility field.

as he later admitted, he was uncomfortable with the notion of a quantitative utility, and hence speculated that one could work in terms of the gradient (the little arrows) without resorting to the potential (the utility levels) (p. 88). That hope, as we shall see, was in vain.

The existence of a scalar field defined over the commodity space is not sufficient to define value or equilibrium – for that, one also needs the notion of constraint. In proto-energetics, the particle moves along the path of (generally) minimized potential, given certain constraints and boundary characteristics. This, of course, is the grand entrance of the variational principle. If Figure 5.3 were to describe curves of decreasing potential to the northeast, and the axes described the boundaries of the system, any particle starting in the northeast quadrant would fall endlessly in the northeast direction. If we replace the description with Figure 5.4, which constrains the particle to fall along the line ABC, then it will instead come to rest at point B, which minimizes the constrained potential. One of the innovations of the neoclassicals was to assert that the fall of consumer choice was toward the maximum of potential instead of the minimum, and to restrict all the constraints to be linear. Calculus only distinguishes between local maxima and minima at the level of second derivatives, so most of the mathematical apparatus of first derivatives could be retained thoroughly unaltered from physics.

If the force components are interpreted as prices, then the interpretation of the integral of forces times displacements follows directly. Displacements along the axes translate into incremental changes in the amount of the corresponding commodity. The integral

$$\int (F_x dx + F_y dy + \cdots)$$

which in physics is interpreted as the kinetic energy or work integral,

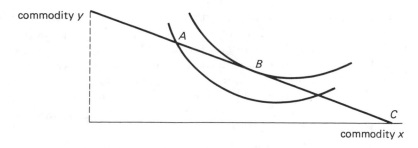

commodity y

A

B

C

commodity x

FIGURE 5.4 Neoclassical equilibrium.

in the neoclassical context becomes total expenditure, the integral of price times incremental changes in quantity. If one were to insist that the price of each incremental quantity of a generic good be a constant – that is, one were to impose the law of one price – then the integral would collapse to a simple summation:

$$\sum \{F_x \cdot x + F_y \cdot y + \cdots\}$$

which, if set equal to a constant, becomes the familiar budget constraint.

The imposition of the law of one price in this context is the major single revision of the proto-energetics model made specifically by neoclassical economists after the appropriation of the energy metaphor. It is the reason why one does not encounter the energy integral in an explicit format in neoclassical textbooks, unlike the ubiquitous first integrals of rational mechanics. Among other results, it accounts for the restriction of all constraints to linear relations and serves to cloud the conception of the relevant conservation principles, as we shall observe below. In practice, it imposes an extra independent restriction upon the vector field, while preserving the explanatory construct of extremal principles and conservation principles.

Recall that the potential function is *defined* by the condition that its partial derivatives with respect to its variables are equal to the forces along the associated axes, that is $F_x = \partial U/\partial x$, $F_y = \partial U/\partial y$, and so on. If one reinterprets the potential function as representative of utility, then the ratio of the marginal utilities of any two goods at a point such as *B* would be

$$\frac{\partial U/\partial x}{\partial U/\partial y} = \frac{F_x}{F_y}$$

(Parenthetically, most physics textbooks of the later nineteenth century, remaining faithful to the notation of Hamilton and Rankine, explicitly inscribed the potential function as $U(x, y, z)$, hence providing a mathematical mnemonic to spur the imagination of any economist enamoured of the notion of utility.) Hence the ratio of the component forces in equilibrium could be conceptualized as their trading ratios, and the ratio of prices would equal the ratio of marginal utilities. In the same way that force was eventually differentiated from energy in the later nineteenth century, price was differentiated from (marginal) utility as a distinct mathematical expression. The metaphorical overtones of this distinction were also seductive: Prices were the forces and the market was the mechanism whereby the maximum of utility was realized.

Patently, at this level the formalism still only describes the comparative static positions of equilibrium or rest, and would also need to coopt the formalism of Hamiltonian dynamics in order to describe movements between equilibrium positions. It is of major importance that not one neoclassical economist was willing or able to take this step until after World War II, a point to which we will return repeatedly in what follows. The culprits in this failure of metaphor will be the inadequate treatment of the conservation principles and the innovation of the law of one price.

Armed with this explicit elaboration of the analogy, we can return to Table 5.1, Fisher's lexicon of correspondences, and evaluate his translations. What appears most striking about such a comparison is that even Fisher, the most sophisticated scientist among the nineteenth-century neoclassical economists, still displayed an inadequate comprehension of the formalism of the energy concept and, as a corollary, a lack of appreciation of the metaphorical dissonances involved.

The indictment that some historical figure was "mistaken" in appropriating a metaphor from another discipline is always a difficult case to prosecute, if only because a metaphor need not bear an identical resemblance to the initial object of comparison in each and every respect. What we must do here is strike a compromise between comprehending Fisher's own understanding of his project and demonstrating how Fisher's view of scientific explanation was skewed in such a way as to misrepresent the understanding of Fisher's scientific contemporaries.

We begin with Fisher's own words, taken from an unpublished retrospective on his career titled "My Economic Endeavors".[5] In that manuscript he produced a list of the innovations to be found in his 1892 thesis as he later saw them:

(1) A concept of utility and marginal utility based on desire and not, as Jevons and others had attempted, on pleasure (gratification of desire) and which leads itself to possible future statistical measurement.
(2) Hydrostatic and other mechanical analogies.
(3) Distinctive price determining equations.
(4) Applications to economics of Gibbs vector concept.
(5) Indifference curves.

One way of understanding the Irving Fisher of the 1890s is that his appreciation of the full physical content of the field concept was deficient, even though he was familiar with Gibbs's formalisms, the most mathematically sophisticated treatment of dynamics at that time. It appears that most of his analogies were taken from hydrostatics rather than from fields of force – although recall there is appreciable overlap, primarily because field theory grew out of hydrodynamics. The comparison of the economy to liquids in vats and cisterns is the primary trope of the *Mathematical Investigations,* and both Fisher and Edgeworth referred to the analytics therein as "the method of liquids."[6] Hence, Fisher frequently had resort to the sophisticated vector calculus of Gibbs without faithfully reproducing the analytic structure of a conservative vector field. This is illustrated by the problems found in Table 5.1.

At the top of the list, the identification of a particle with an individual is incorrect. The individual in this model is only made manifest by his psychology, and his psychology is only portrayed as a field of preferences. It is the energy/utility that provides the only ontological identity of the actor in the mathematics; this is one sense in which the conservation of energy will become important. The individual is to be found nowhere on the graph, just as energy cannot be conceptualized as being located at particular coordinates in a field. The energy is constitutive of the field, and is in the field, but nothing more specific can be said of it. It does not describe a material property; this is where the substance and field conceptions of value collide. Utility is not a "stuff" or liquid and neither is the somewhat spectral neoclassical economic man: both are a field of possibilities that can characterize an empty commodity space.

Fisher's next mistake is the conflation of two incompatible meanings of the term "work". He correctly states that work in physics is defined as force times displacement, but then misleadingly equates it with energy. The integral of forces times displacements is equal to *kinetic* energy, which is only one aspect of the total energy, the other aspect being the potential. The kinetic energy in conjunction with the law of one price, as we have seen, corresponds to total expenditure. Fisher, however, tried to dragoon the work concept to do double duty as disutility as well as the budget constraint, obviously appealing not to the physics definition, but rather to his own further theoretical predisposition to portray human effort as if it were odious, or as negative pleasure. Here we observe the vestiges of Gossen's confusion of the labor and utility theories of value, the confusion of value as substance and value as field, the play upon the dual connotation of energy as utility and energy as human bodily effort.

The metaphorical problem is not merely that Fisher attempted to squeeze some considerations into his table that were not legitimately present in the rational mechanics; the gaps in his lexicon of corre-spondences are more serious that that. He began by asserting that "to construct a positive science, force must be defined with respect to its connection with *space, time* and *mass*. So also . . . when economics attempts to be a positive science, it must seek a definition which connects it with the objective *commodity*" (Fisher 1926, p. 17). But then why not mention the comparison of orthogonal decomposition of forces to prices, which is the heart and soul of the objective part of the metaphor? Could it be that the connection could only be maintained in equilibrium, or that the superimposition of the law of one price might have compromised its objective nature? And further, while space is equated with commodities, how about *time?* Or, more telling-ly, how about *mass,* the invariant in rational mechanics that allows force to be empirically observed? Would prices need some sort of parallel invariant?

Fisher was caught in a clash of conflicting desires: He wished to create an analytical opening for the discussions of production in a pure exchange model, as well as simultaneously abjuring money as representing any species of value invariant, because as he insisted, "money value simply measures utility by a marginal standard which is constantly changing" (p. 87); and to avoid all treatment of utility as a palpable quantity, all the while giving the impression that the marshalling of his appreciable mathematical armory had some firm epistemological basis in the world of social observables. His chosen tactic was to *avoid discussion of the conservation of energy* at all costs, even if it meant some misrepresentation of the model appropriated from physics. The reason for this embarrassed silence can be found in the last row of our augmented Table 5.1. Merely extrapolating the previ-ous development of the physics analogy, we note that the conserva-tion of energy, when translated, means that the sum of total expenditure and the sum of total utility in a closed trading system must be equal to a constant.

The addition of income and utility? The very concept seems absurd. Surely Fisher thought it so. It is probable that Fisher thought he could safely discard this aspect of the metaphor without harm to the rest of his system and replace it with his notion of human labor as disutility, the cost by means of which income is generated. However attractive his solution, Fisher was mistaken, and so, too, are the great majority of neoclassical economists who follow in his footsteps. This suppressed conservation principle, forgetting the conservation of energy while simultaneously appealing to the metaphor of energy, is the Achilles heel of all neoclassical economic theory, the point at which the physical analogy breaks down irreparably. (Does the necessity of Chapter 2 now become somewhat more apparent?) This will become clearer in the next chapter as we trace the development of neoclassical economics in the twentieth century.

For now, only one facet of the argument needs to be sketched out: In physics, there is no such thing as the deployment of a variational principle without the postulation of a corresponding conservation principle. Neoclassicals cannot have their maximum principles without it. If they leave things where Fisher left them, then their mathematics says that *money and utility are effectively ontologically identical*, because they may be extensively added together and conserved in the process. One merely is transformed at determinate ratios into the other, just as potential energy becomes kinetic, and vice versa. The fundamental mathematical identity between utility and money income thus provides the logical metric for value in the proto-energetics model. These implications of the model had to be repressed, however, because they contradicted the entire science-based project of grounding the economy in a "natural" principle beyond money.

Some consequences of a field theory of value

The utility field

However strange it may seem, the consequences and implications of the adoption of the field metaphor in economics have *never* been elaborated in any greater detail than that provided in Fisher's thesis. For this very reason, it might be useful to make them more explicit, in order to reveal how drastic the divorce from the classical economic tradition would become, once the depths of the new physical metaphor were plumbed. An exegesis of the physical metaphor is a prerequisite for understanding how neoclassical economics redefined many of the classical topics to the point where whole subsets of the respective research programs became incommensurable with each other.

Fisher, in his retrospective account of his life's work, "My Economic Endeavors," asserted without guile that he had persistently aspired to "the goal on which my heart has been most set, the goal of economics becoming a true science comparable with physics. I have always believed that one of the best disciplines for an economic novitiate is a thorough course in physical science." But what precisely should that course cover?

If the objective is to comprehend neoclassical economics, then it had better cover the formalisms of the vector field: namely, equations (2.1) through (2.5) in Chapter 2. Translating these into the appropriate economic analogues, let **P** be the vector field of gradients of utility in a commodity space $q = \{q_x, q_y, q_z\}$, as in Figure 5.2. Now, the analogue of the work function would be the expenditure line integral:

$$(5.1) \quad E = \int \mathbf{P} \, dq$$

Without some further structure being imposed on the vector field, analysis would, for all practical purposes, remain paralyzed at this stage. The most important condition is that the vector field be irrotational. In economic terms, this implies that, given any sequence of virtual exchanges that ends up at the same commodity bundle where it started, the utility gradient at that bundle remains unchanged. One would specify this condition in mathematical format at a path integral around a closed curve c:

$$(5.2) \quad \oint_c \mathbf{P} \, dq = 0$$

As observed in Chapter 2, this condition implies a number of isomorphic conditions, (2.2) through (2.5); or, rewriting them in our economic analogue,

$$(5.3) \quad \mathbf{P} = \operatorname{grad} U = \left[\frac{\partial U}{\partial x} \quad \frac{\partial U}{\partial y} \quad \frac{\partial U}{\partial z} \right] = \{P_x, P_y, P_z\}$$

that is, prices are proportional to marginal utilities; and

$$(5.4) \quad \operatorname{curl} \mathbf{P} = \left[\frac{\partial P_z}{\partial y} - \frac{\partial P_y}{\partial z} \quad \frac{\partial P_x}{\partial z} - \frac{\partial P_z}{\partial x} \quad \frac{\partial P_y}{\partial x} - \frac{\partial P_x}{\partial y} \right]$$

Hence $\{\mathbf{P} \cdot dq\}$ is an exact differential equation. and curl $\mathbf{P} = 0$.

These are the neglected and frequently misunderstood integrability conditions in neoclassical theory, which often appear under the rubrics of Antonelli conditions, Slutsky conditions, or the strong

axiom of revealed preference. Finally, as noted, the sum of expenditure plus utility is conserved:

(5.5) $E + U = k$

These are the equations of a conservative vector field of prices,
which can also be expressed as a scalar potential field of utility. Here
utility is a path-independent phenomenon, which means that the
notional sequence of trades will not influence the final outcome: The
outcome is independent of process. If we are serious about the fact
that all trades take time, then the utility field and the accompanying
price vector field must also be *conservative*, – i.e., independent of time.
Otherwise, the entire notion of a unique equilibrium independent of
temporal sequence and location must be relinquished. Another way
of putting it would be that we were no longer dealing with a natural-
law phenomenon.

Finally, the neoclassicals appended the law of one price

(5.6) $\dfrac{dy}{dx} = \dfrac{y}{x}, \dfrac{dy}{dz} = \dfrac{y}{z}, \ldots$

and the requirement that equilibrium be on the linear budget constraint

(5.7) $\sum P \cdot dq = \sum P \cdot q = \bar{E}$

and thus arrived at the full system of neoclassical equilibrium in the
case of pure exchange. This is the full content of what we shall call a
field theory of value.

It is a commonplace that this model displaced value from the
physical world, "out there," embodied in the physical commodity, and
located it in the subjective world, the "in here," in the mind. This
crude portrayal of a leap from one pole of the ubiquitous Western
dualism of mind and body to the other cannot account for the success
of neoclassical theory, unless one also savors the irony of the fact that
the premier model of the external physical world in the nineteenth
century was the vehicle by which it was accomplished. This could
never have been achieved as long as natural science was wedded to an
inert substance concept of motion and causality: the prospect of the
mind "pouring" a value substance into a commodity could not provide a sufficiently compelling narrative for a convincing tale of social
dynamics.

The changing ontology and epistemology of nineteenth-century
physics did alter the rules of the game of scientific debate, and it was
this more than anything else which encouraged the appearance of the

bridging of mind and external world in economics. The neo-Kantian mandate to see number as an outgrowth of the a priori, as well as the growing skepticism over the presence of a single, natural algebra inherent in the world, opened up the possibility that the metric of value might not ultimately reside in the commodity itself. Paradoxically, science itself grew more obscure after the spread of energy physics. Physical phenomena were no longer rooted in the tangible and the prosaic; energy became less and less "there," especially when suffused throughout an infinite immaterial field. The optimal route to an understanding of energy was to realize that it merely was an integral, a mathematical pattern shared in common by the descriptions of a number of phenomena. As Maxwell wrote,

> What I propose now to do is examine the consequences of the assumption that [electromagnetic] phenomena . . . are those of a moving system, the motion being communicated from one part of the system to another by forces, the nature and laws of which we do not even yet attempt to define, because we can eliminate those forces from the equation of motion by the method given by Lagrange for any connected system [quoted in Cantor and Hodge 1981, p. 261].

Utility was likewise prone to dissolve just as one thought one had hold of it; it was merely an integral, determinate only up to a constant of integration, best understood through its mathematical eidolon. The vacillating attitude of all the early neoclassicals toward the measurement of utility provides an apt illustration of the elusiveness of the new field theory of value.

William Stanley Jevons (1970, pp. 81–6) confronted the issue with not one, but three distinct and conflicting rationales. First, he took refuge in Hume's problem of induction: Just because we cannot measure utility *now* is no argument that someday in the future we will not have that ability. Next, reversing gears, he argued we *can* measure utility through measurement of its effects (i.e., prices). Last, acting on the principle that if one contradiction is not enough, two of them in linked sequence should be sufficient, Jevons then claimed that no mind can ever know the motives of another mind. To any lesser mortal, this would seem to preclude the possibility of ever subjecting the neoclassical model to any serious empirical scrutiny. For Jevons, it suggested that the goal of the economist is not to empirically know the mind of a particular individual, but only to describe the average behavior of a collection of individuals.

Walras, imbued to a greater extent with the physicists' predisposition to relinquish intuitive justification of mathematical models, wrote in one place that *rareté* is personal and subjective, whereas elsewhere he merely assumed that utility is measurable without any further justification or explanation (Walras 1965, pp. 117–146). Unlike Jevons, Walras had no Benthamite tradition on the continent to fall back on, and in any event, throughout his life he was openly hostile to any form of Benthamite psychology (Jaffé 1983, p. 318). As continental psychology in the later nineteenth century progressively left utilitarianism behind, and such theories as Freudianism cast doubt upon our knowledge of our own internal motives, not to mention those of other minds, economists relinquished all legitimate pretense to base their theories on subjective psychology. As Fisher (1926, pp. vii, 23) insisted: "The foisting of Psychology on Economics seems to me inappropriate and vicious," and "Utility is the heritage of Bentham and his theory of pleasures and pains. For us his *word* is the more acceptable, the less it is entangled with his *theory*."

The question of the "measurability of utility," which has dogged the neoclassical research program since its inception, was not due to some tempest in a teapot over cardinal versus ordinal utility, contrary to most modern histories of doctrine. To the early neoclassicals, on the contrary, it represented the goal of the final attainment of the status of a science on a par with physics. Such status was doubly desired because it would then dissociate economics from all of the contentious and nonscientific speculations to be found in the low-rent program of psychology. In a simple extrapolation of the metaphor, physicists spent their time measuring energy, so economists should likewise measure utility. Nevertheless, this program was doomed from the start because of the neglect of the meaning and requirements of a conservative vector field. Quite simply, energy was measurable *because* it conformed to certain conservation principles. The prognosis for utility was nowhere nearly so favorable so long as Jevons, Walras, Pareto, Fisher, and others were oblivious to the nature of these conditions. Their diverse, distended, and discordant responses to the question of measurability only served to disclose their confusion to anyone who understood equations (5.1) through (5.5).

Perhaps the most efficient way to comprehend the canonical neoclassical model is to first realize that it has nothing to do with subjective psychology or the mind, as it is understood in the Western dualism of mind and body. In fact, as Fisher said, it has nothing to do with utilitarianism as a political or psychological theory. Neoclassical economists have always been uncomfortable when trying to justify utility theory because it readily becomes clear to any listener that they do not care to know much of anything about human psychology, which they view as a nonscientific field of inquiry, much less to accomodate their theses to it. Often they will assert that they are merely describing an ideal rationality (rational-choice theory), but this is an egregious misrepresention of the issue.

As far back as Gossen, neoclassicals have wavered between claiming that they were describing actual behavior and claiming that they were prescribing what rational behavior should be. Their contempt for psychology has always given the lie to the first claim, so of necessity, they have eventually retreated to the second. This second position is untenable, however, because it conflicts with the ideology of the scientist as detached and value-neutral observer as it commits the transgression of defining rationality in a post-hoc manner in order to conform to the mathematical model of utility. As we shall shortly observe, the metaphor of utility implicitly assumes all sorts of restrictions on what it means to be a human being, and the definition of economic rationality is part and parcel of them. Only if value looks like energy can there be any meaning to neoclassical economic rationality. Man, being recast in the image of physics, is now reprimanded by the economic scientist to shape up and behave like a field of force.

The law of one price

One direct consequence of the adoption of the proto-energetics model was that the classical concern over the trade of equivalents as the benchmark of free and voluntary competition grew muddied (Dennis 1977). The primary conception of equilibrium in the physical analogy occurred in a single individual's utility field when he/she equated the marginal utilities of the final increments of each commodity. As the classicals feared, if every individual possessed incommensurable desires and there were no further restrictions on this theory, then there would be no coherent statements to be made about exchange value within this model. The crucial auxiliary hypothesis, which reintroduced equivalence through the back door, was the further stipulation of the law of one price, equation (5.6). Although each unit of a generic commodity represented a differing quantity of utility, it was forced by nothing more than unjustified fiat to be exchanged at the same ratio as any other unit. As Fisher (1926, p. 14) put it, "for a given purchaser the utilities of [the commodities] A and B, though actually unequal, *would be* equal if every portion of A (and also of B) were rated at the same degree of utility as the last infinitesimal. This [N.B.] hypothetical equality underlies . . . the notion of the equality of the *values* of A and B." (See also Edgeworth [1925, II, pp. 372–3].)

The main problem of any theory of use-value is to explain interpersonal exchange; the alteration of the physics model that accomplished this goal was the restriction of all exchange ratios to be identical, both for the individual and among individuals. This law of one price surreptitiously rendered utilities comparable, and hence equivalent, since the ratio of the marginal utilities of any two commodities for transactor one were translated into the equivalent ratio for transactors two, three, and so on. The innovation vis-à-vis classical value theory was that the translations were generally nonlinear in value terms.

The full rationale for the law of one price was never mooted along these lines, needless to say. The neoclassicals' ambivalence concerning the measurability of utility/energy caused them to deny that any interpersonal comparisons of utility were needed in their theory. Instead, the law of one price was treated as if it were the very definition of perfect competition in a market, although this completely misrepresented the classical theory of competition (Dennis 1977). It was asserted that the existence of two different prices for the same generic commodities in the same market would imply that there were arbitrary gains to be made, and that the price differential would be traded away until one price was restored. This seemingly plausible rationale was so bound up with the metaphor of a conservative vector field that to try to sort it out took many years and much ink.

Its primary flaw was the lack of any plausible specification of how the activity of trading was prosecuted, so that realized prices (as opposed to virtual or notional prices) were uniquely equalized. It is important to recall that utility is a virtual concept, prior to any activity of trade. If the notional calculation of utility allows differential pricing, there is no plausible reason why anyone would acquiesce in the law of one price. In mechanics, forces are not explained; in the economic analogue, prices are not explained, but merely treated as given by the transactors, encouraging a debilitatingly passive interpretation of "competition." Certainly the notion of a unique general equilibrium would be compromised by the existence of strategic considerations, as demonstrated in the later development of game theory. Its next significant flaw was the singular absence of any specification of the institutional structure of the market, so that any price divergence could be rationalized in a post hoc manner by claiming that the apparent previous identity of the generic commodities was spurious, due to some overlooked characteristic or factor, or due to some ill-specified market power. The third flaw was the reliance upon a dynamic arbitrage argument in the context of a static optimization framework in which aggregate utility could, in many cases, be higher if the law of one price were relaxed. The fourth, and most fundamental flaw, was the absence of a reconciliation between the particular subjective conceptions of the commodity and the purportedly objective specifications of its generic identity (Mirowski 1986). All of these controversies served to distract attention from the real function of the law of one price, which was to consolidate the various utility fields into a single metric of value. It was akin to the economists having their cake and eating it too: value was defined as an equivalence relation – or as Edgeworth (1925, II, p. 274) put it, "It is not so much political arithmetic as economic algebra" – and simultaneously it was claimed that equivalence was irrelevant and unnecessary for economic analysis.

Equilibrium

The very term "equilibrium" unabashedly reveals the heritage of physical analogy, so it should not be surprising that a metamorphosis in the physical theory would result in a parallel metamorphosis in the conception of economic equilibrium. Recently, in reaction to histories of economic thought that foster the impression that Adam Smith and Paul Samuelson share the same notion of price determination, Pierangelo Garegnani (1976) has argued that there was a sharp discontinuity between classical and neoclassical economics in the notion of equilibrium. He claims that the classical paradigm of equilibrium was a center-of-gravity concept, where market price was drawn to a natural price whose determinants were predominantly physical; whereas neoclassical economics eventually settled upon a paradigm of temporary equilibrium, a sequence of market-clearing prices that do not display any stability over time. Garegnani has asserted that this relatively unconscious metamorphosis was a defensive response to neoclassical problems in the theory of capital. His thesis is very intriguing, but incomplete, because it does not examine the critical role played by the physical metaphor in the change in the notion of equilibrium. (The specific interaction of the theory of capital and the theory of value will be considered in the next chapter.)

Classical notions of equilibrium conformed to the imperatives of value as substance. Equilibrium in exchange was the trade of equivalent substance for equivalent substance. Equilibrium in production was an equalized rate of growth of the value substance, in the guise of an equalized rate of profit. These two conditions jointly defined natural price. Physics metaphors served a dual purpose here: First, the determinants of natural price were generally physical in nature, and were kept discrete from social variables, which only influenced market price; second, the classical economists used the words "center of gravity" to describe the relationship between natural price and market price. The latter gambit was misleading, because classical economists never used any physical theory of gravitation to actively structure their analogy: not Cartesian impact, not Newtonian action at a distance, nor early proto-field concepts. If anything, the loose implicit comparison seemed to be with hydrostatics (Edgeworth 1925, II, p. 280): If the market price diverged from natural price due to some social change, this would be made manifest by a lack of equivalence in rates of profit and rates of exchange, and resources would flow from low-profit to high-profit industries until equivalence was restored. Because of the necessary interaction of production and exchange in the operation of the response mechanism, the classical notion of equilibrium was not predicated upon market clearing, nor upon the law of one price.

Given that there have been a plethora of attempts to make nineteenth-century classical economic theory lie down on the Procrustean bed of twentieth-century mathematical models,[7] this point deserves some emphasis. Because classical substance theories posited that value was conserved in exchange, exchange value persisted through time, and thus there was no logical imperative that markets be cleared in equilibrium. The accumulation or decumulation of inventories could be consistent with the exchange of equivalent substances; or, alternatively, individual generic units of a commodity might not all trade at the same ratio, but equilibrium might be preserved if the aggregate of embodied value substance were equal to the aggregate of value substance tendered in exchange. The persistence of the value substance through time left many useful degrees of freedom in the exact configuration of the theory of equivalence. As we have already observed, classical economics was in possession of a separate theory of psychology that served to explain when a transactor would participate in the market and when she would abstain. In direct contrast with the later neoclassical theory, the commodities themselves were not endowed with an inherent necessity to be traded at a particular point in time, nor was the transactor analytically forced to acquiesce in a price reigning in a particular market at a particular point in time.[8]

The classical appeal to physical analogy without elaboration of the underlying components of the metaphor led to certain inconsistences, inconsistencies that the neoclassicals were quick to turn to their advantage. The continual classical invocation of science was embarrassed by a lack of participation in the mathematical trappings of science. Among other consequences, this resulted in the absence of any cogent explanation of why market price must necessarily gravitate to natural price, if market price is conceptualized as the resultant of the vagaries of supply and demand: the idiosyncratic presence or absence of an appropriately constituted conjunction of willing buyers and well-stocked sellers (Levine 1980). Another consequence was that the quarantine of the physical determinants of the natural price and the social determinants of market price was breached in practice in the elaboration of classical doctrine: subsistence wages were allowed to possess cultural determinants, mercantile and distributive functions were incorporated as productive, and government taxation became an intermediate case. This raised the specter that market trades might feed back upon the determinants of natural price, and that there might not exist a stable natural price toward which market price might gravitate, because the two fluctuated in tandem.

Neoclassical economics resolved the conundrum by collapsing natural price into market price. The Marginalist Revolution preempted all talk of gravitational metaphors by appropriating the actual mathematical model from physics. Natural price was redefined to be the equilibrium concept in the energetics model, and market price was redefined to be the price that would clear a market at a single point in time. By choosing a static physics model of equilibrium, and avoiding the physical dynamics, the two were conflated and made identical. The market-clearing condition and the law of one price became inseparable in the definition of equilibrium, because without the law of one price, the market-clearing price vector could never be unique. However, the simultaneous imposition of these two conditions destroyed all the previous intemporal links of economic equilibrium: Transactors were not allowed to hold stocks of inventories except for personal consumption; transactors were lobotomized into passively accepting a single price in a market at a point in time; and, as we shall discuss in the next section and in Chapters 6 and 7, outrageously rococo and inconsistent contraptions were postulated to explain out-of-equilibrium behavior.

In a field theory of value, the only phenomenon that can be said to persist through time is the psychology of the transactors; but the first two generations of neoclassicals backed away from any analysis of this persistence as part of their larger self-denying ordinance with respect to psychology. Later, neoclassical economics was said to conform to a supposed sequence of timeless yet somehow temporary equilibria whose interrelation was tenuous – beads on a very unsubstantial string. Many later-twentieth-century neoclassical economists have come to be dissatisfied with the newer equilibrium concept (Hicks 1979; Shackle 1967), but their attempts to ameliorate the situation have failed, largely because they themselves did not understand the fundamental connections between the physical analogy and the entire structure of neoclassical theory. The structure of explanation encapsulated in the physical model could not, and cannot, be simply wished away with impunity.

Finally, the collapse of natural price to market price was rendered acceptable by the earlier reconceptualization of Nature herself as a niggardly paymaster – that is, with the rise of the idea that Nature kept her own set of energy accounts, as described in Chapter 3. Prior to that time, scarcity as some sort of primordial state of mankind did *not* play any significant role in the value theory of classical political economy (Brown 1987). Only with the dominant impression that Nature enforced a general state of dearth, say, rather than the physiocratic notion of Nature's bounty, could it become possible to even think of economic equilibrium as a state of psychological counterpoise, hemmed in by the urgent necessity to clear markets in a state of stringent limitations.

The sciences were never at war?

It would have been extraordinary for so many economists to mangle and misrepresent the energy model so frequently without eventually calling down the wrath of physicists upon their labors. Indeed, one of the skeletons in the neoclassical closet is that around the turn of the century, quite a number of competent physicists turned their attention to this species of upstart proto-energetics and pronounced it wanting (Ingrao and Israel, 1985). It should come as no surprise that their most stinging barbs took the form of criticisms of the misrepresentation of the energy concept itself and the incongruous silence concerning conservation principles. While the ideology of science declares the sciences were never at war, the early neoclassicals who bore the brunt of the physicists' slings and arrows certainly did not end up feeling that way. Time and again they met these inquisitions with hurt incomprehension, bluster, farrago, protests that the physics was irrelevant, and finally, a feeling of betrayal: How did it come to pass that those in the forefront of trying to make economics a science should be so abused by those whom they were only trying to emulate?

The first instance of such a confrontation was the review by Joseph Bertrand of Cournot's *Recherches* and Walras' *Théorie Mathématique de la Richesse Sociale,* which was a compilation of Walras's previously published journal articles (Bertrand 1883). Bertrand was well placed to comprehend the scientific pretensions of the fledgling science: a product of the Ecole Polytechnique, professor at the Collège de France, a specialist in the mathematics of rational mechanics and the editor of the third edition of Lagrange's *Mécanique Analytique.* Most of his review centered on the thesis that the neglect of mathematical political economy in the French academy had been deserved, because the existing attempts had been devoid of any serious empirical content, not to mention their numerous mathematical and conceptual errors. While the preponderance of the review was devoted to Cournot, Bertrand also offered two critiques of Walras's general approach.

In the first, Bertrand observed that in general there would exist what in the modern literature is called false trading – namely, some exchanges are conducted at nonequilibrium prices in the process of trying to discover the market-clearing price. Bertrand pointed out, quite correctly, that the mere existence of false trading, or indeed any mercantile speculation, would obviate the determinacy of Walras's general equilibrium. It is noteworthy that here Bertrand homed in directly on the one emendation that the neoclassicals had made to the proto-energetics model – the law of one price – and demonstrated that it rendered the rest of the model a poor analogy for market activity. Bertrand's second critique centered on the putative path-independence of utility or *rareté.* He suggested that if all actors traded only according to the independently given utility functions, that would give one result, but if they calculated gain and loss over time in price terms, that would give entirely another result. Although he did not phrase it precisely in these terms, this clearly was the tentative probe of the sore spot of conservation principles.

The story of the hostility of the French academic establishment to neoclassical economics is often told as a moral tale of ignorance and backwardness, but as usual, this was not the way things were perceived at the time. Bertrand's critiques were felt to be devastating in fin de siècle France, regularly quoted, and thought to justify the rebuff of Walrasian economics (Bouvier 1901a, 1901b; Zoretti 1906; Boninsegni 1903). The situation was not helped by the fact that Cournot (having died in 1877) could not retort, and Walras never directly answered the criticisms; however, we shall observe below that Bertrand's barb did have a profound impact upon the fourth edition of the *Elements of Pure Economics* (Walras 1954).

We conjecture that the second skirmish probably occurred with

Fisher's thesis in 1892 (Wilson 1912, p. 467). His thesis advisor, J. Willard Gibbs, undoubtedly asked Fisher why Fisher's indifference lines should be able to be integrated into utility surfaces. Far from being a minor technical complaint, Gibbs probably tried to make Fisher aware that the absence of integrability would necessarily mean that there could exist no such quantity as total utility, and path-independence of equilibrium would be compromised. Fisher acknowledged such a possibility in his thesis, and then proceeded to claim that the integrability conditions were entirely inessential (Fisher 1926, p. 89). Perhaps the elder statesman of neoclassical economics felt less confident about this dismissal than the impetuous young thesis candidate: In his retrospective manuscript "My Economic Endeavors" Fisher crossed out the section containing this comment, leaving out of the text all discussions of integrability.[9]

Fisher *never* wrote down condition (5.4) in any of his work, and therefore it is a bit of a sham to credit him with any contribution to the problem of integrability. Fisher's stock reaction to problems of conservative entities within his economic theories was simply to deny the possibility of any serious dynamic theory (p. 104). What he apparently never understood was that Gibbs wanted to know why Fisher did not explore integrability as the next logical step towards a dynamic theory of optimization: Hamiltonians are solved for conservative integrable systems. Fisher, uncomprehending, instead went on to say that he did not need integrability for his theory, and indeed, he did not need utility, period. This statement only served to demonstrate that he was out of his depth. We can date the collective neoclassical neurosis with regard to the physics metaphor from this point.

The third instance of a scientist harassing the new economic science came in 1898, close on the heels of the second. Hermann Laurent, a mathematician at the Ecole Polytechnique and the author of a textbook on rational mechanics (Laurent 1870) as well as treatises on statistics and actuarial science, wrote to Walras about some things, as he later put it, "ce qui choquera un peu moins les mathématiciens purs" [which won't shock pure mathematicians quite so much] (Walras 1965, III, p. 116). Laurent queried Walras on 29 November 1898 as to the appropriate unit of value (Walras 1965, III, letter 1374, pp. 40–1). Walras, after trying to fob him off with compliments, responded by repeating of the thesis in the *Elements* that it is not proper to speak of a unit of value, only an arbitrary *numéraire* (Walras 1965, III, letter 1377). Laurent, a little perturbed at being patronized, wrote back that he was asking about *dynamics* and the essential role of time, but that Walras had only responded with a static argument (letter 1378). Walras, himself getting a little flustered, then accused Laurent of conceptualizing value as an absolute magnitude, in analogy with certain physical magnitudes such as length, weight, and force. He wrote, "A vrai dire, vous tendez à identifier purement et simplement la valeur et la force en prenant pour unité de valeur la valeur de l'unité de force." [To tell the truth, you purely and simply tend to identify value and force by taking as the unit of value the valve of the unit of force] (pp. 47–8). This, of course, began to get at the issue of the analogy to energy invariance. Walras in return went on to say that he thought of value as a magnitude sui generis, and did not expect that there existed any unit of value which was constant over time and space.

Laurent, by this time, was beginning to wonder whether Walras was just playing dumb, was being obstreperous, or perhaps simply did not understand the physics (letter 1380). As might be expected, the correspondance concerning value theory then cooled for a while, but upon a friendly letter from Walras a year later, Laurent decided to try one more time. This letter of 13 May 1900 (letter 1452) is a miracle of compression and lucidity. Laurent wrote [my translation]:

> Let $dq_1, dq_2, \ldots, dq_N$ be quantities of merchandise $A_1, A_2, \ldots, A_N$ consumed during time dt. Their total price is
>
> (1) $p_1 dq_1 + p_2 dq_2 + \cdots + p_N dq_N$
>
> where p_i designates the price of a unit of q_i. If one accepts that there is a standard of measure for utility, then one must also accept that expression (1) is integrable after having multiplied by a factor μ, if it is an exact differential. Then one posits
>
> (2) $d\phi = \mu[p_1 dq_1 + p_2 dq_2 + \cdots]$
>
> and
>
> $$\frac{d\phi}{dq_1} = \mu p_1; \quad \frac{d\phi}{dq_2} = \mu p_2; \quad \ldots$$
>
> and hence these derivatives are proportional to the prices, such that one would be able to call the *raretés* of $A_1, A_2, \ldots$ the partial integrals
>
> $$\int \frac{d\phi}{dq_1}, \ldots$$
>
> which will be the utilities. But there is one difficulty: the measure of *rareté* depends on the factor μ. One could respond that it is just a matter of definition, but that does not mean it is any less interesting to interpret the significance of the factors of integration. If the

differential equation (1) is null then the function ϕ is constant, and after our hypothesis, will there exist *one* relationship between prices and the quantities consumed?

Recall that asking if (1) was an exact differential equation was the same as asking if conditions (5.2) and (5.4) would hold; that is, are we dealing with a conservative vector field?

This threw Walras into a tizzy. In a reply dated 22 May 1900 he compared his work to that of the early progenitors of the calculus, who knew their technique worked, although they were unsure of its principles. Then he insisted that there were other economists who were also good mathematicians (such as "Bortkevitch, Pareto, and Barone"), who also started from the same point of departure without quibbling about these issues and such consensus was rare. (He seemed to be implying that there was safety in numbers.) He then proceeded to reveal his dishabille with regard to the mathematics by suggesting that the integrating factor is equal to the ratios of marginal utility to price, and to rewrite Laurent's equation (1) as a system of individual demand and supply equations. Finally, he reiterated that he did not see any need for a standard or measure of utility (Walras 1965, III, letter 1454).

Amazingly, Laurent doggedly tried one more time, on 24 May 1900, writing that Walras still had not answered his question. Patiently he asked: Why is equation (1) an exact differential, and what is the economic interpretation of the factor of integration? (letter 1455). Exhausted, Walras entirely ignored the question about the exact differential and responded by shifting his premises, insisting that the integrating factor is the marginal utility of the numéraire; he claimed that this was similar to Marshall's discussion of the marginal utility of money (letter 1456). From this point on, Walras started suggesting to others that Laurent was part of a plot against him (letter 1469). Both sides then retired to nurse their bruised egos, and Walras in particular his "tête assez sérieusement malade" [his harrowing headache] (p. 132), never to correspond again concerning this issue.

Because of his avid devotion to getting the content of the physical metaphor correctly specified, Laurent should be considered one of the unsung heroes of neoclassical economic theory. Strange at it may seem, Laurent thought of himself as a supporter of the Lausanne school of economics throughout the entire episode. So just when the Walras correspondence looked to him as if it was going nowhere, he decided to try one of the neoclassicals who might possess a little better comprehension of the issues involved. In an effort clearly above and beyond the call of duty, early in 1899 he composed a number of letters to Vilfredo Pareto, essentially posing the same queries.[10] Pareto's first response was to praise Laurent's mathematical textbooks, and insist that it gave him great pleasure (in his own words, "for the first time") to discuss these questions with a person well versed in mathematics. He then tendered his stock answer: It was not a question of utility being numerically measurable, it was only a rank ordering of greater or less. In the next paragraph, there appeared a jolting non sequitur, in which he stated that the "general economic problem" is to take the prices in equation (1) as variables, and not as constants. If this is the case, pleasure or utility will depend upon the order of consumption. But, he concludes, we can usually ignore this case (Chipman 1976, p. 47).

Laurent must have been perplexed by this further indication of erratic behavior on the part of the avatars of economic mechanics and rational economic man. Not only was Pareto's letter internally inconsistent, it resembled Walras's responses only in its cavalier assertions that the problem was insignificant; yet their respective understandings of the problem had no relation one to another, and worse, both had no connection to the obvious physics metaphor. Laurent chose to press the inquiry with greater insistence, to which Pareto replied with a wholly different defense.

Pareto began by agreeing with Laurent that one can only measure that which is susceptible to being added and equalized. However, Pareto then admitted that pleasure was not susceptible to addition or equalization. This was not a crippling admission, he suggested, because in their early stages all the sciences pretended to measure what was not measurable. There then followed a thoroughly awkward comparison of economics with geometry (Chipman 1976, p. 48). Realizing belatedly that this analogy wanders into a *cul-de-sac,* Pareto then sought refuge in another non sequitur. Shifting gears, he decided that Laurent had mistakenly attempted to derive equilibrium from the single equation (1), whereas both equations (1) and (2) were required to locate equilibrium.

At this point, one is at a loss as to why Laurent wanted to pursue the matter any further, but, as Pareto would undoubtedly say, *chacun à son goût.* Pareto's next letter is more than a little testy, and at one stage he writes, "What you say about the habits of pure mathematics doesn't bother me" (Chipman 1976, p. 56), perhaps reevaluating the joys of a friendly chat with relentlessly logical mathematicians. (We remind the reader that at this same time, Pareto was attempting to intimidate other social theorists, such as Croce, with the supposed precision of his mathematical science.) In the last letter, Pareto tangles himself up further by (a) taking the position that there is no reason to integrate equation (1), since it is merely a budget constraint, and (b) denying that the integral of equation (2) is what he meant by utility (or, in his redundant terminology, *ophelimité*). He then tried to drive this point home by an illustration of the derivation of prices in a two-good system. Of course, the retreat to the two-good model only more clearly displayed Pareto's incomprehension of what was at issue, since the question of integrability only arises in the case of three or more goods.

Chipman (1976, pp. 42–3) has attempted to defend Pareto in this little contretemps by suggesting that it was Laurent who confused the indifference curves with the budget constraint, equation (1). According to Chipman, one should not worry about integrating the budget constraint, because it is always susceptible to summing by definition and in any event is denominated in money, not utility. This retort thoroughly misunderstands the thrust of Laurent's inquiry. The points he was trying to get across were: (a) did price vectors generally conform to the conditions for a conservative vector field, namely, (5.1) through (5.5); (b) without the law of one price, the prohibition of false trading, and a host of other auxiliary conditions, wouldn't the budget constraint end up as not integrable; and (c), if the energetics metaphor were to be valid, the integral of the budget is directly linked to the integral of utility (or *rareté*, or ophelimity, or any of the other redundant euphemisms) through the instrumentality of the conservation principles – In this case, that money is directly transformable into utility in a linear fashion through the integration constant. The explanation of this failure of communication is straightforward: Laurent understood the physics, and Pareto did not.[11]

Perhaps the most incongruous aspect of this particular episode is that Laurent persisted in seeing himself as a partisan of the Lausanne school of mathematical economics. In 1902 he published his *Petit traité d'économie politique mathématique*, which was little more than a pastiche of brief observations on a sequence of mathematical models; nevertheless, it was written with the intention of defending the Walrasian program. Curiously enough, the section on price theory merely recapitulates the contents of his letters cited in this section, minus the parts questioning why equation (1) is an exact differential. His questions along those lines were never adequately answered by the protagonists, and so it appears he just passed them by in his own treatise. Reading between the lines, however, we can discern that he does offer two hints about conservation principles. The first shows that equilibrium at a point in time outside of a Robinson Crusoe world requires the further condition that $\Sigma dq_a = 0$, $\Sigma dq_b = 0$, and so forth, which we would now recognize as "Walras's Law"; a better way of stating it would be that motion in commodity space is a zero-sum game and hence path-independent (Laurent 1902, pp. 10–11). Second, he observes that enjoyment of goods must be independent of time, which we could restate as the condition that the utility function is itself conserved. Here Laurent was one of the earliest, along with Antonelli, to anticipate later neoclassical attempts to simulate the energy-conservation condition by means of an ensemble of auxiliary hypotheses. Finally, in a very brief section, Laurent noted, "There exist between economic facts and those of rational mechanics some analogues which we merely point to without drawing any conclusions" (Laurent 1902, p. 19).[12]

The fourth instance of a scientist taking a neoclassical economist to task was Vito Volterra's 1906 review of Pareto's *Manuale di Economia Politica* (in Chipman et al. 1971, pp. 365–9). The complaint was the same: The mathematics of fields should be used in economics only with caution. Volterra warned that when there are more than two goods, Pareto's expression, which was identical to Laurent's equation (1), would not necesarily be integrable. By 1906 this must have seemed as a déjà vu to Pareto. Moreover, by that time he must have reconsidered his retorts to Laurent, because he relinquished all his later defenses, and returned to his immediate reaction to Laurent's first inquiry: All the fuss must be about the problem of utility depending upon the order in which goods are consumed. This was the gist of his article on "Open and Closed Cycles of Ophelimity," in the *Giornale degli Economisti* in 1906, which was intended as a public reply to Volterra's relatively gentle criticism (in Chipman et al. 1971, pp. 370–85).

The terminology of open and closed cyles reveals that Pareto had begun to grasp what was at issue, namely condition (5.2), although we shall see that he never completely understood or felt comfortable with the critics' concerns or his own replies. The terminology of open and closed cycles, which as appeared so incomprehensible to Pareto's later partisans (see Chipman et al. 1971, p. 324), was intended to evoke the open and closed cycles of the work integral, and thus to directly admit the analogy of energy and utility. In a closed cycle the initial and final states of a system are independent of path; in mechanics, this is isomorphic to a statement of the conservation of energy.

It is not to Pareto's credit that he took the metaphor of a path too literally, associating it with the effect of the temporal order of consumption of particular commodities. His example of the order of consumption of soup and roast beef made the problem sound trivial, an opinion he himself expressed in the first page of the paper. The triviality of the problem derived from Pareto's interpretation, however, and not from the intrinsic character of the problem. In a field theory of value, the actual act of consumption is supposed to be irrelevant to the magnitude of the utility derived from the good, because utility is a virtual notion. Hence, temporal problems of the sequence of consumption are rendered meaningless. Further, we have already observed that neoclassical equilibrium was, of necessity, a static conception, which ruled the passage of time out of consideration. This was well understood by the more sophisticated neoclassicals at the turn of the century. Fisher, for instance, wrote that "total utility is not an experience in time but the sum of increments of utility substitutionally successive . . . the marginal utility to a given individual of a given commodity is the same at all instants at which he buys or consumes it or sells or produces it" (Fisher 1926, p. 19). Hence, in the eyes or most of his contemporaries, Pareto was discussing a nonproblem. It did not help matters that he spent most of his time on a two-good example, when the integrability problem only mathematically arises with three or more goods.

The history of the integrability problem in neoclassical economics is an extremely peculiar interlude. Around the turn of the century, some major figures in neoclassical thought were challenged by some even greater luminaries in the scientific community, and, to a man, they acquitted themselves abysmally. It should have been all the more humiliating since an obscure Italian engineer (Giovanni Antonelli) had already gotten the technical mathematics right (for Antonelli's 1886 work see Chipman et al. 1971, pp. 333–63). Yet the prognostications of Antonelli and Laurent, and indeed, all the embarrassing inquisitions by natural scientists, were forgotten, at least until the 1930s – it was as if it all had never happened. The revival of interest in this problem in the 1930s will be described in the next chapter; for now, our concern is simply to relate this odd fact to the adoption of a field theory of value.

What happened around the turn of the century was really quite simple. A number of mathematicians and scientists stumbled upon some of the writings of the early neoclassicals and immediately apprehended what was going on: These economists were calling energy "utility." Their reaction was to try to see if these economists were merely using the physical mathematics to browbeat and hoodwink their colleagues, or if there actually were legitimate parallels in the two traditions. With their background in the physical sciences, they knew what the really critical attributes of the energy concept were: Was it conserved in a closed system? Was it the core concept in a Hamiltonian-style dynamics? Was it a variable of state, which would then suggest various procedures for its empirical examination? Were prices the gradient of a conservative potential field? These are the questions they asked, but they phrased them in shorthand terms, as would one mathematician to another: Why is equation (1) an exact differential? Why should we expect utility to be integrable, and what is the interpretation of the integrating factor? As we have observed, these questions were met with defensiveness, incomprehension, and farrago. The fact was that all the progenitors of neoclassical economics had been trained as engineers, but their grasp of physics was shallow and superficial. And these were the same individuals who insisted that economics must become a mathematical science in order to instill some discipline and clarity of thought.

The problem of integrability, far from being merely an arcane game played by a small coterie of mathematicians, was (and still is) the key to the understanding and evaluation of the neoclassical cooptation of the physics metaphor. The early progenitors of neoclassicism liked the analogy of utility as energy, but could not be bothered to examine the analogy in sufficient detail to evaluate rationally its strengths and drawbacks. One facet of the analogy from which they persistently averted their gaze was the principle of the conservation of energy, even though that principle was the single most important unifying concept in physics in the third quarter of the nineteenth century. The reason they shunned the concept (when they understood it) is that, as we have seen, the metaphor implied that the sum of utility (the potential energy) and expenditure (the kinetic energy) should remain a constant. Not only was this repugnant and absurd on the face of it, but it also harbored a deeper meaning, one that could potentially undermine the entire neoclassical research program.

The overall thrust of the emulation of physics by economics was to discover the hidden fundamental natural determinants of value that lay behind the veil of everyday phenomena of money prices and incomes. Utility as a field of scalar potentials fit that pattern quite nicely, but the physics metaphor did not stop there. A potential field should have been coupled with a well-defined set of transformation algorithms into kinetic forces, because the field and the forces were just two aspects of the same ontological thing. Strictly and logically interpreted, the analogy would thus suggest that money and utility were the same ontological thing. Even worse, because most newcomers to neoclassicism found it difficult to believe that utility actually existed, would it not have seemed superfluous and redundant to have based a new theory of value upon an intangible and unobservable eidolon, when the other legitimate metric of value was reassuringly tangible, nestled in everyone's pockets?

At the turn of the century and subsequently, many economists who did not know that neoclassicism was reprocessed physics felt that they could assume that money and/or income possessed a constant marginal utility (Marshall 1920, p. 842). Little did they realize that they were simply completing the original physical metaphor by imposing the conservation of energy through the condition that money and utility were identical. Some pointed out that this assumption imposed stringent restrictions on the utility function (Samuelson 1942), but what they did not add was that it rendered the whole contraption of the utility function redundant, because money provided the unique and sufficient direct cardinal measure of utility in that regime. The same comment applies to the habit of interpreting the integrating factor of the differential equation (1) as the Marginal utility of money. This explains why the natural-science critics of early neoclassicism were so insistent upon specifying the interpretation of the integrating factor – if some such constant existed, then the empirical implementation of the physical metaphor would hold some promise, because that aspect of value would have some empirical regularity and stability. Of course, those scientists had no way of knowing that they were prodding a sore spot of the appropriated physics model: If money was a sufficient and credible measure of value, then the whole project of a science-based value theory, which aimed to uncover the fundamental lawlike reality obscured by the blooming buzzing phenomenological diversity, was superfluous.

The question of the extension of the physics metaphor to encompass Hamiltonian dynamics merged all the critical issues of time, process, conservation principles, and integrability into a single, seemingly technical issue. A genuinely rigorous response to this question would by its very nature need to incorporate an evaluation of the suitability of the energetics metaphor to describe social processes. For whatever reasons, neoclassicals have avoided this extension and its attendant evaluation whenever possible. Instead, they have gone out of their way to concoct jerry-built scenarios of dynamic movements between the static equilibria identified by the primitive physics model. Jevons invented a black box, called a "trading body," which magically performed all the dynamic functions of coordination in an unspecified manner (Jevons 1970, pp. 135–8). Walras posited his famous auctioneer, who prevented all trading activity while potential transactors resorted to hypothetical questions about their utility fields. Others attempted a pseudodynamics predicated upon the difference between demand and supply functions, piling one Rube Goldberg contraption atop another. The purpose of all these contrived schemes was to circumvent the dynamics constructed by the physicists within the logic of the appropriated physics model.

Donald Walker has recently shown that, in the case of Walras, the encounter with the physicists plunged the neoclassical general equilibrium model into worse confusion (Walker 1987a). He points out that the first three editions of Walras's *Elements* attempt to construct a model of economic dynamics where purchases of inputs and production of commodities actually occur through time as part of a mechanism of equilibration. However, in the (fourth) edition of 1900 – that is, after Bertrand's blast and Laurent's needling – Walras switched to a different model of *bons* or "pledges," one in which everything is coordinated on paper prior to any and all economic activity: Everything is irredeemably static, trying to make a virtue out of a necessity. This later version, of course, is the one that does not violate the proto-energetics model, because all trades are virtual, ensuring that conservation principles are avoided; this version, of course, is the progenitor of the twentieth-century Arrow–Debreu model. The one unfortunate aspect of all this, however, is that Walras himself never really understood that the problem was one of path-dependence and thus violation of the original energy metaphor; he therefore merely forced the pledges model into the structure of the *Elements* without eliminating or revising the older theorizing that contradicted it (Walker 1987a). As a consequence, generations of neoclassical theorists have felt free to assert anything they pleased about the dynamics of their model, without understanding that their freedom was spurious.

What would the suppressed but valid neoclassical Hamiltonian dynamics have looked like? There would first be the problem that the Hamiltonian formalism is expressed in the format of generalized coordinates. A system with S individuals and N commodities has SN degrees of freedom, which can be reduced to $SN - k$ by the explicit incorporation of the k constraints into the coordinate system. Hence the variables expressing the quantities q_i of the N commodities would be rewritten as functions of the new, artificial coordinates $a_1, a_2, \ldots, a_{N-k}$ and time:

(5.8) $q_1 = q_1(a_1, a_2, \ldots, a_{N-k}, t)$
$q_2 = q_2(a_1, a_2, \ldots, a_{N-k}, t)$
$\vdots$
$q_N = q_N(a_1, a_2, \ldots, a_{N-k}, t)$

These generalized commodity coordinates are somewhat opaque, in that they have no immediate intuitive interpretation; that is, their dimensions are no longer the physical amounts of any particular commodity.[13] Their primary purpose is to make it easier to write down the Hamiltonian equation:

(5.9) $H = E(b_1, b_2, \ldots, b_{N-k}) + V(a_1, a_2, \ldots, a_{N-k})$

Here the b's can be interpreted as generalized prices associated with the ith generalized commodity coordinate. (The analogies with the physics are: The a's are generalized spatial coordinates, and the b's are generalized momenta). Knowledge of the Hamiltonian equation in the most general sense is knowledge of the future evolution of the system. The laws of dynamics are expressed by Hamilton's equations:

(5.10) $\dfrac{db_i}{dt} = -\dfrac{\partial H}{\partial a_i}$ and $\dfrac{da_i}{dt} = \dfrac{\partial H}{\partial b_i}$ $i = 1, \ldots, N-k$

At this juncture, considerations of conservation principles and integrability would enter the picture in a decisive fashion. In physics, the purpose of rewriting the coordinates in a generalized format is so that the Hamiltonian equation (5.9) can be written in the two separable parts: E and V. If energy is conserved in the system, the first part E is interpreted as the kinetic energy, depending only on momenta; and the second part V is the potential energy, depending only upon position. Hence the Hamiltonian is equal to the total energy of the system, which is a constant. A major obstacle to importing the Hamiltonian into neoclassical economics is that the parallel conservation of expenditure plus utility would be blatantly obvious whenever anyone wrote out equation (5.9).

It comes as somewhat of a surprise to find that the "Antonelli conditions" for integrability, frequently cited in the twentieth-century literature (Samuelson 1950; Chipman et al. 1971, p. 347) are nothing more than the conditions for the separability of the Hamiltonian (5.9), augmented with some specification of the law of one price. Indeed, in the more familiar guise of the Slutsky equations, condition (5.4) is regularly imposed without comment in modern neoclassical textbooks. If we just extend the stipulation to time invariance, that would suffice to get us condition (5.9), with the framework for a true neoclassical Hamiltonian dynamics. In other words, under the guise of a merely technical mathematical condition, the assumption of integrability is a surreptitious reimposition of the conservation of expenditure plus utility, as well as the imposition of the conditions for a Hamiltonian dynamics *over and above* any other postulated mechanism for the convergence of prices to equilibrium over time. So much for the bracing influence of mathematical formalism upon the communication of assumptions.

Walras, Jevons, Menger

Only after absorbing the relevant background just provided can we now finally evaluate the biographical particulars of the premier troika of the Marginalist Revolution: Léon Walras, William Stanley Jevons, and Carl Menger. The reason for so much preparation is that, just as in the case of the "simultaneous discoveries" of Helmholtz, Mayer, Joule, and Colding, a close reading of their accomplishments reveals that they did not all "discover" the same thing; more disturbing, no one of them really managed to enunciate the full system that was only retrospectively attributed to them. Yet here there is a marked divergence from the parallel paradigm of "simultaneous discovery" in physics: At least the favored four of physics demonstrated appreciable originality, whereas the economic troika was highly derivative. More important, the level of competence in physics among the troika left so much to be desired that much of the work of the next two generations of neoclassicals consisted of sifting the proto-energetics model back out of the original texts and elevating the formalism of the field to pride of place in value theory.

It is of paramount importance to keep in mind that the proto-energetics model was the physics of energy minus all later developments such as the second law of thermodynamics, relativistic invariants, and so on. As such, it was mostly comprised of rational mechanics and hydrodynamics characteristic of the eighteenth century, even though the *metaphorical* content of energy and fields was only generated in the middle of the nineteenth century. Hence it was entirely possible to be attracted to the metaphorical content of proto-energetics and yet have only a sketchy background in the mathematical formalisms of variational principles and conservation principles and in the formalisms of the field; in the early stages one could get by with dribs and drabs of mechanics and a smattering of calculus if one were inclined to imitate physics, especially if one's audience was paralyzed by the mere suggestion of algebra. This was the case with two out of three of the marginalist troika.

The most obvious and straightforward case is that of the most respected of neoclassical progenitors, Léon Walras. William Jaffe tells us that "after twice failing these [entrance] exams, he was finally admitted upon examination to the Paris School of Mines, [and yet] he still knew nothing about the extreme values of functions . . . After that, as he himself acknowledged, he spent his time reading about the history of calculus instead of working out its problems. He could hardly have learned anything more at the School of Mines, where he was student in name only" (in Black et al. 1973, p. 133). It seems that only later in life, around 1860, did Walras conceive a desire to create a scientific economics, probably at the behest of his father. It was Auguste Walras who had searched for a way to reconcile value with the new metaphors of motion: "Just as speed is the ratio of distance covered to the time taken to cover it, so *rareté* is a ratio of the sum of wants to the total supply of goods available to gratify the wants" (in Black et al. 1973, p. 123). Walras *père's* attempts at value theory were unavailing – he knew no mathematics to speak of – and the prognosis was not all that much more optimistic for the son, whose grasp of mathematics was never formidable and whose acquaintance with physics remained rudimentary.

In his first effort to mathematicize his father's concept of *rareté* in 1860, Walras attempted to implement a Newtonian model of market relations, postulating that the "price of things is in inverse ratio to the quantity offered and in direct ratio to the quantity demanded" (Walras 1965, I, pp. 216–17), the very proposition Cournot had disparaged as meaningless. One observes here an attempt to appropriate the Newtonian force law $F = G(m_1m_2/r^2)$; more important, one observes Walras rummaging through the schoolboy formulas of his youth trying to relate force to price. It is a reproof to all those who insist that neoclassical theory is Newtonian that Walras simply got tangled in the algebra; as Jaffe notes, it was a "sorry performance" (in Black et al. 1973, p. 126). Nevertheless, Walras did not give up, and the motivation that kept him going was not the specific ideas expressed in any particular model, but rather the ideal of the imitation of physics. One observes this, for instance, in his letter of 23 December 1862 to Jules du Mesnil-Marigny, pleading for financial support to develop "an original creation," a "new science . . . a science of economic forces analogous to the science of astronomical forces . . . The analogy is complete and striking" (Walras 1965, I, pp. 119–20).

There was more than a little bravado in this promise, since by that time he had gotten nowhere with the Newtonian force law. Jaffe suggests that a later reading of Isnard inspired Walras with the notion of the general equilibrium of prices, but all that constituted was the algebraic solution of a set of linear equations, similar to a Leontief system, consistent with a substance theory of value (see Chapter 6). Walras was no closer to his promised force analogy in January 1872 than he had been twelve years earlier (Black et al. 1973, p. 128). No model involved the constrained maximization of utility, or even the calculus, until the late autumn of 1872.

At that time, an engineer and professor of mechanics at the Academy of Lausanne, Antoine Paul Piccard, wrote a memo to Walras sketching the mathematics of the optimization of a "quantité de besoin" (Walras 1965, I, pp. 308–11) along the lines of the model in the section of this chapter on the canonical neoclassical model. In Jaffe's notes to the memorandum, he writes that "It is even doubtful whether L. W., who arrived in Lausanne with virtually no mathematics beyond elementary analytical geometry, was able to grasp more than the simple algebraic and geometric aspects of Piccard's explanation," although Jaffe did not see that it was sufficient *for metaphorical purposes*. It took further coaching for Walras to approximate the formalism of the field: in the first edition of the *Elements* (Walras 1969, pp. 567–8) all the curves of *rareté* were drawn as straight lines. This undoubtedly explains Walras's enthusiasm over Gossen – they both made the same mistake. Time and again one observes mathematicians and engineers such as Hermann Amstein (Walras 1965, I, pp. 516–20) explaining some technical aspect of energetics to Walras (such as Lagrange multipliers) and Walras absorbing some vanishingly small fraction of the physics. It gives one pause to realize that Léon Walras was a sort of clearinghouse for energetics metaphors gleaned from various engineers, but a faulty variety of clearinghouse – one where some large fraction of the content got lost in transit to the *Elements*.

The case of Jevons is in many respects equally circuitous and oblique. On his father's prompting to become an engineer, Jevons studied chemistry and mathematics in London. Notes in his journal indicate that he did study mechanics, but hated the professor and found physics uncongenial. However, he did attend some of Michael Faraday's renowned public lectures at the Royal Institution, at which Faraday claimed that magnetic forces did not obey the Newtonian force rule (Jevons 1972, I, p. 82). This is significant because Faraday was one of the very few partisans of field theories in the land of Newton in the 1850s; and it is clear from Jevons's letters that he was very nearly in awe of Faraday. There is some evidence that Jevons was familiar with the writings of Thomson and Joule on the interconvertability of heat and mechanical work, writings which led to the enunciation of the conservation of energy (Jevons 1905a, p. 465), and there is also some evidence that Jevons knew Joule personally when he resided in Manchester.[14]

Another significant influence on Jevons was the writings of James Clerk Maxwell, the premier Victorian physicist in Jevons's Britain, and another innovator of the field concept. There are numerous instances in Jevons's writings of unattributed appropriations of the philosophical writings of Maxwell, who, because he was extremely concerned to reconcile human intellect and will with the laws of inanimate force and matter, must have seemed an attractive figure to Jevons. Indeed, Maxwell once suggested that moral laws could be modeled by a process of analogy with natural laws, making reference to the "attractions of pleasure or the pressure of constraint activity" (Krüger et al. 1987, p. 79). All the various species of laws were to be brought under the single organizing principle of "analogy of Cause"; such conceptual unity permitted Maxwell to invert the more conventional order of metaphorical acknowledgement, locating the source of his new statistical mechanics in social theorists such as Quetelet (Porter 1981a).

Yet none of this would have been sufficient to have acquainted Jevons with the mathematics of fields or rational mechanics. Indeed, all evidence points to the fact that Jevons was inept at the mathematics of rational mechanics. The historian of economics Robert Fisher (in personal communication) has suggested that Jevons came to energetics by way of contemporary controversies in chemistry, where debate centered over whether elements had inherent properties or whether they were governed by mechanical forces. To this must be added the fact that when Jevons was at Owens College, one of his closest colleagues and friends was Balfour Stewart, who was engaged in sunspot research and had written a popular book on the conservation of force, which we discussed in Chapter 3 (Stewart 1883).

It appears that Jevons, much like Walras, was casting about for a physical analogy for exchange and hit upon the simplest possible example for the principle of virtual velocities – namely, the equilibrium of the lever (Jevons 1970, pp. 144–7). From this, he arrived at his initial equations of exchange:

$$\frac{\phi x}{\psi y} = \frac{dy}{dx} = \frac{y}{x}$$

As far as the mathematics went, he never really made any further progress, which explains, among other things, the facts that he always wrote utility as a function of a single variable – this precludes the field formalism – such as $\phi_1(x)$; that he frequently wrote as if utility were a substance (see Chapter 6); and that he was baffled when more sophisticated reviewers kept challenging him to integrate his equations (Jevons 1970, pp. 144, 267; also Marshall's review of *The Theory of Political Economy* in Jevons 1981, VII, p. 145). Of course, the reason they did so was to examine the metaphor of utility as energy more rigorously, something Jevons clearly never understood. If you turn to the derivation of the law of the lever in Chapter 2 (p. 32), you will observe that such a derivation would have forced Jevons to state the variational principle involved explicitly and, more telling, to confront the unsavory conservation of utility plus budget constraint. As it stood, the job was left for later generations.

If there was a difference between Jevons and Walras, it was this: Walras did not evince any deep understanding of mid-nineteenth-century physics, and applied the mathematical techniques and the metaphor in a rather mechanical manner, leaving it for others to plumb the logical and connotative implications of the physical metaphor. Jevons, on the other hand, was an even less facile mathematician than Walras, but did dedicate his life's work to drawing out the meaning of the metaphor of proto-energetics for the metaphorical simplex of body/motion/value. This point is not readily apparent, because Jevons's work is rarely considered as a whole. If one were to list his major achievements, they would be the *Theory of Political Economy, The Coal Question,* his work on sunspots and the business cycle, and *The Principles of Science.* The connection among the four can best be summarized in Jevons's own words, from his paper "The Solar Influence on Commerce" (Jevons 1972, VIII, p. 97):

> Long ago George Stevenson acutely anticipated the results of subsequent scientific inquiry when he said that coal was sunshine bottled up; now it is among the mere commonplaces of science that all motions and energies of life, whether be it that of the windmill, the waterwheel, the steam engine, the beast of burden, or the human operative, are directly or indirectly derived from the sun . . . In a physical point of view it is simply the soul, the fount, the mainspring of life & energy of the planetary system.

The maximization of utility, the prediction that England was rapidly exhausting energy stocks in the form of coal, and the lifelong theme that economic crises must be caused by energy fluctuations exogenous to the social operation of the economy are all direct extrapolations from the energetics movement of the later nineteenth century (Mirowski 1984a). The last point gains credibility when one notes that Jevons recorded in his journal that he attended the lectures where Faraday explicitly discussed the periodicity of sunspots in 1853 (Jevons 1972, I, p. 82). As for the *Principles of Science,* it can be read as a plea for the unity of methodology in all sciences, in the face of the serious upheavals and discontinuities that erupted both in subject matter and in research methods in mid-nineteenth-century physics. The fact that his own conception of scientific endeavor was highly colored by the rise of energetics can be observed in the *Principles'* definition of science: "Science is the detection of identity, and classification is the placing together, either in thought or in the proximity of space, those objects between which identity has been detected" (Jevons 1905a, pp. 673–4).

Those familiar with conventional histories of neoclassical economic theory must, by this point, be impatient to object: What about Menger and the Austrians? Do they fit our thesis, which links the rise of neoclassical theory to the rise of proto-energetics in physics?

Although it has become conventional wisdom to cite the triumvirate of the Marginal Revolution as Jevons, Walras, and Menger, it is important to note that the three actors themselves did not accept this regimentation. Jevons did not mention Menger once in all his writings: – a curious reticence in an avowed bibliophile and one so determined in later life to uncover all predecessors and fellow revolutionaries. Walras did correspond with Menger, but only, to his amazement, to discover that Menger denied the value of Walras's contribution due to its mathematical nature. As for Menger, he said that he had been aware of Walras's work, but hadn't thought there was any similarity in points of view (Walras 1965, I, pp. 768–9). This was sufficient for Walras to drum Menger out of the corps of the revolution, writing in a letter to Bortkiewicz in 1887 that Menger's and Böhm-Bawerk's efforts to describe the theory of *Grenznuten* in ordinary language was unsuccessful, and even painful (Walras 1965, II, p. 232). Walras viewed Menger's 1871 *Principles* as merely an attempt at *translation* of marginalist ideas into ordinary language, and a failed one at that: There was nothing novel or original there, thus denying Menger any status as an equal. (Interestingly enough, this opinion seems to be shared by many modern neoclassical economists. In this regard, see Samuelson [1952, p. 61].) Menger did not conform to Walras's main criteria of a neoclassical theorist: He was not mathematical, he did not adhere to the norms of physical science, and therefore he was not "scientific."

In the reverse direction, historians of economic thought are persistently perplexed by Menger's recalcitrance in being elevated to membership in the triumvirate. Howey, the most careful of these writers, notes:

> [A]lthough Menger talked about the Austrian school, no-one would gather from his words in any of his publications after 1871 down to his death that the Austrian school had the slightest connection with the Marginal Utility school. He either did not admit the connection, or wished to minimise it, or took it for granted. Menger never publicly admitted any kinship with Walras or with Jevons. [Howey 1960, p. 142].

There is much more here than petty squabbles over precedence or methodology, or personality clashes, or nationalistic insularity. There is the possibility that it is an analytical error to include the Austrians, or at the very least Menger, as part of the fledgling movement of neoclassical economic theory. This possibility has already been suggested by some Austrian economists, notably by Erich Streissler in a centenary collection of essays on the marginalist revolution (Black, Coats, and Goodwin 1973, pp. 160–75). Streissler points out that Menger's scales of successive Marginal satisfaction, introduced in the middle of his *Grundsätze* (Menger 1981, p. 127), were not at all central to his conception of economic theory. This contention is indirectly supported by (Kauder 1965, p. 76), who reports that Menger crossed out this table in his author's copy of the book. Howey (1960, p. 40) notes that Menger's "importance of satisfactions" cannot be easily translated into the language of utility because it did not vary in *quantity*. Satisfaction never varied, but its subjective importance could be altered in a regular manner. Streissler maintains that Menger's major concerns – uncertainty, changes in the quality of goods, the absence of a notion of equilibrium, and hostility to the law of one price – were so fundamentally motivated by his radical subjectivism, that he could not be considered as promoting the same theory as Jevons and Walras. From our present vantage point, we can find support for Streissler's thesis by examining Menger's relationship to physical theory.

After a personal visit, Bortkiewicz wrote to Walras that Menger did not have the least idea of mathematical analysis (Walras 1965, II, p. 519). It also seems clear from a perusal of Menger's major works that he was similarly innocent of any familiarity with the physics of his time. It is all the more striking that, in the face of these inadequacies, Menger launched a scathing attack upon the German Historicist school in his *Untersuchungen über die Methode*, mainly consisting of the claim that his opponents did not understand the nature of "exact science" (Menger 1963). In sharp contrast to Jevons's *Principles of Science*, Menger's unfounded claims that he was promoting the methods of "Exact research of a Newton, Lavoisier or Helmholtz" reveal an ignorance camouflaged by bombast. He attempted to extend his radical subjectivism to physics without giving even a single example from the physical sciences. He denigrated empiricism without being specific about the practices to which he objected. His conception of science was severely Aristotelian, without his ever once addressing the fact that this conception had been rejected by the scientists of his day. He merely appropriated their names for credibility.

Menger cannot be considered a neoclassical economist because he rejected the unifying principle of that research program: "Past attempts to carry over the peculiarities of the natural-scientific method of investigation uncritically into economics have led to the most serious methodological errors, and to idle play with external analogies between the phenomena of economics and those of nature" (Menger 1981, p. 47). (How this is reconciled with his later jabs at the Historicists is a problem best left for someone else to figure out.) There is no mention of anyone maximizing anything (Menger 1981, p. 96), and if anything, satisfaction is treated in the rather older tradition of value as substance, which explains the intelligibility of the goods of various "orders." And then, of course, there is the embarrassing footnote that orthodox histories feel the need to explain away:

> The confusion of "use value" with "utility," with "degree of utility" or with "estimated utility" arises from the doctrine of the *abstract* value of goods. A species can have useful properties that make its concrete units suitable for the satisfaction of human needs. Different species can have different degrees of utility in a given use (beechwood and willow wood as fuel, etc.). But neither the utility of a species nor the varying degree of utility of different species or subspecies can be called "value" [Menger 1981, p. 116,fn].

Were it not for the historical accident that the *Grundsätze* was first published in 1871 and the fact that Menger's illustrious student Wieser promoted Menger's claim as one of the originators of neoclassical theory, and himself *did* adopt the new marginalist techniques and language (as well as the fact that Menger's works were largely unavailable outside the German-speaking world), then by all logic Menger would not be considered one of the marginalist revolutionaries today.[15]

Marshall: More discreet than right

I should not wish to make it appear that the entire economics profession was composed of sleepwalkers, stumbling unwittingly into a labyrinth of proto-energetics. Alfred Marshall, for one, certainly discussed some aspects of the adoption of physical metaphors (Marshall 1898), and it cannot be denied that what he saw gave him pause. However, the case of Marshall is actually illuminated by an understanding of proto-energetics.

Marshall's place in the history of economic thought has always been a curious one. He hinted, both privately and in print, that many of Jevons's ideas had been familiar truths to Marshall when they were published, thus intimating that somehow he also deserved discoverer status. Since much of what appears in introductory and intermediate microeconomics texts as the theory of supply and demand is, in fact, an artifact of Marshall's textbook, his claim contains a grain of truth. However, once the actual sequence of events is uncovered, it should become apparent that Marshall's major service in the Marginalist Revolution was as a popularizer and a builder of a stable profession; by no stretch of the imagination was he a serious innovator in theory. As Maloney (1985, p. 24) put it so aptly, "Marshall's outstanding achievement was . . . his success – gained by tactical skill, eloquence and tenacity – in keeping his colleagues' eyes on the goal of an economics whose range, precision and predictive reliability would compare with that of the natural sciences."

Recent study of Marshall's early unpublished writings, especially by Bharadwaj (1978a), reveals that his early work was on the equilibrium of a supply curve with a phenomenological demand curve; at that point he did not much care what lay behind his demand schedule, undoubtedly influenced in this respect by Cournot. Implicitly, movements along the demand curve came from variations in the number of buyers, rather than a posited constrained maximization by an individual buyer. "The word 'utility' itself was used only once in relation to Adam Smith, and not approvingly" (Bharadwaj 1978a, p. 267).

The saga of the journey between Marshall's early *Essay* and his *Principles* is the story of a decision to incorporate the innovations of the marginalist revolutionaries in order to shore up the foundations of the demand blade of the "scissors," while preserving his original concerns with the underlying theory of the supply schedule. Unhappily, the superficial parallels between diminishing returns and diminishing marginal utility could not obscure the fact that the result was more like paper and stone than scissors. For example, much of Marshall's typology of markets involved altering the time frame of analysis and its resultant effects upon the supply schedule. This method produced some embarrassment when applied to the demand side, since either (a) the underlying demand determinants remained constant over time, revealing that the fundamental cause of price was an exogenous posited psychology, as Jevons had maintained, or (b) the demand curve would also be shifted in relatively arbitrary ways, undermining any claim that an equilibrium of demand and supply had been identified. Perhaps it was predictable that the attack would be pressed against the part of the system that was original with Marshall (Sraffa 1926), and that the ensuing retreat would vindicate Jevons's position.[16] Edgeworth, one of Marshall's supporters, saw the problem quite clearly:

> [Marshall] was perhaps deterred by the difficulty of conveying through any physical analogy the distinction between the "long" and the "short" periods . . . We should indeed have to suppose the attraction of the "moon and the sun" in contrast to the terrine forces, to occupy a considerable time in being propagated to the surface of the sea! [Edgeworth 1925, III, p. 9].

It seems plausible to suggest that Marshall sensed that his concerns could be overwhelmed by the zeal of his marginalist allies (Maloney 1985, p. 46) and that this carries us some distance in understanding why he does not conform in style to the characteristics of the marginalist cadre identified above. His defense of Ricardo vis-à-vis Jevons, his soft-pedaling of the mathematics method, his insistence on the basic continuity of economics from Adam Smith to Marshall's time, his persistent praise of organic metaphors – all of these activities were attempts to incorporate proto-energetics into economics while controlling, masking, or perhaps altering some of its more objectionable aspects. Many wave as a banner Marshall's claim that "The Mecca of the economist lies in economic biology," but few bother to quote the next sentence: "But biological conceptions are more complex than those of mechanics; a volume on Foundations must therefore give a relatively large place to mechanical analogies" (Marshall 1920, p. xiv). However much he might protest, the fact remains that Marshall did render the proto-energetics metaphor safe and soothing for a Victorian English audience, which would have been predisposed to oppose the brash revolution of a Jevons, and was nonplussed by an Edgeworth. Further, he can be credited with fostering the illusion that:

"The new doctrines have supplanted the older . . . but very seldom
have subverted them" (Marshall 1920, p. v).

It is important to see that Marshall thought that the physical interpretation could be separated from the mathematical technique,
and that his reservations lay in the interpretation rather than the
technique. Those who happily quote Marshall's dictum to "burn the
mathematics" should read carefully the preface to the eighth edition
of the *Principles:*

> The new analysis is endeavoring gradually and tentatively to bring
> over into economics, as far as the widely different nature of the
> material will allow, those methods of the science of small increments
> (commonly called the differential calculus) to which man owes di-
> rectly or indirectly the greater part of the control that he has
> obtained in recent times over physical nature. It is still in its infancy;
> it has no dogmas, and no standard of orthodoxy . . . there is a
> remarkable harmony and agreement on essentials among those who
> are working constructively by the new method, and especially among
> such of them as have served an apprenticeship in the simpler and
> more definite, and therefore more advanced, problems of physics.
> [Marshall 1920, pp. xvi–xvii].

But of course there was dogma and a standard of orthodoxy. That
was why agreement had been achieved relatively quickly by the
mathematical workers: the standards and ideas had been appropriated during the apprenticeship in physics. As we have seen, the entire
Lausanne school were initially trained as engineers. The first British
neoclassicals all came from an engineering background, or else they
read mathematics at Cambridge, which in those days meant mathematical physics (Harman 1985).

The *Principles* is a book that touts the mathematical method while
attempting to deny that the method could influence the content of
what was being expressed. The clearest manifestation of this tension
occurs in the appendix to the *Principles,* where, in the midst of a series
of abstruse notes concerning the application of constrained
maximization to utility, there is an absolutely incongruous discussion
of the applications of Taylor's Theorem to the webbing between a
duck's appendages (Marshall 1920, pp. 841–2). The purpose of the
digression was to suggest that the calculus was being borrowed from
an organic evolutionary metaphor. Not only did Taylor's Theorem
have nothing to do with the duck's webbing in Marshall's actual
example, but the calculus of constrained maximization was not employed by evolutionary theorists in Marshall's day.

Biological metaphors were also very important in Marshall's *Princi-*

ples, but they were not central to the proto-energetics model of value, and indeed were progressively sloughed off by the subsequent Cambridge school – they were never central in any other outpost of neoclassical mathematical economics. In the British context, the language of biological analogy played three discrete roles. The first consisted of creating the appearance of a synthesis of the three core metaphors of body/motion/value at a level to rival the labor theory of value: Marshall's text is replete with references to Darwinian and Spencerian evolution, eugenics (p. 248), and assertions that economists "have at last established their claim to illustrate a fundamental unity of action between the laws of nature in the physical and the moral world" (p. 240). Second, the references to the "trees of the forest" and so on created the impression of the existence of a dynamic neoclassical theory where none ever existed (Levine 1983). Third, the truck in biological metaphors constituted an important tactic in the defense of the scientific status of economics in the British context. In a little-known incident in 1877, the statistician and eugenicist Francis Galton spearheaded a drive to oust Section F (Statistics and Political Economy) from the British Association for the Advancement of Science on the grounds that (what else?) research had not been conducted and reported in a scientific manner (Pearson 1924, pp. 347–8). In 1878, J. K. Ingram's Presidential Address to Section F initiated a defense that claimed that political economy resembled biology in important respects, thus taking the sting out of Galton's attack. Marshall's recourse to biological analogies can be understood as a continuation of that strategy, as part of his larger project of building a stable professional identity for economics.

Neoclassical economics as a species of energetics

Neoclassical economics was not an object of discovery, either by means of introspection or by some form of empiricism. These hoary myths only serve to hide its real origins. Economists did not exist on some sort of island, cut off from the cultural movements of their time or the metaphors used to rationalize the physical and social worlds. In many collateral fields of inquiry, the linked metaphors of body/motion/value had undergone profound transformations in the nineteenth century, with the physicists managing to prosecute the inquiry from the lineamentric to the syndetic stage. The push to unification held out the promise that body, motion, and value really were seemingly different aspects of the same protyle. The elaboration of the energy concept created a stir in physical theory because it promised the eventual unification of all the natural sciences under one principle. The unification of the theories of rational mechanics, heat, electricity, and magnetism was thought to be merely the first installment in the grand scheme. In the midst of all the excitement, who could really say how far the unification might go? The rise to predominance of energy physics had a vast impact upon philosophy and social theory from roughly the 1850s to the 1930s precisely because it conjured up the image of a science of society on a par with the science of the inanimate world, due to the fact that they were ultimately the same science. In this context, neoclassical economic theory was just one small part of a much bigger movement.

Rankine's conception of a unified general science of energetics discussed in Chapter 2 crops up with increasing frequency from the 1860s onwards. Its next important venue was in the work of Herbert Spencer. While twentieth-century theorists, if they remember Spencer at all, tend to pigeonhole him as an avatar of Victorian social Darwinism, the nineteenth century regarded him as one of the towering polymaths of the era. His *First Principles,* the first edition of which was published in 1862, was read by intellectuals in widely different fields (for instance, Friedrich von Wieser, Francis Ysidro Edgeworth, Irving Fisher, and Vilfredo Pareto all acknowledged the influence of Spencer). Because his *First Principles* is not often read today, it has not been appreciated that it was one of the primary vehicles for the promulgation of energetics in the later nineteenth century (Capek 1961, pp. 100–3).

Employing the already anachronistic terminology of the "Persistence of Force," Spencer discussed the conservation of energy as if it were not only a confirmed physical theory, but also an epistemological necessity verging on a priori truth. In retrospect, this seems extremely bold, given the relative novelty of the doctrine at that time. Not being one to stop there, Spencer then asserted that "the law of metamorphosis, which holds among the physical forces, holds equally between them and the mental forces" (Spencer 1887, p. 217). According to Spencer, there was only one generic energy, and its laws should apply equally to physical and social phenomena. Spencer's grasp of physics, and therefore the physical/social metaphor, was not very secure – he even misspelled "Mayer" as "Meyer" – and this undoubtedly explains his disinclination to actually implement the mathematical facet of the metaphor.

Nevertheless, his system of a hierarchy of energies – the physical giving way to the vital, resulting in the social – captured the imagination of his audience. As a parallel example, we again discover an anticipation of Jevons's later work in economics. Spencer wrote: "If we ask whence came these physical forces from which, through this intermediation of the vital forces, the social forces arise, the reply is of course as heretofore – the solar radiations" (Spencer 1887, p. 219; see also Mirowski 1984a).

At this juncture, the narrative of social theory becomes more tangled as the strands of proto-energetics proliferate. Neoclassical economics was spun off as a restricted and narrow version of energetics, in that the explicit claims to be part of a general unified science were relatively muted. Other versions of energetics were not so modest, did maintain the pretence of a synthetic science, and eventually succumbed to attacks from famous scientists and the rapid transformations in physics itself around the turn of the century. From the 1880s to the 1930s, a social-science version of energetics attracted adherents in many countries: the German tendril sported Helm and Ostwald; the French filament traced its lineage from the Lausanne school and Winiarsky; the Belgian skein found a patron in Ernest Solvay; the British contingent had a champion in Fredrick Soddy. The American odyssey of energetics could itself absorb an entire chapter to trace the filiations through T. N. Carver, Frederic Taylor, and the Technocracy movement. A complete history of the energetics movement would take us too far afield from our present concern with neoclassical economics. Instead, we will conclude this chapter with a brief sketch of the relationship of neoclassical economics to energetics in the period 1880 to 1930.

The most famous branch of the energetics movement flourished briefly in Germany, as we observed in Chapter 2. The prophet of this new science of the spirit was Georg Helm, a schoolteacher who caused a sensation with his monograph *Die Lehre von der Energie* (Helm 1887). He argued that atomism was a superfluous hypothesis, and that all of physics would be greatly simplified by the uniform application of the energy principle. Although most of the book was concerned with physical theory, Helm did append a final chapter on the extension of the energy principle to social theory and, more specifically, to economics, traversing the now familiar hierarchy of physical energy to vital energy through to social energy. He demonstrated how the work of Gossen and Jevons could be incorporated into the pattern of his previous chapters, where every energetic phenomenon was divided into a differential capacity factor and a law of intensity of the general form $dE = J(dM)$. He easily derived the conditions for a maximum of "utility or economic energy," and then noted that the conservation of energy had not been thoroughly explored in the new economics. He ended the chapter and the monograph on the speculation that:

> [I]t should be possible to establish the economic rule upon an axiomatic perpetual motion principle or to develop a concept of energy which combines means and ends into a single analysis. But this is not the place to consider whether such observations are appropriate or fruitful; they are mentioned only as an example of the significance inherent in energy concepts [Helm 1887, p. 75].[17]

Helm's new science of energetics did not provoke much interest among German economists, but it was read widely and attracted the attention of many natural scientists, most notably Wilhelm Ostwald. Ostwald enjoyed much renown as a physical chemist, and was awarded the Nobel Prize in chemistry for his work on catalysis and reaction velocities in 1909. He obviously did not think of himself in such narrow terms, however, and adopted Helm's precept that "In the last analysis everything that happens is nothing but changes in energy" (in Lindsay 1976, p. 339) to argue for an all-encompassing science of energetics. The principles of this science were extended to the *Kulturwissenschaften* in a monograph that located the function of law, commerce, government, and language itself as the transformation of 'crude" energy into "useful" energy with a minimum of waste (Ostwald 1909).

As described in Chapter 2, this ostensibly unified program of science received a blow from which it never recovered in Germany in the form of concerted attacks upon Ostwald and energetics by two of the most respected physicists of the era, Max Planck and Ludwig Boltzmann. Both complained that the energeticists did not sufficiently understand the distinction between a state function like energy and path-dependent quantities, such as physical work. Planck further accused the energeticists of only conceptualizing reversible processes within the ambit of their apparatus of capacity factors and intensity functions: If we restrict the world to such processes, the formalism of the Hamiltonian already performed the function of the unification of all physical science. Finally, in the realm of philosophy, Planck shrewdly observed that "energetics achieves the apparent and surprising simplicity of its proofs by the simple process of pushing the content of the laws to be demonstrated (which must always be known in advance) backward to their definitions" (in Lindsay 1976, p. 361). Planck's indictment of energetics deserves to be read today because, although it was intended to counter the influence of energetics in the physical-science faculties of German academia, it is (unintentionally) one of the most cogent and concise critiques of neoclassical economic theory.

In French-speaking Europe energetics did not generate much interest within the circles of physics and chemistry, but did find some very avid supporters in the social sciences. Ernest Solvay, whose main claim to fame nowadays is the institution of the Solvay Conferences in physics during the 1910s, devoted most of his fortune and his efforts to the promotion of a social energetics (Warnotte 1946; Mehra 1975). He gathered about him many like-minded researchers in 1894 in his *Institut des sciences sociales,* which published many tracts on aspects of energetics well into the 1930s. Solvay himself penned a number of energetics texts, such as *L'Energetique considérée comme principl d'orientation rationelle pour la sociologie* (1904) and *Questions d'énergetiques sociales* (1910). Solvay was persuaded to spend some of his money supporting the Solvay Conferences in Physics beginning in 1911 in part as a way to interest the most respected physicists of the time in his energetic ideas, but of course, they just took the money.

Another Francophone proselytizer for a social energetics was Léon Winiarsky, who wrote for philosophy and legal journals from his base in Lausanne (Winiarsky 1900). The French school of social mechanics, which included such authors as Haret and Barcelo, remained active until the 1930s.

The fact that energetics as an explicit social theory was so multiform and widespread at the turn of the century and yet went into eclipse so rapidly in the 1930s and 1940s, whereas neoclassicism has persisted (if not thrived) down to the present day, is a curious fact that demands some explanation. A tentative analysis consistent with that of this chapter would rest on two pillars: First, neoclassical economics (unintentionally?) managed to segregate itself from the larger program of energetics, to the extent of having no apparent association with it; second, events in physics undermined the pretensions of an unabashed energetics to be based on accepted and credible physical theory, thus rendering pathetic its supposed scientific advantage over other theories.

The first generation of neoclassical economists never completely explored their structural physics metaphor, largely because their understanding of it was so deficient, and hence never 'joined forces' with the energetics movement. At the turn of the century, this was cause for some grumbling on the part of energeticists. Helm, for instance, thought a more careful elaboration of the metaphor would unify German economics. Winiarsky, in a more sardonic mood, wrote, "Cette science [political economy] peut être considerée comme une veritable énergetique sociale. Il est vrai que la plupart des économistes ne savent pas, mais on peut toute la vie parler en prose, sans savoir ce qu'est le mot «prose»." [This science can be considered a true social energetics. It is true that the majority of economists are not aware of it, but one can spend one's entire life talking in prose, without knowing what the word "prose" is.] (Winiarsky 1900, p. 266, fn.). Although we hesitate to impute any rational choice to the phenomenon, this oblivion, this distance from the unsavory cousins, was ultimately the salvation of neoclassical economics. In fact, it is most likely that it was pure historical accident that Jevons and Walras were so ignorant of social energetics that they did not try to make common cause with it.

Physical energetics did come under direct fire from physicists of the stature of Boltzmann and Planck in Germany, but what finished it off was the tremendous ferment in physics at the turn of the century, as outlined in Chapter 2. Neoclassical economics remained unscathed by the general skepticism, however, because by the 1930s no one recognized it as energetics. This, in turn, was due to two trends. One was the "forgetting" of the physics metaphor, largely due to general incomprehension and incompetence, which we have documented in this chapter. The other was the fiasco, in the first third of this century, of value theory, which indiscriminately mixed field theories and substance theories to the point where the physical inspiration of economics would be thoroughly obscured and muddled. It is to this latter trend that we turn our attention in the next chapter.

The syndetic stage?

In Chapter 3 we argued that disciplines go through a sequence of metrological stages and pointed to the development of the energy concept as a paradigm of that process. If one accepts that scenario, the question naturally arises whether the rise of neoclassical value theory constituted progress from the lineamentric value theory of classical economics to the syndetic stage, where various fragmented metrics are consolidated under a single all-encompassing yet reified invariant. Given that neoclassical utility is patterned upon a conservative field of force, one might expect that the parallel transition to the syndetic stage was successfully accomplished in economics.

Clearly, neoclassical theory managed to forge links between the newer concepts of motion and its novel value metaphor; in that sense it was an improvement over classical theory. It also participated in the rhetoric of the unification of the sciences, although as we have seen in the previous section, it did so in an extremely muted voice. Marshall initiated an attempt to incorporate certain biological metaphors of the body, but it was done in such a manner as to subsequently have no profound effect upon the research program. But beyond those achievements, its record was seriously deficient in comparison, say, with the metrological development of physics. Whereas in physics there was a continuous research program whose purpose was to come to understand the nature and limits of the new reified invariant, it seems not one of the neoclassical economists even understood what was at stake in the problem of invariance. When push came to shove, whether in the integrability problem, or the understanding of the prospects for measurability of utility, or serious examination of the premises underlying the formalization of economic theory, the neoclassical economists were dazed into incoherence, blinded by science. These proponents of a scientific economics never got much further than superficial resemblances to science, because they never really understood how to emulate the characteristic behavior of the physicists. One suspects this explains the hostility of many scientists to the program, as well as the fact that, outside of Marshall's dominance of British academic economics, the neoclassical research program made excruciatingly slow headway into professional economics in the period of roughly 1880 to 1930.

There was not just one Marginalist Revolution, there were two. The second wave of scientific neoclassicism had to await fresh recruits from the physical sciences in the second quarter of the twentieth century, as we shall observe in Chapter 7.

The imperatives of proto-energetics

It may seem harsh and unfair to indict the first generation of neoclassical economists for not hewing more closely to their adopted physical metaphor of the field. After all, aren't metaphors merely a tool to suggest novel lines of inquiry without demanding rigid adherence to strict isomorphism? This would seem to be the attitude of Pareto when challenged by Croce to defend his mechanical economics (Pareto 1953, p. 185):

> Evidently it is not a case of identity but of resemblance . . . mechanics can be studied leaving aside the concept of forces. In reality all this does not matter much. If there is anyone who does not care to hear mechanics mentioned, very well, let us disregard the similarity and let us talk directly about our equations. We shall only have to face the drawback that in certain cases we shall have to labor greatly in order to deduce from those equations certain conse-

quences that we would have perceived at once had we kept in mind the fact that mechanics had already deduced them from its own equations, which are similar to ours.

The irony of this situation was that it was precisely the consequences of the mechanical equations that were a major bone of contention and source of hostility to the neoclassical research program. Further, these objections were circumvented and the critics bewildered precisely by the suppression of any further deliberate discussion of the physics. It is certainly true that one need not be obsessed with the exact duplication of all aspects of a metaphor when it is transported from one area of inquiry to another. However, one of the most attractive aspects of analogical reasoning is the prefabricated nature of an interlocked set of explanatory structures and constructs, allowing quickened evaluation of logical coherence. Pareto's response to Croce said, in effect, that it does not matter that the mathematical core of neoclassical economics came from physics, since we can subsequently pick and choose whatever aspects we like and discard the rest. The error of Pareto and every other historically sophisticated neoclassical theorist is to think that every aspect of the physics metaphor is equally expendable. Contrary to the ideology of neoclassicism, we are not so indifferently free to choose.

The essence of neoclassical economics is the appropriation of the physical concept of the field and its elevation to pride of place in the theory of value. While the notion of the field is a very flexible concept, it does possess a modicum of structural regularity that, if absent, undermines its logical integrity. The history of physics teaches that one indispensable element of a field theory is the imposition of some set of conservation principles. In vernacular terms, a field can seem a very nebulous thing: Only certain regularities in its interaction with other theoretical entities would endow it with the status of causal explanation (in the sense of Meyerson). It is the role of conservation principles to define and fix the identity of the system as it undergoes its various transformations, as well as to define the boundaries of discrete systems. One can observe this function in physical field theories, particularly in such situations where fields pervade what appears to be empty space.

The epistemological imperative of conservation principles in field theories is mirrored in their mathematics. As we have repeatedly observed in Chapter 2, variational principles are always married to conservation principles. There can be no such thing as a mathematics of constrained extrema without some corresponding conserved entities or structures. Neoclassical economists, out of neglect or ignorance or blind faith in the trappings of science, have persistently refused to learn this lesson from the history of physics. Time and again they acted as if they could appropriate extremum principles and ignore issues of conservation. Various natural scientists have tried to jar them out of their complacency, but the reminders were met with something less then warm welcome and comprehension.

Lack of self-conscious appropriation, however, did not imply the absence of any and all conservation principles. The physical metaphor was completed in the most exceedingly strange fashion: haphazardly, absent-mindedly, and surreptitiously, generally under the guise of the technical imperatives of the mathematics itself. Indeed, in the medium of the mathematics, the physical metaphor took on a life of its own, reimposing the imperatives of a field concept. Recall that the mathematics of the energy metaphor required that the sum of potential and kinetic energy – which in the neoclassical incarnation should be the sum of total utility and total expenditure – be conserved in a closed system. In a higgledy-piggledy fashion, neoclassical economists effectively imposed the conservation of utility, the conservation of the budget, or their sum, depending on the context and their own ideosyncratic preferences; sometimes they imposed all three within the ambit of the same model, which was redundant. Let us briefly survey the options.

The conservation of utility is one of the least understood unobtrusive postulates in neoclassical theory. It does not mean total utility is constant before and after a trade: Obviously, a major tenet of neoclassicism is that trade increases the sum of *realized* utility. Rather, the conservation of the utility field is invariably posited, independent of any and all exchange activity. This assumption is smuggled into the analysis in a number of ways, all ending up at the same conservation condition. The most common method is simply to posit a mathematical form of the utility function or preference field that is symmetric and path-independent. Another gambit is to rule out the phenomenon of regret in the psychology of choice (Fisher 1926, p. 21; Mirowski 1984b). A third alternative is to rule out any endogenous change of tastes. A fourth option is to model putative taste changes so that they are effectively path-independent and stationary – that is, so that they are really conservative after all. All these options are special cases of the same imperative: There can be no divergence between the anticipation and the realization of utility. More recent innovations that incorporate expectations or probabilistic considerations in utility theory muddy the waters somewhat, but through some artifice or another conservation principles are imposed, and so the results are essentially the same.[18]

The conservation of income and/or expenditure is slightly better understood, if only because it is so very implausible that it has been the nexus of much controversy. It is the second half of the neoclassical litany of "given tastes and given endowments." Most frequently, this conservation principle assumes the format of an assumption that incomes are given, exogenous to the analysis. This assumption is inextricably bound up with a neoclassical version of Say's Law, stating that aggregate incomes in equilibrium are independent of the path of exchanges that produces them. The narrative of the vicissitudes of this principle belongs in the twentieth century, with its vain attempt to fuse macroeconomics and production theory with neoclassical value theory; hence further explication is postponed until the next chapter.

The third option of the conservation of the sum of expenditure plus utility has either made its appearance in neoclassical theory in the format of the assumption of a constant marginal utility of money or income or been smuggled in under the cover of the integrability conditions, the Antonelli conditions, or the Slutsky restrictions. Because it is the closest to the original energetics metaphor, it has been the subject of much historical exegesis in this chapter.

Hence there have been *at least* two inescapable imperatives of the appropriated energy metaphor that was brought over into economics. The first may be stated simply: The metaphor makes no sense without some analogy to the conservation of energy. However much individual economic theorists may not like it, they must have one if they are to retain the field concept. Some have struggled mightily to renounce their dependence by means of the proliferation of alternative conservation principles, only to claim they hold allegience to none. Perhaps you don't like the assumption that tastes are exogenous? We can change that, they smile. But then you object to Say's Law? We can do without it, if you understand the mathematics, they reassure us. Perhaps the integrability conditions sound a little odd? In certain special cases, we can do without them, but this is mainly a technical complication, we are told (Katzner, in Chipman et al. 1971). But in the final analysis this is all just one big shell game, with the offending conservation principles passed from one assumption to another.

The second imperative of the field metaphor is that the nineteenth-century model that spawned it was the very pinnacle of the identification of all explanation with rigid mechanistic reductionism and Laplacian determinism. It is, after all, the physics of the Laplacian

Dream. The beauty of the Hamiltonian is that, once correctly written and supplemented with an exhaustive set of initial conditions, it promises to predict all motion of a closed system ad infinitum. Although the first generation of neoclassicals did not directly avail themselves of the Hamiltonian formalism, they did adhere to the goal of a thoroughgoing determinism that would allow the mapping of the future evolution of the economy on paper. But the neoclassicals warmed to this aspiration with almost no understanding of what it entailed; further, they did so just as physics began its long retreat from the Laplacian Dream.

As we suggested in Chapter 2, the elaboration of the Laplacian Dream led inexorably to its dissolution; that, too, is an imperative of the physical metaphor. But given that the neoclassicals were incapable of confronting the issues of conservation principles, of integrability, and of invariance, it should come as no surprise that they were left high and dry by the retreat of atomistic determinism in science. As long as the Laplacian Dream was their dream, they clutched neurotically at their portrait of persons as irrotational mental fields suffusing an independent commodity space, as science ebbed ever further away toward a world subject to change, diversity, and indeterminacy, and at one with the observer.

But even that is too simple, too neat. There were other imperatives of the energy metaphor, although they might be thought of rather as prohibitions – after all, total freedom in reasoning is no reasoning at all. These imperatives state that if value is to be conceptualized as a field, then with some minor exceptions, it can no longer be conceptualized as a substance. As we shall see in Chapter 6, the metaphor of energy had implications for economics far beyond anything in the simple dreams of a social physics.

CHAPTER 6

The corruption of the field metaphor, and the retrogression to substance theories of value: Neoclassical production theory

> It is the purpose this work to show that the distribution of income of a society is controlled by a natural law, and that this law, if it worked without friction, would give to every agent of production the wealth that agent creates.
> John Bates Clark, *Distribution of Wealth*, p. v

> Until the laws of thermodynamics are repealed, I shall continue to relate outputs to inputs – i.e., to believe in production functions.
> Paul Samuelson, *Collected Papers* [1972a, III, p. 174]

Anyone who makes it their business to keep up with academic economics cannot fail to notice that something strange has happened since World War II. While the exact contours of the altered ambiance are difficult to pin down, it might be characterized loosely as a certain ambivalence about the out-and-out truth (for lack of a more precise word) of the doctrines that comprise neoclassical economic theory. While recantations on the road to Damascus are still relatively rare, there does seem to be a surfeit of retreat to a vague paradigm of sophisticated general equilibrium models whenever a critic seems on the verge of scoring a point at neoclassical expense; or it may show up as a disparaging irony about the plausibility of the assumptions of the model (Klamer 1983). I have also encountered something like this phenomenon in reaction to the theses broached in the previous chapter.

It goes something like this: OK, so maybe the early neoclassicals derived their inspiration from physics. Nevertheless, this fact has no bearing on the content or subsequent evolution of the theory itself, although one might be willing to admit it had some impact upon external considerations, such as the favor of funding agencies or the untutored impressions of the public. Further, metaphors are just metaphors, not scientific research programs. They belong in literature, not in science. Therefore, any attempt to use the structure of the physical metaphor to analyze modern theory is fundamentally misleading and irrelevant. Complaining that economists misunderstand the physics is a waste of time: They had no reason to need to know it, because they were working on economics. The best and the brightest have now wisely left all of that behind.

Karl Popper once gave a somewhat more lofty account of this assertion that bygones are bygones: He called it the separation of the context of discovery from the context of justification. Any poet or raving madman can see a dust mote or atom as a microcosm of the solar system, or all life as various manifestations of a primal entelechy or energeia, but what really matters is the application of the scientific method, or so he claimed. Further, metaphors are tainted by their association with literature – no sober scientific attitude to be encountered in that den of iniquity. No metaphor is premised upon the precise identity between the initial object and the thing compared to it, so there is no point in elaborating the ways the metaphor does and does not fit. A metaphor is just a rhetorical ploy for rousing the emotions of the audience; science is better off without it.

As the reader must surely suspect by now, I think this attitude is profoundly mistaken, and would assert that the history of the concept of value in economic theory and the history of the concept of energy in physics are prime counterexamples. Trying to understand the attractions that render such broad-brush portraits of human nature and physical nature satisfying and fruitful, as well as comprehending what it is that unifies a research program in the midst of the endless revision that constitutes normal scientific activity, is a project to push the program of self-understanding to its very limits. If Chapter 2 is correct and energy was not discovered, and Chapter 5 is correct that utility was not discovered, then it would seem that presumptions concerning the obvious and simple evolution of inquiry might also be at risk. One function of Chapter 3 has been to suggest ways in which metaphors have provided systematic guidance in constructing explanations in our culture.

The purported separation of the context of discovery and the context of justification is a vain attempt to cleanse the theoretical object of any worldly taint and isolate it in a hermetically sealed environment so that the scientist can commune with its essence in splendid isolation. One reason these purification rites are self-defeating is that most scientific reasoning is metaphorical. This has been recognized by numerous historians of science from Duhem to Hesse, including, oddly enough, William Stanley Jevons (Jevons 1905a, pp. 643 ff.). Duhem wrote; "The history of physics shows us that the search for analogies between two distinct categories of phenomena has perhaps been the surest and most fruitful method of all the procedures put into play in the construction of physical theories" (Duhem 1977, pp. 95–6).

I propose that we take Duhem's words seriously here: He did not merely say that metaphors were fruitful sources of inspiration; he said that metaphor was a *method of theory construction*. This suggests that there are methods of the conduct of inquiry that are distinctly metaphorical; that is, metaphors have fundamental consequences for research programs. But how does this relate to the notion of a literary metaphor? Mary Hesse, who has considered the role of metaphor in physics at great length, has attempted to describe the fundamental distinctions between metaphors in science and metaphors in poetry (Hesse 1966, 1974; 1980, pp. 118–23). She claims it is a distinguishing characteristic of successful poetic metaphor that the images chosen be initially striking, unexpected, shocking, or even perverse. (Here one might recall Baudelaire's comparison of his lover's body with a piece of carrion in his poem "Une Charogne.") A poetic metaphor is largely meant to be savored, to be entertained the way one sips a wine, and definitely not to be further analyzed in pedantic detail. (This probably explains the pariah status of literary critics in certain quarters.) The poetic metaphor sports a penumbra of further metaphors and implications, which may themselves clash with the conventional usage and the tacit knowledge of the reader, be flagrantly contradictory with one another, and fly in the face of previous comparisons in the same text. Far from being considered an error, this is part of the calculated impact of poetic language. Finally, only the confused pedant takes a poetic metaphor to be a research program. A poem is intended to be self-contained; it is a rare occurence in the modern world for a poem to recruit missionaries who march out to remake the world in its image.

Scientific metaphors clearly have different criteria of efficacy and success. Although a scientific metaphor may initially appear incongruous, this is not generally conceded to be a point in its favor; and much of normal scientific activity can be interpreted as an attempt to render unseemly aspects of metaphors intelligible and pedestrian. A hallmark of scientific metaphors is the fact that they are deemed failures if they can muster only temporary impact and do not manage to become the object of pedantic explication and elaboration. Here one might cite the instance of mathematicians rooting out the most obscure and arcane implications of the idea of a continuous function, or of the metaphor of infinity (Dauben 1979; 1984). Scientific metaphors should set in motion research programs that strive to render explicit the totality of the attendant submetaphors. They should provoke inquiry as to whether the implications are consistent one with another, as well as consistent with the tacit background knowledge.

There is no such thing as a perfect scientific metaphor that scrupulously sports no nasty aspects. In a curious way, this is a beneficial phenomenon, because it serves to provide guidance and structure in the process of inquiry, which might otherwise be even more rife with rampant individualism and random research than is already the case. What matters for our present purposes is not that any particular metaphor has flaws, but rather that the appropriate research community responds to those flaws in a responsible, systematic, and scientific manner, and acknowledges that metaphors have consequences for the content and conduct of inquiry. As we have attempted to demonstrate in the previous chapter, the progenitors of neoclassical theory did admit that they were asserting that something in economics was like potential energy in physics, but not one of them ventured beyond coy references to examine the consistency of the metaphor in any detail. When various physicists and mathematicians challenged the consistency and adequacy of the mathematical metaphor, particularly with repect to what they considered to be the fundamental property of energy (i.e., its conservation), the neoclassicals responded with nonsense and incomprehension.

What this chapter and the next will attempt to demonstrate is that this situation did not improve over time. Subsequent generations of neoclassical economists became less intimately acquainted with the metaphor, but that did not banish its negative or unsavory components – it merely resulted in progressively more disorganized and rudderless attempts to render the theory more "realistic." Perhaps even more incongruously, we shall in Chapter 7 witness some twentieth-century neoclassicals such as Paul Samuelson trying to suppress the negative components of the energetics metaphor by attempting to suppress the metaphor itself. This goes some distance in explaining the fact that contemporaries are still surprised and a little shocked when confronted with the fact that their economic theory was appropriated from nineteenth-century physics. Nevertheless, the metaphor still has had profound consequences for the neoclassical research program. To deny that this has been the case is to deny the possibility of scientific metaphor – and, quite frankly, the constrained maximization of utility never was passable poetry.

The physics metaphor, even in its generally repressed state, provided such a powerful inertial guidance system for research that we shall claim it was a major determinant of the outcome of some critical controversies in twentieth-century economic theory. Of paramount importance for the present chapter is the critical observation that neoclassical theorists have attempted in vain to absorb the classical concept of production into the ambit of the physics metaphor, for the very straightforward reason that classical production is predicated upon a substance theory of value, whereas neoclassical price theory is predicated upon a field theory of value. The two theories of value cannot be reconciled within any uniquely comprehensive or attractive synthesis; the problem evokes a parallel from Chapter 2, where the failure of the energetics program *within physics* was due, in part, to the irreconcilability of substance and field conceptions of energy.

Consequently, in economics there was a proliferation of many competing neoclassical theories of production, beginning soon after the original appropriation of the energetics metaphor. No one theory swept the profession at any point in the last century, even though the proliferation is masked in modern texts by the frequent claim that production and exchange are treated symmetrically in the neoclassical tradition. As a result, there has been a pronounced retreat to the classical substance theories of value in two areas of economic theory most concerned with questions of production: capital theory, and Keynesian macroeconomics. Nevertheless, the incompatibility of the earlier substance metaphor with the later field metaphor festered in a latent state until it erupted in both of those areas in the third quarter of the present century, in the guises of the Cambridge Capital Controversies and the quixotic search for the "microfoundations of macroeconomics." From the vantage point of the late 1980s one can observe that the later physics metaphor of the field finally superseded the earlier substance metaphor, in that late-twentieth-century Walrasian neoclassicals eventually claimed that capital was an expendable concept in their system, and that Keynesian theory was logically flawed. Perhaps it is just the wisdom of hindsight, but it is now clear that once economists became wedded to the metaphor of utility as energy, then eventually all vestiges of value substances just had to go.

A dybbuk named production

The neoclassical appropriation of nineteenth-century energetics hinged upon a comparison between mass points coming to rest in a space permeated by a field of force and commodities coming to rest in a configuration of fields of utility. This was the common denominator of the writings of each of the early neoclassicals. Their books would invariably begin with some homiletic references to science, and then summarily move on to the determination of equilibrium prices with reference to a given field of utility and given endowments, generally in a situation of isolated or virtual trade. This much they could all agree upon. The diversity, discord, and even dissembling came next, with the attempt to treat such topics as "production" and "distribution." The physics metaphor provided a ready means to conceptualize prices, but did not provide an equally ready-made strategy for extending the Marginalist Revolution to the rest of economic theory. Here the early neoclassicals had to display their own prowess in the innovation of economic theory, and here we find the most controversy, calumny, and cacophony well into the twentieth century. As the early neoclassicals strove to differentiate themselves from the discredited classical theory and simultaneously extend their competence to areas previously deemed the province of classical political economy, they discovered that the maximization of utility was not the philosopher's stone for which they had hoped, and in a few cases began to suspect that it was rather a millstone.

The tension between the physics metaphor and the aspirations of the early neoclassicals emerged in the question of the proper specification of the nature of production in the 1880s. Indeed, a telling bit of evidence in favor of the thesis that the protoenergetics model set the agenda for the subsequent evolution of neoclassical economic theory is the fact that *every* neoclassical discussion of production postdated the specification of the model of exchange. Such an order of inquiry would have been an anomaly in classical political economy. The classical substance theory clearly privileged production as the font of all value, whereas circulation merely transmitted value and consumption destroyed it. This very insistence of classical political economy upon the primacy of production dictated that the neoclassicals must confront the issue. Most were familiar with John Stuart Mill's distinction between laws of production and laws of distribution. The former were given ineluctably by our natural physical environment and therefore immutable, whereas the latter were deemed the product of human institutions, and hence by contrast eminently mutable. Most were also cognizant of the Ricardian predisposition to ground prices in the physical relations of production, with the attendant appeal to the stable determinate character of the external world. As might be expected, the early neoclassicals felt it their vocation to distinguish their price theory as sharply as possible from the Ricardian (and Marxian) versions. Their ambitions to supplant classical economic doctrines led them to make numerous disparaging statements concerning cost prices or the prices-of-production framework. However, once they opened their own brief on production, they discovered some unsavory implications of the physics metaphor.

Every protagonist in the first phases of the marginalist revolution had some harsh words for the classical doctrine of price as a reflection of production costs. Walras, for one, wrote:

> The selling prices of products are determined in the market for products by reason of their utility and quantity. There are no other conditions to consider, for these are the necessary and sufficient conditions. It does not matter whether the products cost more or less to produce than their selling prices . . . It is not the cost of the productive service that determines the selling price of the product, but rather the other way round . . . Is it possible for the prices of productive services to affect the prices of products? Of course it is, but only through their influence on the quantity of products. [Walras 1969, pp. 399–400].

Jevons had his famous catena about "cost of production determines supply/ supply determines final degree of utility/ final degree of utility determines value"; and just in case anyone found that a little cryptic, he went on to insist that the "value [of labour] must be determined by the value of the produce, not the value of the produce by that of the labour" (Jevons 1970, p. 187).

Many of the next generation of neoclassical economists carried the rejection of cost-of-production arguments to even wilder extremes. Fisher (1919, p. 173) wrote: "We have found, in using the method of couples, that every objective item of cost is also an item of income, and that in the final total, no objective items of outgo survive cancellation . . . in a comprehensive view of production there is no cost of production in the objective sense at all." Böhm-Bawerk, as usual, stated the neoclassical case with exemplary clarity:

> Value is not produced at all, and cannot be produced. We never produce anything but forms, shapes of materials, combinations of material, that is to say, goods. These goods . . . only acquire value from the wants and satisfactions of the economic world . . . The most that production can do is create goods in the hope that, according to the anticipated relations of demand and supply, they will be of value [Böhm-Bawerk 1959, p. 90].

However much modern neoclassical historians of economic thought find these statements baffling and dismaying (Stigler 1941, p. 187), it should now become apparent that they are straightforward extrapolations from the original physics metaphor. If utility looks like potential energy, then prices are determined by the introduction of a given set of commodities into the potential field. Asking where the given commodity endowments came from was a meaningless question, just as senseless as asking where the initial conditions come from in any mechanics problem: Of course they came from another mechanics problem, but thanks to the various conservation principles those previous problems have no bearing upon the solution of the present problem. In other words, there was no sensible analogue of production in the energetics metaphor.

This absence of metaphorical inspiration was exacerbated by a renegade interpretation of the concept of utility, which aimed to rule production entirely out of the bounds of discourse. Given the methodological individualist and mentalist cast of early versions of utility, there lurked in the interstices of neoclassical theory the potential for an extremist version of idealism. Were one to entertain seriously the notion that value is whatever Ysidro thinks it is, and then to observe that the formal mathematical expression of this doctrine blocked any further investigation of just how Ysidro came to think as he did, then one obvious inference is that costs can have no influence on value by construction. It is only a short and unimaginative leap to further conclude that value expands and contracts with Ysidro's moods. Indulging in the luxuriant monomania of idealism, the economy only amounts to whatever any individual deems appropriate. It was precisely these sorts of tendencies that convinced the classical economists that usefulness could not account for value.

Some of the second generation of neoclassicals flirted with this extreme species of solipsism – no objective cost, no production of value, no production of commodities at all. (The incongruous marriage of this solipsism to physics is discussed in the next section on the conservation of matter.) Nevertheless, as a research tradition, they did not entirely succumb to it. Why not? Again, the rosetta stone is the physics metaphor. Above all, neoclassicals appropriated the physics metaphor in order to appropriate its scientific legitimacy: the image of the mathematical comprehension of the deterministic laws of a stable external world. The resulting redefinition of potential energy as utility, however, involved a neat dialectical juggling act. A deterministic portrayal of the physical world had to be transmuted into a similar portrayal of the psychic realm, which then lacked any physical determination. But in the later nineteenth century, the absence of any physical determination was tantamount to the absence of any deterministic explanation *tout court*. In effect, full acquiescence in the energetics metaphor would have been a self-defeating program for the fledgling economic theory, neutralizing its proud new claim to the status of a science.

Cost-of-production theories of a physical cast were in direct conflict
with the original utility theories of price. This conflict was of the most
vexatious character, the kind that insistently reminded the early neoclassicals of their own conflicting motivations in adopting the physics
metaphor. The wringing of hands and the gnashing of teeth whenever the topic of production was broached was not a semantic tempest in
a teapot, as was claimed by both Marshall and Schumpeter. On the
contrary, it was the dybbuk of classical economics, and it had to be
exorcised.

The dybbuk grew more imposing and insistent in the period from
1890 to the late 1920s. The broad outlines of the ideal solution were
fairly clear, even at that time: The anomaly of production should be
isolated and downgraded in significance. What was needed was a
redefinition of the production concept more in line with the physics
metaphor; the concept should appear to subsume earlier substance
notions of value, but at the same time it should unquestionably subordinate production to consumption in its new sense, – i.e., the field
metaphor of utility as energy.

Of course, knowing the name of the dybbuk is not the same as
knowing how to banish him, and success eluded the neoclassicals for
over a century. The problem has been that the classical conception of
production just refuses to die, or perhaps it is the capitalist culture
that is reluctant to give up the ghost. In any event, neoclassicals
persistently found themselves backsliding into a substance theory of
value wherever considerations of production became overly pressing
or paramount. The dybbuk lived on, and from time to time managed
to make an embarrassing appearance. Contretemps over marginal
productivity, periodic shouting matches over capital theory, pothers
over supply curves and empty boxes, and pouts over the superfluity
of the firm and the entrepreneur were symptomatic of the generic
problem. While we shall not take the temperature of each individual
tiff and squabble, it is necessary to summarize in some detail the basic
issue: Production, as conventionally understood, does not "fit" in
neoclassical value theory.

To get a trained economist to entertain this thesis is as easy as
getting a Catholic priest to entertain the notion of the fallability of the
Pope. Because of the great diversity in the beliefs of theologians and
neoclassical economists, perhaps all that we can aspire to in this venue
is a Cook's Tour of the landscape with some brief asides as to where
historians might further till this shamefully neglected patch of turf
and skeptics might retreat to test their faith. The problem is that
every economist is taught that there exists but one neoclassical theory

of production. Nothing could be further from the truth. Purely from an historical vantage point, there are at least eight different ways of trying to incorporate production into neoclassical theory. They are, in rough chronological order of their first appearance:

1. The identification of human labor with negative utility, which in turn somehow generates commodities *de novo*. (Gossen, early Fisher)
2. The backward imputation of the utility of final goods to their antecedent intermediate inputs through time in order to consolidate the maximization calculations into a single calculation. (Gossen, Menger, the Austrian school, the later Irving Fisher)
3. Reversion to a classical substance theory of value similar to the labor theory of value, but with little or no serious attempt to reconcile it with the neoclassical field theory of value. (Jevons, Böhm-Bawerk, J. B. Clark, Frank Knight, and naive capital theorists)
4. Reduction of produced goods to unexplained primitive endowments by means of a linear transformation. (Walras, Wieser, Leontief)
5. Marshallian supply curves.
6. Pareto's general theory of transformations.
7. Postulate the existence of an entirely novel value substance in order to bypass all previous production controversies and to finesse reconciliation with the neoclassical field theory. (Keynes)
8. Render production formally symmetrical to exchange by projecting the metaphor of the field onto "technology." (Wicksteed, Johnson, Douglas)

At the very outset, one might well wonder: Why are there so many production theories? The simple answer is that the very concept of production rests so uneasily within the ambit of a field metaphor. In Chapter 5 it was asserted that the conservation of energy would have as a legitimate analogy the conservation of utility plus the budget. The meaning of such an artifice would be that trade could be effectively decoupled from production so that value would be altered purely by the act of exchange. If one then allowed some alternative option for the increase of value strictly by means of the increase of commodities, it should be apparent that the whole notion of a path-independent equilibrium is severely compromised, not to mention the bedrock intuition of scarcity as a natural state. The incongruity of it all may be rendered more apparent by projecting the problem back onto the physics for a moment. If there were such a thing as production in energy physics, then there would be two different ways to get to any spatial location: the first, the conventional locomotion by means of impressed forces, and so on; and the second, a noncontinuous leap by means of some new power, perhaps transmigration or telepathy.

The problem – is the reader beginning to weary of this repetition? – is that the neglect of the implications of conservation principles for the original models of exchange made it impossible to make any coherent statements about the problem of production. One myth that has serves to garble the discourse for over the century is the refrain that the correct portrayal of production should not be an issue because it was dictated by considerations outside of the economics discipline. In other words, it was given to economists by engineers, or perhaps directly dictated by the laws of physics, as Samuelson claims at the beginning of this chapter. Such claims are false in every respect, as we shall soon see, but first, it should be noted that this attempt to pass the buck is just another instance of the denial of the pervasive character of metaphorical reasoning in economics. There is no single correct way to conceptualize production in all its myriad splendor; hence, some framework must be imposed upon the phenomenon in order to render it amenable to the purposes and perplexities of the neoclassical project. Historically, what happened was that certain classes of invariants had to be projected upon what was, at best, a mixed legacy from classical political economy. No engineer qua engineer had any clue about what these requirements were, and none would find out without actually becoming a neoclassical economist.[1]

Putting square pegs in round holes: Flirting with the conservation of matter

The ontology of the commodity has been sadly neglected in the history of economic thought, a fact observed by such noneconomists as Douglas and Isherwood (1979) and Sahlins (1976). In classical economics, the commodity was preeminently substantial in the sense discussed in Chapter 4. Value was itself a homogeneous substance, an undifferentiated "stuff" that embodied any economic phenomenon in its motion. This preoccupation with substance dictated the priority of the theory of production, since the creation (and destruction) of the value substance was of unsurpassed importance in accounting for economic "motion." The triumvirate of physical substance, physical production, and physical science summed up for the classical economist all that was objective and lawlike in the determinants of social behavior. From there it was only a short distance to the materialist interpretation of history, which insisted that all human interaction was merely a reflection of the material/technical substratum. The distinction between productive and unproductive activities so dear to the classical tradition was rendered coherent by this connection to the putatively stable physical world. Classical economists were fully in sympathy with Samuel Johnson in his refutation of Bishop Berkeley: Kicking a stone should be sufficient to bring a reasonable man to his senses.

This world was lost upon adoption of the novel energetics metaphor. As observed in Chapter 5, forces became prices and spatial coordinates became quantities of goods. At first, it seemed that commodities had retained their palpable *thing*ness as marking off the metric of the commodity space of the utility field. The firm cadence of "one apple, two apples, three apples, . . ." seemed to provide secure moorings for a materialist interpretation of social life. However, whenever the early neoclassical economists gave a little thought to the brute physical nature of commodities, they commenced to squirm in a most apprehensive and guilty manner. Witness, for example, Jevons discussing the mathematical foundations of economic dimensions:

> Beginning with the easiest and simplest ideas, the *dimensions of commodity*, regarded merely as physical quantity, will be *the dimensions of mass*. It is true that commodities are measured various ways – thread by length, carpet by length, corn and liquids by cubic measure, eggs by number, metals and most other goods by weight. But it is obvious that, though the carpet be sold by length, the breadth and width of the cloth are equally taken into account in fixing the terms of sale. There will [N.B.] generally be a tacit reference to weight, and through weight to mass of materials in all measurement of commodity. Even if this be not always the case, we may, for the sake of simplifying our symbols in the first treatment of the subject, assume that it is so. We need hardly recede to any ultimate analysis of the physical conditions of the commodity, but take it to be measured by *mass*, symbolized by M, the sign usually employed in physical science to denote this dimension. [Jevons 1970, p. 118]

It appears that Jevons felt that physics and economics were so indistinguishable that it would be effortlessly possible to extend the language of one to that of the other. Here, his terminology is lifted directly from Rankine and Maxwell: "The dimensions of this quantity are ML^2/T^2, where L, M and T represent the concrete units of length, time and mass" (quoted in Smith 1978, p. 249). Yet even Jevons felt compelled to admit that "commodityness" had not yet been abstracted out of phenomenal massy bodies. The reversion to the language of classical substance theories and the appeal to the physical sciences presaged the quandries and reactions of later neoclassicals when forced to confront their materialist presuppositions with the metaphor of the utility field. As time went on and no easy reconciliation of field and substance appeared on the horizon, the appeals to physical science grew ambagious and deceptive.

Patently, commodities were not givens in classical economic analysis in quite the same way that coordinate systems were givens in nineteenth-century physics. Prior to the spread of non-Euclidean geometries and the theory of relativity, rational mechanics was premised upon the certainty that the Euclidean coordinate system was a true representation of the mathematical substratum of the world. When this physics was imported into economics, the corresponding attributes were attributed to commodities. Commodities were simply "there," independent of social activity, and particularly, independent of trading activity, the analogue of motion. These commodities were ontologically inert, isolated from the theory of exchange, characterized as unexplained endowments. The fact that generic commodities were capable of comparison was attributed to the existence of the utility field, a kind of a priori knowledge in the mind, rather than any embodied value substance.

Contrary to the claims of neoclassicals such as Marshall (1947, p. 64), in this scenario consumption is *not* negative production. That doctrine is the province of classical political economy. Rather, neoclassical theory is characterized by the absence of true classical consumption *and* true classical production. Actors come equipped with a field of preferences that indicates what they *would* prefer if they possessed a virtual basket of commodities and were constrained to operate in a certain subset of their field. Consumption, in the common classical connotation of a process of experiencing satisfaction through use that destroys the substance of the commodity, is abnegated because of the postulate of the conservation of utility, as discussed in Chapter 5. After all, spatial coordinates do not disappear when a field is introduced into that space. The question of the disappearance of value had itself been effectively banished from the analysis: One could speak of it, but it was nowhere to be found in the mathematics. On the other side of the analysis, production in the sense of the process of the generation of commodities *de novo* had also been abnegated by the assumption of the conservation of the endowment and/or that of income. By this reckoning, there was no room left for classical ideas of production and consumption in neoclassical theory because they were blocked by the mathematical conservation principles.

If the neoclassical model of exchange was not a theory of production or consumption, then what was it? A neutral exegesis of the mathematical metaphor would suggest that all that could be portrayed would be virtual motions of unexplained commodities in a conserved mental field. All specification of process is absent, including such primary considerations as the acts of perception and interpretation inseparable from the behavior of an economic actor. It was precisely for this reason that there was no guarantee that it should be the *physical* essence of the commodity that would ultimately be economically relevant. As one commentator put it, "If 'consuming' means 'extracting utility from', then we may expect, by symmetry, that 'producing' must on the face of it consist, not in making or creating *things,* but in creating utility" (Fraser 1937, p. 178).

This tergiversation over the physical status of the commodity resulted in one of the more curious episodes in the history of economic thought – namely, the invocation of physical conservation principles in order to argue that physical science dictated that production did not really exist in a physical sense, thus absolving the new economics from having to deal with the questions of material production processes that had so occupied the classical economists. We have previously mentioned that Jean-Baptiste Say made reference to the law of the conservation of matter to support his argument that physical goods were not created, and that changes in value resulted primarily from spatial reorganizations of existing matter.[2] In retrospect this would have appeared an attractive doctrine to a neoclassical economist, and it is interesting to observe that as late as the 1890s many of the neoclassicals concerned to absorb some notion of production into the theoretical structure were drawn to this idea as bees to honey. The explicit invocations of physics must be sampled to be appreciated.

W. S. Jevons, in his posthumously published fragment *Principles of Economics,* mused:

> We speak, indeed, familiarly of *creating wealth,* but we must always understand this expression to mean only *creating utility.* There is no law better established in physics than that man can neither create nor annihilate matter . . . Our labour, then, only appropriates things, and by changes of form and place renders them useful for the satisfaction of our wants . . . Since most of these economists [such as Say] wrote, the truth of their remarks has been extended by the establishment of the principle of the conservation of energy. Not only matter, but of energy we may say that it can neither be created or annihilated. All change, then, is apparent rather than real change, and that changes not, but is itself a constant change [Jevons 1905b, pp. 68–9].

It makes one wonder whether Jevons might have been dipping into Hegel in his dotage.

Böhm-Bawerk likewise felt it prudent to insist that economic processes could violate no natural laws. To a scientifically literate person in the 1890s, such a statement would imply that the speaker was concerned that the laws of thermodynamics acted to severely limit the economic pretensions of the human race, but this was not Böhm-Bawerk's intention. The only extended reference he made to the laws of science in his three-volume work on capital and interest was to define production as "only a conversion of indestructable matter into more advantageous forms, and it can never be anything else . . . [man's] sole but completely adequate activity lies in the spatial control of matter. The ability to move matter is the key to all man's success in production, to all his mastery over nature and her forces" (Böhm-Bawerk 1959, II, p. 7).

While there might be a temptation to discount these passages as the idiosyncracies of two of the theorists most hostile to real-cost doctrines, the same excuse will not suffice for the self-proclaimed great peacemaker of utility and cost theories:

> Man cannot create material things . . . when he is said to produce material things, he really only produces utilities; or in other words, his efforts and sacrifices result in changing the form or arrangement of matter to adapt it better for the satisfactions of wants [Marshall 1947, p. 63].

The repeated citation of the law of the conservation of matter by the major progenitors of neoclassical production theory is one of the most revealing bits of evidence that physics and economics were restive bedfellows at the turn of the century. The primary allure of the law of the conservation of matter for the early neoclassicals was its service in repudiating the classical doctrines of production as the creation of value and of the conservation of the substance of value in exchange.

Neoclassical theorists wanted to assert that value was increased by the act of exchange; it was appreciated that the cause and extent of this increase would be extremely difficult to isolate and identify if the volume of production also increased as a simultaneous consequence. In order to render dramatic and unambiguous the purported increase of value attributable to market exchange, the early neoclassicals alit upon the expedient of neutralizing production by projecting the conservation principle from Nature itself, asserting that man could neither create not annihilate any physical substance. (In this respect, their tactic was precisely the reverse of Marx's abstraction from the transformation problem in Volume I of *Capital* in order to highlight the conservation of value in exchange.) They claimed that because Nature was immutable, changeable values could not in any way, shape, or form reside in the external commodity, and therefore must reside in the mental apparatus of the beholder. The conservation of matter seemed the perfect Trojan Horse to trundle into the midst of classical economics; it traded in the classical idiom of the reduction of phenomena to undifferentiated matter in motion, but coopted the legitimacy of physics for the neoclassical side, countering that material substance could not be increased as the classical corn model said it could.

However salutary as a neoclassical doctrine the conservation of matter initially appeared, its charms palled rapidly, to the extent that no self-respecting neoclassical dared to mention it after roughly 1920. The metaphor of an economic world of conserved matter was subverted from many different directions. The first and most unforseen reversal was the bad news from the physicists that the world had changed: Matter qua matter could be annihilated according to the theory of relativity and the later particle physics, and there was the discovery that some elements spontaneously decayed into elements of lesser atomic weights. Marshall's famous quotation that *Natura non facit saltum* was looking decidedly old hat, especially to those who understood some of the implications of the new quantum mechanics. To the twentieth century, matter just did not appear all that static and immutable.

The second bit of bad news was that, strictly speaking, the utility field was neither created nor destroyed in the mathematics imported from physics, and so, ill-founded assertions that trade created utility had to be relinquished. This put on the pressure to admit the expansion of endowments as the ultimate cause of the increase of utility.

Third, try as they might, neoclassical economists could not banish the popular conviction that *physical* expansion was the hallmark of economic progress. Every attempt to bury the notion of value as substance was met with two more novel variants, often from within the neoclassical camp.

Finally, because (as documented in the last chapter) the neoclassicals' own grip on the significance of conservation principles was tenuous, they frequently had a muddy conception of the relationship between the conservation principles imbedded in their physics metaphor and their advocacy of the conservation of matter. The major drawback was that the latter was redundant when coupled with the conservation of the endowment and/or income dictated by the physics metaphor. The result was that, by 1920, the neoclassicals had repudiated the one natural law they had been willing to claim was identical to an economic law.

Production would not be seduced onto the Procrustean bed of the physics metaphor; natural laws would not openly cohabit with natural metaphors; the energy metaphor was being frustrated by a refractory Nature. The situation was embarrassing, but no neoclassical was willing to come right out and say that production was superfluous or irrelevant in their scheme of things. (Lionel Robbins came the closest.) What happened instead was that the infelicity of the production concept in the first half-century of neoclassical theory was given vent through innuendo: One notices an inordinate number of slurs cast upon cost-of-production theories of price, or incongruous assertions that production was really just an exotic form of trading with Nature, or bizzare comments *en passant* such as: "We have all felt, with Professor Schumpeter, a sense of almost shame at the incredible banalities of much of the so-called theory of production – the tedious discussions of various forms of peasant proprietorship, factory organization, industrial psychology, technical education, etc." (Robbins 1952, p. 65). But production would not be conjured away; that went too much against the grain of a discipline which still prided itself on its tough-minded materialism. The paramount task was to find some plausible version of production that would fit snugly into the model of exchange.

At this juncture it is important to recall that the concept of production is not and has never been an eternal category in political economy, nor does it possess a fixed or immutable referent. Cannan (1917, pp. 32–40) claimed that a theory of production could only to be said to have existed by the second half of the eighteenth century, and that production as a broad division of the subject matter of political economy dates from 1821 in England. Production then quickly grew to dominate classical political economy, given the place it occupied in the context of the parallel evolution of substance theories of value, as described in Chapter 4.

As a simple rule of thumb, the locus of the generation of the value substance was defined to be the sphere of production, and the locus of the destruction of the value substance was defined to be the sphere of consumption. In classical economics everything else in between these two poles was defined as the sphere of circulation, in the sense that the conservation of value and the attendant exchange of equivalents reigned as the normal and just state of affairs. Depending upon a particular theorist's preferred incarnation of the substance of value, theories of production tended to exhibit a more or less overt concern with what we would now call technological questions. However, with the elaboration of the labor theory of value, a reaction had already begun to set in, to the extent that Marx felt it necessary to remind himself that "political economy is not technology" (Marx 1973, p. 86). Hence the concept of production that was the legacy of classical economics was in considerable flux when neoclassical theory appeared on the scene in the 1870s.

Situated a century later, we might now think it obvious what the physiognomy of the viable offspring of the marriage of neoclassical price theory and the classical theory of production would look like; or do we? Once it is understood that the raw material, the genetic endowment as it were, was the classical substance triad of production/circulation/consumption, and the environmental pressure was the energetics metaphor, then the possible outcomes do sort themselves into a limited number of categories; we shall now tour the taxonomy of those categories.

Getting more and more out of less and less: The neoclassical production metaphors

There is a good reason why the Marginalist Revolution made its first beachhead in the area of exchange rather than production. The metaphor of utility as potential energy was predicated upon a Weltanschauung of a closed, bounded system that exemplified the natural state of mankind as enduring ineluctable scarcity. If and when production was to be introduced into this morality play, it had to be done in such a way as to prevent the contravention of the scarcity principle, all the while maintaining the field theory of value. After all, in the Laplacian dream, can you really get something for nothing?

In retrospect it is painful to observe how the neglect of conservation principles doomed the neoclassicals to misunderstanding each other once they came to the problem of production. The most frequent mistake was to sow confusion in the value principle by reintroducing a substance theory of value. One can see why this might have initially seemed an attractive option: For instance, one could claim some continuity of doctrine with classical political economy, with its portrait of production as the generation of a surplus value substance, or one could seemingly effortlessly incorporate capital as an analytical term, or one could fudge all problems with the absence of any serious dynamics in the price theory. Nevertheless, in the end it was nothing more than mass confusion. The greatest source of discord in the history of neoclassical theory has been due to the lack of consensus concerning the meaning of production.

Because even today one rarely gets an inkling that neoclassical production theory is plural rather than singular, it is necessary to run down the list of production theories for the purpose of indicating: (i) the earliest progenitors of a particular option, (ii) its relationship to the primal physics metaphor and its treatment of conservation principles, and (iii) a brief indication of some of its drawbacks. Once one gets the scorecard straight, then it will become apparent that twentieth-century neoclassical theory resembles nothing so much as the child's game of Mr. Potatohead – the fun comes in mixing and matching components with little or no concern for the coherence of the final profile.

1. The earliest attempt to formalize a notion of production within neoclassical economics was the *identification of human labor with negative utility, which was then transformed into new quantities of existing commodities,* usually in some unspecified fashion. Gossen was the first to do so, as we have indicated in the previous chapter. One can also find this option in Irving Fisher's doctoral thesis of 1892; Edgeworth, too, flirted with the idea in 1881, but did not go so far as to formalize it (Creedy 1986, p. 87). The inspiration for this option is transparent: It is a superficial rendering of the labor theory of value appended to the neoclassical field equations. In this option, one posits a single activity called labor, which, for unexplained reasons, has a negative potential. However, said negative potential may be transformed at some fixed rate (immediately?) into a new position in the positive orthant of commodity space. The primary mode of visualization (or vitalization?) is to think of labor time as a fixed, naturally scarce endowment, conserved in its transformation into some set of commodities in a preset commodity space.

The primary drawback of this option is that labor is being formalized as a surrogate value substance, which is not consistent with the field specification of value. For instance, if labor takes time, the static character of the field is compromised. Or, generally the potentials in the original energetics metaphor all have the same sign; combinations of negative and positive potentials (such as electromagnetic theory) require a much more complicated formalism. If the conservation of labor in production is thought to hold strictly, then the entire system collapses to an embodied labor theory of value. What is missing is an explicit treatment of factors other than labor time, as well as their temporal location vis-à-vis the purported duration of labor "hours."

No neoclassical theorist has entertained this theory long enough to seriously develop it, but latent vestiges still remain in the guise of opportunity costs (Vaughn 1980).

Although its history is forgotten, the concept of opportunity costs was introduced into economics by Green (1894) in order to justify the earliest incorporations of production and labor cost into neoclassical theory by means of the artifice of negative utility. Subsequently, it maintained a subterranean existence in introductory neoclassical text-books, shorn of much of its subjectivist content and all of its negative utility, sporting a dowdy air of irrelevance as it disappeared from more advanced treatments of the theory. Indeed, it is the closest thing to a purely mental theory of production and exchange, repudiated because of its incipient solipsism and distance from materialist rheto-ric. That is not to say the temptation to reinvent the wheel is not endemic: It has been kept alive in the twentieth century by the neo-Austrian school and by certain partisans of a neoclassical "welfare economics." Practically, it has become one of the primary tools for the immunization of neoclassical theory from adverse falsifications: One can always maintain that the true costs in any given situation did not correspond to observed costs, and no one will feel impelled to object too strenuously. The fact that the mind/body separation has never been bridged in neoclassical theory allows such analytical in-determinacy to persist indefinitely.

2. Another attempt to subordinate production to the utility field is the *backward imputation of utility from final goods to intermediate inputs or goods of "lower order."* The hallmark of this option is the relative neglect of the field formalism and the treatment of utility entirely as if it behaved like an embodied value substance. Carl Menger is the premier advocate of this option; his "innovation" is explained by the fact (mooted in Chapter 5) that he was not a neoclassical theorist, in the sense that he had no comprehension of physics; indeed, this theory is little more than a classical substance theory with a different label. Menger believed that value exhibited a sort of temporal and situational integrity that would allow the analyst to impute it back from final use through to the original factors of production. Such an analysis hinges critically upon an unstated conservation principle that posits satisfaction as invariant with respect to processes of production and exchange, a principle patently at odds with the field concept.

Curiously enough, Irving Fisher also resorted to this option later in life, even though he was one of the early neoclassicals most familiar with the field metaphor. Although Fisher's thesis advocated option #1, he was careful there to include a list of ten caveats and disanalo-gies thrown up by the production concept (Fisher 1926, p. 105). As

Fisher became increasingly embroiled in debates over capital theory with Böhm-Bawerk and others, he began to speak more and more in substance language. Runyon (1959, p. 18) reports that Fisher experienced his epiphany in this regard during a trip through Bavaria, where he claims to have gotten his idea of distinguishing between capital and income by observing a spigot over a watering trough. Even in modern textbooks, there is no more prosaic illustration of a conserved value substance than the metaphor of water in a bathtub.

The fruit of his inspiration, the book *The Nature of Capital and Income,* is a work that preaches the importance of the distinction between a stock of capital goods and a flow of capital services. These services are the imputed utility under a different name. Because the utility had to be imputed through time, Fisher grew uncharacteristically vague when it came to measuring the stock of capital goods (Fisher 1919, pp. 10, 67). To deflect such problems, Fisher's later work moves with breathtaking freedom back and forth between income and utility, as if they could be treated as identical. The only cogent interpretation of this work is to deduce that Fisher ended up treating utility as if it were a conserved value substance, especially when committing such atrocities on the field metaphor as discounting back future utility using a single rate of interest.

The primary drawback of this option is that, although it displays a poignant sensitivity to the fact that production takes time, it cannot be reconciled with the way the field formalism treats time. A field expresses a virtual state, which can only be extended through time by means of the conservation of tastes and incomes. Utility is not inherent in the commodity, but in the mind, and therefore it cannot be passed from one commodity to another.

3. A third option was to *revert to a classical embodied substance theory of value* when discussing production *without any attempt to reconcile it with the field theory of value.* Although this seems the shoddiest option of all (Why bother to posit one value theory in one sphere, when a wholly separate one is thought to hold sway in another?), it certainly was a quick and dirty way to make neoclassical theory look as if it were reconciled with classical political economy.

The earliest progenitors of this option were some of the neoclassical theorists most prone to expressing anguish over the production concept, although most of the problems were of their own making. Stanley Jevons, for one, wrote: "There is no close or necessary connexion between the employment of capital and the process of exchange. Both by the use of capital and by exchange we are enabled vastly to encrease the sum of utility we enjoy; but it is conceivable that we might have the advantages of capital without those of exchange" (Jevons 1970, p. 225). The void that yawned between capital and exchange was the rupture between classical and neoclassical value theory, and Jevons could not bridge the chasm. Jevons initially defined capital as identical with the subsistence goods forwarded to laborers, but in his mathematical lucubrations proceeded to conflate this idea with the numerical expression of the hours worked multiplied through by the time duration of the investment. There was no way this hodgepodge could have been related to the utility field, although it did bear a passing resemblance to an embodied-labor-theory of value.

Another pitfall in the history of neoclassical economics is to assume all Austrians are alike. Böhm-Bawerk's theory of production was not the same as that of Carl Menger; rather, the scourge of the Marxian labor theory expressed his own preference for a concept of capital measured by its average period of production, defined much the same as in Jevons's theory – the product of labor hours expended multiplied through by the duration of investment (Böhm-Bawerk 1959, II, pp. 86–7). He opted for this mathematical definition despite his earlier claim that capital is reducible to the two primary factors of land and labor. Knut Wicksell (1938, p. 150) follows Böhm-Bawerk in this respect, insisting that capital was "a single coherent mass of saved-up labor and saved-up land," only to discover that a substance is not a substance (and certainly is not a mass) once its heterogeneous components are permitted freely varying relative prices determined by the field metaphor.

J. B. Clark, the all-time slipperiest proponent of this doctrine, regularly dealt in the language of transmigration (Clark 1938, p. 119) in order to give life to a substancelike fund that managed to rival the Deity in both Being and Not-Being identical to the heterogeneous commodities that constituted the inputs to production. Clark deftly played upon the numerous connotations of the word "capital" while making vague references to the utility theory of value; disparaging mathematics, Clark was never held to the rigors of the formalisms of the field metaphor. Energy looked more like Spirit in Clark's system, and this resonated with his zeal for a moral economics. However, the key to understanding the mundane side of Clark's economics is to note that he, too, had to revert to units of labor hours in order to measure his capital, although he did manage to postpone the admission until the end of his book (Clark 1938, p. 346).

This option, however slipshod, took root in the neoclassical tradition, and began to turn up in all sorts of exotic guises, such as Frank

Knight's "Crusonia plant" (Buechner 1976) and "jelly," "schmoos," and "protoplasm." Acceptance of these cartoon caricatures was probably encouraged by the *appearance* of consistency with the field metaphor fostered by the repeated invocation of some "marginal product of capital". A moment's reflection should reveal that nothing prevents the application of calculus to a substance theory of value; but mere use of calculus is not tantamount to deployment of the field metaphor. This was a fine point easily overlooked in the early days of neoclassicism, when calculus struck terror in the average social theorist.

The drawbacks of this options should be obvious. Value cannot reside in the goods in a field theory of value, nor can it exist independent of the prices determined by the field formalism. A simple point, but one lost in the shuffle of production options soon to follow in the twentieth century.

4. Another possible conceptualization of production was as a *reduction of "produced goods" to their ultimate constituent endowments by means of a linear transformation.* This option was first innovated by Walras in his *Elements,* in Wieser's *Natural Value,* and in the more well-known endeavors of Wassily Leontief. The use of the term "production" here is little more than an elaborate pun, since all this gambit does is project one set of axes into another set in commodity space as a prelude to the conventional optimization over the utility field. If the matrix operator is square (the most frequent case), then the commodity space is uniquely mapped onto itself. Although this option has a clearer notion of how to subordinate production to the physical metaphor than the previous cases, it has close connections to the substance theory of value, a fact rendered apparent by the work of Sraffa, discussed later.

From the neoclassical viewpoint, one major drawback of this option is that it portrays a situation where relative prices could be inferred from a square matrix without recourse to the utility fields: These are the infamous nonsubstitution theorems, also to be discussed later. Another drawback is that the very notion of surplus is inscribed in the structure of the transformation matrix independent of any economic activities, in the guise of the Hawkins–Simons conditions.

5. A more familiar option, if only because it is a ritual part of the initiation rite of tyro economics students, is the *Marshallian supply curve.* Marshall's role in the pasteurization of the physics origins and the mathematical consequences of neoclassical theory has been sketched in Chapter 5. It is worthwhile in the present context to recall that one of his techniques of rendering neoclassicism palatable was to create the impression of strong continuity between classical and neoclassical theory. The classical concern with the process of production was to have been retained in the new theory by means of his supply curve. Combining the supply curve with Cournot's phenomenological demand function, he identified in their intersection a novel concept of equilibrium, one nowhere to be found in the physics metaphor. The task of the reconciliation of this novel artifice with the original field metaphor is the key to understanding the meaning of the supply curve.

As is well known, Marshall, initiated the practice of distinguishing types of analysis according to the duration of "abstract time," which is conceived to elapse during the analysis (Blaug 1985, p. 371). He posited a market period that was essentially the instantaneous equilibrium of the physics metaphor; a short run in which production of output could be augmented but the expansion of productive capacity is prohibited, and a long run in which productive capacity can be augmented but original natural endowments are still fixed. The purpose of this distinction was twofold: to suggest that certain economic adjustments were prior to others through a ranking dependent upon freezing certain variables, and to accomodate the temporal character of production by creating a category of irreversible phenomena identified with fixed capital.

As was standard with Marshall, the narrative told one story, the mathematics another. The narrative claimed that the artifice of temporal frames would heal the rift between classical and neoclassical theories, or, as Marshall (1920, p. 349) put it,

> [A]s a general rule, the shorter the period we are considering, the greater must be the share of our attention which is given to the influence of demand on value; and the longer the period, the more important will be the influence of cost of production on value. For the influence of changes in cost of production takes as a rule a longer time to work itself out than does the influence of changes in demand.

But the mathematics in the footnotes and appendixes said no such thing, given that equilibrium was expressed as a solution of simultaneous equations and that most feedback effects were frozen in the ceteris paribus conditions. With no mathematical contrivance for making temporal distinctions, production effectively remained instantaneous, a fact that led to an acrimonious exchange with Böhm-Bawerk.

Apparently Marshall's intention was to subsume the structure of a production field in his two-dimensional supply curve by means of his "principle of substitution" (Marshall 1920, p. 356). As in a field formalism, he wanted the composition of factors of production to be altered with changes in factor prices, thus coopting the language of marginal productivity, but he also wanted to assert that certain substitutions could only be effected slowly, a notion antipathetic to the field formalism. In some contexts he further fudged the logic of a field by conflating substitution in the long run with technical change, a revision that compromised the mathematical integrity of the field. The purpose of these slapdash amendments was to represent the passage of time in production as a change in the slope of his supply curve. In Marshall's terminology, the short-run supply curve was inelastic. Here the scarcity of endowments was the primary constraint, and therefore price was predominantly demand-determined, as indeed was the case in the original physics metaphor. In the long run the supply curve was more elastic and output could be expanded, partially ameliorating the primal scarcity. In retrospect, or at least after reading Sraffa's 1926 article, it should have been apparent that such supply-mediated price adjustments must have implications for other prices and thus the supposedly fixed input prices that constituted the underlying cost curves. Marshall clearly hoped all these problems were swept under the rug by the partial equilibrium method, but later Marshallians could not leave them be. Empty boxes, representative firms, internal external economies and all sorts of clutter began to crawl out of the woodwork.

Marshall has often been praised for relegating his mathematics to the back of the book, but that practice does have its drawbacks. For example, when it came to actually writing down the expression for marginal products, Marshall promptly forgot all the paraphernalia of his temporal schemes, and essentially reproduced the same static field equations as found in the theory of the consumer (Marshall 1920, pp. 852–3) All his avuncular warnings about not taking the theory of marginal productivity too seriously (pp. 410, 518, 519) might be interpreted as the prudence of a scholar who tempered the mathematical enthusiasms of the theorist with a respect for the complexity of experience – or it could just have been the judicious covering of tracks after a messy bit of work.

The Marshallian juggling of time frames did not successfully reconcile the classical conception of production with the field formalism. His amphilogisms, however, do project in bold relief precisely what one can and cannot do with field formalisms as a metaphor for production. His first amphilogism was to posit substitution in the long run. This contrasts sharply with a field formalism, which deals in *virtual* adjustments. To allow the passage of time to influence the outcome of production is to relinquish path-independence and the stability of the field.

Now, some readers may think this is carrying faithfulness of metaphorical representation too far – why not alter the metaphor to make it conform to what is clearly an important consideration in reality? The problem in this case is that these temporal amendments destroy the internal coherence of the metaphor and violate its mathematical consistency, rendering it useless as a paradigm of research. Here, one cannot logically have it both ways by having a short-run field theory and a long-run system that exhibits hysteresis. After all, if the short run is really short, how can there be any substitution, and therefore a field formalism at all? Some may try to justify the oxymoron of a short-run field by claiming that adjustments in capacity utilization fulfill this role (Blaug 1985, p. 447). But this has all sorts of unsavory consequences: It confuses technological and organizational specifications; it tries to graft another variable time frame upon a static formalism; it conflates stocks and flows; and it neglects to explain how anything less than full utilization can be reconciled with constrained optimization and the putative "envelope" character of the production surface (Mirowski 1985, chaps. 5, 6). Independent of all those consequences, the Marshallian revision has one further fatal flaw: The specification of the relative time frames of what can be substituted how rapidly for whatever else must itself be entirely exogenous to the operation of the economy. If relative price changes also alter the rankings of the fixity of factors, as they do in reality (alterations in capacity utilization being a prime example), then the supply curve cannot even be considered a function (Mirowski 1981).

The second amphilogism is Marshall's insistence that the supply curve is irreversible: That is, once a firm started to move along it, it would set in motion a sequence of events that would prevent a return along the same path (Bharadwaj 1978b, p. 50). This obviously violates the path-independence condition, which is one of the distinguishing characteristics of a field. Without the field formalism, all that is left of Marshall's theory is some statement that production systems have some inertia, but beyond that nothing intelligible can be said about firms' reactions to price fluctuations. Marshall, never one to do things by halves, killed the supply curve twice over.

The third amphilogism was Marshall's equilibrium of demand and supply functions. While the rhetoric of symmetry was obviously important to him, he was unable to carry through that symmetry in his melding of the theories of demand and supply. The slapdash scaffolding of the short run and the long run were used to prop up the supply side of the analysis, but some noticed that Marshall never chose to symmetrically differentiate a short-run and long-run demand curve. The reason was simple: Insofar as the demand curve is derived from the utility field, it is static and cannot accommodate the passage of time. These two curves, advertised as purportedly commensurate, in fact should not be inscribed on the same axes (Souter 1933; Wicksteed 1950).

Further, recall the importance of the conservation of utility/energy metaphor from Chapter 5. Marshall was probably unfamiliar with this condition, and his differential time frames repeatedly violated it. For instance, were the demand curve extended into the long run in symmetry with the supply curve, then both the conservation of utility and the conservation of income would be violated. Increased production would generate increased incomes and altered prices, and tastes would be required to persist unaltered even through the innovation of new commodities and commodity uses. The more one considers it, the more incoherent appears Marshall's long run. However, after these first tentative steps down the primrose path, there was no real alternative. A retreat to the short run, by his own admission, would forestall any significance of production and the reconciliation with classical theory. There was no solution, so Marshall papered the whole thing over with a florid pattern of Victorian common sense.

The supply curve was the Achilles heel of the Marshallian system, the locus of numerous attacks upon Marshallian theory in the 1920s and 1930s (Robbins 1928; Sraffa 1926; Clapham 1922; Schumpeter 1954, p. 922). The response in the world of English theory assumed two formats: the first a redoubled concern with the definitions of perfect and imperfect competition, the second a reversion to the pure symmetry thesis. The first research program was eventually a failure, and was admitted to be such by its most perceptive protagonist, Joan Robinson. The second program, initiated by Wicksteed, Berry, and Johnson, essentially prepared the ground for the eventual repudiation of the long-run supply curve in favor of the metaphor of technology as a static field (option [8]).

The story of the rise and fall of the supply curve still awaits its historian, although an admirable beginning on its genesis has been made by White (1989). The supply curve as a loose phenomenological expression of costs was in fact invented by Fleeming Jenkin in 1870, well before Marshall's appearance on the scene.[3] A case can be made that, whereas in Jenkin's hands it had nothing to do with the neoclassical field model, Marshall, upon reading the paper, saw that he might graft it onto neoclassical price theory in order to heal the rupture between the field theory of value and the classical substance theory, which had remained dominant in discussions of production.

6. One neoclassical theory of production that seems to have had no further partisans other than its original author is *Pareto's general theory of transformations.*

Pareto's strictures on production are one of the important repressed episodes in the history of neoclassical economics. In Stigler's otherwise comprehensive survey of early production theories, Pareto's own theory is not even described, the only attention he merits being a curt dismissal of his critiques of theories of marginal productivity (Stigler 1941, pp. 364–8). Hutchison (1953, p. 221) likewise opts out of actual description by tendering the excuse that Pareto's theory of production is "one of the most difficult to follow in detail." Even Edgeworth (1925, II, p. 379) admitted that he might not fully understand it. The difficulty that most orthodox neoclassical historians have with Pareto's writings is that he rejects precisely the production theories that they hold dear, and yet claims for his own ideas a generality to which they cannot aspire.

Pareto, employing an insight that would still repay sustained attention, desired to reduce all economic interactions to the status of special cases of a single generic mathematical transformation. He proposed that when an individual relinquishes a certain quantity of good A in order to procure good B, this can be interpreted as a species of transformation of good A into good B. In an economy, a number of alternative paths of transformation from A to B exist: one such path is predicated upon direct exchange of A for B in a market; another such path starts with A and subjects it to a production process that results in B; a third path involves giving A to some third party who implements some combination of production and exchange and returns B to the original owner of A (Pareto 1971b, p. 124). Pareto then proceeded to differentiate three broad classes of transformations: physical transformations, transformations in space, and transformations in time. Endowments that are not already in their optimal physical manifestations of spatial/temporal locations are what Pareto calls "obstacles of the first kind." "Obstacles of the second kind," in direct analogy with Ostwald's energetics, are constraints that hinder or prevent the transformation of commodities from occuring in the most direct or efficient manner. Judging from his figure number eight (p. 125), it seems that obstacles of the second kind arise because *economic transformations are not generally path-independent.* This interpretation is supported by Pareto's sensitivity to such issues after being chided for their neglect by Vito Volterra (Volterra, in Chipman et al., eds., 1971), as well as the statement concerning obstacles of the first kind in the Appendix to the *Manuale:*

> [I]n assuming the existence of the integral functions F, G, . . ., we implicitly assume that the quantities of A, B, C, . . . employed in production do not depend on the path followed to reach the point under consideration. This is indeed just how things take place in reality [p. 444].

Hence, we begin to divine the reasons for Parero's scorn for all other competing neoclassical theories of production, from those attempting some minor addendum to the utility field (options 1, 2, 3, and 5) to those that purported to specify an entirely distinct technological relation (4 and 8). He poured abuse on those who "believed that they had found a law in political economy analogous to the law of definite proportions in chemistry," and insisted that "it is necessary to get rid of such vague conceptions as the *utility* of production . . . and replace them with precise notions, such as those of minimum cost of production and maximum profit. Next it must be clearly understood that the determination of the coefficients of production is not solely a technical operation" (Pareto 1971, p. 466).

Fortified with an understanding of the tensions that beset the appropriation of the energetics metaphor, it should become apparent that Pareto's theory of production was intended to parlay the formalism of energetic transformations into a solution of the mind/body problem and simultaneously to circumvent all the conundrums of absorbing production into the physics formalism. In physics, heat and light are not really identical, but rather share some profound similarities and symmetries, which are expressed by means of the formalism of energy transformations. In Pareto's theory, again commodities are not identical, but rather exhibit certain similarities that should be analogously expressed in the formalism of transformations. But here we run into logical difficulties, most notably the specification of the analogous standard of comparison that allows us to see the symmetries.

The proto-energetics metaphor originally appropriated by Jevons, Walras, and others suggested that it was the ontological stability of mind itself that warranted the stability of the various transformations of utility: All commodities are alike in that they are objects of our independent esteem. Pareto, in attempt to absorb production within the ambit of neoclassical theory, wanted to stretch the concept of esteem by including within it an a priori estimate of whether a given commodity could potentially be used to produce another. But these two versions of similarity are not congruent one with another: Is it the mind that judges whether production is possible, or is it the natural-law dictates of the objective natural world that deem whether and how commodities are to be compared? Are all obstacles primordially present in the mind, or do they vary with physical conditions? The former option was embodied in the early radical solipsism of neoclassical theory described in the previous section, while the best representative of the latter was, *mirabile dictu,* classical economic theory.

Pareto, of course, thought he could innovate a third way, a passage between Scylla and Charybdis. Just because neoclassicals posited mental relations that resembled natural law, it did not follow that the relations were identical with natural law. Pareto alone among all the neoclassicals eschewed any specification of technology, because he understood that the reification of a necessary relationship between inputs and outputs would entail an additional specification of commodity identity, another invariance condition over and above the conservation of utility. This explains the fact that so perplexes neoclassical historians of economic thought, the fact that Pareto was contemptuous of all theories of marginal productivity. In lieu of all that, Pareto proposed to subsume all trade and production under the single formalism of "indifference lines of obstacles" (Pareto 1971, pp. 126 ff.), where all of the paths by which good A could be transformed into good B were plotted as if on a gradient. This gradient abstracted away the process by which one arrived at B from A; trade and technology were treated as an inextricably unified and homogeneous phenomenon.

Pareto's general theory of commodity transformations was undeniably ambitious and yet fatally flawed. Pareto's admission that economic transactions are not in general path-independent results in a serious internal contradiction. Because one could potentially get from A to B by a myriad of paths that are neither transitive or reversible, it follows that Pareto's indifference lines of obstacles could not be integrated to a functional surface in commodity space (Neisser 1940). When Pareto acknowledged the prevalence of economic path-dependent transformations, his "obstacles of the second kind," he did not comprehend that this was tantamount to an admission that there existed no identity relation for the operation of transformations. No identity relation means no conserved-value principle, which implies no legitimate constrained optimization. Hence all Pareto achieved was to get further tangled in the already convoluted problem of the conservation of value in neoclassical theory.

If commodities exhibited no identity through time (a route foreclosed by allowing an apple at different temporal locations to be a different commodity), then the concept of production was bereft of significance. Lacking a conservation principle that structured the interpretation of the very notion of an optimal transformation from commodity A to commodity B, the very existence of any commodity is necessarily an adventitious proposition, without rhyme or reason. Apples could just as well have been dropped from the sky as been the fruits of conscious cultivation, for all it mattered to the theory.

7. A generally unrecognized alternative to the above options is to *posit a novel value substance,* which has no previous relationship to any of the other options or to the field theory of value, *in order to circumvent existing controversies over the concept of production.* John Maynard Keynes was the premier advocate of this option, with his postulation of an entity called national income, which exhibited all of the attributes of a value substance in his new system of macroeconomic theory.

The rise of a separate macroeconomics in the 1930s and 1940s was a direct consequence of Keynes's renunciation of all of the previous options for the conceptualization of production in neoclassical theory. Although a goodly proportion of the recent deforestation of our planet may be attributed to the surfeit of books published on *What Keynes Really Really Really Meant,* it does seem odd that the paramount importance of the rise of the national income concept in the context of the problems of the neoclassical research program has been neglected. The notion that a nation as an entity could be thought of possessing a wealth or an income is an old idea, dating back to William Petty and Gregory King in late-seventeenth-century England (Studenski 1958; Kendrick 1970). However, the coherence of such concepts was in doubt, as explained in Chapter 4, because there was much confusion over the underlying value theory. Later attempts at gauging national wealth, such as Giffen's (1889) were more directly linked to the substance theory of value by being cast in terms of capital. It was only around World War I that some economists set about the task of collating reams of statistical series of physical volumes of output for the purpose of creating indexes of national production, partly to discuss the phenomenon of business cycles (Copeland 1915; Persons 1919).

Wartime mobilization requirements were one stimulus to this activity, but another, underrated, impetus was the rival school of American Institutionalist economics. The Institutionalist school held as one of its tenets that orthodox neoclassical theory was useless for the discussion macroeconomic contractions (Mirowski 1985, chap. 3).

The most prominent spokesperson for this position in the United States was Wesley Clair Mitchell, the prime mover behind the foundation of the National Bureau of Economic Research (NBER). It was under his tutelage that the very first research report of the fledgling NBER was a statistical estimate of the newly defined concept of national income. Significantly, Mitchell was not prompted to define the concept by any prior economic theory; instead, he based its legitimacy on the common practices and everyday parlance of businesspeople.

Mitchell's NBER, Colin Clark, and some others invested the national-income concept with empirical legitimacy, creating a distinct theoretical entity in its own right. This undoubtedly set the stage for Keynes's decision to base the *General Theory* upon it; and indeed, there are even a few documented links between Mitchell and Keynes (Mirowski 1985, pp. 42–5; Stoneman 1979). While we cannot attempt a summary of the Keynesian system here, it may suffice to highlight the fact noticed by others (Mehta 1978; Cencini 1984) that the path from Keynes's *Treatise on Money* to the *General Theory* was marked by a profound change in the attitude towards national income. Along the way the national-income concept was effectively severed from capital, permitting the rate of increase of income to be analytically divorced from the rate of profit on capital. This breach was a very subtle rhetorical trope, for it shifted the index of production from the more conventional capital to the new device of income:

> Let us mean by current *income* the value of current output, which, I understand is what Mr. Robertson means by it. If we define savings as the excess of income during a period over expenditures on consumption during that period, it follows that savings are exactly equal to the value of output added to accumulated wealth, i.e., to investment [Keynes 1973, XIII, p. 327].

Much confusion is dispelled if one notes that the putative equation of the concept of income and the concept output is the font of most of the theoretical novelty of the *General Theory*. From this premise, it was only a short step to Kahn's multiplier and the marginal propensity to consume. After that epistemic rupture, one found oneself with a theory of the magnitude of output independent of production functions and technological specifications, free of all those nagging transtemporal considerations, free from all utility fields, and, for all practical purposes, unencumbered by any binding commitment to any specific theory of capital. One can document this freedom by noting that all of the discussions of the "marginal efficiency of capital" in the *General Theory* never explicitly advocate any of the theories of production outlined above. Indeed, Keynes was famous for his democratic willingness to sneer at any and all theories of production: for instance, "God knows what the Austrians mean by the 'period of production'. Nothing, in my opinion" (p. 517). Or, for those who insist that the vintage of a Keynesian apercu is an important test of its validity, there are his lecture notes of 1937:

> Those who are old enough and attended in 1931–32 may remember a contraption of formulas of processes of all sorts of lengths depending on technical factors with income emerging at a given date corresponding to input at an earlier date. My distinction then was between input and output. I would lecture on this at considerable length and at one time it occupied several chapters of my book. But I discarded it partly because it was frightfully complicated and really had no sense to it, but mainly because there was no determinate time unit . . . When one is dealing with *aggregates*, aggregate effective demand at time A has no corresponding income at time B [XIV, p. 180].

One of the numerous charms of the *General Theory* was that, like its contemporary work of art *A la recherche du temps perdu*, it played upon the nostalgia of its audience, in this case a return to the substance theory of value while maintaining the outward trappings of modern (or, at least, Marshallian) analysis. The initial vituperative attacks upon its curious "tautologies," such as savings equals investment, or $Y = C + I = C + S$ were in fact right on the mark: The real departure of the Keynesian system occurred at the level of definition, the level of value theory, the level of fundamental conservation principles (Cencini 1984, chap. 1). The disparaging terminology of Hydraulic Keynesianism of later years can also be understood in the same manner.

However much Keynes claimed that he was motivated by concerns over the problems of uncertainty, disequilibrium, interdependence, and the deficiencies of classical economics, the fact remains that in Keynesian theory national income = national output is treated as a conserved value substance outside of the sphere of the multiplier; yet in neoclassical theory both the level and composition of national income are subject to unpredictable changes in magnitudes due to changes in relative prices. National income would not be expected to be conserved anywhere by a card-carrying neoclassical theorist, which goes quite a distance in explaining the ire of such theorists as Hayek, Haberler, and Robertson. Yet Keynes held one advantage over those critics: He was free to posit the existence of an analytical term called national income that acted just like a classical value substance. When the inevitable challenges arose, he could point to actual compendia of statistical national accounts provided by the NBER, Colin Clark, and others. The fact that those compendia were constructed according to principles that had nothing to do with his own theoretical pronouncements evoked no more than a moment's discomfort, since no economist (and especially no neoclassical economist) would be willing to become embroiled in the distinctly low-status controversies in the construction of the relevant accounts, much less actually accept tutelage from accountants (Palmer 1966; Tew 1953; Copeland 1958, chap. 10; Keynes 1964, chap. 6). And finally, if all else failed, Keynes proved remarkably willing to redefine national product to be anything his critics wanted it to be.[1]

8. We have saved the most popular option, if not actually the best option, for last. In this representation of production, it is asserted that an *exogenously given technology can be portrayed as a field in commodity space.* Another common way of referring to this option is to assert that technology may be treated in a manner fully symmetric with preferences; we should now observe that this means that the physics formalism of the field equations can be applied to production as well as consumption. The role of the proto-energetics metaphor is more direct here than elsewhere: Potential energy, once projected onto the mind, is now reflected back onto the physical world. The unsung original progenitor of this option was Hermann Amstein, who sketched out its possibilities in a letter to Leon Walras in January 1877 (Walras 1965, I, letter 364). Walras, always incapable of really understanding field metaphors, put it aside, only to have the option revived at the turn of the century by Philip Wicksteed, Enrico Barone, W. E. Johnson, and a host of others. Johnson, the most sophisticated mathematician as well as the inventor of the term "production function," explicitly made the connection to an "analogy to a line of force cutting across equipotential surfaces" (Johnson 1913, p. 509).

The portrait of technology as an exogenous equipotential field *may* evade dependence upon a substance theory of value, but that is neither necessary nor inevitable. Indeed, Wicksteed's advocacy of the doctrine that all production functions must a priori be homogeneous of degree one was a direct attempt to make production fields behave like value substances. The waters are further muddied by the fact that many early users of the production function, such as Paul Douglas, persistently tried to introduce substance concepts into the field by proposing that such analytical artifacts as capital be introduced as arguments of the production function.

Because of the range, diversity, and sloppiness in the use of neoclassical production functions, the option of treating technology as if it were a field is one of the most tangled and intransigent phenomena in the history of neoclassical economics. It will take special effort to sort out the historical and analytical issues in this case, not in the least because economists have gotten accustomed to illegitimately attributing its peccadillos to outsiders, such as engineers. Let us begin to clear away the underbrush by starting with a representative modern textbook treatment.

The spurious symmetry of neoclassical theories of production and consumption

If we take a recent graduate microeconomic theory textbook (Varian 1978) as paradigmatic, the student's initiation into the mysteries of neoclassicism now begins with the "theory of the firm", taking prices as given. A critical assertion is made that costs of production are a direct function of the level of output of the firm; then a number of quaint Marshallian notions are introduced, only to be unceremoniously dropped once one arrives at Walrasian general equilibrium. The impression is thus created that the technical aspects of the theory are firmly rooted in the real-world phenomena of physical goods and technological blueprints. Only then is the novice introduced to the theory of the consumer, which is, of course, the original physics field metaphor. Utility functions are broached gingerly as hypotheses (thus fostering the impression that they would or could be relinquished at the drop of a hat, the minute some crucial experiment called them into question), which are nonetheless lent credence by the observation that the problem of the consumer is symmetrical with the problem of the producer (Varian 1978, p. 85). Both are conjoined as one general problem of the constrained maximization of an objective function, both subordinate to the same general logic of rational choice.

This assertion of symmetry is one of the primary rhetorical tools of neoclassicism in the twentieth century, judging by the frequency with which it is met (Marshall 1947, p. 820; Fisher 1926, p. 55; Hicks 1946, pp. 78–9). Earlier generations of neoclassicals were pronouncedly less ingenuous about this fact, though, since some, such as Edgeworth (1925, II, pp. 468–9) explicitly admitted what they were doing:

> The analogy between consumption and production, between maximizing utility and minimizing cost, is calculated to elucidate one or other of the phenomena, whichever is less clear and familiar. It is usually the more subjective of two compared phenomena which gains in clearness by the comparison. Yet the poets, those masters of allegory, occasionally illustrate things of sense by things of the soul.

Varian and the other modern textbooks, of course, want to suggest that the more "objective" problem of choice of production technique is an allegory for an analogous choice on the part of the consumer.

This presentation of the structure of neoclassical theory is stubbornly and willfully backwards: The physics metaphor of the soul came first, and the production theory was grafted onto it much later. To stare into this house of mirrors is dizzying; the physics of the external world was reified as an allegory of the human soul, only to be turned around and projected back in a further reification onto physical production. From our historical perspective, temporal primacy also dictated theoretical primacy: The standards of an adequate scientific explanation of the economy were first reified in the physics metaphor, and consequently the concept of production had to be recast in order to conform to its imperative. But the reconceptualization of the classical notion of production was never entirely complete and never thoroughly successful, and it is those deficiencies that the allegory of the symmetry of the producer and the consumer is intended to ameliorate, or perhaps to camouflage. Superficial resemblances between isoquants and indifference curves serve to obscure the more profound incompatibilities in theoretical exegesis.

Theoretical disharmonies between the demand and supply perspectives were recognized early in this century, and have provoked some heated, though obscure, debates (Suranyi-Unger 1931, pp. 91–104, 171–85; Sraffa 1926; Veblen 1969; Souter 1933; Eatwell 1975; Bharadwaj 1978b; Roncaglia 1978). Perhaps the preeminent failure on the part of the critics was not to understand that the inspiration for the demand tradition was the physics of energy, and that the theory was sufficiently characterized by the mathematics of variational principles and conservation principles in a field of potentials. Because the physics origins of neoclassical economics were mislaid in the twentieth century, no critic has ever completely succeeded in explaining why production is asymmetric with consumption in neoclassical theory, although there have been a number of obliquely informative attempts (Georgescu-Roegen 1976; Bharadwaj 1978b; Eatwell 1975; Walsh and Gram 1980; Pasinetti 1981; Baranzini and Scazzieri 1986). Because the reader who has persevered to this point may be assumed to have become familiar with many of the fine points of the physics metaphor, we may now proceed to demonstrate the asymmetry of production and consumption theory as a bill of particulars:

THE FIELD METAPHOR. The first and most fundamental asymmetry between the neoclassical theories of the firm and of the consumer is that the quotidian notion of production lends itself less felicitously to expression by means of the metaphor of a field than does the notion of an ordering of preferences. Let us compare the two metaphors, making use of Figure 6.1.

It is not at all clear, or even a metaphorically compelling statement, that physical inputs have a potential to metamorphose into other physical objects in precisely the same sense in which commodities are asserted to possess a potential to either provoke or metamorphose into utility. We are tendered explicit warrant to ignore the process through which commodities summon utility by the conservation principles that define the ontological stability of the utility field: The utility index associated with any commodity bundle is a metric putatively independent of the commodity metric; the utility is virtual in the sense that it is purportedly identical *ex ante* and *ex post;* and the field is conserved, in the sense that the magnitude of utility is path-independent. The translation of commodities into their utility poten-

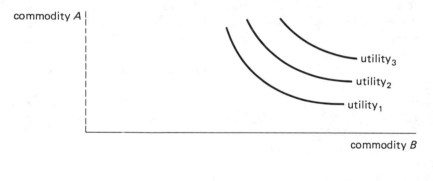

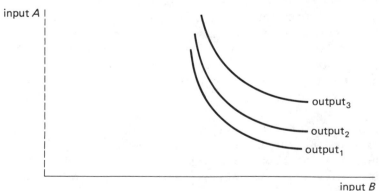

FIGURE 6.1   Utility fields and technology fields.

tial is a one-way street, implying that the issue of the reverse translation of utility into commodities need never arise in the course of
theoretical explanation. In brief, the utility field is portrayed as analytically prior to the economic process. The metaphorical failure of
textbook theories of production is that there is no comparable warrant when it comes to the portrayal of a "technology field."

Taking the symmetry thesis at its face value, we could write the
technology field as a set of equations in exact parallel to the equations
of the preference field developed in the previous chapter. Let **P** be a
vector field of gradients of greatest increase of output in factor space
$q = \{x, y, z\}$. Now, the legitimate analogue to the work function in
energy physics would be the expenditure line integral:

(6.1) $E = \oint \mathbf{P} \, dq$

Further analysis requires further specification of the character of
the vector field. The most significant condition, once again, is that the
vector field be irrotational: In economic terms (and here we venture
onto strange metaphorical terrain), any sequence of virtual productions will end up at the same bundle of factors from whence it
started, so that output gradient remains unchanged by any particular
path of production. This condition, as we shall shortly observe, is (if
possible) even more counterintuitive than in the consumer case; but it
is an indispensable prerequisite for describing the neoclassical notion
of substitution in production. One specifies the condition in mathematical terms as:

(6.2) $\oint_c \mathbf{P} \, dq = 0$

As observed in Chapter 2, this condition is isomorphic to conditions
(2.2) through (2.5); or, rewriting them in this new context,

(6.3) $\operatorname{grad} Y = \left[\dfrac{\partial Y}{\partial x} \quad \dfrac{\partial Y}{\partial y} \quad \dfrac{\partial Y}{\partial z} \right] = \{P_x, P_y, P_z\} = \mathbf{P}$

or, in other words, prices are proportional to their marginal products,
while

(6.4) $\operatorname{curl} \mathbf{P} = \left[\dfrac{\partial P_z}{\partial y} - \dfrac{\partial P_y}{\partial z} \quad \dfrac{\partial P_x}{\partial z} - \dfrac{\partial P_z}{\partial x} \quad \dfrac{\partial P_y}{\partial x} - \dfrac{\partial P_x}{\partial z} \right]$

and curl $\mathbf{P} = 0$.
Hence $\mathbf{P} \cdot dq$ is itself an exact differential equation.

If the symmetry thesis is to be taken at all seriously, then there must
exist integrability conditions for each and every technology field on a

par with those for the preference fields. Please note that this is entirely an a priori restriction, independent of any information actually derived from technological specifications, the laws of physics, and so forth. Finally, there must also exist a conservation principle in parallel to the principle of the conservation of energy, which here translates into: The sum of output plus costs must equal a constant; or

(6.5) $E + Y = k$

These are the equations of a conservative vector field of factor prices that can also be expressed as a scalar field representation of an output index. Above all, in this particular representation, output is a path-independent phenomenon, which implies that the manner of the combination of the inputs does not influence the magnitude of the final output. If we were also to take to heart the observation that production takes time, then the factor prices and the output field must be *conservative* (i.e., independent of time). (Otherwise, merely slowing down the production process would alter the resulting output.) Now, one musn't immediately cavil at the misguidedly excessive devotion to metaphoric symmetry without remembering one pertinent fact: Without a conservative vector field, the entire framework of a unique equilibrium independent of temporal sequence and location must be relinquished – that is, we would no longer be describing Laplacian natural-law phenomena in a deterministic setting.

Finally, to complete the symmetry, neoclassical theorists generally append the law of one price,

(6.6) $dy/dx = y/x, \quad dy/dz = y/z, \ldots$

and the constraint that equilibrium must fall on a linear budget constraint,

(6.7) $\sum \mathbf{P} \cdot dq = \sum \mathbf{P} \cdot q = \bar{E}$

These, in a nutshell, are the correct equations for the representation of technology as a field in input space.

Now, the trick to metaphorical evaluation is an ability to sense when one has finally ventured beyond the pale, so that the coherence of the metaphor is strained to the point of dismemberment. It is, of course, possible to sympathize up to a point with some of the motivations behind the original comparison of a person's preferences to a field of force. The energetics movement had already asserted that mental events were just another manifestation of energy transfer; the work of Meyerson suggests that the postulation of a causal invariant is often conflated with scientific explanation *tout court;* Mary

Douglas suggests that social order is promoted and conceptualized as a projection of natural order; and finally, an irrotational conservative vector field does embody the insight that under some circumstances a price system is connected and transitive. But the comparison of the technology of a production process to a field of force is surely gratuitous and meaningless, a mere artifact of the *problems* thrown up by the original proto-energetics metaphor, a rhetorical ploy to make it appear as if production had been subsumed under the same structure of explanation as the equilibrium of the consumer.

At the most fundamental of levels, neoclassical consumer theory is premised upon the deep presumption that trade alters neither the commodity nor the consumer (Sohn-Rethel 1978); one supposes most denizens of our culture would find this assertion more or less unobjectionable. However, when it comes to the supposedly symmetric theory of production, would everyone acquiesce in the symmetric thesis that production alters neither the factors nor the process if they understood it?[5] This is the Meyersonian problem in spades: To discuss change, we feel we must posit some invariant, but what are the appropriate invariants to discuss the *process* of production? The neoclassical answer, variant #8, says that substitution possibilities prevent us from associating the invariant with any specific commodity or vector of factor inputs, but that there must exist some virtual field of possibilities, some book of blueprints in which resides the integrity and identity of the production process. Yet to further assert that firms are *symmetric* – that is, that they also carry out a virtual calculation of a constrained extremum, which implies to the neoclassical mind that they represent something more than a concatenation of time-specific accidents – economists must presume that the technology field is path-independent, so that the firm can go anywhere in the field (within the stated constraints) from any other point, and actually end up producing the anticipated output. Further, this has to be true for each and every technology, past, present, or future, independent of any other considerations.

On the simplest possible level, a production field such as that portrayed in Figure 6.1 cannot adequately capture any production process that is more complicated than the bundling together of inputs A and B – similar to, say, the packing of a picnic basket (Arrow and Hahn 1971, pp. 169–73). This is primarily an artifact of the metaphor: Movements in factor space don't alter the axes. The tacit presumption that the process of production might be adequately captured by a spatial metaphor is the deepest unobtrusive postulate in modern economic theory (Georgescu-Roegen 1976, pp. 271–96; Mirowski 1986).

> This tacit connection between a property [of spatial separation and combination] and one of processes implies a particular view of natural phenomena . . . The view boils down to this: In nature all transformations consist of mere reshuffling of some primary substances; such reshuffling can bring about no qualities other than those inherent in the primary substances [Georgescu-Roegen 1976, p. 288].

The language here is reminiscent of Meyerson; this, of course, is no coincidence. Of all of the nasty conundrums encountered in economics, the problem of production most immediately conjures the hobgoblins of change versus invariance that haunt Western scientific thought. What comes out of a production process must have some relationship to what went in – this, the very essence of business – but an economic theory based upon an invariant mental field in a space of independently constituted commodities has no resources to dictate what the relationship should be. One could posit that some primary substance can be used to characterize both inputs and outputs, which is the solution of classical political economy, as well as options #1 through #5 and #7. Or else, one might emulate the nineteenth-century notion of invariance embodied in the field concept by projecting it onto a representation of a technology field. Nonetheless, the problems of describing change vis-à-vis invariance have just been shoved aside, and not resolved.

Equations (6.1) through (6.7) describe a world where the configuration and character of output is indifferent to the way it is made, where understanding of production processes is independent of experience, and where the independently postulated commodity space sets the boundaries for any and all possible reactions to a change in economic circumstances. Yet one might aver that production is the realm of the creation of *differences* instead of invariants. This seems to be the nature of the complaint of those economic historians concerned to describe the evolution of technology – such as Paul David (1975), Nathan Rosenberg (1982) and Avi Cohen (1984). In their texts they assert that the neoclassical phenomenon of factor substitution is difficult to discover in the historical record: In general, changes in inputs result in a qualitatively different output as well as a qualitatively different production process. The neoclassical field theorist would surely retort that this was merely a shift in the isoquants rather than a movement of pure substitution along a fixed set of isoquants. But this evades the crux of the issue, which is the observation that no actual production process exhibits enough invariance to justify the metaphor of the field formalism in the first place.

The field metaphor commits the dual transgression of positing much more invariance than can be inferred from the physical phenomena, but less invariance than might be inferred from a concern with the social manifestations of the production process. Suppose the boundaries of any given production process were platted by their social structures – the firm as social institution rather than embodiment of a technology, or a social definition of the commodity rather than a putative dependence upon its physical specifications – then the entire problem of invariance would appear in a new light; in particular, the field formalism would be easily recognized as inappropriate. It would have been much more candid simply to admit that engineering blueprints cannot describe much that constitutes the process of production, and further, that the characterization of production as motion in a field ignores or surpresses much that can be found in engineering blueprints.

A physical production process cannot be mapped one-to-one and onto a field formalism, primarily because natural physical relationships are not isomorphic to social relationships. For instance, the analytical boundaries of a production process are frequently indeterminate from a physical point of view: Does the process of producing tables include the truck that brought the lumber from the sawmill? the sawmill itself? the forest? the carrying aloft of the seeds by the wind? Such analytical distinctions are not at all resolved by recourse to physical considerations, but rather by the social and economic definitions of the firm and its accounts. Or, take the efficiency of inputs. The metrics of the efficiency of inputs in a production process are rarely identical with the units in which the commodities are bought and sold. Oil is sold by the barrel, but its efficiency as an input depends on its BTU rating, or perhaps its sulfur content in milligrams per liter, or its Reynolds number, and so on. Further, this metric will vary from process to process, even if one is looking at the same barrel of oil. (Not every barrel of Saudi Light No. 6 is identical.) Such distinctions are critical for any serious representation of a production field, because they raise the possibility that, as long as the axes of the field formalism are confined to *commodity* space, the field cannot be analytically defined (Georgescu-Roegen 1976, pp. 61–9; Eatwell 1975, p. 174).

We hasten to add that this entire discussion is a disquisition on the problems of neoclassical economic theorists, and *not* the practical actors in the actual economy. They do not separate their world into airtight divisions of substitution versus innovation; nor do they keep tabs on marginal products (unless they have been to business school); nor do they have difficulty keeping track of the boundaries of their economic activities. Instead, they actively constitute the identity of their economic roles and artifacts as they go along.

The reason that neoclassical economists have proved incapable of serious confronting these facts is that they would then have to face up to the futility of their entire research program: Physical metaphors used to describe social processes are spuriously grounded in the natural phenomena. To admit that the metaphor was a failure in the very area it should seemingly be most natural, the description of putatively physical processes, would be the last straw, and perhaps even encourage doubt that the metaphor was adequate in the sphere of psychology, i.e., utility.

Acknowledging the logical untenability of the technological/ economic separation in production theory would drive a wedge into the much-touted symmetry of diminishing marginal utility and diminishing marginal returns to a factor. The idea of an exogenous ordering might be plausible in the case of mental phenomena (although, it must be admitted, only because it is de facto inaccessible to empirical research), but it would clearly be illegitimate in the case of production if the technological ranking could not be carried out prior to and independent of the process of economic definition and economic valuation (Bharadwaj 1978b, p. 53). It is conceivable that what is deemed to be the output of a production process is socially determined, as witnessed by the cavalier treatment of waste, by-products, discharges, effluents, and joint products in neoclassical theory, often rendered harmless and invisible by the assumption of free disposal (Kurz 1986). These have been ignored in the past because they were deemed to be economically irrelevant. This, of course, puts the cart before the horse: There can be no unique ranking of technological productivity in the absence of a single prior stable metric of economic output, and hence there should be no such thing as a general *technological* phenomenon of diminishing marginal productivity.

These objections can be expressed more concisely within the formalism of the field metaphor. It is impossible to legitimately abstract away the processes whereby inputs are transformed into outputs, because the conservation principles that define the stability of the technological field are absent. There is no symmetry of the process of production such as (6.4) that can be represented by an output index; neither can the output index be defined prior to the economic process. Output is not virtual in the sense of being identical *ex ante* and *ex post*, and therefore the output index is not path-independent. Further, the transformation of input commodities into output commodities is not generally a one-way street. In the language of field formalisms, such a process would be analogous to a relativistic field that is self-acting and self-generating. As discussed in the section on the theory of relativity in Chapter 2, such fields possess no general global conservation principles. This problem of outputs that, directly or indirectly, become inputs of the same production process has been a particular bugbear in neoclassical theory, as shall be further discussed later in the section on "time" below.

One should not infer from these criticisms that it is impossible to write down some such technological field equation as $Q = F(x, y, z)$ and proceed to employ the variational techniques already applied to the analysis of the utility field $U = G(x, y, z)$. Obviously, numerous economists alive today make their livelihoods doing precisely this. The point to be made is that the desperation to cling to the physics metaphor come hell or high water in conjunction with the attendant assertion of the symmetry of consumption and production has severely limited and crippled any pretense of cogent description and discussion of actual physical production processes. Rather, from the neoclassical point of view, the production side of the analysis should ideally be more effectively subordinated to the utility/exchange side, serving only to net out any intermediate processes and to reduce produced goods to the status of unexplained (and conserved) endowments. "Assuming equilibrium, we may even go so far as to abstract from entrepreneurs and simply consider the productive services as being, in a certain sense, exchanged directly for one another, instead of being exchanged first against products, and then against productive services" (Walras 1969, p. 225; see also Walsh and Gram 1980, p. 153). Hence, we have come full circle to where the only truly external determinants of equilibria are the utility fields and the exogenous endowments of commodities, be they dubbed productive services, or whatever. The problem of production has been reduced to a matter of semantics. Nothing captures the exigencies of the physics metaphor in neoclassical theory as well as the figure of speech that equates production with "trading with Nature."

TIME. The second major asymmetry between the neoclassical theories of production and of the consumer transpires in the treatment of time. In the neoclassical version of proto-energetics, trade is conceptualized as instantaneous for reasons discussed in Chapter 5.

Chapter 2 has outlined how the twentieth-century understanding of energy sees it as imposing temporal symmetry and hence the condition of reversibility upon certain analytical processes. Put the two observations together, and one can see that the utility field expresses the presupposition of the temporal reversibility of transactions. Now, entertain the notion that technology should be treated as analogous to utility, and one is then brought face to face with a dilemma: Should production also be treated as instantaneous and reversible in time, or should one instead explicitly make separate allowance for the passage of time?

The repugnance felt by many neoclassical economists around the turn of the century for the conceit of instantaneous production was a consequence of this dilemma, as was the widespread fascination with Austrian conceptions such as the period of production (Wicksell 1938, I, p. 98). The physics metaphor in this respect proved a harsh taskmaster. A thoroughgoing symmetry between production and consumption theory dictated that production should be portrayed as instantaneous, virtual, static, and path-independent, or, more prosaically, fully reversible in time. This conception offended commonsense images of production; even worse, it violated and subverted the very message of the proto-energetics metaphor on the side of consumer theory – namely, it made a joke of the primal parable of neoclassical theory, the stern moral tale of scarcity and constraint. If production were instantaneous and fully reversible, it is difficult to see how there would ever be a shortage of anything. Silk purses could be made from sows' ears, but if we then conceived a craving for pork, we could just temporarily take the silk purse from the closet and presto! pork chops. When production is akin to prestidigitation, the economic problem becomes a sideshow.

This dilemma is not some crumbling relic from the turn of the century. It still is a skeleton in the neoclassical closet, admittedly a closet big enough to hold a cemetary. The most up-to-date versions of the symmetry thesis, such as those found in Varian (1978, p. 3), Fuss and McFadden (1978, p. 61), and Arrow and Hahn (1971, p. 52), regularly represent the production side of their models as a vector, with inputs expressed as negative real numbers and outputs expressed as positive real numbers. Even if the vector entries are time-dated, the mathematics still (surreptitiously? inadvertently?) portrays an instantaneous reversible process. This is due to the fact that whenever a single process or an aggregation of processes uses at least one of its outputs as an input ("production of commodities by means of commodities") only the net result appears in the vector formalism;

hence the jargon of "netput vectors." The convex cones so instrumental in modeling general equilibrium are constructed from netput vectors. A netput vector implicitly states that *a producer does not have to wait for his own output* and, in the presence of adequate "nonproduced" inputs, production is temporally symmetrical. This is a straigtforward consequence of treating production like addition, or similar to spatial contiguity and separation. Netput vectors also surreptitiously define away the circular nature of production processes mentioned in the previous section. Hence, even in the most high-tech, up-to-date neoclassical models, there is no real scarcity of produced goods as such. The scarcity of commodities, such as it is, is shifted back to the unexplained fixity of the natural endowments of productive services and the like.

Dissatisfaction with a portrait of production that is powerless to express its purported raison d'être – the partial abatement of scarcity – prompted many neoclassical theorists to break the symmetry of production and consumption by explicitly introducing the lapse of time into their production models. This has not proved to be a happy solution, since it lifted these theorists off one horn of the dilemma only to impale them on the other. The problem, put in simple terms, is that there is no unambiguously correct or convenient way to introduce the passage of time in production theory in such a way as to maintain consistency with the original physics metaphor on the consumer side (Kennedy 1968; Landesmann, in Baranzini and Scazzieri 1986). Some methods retain the mechanical conception of time; some attempt to introduce hysteresis and historical time. Those that retain mechanical time discover to their discomfort that they have not escaped the drawbacks of instantaneous production without simultaneously undermining critical duality properties. Further, the second law of thermodynamics plays havoc with point-input point-output models and the idea that more roundabout is more productive (Georgescu-Roegen 1971). On the other hand, those methods that claim to eschew mechanical time end up hopelessly tangled in contradictions. A premier example of this conundrum is Alfred Marshall's own amalgam of partial equilibrium analysis, the principle of substitution, and the resort to biological metaphor.

THE IDENTITY OF THE COMMODITY. The third major asymmetry of neoclassical theory vis-à-vis production partakes more of the texture of a philosophical problem than of a mathematical infelicity. As long as one cleaves strictly to the physics metaphor, the last recourse for defining the commodity is to the mind of the individual. However, as soon as an attempt is made to graft production onto the theoretical system, there are thenceforth two conflicting standards of the identity of the commodity: that provided by individual psychology, and that inferred from the physical integrity of the production process. As Pareto (1971b, p. 224) noted, "the physical identity of things does not entail their economic identity." In the same vein, Böhm-Bawerk (1959, I, pp. 74, 170) thought he saw the possibility for two distinct kinds of productivity – physical versus value – and that the legal fiction of the identity of commodities through time may factually hold for the former, but cannot legitimately be said to hold for the latter. (See also Robbins [1952, p. 11, fn.])

This dichotomy is not peculiar to economic theory; it is a legacy of the time-worn Cartesian mind/body problem. Given that one proceeds from the premise that individuals know their own mind better than they know anything else, then the question must surely arise how they do come to know the putatively external world, and indeed, how they authenticate that knowledge. In classical economics this question rarely arose because value was posited to be a substance eminently physical and external and accessible to all; mental considerations were definitely secondary. Neoclassical economics shifted the onus of invariance onto individuals and their preferences, but in doing so neglected to elaborate the mechanism whereby the physical world retained its identity for the economic actor. Hence the possibility exists that the economic identity of goods may clash with their physical identity, with dire consequences for the theory of value.

Few neoclassical theorists went as far as Pareto in trying to reconceptualize all economic phenomena as generic commodity transactions. Nevertheless, their less sweeping responses to the problem of production still could not crack the enigma of the identity of the commodity in the presence of production. In an anthropomorphic attempt to accomodate the notion of one commodity being transmuted into another, it has become fashionable to resort to the figure of speech of an input "performing a service" (Georgescu-Roegen 1976, p. 86; Ellerman, in Mirowski 1986). This rhetorical practice does not achieve its aim of neutralizing the mind/body problem, and indeed, from a certain point of view, exacerbates it. The metaphor of service insinuates that physical relationships have been subordinated to mental preconceptions and desires (read, the utility field), but this is merely wishful thinking, since there are no grounds for such a hierarchy in the mathematical formalism. If a commodity may be enjoyed for its ontological identity within the utility field and simultaneously be exploited as a source of services in the transmutation of other commodities, we are clearly confronted with the possibility of double and even triple counting of value. For instance, is it possible that the owner of an input might derive utility from its use in some production process over and above the utility derived from simple possession? If so, utility is no longer abstracted from the process of enjoyment, the conservation principles are violated, and the utility field breaks down. Both Walras and Wicksell felt impelled to introduce ad hoc assumptions in order to prohibit this eventuality (Stigler 1941, p. 230; Wicksell 1938, p. 103). The Austrian school resorted to the alternative of the imputation of the utility of final goods back to the inputs in order to evade the specter of double counting, but this option also violated the integrity of the utility field, confusing the conservation of the field with the conservation of an embodied value substance (Pareto 1971b, p. 220).

The mind/body problem persists in neoclassical production theory down to the present in the guise of the concept of "opportunity costs" and the predisposition to import subjective cost notions into the existing formalism of constrained optimization (Vaughn 1980).

CONSERVATION PRINCIPLES AND THE MEANING OF COST. The fourth major asymmetry between neoclassical theories of the producer and of the consumer may be discovered in the pattern of conservation principles imposed in order to operationalize the variational principle. On the consumer side, the conserved ontological entity that insures that the analyst can identify the "same" phenomenon is the conserved utility field. Change the preferences and for all practical purposes the world has been turned upside down, for any continuity with the previous situation has been lost. On the production side, by contrast, the conserved entity that defines the continuity and integrity of the world is not avowedly the technology field, since it is commonly acknowledged (and indeed fervently hoped) that the field will change even over short periods of time as a normal consequence of the operation of the capitalist system. If the firm has no independent existence in neoclassical theory beyond a description of its cost structure, then its identity must somehow be bound up with that cost structure (Levine 1980).

The analogy between the consumer and the firm breaks down in neoclassical theory because costs have such a tenuous existence within its ambit. When production is tethered to the physics metaphor of the consumer, one of the ties that bind them is the requirement that prices be *market-clearing prices*. In the absence of some very restrictive conditions, there is absolutely no reason to expect such prices to have any temporal continuity from one time period to the next (Garegnani, in Brown et al. 1976; Milgate 1979). Even without the complications of changing preferences or technologies, the impact of last period's transactions upon endowments and prices should result in a new set of market-clearing prices in the present period. Some neoclassical economists touted the market-clearing assumption as exhibiting supreme virtue in combating earlier theories of value because it dictated that bygones are bygones and that past prices should have no bearing upon future prices (Stigler 1941, p. 62; Robbins 1952, p. 62). These authors ignored the far-reaching and disturbing implications this thesis had for the conception of the production process.

If it is acknowledged that the act of production requires the passage of time, or that output appears on the market later than inputs are purchased, then it is a foregone conclusion that in neoclassical theory costs have no necessary relationship to the price of the product. This merely restates the first generation of neoclassicals' repudiation of cost-of-production theories, but as in many other instances, it took some time for the unsavory implications to sink in. Also as usual, Marshall caught whiff of the corruption, but stoically passed it by, for "the value of a thing, though it tends to equal its normal (money) cost of production, does not coincide with it at any particular time, save by accident" (Marshall 1920, p. 401).

If there is no rational reason to expect any shred of temporal continuity of input and output prices, then it seems a singularly unattractive proposition to be the one stuck playing the role of the neoclassical firm. More to the point, if the only identification of the firm is by means of its cost structure, and the very idea of a cost structure is adventitious, the entire symmetry of production has vanished into thin air. Try to then superimpose technological progress upon this insubstantial structure, and one can draw no other conclusion than that there are no regularities left to justify a theory of production (Winter 1982).

Attempts have been made to mollify these contradictions by appending additional conservation principles to the physics metaphor, particularly under the guise of the adding-up problem. Lacking a guarantee that the sum of input prices have some calculable relationship to the price of output, the neoclassical theory of production is potentially decoupled from neoclassical consumer theory. The first neoclassicals avoided the problem by adding an unjustified assumption that the sum of costs equaled the value of production – hence Walras's famous no-profit condition. Although never stated coherently, this condition was a conservation principle: Value is globally conserved in the production process, turning the classical conservation principle on its head.

The assertion that "this law, if it worked without friction, would give to every agent of production the wealth that the agent creates" (Clark 1938, p. v) served a much larger function than simple apologetics: it was an attempt to reconcile market-clearing prices, the physics metaphor, and the classical legacy of production theories. Puzzles proliferated when Wicksteed and Flux noted that even in rudimentary production models the exhaustion-of-product condition would only hold for processes that exhibited constant returns to scale. From our present vantage point, we would reinterpret this condition to state that conservation of value in production requires a substance theory of value, which is closely approximated by production functions that are homogeneous of the first degree. Further commentary by Wicksell and Barone suggested that if cost curves exhibited a U shape, in the sence that average total costs would first diminish and then increase over the relevant range of output, then the sum of costs would equal the value of output at the point of minimum costs. Despite the sighs of relief this reconciliation evoked in certain neoclassical quarters, this "solution" did not come to grips with the real meaning of the imposed conservation principle. Most of the discussants missed the crucial condition of the temporal continuity of costs and prices, mainly because their production models treated costs as independent of prices set on the consumer side. It was only with the revival of the Walrasian tradition and the advent of the work of Arrow and Hahn (1971, p. 77) the neoclassicals began to glimpse what was really at stake.

The full Walrasian general equilibrium model revealed that if all production processes exhibited constant returns to scale *and* if all the resultant incomes were simultaneously spent, then a stable definition of costs (and hence firms) was conceivable. If, however, the assumptions on scale economies were loosened to encompass increasing returns to scale, then it became imperative to append further assumptions requiring that any divergences of output values from costs be allocated to consumers, generally through some artifice of shares of ownership of the firm. It should be noted that the function of such schemes is to render costs determinate by directly linking them to the primal physics metaphor. The artificial character of this further conservation principle – here the total value of production is constrained to be equal to the total value of consumer incomes and consumer expenditure through the shares assumption – can only be recognized when it is made clear that this allocation scheme is inconsistent with the rest of the Arrow–Debreu model. No provision is made for the market arbitage of the shares (Ellerman, in Mirowski 1986, p. 87). Were such a provision present, then the value of output would no longer correspond to the value of inputs, and production would once more become decoupled from consumer price determination. Further, the shares assumption robs the firms of their independent raison d'être, reducing them to mere reflections of consumer preferences.

Such attempts to jury-rig conservation principles under the guise of profit payouts merely obscures the real conundrum of neoclassical theory: Costs have no temporal continuity and therefore production bears none of the actual theoretical weight in the determination of prices. Ultimately, the inner logic of neoclassical theory requires that, even in the extremely artificial case of instantaneous and simultaneous purchase of inputs and outputs, the analyst must impose the counterintuitive restriction of Walras's Law, a condition which we should now comprehend not at all as a law, but rather as a conservation principle, constraining costs and the value of output to conform to a fixed relationship. This conservation principle is not an empirical proposition but rather an analytical device that constrains the production side of the analysis to be subordinate to the primal physics metaphor on the consumer side. In order to achieve this subordination, the analytical device robs the firms of any separate economic identity.

The postulation of the equality of the value of inputs and outputs is absolutely essential to any neoclassical model that claims to encompass the phenomenon of production. It is not just one of those assumptions that can be shed with the cool agnosticism affected by neoclassical theorists; it must be retained even in the most advanced versions of the so-called disequilibrium dynamics. "In models with households only, Walras' Law comes simply from summing the budget constraints. Firms, unlike households, have no budget constraints but do have balance sheets. Hence Walras' Law in models with firms requires us to use the fact [sic] that the profits of the firms ultimately belong to the shareholders" (Fisher 1983, p. 159). One notices the disingenuous tone used in discussing the problem: The analytical requirement has little to do with any specification of the legal mechanisms of ownership; it is instead an unsubstantiated assertion that costs and incomes are conserved in the process of production. The only alternative to the explicit specification of the conservation principle is the equally unwarranted assumption of constant returns to scale in all processes of production, a condition that achieves the same analytical result. The widespread use of the constant-returns assumption plays an important role in the natural history of the physics metaphor, because the retreat to constant returns is tantamount to a retreat to the classical substance theory of value.

In neoclassical production theory constant returns to scale is frequently represented by a production function $Q = F(x, y, \ldots, x)$, which is homogeneous of degree one – that is, if l is an arbitrary positive constant, then $F(lx, ly, \ldots, lz) = lF(x, y, \ldots, x) = lQ$. Such a function represents a perfectly symmetric gradient in input space, and those symmetry properties render it an effective analogue of a one-good economy. Optimal factor proportions are independent of output levels, and relative prices (under certain common assumptions) are independent of demands: This is the neoclassical nonsubstitution theorem. Specifications of stock and flow conditions are indistinguishable for analytical purposes (Georgescu-Roegen 1976). Together, these conditions endow costs with a physicalist existence reminiscent of a substance theory of value. The irony of the situation is that the very assumption that invests production with a persistence and integrity that fully justifies the link between the value of inputs and the value of outputs is precisely the same assumption that abnegates the primal physical metaphor of utility as potential energy. Production squirms upon its Procrustean bed.

The myth of the engineering production function

In order to foster the impression that the production field is somehow analytically prior to the economic problem, one finds it frequently asserted that it represents a purely technological relationship, "taken from disciplines such as engineering and industrial chemistry: to the economic theorist they are the data of analysis" (Stigler 1949, p. 109). One further example graces the beginning of this chapter, with Paul Samuelson swearing undying fealty to production functions because they are the very embodiment of the laws of thermodynamics. However many times this litany is repeated, the laws of physics still resist being dragooned into the defense of the neoclassical metaphor for production (Georgescu-Roegen 1976, pp. 61–9, Baranzini and Scazzieri 1986, pp. 260–72). The idea of a path-independent transformation of one set of physical objects into another violates so many physical laws that one can only marvel at the audacity of those who wrap themselves in the banner of physics before marching off to do battle with the opponents of production functions (Ayres and Nair 1984).

Examine once more equation (6.4), the curl conditions for an irrotational field. First, they assert that input combinations are characterized by continuous substitution; this is an artifact of the continuity of
input space. The earliest complaints about production functions centered on the unreality of this representation. Second, they assert that
the technology must be symmetric, in the sense that a change in the
marginal product of steel given a change in labor inputs must be
equivalent to a change in the marginal product of labor given a
change in steel inputs. There is no warrant from any known law of
physics to justify that this condition holds in a global sense. Indeed,
here we find the neoclassical economist dictating the laws of physics to
the physicist! Third, as already noted, the field metaphor portrays
each and every process as if it were fully reversible in time. Not only
does this directly violate the second law of thermodynamics, it makes
a mockery of most of what an engineer is paid to do for a living.
Engineering is taken up with problems of turbulence, metal fatigue,
changes of state, friction, and the like – all problems found in a world
of irreversible change. Engineers deal with path-dependence, the
particularities of the specific material, and so forth – all differences
and distinctions blithely assumed away by the field formalism. And, to
top it off, equation (6.5) says that output and money are ontologically
identical. That statement will never be found in an engineering textbook.

Very infrequently in the modern neoclassical literature can one
find a discussion of any tangible production *process*, much less any of
the issues responsible for the asymmetry of neoclassical production
and consumption. Indeed, research into the analytics of production
processes has been flagging since the 1930s and 1940s, when issues of
returns to scale and the organization of production were thought to
have profound consequences for neoclassical economic theory. Residual concern over such issues has been deflected into the sub-
discipline known as industrial organization, by general consensus an
elephant's graveyard of little theoretical consequence.

All this is not to say that there haven't been *attempts* to make good
the promise that field-type descriptions of technologies could potentially be derived from the laws of physics, or at least those of engineering. There exists a small body of literature on neoclassical "engineering production functions," which even its enthusiasts admit has had
little impact upon the conceptions and practices of their neoclassical
bretheren (Wibe 1980, p. 40). The lack of efficacy should not surprise
us, given the rather disparate attitudes toward the concept of production documented in this chapter. What is important to note about this

literature, however, is: (a) It is conventionally the last resort of those confronted with the inadequacies of the production field metaphor – that is, it allows them to claim that someone has dealt with these issues, even though they themselves have felt no compunction to take physical issues into account – and (b) upon actually reading this literature, it becomes apparent that these authors have achieved no such advance over the conventional field metaphor in accomodating neoclassicism to the laws of physics. Indeed, the reverse is the case (if the reader is not yet fed up with the irony of it): All they have achieved is a further retreat into neo-energetics. Because they have opted for an proto-energetics framework, they misrepresent the content of modern physics just as surely as did Ostwald and Helm.

The concept of the engineering production function dates back to the work of Chenery (1949; 1953), and has been elaborated in the writings of Marsden, Pingry, and Whinston (1974), Wibe (1980), and Pearl and Enos (1975). There has been no clearer statement of the problem since Chenery (1953, p. 302): "The central analytical problem of using engineering results is to transform a set of design laws describing a process into an economic production function involving only economic quantities." This problem arises on many levels. First, it is a bit of a capitulation to appeal to design laws, since that already involves an appreciable abstraction from physical laws, and further, it betokens a naive conception of what it is that engineers do. (In my experience, they often look up certain calculations based on crude empirical techniques rather than explicit physical laws, and then arbitrarily multiply the requirements by ten for safety's sake.) Second, and more important for our purposes, using engineering results ignores the fact that economics operates with a single common denominator (i.e., value) whereas engineering equations generally do not (i.e., friction, tensile strength, viscosity, heat transfer, etc.), and therefore, one would not expect that it would be possible to come up with a one-to-one mapping from design laws to economic production functions of a neoclassical field character.

Indeed, once these economists gain some acquaintance with the practices of engineers, it is interesting to see how they respond to the cognitive dissonance. Three broad responses can be taxonomized: (i) to pick production processes to formalize that do not involve actual physical transformation of the product; (ii) to ignore any design laws that are intrinsically incompatible with the metaphor of the field; and (iii) to pretend that all engineering laws also may be reduced to a single common denominator, namely (what else?) energy.

Chenery (1953) provides a paradigm example of all of these practices, even though his is the most careful and circumspect of the studies just cited. First, in order to demonstrate the possibility of translation from physical relationships to the neoclassical production function, he chooses a very nonrepresentative production process – namely, the delivery of natural gas through pipelines. The significance of this judicious choice is that the output of the process is the mere geographical movement of gas from one location to another: No physical input actually undergoes transformation into a previously nonexistent physical output. The reason for choosing such a process should be apparent: Neoclassical field theory can only encompass production that resembles the spatial joining and separating of conserved inputs. Field theories cannot express qualitative change, which is one reason why most engineering relationships are not derived directly from the laws of classical physics.

Second, Chenery then ignores almost everything that distinguishes the engineer from the physicist. He simply assumes that natural gas behaves like an ideal gas, he makes an outrageous assumption that the compression of the gas is adiabatic, he presumes a steady isothermal flow at an essentially infinitely slow speed (in layman's terms – no perceptible movement in the pipeline), assumes that the work done is proportional to the difference between the initial and final pressures (and hence is path-independent), . . . the list goes on and on. It may all seem gobbledygook to the average economist, but there is a pattern here that would be apparent to an engineer. Chenery is assuming away anything that would make the process path-dependent. In other words, he is chopping off every physical phenomenon that cannot be represented by a field formalism. This includes banishing the second law of thermodynamics, something an engineer would never be allowed to even contemplate without risking his diploma. Just as in every other instance, it is physics itself which is forced to lie upon the Procrustean bed of the neoclassical metaphor, and not vice versa. To claim this represents engineering relationships simply betrays a lack of familiarity with the science involved.

As if this were not enough, the movement from the putative physical relationships to the putative economic production function is handled with something less than candid disgression. At one point Chenery (1953, p. 306) admits that physical laws mostly underderdetermine engineering relationships, so that these are settled in practice by trial and error over a limited experimental range. Of course, this has dire consequences for the neoclassical production function, both in that there is no longer any coherent separation between the process of technological change and a given specification of technological possibilities, and because a local definition of production possibilities is not a field and cannot be used to justify substitution of inputs.

Worse than that, the proof of the transition between physical relations and economic relations is implemented as nothing more than an assumption: "The selection of variables to appear in an engineering production function is partly a matter of analytical convenience. The variables should be those which are most readily related to the dimensions of the input which determines its cost" (p. 306). This renders the entire exercise meaningless. Oil does not enter into engineering relationships by the barrel; it enters as a vector of characteristics such as BTU rating, viscosity at a certain Reynolds number, sulfur content in milligrams per liter, and so on (Mirowski 1986). This vector *cannot* be collapsed to a scalar without losing all the physical information that was central to the original purpose of the analysis – viz., to model engineering processes. As this chapter has repeatedly demonstrated, physical magnitudes are not isomorphic to economic magnitudes; the analytical unit of the physical process is not identical to the analytical unit of the economic process; physical metaphors are not the same thing as practical physics.

Even in this most artificial of cases, Chenery must have been confronted with the fact that the multiplicity of engineering considerations would resist reduction to a single production function unless something could be found in physics that corresponded to value in economics; now what could that be?

> To an economist "production" means anything that happens to an object or set of objects which increases its value. This action is most often a change in form, but it may be merely a change in space or time. The basic physical condition necessary to effect any of these changes (except the last) is that energy must be applied to the material in some form . . . The application of energy is one element common to both the economist's and the engineer's conception of production . . . From an analytical point of view, production might be broken down into single energy changes. . . .
>
> In one sense, a production function measures the effectiveness of various combinations of factors in producing a specified energy change . . . The output of any productive process may be measured in terms of any of these forms of energy, using units of either work (force × distance) or heat (calories). . . .
>
> In the present case, horsepower may be treated as if it were an economic commodity because, to a first approximation, it de-

termines the amount of each of the joint factors used in the compression station" (pp. 299, 301, 317).

Finally, we have before us the actuality of engineering production functions: How neoclassical economics proves incapable of resisting the siren song of energetics. In practice, it is common in this literature to simply equate capital with energy, and to then assert that there is no problem in the translation of physical terms into economic terms. Yet it does no end of violence to science to maintain that physical relationships are nothing more than multiform manifestations of embodied energy. But the authentic representation of science and the physical production process has never really been the issue in neoclassical theory; instead, the governing consideration has been the *metaphor* of value/energy. Utility is reified as the proto-energy of economic science; and then the metaphor is projected back onto the production process. The adopted formalism demands a certain format of quantification, and persistently the neoclassicals return to find the energy concept, over and over and over.

Abandoning the field

Perhaps it is not so very astounding that when adherents to an intellectual discipline find that a metaphor so fires their imaginations and so resonates with their self-image as scientists, they feel impelled to return to the same metaphor again and again. What is perhaps harder to understand is the tenacity and longevity of the metaphor of technology as a conservative vector field in the face of widespread doubts and dissension concerning its fitness as a legitimate description of a production process.

Production is one of the three or four central concepts in the ongoing inquiry now dubbed economics. It is the expression par excellence of the conviction that there is progress in material life. Superimposed upon that connotation was the classical concern to explain social order; to achieve that goal the concept was expanded to encompass *reproduction*. In this way of thinking, production was the central fact of human experience because it was the means whereby the society reconstituted itself through time. The fate of the capitalist producer was to guarantee the continuity of civilization itself, not, as Smith was to insist, out of benevolence, but rather out of a drive to accumulate. The notion of reproduction was the touchstone of the classical theory of value. Once a system was conceptualized as returning to its point of departure and reattaining its identity, the analyst had found the benchmark against which to measure both expansion and transformation.

The neoclassicals were inheritors of this tradition, but their metaphor of the field would not let them sustain it. The conservative vector field was predicated upon a situation sui generis, a configuration of commodities without rationale and therefore incapable of reconstitution. All economists had to acknowledge that there was an objective "necessity" for production, but because that necessity could not be derived from the model, there could be no agreement as to why production was necessary, or as to what (if anything) must be preserved from the classical conception.

The diminished stature of production in a neoclassical world was an unintentional artifact of the proto-energetics metaphor. The identity of the commodity in time was rapidly being eroded by the dual abrasives of the mind/body problem and the tendency of the Arrow–Debreu tradition to define generic toothpaste on different days as qualitatively and quantitatively different commodities. It seems clear in retrospect that the very notion of reproduction was being eased out of the picture. With no reasons for stability of costs over time, the neoclassical shell called the firm had no rationale for persistence. Indeed, the production unit was also slated for obsolescence, a phenomenon noted by Schumpeter, Knight, and the Austrian school. The entrepreneur became the odd man out; few economists expressed an interest in bringing him back in. All of these phenomena were direct consequences of the imitation of nineteenth-century physics.

To add insult to injury, according to the Lausanne school, entrepreneurs would gladly assume the thankless task of refraining from present consumption only to let themselves be held hostage to an intrinsically incomprehensible future, in full knowledge that in equilibrium (the only state described in the theory) they would earn no profit! It is hard to argue with the assessment of Edgeworth (1924, II, p. 470):

> The entrepreneur is transformed, like the father of the Bourgeois Gentilhomme, who, it was discovered, had after all not been a shopkeeper. 'Tis true he was a very good-natured and obliging man, and as he was a connoisseur of drapery he used to get together goods of that sort and make presents of them to his friends – "*pour de l'argent.*"

It is significant that it was the Marshallian school, doggedly disregarding mathematical anomalies and consistency, that managed to nurture some sustained discussion of the nature of the firm. It was

the tough-minded Walrasian tradition, the tradition of blind reproduction of the proto-energetics metaphor, that persistently marginalized and mangled the producer. For Walras, the purchase and sale of
existing capital goods was irrational precisely because no gain could
come of it. His metaphoric solution was to conjure a market for new
capital goods by assuming that all people saved a portion of their
income even though in the model there really was nothing they could
do with it. Even then, true production could not be incorporated into
his model, because that would introduce hysteresis and compromise
equilibrium. Hence, as already described in Chapter 5, all production
activity in the later editions of the *Elements* was entirely virtual (Jaffe
1983, p. 353; Walker 1987a).

The peripheral status of the producer has not been upgraded in
the century of further elaboration of Walrasian general equilibrium.
The Walrasian model is congenitally incapable of depicting reproduction in the classical sense, given that it must assume a priori that all
actors possess adequate endowments to guarantee their own subsistence independent of any trading activity (Koopmans 1957, p. 59;
Walsh and Gram 1980, pp. 175, 404). Perhaps just as telling is recent
work on the so-called non-Walrasian neoclassical theory, which demonstrates that a prerequisite of stability is an assumption that no actor
ever runs out of *any* commodity during the process of convergence to
equilibrium (Fisher 1983).

What is there left to reproduce? Who really needs produced goods
in these models? What can a problem of the reproduction of a set of
effectively autarkic actors mean? The Wealth of Nations has obviously
been debased to a Wealth of Rations.

The unintelligibility of production and reproduction in neoclassical
value theory is responsible for the unchecked proliferation of alternative conflicting conceptions of production within the neoclassical research program. It also accounts for the penchant of neoclassical
economists to revert to substance theories of value when the going
gets tough, especially under the rubric of capital theory. Neoclassical
capital theory is the main theater of action where substance and field
theories of value battle it out for the hearts and minds of neoclassical
economists.

Every man his own capital theorist

Etymology is not very often a fruitful mode of inquiry in economic
research, but in the case of capital it is fairly revealing. The term
"capital" entered economic discourse in the English language de-

scending from the Latin *capita,* meaning "head" or "chief" or "principal." As an economic term, it first appeared in the sixteenth-century translations of Italian manuals of double-entry accounting techniques. There it was given one meaning that it has preserved down to the present day: A sum of money equal to the difference between assets and liabilities (Cannan 1921; Richards 1922; Hatfield 1922). Significantly, in sixteenth-century England it was deemed that the nearest vernacular term to this foreign import was the word "substaunce," as in the later "man of substance" (Richards 1922, p. 331). The word "capital" retained this connotation of "substance" well into the eighteenth century. Hence, it already bore a dual meaning when the classical economists pressed it into service to express both their own substance theory of value and their conception of the accumulation of net worth. The fact that the dual connotations blurred the distinction between accounts in monetary terms and physical substance was not detrimental for classical economists, because their substance theories of value were intended to provide the stable underpinnings of monetary expressions of value.

Capital, then, was also part of the heritage of neoclassical economics in the 1870s, but its connotations by that time were not consciously tailored to fit the new corpus of value theory. The connotations of value substance were still paramount, and of course these clashed sharply with the new imperatives of value as utility field. However, the primal physics metaphor did not specifically dictate the format in which production was to be incorporated into neoclassical theory, and there was a legacy of classical theory that, even from the vantage point of the marginalist cadre, did seem to be strongest in the area of production theory. Many who held Marshall as spokesman felt that the preferred response was to coopt classical production theory to the greatest possible extent, which was another argument in favor of trying to absorb classical production concepts. Hence the term "capital" appears in all of the early neoclassicals' manifestos, but it never means the same thing twice.

Bliss (1975, p. 3) provides a definition of capital theory as being "concerned with the implications for a market economy, for the theory of prices, for the theory of production and the theory of distribution, of the existence of produced means of production." Precisely so. It is this issue of produced means of production that so bedevils the coherence of the original physics metaphor of utility as potential energy. And it is the fervently desired reconciliation of the physics metaphor with the concept of produced means of production that so preoccupies neoclassical capital theorists. The reason their project has been so conspicuously lacking in success over the course of a century has been that each successive capital theorist pretends to start anew, thoroughly oblivious to the fact that there have existed at least seven distinctly different definitions of production within the neoclassical paradigm (eight if you count Pareto, but no one does), and because those determined to forget history are destined to repeat it, the result is some Frankenstein's monster of stitched-together discards. Ignorant of the relative characteristics of the options, each tyro capital theorist proceeds to trample over substantive distinctions, scaring the townsfolk and provoking a posse to try and corral the abomination. Thus begins yet another round of capital controversies.

The middle of the twentieth century, and particularly the decades of the 1930s through the 1970s, was the heyday of this brand of mix-and-match capital theory. This indiscriminate permutation of production concepts was sometimes mistaken for an uncontrolled proliferation of economic theories: Keynesian macroeconomics appeared for as while as if it were an autonomous subject, growth theory had a brief day in the sun as a separate fad, the study of production functions became a speciality unto itself, and subfields such as welfare theory and the theory of the firm initiated a long internal dialogue. From the viewpoint of a few key neoclassical theorists, it seemed imperative to rein in the luxuriant speculation and proliferation by demonstrating that all the strands of production theory nominally associated with neoclassical price theory actually were components of a single overarching framework.

Two of the most important protagonists in this drive towards theoretical order and conceptual clarity in this period were Paul Samuelson and John Hicks. Hicks came from an unusually diverse set of influences including Paretian economics, Austrian theory, and a favorable inclination toward Keynesian concerns. Samuelson combined a crusading fervor for Keynesianism, some training in physics, early exposure to the Chicago variant of capital theory as well as Paul Douglas's production functions, and finally, a respect for Schumpeter's conviction that Walras was the greatest economist of all time. From our present perspective, the careers of both Hicks and Samuelson are conveniently divided up according to which of the variants of neoclassical production theory they were attempting to synthesize.

Take, for instance, Hicks's *Value and Capital* (Hicks 1946). This book begins, as all good neoclassical books should, with the physics metaphor of the field theory of value; it then proceeds in Chapter 6 to assert the symmetry thesis of a parallel field theory of technology. In Chapter 14 the concept of a social income is mooted with some circumspect caution, and by the time we get to Part IV we are confronted with a full-fledged substance concept of capital – accompanied, without apology, by a theory of backward imputation – in the course of a discussion of Böhm-Bawerk. Elsewhere, under the rubric of the composite commodity theorem (Hicks 1946, pp. 312–13), aggregates of commodities are assumed to behave as if they were a homogeneous value substance. The marvelous thing about the book is that Hicks's elegant and genteel prose does create the illusion that it is all one seamless whole, even though certain liberties are taken with the conceptualization of the passage of time in order to marry a field value theory to a substance theory of capital.

Hicks did not remain satisfied with this first attempted reconciliation of the various versions of neoclassical production theory. In his infamous IS-LM model, he conflated the Keynesian value substance of national income with a separate and distinct capital substance, even though this would appear to violate his own warnings in Chapter 14 of *Value and Capital*. Later in life, he tried repeatedly to pasteurize chalk and cheese by generating hybrids of the Austrian imputation theory and the neoclassical field theory (Hicks 1970; 1973). These hybrids of neoclassical production theories were subject to scathing attack from many quarters in the 1970s – IS-LM was ridiculed and highbrow theorists lectured Hicks on the superfluity of his Austrian models – and Hicks subsequently entered a more reflective phase, recanting on IS-LM and suggesting that something was wrong in how neoclassical theory incorporated the passage of time (Hicks 1975; 1979).

The other ambitious attempt to reconcile all of the versions of neoclassical production theory can be found in the collected work of Paul Samuelson. First, there was the attempted reconciliation of the capital substance (#3, #4) with the portayal of technology as a field (#8): Here one finds Samuelson's nonsubstitution theorems and his surrogate production functions. Second, there was the attempted reconciliation of the substance theory of capital (#3) with the Keynesian national income substance (#7): Here one discovers Samuelson's program of the neoclassical synthesis (Feiwel 1982). Third, there was a conflation of capital as the temporal imputation of utility (#2) with capital as a homogeneous value substance (#3): Here one thinks of his work on turnpike theorems, and Ramsey growth models, and his work with Robert Solow on linear models and capital vintages (Dorfman, Samuelson, and Solow 1958). Fourth, there was his early attempt to reconcile Marshallian concepts (#5) with Walrasian theory by means of the correspondence principle (discussed below in Chapter 7). One of the few permutations of the neoclassical production concepts missing from his extensive oeuvre is an explicit attempted reconciliation of the portrayal of production as a technology field with the Keynesian income substance. This was probably due to the fact that he often regarded Keynesian models as vague aggregates of an orthodox Walrasian system, therefore relegating any problems in this area to the black hole of the theory of aggregation. Later theorists took this problem much more seriously, calling it the question of the microfoundations of macroeconomics.

All of Samuelson's hybrids of production theories appear consistent because they all involve the use of neoclassical production functions, but it takes a keen eye to discern that the resemblances are only superficial. Capital, income, and the formalism of the field often change their stripes between one hybrid and the succeeding one; not once does Samuelson explore the conditions under which (for example) the field formalism is violated, say, by the passage of time. The thrust of his research program appears to be a mandate to reduce all the variants of the conceptualization of production to a single canonical model under the guise of the seemingly general concept of the production function, and finally to subordinate the lot to the physics metaphor on the side of the theory of the consumer. Hence Samuelson and Hicks are the primary culprits in spreading about the impression that there is only a single neoclassical theory of production.

The siren song of the consolidation of the neoclassical production theories has been heard only by a few, and fully comprehended by even fewer. The economist who displayed the greatest perception and clearest grasp of the issues involved was Joan Robinson. She, to a greater extent than anyone else, realized that capital theory, Keynesian theory, and Marshallian neoclassicism were jointly inconsistent propositions. Although it cannot really be said that she succeeded in making clear the proposition that the Cambridge Capital Controversies of the 1960s and the critique of a Walrasian microfoundation for Keynesian macroeconomics were really two sides of the same coin, others have begun to reinterpret her work in that light (Walsh and Gram 1983). Her one-woman crusade to expose the flaws of the conflation of the various neoclassical theories of production began with the classic 1953 article, "The Production Function and the Theory of Capital" (in Harcourt and Laing 1971). At first, her objections were misconstrued as a rather niggling complaint about the units of measurement of capital in the neoclassical production function. Yet, as we have persistently observed in this narrative, behind every measurement controversy lies a deep problem of metaphoric interpretation. This case was no different. Subsequent controversy led her to state rather adamantly that the "real dispute is not about the *measurement* of capital but the *meaning* of capital" (Robinson 1980, p. 115). By the 1970s, she had differentiated at least three different uses of the term "capital" by neoclassicals:

> The first derived from the Walrasian theory of the general equilibrium of exchange. The economy has an endowment of various items of productive equipment which appear to be man-made machines but play the role, in the argument, of scarce natural resources, like Marshall's meteoric stones. The second conception, which Professor Samuelson attributes to J. B. Clark, is of a one-commodity world . . . The third conception is that of Irving Fisher, for whom saving is merely a means of transferring consumption from an earlier to a later period . . . Of these conceptions, [J. B. Clark's] putty capital has been the most fully developed . . . Say's Law is restored and household saving governs industrial investment . . . Thus every objective of Keynesian and post-Keynesian analysis is ruled out of court. This conception of capital, mixed with some elements of the other two (Walras and Fisher) was straddling like the impenetrable Boyg across the path of reasoned argument [Robinson 1980, pp. 108–9].

Here, in a nutshell, she identifies much of our taxonomy of the alternative neoclassical attempts to tame the production concept. There is the technology field (#8), the reduction to unexplained endowments (#4), the reversion to the classical substance concept (#3), and the Fisherian imputation of a value substance through time (#2). Perhaps her life-long allegience to Keynes clouded her perception of the exact nature of option #7, but she does clearly indicate in this quote that Keynesian theory is inconsistent with the options just listed. She also puts her finger directly upon the indescriminate mix-and-match character of neoclassical models of production.

As she acknowledged on numerous occasions (Robinson 1973; 1980; Kurz 1985), it was the work of Piero Sraffa that opened her eyes to the meaning of productivity and accumulation in a one-good, corn model. In the terminology of the present book, Sraffa's *Production of Commodities by Means of Commodities* (PCMC) is the most highly developed mathematical model of a substance theory of value, and as such serves as the most appropriate polar comparison with the neoclassical field theory of value. This interpretation renders many of Sraffa's more cryptic comments comprehensible, such as the claim that he was concerned with production processes that were circular rather than with a conception of production as a one-way street (Sraffa 1960). It also explains Joan Robinson's contention that PCMC served to illuminate the nature of neoclassical theory, a claim regarded as impenetrable by her opponents.

The ensuing convulsions and coruscations provoked by Joan Robinson's poison-tipped barbs were dubbed the Cambridge Capital Controversy (CCC) by one of her supporters (Harcourt 1972) and the name stuck. It just so happened that most of the critics of neoclassical theory had some affiliation with Cambridge University, U.K., whereas most of the defenders had affiliations (or were frequent visitors at) MIT in Cambridge, Massachusetts. Various blow-by-blow accounts of the controversy can be found in Harcourt (1972; 1982), Blaug (1974), Bliss (1975), Feiwel (1985), Brown and Solow (1983), and Burmeister (1980), and therefore we shall not dally over the fine points of who said what to whom. It is more critical for present purposes to understand the underlying determinants of the debate and to suggest an explanation of why it ended on such a sour note for both camps.

Our starting point is to reiterate that there was no single paradigmatic neoclassical theory of production in the period 1890 to 1970; the reason for this state of affairs was that the physics metaphor of utility had no obvious or optimal way of encompassing the classical notion of production. While neoclassicals assiduously generated production-theory options #1 through #8, none really swept the profession, and this equivocation encouraged a rather promiscuous miscegnation of concepts. No neoclassical economist was willing to interpret this situation as an indication that the physics metaphor was fundamentally incompatible with any plausible comprehensive notion of production, and so, in the absence of any further irritant, the neoclassical school was basically content to muddle through. In practice, this meant moving back and forth peripatetically between classical substance notions of value (mainly but not exclusively imported through the capital concept) and the physics-oriented field metaphors.

On the other hand, the truly single-minded substance theorists – namely, the Marxists and the Keynesians – would naturally feel that this neoclassical sliding in and out of "their" value theory misrepresented and cynically parodied their conception of the primacy of production. Contrary to the assertions of authors such as Harcourt (1972), Hahn (1975), Bliss (1975, ch. 5), Blaug (1974), and Stiglitz (1974), it was not merely political intransigence or bone ignorance that prevented each side from seeing the other's point of view. True, there were political overtones of Left versus Right, but by and large, those were incidental to the real division, which was between the physics of the eighteenth century and the physics of the mid-nineteenth century. This explains the oft-repeated lament that the CCC shed more heat than light.

This Battle of the Metaphors had to be baffling and frustrating for both sides, because without knowing it – that is, having each lost touch with the core inspirations of their respective theories – they were speaking different languages: The models and the abstractions were similar enough to hold out the promise of communication, but differed just enough to thwart it. The United Kingdom contingent did manage to briefly discomfit the Massachussetts contingent in the November 1966 *Quarterly Journal of Economics,* mainly by showing that Samuelson's attempted reconciliation of the metaphor of technology as a field and a homogeneous capital substance was mathematically incoherent. Nevertheless, Cambridge, Massachussetts, quickly recovered from what their opponents felt was a coup de grâce, because the classical substance theory of production was perceived to be expendable within the neoclassical scheme of things. Not surprisingly, the United Kingdom cadre felt betrayed by the ease with which the neoclassicals sloughed off the offending production concept, betrayed by the way the paragons of scientific rigor shrugged off mathematical mistakes, and disgruntled because they (rightly) suspected that a concept that had been so instrumental in many key neoclassical arguments could not be given up lightly.[6]

Let us briefly recapitulate how the CCC demonstrated that the concept of production predicated upon value as a substance clashed with the physics metaphor, the core of neoclassical theory. Early in the controversy, it was shown that four neoclassical "parables" would not hold in general: (i) a negative association between the rate of profit and the magnitude of capital per person, (ii) a negative association between the rate of profit and the capital/output ratio, (iii) a negative association between the rate of profit and steady-state consumption per head, and (iv) the distribution of income explained by technologically determined marginal productivity in conjunction with given factor supplies (Harcourt 1972, p. 122). Those who had only enough patience to follow the controversy this far and no further were inclined to believe that only the special case of the aggregate neoclassical production function was punctured by the brickbats hurled by the United Kingdom cadre.

Far from such localized damage, the United Kingdom Cantabridgians were convinced that more was at stake. Their subsequent challenges did seem to be framed in manners more philosophical than strictly technical: Is there a unit of capital independent of its price? Is it possible to analytically eschew capital and yet coherently preserve the notion of a rate of profit? What are the ultimate determinants of growth? What is the meaning or implication of scarcity if the amount of capital employed is not inversely related to its price? Can one seriously use the neoclassical framework to describe the actual historical evolution of an economic system? Did neoclassicals rigorously hew to an identical notion of equilibrium over the last century? The great weakness of the Cambridge, U.K., critics was that they were incapable of seeing the single thread that ran through all of their queries, the acknowledgment of which would have united their research program. If only they had been acquainted with a little history of physics, they would have seen that their mandate was to explore all of the ways in which a substance theory of value was inconsistent with a field theory of value.

What the CCC made clear (but only in the cold flat light of hindsight) was that the production function was imported into neoclassical theory as a parallel analogue of the utility field, but rapidly became conflated and confused with the erstwhile substance theory of value as neoclassicals immediately began to incorporate a homogeneous substance, capital, as one of its functional arguments. This was logically fallacious, as Joan Robinson and her comrades demonstrated, because it confused value terms with supposedly exogenous technological specifications.

> When marginal products are spoken of as key determinants of equilibrium values, what is meant is that the relationships which are being partially differentiated in order to obtain marginal products need to be technical relationships, formally akin to psychological ones like utility functions, so that they exist before and *independent* of the equilibrium values which are the solutions to the sets of simultaneous equations [Harcourt 1982, p. 250].

In other words, the Samuelson–Hicks program of the reconciliation of the metaphors of value as substance and value as field was illegitimate, in the same sense that the Helm–Ostwald program to reconcile energy as a substance with energy as a field was illegitimate. The drive to reconcile such immiscible notions in economics was understandable; after all, there were huge areas of economic experience in which the pure field metaphor was not plausible, production theory was just the most naggingly insistent case. The growth of a value substance is a readily acceptable notion; the growth of a field of value is not. The expansion of commodities is the expansion of value in the substance metaphor; the expansion of commodities is without rationale in the field metaphor.

The incident that raised the temperature of the CCC was the

attempt by Samuelson's student Levhari (1965) to extend Samuelson's nonsubstitution theorems to proofs of the four parables for a general model of an economy. Subsequently, a symposium in the November 1966 *Quarterly Journal of Economics* embarrassed Samuelson into admitting he had made mathematical errors, an admission rendered doubly grievous by previous statements by MIT economists that Cambridge, U.K., did not understand their basic maths. It was noted afterward with glee by Marxist economists that the critical error of Samuelson and Levhari was to assume uniform capital/labor ratios in all industries, the very same assumption derided by neoclassicals in their condemnation of Marx's solution of his transformation problem (Bhaduri 1969). The significance of this observation from the present vantage point is that it reveals the true nature of Samuelson's project, which was to reconcile classical substance theories of value with the neoclassical field theory of production. Although inadvertently, he obviously posited a system which acted *as if* it were a one-good economy, the very paradigm of classical substance theories since the physiocrats.

The response of the neoclassicals to their November 1966 debacle was also very instructive. At first, disoriented and disorganized, some retorted that the critics had a point, but that the putative prevalence of perverse behavior of capital was really an empirical issue (Ferguson 1969; Blaug 1974). This response betrayed a tenuous grasp of the real issues in the CCC. The CCC was first and foremost the confrontation of two rival physics metaphors, the clash of two separate conservation principles. Chapter 2 proffers evidence from the history of physics that conservation principles are not ultimately falsified by empirical evidence per se; there is absolutely no reason to think the situation in economics would be any different.

Another early neoclassical response was to claim that the CCC was a tempest in a teapot, a misplaced concern over problems of aggregation. This also missed the point because although it was true that all other factors such as land and labor also were aggregated in most production functions, it was capital alone that was performing the role of the value substance in many variants of neoclassical production theory. If it were to serve as a viable value substance, then it was imperative that it be homogeneous, conserved in trade, the unique index of growth, and so on. It was specifically these functions that Cambridge, U.K., had demonstrated were untenable within the original physics metaphor.

With the passage of (historical) time, the neoclassical responses grew more subtle and sophisticated. The orthodox history of the CCC now goes something like this (Bliss 1975; Hahn 1975; Brown and Solow 1983): Granted, some neoclassical economists had grown sloppy in their employment of the capital concept, and the Cambridge, U.K., critics did catch them out. Nevertheless, this in no way impugned the real logic of neoclassical economic theory, embodied in the model of Walrasian general equilibrium. This model has no need of the concept of capital (although Walras himself might have messed up a bit here), because it explicitly accounts for every commodity and productive input separately. Further, there is no requirement for an equalized rate of profit in this model; in any event, one would not expect it in intertemporal general equilibrium. The accomplishment of the Cambridge, U.K., critics was ultimately small potatoes, because each and every one of their results were already known by sophisticated neoclassicals prior to the CCC (Solow, in Brown and Solow 1983, p. 184). In conclusion, how did everyone manage to get so worked up over so trivial an incident?

Let us propose another interpretation of what really happened. The primary outcome of the CCC for neoclassical theory was to render unattractive (although, it must be admitted, never really bring to a halt) the practice of indiscriminately mixing and matching options #1 through #8 in the portrayal of production. Option #3, the reversion without apology to classical substance theories of value, was more or less repudiated by the highbrow segment of the profession. One symptom of this self-denying ordinance was the nearly immediate loss of interest in growth theory and capital theory in the American neoclassical economics journals in the 1980s. The retreat from option #3 was primarily in the direction of options #4 and #8, the formalism of technology as a field in the guise of netput vectors and production sets – in other words, to the symmetry thesis. The advocates of the Austrian option #2 initially seemed to derive succor from the demise of J. B. Clark–style parables, but they too were repudiated by the high theorists. The fallout from the CCC made many neoclassicals painfully aware that option #5 was inconsistent with their underlying price theory; they even began to regard option #7 with a newfound skepticism. The symptom of this latter response was the heightened concern over what came to be called the microfoundations of macroeconomics (Weintraub 1979).

In the 1980s it became fashionable among neoclassicals to repudiate and disparage Keynesian macroeconomics; the reasons for this profound change are too numerous and involved to go into here (cf. Klamer 1983). While one must acknowledge the role of the rational-expectations movement and the coincidence of high inflation and high unemployment in the 1970s, in our present context we merely wish to add to this list the important consideration of the general breakdown of neoclassical substance theories of production as a consequence of the CCC.

As we have tried to suggest here and elsewhere (Mirowski 1985), Keynesian theory and neoclassical theory have always been uneasy bedfellows. During the composition of the *General Theory*, Roy Harrod continually pleaded with Keynes not to renounce neoclassical theory (Keynes 1972, XIII, pp. 533–4). It appears that Keynes took Harrod's advice to heart, but not in the way that Harrod had envisioned. Keynes simply neutralized the problem of price theory by the artifice of a homogeneous value substance called national income, attaching to it various trappings such as the marginal efficiency of capital and the marginal product of labor. Critics of the late 1930s and 1940s had an easy time isolating this or that particular inconsistency between Keynesian macroeconomics and neoclassical theory; however, the orthodox wing of Hicks, Samuelson, Tobin, Modigliani, and others took it upon themselves to produce a neoclassical synthesis, rendering unto Keynes the things putatively Keynesian, and this became the textbook wisdom of the 1960s.

The heart of this neoclassical synthesis was the most elaborate conflation of all of the various neoclassical theories of production in the history of neoclassical theory. First, there was a by now familiar reversion to capital as a homogeneous value substance, in a throwback to classical theories of value. Next, this homogeneous capital was thrust into a conventional neoclassical production function, so that the field theory of technology might be made to seem to receive its due; but then, incongruously, the index of output was conflated with the Keynesian value substance of national income, and this was cojoined with a Keynesian multiplier. Finally, to guarantee pandemonium, the whole lot was to be held subject to various arbitrary optimization algorithms, predicated upon the prior existence of an aggregate utility field. Ignoring for the moment all of the various ways the superposition of substance theories of value upon value fields engender logical difficulties, the proponents of the neoclassical synthesis still found themselves beset with a surfeit of value substances in their new model. Their resolution of this dilemma, such as it was, consisted of reducing two substances to one by defining capital as the sum of past national income devoted to investment, corrected by some exponential decay factor, namely

$$K_t = \sum_{i=1}^{\infty} \gamma^i I_{t-i} \qquad 0 < \gamma < 1$$

As long as this indiscriminate hybrid of substance and field conceptions of production went unchallenged, the neoclassical synthesis held sway in orthodox macroeconomics. Retrospectively, many have noticed that when the substance value theory was brought into question by the CCC, the neoclassical synthesis went into decline (Tobin, in Brown and Solow 1983, p. 197; Feiwel 1982, pp. 211–12). Interestingly enough, the nature of the neoclassical retreat was similar to the sophisticated response to the CCC itself. Neoclassical economists intending to retain certain Keynesian propositions felt compelled to reconceptualize their problem as the reconciliation of those propositions with a field theory of production and a field theory of value, a project they dubbed the microfoundations of macroeconomics.

The first inclination of this microfoundations research program was to drop the Keynesian analytical device of national product/income and to work strictly in terms of a vector of commodities, a utility field, a technology field, and a proliferation of conjectures about how the process of trading might result in inefficiencies. More than a decade of this sort of work has yet to produce any consensus, or even any striking results (Drazen 1980; Fisher 1983). This is probably due to the fact that no one was particularly impressed by demonstrations that the external imposition of arbitrary rigidities upon a Walrasian system would result in divergences from optimality (Weintraub 1979, p. 66).[7]

The closest the microfoundations research program got to a novel insight was the insistence by Robert Clower that the conflict between Keynes and neoclassical general equilibrium was due to an incompatibility between basic presumptions about conservation principles. His intuition was correct: It is true that the Keynesian conservation of income substance outside of the multiplier directly contradicts the assumption of the competing metaphor that income is conserved in the act of trade; both cannot be true simultaneously. As Clower (1984, p. 41) phrased it: "either Walras' Law is incompatible with Keynesian economics, or Keynes had nothing fundamentally new to add to orthodox economic theory." Unfortunately, though, Clower did not follow through on the physical metaphor, as revealed in the following representative quote:

> [N]o transactor consciously *plans* to purchase units of any commodity without at the same time *planning* to finance the purchase either from profit receipts or from the sale of some units of some other commodity . . . I shall call the last and very general proposition *Say's Principle*. This is essentially a rational planning postulate, not a

bookkeeping identity or a technical relation. Unlike the market principle known as Walras' Law, moreover, Say's Principle does not depend on the tacit assumption that values are calculated in terms of current market prices, or on the equally tacit assumption that market prices are independent of individual purchases and sales. Neither does it presuppose that individual behavior is in any sense optimal. Thus, Say's principle may indeed be regarded as a fundamental convention of economic science, akin in all relevant respects to such basic ideas of physical science as the second [sic] law of thermodynamics [Clower 1970, p. 285; 1984, p. 47].

The reason why the work of Clower and other perceptive theorists has not been sufficiently appreciated is that the microfoundations literature harbors a paradox at its very core that will persist in crippling the research program. Keynes generated a theory of an unstable economic *process* by the instrumentality of his reversion to a substance theory of value, a tactic that allowed the joint conceptualization of production, growth, and the passage of time in a (relatively) internally consistent manner. In contrast, it is the avowed intention of the microfoundations school to renounce all value substances and to recast all macroeconomic analysis in the format of production and utility fields. It is precisely this choice that prohibits the logical modeling of process in production, in growth, and in exchange, as explained earlier in this chapter. The field metaphor cannot represent a circular economy where outputs become inputs and so on, ad infinitum. It cannot specify precisely what it is that grows in an economy. All such recent exercises, such as the postulation of an Edgeworth process or a Hahn process, that attempt to describe the temporal sequences of exchange within the neoclassical framework are contradictions in terms, mathematical oxymorons. If they could have been enticed to read a little intellectual history, these theorists would have realized that the formalism of the field is useful only in cases where one can safely abstract away all considerations of process and the passage of time. Path-dependence violates the necessary conservation principles and undermines the coherence of the field formalism. Neoclassical economists needlessly shoulder the Sisyphean task of coopting a natural metaphor and then rendering it devoid of all logic and sense in the name of realism.

So much for the defenders of neoclassicism. What about the critics? Their sympathy for the substance metaphor led the Cambridge, U.K., contingent to research the conceptualization of growth and to stress the necessity of a single overall rate of profit as an index of economic expansion. Sraffa's "standard commodity" was a pivotal innovation in this respect, because it developed a scheme of weights that allowed the analyst to invoke a virtual variation in the rate of profit while holding certain value parameters invariant, revealing in a most concise manner the strengths and weaknesses of a substance theory of value in the context of a many-good economy (Sraffa 1960. p. 20). The strength of the standard commodity was that it reconceptualized the uniform expansion of value at a point in time such that it could be well-defined[8]; and clarified the meaning of a static commodity system.

Much ink has been spilled over the issue of whether Sraffa did or did not assume constant returns to scale and no substitution of inputs in production technologies (Salvadori 1985), but the real thrust of the standard commodity is to undermine the portrayal of technology as a field. Recall from earlier in this chapter that the production field must be static and path-independent if it is to be symmetrical with the utility field. Sraffa from the beginning was adamant that the path-independence condition was fallacious, as witnessed by his insistence in his seminal 1926 article that changes in technique brought in train irreversible consequences. *Production of Commodities,* with its fixed input coefficients, was the direct offspring of this conviction. Field theory purports to model a static, virtual, atemporal economy, but the *only* legitimate way to model such an economy is as a *point* in input space – that is, all that can be said about such an economy is to make a list of all of the quantities of inputs used to make a fixed quantity of outputs *now*. Most further specifications would presume path-independence at a point in time, and that presumption is simply false. At a point in time, in the absence of path-independence, there can be no countenancing the portrayal of technology as a field. The weakness of Sraffa's standard commodity – the attribute that rendered it nothing more than the "prelude to a critique of marginalist theory" – was its demonstration that, in general, there exists no principle of conservation of value that may be derived from technological information alone. In general, there is no natural continuity between one production situation and the one immediately subsequent to it, as revealed in his analysis of the reduction of value to dated labor, as well as in his notes on the problems of joint production. From this vantage point, *Production of Commodities by Means of Commodities* was the mathematical culmination of the classical tradition of substance theories of value, but it was also its swan song.

The CCC demonstrated that there is no technologically based value substance independent of the pricing process except in some very unusual and unlikely circumstances, and hence the preeminent connotation of production (i.e., the expansion of value, or "growth") could be given no plausible interpretation in neoclassical economics.

At this juncture, the Cambridge, U.K., critics branched out in two directions: One, associated with Pierangelo Garegnani, John Eatwell, and Murray Milgate, asserted that this impotence of neoclassicism had been turned into a supposed virtue by the surreptitious reconstruction of the meaning of equilibrium in the twentieth century. They argued that the neoclassical mathematical models had been weaned from a center-of-gravity interpretation of equilibrium to the contrivance of temporary equilibrium (Garegnani, in Brown, Sato, and Zarembka 1976; Milgate 1979). The other branch, associated with Joan Robinson and the post-Keynesians, insisted that neoclassical theory was unable to describe how an economy ever got into an equilibrium because it had abstracted away from the actual passage of historical time (Robinson 1980, pp. 86–96). Both branches would have benefited immensely from an understanding of the underlying physics metaphors.

The Garegnani/Eatwell group have in the interim taken to advocating use of the Sraffian system as a legitimate alternative to neoclassical theory, dubbing their price theory the center-of-gravity approach. A familiarity with physics would suggest that the gravity metaphor is misleading, in that it somewhat obscures the fundamental differences between Sraffa and the orthodoxy. The transmutation of equilibrium concepts from "center of gravity" to "temporary equilibrium" was a direct consequence of the passage from a metaphor of value substance to value field. In classical economics, since the value substance is conserved in exchange through time, the equilibrium has a persistence and integrity that allows the convergence of price to its magnitude. (Yet, ironically, this is precisely the idol smashed by Sraffa's PCMC.) In neoclassical theory, value is conserved only through the arbitrary imposition of conservation principles such as those discussed in Chapter 5; when endowments are permitted to vary as the result of previous trades, prices exhibit no temporal integrity or persistence, as we have discovered in this chapter. Hence, the move to temporary equilibrium was a foregone conclusion. The post-Keynesian branch could also derive some enlightenment from a familiarity with physics. Their complaints about the absence of historical time from neoclassical models is correct, because neoclassical theory is the physics of the Laplacian dream. What they do not seem to comprehend is that as long as neoclassicism is unwilling to part with its Ur-metaphor of utility as potential energy, then there can never be anything other than mechanical time in their models, however much this restriction clashes with commonsense notions of production or social interaction.[9]

In sum, the CCC has been an unfortunate comedy of errors. Neo-classicals were embarrassed into retreating to their pure physics metaphor of the field, only to run it into the ground because they misunderstood its imperatives and significance. The critics felt betrayed by this rejoinder, and because they also were oblivious to the physics metaphor, they did not understand the futility of a return to an even earlier vintage of physics metaphor.

Has there been any progress in the theory of value in the twentieth century?

Most of the commonsense conceptualizations of production still derive from classical substance notions of value, a fact attested to by recent clarifications of the theory of value by Sraffians and Marxists. This clarification traces its genesis back to Cournot (1897, chap. 3), where the question was first broached: In a world of more than two commodities and two traders, what is it that guarantees that a price system is coherent – that is, that consecutive binary trades of A for B and B for C are transitive, such that

$$p_{A,C} = [p_{A,B}] \times [p_{B,C}] \, ?$$

Of all the early neoclassicals, only Walras even acknowledged the problem, but he avoided it by simply assuming that the conditon would always be fulfilled (Howitt 1973). To be fair, however, the reason that such a fundamental problem could be ignored was that the algebraic properties of the price system were already built into the appropriated physics metaphor. Reflexivity, transitivity, and symmetry of forces are already built-in characteristics of the irrotational field. As the formalism of the field was adopted without rationale or scrutiny, an equivalence relation between commodities was smuggled in at the initial stages of the analysis. Also, since the field formalism abstracts away process, any discussion of the means whereby transitivity might be brought about or enforced was likewise blocked.

In the 1960s, there was a revival of interest in these issues amongst monetary economists. In seminal articles, such as Clower (1984), Ostroy and Starr (1974), and Ellerman (1984), the mathematical properties of exchange were mooted without dependence upon the neoclassical physics metaphor. Given that these theorists' point of embarkation was still neoclassical economics, certain elements of the tradition were still in evidence: Transactors were presumed to possess an unexplained endowment of commodities that did not fulfill their desired objectives from a personal vantage point. The divergence from the physics metaphor came in an eschewal of the field formalism and its preemption by a model of an explicit search for an appropriate sequence of pairwise barter trades which would result in the desired commodity bundle. Even in the unlikely case where all relative prices were given a priori and enforced by some unspecified authority, these papers showed that the problem of constructing a chain of pairwise trades in order to arrive at a preconceived objective was intractable without the artifice of a specific money commodity and the prior existence of appreciable stocks of inventories. Unfortunately, this profound insight subsequently languished undeveloped within the context of the neoclassical research program.

From our present perspective, we might suggest two reasons for this shortcoming. First, as we have seen time and again, when given the choice between preserving their physics metaphor and innovating a truly indigenous economic theory, neoclassicals have invariably opted for the former. Second, the mathematical results initially achieved in these papers hinged crucially upon the dual assumptions of the conservation of commodities and the full equivalence of trade (Ostroy and Starr 1974, pp. 1095–96). These assumptions embody postulates that have never rested securely in the core of neoclassical doctrine (see Chapter 5), and moreover, that preclude the existence of production. Had these theorists attempted to bring production within the ambit of their research agenda, they would have rapidly discovered that in this context, production implies autarky, in the sense that demand for good A could not only be met by a chain of pairwise trades arriving at A, but also by any combination of goods X, . . . , Z that might be employed to produce A. The condition of sufficient inventory stocks of most commodities would then imply that almost everyone could potentially produce all of their desired commodities, refraining from all trade. End of promising research program.

Serious inquiry into the formalization of the interplay between production and exchange was then taken up by the Sraffian/Marxian contingent, probably because neoclassicals could not seriously entertain the notion of relinquishing the metaphor of production as a field. The issues involved were clearly laid out by Krause (1982) in *Money and Abstract Labour*, one of the most important works in the tradition of the substance theory of value after Sraffa's *Production of Commodities by Means of Commodities*. Krause recapitulated Cournot's insight that: "Regarded merely as events, individual acts of exchange have no connection with one another and are simply fortuitous happenings" (Krause 1982, p. 28). If there is structure to be found in the world of exchange, then it can only be made manifest by resisting the temptation to see the structure as fully determined by relations of final use.

Krause (1982, p. 31) initiates the inquiry by positing a matrix $\mathbf{E}$ whose elements e_{ij} correspond to the number of units of commodity j which are exchanged for one unit of commodity i in a particular pairwise exchange. He then observes that one might be tempted to assume that $e_{ji} = (1/e_{ij})$, but that, in general, there is no guarantee for it to be true in comparisons of any two chains of pairwise exchanges. The likelihood of arriving at a particular commodity bundle starting with an arbitrary endowment of commodities can hence be reduced to the problem of determining whether the matrix $\mathbf{E}$ is indecomposable, or in his terminology "connected" (Krause 1982, p. 164). The link to Sraffa's work immediately becomes apparent. In PCMC, basic commodities are defined by partitioning a technology matrix into decomposable and indecomposable subsets, in effect defining a sub-economy where every member commodity can be produced directly or indirectly using every other member commodity; in other words, you can always get there from here. His artifice of the basic commodity explains what Sraffa can define prices of production without considering the actual structure of exchange. Krause perceptively notes that, in general, neither production alone nor exchange alone would exhibit the necessary characteristic of indecomposability or connectedness. If they did, then economists would be justified in postulating a dichotomy between real and monetary phenomena. We might add that the reason neoclassical theory appears to be so enamoured of that dichotomy is that the indecomposability of the exchange system is an unobtrusive postulate of the metaphor of utility as a conservative field.

Krause also profoundly clarifies the significance of the structure of a substance theory of value by observing that the connectedness of exchange is a necessary but not sufficient condition to define a system of transitive prices – that is, Cournot's problem revisited. In order to attain transitivity, one must also posit that the exchange matrix is symmetric and, strikingly, this can be accomplished by the addition or imposition of a specific money commodity. What Krause does not notice, but what should now be apparent from our long sojourn in the histories of physics and economics, is that *this imposition of symmetry is isomorphic to the imposition of the conservation of value in exchange*. Thus the theory of value is brought full circle in a realization that the analytic significance of substance theories of value has been to explain and guarantee the existence of a transitive, connected system of prices. Once this has been achieved, having guaranteed the conservation principle assuring the general quantitative coherence of the price structure, then a separate system bearing the title "production" is posited. Production is characterized by the fact that it is *not* symmetric and *not* transitive with respect to economic value. Once appended to the system of exchange, production induces the breaking of symmetry, which in turn explains the expansion of value. In classical substance theories, value is conserved in exchange and is not conserved in production; value in exchange is attemporal, allowing production to have a temporal aspect. The "connectedness" of an isolated production system may influence the magnitude of prices, but in classical economics it is incapable of accounting for the coherence of the price system (Levine 1980). The analogy with the use of the concept of broken symmetry in twentieth-century physics is both enlightening and instructive.[10]

For all practical purposes, Krause has demonstrated that it was a vain hope of classical economics to look solely to the production process to adequately define a substance theory of value. In other words, recourse to physical science (or scientific metaphor) is insufficient to render an economic theory fully determinate. If only those who saw themselves as preserving the legacy of Sraffa could embrace this precept, then perhaps that legacy would finally prove a powerful rival to the neoclassical orthodoxy.

CHAPTER 7

The ironies of physics envy

I perfectly agree with those who object to the practice of some economists, simply to copy out what they believe is an economic argument from textbooks of pure mathematics or theoretical mechanics or physics, and I hope you will not interpret what I am to say in the sense of that practice. . . . We must not copy out actual arguments but we can learn from physics how to build up an exact argument. . . . Most important of all is the consideration that there are obviously a set of concepts and procedures which, although belonging not to the field of pure mathematics but to the field of more or less applied mathematics, one of so general a character as to be applicable to an indefinite number of different fields. The concepts of Potential or Friction or Inertia are of that kind. . . . [Letter of Joseph Schumpeter to Edwin Bidwell Wilson, 19 May 1937, in Harvard University Archives, Wilson Correspondence, HUG 4878.203]

[Schumpeter] asked me: "Are you not reminded, dear colleague, of general equilibrium theory in economics when you read modern mathematical physics?" I doubt that I had the courage to admit that I had sadly neglected mathematical physics, and I surely did not dare tell him that I doubted his own knowledge of that area. [Stigler 1988, p. 101]

My impression is that the best and the brightest of the profession proceed as if economics is the physics of society . . . If the project of turning economics into a hard science could succeed, then it would surely be worth doing. [Solow 1985, pp. 330–1]

In 1942, enjoying the zenith of his prestige among economists, Friedrich von Hayek chose to do a very unusual thing. In a series of papers in *Economica,* he scathingly denounced the phenomenon of what he called "scientism" in social theory, which he proceeded to define as "slavish imitation of the method and language of science." Whereas he regarded these articles as a counterblast to socialism and the engineering mentality, from the point of view of neoclassical economists, this was regarded as rather a bit of unforgivably uncouth behavior. This little outburst earned Hayek a modicum of opprobium, precipitating a decline in his reputation as an economic theorist throughout the Anglophone world.[1]

354

What was not well understood at the time was that Hayek was a rare bird in the Anglo-American economic aviary: He was one of a very few remaining representatives of the Mengerian tradition of Austrian economics. That tradition, as I argued in Chapter 5, in fact opposed the importation of physics metaphors into economic theory. Hayek, in contrast to his British and American colleagues, actually had first-hand experience with the writers of the German Historicist school, and was familiar with their claims that economics, and indeed all the *Geisteswissenschaften*, were incapable of legitimate implementation of the concepts and techniques of the natural sciences.

Anglophone economists were oblivious to these undercurrents in Hayek's economic influences, and only noticed his implacable vigilance against any and all tendencies to socialist thought. So when Hayek sounded the alarm in the 1940s that creeping scientism and the engineering mentality were sapping the moral fiber and jostling the West down the road to serfdom, it is perhaps not surprising that more than one neoclassical economist suspected he was dealing from something less than a full deck.

At this juncture, failures of communication became endemic to twentieth-century economics. In one corner were the orthodox neo-classicals, unwittingly intent upon the reinvention of energetics from scratch. The irony of their situation can only be compared to the irony of Jorge Luis Borges's Pierre Menard who "did not want to compose another *Quixote* – which is easy – but *the Quixote itself*. Needless to say, he never contemplated a mechanical transcription of the original; he did not propose to copy it. His admirable intention was to produce a few pages which would coincide – word for word and line for line – with those of Miguel de Cervantes." In the other corner was Hayek, tilting at scientific socialism in blissful ignorance of the other brand of scientism coming to be embraced by his LSE colleagues (de Marchi 1988).

The purpose of this chapter is to gain some further insights into "the place of science in modern civilization" (to echo a famous title of Veblen), and from that perspective, Hayek does hold some intrinsic interest. His indictments of scientism display brief flashes of brilliance, interspersed with long patches of gloomy oblivion as to the true character of the persistent symbiosis of economics and physics. For instance, he quotes a German work that observes piquantly that "the characteristic Weltanschauung of the engineer is the energetics world-view" (Hayek 1979, p. 171, fn.). He also sketches the roles of Saint-Simon and Auguste Comte in popularizing the idea of a social physics, a set of influences central to the history of the dominance of physics over all Western social thought, a history that remains to be written.

Yet these insights pale in comparison to Hayek's superficial references to physical theory and his deficiencies in understanding how physical metaphors have driven the evolution of neoclassical thought. Further, there are the patent misrepresentations of the history of economic speculation, such as the absurd claim that in the eighteenth and nineteenth centuries "the study of economic and social phenomena was guided in the choice of its methods in the main by the nature of the problems it had to face" (Hayek 1979, p. 19), implying that the mimesis of science is only a relatively recent phenomenon. In an area where he should have known better, he also attempted to smear the German Historicist school with the scientistic label, even though they were the only group to correctly identify neoclassicism with the slavish imitation of physics (Sombart 1929). Finally, it was misleading (to say the least) to insist that scientism was associated with a specific political position, much less an explicitly socialist orientation, as Hayek did. Physics metaphors have been at least as instrumental in reifying the image of a natural self-regulating market as they have been in encouraging engineers to believe in their own capacities to successfully plan economic activity.

Is economics a science?

Without exaggeration, one may say that there has been a surfeit of breast-beating, wailing, crowing, and soul-searching over the question of whether economics is a science. In the modern era, this has mainly served as a prelude to a round of smug satisfaction and self-congratulations. What made the Hayek incident so refreshingly different was his assertion that economics was not a science, should not strive for scientific status, and should revel in its exclusion from the ranks of the sciences. The poverty of economics is revealed by the fact that the debate has not moved beyond those mutually exclusive poles in the subsequent half-century. Perhaps the next step is to dissolve both poles in the acid bath of their own irony.

Let us begin by admitting that there exists no scientific method, no set of timeless criteria that the program of economic research could adopt and embrace in order to guarantee its own scientific status and legitimacy. This lesson is the legacy of the decline of positivist philosophies of science in the late twentieth century. Juxtapose this fact with the hypothesis that economic research has always met with the greatest difficulties in establishing the credibility of its results and in fending off charges of charlatanism and quackery. Consequently, the pressure to usurp the legitimacy of science has always weighed down economic research; further, there is no sign on the horizon that this weight will be lifted any time in the foreseeable future.

From a certain point of view, the neoclassical economists' response to this pressure has been particularly resourceful, especially in comparison with other branches of social theory. The neoclassicals opted to become scientific by ignoring what the physicists and the philosophers of science *preached,* and to cut the Gordian knot by directly copying what the physicists *did.* There can be no more pragmatic definition of science than this: Imitate success.

Nevertheless, imitation bears its own ironies and discomforts, as any reader of this volume now undoubtedly senses. First, there are those imperious role models, the physicists, who have a most disconcerting habit of spurning the social scientists most in awe of their exalted persons. Time and again in the twentieth century, prominent physicists have chastised their economist colleagues in no uncertain terms:

> The success of mathematical physics led the social scientist to be jealous of its power without quite understanding the intellectual attitudes that had contributed to the power. The use of mathematical formulae had accompanied the development of the natural sciences and become the mode of the social sciences . . . The mathematics that the social scientists employ and the mathematical physics that they use as their model are the mathematics and the mathematical physics of 1850 . . . Their quantitative theories are treated with the unquestioning respect with which the physicists of a less sophisticated age treated the concepts of Newtonian physics. Very few econometricians are aware that if they are to imitate the procedure of modern physics and not its mere appearances, a mathematical economics must begin with a critical account of these quantitative notions and the means adopted for collecting and measuring them [Wiener 1964, pp. 89–90].

Then there are the disturbing and insistent questions about the nature of the success of neoclassical economic theory. Why should scientific success in one sphere of inquiry carry over into another sphere? Is mimesis an irredeemably cynical ploy, or is there some sense in which it can serve as a gyroscope for a floundering research program? Once instituted, is imitation a persistently pragmatic operation? In other words, once they have begun, should economists continue to emulate and simulate physics as physics itself evolves? How can this mimesis be effective if many of the individual neoclassical economists are personally unaware of it? And – and this is the particular relevance of the Hayek incident – isn't there a danger that imitation might breed contempt as well as respect? Could the physics metaphor generate more heat than light?

This chapter contrives to bring evidence to bear on the question of the uneasy coexistence of neoclassicism with twentieth-century physical theory. A little-understood predicament of neoclassical economics in the twentieth century is that it has been obliged to acknowledge that physics itself has undergone some profound transformations since the consolidation of the energy concept.

Although the meaning and significance of the twentieth-century innovations of thermodynamics, quantum mechanics, relativity theory, and the unified forces theories are matters of extensive debate and contention, Chapter 2 argued that no one who understands these developments expects a return to the cozy world of the Laplacian Dream or a reversion to a simple notion of natural law. Instead, we live in an era where eminent physicists such as John Wheeler can go around claiming: "There is no law except the law that there is no law." This change in the character of physics (not to mention physicists) puts new pressure on neoclassical economic theory, but pressure from an unexpected direction. The criteria of scientific success in the physicists' camp have clearly changed, and the new models are not always congruent with the earlier formalisms of energy. Hence neoclassical economics finds itself caught in a pincers movement: By how much should it revise its nineteenth-century metaphor in order to accommodate the new understanding of the physical world?

Revise too much, and then the program is vulnerable to the complaint of slavish and mindless imitation. Revise too little or not at all, and neoclassicism grows quaint, dowdy, and anachronistic, effectively withering on the vine along with its scientific pretensions. Hesitation and equivocation also have their drawbacks, because it is a fact of Western life that *there are always new pretenders to the title of social physics*, in effect trying to beat neoclassical theory at its own game. Challengers to neoclassical hegemony have never relented in their attempts to appropriate more up-to-date physics metaphors. The question of the scientific character of economic theory cannot be understood without savoring the vulnerabilities of an aging social physics, surrounded by jeering scientistic upstarts, and the responses of late neoclassical theory to meet the challenges.

Rediscovering the field: Integrability and revealed preference

Once neoclassicals appropriated their core physics metaphor of utility as potential energy, it had profound and persistent implications for the further evolution of their theoretical endeavors far into the twentieth century. When it came to the proto-energetics metaphor, to coin a phrase, the expropriators were expropriated.

The time has now arrived to briefly revisit the core metaphor of utility as a conservative vector field of potential energy in its twentieth-century incarnation. The rationale for this rendezvous is to provide one last piece of evidence that the physics origins of neoclassical theory still matter for neoclassical economics, in the sense that the motives behind many otherwise untoward behaviors of neoclassical theorists in the twentieth century can only be comprehended in light of the proto-energetics metaphor.

As difficult as it may be to imagine it now, the rise to predominance of the proto-energetics metaphor of utility as potential energy was neither smooth nor unhindered. In the decades from 1910 through 1940 it seemed, on the contrary, that most economists looked askance at the physics metaphor, finding it cumbersome, unwieldy, perhaps a trifle silly, and maybe even a little embarrassing. Veblen and the American Institutionalist school had been particularly scathing when it came to utility, and in that period they were at the zenith of their influence in American economics. The Lausanne school had yet to become household names in the French and English economic professions, blocked in the former case by political hostilities and in the latter case by Marshall's version of neoclassicism (Maloney 1985). One need only to glance at Schultz (1931) or at Jacob Viner's impassioned 1925 defense of utility to detect the profound pessimism that surrounded the question of the legitimacy of the physics metaphor at that time; Viner (1925, p. 382) resorted to the expedient of claiming that economists' understanding of utility was comparable to the "knowledge of heat prior to the discovery of the thermometer." Samuelson (1972b, p. 255) was told a similar story:

> Prior to the mid-1930s, utility theory showed signs of degenerating into a sterile tautology. Psychic utility or satisfaction could scarcely be defined, let alone measured . . . Just as we can cancel two from the ratio of even numbers, so one could use Occam's razor to cut utility completely from the argument, ending up with the fatuity: people do what they do.

It cannot be said that, prior to the 1930s, the partisans of the field metaphor had much cause for enthusiasm with regard to the proto-energetics research program. A perfect example of a dejected economic scientist was Henry Schultz:

> But what equations of motion and what laws of conservation of comparable scope do we have in economics? To ask the question is to

> answer it. There are none that have the definiteness and universal
> demonstrability of the corresponding physical laws . . . we can think
> of the total utility function – if it exists – as corresponding to the
> energy potential whose partial derivatives measure the forces which
> guide the movements of the individual. But unfortunately, we know
> neither the values nor the forms of the required functions [Schultz
> 1938, p. 57].

The wild swings in attitude toward the measurability of utility
provide another perspective upon the vulnerability of the physics
metaphor in this period. Early in his career Irving Fisher was vehe-
ment that utility should be quarantined off from any intercourse with
any psychological research program, maintaining that it was intrinsically incapable of measurement. Later in his career he reversed
his position and claimed that utility was measurable; such equivocation did little to promote confidence in his grasp of the issues involved. Again, Vilfredo Pareto evolved from an openness to the idea
that utility might eventually be empirically accessible to a strong
conviction that it would never be empirically measurable; along the
way he tried to change the name of utility to ophelimity to foster the
impression that his assumptions concerning utility were somehow less
restrictive than those made by others. It is worth noting for future
reference that, for both Fisher and Pareto, the issue of the empirical
accessibility of utility was intimately bound up with the question of the
integrability of a sequence of points in commodity space, an important issue in the physics analogue that got lost in subsequent discussions. A third example of neoclassical ambivalence was Gustav
Cassel's *Theory of Social Economy*, which claimed that it was possible to
derive all the substantive propositions of neoclassical theory without
resort to that suspicious entity called utility.

The orthodox version of the history of economic thought has
conveniently forgotten just how pervasive was the skepticism over the
legitimacy of utility on the part of those later to be considered its
staunch defenders. Milton Friedman, for instance, thought in 1934
that utility functions might be empirically recoverable (see Schultz
1938, chap. 19), whereas by 1942 he repudiated the possibility of any
such measurement (Friedman and Wallis 1942). There arose an attitude, particularly at the University of Chicago in this era, that neoclassical economists were in fact not constrained by any analytical imperatives dictated by the utility concept; they could go wherever their
inclinations led them:

> The attempt of science to find what is real in human behavior
> reduces it first to mechanical movements and physiological processes

. . . But physiology just as inexorably dissolves into chemistry, and chemistry into physics, and all that physics leaves of reality is electric charges moving in fields of force – things far more unreal than the characters in the most fanciful works of fiction. Moreover, the experts in science and scientific method (Mach, Pearson, Russell) are frankly skeptical of the reality of any of it, and talk in terms of concepts useful for the purposes of analysis, and of the simplification of our thought processes. The answer at the end of every line of inquiry is instrumentalism [Knight 1925, p. 94].

The view from outside Chicago was less tolerant, and more biting:

> In the closing quarter of the last century great hopes were entertained by economists with regard to the capacity of economics to be made an "exact science." According to the view of the foremost theorists, the development of the doctrines of utility and value had laid the foundation of scientific economics in exact concepts, and it would soon be possible to erect upon the new foundation a firm structure of interrelated parts which, in definiteness and cogency, would be suggestive of the severe beauty of the mathematico-physical sciences. But this expectation has not been realized . . .
>
> The explanation is found in the prejudiced point of view from which economists regarded the possibilities of the science and in the radically wrong method which they pursued. It was assumed gratuitously that economics was to be modeled on the simpler mathematical, physical sciences, and this assumption created a prejudice at the outset. Economics was to be a "calculus of pleasure and pain," "a mechanics of utility," a "social mechanics," a *"physique sociale"* . . . The biased point of view implied in these descriptions led to an undue stressing of those aspects of the science which seemed to bear out the pretentious metaphors [Moore 1914, pp. 84–6].

In such a hostile atmosphere, it might have been regarded as prudent to eschew the utility concept, but recall this would be tantamount to renouncing the fundamental physics metaphor. Indeed, from the decade of the 1910s there does appear a neoclassical tradition that claimed it was repudiating the utility concept, but it strained mightily to have its cake while feasting on it too: Time and again all that was achieved was to restate the field formalism in other, less intuitively accessible terms. One observes this trend beginning with Johnson (1913) and Slutsky's well-known 1915 paper on the "balance of the consumer" (in Boulding and Stigler 1952). Johnson's paper asserted: "The impossibility of measurement does not affect any economic problem" (Johnson 1913, p. 490), but that was only empty bravado. Energy/utility was an integral and was therefore only unique up to a monotonic transformation, and hence Johnson's self-denying ordinance to restrict all economic analysis to ratios of marginal utilities was hardly a call to liberation. Although the paper by Hicks and Allen (1934) garnered more attention, it provided no further advance upon Johnson's original thesis: The claim that indifference curves were an advance upon utility functions, or that they embodied less restrictive or onerous assumptions, was simply false.

Having forgotten that utility was a field of potential energy, neoclassicals frantically occupied themselves with rediscovering the energy concept. The paper by Slutsky is a paradigm in this respect. He began by bemoaning the tribulations of the "hedonic school," plagued as it was by detractors. In a burst of enthusiasm (anticipating later positivist and operationalist manifestos), he asserted that "if we wish to place economic science upon a solid basis, we must make it completely independent of psychological assumptions and philosophical hypotheses" (Slutsky, in Boulding and Stigler 1952, p. 27). Slutsky then embarked upon a breathtaking parade of non sequiturs. First, he conflated the definition of neoclassical consumer equilibrium with the requirement of stable budgets; he did not clearly recognize the mathematical format of the relevant conservation principles, here in particular the conservation of income. Second, he admitted that utility is never accessible to empiricism, in the sense of direct observation of preferences. Third, he asserted the mathematical condition for the continuity and symmetry of the utility field, namely equation (5.4).

This should now be familiar to the reader as the condition for the conservation of utility and the path-independence of preferences. It is isomorphic to an assertion of the transitivity of preferences, in the sense of the strong axiom of revealed preference. It is also isomorphic to the imposition of the condition of the integrability of a preference structure, as discussed in Chapter 5 (see Hurwicz, in Chipman et al. eds. 1971, p. 177). Slutsky seems to have conflated points one and three above in his own mind, perhaps because in the original physics metaphor the conservation of energy would translate as the conservation of income plus utility. Fourth, he then proceeded to admit that "when all the marginal utilities are functions of the quantities of all the goods, unequivocal determination becomes impossible." Fifth, he then testified to his conviction that diminishing marginal utility "can be founded upon some sort of *internal evidence*, not on the facts of economic conduct. The generality of this conviction authorizes us to call it *faith in the consciousness of economic conduct*" (Slutsky, in Boulding and Stigler 1952, pp. 54–5).

This much-cited, much-praised, but little-read paper is often asserted to be the seminal text in the modern neoclassical theory of the consumer. The fact of the matter is that it was a rehash of the same equivocations that have characterized proto-energetics since its inception, leavened with an explicit inscription of the equation of the integrability condition for a field of force. The utility function had to be symmetrical and path-independent in order to qualify as a field formalism, as physicists such as Volterra and Laurent had persistently reminded neoclassical economists such as Walras and Pareto, but it seems the meaning of the field formalism never quite sunk in, to the extent that a later generation of neoclassicals could retrospectively credit Slutsky with a "discovery" of something. The much-touted Slutsky conditions can, of course, serve to clarify the slope of the demand curve – hence the income and substitution effects so favored by intermediate price theory texts (Green 1971, pp. 65–9) – but here recall that the demand curve is only a Marshallian gloss upon the original physics metaphor, one that is freely disposable from the viewpoint of modern Walrasian theory. The Slutsky conditions added nothing to the structure of neoclassical price theory per se.

In retrospect, neoclassical economists were itching to repudiate the utility concept, but could not figure out how to simultaneously retain the physics metaphor. This version of the neoclassical research program was given a new lease on life in the 1930s, and the person most responsible for breathing life into it was Paul Samuelson. As he put it in his Novel Prize lecture, "From the beginning I was concerned to find out what *refutable* hypotheses on the observable facts on price and quantity demanded were implied by the assumption that the consumer spends his limited income at given prices in order to maximize his ordinal utility" (Samuelson 1972b, p. 256). A different interpretation of Samuelson's role (at least in this particular context) was instead as the Slutsky of his generation. In other words, Samuelson also intended to deflect dissatisfaction with neoclassical utility by exiling psychology, banishing metaphysics, and plumping for a putatively pristine empiricism; however, just like Slutsky, all he succeeded in doing was to restate the energy field equations in yet another mathematical idiom.

The case that Paul Samuelson's defense of neoclassical value theory was a failure has been argued with great verve and brilliance in the superlative unsung classic by Stanley Wong (1978). There is no substitute for the reading (and rereading) of this book as an antidote to the conventional wisdom that the neoclassical research program of the theory of revealed preference (TRP) has managed to shed its concept of utility/energy. Briefly, Wong's case is this: Samuelson was originally motivated by a desire to dispense with all psychological overtones of the utility concept, and perhaps as well a conviction that utility could be excised from the neoclassical program altogether. However, as his extraction of a pure empirical theory of value ran into snags, Samuelson's reaction was to revise the objectives rather than the actual content of the revealed preference concept.

In 1938, Samuelson claimed that the theory of revealed preference would permit the derivation of *all* the principal results of ordinal utility theory (i.e., the original physics metaphor) without any recourse to any nonobservable concept. This interpretation rapidly became impaled upon the horns of a dilemma: Either the appeal to revealed preference was an appeal to a vicious circle – observations are used to construct a preference ordering which is then turned around to explain those same observations – or else a critical auxiliary postulate of consistency is appended to the TRP, a postulate that is not at all observational, unless one admits that it is continuously falsified (Wong 1978, p. 57). This conundrum forced Samuelson to shift his ground in 1948, and claim that the TRP was only a method of constructing an individual's indifference map from observable market behavior. The 1948 position was a pronounced retreat from that of 1938, because it tacitly acknowledged that ordinal utility theory was the canonical neoclassical theory, and therefore the TRP could hardly be regarded a repudiation of or replacement for that theory (Wong 1978, pp. 73–4). Nevertheless, the watered-down 1948 program still was a failure for a number of reasons.

The failings of the TRP still bear repetition. First, it is intrinsically impossible to actually implement it as an empirical program:

> Not only is the ratio of observations to potential choices equal to zero, but moreover the absolute number of cases investigated is also fairly small. Comparisons have to be made within a fairly short time to avoid tastes change, but the time elapsed must also be sufficiently long so that the mutton purchased last time is not still in the larder, making the choices non-comparable [Sen 1973, p. 243].

Second, it confuses and conflates preferences and behavior (Wong 1978, pp. 86–7), or, as we should prefer to phrase it in the present work, it surreptitiously *assumes* the "metaphysical" principle of the conservation of utility. As if this were not enough bad news for a program of pristine empiricism and purely operational concepts, it turned out that Samuelson's "weak" version of the TRP was not formally sufficient to guarantee the existence of a preference gradient. This was made evident when Houthakker found the necessary observational conditions for the indifference map in 1950. These were – voilà – those very same integrability conditions dating back to the earliest controversies over the original physics metaphor!

At this juncture, Samuelson hailed the Houthakker result as a demonstration that, "The 'revealed preference' and 'utility function' (or 'indifference surface') approaches to the theory of consumer behavior are therefore formally the same" (in Wong 1978, p. 111). Trying to snatch victory from the jaws of defeat, Samuelson (1972b, p. 250) touted this as some sort of seminal breakthrough in neoclassical theory; yet it seems that Wong's assessment is the more prudent and perceptive one when he concludes that the TRP is not a new theory of consumer behavior nor is it an observationally based means of constructing consumer indifference maps. Instead, it was a long detour that ended up right where it started. Readers of the present volume should note the implicit rider attached to Wong's conclusions: Samuelson began with energy and the field formalism and ended up with energy and the field formalism. Or, as Sen (1973, p. 242) put it, the very idea that the TRP freed neoclassical demand theory from utility is "an elaborate pun."

If Samuelson's TRP really was wordplay, then how did it come to pass that neoclassical theory managed to get a new lease on life? This is a devilishly difficult question, and our answer will necessarily be conjecture as we cannot poll every individual neoclassical theorist on the reasons for their allegience to the basic theory. However, there are some important clues to the answer. One clue is to note that not one single neoclassical economist today acknowledges that TRP was an abortive or futile program. Even Amartya Sen, a most perceptive critic, still finds it profitable to conduct various TRP exercises. Further, as far as the present author can attest, a deafening silence greeted the appearance of Wong's book. A second clue (documented below) is the habit of Samuelson and his protégés to deprecate and abjure any affiliation with physics analogies when cornered by critics, but to freely traffic in them in internal discussions of neoclassical theory. The third clue is to take note of the way in which advanced neoclassical textbooks treat the issues of utility and the TRP.

Take Varian (1978) as an example. After the student is put through the thoroughly conventional paces, on page 101 there is a suggestion that the TRP is an "alternative approach [that can] take demand functions as a primitive concept and derive preferences that are consistent with such functions." The wording here is a bit tricky, but if this means to insinuate that the TRP renders preference maps⁻ recoverable from market observations, then, as we have observed, it is false. In contrast, Varian (pp. 80–2) introduces the theory of the consumer as if it were based on a set of axioms: completeness, reflexivity, continuity, strong monotonicity, local nonsatiation, and convexity. It is then admitted that these combined axioms are isomorphic to the postulation of the conventional utility function – i.e., the physics metaphor of potential energy, although, of course, this is nowhere mentioned. The student is then cautioned: "A utility function is often a very convenient way to describe preferences, but it should not be given any psychological interpretation. The only relevant feature of a utility function is its ordinal character." Again, these last two sentences are dubious interpretations, if not willfully misleading.

Bringing together all of these clues, I should like to argue that the reason that the physics metaphor of energy/utility was able to overcome the antipathy and powerful critique trained upon it in the first half of the twentieth century was that the TRP and the subsequent set-theoretic approach to preferences managed to disguise the physics metaphor beyond all recognition. The impression was thereby created that neoclassical preference structures were in principle (if not in fact) empirically recoverable. Hence, neoclassical theory succeeded in disarming many of its most strident critics. I do not mean to argue, however, that in most cases this was done with a conscious intent to deceive.

Explorations of the possible expendability of the assumptions of continuity and convexity, and the promulgation of important counterexamples such as lexicographic preference orderings (Green 1971, p. 81) demonstrate that most neoclassical economists had no idea where the original utility framework had come from and were genuinely curious as to the minimum assumptions needed to preserve their well-behaved results. But since the "nice" results had earlier been defined by the proto-energetics metaphor, is it any wonder that the neoclassicals eventually converged on just that right set of assumptions that – *mirabile dictu* – were necessary and sufficient to formalize the metaphor of a field of potential energy?

At this point in the proceedings, the reader might expect that such a strong claim should be backed up by a demonstration that the axioms of revealed preference are those sufficient to formalize the potential energy concept. Normally, the author would oblige, except for the fact that it would be superfluous, since *it has already been accomplished* by both economists and by physicists! First, let us examine the track record of the neoclassical economists. As a recent example, Hurwicz and Richter (1979) provide a formalization of neoclassical consumer theory employing the Ville axiom, which can be intuitively grasped as an assumption that there exists no sequence of revealed preference relations that could return to its starting point; in such a situation the axiom of transitivity would dictate that commodity bundle Z would end up being preferred to itself. Then, rather innocently, Hurwicz and Richter note that the very same theorem can equally well be used to describe a thermodynamic system, but a thermodynamic system of a very special kind (and this is crucial) – a system in which there is no entropy increase, and hence, one in which there are no irreversible paths. As any reader of Chapter 2 will realize, this is precisely the mid-nineteenth-century model of the field of potential energy prior to the rise of the second law of thermodynamics, or to be blunt about it, the original neoclassical physics metaphor. This fact should be compared with the coy and disingenuous statement that concludes this article, that "it is clear there are close formal similarities between thermodynamics and utility theory" (p. 13).

So some neoclassicals have already proven that the mathematical formalism of revealed preference is isomorphic to that of potential energy. A certain piquancy is added to this situation by the fact that similar demonstrations have also come from the other side of the fence, from the camp of the physicists. For example, Bordley (1983) makes use of the mathematical formalism of preferences appropriated from his reading of the works of Debreu and Marschak. It may be apposite to let him describe his conclusions in his own words:

> When I choose that function to be the potential energy minus the kinetic energy and add a single probabilistic constraint on the particle's motion, I can derive the Schrödinger equation. By neglecting this constraint (which corresponds to saying that Planck's constant is negligible), I can derive Hamilton's principle ... Economic theory is similarly based on the idea that an individual's behavior is rational and hence he acts as if he maximized the expected value of some function (called his utility function). Thus the results of this paper show that there is a common foundation underlying physics and economics. This is hardly surprising inasmuch as both are rational attempts to understand behavior – in the case of physics, the behavior of nature; in the case of economics, the behavior of individuals [pp. 803–4].

Perhaps one is forgiven if one wonders just how many times the wheel can be reinvented and the results attributed to rationality. Probably the answer is that it will continue on into the indefinite future, because neither the scientists nor the neoclassical economists will be willing to face up to the nature of their theoretical practices.

The ramifications of the idea, first broached in Chapter 3, that mathematical formalization in physics and economics has by and large consisted of the passing back and forth from the social to the physical world of a very few key metaphors, would probably shake the foundations of many cherished beliefs concerning the nature of science. It would also have major repercussions on the way societies generally constitute their legitimations of social order, but examination of these far-reaching issues must be postponed for a later volume.[2] The narrower question in the present context is how to understand the ascendancy of the neoclassical research program within economics.

Neoclassical economics kept itself aloof from the larger energetics movement in the late nineteenth century (as explained in Chapter 5), and that reserve stood it in good stead when the energetics movement fell into disrepute at the turn of the century. Likewise, neoclassical economics kept itself aloof from any complete identification with the energy metaphor whenever serious challenges arose in the twentieth century. In Chapter 6 we observed the outlines of that ambivalence in the specific instances of the problem of the incorporation of the production concept, and now, with the on-again off-again repudiation of any utilitarian psychology; this tergiversation has likewise stood the program in good stead. But in the final analysis, however coy and ambivalent neoclassicals may appear to be about their physics metaphor, it cannot seriously be repudiated or relinquished, because *there is nothing else that can hold the neoclassical research program together.* In the absence of the metaphor of utility as nineteenth-century potential energy, there is no alternative theory of value, no heuristic guide to research, no principle upon which to base mathematical formalism, no causal invariant in the Meyersonian sense, and most threatening, no basis for the claim that economics has finally become scientific. Ultimately there is no practical substitute for unabashed and shameless imitation, when it comes to neoclassical economic theory. The nature of science is far too elusive for any adherence to some rote method to be an effective or plausible substitute.

The only proof of this statement can be historical, irredeemably inductive. Whenever neoclassical theory has been perched upon the brink of breaking with the original physics metaphor in a fundamental or profound way – in the theory of production, or Keynesian macroeconomics, or the repudiation of a utility theory of value, or even in the innovation of game theory (Mirowski 1986) – there has *always* sprung up a powerful revanchist movement that succeeded in either coopting the rival metaphor or else amputating the new offending doctrines as unsound and unscientific. In this narrow sense the neoclassical research program has proved exceedingly flexible. Yet from the vantage point that comprehends the brute necessity of the nineteenth-century physics metaphor for the very identity of the neoclassical research program, it appears that economics has been the most rigidly doctrinaire of all the social sciences. It has ruthlessly barred any discussion of the legitimacy of a social physics, and yet paradoxically preserved itself from any contamination by subsequent intellectual developments in twentieth-century physics, all the while basking in the general impression that neoclassical economics was more scientific than sister disciplines such as sociology or anthropology. This precarious balancing act will be the subject of detailed examination shortly.

The integrability problem and the misunderstood conservation principles

One more revanchist tendency in neoclassical economic theory merits brief mention, the one that travels under the rubric of the integrability problem and the related confusion over the measurability of utility. Requiring the integrability of utility functions has been a nuisance for neoclassical theory since its very inception, as we saw in Chapter 5. The reason for this is quite simple: In classical physics, all the relevant properties of energy are captured by its representation as an integral; therefore, the first test of the intelligibility and coherence of the transfer of a metaphor of energy is to inquire whether utility should be expressed as an integral. From the point of view of physics this all seems straightforward, but because of the love-hate relationship of neoclassicism with its origins, this issue in economics has been permeated by a great fog of mystery.

In 1938, Samuelson wrote on the integrability problem: "I cannot see that it is a really important problem . . . I should strongly deny, however, that for a rational and consistent individual integrability is implied, except possibly as a matter of circular definition" (quoted in Wong 1978, p. 47). He was forced to change his mind in 1950, however, when it became apparent that his theory of revealed preference did not constitute an alternative to the conventional neoclassical theory of utility. Henceforth he admitted that integrability is an inescapable requirement of neoclassical theory, but he chose to portray it as some sort of exotic and abstruse technical condition, about which the average economist should not worry her head: "I do not think there is any single way of picturing integrability conditions so that we can easily grasp their meaning in common-sense intuitive terms . . . This involves the purely mathematical properties of partial differential equations" (Samuelson 1950, pp. 358, 365). In this particular article he asserted that the integrability conditions had nothing to do with the prohibition of hysteresis or with the path-independence of the order of consumption, both statements that are immediately revealed as false by comparison with the relevant energy metaphor.

The treatment of the neoclassical integrability problem has not improved in the interim. Textbooks regularly indicate to students that they can skip the section devoted to it (Green 1971, p. 127) or give it short shrift as if it were an artifact of the Slutsky restrictions (Varian 1978, pp. 100–1). More advanced treatments also approach the integrability conditions gingerly, referring to the "rather unmotivated requirement of symmetry of the Slutsky or Antonelli matrix" (Hurwicz and Richter 1979, p. 7) or, with somewhat more charming candour, stating that:

> [T]he integrability conditions are quite familiar. They are simply the symmetry and negative definiteness of the Slutsky matrix . . . The negative definiteness condition has a clear economic interpretation; it is simply the law of demand for a compensated demand function . . . Whether this should be looked at as a rationality or a stability condition is a question we shall not get into. The point is that it has an obvious economic meaning. The same cannot be said about the symmetry condition . . . to impose it as a primitive axiom of the theory is economically quite opaque. In fact, in the 1930s a number of researchers hesitated to do so and entertained a notion of nonintegrable preferences that, once all is said, led to a dead end [Mas-Collel, in Feiwel 1982, p. 79].

Now, what *is* the economic meaning of the obscure, abstruse, deep, complex, opaque principle of integrability? It is simply this: The utility gradient must be a conservative vector field if it is subject to deterministic constrained maximization. This in turn dictates that utility must be path-independent – that is, by whatever sequence of events one arrives at a particular commodity bundle, one must always experience the identical level of utility. Contrary to Varian (1978), this is the principle that guarantees that there is something more than a mere preference ordering being represented by a utility function. It is beyond the ken of most orthodox economists that this is the one principle that guarantees that, in principle, energy (and therefore utility) should be measurable. Why? Because conservation principles dictate that phenomenon W remains the "same" under transformations $A, B, \ldots, N$ and therefore will report the same measurement under repeated examination. Precisely because it is constant under specified controlled conditions, a scale may be constructed that numerically relates changes in phenomenon W to changes in external conditions X, Y, Z such that every alteration of $\{X, Y, Z\}$ will map into an alteration of W. In other words, it states that the conditions for an algebra are met by the phenomenon.

So, then, why are neoclassical economists so bashful about their integrability conditions, and so coy when it comes to their economic interpretations? There are at least two reasons. The first is that the conditions for such an algebra are not met in the empirical world of markets and psychology. A little bit of introspection should normally suffice to reveal the outlandish character of neoclassical preferences, but for the true believer there also exists a vast literature based on controlled experimentation that testifies to their spurious character (Shoemaker 1982; Tversky and Kahneman 1981). The integrability conditions insist that your preferences are not at all affected or influenced by what goes on around you, and especially not by the process by which you attain your commodities. It dictates that your preferences are purely time-symmetric. It demands that any change in your preferences inexorably alters your identity. Were neoclassical economists to openly admit the meaning of the indispensable integrability conditions, it would be tantamount to an admission that they refuse to entertain the overwhelming evidence that utility is not conserved in everyday experience.

There is a second reason why neoclassical economists are reticient when it comes to the integrability conditions. The integrability conditions are the core of the analogy that equates utility and energy; they are the very essence of neoclassical economics. If the integrability conditions were legitimate when transported into the sphere of economic life, then it was not unreasonable to hope that economics could develop in the same manner as physics. As Pasquale Boninsegni put it in a letter to Leon Walras early in the twentieth century:

> If a day comes when we can find an entity resembling acceleration in mechanics, the problem which occupies you [i.e., the measurement of utility] will be solved. You have found the fundamental equation of static equilibrium; we hope that one of your students will be able to find an equation similar to that of d'Alembert" [Boninsegni to Walras, letter 1708, in Walras 1965, III, p. 376; my translation].

But that longed-for day never arrived (English 1974, p. 282). Instead, Walras's progeny arbitrarily imposed an analogue of d'Alembert's equation under the rubric of the technical requirement of integrability. Without an acceleration constant, there could be no mechanical energy; without a value constant, there was no sense in pretending that there existed something called utility.

The befuddled treatment of the neoclassical integrability conditions should call into question the entire project of portraying utility as potential energy; in other words, they should undermine the entire neoclassical project of imitating physics. This, more than any other consideration, accounts for the bizarre claims that the integrability conditions are unintelligible, merely technical considerations. To discuss and evaluate economic integrability conditions is to discuss and evaluate the intellectual credibility of the neoclassical physics metaphor. If preferences do not approximate a field, then it is pointless for economists to pretend they can use the mathematical formalisms and conceptual frameworks of nineteenth-century physicists.

The age of technique

Something happened to neoclassical economics around 1930 or so. I am not referring to the Great Depression that spread to almost every Western industrial economy in the course of the decade, although it loomed menacingly in the background, a dark reproach to the purported expertise of every neoclassical economist. Instead, I should like to draw the reader's attention to a watershed in the style and substance of argumentation among neoclassical economists that is situated in this period.

Prior to this watershed, the explicit imitation of the mathematical practices of physicists was not exactly absent, but was regarded with a certain diffidence. In a paradigm that traced its genesis to the expropriation of a physics formalism, such reticence might seem strange, yet it may have been linked to certain cultural attitudes characteristic of scientists around the turn of the century, especially when it came to issues of imagery and metaphor in scientific reasoning. In France, Pierre Duhem was ridiculing various national styles of scientific exegesis, insisting that only the most literal of minds would need the crutch of a model from another discipline. In Britain at that time, most British scientists considered the lines of force in the field formalism to be chiefly useful for pedagogical purposes, rather than descriptive of some underlying reality. This attitude also was characteristic of the British orthodox economics profession, imitating Marshall's preference for geometrical exposition, as well as his disregard for mathematical consistency. In direct contrast, German scientists regarded lines of force as a fundamental *Anschauung*, an intuition held in the mind's eye derived from a previous visualization of physical processes (Miller 1984, p. 110). The poverty of intuitive visualizability of formal neoclassical models may have had some bearing on the repugnance for neoclassical theory expressed by most German academic economists.

In any event, all of this began to change around 1930. The previous philosophical attitude toward models and formalism started to break down, and a newer generation of economists appeared to warm to the task of more closely imitating the physicists. In 1912, Irving Fisher had tried to found a society dedicated to the promotion of research into quantitative and mathematical economics, and had found few takers. Yet by 1930 Fisher, Ragnar Frisch, and Charles Roos were able to convene the founders' meeting of the fledgling Econometrics Society (with Joseph Schumpeter elected the first chair). The Cowles Commission was founded in 1932, and promptly became the leading source of financial support for the new movement. The first issue of *Econometrica* appeared in January 1933, and it contained a manifesto written by Schumpeter claiming: "We do not impose any credo – scientific or otherwise – and we *have* no common credo beyond holding: first that economics is a science, and secondly, that this science has one very important quantitative aspect." Of course, scientific economics was promptly equated with neoclassical theory, but even so, the style of economic discussion underwent further transformation. The discursive and ruminative format of the book gave way to the terse journal article structured around a formal mathematical model, in clear mimesis of *Zeitschrift für Physik* or *Physical Reviews*. Interest was revived in the research program that later became known as general equilibrium analysis (Weintraub 1985, chap. 7).

This change in the tenor of economic discussion can be directly traced to an influx of engineers, physicists manqués, and mathematicians during the Great Depression and after (Harcourt 1984; Craver 1986; Craver and Leijonhufvud 1987). When money for any sort of research was tight, the powerful Rockefeller Foundation decided to redirect economics in a scientific direction (Craver 1986). American scientists and engineers with dim prospects in their original fields of endeavor were drawn toward these new opportunities, as were many Europeans fleeing the political disruption and persecution of that decade.

Given this infusion of fresh scientific talent, one might think that a third generation of neoclassical converts would have updated and revamped the original physics metaphor, perhaps incorporating the new insights of thermodynamics or the theory of relativity or quantum mechanics. That is not to say that any specific subset of the newer physics should have been appropriated by the third-generation neoclassicals: No subset of the new physics was naturally any more an "ideal" description of the economic sphere than was the original energetics metaphor. However, scientists will be scientists, and if the incipient allure of the original metaphor had derived from its similarity to the practices of contemporary physicists, then one might infer that the more modern physical models would have been no different in that respect.

Yet, curiously enough, the third and fourth generations of neoclassicals, spanning the period from roughly 1930 to 1980, did not really assimilate the pith and grit of twentieth-century physics and reprocess it into novel metaphorical descriptions of the economy. The tyro recruits did bring a new expertise to economics, but this expertise did not get parlayed into novel physical/economic metaphors. In lieu of that, what economics received from the new generation were new mathematical techniques and a patina of superficial references to the physics of the twentieth century. This is a subtle distinction, lost on those such as Hayek who pronounced a plague on all scientistic economics.

Thermodynamics, general relativity, quantum mechanics, chaos theory, and the grand theories of unified forces are all characteristically *modern* physics; they have fundamentally revised the very structure of explanation in physical theory. The survey of physical theory in Chapter 2 attempted to give a flavor of this novelty by tracing the concomitant transformation in the energy concept. Thermodynamics introduced irreversibility into Laplacian determinism; quantum mechanics extirpated continuity at the micro level; relativity and cosmology reconceptualized energy conservation merely as a mathematical symmetry, an expendable analytical convenience; chaos theory reconciled determinism and indeterminism by revealing the nightmare underneath the Laplacian Dream. Each innovation reinvented the boundaries of our experience. Nevertheless, the dowry that the displaced scientists brought with them to neoclassical economics did not include these fundamental reconceptualizations; at most, it consisted of some of the new mathematical formalisms that had been cultivated within the modern physics community.

Consequently, neoclassical economics has remained wedded to a straw man of a physical metaphor of vintage circa 1860, with some minor alterations. In a tale reminiscent of Dorian Gray, neoclassicals, by imbibing some mystical elixir of modern mathematical techniques, have maintained the figure of vibrant youth, while hidden away somewhere in the attic is the real portrait, the original metaphor of a conserved preference field in an independently constituted commodity space, growing progressively desiccated and decrepit. The irony of neoclassical economics in the twentieth century is that, just as it reached the pinnacle of self-confidence in its scientific status, spurred onward by such glittering prizes as its own Nobel and access to funding from scientific agencies, its own science was looking increasingly démodé.

The first perceptible consequence of the influx of physicists and engineers into economics during the 1930s was the concerted application of the vastly improved mathematics of the field formalism to problems of equilibrium within the utility field. Paul Samuelson was in the forefront of the application of variational principles to neoclassical questions in the 1930s, urging the position that the entire operational content of neoclassical economic theory could be expressed solely by the techniques of constrained optimization. Jan Tinbergen (1929) wrote his thesis under the physicist Paul Ehrenfest on the use of variational principles in physics and economics. Ragnar Frisch tutored the members of the Cowles Commission on the finer points of field theory (Frisch 1937). Tjalling Koopmans (1957, pp. 175–6) showed that field theory could even eschew calculus.

There were some problems, but they were rendered harmless by their consideration being restricted to a small coterie seemingly concerned with abstruse technical questions (the integrability problem discussed in the previous section provides a paradigm of the type of questions that occupied the new generation). Recognizing the obvious extensions of the physics of energy, some strove to incorporate Hamiltonian dynamics under the misleading rubric of optimal control theory (Burmeister and Dobell 1970, chap. 7; Burmeister 1980, chap. 6; Magill 1970; Cass and Shell 1976).

One can't help but notice the carnival atmosphere of these appropriations. How easy it was to be a neoclassical if you just had the mathematical physics background! There were all the standard techniques of the analysis of potential and kinetic energy, just waiting to be transported bodily into the economics context. The elaborations seemed obvious, but of course they were not effortless. As we have observed, certain specific concepts by their nature were not interchangeable between the two contexts. Frequently, there were mathematical puzzles to be solved, puzzles thrown up by the sheer inappropriateness of the energetics metaphor in the economic sphere: for instance, the pesky phenomenon of negative forces/ prices, or the mathematical fact that money was patently superfluous in the proto-energetics metaphor, and so on. Yet it was a joy to be young and mathematically gifted once it dawned on you that you had seen this stuff before, probably in Mechanical Engineering 14a, and it was just a matter of digging out those old notes. A veritable industry sprang up after 1930, giving the old physics metaphor a new shot of rigor, tinkering with it in a million ways to make it more respectable, more scientific.

Now, the question naturally arises whether all this effort could make neoclassicism better? One thing can be said about the period from 1930 to roughly 1980: Chapter 6 has documented that the neoclassical literature did not succeed in reconciling the original physics metaphor with one of its more egregious disanalogies in the economic sphere, nor did it succeed in expropriating a more contemporary metaphor of the physical world. If anything, the neoclassical research program became rudderless, held together by the implicit proto-energetics metaphor, but bereft of any conception of how to firmly transcend the notion of utility. Value theory essentially was stagnant, and the escalating importation of mathematical techniques from physics increasingly seemed devoid of consistency or rationale. Nowhere was this more apparent than in the rush to the mathematics of Hamiltonians after circa 1945.

The drive to incorporate the formalism of Hamiltonian dynamics is one pertinent example of the triumph of technique over theoretical insight. If the neoclassicals had consciously appropriated a legitimate Hamiltonian dynamics from the physicists, they would have had to take a tack similar to that sketched out in Chapter 5. They would have to express the amounts of the N commodities possessed by S individuals subject to k constraints in terms of $SN - k$ generalized commodity coordinates a_i, hence defining $SN - k$ generalized prices b_i. This would lead to the inscription of a Hamiltonian function such as:

$$H = E(b_1, b_2, \ldots, b_{N-k}) + V(a_1, a_2, \ldots, a_{N-k})$$

The function H would have to represent a conserved quantity if the function $V(\cdot)$ were to be integrable. In other words, the sum of utility and expenditure would have to be conserved if the Hamiltonian were to be used to describe the path of the system over time. There is no point developing the metaphor any further, because it is clear that these implications of Hamiltonian dynamics were anathema to neoclassicals for a myriad of reasons. Some may have scoffed at the idea of a conserved utility field over an infinite time horizon–something akin to an immortal entity who never experiences an alteration of tastes – others might balk at the explicit acknowledgement of the ontological identity of utility and money income; still others might look askance at a putatively dynamic system that abstracted away production. This cavalcade of incongruities might be interpreted as indicating that the entire metaphor was incoherent: After all, what is the sense of a super-optimization problem that could never be performed by any human being over a field most doubted the existence of, and that was in any event probably not a conservative field, bounded by constraints that no one seriously thought were strictly binding, evolving towards some terminal point no one ever thought to be a reasonable characterization of the future or of our beliefs about it?

So what did the neoclassicals fresh from their engineering classes do? Basically, they never ventured to evaluate the entire physical metaphor and its attendant formalism, but rather just began to write down any old Hamiltonian that attracted their passing fancy, motivating or justifying it (if at all) by claiming they were solving some isolated mathematical infelicity. After neoclassical θ had written one idiosyncratic Hamiltonian paper, then neoclassical Γ would publish another one, without making any effort to render the two compatible or consistent. The problem, as usual, revolved around neglect of the meaning and significance of conservation principles.

For example, some thought it would be nice if the utility function snatched out of the air would take account of the temporal location of commodities, so they wrote down a Hamiltonian like:

$$H = \int_{-\infty}^{0} U(c_t)e^{-gt}dt + E(b_1)$$

Far from being a deep theoretical innovation, all this accomplished was to render the math tractable at the expense of reducing utility to a homogeneous value substance that could be discounted back from the future to time t at rate g. The fact there was only one price b_1 should have been a dead giveaway that the problem was solved by neutralizing the question, collapsing a field theory to a value substance. Another unrelated attempt to appropriate Hamiltonians might superimpose a production function that translated endowments into a single consumption good, but this also would be a surreptitious reversion to an embodied-substance theory (Burmeister 1980, pp. 238–45). Still others totally inverted the meaning of the Hamiltonian by taking the initial coordinates as arbitrarily fixed and applying variational principles to undetermined "final" future coordinates (Magill 1970, p. 75). Finally, some went so far as to express prices in conserved utility units. The engineer economists were lost in the fun house, because there were no guiding principles to exert control over their research other than the single overriding mandate: Copy the physics. Hamiltonians were legitimate largely because they were copied from physics; otherwise, why imitate a field theory when you have effectively assumed away the structure of a field formalism?

The mathematics of Hamiltonians, Ville axioms, fixed-point theorems and all the rest might seem novel to economists, but at bottom it is still nineteenth-century physics. The shiny toys might distract attention, but the knowledgeable players understood that it all never ventured outside the world of the Laplacian Dream equations. The newer generation had some acquaintance with the profound upheavals in twentieth-century physics, and they felt some inclination to make reference to it: but how, given their allegiance to the neoclassical paradigm? This new generation of neoclassicals did make reference to the ferment in modern physics, but to a man, they stopped well short of ever actually appropriating any substantive twentieth-century physics metaphor. Let us consider a premier example.

Paul Samuelson, scientist

Paul Samuelson has already made numerous appearances in this narrative: the true believer in production functions and the immutability of the laws of thermodynamics; the failed synthesizer of the numerous versions of the neoclassical theories of production; the latter-day Slutsky; and an unwitting rediscoverer of energetics. It is a testimony to his verve, his breadth, and his lucid writing style that his opinions were to be found in nearly every corner of neoclassical analysis from roughly the 1930s to the 1980s. But there is another way in which Paul Samuelson was the very model of a man neoclassical in twentieth-century economics: He set the tone for the appropriate demeanor to be displayed before the altar of Science in the twentieth century, innovating an elaborate rapprochement with the developments in twentieth-century physics. However much hoi polloi paid obeisance to Milton Friedman's incoherent 1953 essay on method, it was Samuelson, and not Friedman, who by both word and deed was responsible for the twentieth-century self-image of the neoclassical economist as scientist.

This definition of neoclassical virtue happened on many levels, from a simple shift toward the style of the terse physics journal article and away from the discursive and self-reflexive book, to an insistence upon the absolutely inviolate character of the method of explanation premised upon variational principles. These attributes have been the subject of intermittent comment throughout this volume, and so require no further examination here. What does merit attention is a characteristic Samuelsonian quirk that has set the standard for the coexistence of the nineteenth-century neoclassical crypto-physics with twentieth-century physical theory, a practice that has not drawn any comment in the numerous *Festchriften* and evaluative volumes dealing with Samuelson's career (Brown and Solow 1983; Feiwel 1982). This curiosum is Samuelson's habit of making reference to modern physics in superficial and rhetorical ways while persistently misrepresenting both its content and its relationship to neoclassical theory.

Let us begin with a simple example. In the days of the "old" quantum mechanics, Niels Bohr proposed a heuristic guide for attempts at understanding the structure of the atom, which he called "the Correspondence Principle" (d'Abro 1951, pp. 499–509). Crudely stated, this principle suggests that the behavior of atomic systems should be approximated by the predictions of classical (i.e., nonquantum) physics in certain specific circumstances where quantum effects would be expected to be unimportant. In a broad interpretation, it was a directive not to abandon previously held mechanistic theories unnecessarily.

Paul Samuelson (1941; 1947) also proposed a "Correspondence Principle," with the transparent yet unstated intention of evoking resonances with Bohr's principle. Nevertheless, similarities in terminology did not extend to similarities in theoretical content. The stated purpose of the Samuelson correspondence principle was to suggest that dynamic stability analysis in a neoclassical context could lend some structure to the comparatively static results in neoclassical price theory (Samuelson 1947, p. 258). Of course, at that time there were no dynamic results in neoclassical theory, and so Samuelson proceeded to mix in some Marshallian themes by tying convergence to equilibrium to the distance between quantity demanded and quantity supplied. Now, given his actual results, why would Samuelson want to evoke the spirit of Bohr?

At the most prosaic level, Samuelson's mathematical model had no connection with those of Bohr, either in the old or the post-1925 quantum mechanics. Patently, Samuelson's mathematics were the same old proto-energetics minus the "correct" Hamiltonian and plus the Marshallian apparatus: nothing new there, and no further appropriation of a more up-to-date mathematical analogy, unlike, say, that in Arrow, Block, and Hurwicz (1959). On a more abstract plane, the Samuelson principle was not so much a research heuristic as a device to evade the unsavory implications of the original static proto-energetics metaphor. It is now widely acknowledged that the Samuelsonian version of dynamics violates the integrity of the Walrasian model of general equilibrium (Hahn, in Brown and Solow 1983, p. 35). Even from the most Olympian heights there are no plausible analogies between Bohr's and Samuelson's Correspondence Principles. In the case of Samuelson, there existed no predictions of any classical theory that economists were exhorted to retain while exploring a different scale of research. What, then, are we to learn from Samuelson's rhetoric, his recourse to innuendo?

One way to understand this reference is to see Paul Samuelson as straining to evoke parallels between neoclassical theory and *twentieth-century* physics, while simultaneously maintaining an assured cleared distance from the substantive content of modern physics, and avoiding any direct acknowledgement of the fact that utility is functionally identical to potential energy. This is a precarious posture, as readers of this volume should now understand. It combines intrinsically incompatible objectives: the disguise of the nineteenth-century-physics origins of neoclassicism, the maintenance of the appearances of a science, and a suppression of the dissolution of the utility concept (similar to the dissolution of the energy concept in modern physics), all the while emulating the outward behavior of the physicists. It was a tough act to get past the critics, but Samuelson pulled it off time after time.

Let us examine another example in Samuelson (1972b). In the thermodynamics of the turn of the century, there existed a qualitative guide to understanding the direction in which an equilibrium would be shifted when a parameter of the system had changed, which was known as the Le Châtelier Braun principle.[3] The principle, which had only the loosest of formulations prior to Paul Ehrenfest's landmark paper of 1911 (Klein 1970, pp. 156–61), went roughly as follows: If a system in thermodynamic equilibrium is constrained so that only two parameters, r and s, can vary, let r be acted upon by an external influence, first holding s constant and then allowing it to vary. The Le Châtelier Braun principle asserts that, if δ_I is a variation holding s constant, while δ_{II} is a variation with s free to adjust, then

$$| \delta_{II} r | < | \delta_I r |$$

In a loose interpretation, letting parameter s float free increases the ability of r to resist the change exerted by the external influence. In 1911, Ehrenfest demonstrated the weakness of the principle by coming up with counterexamples that reversed the inequality sign. He speculated that the principle could only be saved by reformulating it in terms used by the energeticists – namely, the inequality would only hold when the two parameters s and r were both intensive or both extensive quantities, but not when they were mixed.

Although it was never mentioned by Samuelson, the Le Châtelier principle was picked up rather early as a metaphor for the reactions of a social system to outside stresses (Lindsay 1927), and imported into economics as a metaphor for monetary stability by Divisia (1925;

see also Pikler 1951a, p. 94). Samuelson appropriated it in 1941 and applied it to the slopes of Marshallian demand curves in the relative instances when other prices were fixed, and then are allowed to vary. As in the previous bit of physics mongering, the actual mathematical model in the thermodynamics had little relationship to Samuelson's mathematics, and therefore Samuelson was not evoking an exact metaphor. Both the central issues of the relevant conservation principles and the irreversability of phenomena dictated by the second law of thermodynamics were ignored, and therefore the Samuelson/Le Châtelier principle had little connection to the content of the thermodynamics (Mirowski 1984b). As one physicist has commented, Samuelson's discussion "is entirely devoid of dynamical considerations" (Gilmore 1983, p. 742).

Most careful expositions of the Le Châtelier principle made it clear that the principle's usefulness hinges upon the direct and explicit postulation of the relevant potentials, as well as careful separation of extensive from intensive variables. Given these preliminaries, the precise statement of the principle would be:

1. When a small external force is applied to a system in locally stable equilibrium, the system is initially displaced in the direction of the applied force.
2. After the secondary forces generated by the perturbation have established a new equilibrium, (a) the external force is reduced if the displacement is held constant, or (b) the displacement is increased if the external force is held constant.

The striking aspect of Samuelson's restatement is how much it equivocates when it comes to stating these principles directly. Instead of specifying the Le Châtelier principle in terms of the utility functions, Samuelson instead has recourse to the Marshallian framework of demand and supply functions, which, as we have argued in Chapter 6, are fundamentally incompatible with the proto-energetics metaphor, and in any event are certainly inappropriate in any context of the discussion of *stability*. Indeed, the correct specification of a neoclassical Le Châtelier principle should read:

$$\Delta P_b(\text{initial})\Delta Q_b(\text{final}) = \mathbf{L}_{ab}\, \Delta P_a(\text{final})\Delta Q_a(\text{initial})$$

where a and b are commodity indicies, P represents price, Q quantity, and $\mathbf{L}_{ab}$ is a matrix of terms derived from the utility function and defined in Gilmore (1983, p. 740).

More relevant to the question of metaphor, Samuelson also ignored Ehrenfest's clarification of the principle, which stated that mixed extensive and intensive terms would undermine the inequality. Recall from Chapter 5 that in neoclassical proto-energetics the price/force variable is an intensive magnitude and the commodity/space variable is an extensive or capacity magnitude. Samuelson wanted the r and s variables to be price and quantity respectively, but that would mean mixing types of parameters, and therefore in a fully specified Walrasian model there would be no guarantee that the slopes of the demand curves will always stand in the same relationship. In other words, if Samuelson really had done his physics homework, he would have noted just how tenuous his own metaphor of the Le Châtelier principle was.

Again, the reference to a physical principle was *not* being seriously used as a heuristic research device. In noticing this, some have attempted to preserve Samuelson's example by turning the vice of the misrepresentation of the physics into a virtue, averring that "the only merit in Samuelson's use of Le Châtelier's Principle as against Winiarski's wild statistical speculation is that Samuelson was not consciously seeking isomorphisms, while Winiarski was" (Proops, in van Gool and Bruggink 1985, p. 158). So what was Samuelson seeking to achieve?

Throughout his career, Samuelson has been the master of scientific rhetoric, continuously and consciously hinting at parallels between neoclassical theory and twentieth-century physics, and just as consciously denying them, usually in the very same article. A striking instance of this balancing act can be found in his Nobel Prize lecture, just before his discussion of the Le Châtelier principle:

> There really is nothing more pathetic than to have an economist or a retired engineer try to force analogies between the concepts of physics and the concepts of economics. How many dreary papers have I had to referee in which the author is looking for something that corresponds to entropy or to one or another form of energy" [Samuelson 1972b, p. 8].

Nevertheless, Samuelson's *Collected Scientific Papers* are chock-full of titles such as "A Quantum Theory Model of Economics," "The Law of the Conservation of the Capital-Output Ratio," "Two Conservation Laws in Theoretical Economics," and "A Biological Least-Action Principle." Papers with less misleading titles such as "Causality and Teleology in Economics" and "Maximum Principles in Analytical Economics" contain at least as many explicit references to physics as they do to economics. Nevertheless, the single most salient aspect of all of these papers is that their scientific rhetoric is entirely decoupled from their paltry substantive physics content. The "Quantum Theory" paper (Samuelson 1977, pp. 104–10) has nothing whatsoever to do with quantum mechanics; the "Conservation Law" papers never actually come to grips with the problem of what neoclassical theory actually assumes to be conserved in its proto-energetics model. The "Causality" paper (Samuelson 1972a, pp. 428–72) never confronts the various conceptions of cause that have been argued out by physicists and philosophers, and never explains why he is so very unwilling even to entertain hysteresis phenomena. Wandering through this thicket of jumbled physics references, we are then brought up short:

> Why should a person interested in economics . . . spend time considering conservative oscillations of mechanics? Experience suggests that our [N.B.] dynamic problems in economics have something in common with those of the physical and biological sciences. But, as I long ago indicated, it is not useful to get "bogged down in the research for economic concepts corresponding to mass, energy, momentum force and space." And I may add that the sign of a crank or half-baked speculator in the social sciences is his search for something in the social system that corresponds to the physicist's notion of "entropy" [p. 450].

There can be no doubt that we are being warned away from something that is pregnant with significance. The key to the comprehension of Samuelson's meteoric rise in the economics profession was his knack for evoking all the outward trappings and ornament of science without ever once coming to grips with the actual content or implications of physical theory for his neoclassical economics. One might dub it the "having one's cake and eating it, too" gambit – enjoying all the benefits that accrue to science in our culture without actually being vulnerable to a Hayekian charge of scientism. The net result, rapidly appreciated by neoclassicals in general, was a nearly impervious defense of the legitimacy of the neoclassical research program, one that managed to dodge all the substantive issues, such as the wisdom of the appropriation of the original proto-energetics metaphor, the uneasy coexistence of such a nineteenth-century social physics with twentieth-century physical theory, and the impact of mathematical formalism upon the substance of twentieth-century economic thought. Samuelson became the standard-bearer, the first to counterattack when neoclassicism was intellectually threatened.

There is a relatively obscure and overlooked early paper of Samuelson that neatly displays these idiosyncratic uses of physics in the defense of neoclassicism. In "A Negative Report on Hertz's Program for Reformulating Mechanics" (Samuelson 1972a, pp. 316–23), we are confronted with a respected economist dabbling in the history of science, and more unusual, in an area most historians would consider an obscure cul-de-sac in the history of physics. The background to this paper is roughly: The physicist Heinrich Hertz, Helmholtz's favorite pupil, late in life conceived of an aversion to the very notion of potential energy. He claimed that potential energy was not observable and in a sense violated the overall concept of mechanical explanation. Using some results of Helmholtz, in 1893 Hertz actually went to the extraordinary length of constructing an axiomatic alternative to the energetics formalism of mechanics replacing the potential energy function with a function interpreted as representing the kinetic energies of "hidden masses." The full elaboration of Hertz's model is not important here; we are only concerned to divine what it was about Hertz's project that attracted the attention of Samuelson.

Samuelson (p. 319) claimed that his paper demonstrates that "Hertzian methods are incompatible with classical mechanics," but in fact, his paper does no such thing. All Samuelson's little calculation actually shows is that restricting oneself to Hertz's formalism involves some minor inconveniences, mainly having to do with the postulation of a scale factor for kinetic energy, but they are commensurate with the inconveniences which accompany the more conventional proto-energetics formalism. So what was this relatively insubstantial exercise really about? Samuelson was motivated to defend the conventional analytical artifice of the potential-energy function from the scorn of a brilliant and imaginative (but dead) physicist. Who cares? In effect, Samuelson has embarked upon a defense of nineteenth-century energetics from the depredations of a critic of the mechanistic school – and then, all of a sudden, it all falls into place. Since utility really is potential energy, and neoclassicism really is a species of proto-energetics, then Samuelson is really defending the intellectual legitimacy of utility theory without once letting on that is his motivation!

The conjuration of scientific legitimacy by means of vague innuendo abounds in Samuelson's oeuvre (e.g., Samuelson 1983b); we shall leave it to the interested reader to engage in the further sport of the deconstruction of Samuelson's rhetoric. It only remains to inquire whether and to what extent Samuelson is consciously using physics to obscure the very meaning of the neoclassical research program. I have only been able to find *one* very brief passage that that confronts this issue, and I quote it in its entirety:

> There have been those who thought that my fooling around with thermodynamics was an attempt to inflate the scientific validity of economics; even perhaps to snow the hoi polloi of economists who naturally can't judge the intricacies of physics. Actually, such mathematical excursions, if anything, put a tax on reputation rather than

enhancing it. So what? Taxes are the price we pay for civilization. Such work is fun. And I perceive it adds to the depth and breadth of human knowledge [Samuelson 1986a, p. 74].

I think almost everyone would agree this is ingenuous in the extreme: People generally are not given Nobel Prizes for "fun." Instead, Samuelson's role in twentieth-century economics has been to effect the *appearance* of a reconciliation between the nineteenth-century proto-physics neoclassical tradition and twentieth-century science, which means twentieth-century physics. In order to foster this impression, it has been necessary to bolster the dependence upon mathematical technique to the relative exclusion of philosophical and other evaluative discussions – or, as he put it, "philosophers are rarely physicists and physicists rarely philosophers" – and to persistently misrepresent the fact that such twentieth-century innovations as thermodynamics and quantum mechanics are fundamentally incompatible with the nineteenth-century energetics that spawned neoclassical theory. This difficult task has been rendered manageable essentially by making superficial references to twentieth-century physics while simultaneously avoiding their characteristic formalisms and content. Of course, anyone au fait with the physics would notice what was going on, so that dictated that Samuelson must simultaneously ridicule anyone else who might encroach upon his turf (that is, others who might purvey "spurious imitations of natural science concepts"). There is the further fringe benefit that Samuelson is then able to deride scientism while being its most vigorous proponent.

Hence, far from exacting a tax upon his reputation, Samuelson's repeated forays into spurious metaphors with modern physical theory have cemented his renown, not to mention the neoclassical research program, always in danger of splintering due to its own inertial and centrifugal motions. Once Samuelson had set the tone, the floodgates were opened to a multitude of misleading references to Lyapounov methods (Bausor 1987), the Noether theorem (Sato 1981; 1985), chaos theory (Day 1983), catastrophe theory (Varian 1979), and so on. This wretched excess of emulation of technique essentially served to hide the fact that neoclassical economists were maintaining a cool distance from the profound innovations of twentieth-century physics, and that each apparent new wrinkle made absolutely no difference to the basic neoclassical metaphor of utility as a conservative potential field. Nineteenth-century energetics was being reheated, reprocessed, and served up time and again with a little metaphoric twentieth-century white sauce.

In the technical literature, Samuelson's non sequiturs have become a way of life. High mathematical rigor is regularly forced to cohabit with low semantic comedy:

> Early attempts to quantify economic phenomena and to propose suitable mathematical models were based on analytical and quantitative techniques used in the investigation of mechanics. These techniques, which had proved successful in the description and study of the properties of the physical world, were then critically adapted to the study of economic phenomena. Clearly no claim was ever made about an identity of economics with mechanics. Indeed, no basic principle of mechanics, and in particular of dynamics, was ever shown to hold for economic phenomena involving one or more decision makers. Contrary to the situation in mechanics, no invariant law of conservation or variational principle seems to hold for economic systems. On the other hand, disregarding the doctrinal aspects, the mechanics approach seemed to produce very satisfactory, promising results in a variety of special cases. Furthermore, in spite of the lack of a general theory, these early scattered results had the positive effect of inducing a certain quantification in economic thought and allowing the emergence of more generally valid theories, the derivation of more realistic models, and most importantly, the formulation of more relevant, correct, and precise questions [Szegö 1982, p. 3. Copyright © 1982 by Academic Press. Reprinted by permission of the publisher.].

It must be admitted that the imitation of the letter but not the spirit of modern physical theory did manage to provide employment for many displaced engineers and previously unemployed mathematicians within the expanding purview of economics departments, and, Veblen's conspicuous consumption playing an overriding role in a profession with money to burn and ideas at a premium, even provincial universities felt impelled to hire at least one. However much certain respected neoclassicals might complain that this research program was verging upon sterility (Morishima 1984; Leontief 1982), their complaints were written off as the sour grapes of over-the-hill theorists.

Why did neoclassical economics cease to seriously emulate modern physical theory?

On March 19, 1986, the polymath Benoit Mandelbrot delivered a lecture in the political economy series at Harvard University. At that time, Mandelbrot had recently been the focus of much publicity concerning his mathematical innovation of fractals (Mandelbrot 1977); for instance, he had just appeared on the cover of the *New York Times* Sunday magazine, the very acme of American intellectual notoriety. The structure of fractals is not relevant to this anecdote, although it is relevant to note that they grew out of Mandelbrot's original work in economics, where he was concerned to produce phenomenological non-Gaussian models of the distribution of price movements (Albers and Alexanderson 1986, pp. 213–15; Mirowski 1989a). It appeared from the lecture that Mandelbrot was fretful and galled by years of being treated as an eccentric by other economists, which had consequently only served to harden him in his convictions. The lecture was noticeably ill-attended, and his talk rambled, consisting of equal parts explication and self-justification. He did, nonetheless, make one very telling point: In the history of economics there have existed a small but significant band of innovators of mathematical techniques and theories who drew their inspiration directly from social and economic phenomena, and whose mathematical techniques and models subsequently turned out to be useful in a physics context. He cited the work of Bachelier (1900) on stock prices as random walks, which anticipated Einstein's 1905 model of Brownian motion, and R. A. Fisher's 1922 invention of probability amplitudes, which later became central to quantum mechanics, in the context of his work on eugenics and crop variations. Mandelbrot suggested that his own work was another example of that tradition, claiming that fractals had found applications in physics only some years after he had generated them to deal with descriptions of economic phenomena. In a querulous aside, Mandelbrot then said: Wouldn't you expect that economists would find it a source of pride that techniques tailored to economic concepts were generated by economists for the express purpose of economic analysis? But no, he said with some bitterness, that had not ever been the case in this particular tradition. His predicament had been explained to him by an eminent orthodox economist as follows: *No* mathematical technique ever becomes prominent in orthodox (read, neoclassical) economic theory without having first proved itself in physics.

This anecdote reveals the predicament of neoclassical theory in the twentieth century. The imperatives of the orthodox research program leave little room for maneuver and less room for originality; the individual elements of the mandate do not add up to a coherent research program. These mandates are:

1. Appropriate as many mathematical techniques and metaphorical expressions from contemporary respectable science, primarily physics, as possible.
2. Maintain the explanatory structure of the nineteenth-century metaphor of utility as potential energy intact and unaltered, because it is thought to represent scientific explanation.

3. Preserve to the maximum extent possible the attendant nineteenth-century overtones of "natural order." This is generally deemed to include the defense of a Laplacian determinist and atomist world view, even though the original energetics movement that spawned neoclassical theory was hostile to atomism and was later premised upon a phenomenological macroscopic version of thermodynamics.

4. Deny strenuously that neoclassical theory slavishly imitates physics. Barring that option (when confronted with evidence to the contrary), insist that neoclassical theory may once have imitated physics, but that has all been left behind, and neoclassicism now prosecutes an idependent research program with its own integrity and indigenous standards of explanation.

5. Above all, prevent all rival research programs from encroaching upon neoclassical preeminence through imitation of the pattern of behavior of a Walras, Jevons, Edgeworth, Pareto, et al. – that is, any rival attempt to coopt contemporary physical models. Do this by ridiculing all external attempts to appropriate twentieth-century physics metaphors.

Any research program adhering to these mandates will find itself in trouble. Taken as a whole, these heuristics are self-contradictory. It is effectively impossible to have recourse to twentieth-century physics as a reservoir of novel and fruitful theoretical metaphors if all theorizing is held hostage to nineteenth-century concepts of energy. On the other hand, if most of a program's integrity, credibility, and self-image depend upon comparisons with physics, there is effectively only one place to look for cues as to evolving standards of legitimacy in explanation. All that is left is to mimic the superficial appearances of modern physics, as suggested above.

It might seem that there exists a relatively easy way out of this impasse: Drop mandate 2 and freely assimilate the substantive explanatory metaphors of twentieth-century physics along with their attendant mathematical formalisms. At this point, the thesis of the last sections of Chapter 2 (finally!) comes into play. The possibility of dropping mandate 2 is *not* a viable option from the vantage point of the internal logic of the neoclassical research program, but one can only understand this upon contemplating the history of the energy concept in twentieth-century physics. In brief, the practical dissolution of the energy concept in advanced twentieth-century physics has painted neoclassical economics into a corner. Arrogation of the status of a twentieth-century science through appropriation of twentieth-century physical metaphors would necessarily involve the repudiation of the utility or field theory of value, the only persistent common denominator of the neoclassical paradigm. Either neoclassicism must relinquish its only vinculum, and subsequently fragment due to its inherent centrifugal forces, or else it must remain solidly mired in an unalterably anachronistic structure of explanation. Neoclassical economics is metaphorically boxed in, and cannot extricate itself.

For neoclassical economics, mandates 1 through 5 have many layers, rather like an English trifle. The frothy coverings are the ingenuous repudiations of scientism with which we began this chapter. The next layer, of crumbled spongecake, is the problem that the concept of energy has fragmented and dissolved in the overall scheme of the evolution of twentieth-century physics, and therefore any attempt to update the utility/energy metaphor would dictate a rather distasteful parallel disintegration of the utility concept. As if the confection were not already repulsive enough, further down in the dish one discovers an odd assortment of hard and sickly sweet fruits of the fragmentation of twentieth-century physics, each in its own inimitable manner calculated to ruin the appetite of any neoclassical economist. Thermodynamics, general relativity, quantum mechanics, subatomic theory, chaos theory – wherever one turns, one is confronted with an unsavory and repugnant sludge. Swallowing our bile, let us quickly tour the contents of the bottom of the bowl.

Going roughly chronologically, let us begin with thermodynamics. The real impediments to the neoclassical embrace of thermodynamics are the concept of entropy and the implications of the second law. First, most superficially, there are the older cultural connotations of the entropy concept.[4] At the end of the nineteenth century the popular image of the entropy law was of a universe that was running down, growing more diffuse with less useful energy, ever more inhospitable to human life and endeavor, heading for an inevitable "heat death" at an indeterminate rate (Brush 1978). That sort of thing might be serviceable in Spenglerian jeremiads, but would never do for neoclassical theory, committed as it was to a conception of natural order as intrinsically hospitable to human endeavor and conducive to human progress. As Bausor (1987, p. 9) put it, whereas classical thermodynamics "approaches entropic disintegration, [neoclassical theory] assembles an efficient socially coherent organization. Whereas one articulates decay the other finds constructive advance." Recalling from Chapter 6 that existing neoclassical doctrine had its hands full trying to coherently coopt the concept of economic growth, we see that the superimposition of entropy would make that project nearly impossible. As observed in Chapter 6, the entropy concept already plays havoc with the various neoclassical theories of production.

Second, there would potentially be the loss of the atomist perspective. Classical thermodynamics adopts a phenomenological stance in explaining the macroscopic behavior of systems without appeal to supposed underlying causes at the micro level.[5] It doesn't take much to see that this would clash with the cherished neoclassical tenet of methodological individualism. Third, there is the disturbing technical consideration that the entropy law induces a distinct orientation for time's arrow, formalizing the irreversability of experience. The metaphor of a system fundamentally dependent upon its temporal location does not harmonize well with the concept of natural law and natural order favored by neoclassical theory. Indeed, neoclassical economics has always championed the existence of an economic rationality independent of historical situation. Paul Samuelson, as usual, gave the clearest statement of this fundamental research heuristic:

> [A]s an equilibrium theorist he [the economic scientist] naturally tended to think of models in which things settled down to a unique position independently of initial conditions. Technically speaking, we theorists hoped not to introduce hysteresis phenomena into our model, as the Bible does when it says "We pass this way only once" and, in so saying, takes the subject out of the realm of science into the realm of genuine history [Samuelson 1972a, p. 540].

Incidentally, one anticipates that, once neoclassicals truly come to understand it, the same objection will block the wholesale embrace of chaos theory.

Moreover, serious consideration of the notion of irreversibility would clash with the dictum that the market can effectively undo whatever man has wrought. Finally, and most pertinently from the vantage point of a discipline seeking to emulate physics, the concept of energy in thermodynamics is thoroughly unpalatable when cooked down into the parallel concept of utility in neoclassical economic theory. For example, the parallel would dictate that utility/value should grow more diffuse or inaccessible over time, a figure of speech possessing no plausible allure for the neoclassical research program.

However indigestible the thermodynamic metaphor, the metaphor of relativity theory would seem to send neoclassicals running for their Alka-Selzer. Again, begin with the superficial cultural connotations of relativity theory. At first, these might seem to resonate with the neoclassical Weltanschauung: Irrespective of the error involved, the man in the street understands relativity as the proposition that one's position or reference frame determines how one sees the world, and on a superficial level, neoclassical theory places its emphasis on individual tastes, if not exactly individual perceptions. Nevertheless, neither of these impressions corresponds to the true state of affairs. In physics, the theory of relativity is a far cry from the doctrine of relativism; in neoclassical economics, the economic activities of a trader are prohibited from influencing their preference set, this being one of the relevant conservation principles. Instead, the general theory of relativity extends the field formalism to encompass all possible phenomena, banishing all residual substance concepts from physical theory. From a practical point of view this would not be palatable for neoclassical economists – it would exacerbate the tendency to solipsism already present in the metaphor, and it would forestall the numerous instances of the surreptitious reinstatement of substance concepts in production theory described in Chapter 6. It would be as if there were nothing in the world but preference functions.

Both special relativity and general relativity depend crucially upon the existence of a global invariant (namely, the speed of light in a vacuum) so that the specification of energy may be permitted to vary. There exists no plausible parallel analogue of a global invariant in neoclassical economic theory that would permit utility specifications to vary. Were neoclassicals to appropriate the metaphor of general relativity, time itself would be dependent upon the reference frame, a requirement that would certainly clash with the modern Arrow–Debreu practice of predicating commodity identity upon temporal location. Finally, in general relativity, fields frequently exhibit a non-zero divergence. Roughly translated, this means that a field is considered to be self-generating, resulting in "something for nothing." This consideration accounts for the compromised status of the principle of the conservation of energy in relativity physics. Insofar as neoclassical economics is committed to the doctrine of scarcity and the denial of a free lunch, then it is bound to renounce the mathematical metaphor of a relativistic field.

Given that even physicists themselves find the ramifications of quantum mechanics profoundly unsettling, perhaps we need argue less strenuously that neoclassical economists might find the quantum metaphor repugnant. Quantum mechanics drags in a train of cultural images that an orthodox economist would shudder to entertain. It preaches fundamental and irreducible indeterminism at the micro level, wreaking havoc with the neoclassical penchant for Laplacian determinism and methodological individualism. Were the quantum metaphor to be imported into economics, it would precipitate mistrust and perhaps full dissolution of the vaunted neutrality of the economic scientist with respect to the social object of his research, and hence force consideration of the interaction of the economist with the pecuniary phenomenon (at least under the Copenhagen interpretation).

On a more technical plane, importing the mathematics of the quantum metaphor would actually impair neoclassical analysis. At the most basic level would be the obvious objection that there is no plausible reason to posit the existence of a discrete irreducible quantum of value, or to posit that utility is necessarily discrete rather than continuous. (Early flirtations with the Weber–Fechner "just-noticeable difference" were never followed up by neoclassicals, and have also been consigned to oblivion in psychology.) Further, the abjuration of continuity in physics was directly responsible for the recourse to an irreducibly stochastic conception of nature where causality itself had to be redefined, an ensemble of concepts blithely ignored by neoclassicals enamored of introducing stochastic theory into neoclassical formalisms. Other, more superficial analogies also appear equally unpalatable. Wave functions in commodity space have no profound metaphorical attractions. Attempts at invoking the Heisenberg indeterminacy principle would seem to fall through as soon as one acknowleged that random fluctuations in utility through time would hold no promise to illuminate any particular economic phenomenon. Finally, the quantum analogy must ultimately stand an anathema to the entire thrust of the neoclassical research program because it also premises the existence of "something for nothing" in the most explicit sense possible. Here we need only recall the statement of Guth (1983, p. 215): "I have often heard it said that there is no such thing as a free lunch. It now appears possible that the universe is a free lunch." The neoclassical Weltanschauung of a materially dictated world of fixed scarcity and determinate allocations could not easily be reconciled with such a radical shift of metaphor.[6]

Thus, the overarching theme of Chapter 2 is the key to understanding the predicament of orthodox neoclassical economics in its eleven decades of existence. In physics, the energy concept embodied the golden promise of the unification of all science under the banner of variational principles and the conservation of energy. Yet, try as they might, the physicists could not render the Laplacian dream a reality; mostly, this was due to the fact that such a rigidly deterministic world could not encompass the experience of change. Consequently, physics after 1860 or thereabouts underwent meiosis into partially overlapping and yet partially irreconcilable subfields – thermodynamics, general relativity, quantum mechanics, and so forth.

As part of this process, the symbol and currency of the perfect unity of the sciences − namely, the conservation of energy − had to be debased, as explained in Chapter 2. However, according to the argument in Chapter 3, value in economics has always held an intimate relation to the energy concept and its precursors, and thus this bifurcation of the energy concept placed economics in a quandary. Twentieth-century physics should have deeply disappointed the faithful devotees of economics as social physics: Upon tendering their promissory notes for the unification of all science, they were offered not one, but many different energies; not one, but many different sciences; not a single nature law, but a disquieting motley of natural laws. The neoclassicals had placed all of their bets on the energy metaphor, and just at that point the energy metaphor began to unravel.

Nevertheless, the chosen strategy of slavish imitation of physics certainly was not a total failure. It is a matter of historical record that neoclassical economic theory has indeed managed to displace all rival schools of economic thought, with the single exception of Marxism. Furthermore, neoclassical economics has successfully arrogated the aura and trappings of science, if only because a greater part of the populace excluded by the rigors of mathematics in science are convinced by superficial resemblances, whereas many others of modest technical skills are convinced because they recognize the physics of Engineering 101 as of the same character as that found in economics. Be that as it may, the influx of mathematicians and engineers into economics departments after 1930 created a problem.

The comparative advantage of the sophisticated new recruits lay obviously in the further elaboration and appropriation of physics metaphors. However, for the reasons outlined above, the appropriation of new metaphors from physics was not a viable or practical option, essentially because it would entail the relinquishment of the original metaphor of utility as the unique protean energy that would serve to unify and rationalize all social theory. On the other hand, further elaboration of the original metaphor was a possibility, but one severe impediment was the awkward metaphorical implications of Hamiltonian dynamics, and another was the dissolution of the energy concept in physics. The new recruits, the self-conscious scientists of social life, had no choice but to prosecute the neoclassical research program. The rapprochement that was finally worked out (consciously or unconsciously) was the curious combination of repression and denial embodied in he five research heuristics listed earlier in this chapter.

However incongruous it may seem, the neoclassical research program was *forced* to regulate and prohibit the further substantive importation of novel physics metaphors, just as it had to discourage any other conception of value. Consequently, by the 1960s the neoclassical research program became helplessly locked into the physics of circa 1860, and persists in this predicament to the very present.

Reprise: The underworld of social physics

Just because the neoclassical research program prohibited the further appropriation of metaphors from twentieth-century physics, it did not follow that this ukase extended to other economic research programs. Indeed, the second irony of economics in the twentieth century was that people from Nobel Prize winners to two-bit streetcorner dictators were advocates of new economic theories that appealed to physics for legitimation. As if this rush to physics were not sufficiently incongruous, the irony was rendered more pointed by a subset of these anti-neoclassicals specifically rallying around an energy theory of value, all the while oblivious to the fact that the energy metaphor was already the core proposition of neoclassical economics. Admittedly, an energy metaphor is not identical to energy, and many of these challengers to the neoclassical program were eccentrics and cranks, and their systems were mostly Rube Goldberg contraptions – and yet, that is not reason enough to ignore this pervasive phenomenon, nor is it enough to explain the shrill response of the neoclassical orthodoxy to this seditious (and sedulous) underworld of economic theory. In this instance, the amalgam of disgust, fascination, disdain, and compulsive denunciation reminds one of the behavior of zealots opposed to pornography who fixate upon the sordid details of the material. Did the neoclassicals sense that it was their opponents who held some unspoken advantage, because they were free to coopt some modern physics metaphor and parlay it into a scientific research program? Were they uncomfortable with the fact that it was their rivals who were free to choose?

One of the most striking and least noticed aspects of the history of anti-neoclassical thought in the twentieth century is the sheer volume of scientists – that is, research workers trained in physics, chemistry, and biology – who have been under the impression that they were the first to believe that the only true economic value is energy. In fact, the variants on this theme are more luxuriant that the biological metaphors with which they are sometimes entwined.

The history of non- or anti-neoclassical programs of the appropriation of physics metaphors itself remains to be written; we shall decline that task here.[7] However, for the edification of the curious reader, we have included in our bibliography all examples of such activity as we have stumbled across in our researches: from neo-energeticists such as Podolinsky (Alier and Naredo 1982) and Frederick Soddy (1961) to Costanza (1980) and Cleveland et al. (1984); as well as the further out neosimulators such as Lisman (1949a; 1949b), Lichnerowicz (1971), Pikler (1951a, 1954b, 1971), Bryant (1982), Jaynes (1983), and Palomba (1968).

Although we shall not grapple with these texts in this volume, it is imperative that the reader not write them off as irrelevant or simply quirky. In order to truly understand the impasse of neoclassical economic theory, we must appreciate that the importation of physical metaphors into the economic sphere has been relentless, remorseless, and unremitting in the history of economic thought. Simple extrapolation of this trend suggests that it will continue with or without the blessing or imprimatur of orthodox neoclassical economic theory. In a sense, this is just a restatement of our thesis in Chapter 3: Value as a concept is inseparable from our metaphorical understandings of motion and of our body. Metaphorical appropriations will continue under the banner of science; orthodox economists will not be able to stop them.

CHAPTER 8

Universal history is the story of different intonations given to a handful of metaphors

Energy is the only life and is from the Body
And Reason is the bound or outward circumference of Energy,
Energy is Eternal Delight.
William Blake, "The Marriage of Heaven and Hell"

As for himself, according to Helmholtz, Ernst Mach, and Arthur Balfour, he was henceforth to be a conscious ball of vibrating motions, traversed in every direction by infinite lines of rotation of vibration, rolling at the feet of the Virgin of Chartres or of M. Poincaré in an attic in Paris, a centre of supersensual chaos.
Henry Adams, *The Education of Henry Adams*

Whenever I have lectured on the material found in the previous pages, or on the occasions when I have had sympathetic readers of this manuscript seek to discuss its contents, the first reaction is invariably: But do you *really* mean to say that physics is the dog and economics is the tail throughout the whole of the history of economic thought? The short, sharp, wicked answer would be "yes," but that answer would not be worthy of an historian. Clearly, many concepts in the history of economic thought have been prompted by any number of other intellectual concerns; entire schools of economic thought have denounced and resisted the siren song of a social physics: the German Historicist school for one, and the first two generations of the American Institutionalists for another (Mirowski 1988a). Nevertheless, I do assert that within the ambit of the dominant schools of Western economic thought – classical political economy, neoclassical economics, and Marxian economics – the theory of value, the very core of the explanatory structure, has been dictated by the evolution of physical theory. Indeed, this has necessarily been the case for the dominant schools in Western culture, for their dominance is due to their emulation of physical explanation and their resonance with the primal metaphors of body/motion/value.

This assertion is, if anything, more far-ranging and hence more controversial than any of the previous assertions in this volume;

396

prudence and a concern for the reader's threshold of cognitive dissonance suggest that the full argument be postponed till a future volume, tentatively titled *The Realms of the Natural*. But some brief indications of the seriousness of this claim may indicate that this book is not purely iconoclastic and destructive, but that it also intends to point the way toward a reconceptualization of the project of a future economics.

The drive to construct a social physics is not the idiosyncratic compulsion of a few technocratic individuals. It has systematic determinants, causes that must be understood by any serious social theory. Others have already realized this fact, particularly those associated with the work of the anthropologist Mary Douglas and the sociologists of science David Bloor and Bruno Latour. Douglas (1986 p. 58) has written that "it is naive to think that the quality of sameness, which characterizes members of a class, as if it were a quality inherent in things or as a power of recognition inherent in the mind." Stated abstractly, the historical narrative in this volume is intended to illustrate this fact in two realms of intellectual discourse often thought to stand as counterexamples to such cultural relativism. We have shown that the conservation principles found in physics and economics are hardly the epistemological rocks of Gibraltar that they are often made out to be; and more important, their justification depends crucially upon metaphoric reasoning, for the simple reason that all such foundational conservation principles are factually false. No posited invariance holds without exceptions or qualifications. We live in a world of broken symmetries and partial invariances.

However imperfect the world, human reason operates by means of assigning samenesses and differences, as Meyerson argued. Under the mandate of causal explanation, invariance and sameness are assigned by human institutions.

> Equilibrium cannot be assumed; it must be demonstrated and with a different demonstration for each type of society . . . Before it can perform its entropy-reducing work, the incipient institution needs some stabilizing principle to stop its premature demise. That stabilizing principle is the naturalization of social classifications. There needs to be an analogy by which the formal structure of a crucial set of social relations is found in the physical world, or in the supernatural world, or in eternity, anywhere, so long as it is not seen as a socially contrived arrangement [Douglas 1986, p. 48].

Hence, the possibility arises that causal explanation requires invariance, but plausible invariance requires institutional stability, and institutional stability in turn is derived from physical metaphor. If this is indeed the case, then the penchant of economics for appropriating physical models becomes rather more comprehensible, and seemingly inexorable. Any individual or group may in fact decry social physics or advocate a theory based on social contingency, but they will inevitably be descried as failing to provide satisfactory *causal* (mathematical, scientific, etc.) explanations, mainly because they renounce the social grounding of invariants in the metaphors of body/motion/value.

From this vantage point, the critique of neoclassical economics found herein operates on at least three different levels. The first, and most prosaic, might be considered an "internalist" critique. One version of this approach was broached by Bruce Caldwell, who has written (private correspondence, 29 January 1987): "The economists who borrowed the metaphors didn't understand them very well. My initial reaction was: So what? It doesn't matter if they completely misunderstood the metaphor as it was used in physics, or if they took an outdated one . . . What matters is not the status of the metaphor in the originating science, but its usefulness in the one that appropriates it." From the present perspective, ignoring the whole problem of appropriation, it still makes quite a difference to our theoretical comprehension of the questions at issue that neoclassical utility is patterned after a potential in a conservative vector field, because one can readily understand the botch made of the postulation of conservation principles in the neoclassical framework simply by comparing it with the parallel model in physics. Issues of fixed endowments, the integrability conditions, the meaning of revealed preference, the putative path-independence of trade, the uneasy status of production and a myriad of other issues in the history of neoclassical theory are rendered easily comprehensible in this manner. On this level, the present volume is critical of neoclassical theorists because they did not avail themselves of this tool of metaphorical reasoning. The metaphor might indeed have been more useful if the protagonists had used it for this purpose. But there are uses and there are uses, which brings us to the next level of critique.

At the second level, one might observe that the neoclassical research program found the proto-energetics metaphor useful in displacing classical political economy and the Marxian program in the West. However, some acquaintance with the historical record reveals that this displacement occured because of rather superficial aspects of the metaphor: the deployment of mathematical formalisms, vague resemblances to more up-to-date science, unfounded appeals to psychology and methodological individualism, and so forth. The most important aspect of the rival schools, the theory of value, has never

been compared on a point-by-point basis such that one could evaluate
the relative attractions and drawbacks of the competing physical
metaphors for value. This is a separate class of criticism of neoclassical
theory: The program has misled generations of students by suggesting that it has relinquished all attachment to theories of value, when
in fact the theory of value patterned on a conservative vector field is
the only thing that holds the program together.

To reiterate a major economic thesis: The theory of value is the
indispensable foundation of any economic theory that answers the
three questions discussed in Chapters 4 and 5.

1. What about markets renders commodities commensurable?
2. What conservation principles formalize the answer to 1,
    allowing quantitative causal analysis?
3. How are the conservation principles identified in 2 linked to
    metaphors of body/motion/value in order to provide them
    with justification (given that all conservation principles are
    radically unjustifiable)?

Classical political economy, neo-Ricardian theory, and Marxian
economics are generally based upon what we have called a substance
theory of value, itself patterned on earlier substance conceptions of
motion. The chief characteristics of the substance theory of value are
stipulations such as: the conservation of value in exchange (i.e., the
trade of equivalents); a productive/unproductive distinction; production defined as the locus of the augmentation of value; the external
residence of value in the commodity and as such conserved through
time; some naturalistic justification of value by means of tautologies
such as: "You are what you eat" (physiocracy), "Things are valuable
because people made them" (Marx), and so on. Conversely, neoclassical theory is predicated upon what we have called a field theory of
value, patterned on the formalism of the field developed in physics
after the rise of the energy concept. The chief characteristics of a field
theory are stipulations such as: the virtual conservation of preferences plus endowment, either jointly or severally; the law of one price
and a market-clearing conception of equilibrium; the specification of
a conservative vector field suffused throughout an independently
given commodity space; the locus of value in the field and not in the
commodities; some justification of value by means of the tautology
that: "Things are valuable because people think they are."

There have been two other classes of alternative value theories in
the history of economic thought. We have called one of them the
full-scale denial of value, and have illustrated it with the writings of

Samuel Bailey. This position argues that no economic phenomenon is conserved through time, and therefore scientific analysis is impossible. Whatever one might think of the truth of this option, it should be clear that the nihilism inherent in the program assures that in this instance there can be no legitimate research program called economics. The last alternative, which we have not described in this volume, might be called a "social theory of value". The reason we have not described it herein is because its characteristic feature is that this program refuses to ground any invariant or conservation principle in natural or scientific metaphors. That does not mean that this theory of value eschews all invariants; instead, it tends to locate them in social institutions, such as the institution of accounting conventions (say, Werner Sombart or David Ellerman) or in the legal definition of property rights (John R. Commons), or else in money itself (Knapp and the German Historicist school).

Given an understanding of the alternatives of substance, field, and social theories of value, the second level of criticism in this volume would hinge upon the assertion that the neoclassical research program has served to obscure and muddle these options, rather than to set itself off sharply in contrast to competing frameworks. This has been particularly the case in its treatment of production, as discussed in Chapter 6.

Finally, a third level of criticism brings us full circle to the theses of Mary Douglas. The question here transcends existing theories of value, asking: Is it possible to adjure all dependence upon physical metaphors when constructing a theory of value? One might be inclined to indict the neoclassical economists for having recourse to physical metaphors in the first place, irrespective of their use or misuse. However, the work of Douglas, Bloor, Latour, and others forces us to acknowledge that the problem, is much larger and more complex than a narrow concern with the discipline of economics. If science is not some mechanical method but instead a social process intertwined with all social organization, then it is a waste of time to speculate whether economics has this or that clear-cut analytical choice. Perhaps all viable explanation must cement conservation principles with reinforced interlocking social and physical metaphors. In such an eventuality, neoclassical theory still lacks vindication, because as we have argued in Chapter 2, the vintage of physics appropriated by neoclassical theory is that of the most rigid and implacable determinism, the physics of the Laplacian dream. In the ensuing century, physics has largely repudiated this image of explanation. New forms of explanation have taken their place: stochastic forms, forms allowing for interaction with the observer, forms allowing for emergent novelty arising out of apparent chaos, forms allowing "something for nothing." In such a cultural climate, neoclassical economics must appear atavistic, if not irrelevant.

Toward the end of her career, Joan Robinson, wrote an article titled "What Are the Questions?" If I have been able to convince the reader that these are indeed the questions, then this book will not have been in vain. Work on these questions cannot simply be a matter of individual research, precisely because they are intended to set into motion an entire research program. Far from promising pie in the sky, I have already made an effort to gather together some work by economists that seems to me to demonstrate an approach orthogonal to the orthodox social physics in Mirowski (1986). In my article "Mathematical Formalism and Economic Explanation" in that collection, I have made a first tentative argument about the role of conservation principles in the determination of exchange ratios, building upon the observations of modern theorists of value discussed in Chapter 6. In a sense, that work takes the moral of the dissolution of the energy concept to heart, in that the conservation of value is not premised upon any natural relationship, but rather upon the imposition of symmetries and identity on phenomena that are factually heterogeneous and asymmetric. Perhaps in this manner we may learn from physics without feeling that we must be physics.

Finally, it should be indicated that this program of research does derive from a tradition of economic writings that are now (perhaps not surprisingly) held in some contempt by the orthodox economics profession. There has been a striving for the kind of social theory herein described by the school generally called the Institutionalists. One finds it in Thorstein Veblen's writings on "The Place of Science in Modern Civilization" at the turn of the century, and in Gunnar Myrdal's *An American Dilemma,* which attempts to uncover "countless errors . . . that no living man can yet detect, because of the fog within which our type of Western culture envelops us. Cultural influences have set up the assumptions about the mind, the body and the universe with which we begin; pose the questions we ask; influence the facts we seek; determine the interpretation we give these facts; and direct our reactions to these interpretations and conclusions." Perhaps we have made a beginning at convincing a few readers that such concerns really must be central to any logical economic theory.

The mathematics of the Lagrangian and Hamiltonian formalisms

There are numerous good introductions to the mathematics of rational mechanics and hence variational principles. My favorite is Lanczos (1949), mainly because it incorporates many historical and philosophical asides as it goes along – a practice now discarded in more modern textbooks such as (Goldstein 1950) and (Percival and Richards 1982).

Suppose that we are given a definite integral:

$$I = \int_{t_1}^{t_2} L(q_1, q_2, \ldots q_n; \dot{q}_1, \dot{q}_2, \ldots, \dot{q}_n; t)dt$$

with the boundary conditions given at the two endpoints t_1 and t_2. The $q_1, \ldots q_n$ are unknown functions of t, determined by the condition that the integral I will be stationary, or that is, $\delta I = 0$ for any arbitrary variations of the q_k. The problem of finding the stationary value of I can be reduced to finding the solution of the following system of simultaneous differential equations:

$$\frac{d}{dt}\frac{\partial L}{\partial \dot{q}_k} - \frac{\partial L}{\partial q_k} = 0, \; (k = 1, 2, \ldots, n)$$

These are called the Lagrangian equations of motion in rational mechanics. If there are also auxiliary conditions or constraints on the variation of the form $f_m(q_1, \ldots, q_n, t) = 0$, then one simply augments the Lagrangian equations of motion as follows:

$$\frac{\partial L}{\partial q_k} - \frac{d}{dt}\frac{\partial L}{\partial \dot{q}_k} + \lambda_1 \frac{\partial f_1}{\partial q_k} + \ldots + \lambda_m \frac{\partial f_m}{\partial q_k} = 0$$

Here the λ's are the notorious Lagrangian multipliers so mysteriously introduced to tyro students of neoclassical economic theory. Translating this into the physics of energy, letting T stand for kinetic energy and U stand for potential energy, we can then observe that the conservation of energy may be rewritten as:

$$\frac{d}{dt}\frac{\partial T}{\partial \dot{q}_i} - \frac{\partial T}{\partial q_i} = -\frac{d}{dt}\frac{\partial U}{\partial \dot{q}_i} + \frac{\partial U}{\partial q_i}$$

The formalism of Hamiltonian dynamics grew out of an appreciation of the regularities and invariants of Lagrangians in the context of conservative systems. Suppose q is a displacement of a particle of mass m, and define p to be the linear momentum in that direction; the corresponding force on the particle is expressed by the function $F(q,t)$. Hence, $\dot{q} = p/m$ and $\dot{p} = F(q,t)$. If the forces can be derived from a potential function $U(q,t)$, then we can define a Hamiltonian function:

$$H(q,p,t) = p^2/2m + U(q,t)$$

Hamilton's equations of motion are then written as:

$$\dot{q} = \frac{\partial H(q,p,t)}{\partial p}; \quad \dot{p} = -\frac{\partial H(q,p,t)}{\partial q}.$$

The Lagrangian equations of motion may be derived from the Hamiltonian, and vice versa, since they are linked by the relationship:

$$L(q,v,t) = p \cdot v - H(q,p,t)$$

where $v = \partial H/\partial p$.

Notes

Chapter 1

[1] In Ivor Grattan-Guiness's superb recent article "Work for the Workers," he adds "force" to my own humble impressions: "It is clear that this story involved much more than a simple piece of applied mathematics: rather, it is an extraordinary *potage* of mathematics, mechanics, engineering, education, and social change. Yet, despite its importance, it is little known and has been poorly researched" (Grattan-Guinness 1984, p. 31).

[2] The importance of Bloor, Latour, and Douglas for the theses of this book, as well as those of the philosophical anthropology of Emile Durkheim and Marcel Mauss, are so extensive that they require a separate screed. Some indication of their significance can be found in Mirowski (1988a).

[3] "Something must persist, the question of knowing what persists being of relatively little importance. Our mind, conscious of the difficulty involved in causal explanation, is, so to speak, resigned in advance and consents to accept almost anything, even something unexplained and radically unexplainable, if only the tendency to persistence in time is satisfied" (Meyerson 1962, p. 102). I can think of no better brief statement explaining why anyone should be inclined to believe in so implausible a concept as "utility."

[4] As an example, there is the forthcoming multivolume work by Martin Shubik on the implications of game theory for money and financial institutions, as part of his larger project towards a mathematical institutional economics.

[5] This refers to the work of David Ellerman on his labor theory of property and its implications for the connection between accounting and economic theory. An introduction can be found in Ellerman's chapter in Philip Mirowski, ed., *The Reconstruction of Economic Theory.*

[6] The question of formalism is addressed in Donald Katzner's *Analysis Without Measurement.* Dimensional analysis was introduced into economics by Frits de Jong (1967).

[7] The reconceptualization of the role of stochastic concepts in economics began with the early pre-fractals work of Benoit Mandelbrot. A discussion by the present author of the importance of this neglected work will appear in a forthcoming issue of *Ricerche Economisti* in an article entitled "Tis a pity econometrics isn't an empirical endeavor," and in a forthcoming book tentatively titled *Who's Afraid of Random Trade?*

Chapter 2

[1] The alert reader will note that this narrative steers clear of the Newtonian tradition and the habit of English-language texts of referring to classical mechanics as Newtonian physics. This is not to slight Newton, but rather to recognize that conservation principles were only implicit in Newtonian mechanics (Elkhana 1974, pp. 47–8), and the conservation of energy not there at all, no matter how hard British chauvinists searched for it (Elkhana, 1974, p. 49). Indeed, in Newton's *Opticks* (4th ed., 1730, p. 399) one discovers the statement: "the variety of Motion which we find in the World is always decreasing." This is not a promising start down the road to the reification of invariants. Hence, strictly speaking, Newtonian mechanics is just *irrelevant* for much of the story to be told in this book.

[2] Yourgrau and Mandelstam (1955, chap. 2) give priority to Fermat's "Principle of Least Time," But this principle was intended only to describe the path of a ray of

light upon reflection or refraction. Some historians such as Goldstein (1980, pp. 67–8) begrudge Maupertuis any credit at all for the principle of least action in favor of Euler, because of the lack of sophistication of the former's mathematical work. To further muddy the waters, there was a vicious controversy during Maupertuis's lifetime, where it was claimed that Leibniz himself deserved credit for the discovery of the principle (Helmholtz 1887). The present author believes the only moral to be drawn from this cacophony of claims and counterclaims is that the Leibnizian tradition was destined to give rise to variational principles.

3 An exception was (Poisson 1811, II, pp. 286–306). However, Lagrange's method was treated as a curiosity, rather than as a central tenet of mechanics. For a later textbook discussion of Lagrange's method, see Laurent (1870, pp. 86–89).

4 For some contemporary textbook approaches, see Poinsot (1842, pp. 393 ff.), and Laurent (1870, pp. 196 ff.). For a survey of the state of early nineteenth-century textbooks in England and France, see Crosland and Smith (1978).

5 Helmholtz himself later realized this, and worked it into the popular lectures he gave on epistemological topics. We quote from some notes left at his death in 1894 (Koenigsberger 1965, pp. 431–3):

"In its older sense the concept of substance was more comprehensive. It corresponded more to the etymology of the term *id quod substat*, that which subsists in the background, or behind the mutable phenomena; in Greek Being or Essence, by which was understood not merely material things, but the concepts of categories of things, subject to one common law, of which, indeed, nothing very definite could be said, and the attributes of which depended principly on the play of the fancy . . . Intangible as might be this concept of immaterial substance, and as obscure as were its attributes, it was none the less firmly believed in, and the dispute over the substantiality or insubstantiality of the human soul is vigorously kept up to the present day. And there is no mistaking the cardinal point of the discussion, the essential attribute of substance, its indestructability, the immortality of the conscious soul . . . How far the form given to these ideas among the different nations and sects of the human race, has been arbitrary, fantastic, contradictory, and tasteless, need not here be dwelt on . . . But some actual knowledge of magnitudes, so far agreeing with the old conception of immaterial substances, that they are indestructable, incapable of being added to, active in space, but not necessarily divisible with it, has been obtained in the last century . . . I mean the supply of energy, of effective working power, which is operating in the world, a Proteus capable of being manifested under the most various forms, and of changing from one to another while still unalterable in its quantity, indestructable, incapable of being added to."

6 All translations of Helmholtz (1887) courtesy of Pamela Cook. My italics.

7 See Chapter 5 for more on Ostwald's Energetics. The best source in English on the energetics movement is Deltete (1983).

8 While the strategy of trading historical narrative styles in mid-stream is not the most laudable of narrative maneuvers, it does have the slightly redeeming feature that it parallels a shift in attitude which occurred soon after the triumph of the energy concept. The nineteenth century was of course the era of "realistic" representation and linear narrative, which, of course, mirrored the faith in determinism. The twentieth century ushered in the age of impressionism, cubism, and montage, as form followed fragmentation in the intellectual sphere. Hence it makes some sense for our narrative to grow more diffuse just as we consider the impact of the entropy concept upon energy conservation.

9 (Prigogine and Stengers 1984, p. 116) make the very interesting observation that many fields of intellectual endeavor became concerned with the issue of long-term change in the later nineteenth century, but only in physics did this take the format of a movement towards homogeneity and death. No one to my knowledge has suggested that this predisposition was anticipated in early- to mid-nineteenth-century classical economics, which predicted a Ricardian stationary state where the rate of profit was zero and all capitalist accumulation would cease.

[10] The mathematical expression for entropy is dQ/T, where dQ is the heat transfer and T is the initial temperature of the system in units of degrees Kelvin. For a discussion of entropy as a variable of state, see Sussman (1972, p. 128). For a discussion of the relationship of the entropy concept to the formalisms of a conservation principle and a variational principle, see Brush (1983, p. 268).

[11] An exception may be found in the *New York Times* of April 14, 1987, sec. 3 page 1, where a group of MIT physicists are described as being engaged in the ultimate research program, that of creating another universe.

[12] A good introduction to the mathematical aspects of quantum mechanics that serves as a drug and an antidote to the luxuriantly speculative popular literature is by Landshoff and Metherell (1979). An excellent discussion of the philosophical issues may be found in Gibbins (1987).

[13] Another, speculative, reason could be that the importance of the metaphor of energy for the culture at large (something explored in the next chapter) creates a situation where two different versions of "energy" are maintained simultaneously: one, reserved for popular consumption, which is conserved; and the other, for the more sophisticated, which stands in an ambiguous and ambivalent relationship to conservation principles.

Chapter 3

[1] On the Hessen thesis, see Hessen (1931); for commentaries, see Barnes (1974) and Young (1985). Barnes is one of the very few sociologists of science to recommend Veblen over Marx as a superior source on the interplay of science and the economy, an influence central to most of the subsequent chapters in this book. If I may be permitted to put in a plug for that most misunderstood of social theorists, I would like to assert that the broad outlines of this chapter have already been anticipated by that economist as early as *1900:*

> It had come to be a commonplace of the physical sciences that "natural laws" are of the nature of empirical generalizations simply, or even of the nature of arithmetical averages. Even the underlying preconception of the modern physical sciences – the law of the conservation of energy, or the persistence of quantity – was claimed to be an empirical generalization, arrived at inductively and verified by experiment. It is true the alleged proof of the law took the whole conclusion for granted at the start, and used it continually as a tacit axiom at every step in the argument which was to establish its truth; but that fact serves rather to emphasize than to call into question the abiding faith which these empiricists had in the sole efficacy of empirical generalisation. Had they been able overtly to admit any other than an associational origin of knowledge, they would have seen the impossibility of accounting on the mechanical grounds of association for the premise on which all experience of mechanical fact rests [Veblen 1969, p. 160].

> I doubt if anyone who read that passage in 1900 really understood it; I hope that the audience is somewhat more sophisticated today.

[2] Or pure browbeating: "Who cares to enter into interminable arguments with the squarers of the circle, or the contrivers of mills to work themselves and pump their own water-power? If it is folly to propose such impotent labors, it is equally folly to discuss them" (Dircks 1870, p. xxxi).

[3] See also Chapter 4 on Marx's economics and its relationship to his conception of science.

[4] "Hermeneutics, of course, emerged as a philosophical discipline . . . in the struggle of the human sciences for methodological and epistemological independence from the model of natural scientific inquiry. Modern post-Heideggerian hermeneutics, however, has sharply attacked this restrictively methodological conception" (Markus 1987, p. 6). I would wish that the following account might be regarded as a contribution to this tradition.

[5] The mathematics of prices that do not conform to the algebraic structure of a group are discussed in some detail in Mirowski (1986, pp. 204–32). The stages of value theory there outlined are closely associated with the stages of metrology in this chapter.

[6] In 1983, during my visit to the University of Manchester Institute of Science and Technology, Professor Joe Marsh informed me that the historian Keith Hutchinson had mentioned to him the connections between Carnot and the Physiocrats. Subsequently, Professor Robert Fox in his writtings has made numerous citations to a draft manuscript of his on the influence of economics upon Carnot; but in a letter to the author dated 5 January 1987, Professor Fox insisted that this manuscript is not yet ready for circulation.

Quesnay and his *Tableau Oeconomique* are discussed in Chapter 4, with the Tableau itself reproduced as Figure 4.1. A more painstaking reconstruction of the Tableau can be found in Meek (1962).

[7] Whewell's conception of value is characteristic of a substance theory of value, defined in Chapter 4. Whewell's own discomfort regarding the exact structure of the accounts is revealed in a letter of 23 October 1856 to Forbes: "That part of your history where I cannot help having some misgivings about an alleged discovery, is that about the mechanical equivalent of heat. I believe it rather on Wm. Thomson's authority, than because I have satisfied myself" (Todhunter 1876, II, p. 409).

[8] Balfour Stewart was a professor of physics at Owens College in Manchester, whose scientific reputation rested mostly upon research intended to reconcile the effusions of solar radiations with the conservation of energy and the entropy law; he also was one of the most widely known researchers on sunspots. Last, but for our purposes hardly least, during his tenure at Owens College he was an intimate of William Stanley Jevons, a fact of no little significance for the topic of Chapter 5.

[9] The problem of profit is equally central to the evolution of economic thought. See Chapters 4 and 6.

Chapter 4

[1] Zero-sum game is a term from game theory. It refers to a set of players, a set of rules, specifications of all possible payoffs and of all possible strategies; zero-sum indicates that in all possible moves in the game, the sum total of payoffs for all players remains fixed. The best discussion of zero-sum games may be found in Shubik (1982, chap. 8). For a further discussion of the presuppositions of game theory, see Mirowski (1986).

[2] I hope this serves to document one of the more egregious flaws in the *History of Economic Analysis* by Joseph Schumpeter, a text that goes out of its way to insist that early economic analysis was not profoundly influenced by contemporaneous developments in science (Schumpeter 1954, pp. 17, 30, 119, 211). One commentator who has noticed the influence of metaphors of motion and the body is Pribram (1983, p. 37). One other important influence that should be included in any comprehensive natural history of value is the importance of the appearance of double-entry bookkeeping techniques in northern Europe by the mid-sixteenth century, an influence first noted by Sombart (1902, I, p. 319) and discussed in Mayr, (1986, pp. 146 ff.).

[3] Comments such as those found in (Schumpeter 1954, p. 237) and (Blaug 1985, p. 25) reveal a misunderstanding of the context in which these theories are generated, as well as a lack of appreciation of the logical requirements of a set of value accounts predicated upon a substance theory of value, which differentiates, as it must, the spheres of conservation and nonconservation of the value substance.

[4] There exists a literature that attempts to claim that Newtonian physics had some influence on Smith: (Llobera 1981; Mayr 1971; Hetherington 1983). However, it is of neccessity misguided because Newton was not the conduit through which Smith imbibed his scientific influences. The first to point this out was Foley (1976), and this

section owes much to that superb work. A somewhat earlier suggestion of the Cartesian influence was by Mini (1974, chap. 4).

By the way, the first appearance of Smith's famous "invisible hand" was in a *physics*, and not an economic context: "heavy bodies descend, and lighter substances fly upwards by the neccessity of their own nature; nor was the invisible hand of Jupiter ever apprehended to be employed in these matters" (Smith 1967, p. 49).

5 An example of the restriction to best-practice techniques may be found in Marx (1977, I, p. 295) where he suggests that the use of gold spindles rather than the conventional, and cheaper, steel spindles would not enter into the value accounting scheme. The question of effective demand as a neccessary prerequisite for "counting" only particular labor values appears in the same work (p. 202): "If the market cannot stomach the whole quantity at its normal price . . . the effect is the same as if each individual weaver had expended more labor time on his particular product than was socially neccessary." This has profound consequences for the conventionally presumed separation of natural price and market price in the Marxian literature; it is striking that no Marxist has commented upon its significance. It seems this is another example of how the *portmanteau* concept of "socially necessary labor time" conceals all problems.

6 Gauss also fired an early shot in the war between the scientists and the philosophers: "If a philosopher says something that is true, it is trivial. If he says something that is not trivial, it is wrong" (quoted in Lanczos 1970, p. 84). Here he was referring to Kant's defense of Euclidean geometry as being true a priori.

7 It may be of some use to give another example of just how misleading Schumpeter's *History* can be. In (Schumpeter 1954, pp. 486–7, 599), praise is lavished upon Bailey as a precursor of neoclassical economics. Bailey, as would be evident to anyone who read the book, was not a partisan of the utility theory of value. For example, on page 168 of the *Critical Dissertation* he writes: "With regard to heterogeneous commodities, there are in fact only two conceivable criteria of riches; one, the utility of any possessions; the other, their value. The first is in the highest degree unsteady and indeterminate, and altogether inapplicable."

It is clear that Schumpeter has decided to praise Bailey because in the first few pages of the *Critical Dissertation* Bailey states that value is an effect in the mind and that the labor theory of value is faulty. However, Schumpeter writes, "He was before his time, and was wilfully ignored, since he offered a positive alternative to the labor theory of value." Bailey, as we have argued, did no such thing.

8 This issue is discussed further in Chapter 6, and in Mirowski (1986, pp. 200–21).

9 One should acknowledge the possibility that Bailey might not have actually wanted to advocate the negation of all value theory. Much of what Bailey writes is already in Ricardo, the only change being that Bailey pounces on the marginalized and defocused problems in Ricardo and thrashes them over and over. One might say that Bailey turned Ricardian economics on its head in order to expose its soft underbelly. Yet, upon reading his philosophical essays, one instead discovers a sort of nineteenth-century version of Paul Feyerabend:

> The world is full of ignorance and error, and I am glad to see a zealous pursuit of even singular and eccentric views, as the means of ultimately lessening the evil. Tentative processes of this kind are indeed indispensable steps. The grand experiment which Mr. Owen is making in America, even if it miscarry, is sure to throw light on the principles of human nature. Even the modern phrenology, should it prove utterly unfounded, will be of use" [Bailey 1829, p. 175].

Chapter 5

1 Ted Porter informs me that on the continent in the eighteenth century chemists had made great strides in the conceptualization of a "simple substance" and had moved

away from pure taxonomy; he discusses this phenomenon in Porter (1981b). While that was the case, it is doubtful that Bentham's British sources would have made him aware of those developments.

[2] The fact that Cournot's epistemic basis for the mathematicization of economic theory was so very confused seems to contradict the general impression that he is the first reigorous mathematical economist (Schumpeter 1954, p. 959; Baumol and Goldfeld 1968, pp. 162–3). For an argument that, at least with regard to value theory, it was Marx who deserves the palm, see Mirowski (1986). The mere use of the calculus to find an extremum of some function is no great virtue. To see the efforts of a contemporary to critically evaluate such celestial analogues, see Adolphe Quetelet, "Principles de Mécanique qui sont Aussi Susceptible d'application à la Société" Quetelet MS 110, Bibliothèque Albert Iea, Brussels.

[3] Gossen's English translators replace "pleasure" with "intensity of pleasure" on the vertical axis, in order to repair the later confusion in *The Laws* between the value of a function and its first derivative. These emendations are perhaps a little too generous in hindsight, since they give the impression that Gossen had a clearer conception of neoclassical utility than is actually to be found in his writings.

[4] Letter of Vilfredo Pareto to Irving Fisher, 11 January 1897; in the Irving Fisher papers, Sterling Library, Yale University. My translation from the French original.

[5] Irving Fisher's "My Economic Endeavors" is an unfinished manuscript composed in the early 1940s, and preserved in the Fisher collection, series III, box 26, Sterling Library, Yale University. The following quotes are all from Chapter 1 of the manuscript.

[6] See Irving Fisher to E. W. Fisher, 11 February 1894; Irving Fisher collection, Yale University, series I, box 2, folder 16.

[7] See, for instance, Samuelson (1986b, V) and Eagly (1974).

[8] The reception of Albert Hirschman's *Exit, Voice and Loyalty* (Hirschman 1970) shows how myopic economics has become about its past. The simple statement that there might exist mechanisms in the market other than market-clearing price, and that these might be dependent upon a nonutilitarian psychology, was hailed as a novel insight as late as the 1970s.

[9] Irving Fisher, "My Economic Endeavors," op cit., series III, box 26.

[10] Unfortunately, only Pareto's side of the correspondance has survived and has been conveniently published in Chipman (1976, pp. 45–62). Due to this fact, we have inferred the content of Laurent's letters from those he sent to Walras, as well as Pareto's replies.

[11] In Chipman (1976), Laurent is made to appear as if he did not understand the implications of neoclassicism, which Pareto had under complete control. Moreover, the entire incident is written off as a mere technical confusion of (i) whether $\Sigma \phi_i \, dx_i$ was an integrable equation; (ii) whether $\Sigma \phi_i \, dx_i$ was an exact differential; (iii) whether utility was a path-independent variable (i.e., independent of the actual order of consumption); and (iv) whether utility was in fact measurable. While from a merely mathematical standpoint these issues might be given separate answers, once one realizes that they all are questions about the viability of the physics metaphor in economics and particularly revolve around the conservation of energy/utility and the existence of a conservative field, one sees that they really are all the same question.

[12] The only review of Laurent's book that I have been able to find, by Boninsegni (1903), makes all the same mistakes found in Pareto's letters: The reviewer argues from a two-good world, thus begging the question of integrability, and misses the point of Laurent's query about what renders commodity prices transitive (Boninsegni 1903, p. 334). One suspects that Boninsegni was a student at Lausanne, and hence acted as a stand-in for Pareto in a final parting shot at Laurent.

[13] They do have a passing resemblance to Sraffa's "standard commodity," however, in the sense they are an artifical weighted average of all the commodities in the economy at a point in time. See Sraffa (1960).

[14] In the Royal Society Library folder HS 10.328 is a letter of W. S. Jevons to J. Herschel, 29 Oct. 1870 that states:

> It has been felt by several scientific men of Manchester – Mr. Joule, Mr. Balfour Stewart, Dr. Roscoe especially, that there is no sufficient influence possessed by men of science in national affairs, and that the total want of common action in matters relating to government is the cause of this. They therefore wish to ascertain how far it would be possible to draw together the influence which rightfully belongs to the leading scientific men . . .

[15] A letter from Friedrich Hayek to Wesley Clair Mitchell, dated 15 December 1923, sheds a little further light on this topic. Hayek there claims: "Wieser and Böhm-Bawerk (probably also Menger) had originally only a rather superficial acquaintance with Bentham. Later on however, one of Böhm's pupils, Oskar Kraus . . . took the matter up and published two monographs [in 1894 and 1901] which made Bentham pretty popular among the Austrian school." This letter is in the Wesley Clair Mitchell collection in the Columbia University Manuscript archives.

[16] This claim is elaborated upon in Chapter 6, where the problem of "supply and demand" as a nonviable graft onto the neoclassical metaphor is discussed further.

[17] Translation courtesy of Pamela Cook.

[18] The issue of the penetration of probability theory into economics deserves much attention in its own right, too much to give it here. It will be dealt with in detail in my forthcoming book from Princeton University Press, tentatively entitled *Who's Afraid of Random Trade?*

Chapter 6

[1] The endemic character of this problem in neoclassical theory is illustrated by a letter from R. S. Berry to Tjalling Koopmans, January 6, 1981:

> I am acutely aware of the difficulties in doing the kind of work you describe. As yet, I have not been successful in persuading economists to learn the vocabulary of the physical sciences. Only those like yourself, Geoffrey Heal, Paul Samuelson, and a few others who began as mathematicians or physical scientists seem willing to make the effort. There aren't a lot of physicists or chemists who can talk haltingly in the jargon of economics . . . while the economists have no recognized need and therefore little or no interest in learning physics. (I would exclude from this description the very mathematical folks who treat economic and mechanical systems with the same sorts of elaborate modern mathematics). [Letter in the Tjalling Koopmans collection, Sterling library, Yale University.]

[2] The relevant passages are to be found in (Say 1821, pp. 4–5). The relationship of Say's advocacy of the conservation of matter to his value theory was discussed in Chapter 4.

[3] "The Graphic Representation of the Laws of Supply and Demand," in Alexander Grant, ed., *Recess Studies,* Edinburgh, 1870; reprinted in Jenkin (1887, pp. 76–93). Although Marshall vehemently denied it, it seems fairly clear to the present author that Marshall derived all the important parts of the demand/supply apparatus from reading Jenkin. In a letter from Marshall to Edwin Seligman dated 6 April 1896, Marshall denies that Jenkin influenced him, even while admitting: "His paper in Recess Studies was a good deal talked about and I heard of that quite early." Upon gentle chiding from Seligman, Marshall wrote another letter dated 10 July 1896, in which he calls Seligman's suggestion of influence "most unnatural," and states: "I purposely worded my reference to Jenkin so as to imply I was under no obligation to him." Methinks he protesteth too mightily. These letters are in the Seligman collection, Columbia University manuscripts archive.

[4] An example of such a willingness can be discovered in the recently uncovered Keynes

papers at Tilton (Keynes 1979, pp. 240–7). Hugh Townshend, a spectacularly perceptive critic, challenged Keynes in private communication about the meaning of effective demand as an algebraic quantity, reminding Keynes of the "pack of perplexities attending the definition of income." In particular, Townshend called into question whether D could be used as an expression of *output*, especially in Chapter 20, which rather breezily links expenditure with employment. Keynes's response is revealing:

> I am inclined to think that your first point relating particularly to Section I of chapter 20 could be dealt with, though clumsily, by writing $D + U$ [effective demand *plus* user costs!!] in place of D wherever the latter occurs; so that the definitions of the various elasticities will be correspondingly altered. This is undoubtedly artificial and does not fully meet your point, but the whole thing is fundamentally artificial. I have got bogged in an attempt to bring my own terms into rather closer conformity with the algebra of the others than the case really permits. When I come to revise the book properly, I am not at all sure that the right solution may not be in leaving out all this sort of stuff altogether . . .

This is a devastating bit of candor, since once one began to slough off the income = output concept, it is not at all clear what would be left of the Keynesian organon.

5   A good introduction to the subject may be found in Nicholas Georgescu-Roegen, "Man and Production," in Baranzini and Scazzieri (1986) and a further discussion of it in Mirowski (1986). The points made in this section owe much to Georgescu-Roegen's summary, found on page 261 of his article:

> Mathematical theorists of production, although they are not aware of it, have been speaking dialectics all the time. Of course the product changes from one recipe to another, hence we may say that the product is a "function" of the factors. But we commit a crucial infraction if we take that "function" to mean a non-degenerate function in Euclidean space, as in the tradition set by Wicksteed. Surprizing though it may be, the same semantic sin is absent from the theory of consumer behavior. The individual's identity does not change if some commodity is substituted for another, and to say whether that substitution is a compensation or not is a fundamental human faculty . . . Mathematics is more at home in the utility than in the production theory.

6   It was further galling to Cambridge, U.K., to observe that even though the MIT theorists repudiated the J. B. Clark–style capital substances, every single neoclassical journal continued to publish vast quantities of articles, freely using hybrid neoclassical production functions and aggregate capital concepts. This led Joan Robinson to exclaim: "I was delighted to find in a dictionary the word *mumpsimus*, which means stubborn persistence in an error that has been exposed" (quoted in Feiwel 1985, p. 79).

7   "One should now ask how the present mess came into being. For macroeconomics today is in a state which astronomy would be if Ptolemaic theory once again came to dominate the field. There can in fact be few instances in other disciplines of such a determined turning back of the clock. A great deal of what is written today as well as the policy recommendations which have been made would be thoroughly at home in the twenties. So something needs explaining and I hope that some good intellectual historian will attempt to do so soon" [Hahn 1985, p. 18].

8   Here we must caution the reader to keep in mind the distinction between the expansion of value and physical expansion. The von Neumann growth model, which only superficially resembles the Sraffian system avoids the problem by identifying an equilibrium growth rate wherein every single commodity grows physically at the same rate. This, of course, is nothing but an extended analogue of a one-good economy. In the Sraffian system, the maximum rate of profit measured in terms of the standard commodity is invariant to any changes in the reigning rate of profit.

9 It should be recognized that Hicks had progressively come closer and closer in the 1970s and eighties to Robinson's position that history matters, but still seemed oblivious to the fact that the introduction of hysteresis would sink the entire neoclassical science-based project. See, for instance, Hicks (1975, p. 367): "Substitution, the most important substitutions at least, are irreversible." If that really is the case, then technological relations cannot be represented as a field, and therefore the entire analytical engine of constrained maximization is impotent – in other words, Hicks's entire life's work should be scrapped.

10 This thesis about the intimate connections of symmetry and value theory using the formalisms of group theory is briefly sketched in Mirowski (1986). A more thorough elaboration of this point is the obvious next step implied by this historical narrative. A basic description of broken symmetry in physics can be found in Crease and Mann (1986, chap. 13).

Chapter 7

1 These essays were published in an expanded version in Hayek (1979). He was awarded the Nobel Prize in Economics in 1974, which initiated his rehabilitation in polite circles. Under the insistent prodding of Hayek scholars, and particularly of Bruce Caldwell, I am forced to acknowledge that my reading of the Hayek incident in this section is prejudiced in the Gadamerian sense: It tells the story from the vantage point of someone situated in the Anglo-American context, whose understanding of scientism would not have corresponded to that of Hayek. Strangely enough, I then came across a passage of Richard Rorty, discussing of all people, Michel Foucault (!), which captures the disjuncture between the Continental and Anglo-American perspectives. I reproduce it here, just replacing every appearance of "Foucault" with "Hayek":

> Most of us are products of postwar Anglo-Saxon training in philosophy, and so Hegelian historicism looks to us about as far as one can go. It takes us a while to grasp a point that Hacking has patiently tried to teach us – that historicism is as old hat on the Continent as positivism is over here. For philosophers brought up (as most of us were) to smile condescendingly at the mention of Collingwood or Croce, the suggestion that there is no such thing as an ahistorical nature of knowledge or of rationality to be discovered by philosophical analysis is so titillating that we assume that [Hayek] must be getting the same kick out of it that we are. But in fact [Hayek] thinks of historicism as just a variant of Cartesianism. He sees the mighty opposites in contemporary *Wissenschaftslehre* as both so completely subservient to the "will-to-truth" that their differences count for nothing. Whereas we think it daring to suggest that Hegelian history of ideas might replace Cartesian epistemology, [Hayek] thinks that Hegelian "progressive" histories are just a self-deceptive continuation of the original Cartesian project [Rorty 1986, p. 45].

2 The importance of the work of Emile Durkheim, Marcel Mauss, and Mary Douglas has been mentioned *en passant* throughout this volume; however, the author acknowledges that the curious reader must look elsewhere for a summary of their ideas. One good place to start is Bloor (1982). The present author is engaged in a project to expand their insights on the interdependence of social and natural concepts, tentatively titled *The Realms of the Natural*.

3 Le Châtelier's connection with the energetics movement is mentioned in Deltete (1983).

4 Martin O'Connor has pointed out to me that there actually are two widely disparate cultural interpretations of the entropy concept: the older, pessimistic version cited in the text, and a newer, more optimistic version, associated with Prigogine and Stengers. This latter Weltanschauung praises thermodynamics for contemplating the

possibility of describing the emergence of order out of chaos. The Prigogine interpretation has yet to catch on among neoclassical economists.

[5] This is not the case with statistical mechanics, but the reconciliation of statistical mechanics with phenomenological thermodynamics is not as straightforward as the textbooks make out. This has been indicated in Chapter 2 and by Georgescu-Roegen (1971, chap. 6).

[6] I do not wish to claim that neoclassical economics *never* came to any sort of rapprochement with statistical mechanics and quantum mechanics. The actual course of events was much more complex than the bald prohibition stated in the text. In a strange sequence of events, the genesis of the subfield of econometrics in the 1920s and 1930s served to make it appear that neoclassical economics had followed the lead of physics into explicitly stochastic concepts, even though that was not actually the case. This argument is too labyrinthine to include here; the reader is referred to Mirowski (1989d) for the full narrative.

[7] (Martinez-Alier, 1987) would be a good beginning, if it did not persistently gloss over the profound difficulties of an energy theory of value that resists clear differentiation of substance and field conceptions, as well as lacking sensitivity to the various ways the metaphor of energy has been used in the history of economics. I have made an initial foray in outlining the history of the neo-energeticists in (Mirowski 1988b), a paper that could serve as a phantom Chapter 7½ for the present volume.

Bibliography

——. "1980 Nobel Prize in Physics to Cronin and Fitch." *Science* (210):619.

Adams, R. 1975. *Energy and Structure: A Theory of Social Power*. Austin: University of Texas.

Adams, R. 1982. *Paradoxical Harvest: Energy and Explanation in British History*. Cambridge, U.K.: Cambrige University Press.

Alier, J., and Naredo, J. 1982. "A Marxist Precursor of Energy Economics: Podolinsky." *Journal of Peasant Studies* (9): 207–24.

Agassi, Joseph. 1971. *Faraday as a Natural Philospher*. Chicago: University of Chicago Press.

Agassi, Joseph. 1981. *Science and Society*. Boston: Reidel.

Airy, George Biddell. 1830. "On Certain Conditions Under Which a Perpetual Motion Is Possible." *Transactions of the Cambridge Philosophical Society* (3):369–72.

Albers, Donald, and Alexanderson, G. L. 1986. *Mathematical People*. Boston: Birkhauser.

Angel, Roger. 1980. *Relativity: The Theory and Its Philosphy*. New York: Pergamon.

Antonelli, G. B. 1971. *Sulla Theoria Mathematica Della Economia Politica*. Orig. pub. 1886; trans in J. Chipman, L. Hurwtiz, M. Richter, and H. Sonnenschein, eds. *Preferences, Utility, and Demand*. New York: Harcourt, Brace, Jovanovich.

Akatz, D., and Pagels, H. 1982. "Origin of the Universe as a Quantum Tunnelling Event." *Physical Review D* (25):2065.

Amoroso, L. 1940. "The Transformation of Value in the Production Process." *Econometrica* (8):1–11

Amoroso, L. 1942 *Meccanica Economica*. Castello: Instituto Nazionale Di Alta Mathematica.

Anderson, B. 1966. *Social Value*. New York: Kelley.

Appleby, Joyce. 1978. *Economic Thought and Ideology in Seventeenth-Century England*. Princeton: Princeton University Press.

Arrow, K., Block, H., and Hurwicz, L. 1959. "On the Stability of Competitive Equilibrium II." *Econometrica* (27):265–90.

Arrow, Kenneth, and Hahn, Frank. 1971. *General Competitive Analysis*. San Francisco: Holden Day.

Arrow, Kenneth, and Intrilligator, Michael., eds. 1982. *Handbook of Mathematical Economics*. Vol. 2. Amsterdam: North Holland.

Atkins, David. 1942. *A Dimensional National Economy*. Westminster: King and Staples.

Atkins, David. 1925. *The Measurement of Economic Value*. San Francisco: Lantern Press.

414

Aumann, Robert, 1985. "What Is Game Theory Trying to Accomplish?" In K. Arrow and S. Honkapohja, eds. *Frontiers of Economics*. Oxford: Blackwell.

Auspitz, R., and Lieben, R. 1889. *Untersuchungen Ueber der Theorie des Preises*. Leipzig: Duncker & Humblot.

Ayres, Robert. 1978. *Resources, Evironment and Economics*. New York: Wiley.

Ayres, R., and Nair, I. 1984. "Thermodynamics and Economics." *Physics Today*. (37):62–71

Bachelier, L. 1900. *Théorie de la Spéculation*. Paris: Gauthier-Villiers.

Bailey, Samuel. 1829. *Essays on the Pursuit of Truth*. London: R. Hunter.

Bailey, Samuel. 1967 [1825]. *Critical Dissertation on Value*. London: Cass.

Baranzini, M., and Scazzieri, R. 1986. *Foundations of Economics*. Oxford: Blackwell.

Barbour, Violet. 1963. *Capitalism in Amsterdam in the 17th Century*. Ann Arbor: University of Michigan Press.

Barnes, Barry. 1974. *Scientific Knowledge and Sociological Theory*. London: Routledge and Kegan Paul.

Barnes, Barry, and Shapin, S., eds. 1979. *Natural Order*. London: Sage.

Barrow, John, and Tippler, Frank. 1986. *The Anthropic Cosmological Principle*. New York: Oxford University Press.

Baumgardt, David. 1952. *Bentham and the Ethics of Today*. Princeton: Princeton University Press.

Baumol, William. 1977. "Say's (at Least) Eight Laws." *Economica* (44):145–161

Baumol, W., and Goldfeld, S., eds. 1968. *Precursors in Mathematical Economics*. London: LSE Reprints.

Bausor, Randall. 1986. "Time and Equilibrium." In P. Mirowski, ed., *The Reconstruction of Economic Theory*. Hingham, Mass.: Kluwer.

Bausor, Randall. 1987. "Liapounov Techniques in Economic Dynamics and Classical Thermodynamics." Paper presented to meetings of American Economic Assn., Chicago.

Becher, Harvey. 1971. "William Whewell and Cambridge Mathematics." Ph.D. thesis, University of Missouri.

Becker, Gary. 1976. *The Economic Approach to Human Behavior*. Chicago: University of Chicago Press.

Bentham, Jeremy. 1952. *Jeremy Bentham's Economic Writings*. 3 vols., W. Stark, ed. London: Allen & Unwin.

Berkson, William, 1974. *Fields of Force*. London: Routledge and Kegan Paul.

Berndt, Ernst. 1985. "From Technocracy to Net Energy Analysis: Engineers, Economist, and Reoccuring Energy Theories of Value." In Anthony Scott, ed., *Progress in Natural Resource Economics*. Oxford: Clarendon Press.

Berndt, Ernst. 1978. "Aggregate Energy, Efficiency, and Productivity Measurement." *Annual Review of Energy* (9):409–26.

Berndt, E., and Wood, D. 1979. "Engineering and Econometric Interpretations of Energy-Capital Complementarity." *American Economic Review* (69):342–54

Berry, R., Salomon, P., and Heal, G. 1978. "On a Relation Between Economic and Thermodynamic Optima." *Resources and Energy* (1):125–37

Bertrand, Joseph. 1883. "Compte Rendu" of Cournot and Walras, *Journal des Savants* (   ):499–508.

Bhaduri, Amit. 1969. "On the Significance of Recent Controversies in Capital Theory." *Economic Journal* (79):532–39.

Bharadwaj, Krishna. 1978a. "The Subversion of Classical Analysis: Alfred Marshall's Early Writings on Value." *Cambridge* [U.K.] *Journal of Economics*, Sept. (2):153–74.

Bharadwaj, Krishna. 1978b. *Classical Political Economy and the Rise to the Dominance of Supply and Demand Theories.* New Delhi: Orient Longmans.

Black, R., Coats, A., and Goodwin, C., eds. 1973. *The Marginal Revolution in Economics.* Durham: Duke University Press.

Blaug, Mark. 1974. *The Cambridge Revolution: Success or Failure?* London: IEA.

Blaug, Mark. 1978. *Economic Theory in Retrospect,* 3rd ed. Cambridge, U.K.: Cambridge University Press.

Blaug, Mark. 1980. *The Methodology of Economics.* Cambridge, U.K.: Cambridge University Press.

Blaug, Mark. 1985. *Economic Theory in Retrospect,* 4th ed. Cambridge, U.K.: Cambridge University Press.

Bliss, Christopher. 1975. *Capital Theory and the Distribution of Income.* Amsterdam: North Holland.

Bloor, David. 1982. "Durkheim and Mauss Revisited: Classification and the Sociology of Knowledge." *Studies in the History and Philosophy of Science* (13):267–97.

Bloor, David. 1976. *Knowledge and Social Imagery.* Boston: Routledge & Kegan Paul.

Boas, George. 1930. *A Critical Analysis of the Philosophy of Emile Meyerson,* Baltimore: Johns Hopkins University.

Böhm-Bawerk, Eugen von. 1959. *Capital and Interest.* South Holland: Libertarian Press.

Bohr, Niels, Kramers, Hendrik, and Slater, John. 1924. "The Quantum Theory of Radiation." *Philosophical Magazine* (47):785–802.

Boland, Lawrence. 1982. *The Foundations of Economic Method.* Boston: Allen & Unwin.

Boltzmann, Ludwig. 1974. *Theoretical Physics and Philosophical Problems.* Boston: Reidel.

Bolza, Hans. 1940. "The Conception of Invariants in Dynamic Economics." *Econometrica* (8):86–94.

Bolza, Hans. 1935. *Ein Neuer Wea Zur Erforschung Und Darstelluna Volkswertschaftlicher Vorgange.* Berlin: Sprwaer.

Bolza, Hans. 1932.. *Die Wirtschafiskrise.* Berlin: Mittler.

Bolza, Hans. 1936. *Dialektische Oder Rationale Methoden In Der Nationalökonomie?* Munich: Duncker & Humblot.

Boninsegni, P. 1902. "I Fondamenti del l'Economia Pura." *Giornale degli Economisti* Feb. (29):106–33.

Boninsegni, P. 1903. "Un Nuevo Tratto D'Economia Mathematica." *Giornale Degli Economisti* (30):327–36.

Bordley, Robert. 1983. "Reformulating Classical and Quantum Mechanics in Terms of a Unified Set of Consistency Conditions." *International Journal of Theoretical Physics* (22):803–20.

Borges, Jorge Luis. 1962. *Labyrinths*. New York: New Directions.

Born, Max. 1969. *Physics in My Generation*. New York: Springer.

Bos, H. 1980. "Mathematics and Rational Mechanics." In G. Rousseau and R. Porter, eds, *The Ferment of Knowledge*. Cambridge, U.K.: Cambridge University Press.

Boss, Helen. 1982. *Productive Labor, Unproductive Labor, and the Boundary of the Economic Domain*. Ph.D. thesis, Economics, McGill University.

Boulding, Kenneth, and Stigler, George, eds. 1952. *AEA Readings in Price Theory*. Homewood: Irwin.

Bouvier, Emile. 1901a. "L'Economie Politique Mathématique." *Revue Critique de Legislation et de Jurisprudence* (30):623–29

Bouvier, Emile. 1901b. "La Méthode Mathématique en Economie Politique." *Revue d'Economie Politique* (15):817–50; 1029–86

Bowley, Marion. 1973. *Studies in the History of Economic Thought Before 1870*. London: Macmillan.

Brannigan, Augustine. 1981. *The Social Basis of Scientific Discoveries*. Cambridge, U.K.: Cambridge University Press.

Braudel, Fernand. 1982. *The Wheels of Commerce*. New York: Simon & Schuster.

Breger, Herbert. 1982. *Die Natur Als Arbeitende Maschine*. Frankfurt: Campus Verlag.

Brewer, J., and Smith, M. 1981. *Emmy Noether*. New York: Marcel Dekker.

Bridgeman, Percy. 1927. *The Logic of Modern Physics*. New York: Macmillan.

Brody, A., Martinas, K., and Sajo, K. 1985. "An Essay in Macroeconomics." *Acta Oeconomica* (35):337–43.

Bromberg, Joan. 1971. "The Impact of the Neutron:Bohr and Heisenberg." *Historical Studies in Physical Science* (3):307–41.

Bronsted, J. N. 1955. *Principles and Problems in Energetics*. New York: Wiley.

Brown, E. C., and Solow, R., eds. 1983. *Paul Samuelson and Modern Economic Theory*. New York: McGraw-Hill.

Brown, Laurie, and Hoddeson, Lillian. 1983. *The Birth of Particle Physics*. Cambridge, U.K.: Cambridge University Press.

Brown, Murray, Sato, K., and Zarembka, P., eds. 1976. *Essays in Modern Capital Theory*. Amsterdam: North Holland.

Brown, Theodore. 1981. *The Mechanical Philosophy and "Animal Oeconomy."* New York: Arno.

Brown, Vivienne. 1987. "Value and Property in the History of Economic Thought." *Economies et Sociétés* (21):85–111.

Brunet, Pierre. 1938. *Etude Historique sue le Principe de la Moindre Action*. Paris: Hermann.

Brunhes, Bernard. 1908. *La Dégradation de l'Energie*. Paris: Flammerion.

Brush, Stephen. 1976. "Irreversibility and Indeterminism: Fourier to Heisenberg," *Journal of the History of Ideas* (37):603–30.

Brush, Stephen. 1978. *The Temperature of History*. Philadelphia: Franklin.

Brush, Stephen. 1983. *Statistical Physics and the Atomic Theory of Matter*. Princeton: Princeton University Press.

Bryant, J. 1982. "A Thermodynamic Approach to Economics." *Energy Economics* (1):36–50.

Buechner, M. Norton. 1976. "Frank Knight on Capital as the Only Factor of Production." *Journal of Economic Issues* (10):598–617.

Bukharin, Nikolai. 1927. *Economic Theory of the Leisure Class*. New York: International.

Burlamqui, J.-J. 1820. *Principes du Droit de la Nature et des Gens*. Paris: Waree.

Burmeister, Edwin. 1980. *Capital Theory and Dynamics*. New York: Cambridge University Press.

Burmeister, Edwin, and Dobell, A. 1970. *Mathematical Theories of Economic Growth*. New York: Macmillan

Bynum, W., Browne, E., and Porter, R., eds. 1981. *Dictionary of the History of Science*. London: Macmillan.

Cairnes, J. E. 1875. *The Character and Logical Method of Political Economy*. New York: Harper and Bros.

Caldwell, Bruce. 1988. " 'Hayek's Transformation' *History of Political Economy*." (20):513–41.

Campbell, Joseph, 1959. *The Masks of God: Primitive Mythology*. New York: Viking.

Canard, N.-F. 1969 [1801]. *Principes d'Economie Politique*. Rome: Edizioni Bizzarri.

Cannan, Edwin. 1917. *History of the Theories of Production and Distribution*. London: King.

Cannan, Edwin. 1921. "Early History of the Term Capital." *Quarterly Journal of Economics* (25):469–81.

Cannon, Susan F. 1978. *Science in Culture*. New York: Science History Publication.

Cantor, G., and Hodge, M., eds. 1981. *Conceptions of Ether*. Cambridge, U.K.: Cambridge Univeristy Press.

Capek, Milac. 1961. *The Philosophical Impact of Contemporary Physics*. Princeton: Van Nostrand.

Cardwell, D. S. L. 1971. *From Watt to Clausius*. Ithaca: Cornell University Press.

Carnot, Sadi. 1960. *Reflections on the Motive Force of Fire and Other Papers*. New York: Dover.

Carnot, Sadi. 1978. *Réflexions sur la Puissance Motrice du Feu*. ed. Robert Fox. Paris: Vrin.

Cartwright, Nancy. 1977. "The Sum Rule Has Not Been Tested." *Philosophy of Science* (44):107–12.

Cartwright, Nancy. 1983. *How the Laws of Physics. Lie*. Oxford: Oxford University Press.

Carrothers, Gerald. 1956. "An Historical Review of the Gravity and Potential

Concepts of Human Interaction." *Journal of the American Institute of Planners* (17):94–102.

Carver, T. N. 1924. *The Economy of Human Energy.* New York: Macmillan.

Cass, David, and Shell, Karl. 1976. *The Hamiltonian Approach to Dynamic Economics.* New York: Academic Press.

Cassirer, Ernst. 1953. *Substance and Function.* New York: Dover.

Cassirer, Ernst. 1956. *Determinism and Indeterminism in Modern Physics.* New Haven: Yale University Press.

Cencini, Alvaro. 1984. *Time and Macroeconomic Analysis of Income.* London: Francis Pinter.

Centre National de la Recherche Scientifique. 1976. *Carnot et la Essor de la Thermodynamique.* Paris: CNRS.

Charlesworth, Brian. 1980. *Evolution in Age-Structured Populations.* Cambridge, U.K.: Cambridge Univeristy Press.

Chatfield, Michael. 1977. *A History of Accounting Thought.* Huntington, New York: Krieger.

Checkland, Sidney. 1951a. "Economic Opinion in England as Jevons Found It." *Manchester School* (19):143–69.

Checkland, Sidney. 1951b. "The Advent of Academic Economics in England." *Manchester School* (19):43–70.

Chenery, Hollis. 1949. "Engineering Production Functions." *Quarterly Journal of Economics* (63):507–31.

Chenery, Hollis. 1953. "Process and Production Functions from Engineering Data." In W. Leontief, ed., *Studies in the Structure of the American Economy.* New York: Oxford University Press.

Chipman, J., Hurwicz, L., Richter, M., and Sonnenschein, H., eds. 1971. *Preferences, Utility, and Demand.* New York: Harcourt Brace.

Chipman, John. 1976. "An Episode in the Early Development of Ordinal Utility Theory: Pareto's Letters to Hermann Laurent." *Cahiers Vilfredo Pareto* (14):37:39–64.

Clagett, Marshall, ed. 1959. *Critical Problems in the History of Science.* Madison: Universtiy of Wisconsin Press.

Clapham, John. 1922. "On Empty Economic Boxes." *Economic Journal* (32):305–14.

Clark, John Bates. 1938. *The Distribution of Wealth.* New York: Macmillan.

Clarke, Desmond. 1982. *Descartes' Philosophy of Science.* University Park: Penn State University Press.

Clausius, Rudolf. 1867. *The Mechanical Theory of Heat.* London: Van Voorst.

Cleveland, C., Costanza, R., Hall, A., and Kaufman, R. 1984. "Energy and the United States Economy." *Science* (225):890–7.

Clower, Robert. 1970. "The Keynesian Counterrevolution." In R. Clower, ed., *Monetary Theory.* Baltimore: Penguin.

Clower, Robert. 1984. *Money and Markets.* New York: Cambridge University Press.

Coats, A. W. 1954. "The Historist Reaction in English Political Economy 1870–90." *Economica* (21):143–53.

Coats, A. W. 1976. "Economics and Psychology." In Spiro Latsis, ed., *Method and Appraisal in Economics*. Cambridge, U.K.: Cambridge University Press.

Cohen, Avi. 1984. "Technological Change as Historical Process." *Journal of Economic History* (44):775–99.

Cohen, Esther. 1986. "Law, Folklore and Animal Lore." *Past and Present* (110):6–37.

Cohen, I. B., ed. 1981. *The Conservation of Energy and the Principle of Least Action*. New York: Arno.

Cohen, I. B. 1985. *Revolution in Science*. Cambridge, Mass.: Harvard University Press.

Collins, Harry. 1985. *Changing Order*. London: Sage.

Cooter, R., and Rappoport, P. 1984. "Were the Ordinalists Wrong about Welfare Economics?" *Journal of Economic Literature* (22):507–30.

Copeland, Morris. 1958. *Fact and Theory in Economics*. Ithaca: Cornell University Press.

Costanza, Robert. 1980. "Embodied Energy and Economic Valuation." *Science* (210):1219–24.

Cottrell, Frederick. 1953. *Energy and Society*. New York: McGraw-Hill.

Cournot, A. A. 1897. *Research into the Mathematical Principles of the Theory of Wealth*. Trans. by N. Bacon. New York: Macmillan.

Craver, Earlene. 1986. "Patronage and the Direction of Research in Economics." *Minerva* (24):205–22.

Craver, Earlene, and Leijonhufvud, Axel. 1987. "Economics in Amerca: The Continental Influence." *History of Political Economy*, (19):173–82.

Crease, Robert, and Mann, Charles. 1986. *The Second Creation*. New York: Macmillan.

Creedy, John. 1980. "The Early Use of Lagrange Multipliers in Economics." *Economic Journal* (96):808–11.

Creedy, John. 1986. *Edgeworth and the Development of Neoclassical Economics*. Oxford: Blackwell.

Croll, James. 1876. "On the Transformation of Gravity." *Philosophical Magazine* Series V (2):241–54.

Crosland, M., and Smith, C. 1978. "The Transmission of Physics from France to Britain." *Historical Studies in the Physical Sciences* (4):89–136.

Crowe, Michael. 1967. *A History of Vector Analysis*. South Bend: Notre Dame University Press.

d'Abro, A. 1951. *The Rise of the New Physics*. New York: Dover,

Dahl, Per. 1963. "Ludwig A. Colding and the Conservation of Energy." *Centaurus* (8):174–88.

Daly, Herman. 1968. "On Economics as a Life Science." *Journal of Political Economy* (76):392–405.

Daly, Herman. 1980. "The Economic Thought of Fredrick Soddy." *Hsitory of Political Economy* (12):469–88.

Daly, Herman, and Umaña, Alvaro. 1981. *Energy, Economics and the Environment*. Boulder: Westview Press.

Dauben, Joseph. 1979. *Georg Cantor.* Cambridge, Mass.: Harvard University Press.

Dauben, Joseph. 1984. "Conceptual Revolutions and the History of Mathematics." In E. Mendelsohn, ed., *Transformation and Tradition in the Sciences.* Cambridge, U.K.: Cambridge University Press.

David. Paul. 1975. *Technical Choice, Innovation, and Economic Growth.* New York: Cambridge University Press.

Davidsen, T. 1986. "Westergaard, Edgeworth, and the Use of Lagrange Multipliers in Economics." *Economic Journal* (96):808–11.

Davies, Paul. 1979. *The Forces of Nature.* Cambridge, U.K.: Cambridge University Press.

Davies, Paul. 1980. *Other Worlds.* New York: Simon & Schuster.

Davis, Harold T. 1941a. *Theory of Econometrics.* Bloomington: Principia.

Davis, Harold T. 1941b. *The Analysis of Economic Time Series.* Bloomington: Principia

Day, Richard. 1983. "The Emergence of Chaos from Classical Economic Growth." *Quarterly Journal of Economics* (98):201–13.

Debreu, Gerard. 1959. *The Theory of Value.* New Haven: Yale University Press.

Debreu, Gerard. 1972. "Smooth Preferences." *Econometrica* (40):603–15.

De Jong, Frits. 1967. *Dimensional Analysis for Economists.* Amsterdam: North Holland.

Deltete, R. 1983. *The Energetics Controversy in Late 19th Century Germany.* Ph.D. thesis, Yale University.

de Marchi, Neil. 1970. "The Empirical Content and Longevity of Ricardian Economics." *Economica* (37):257–76.

de Marchi, Neil. 1988. "Popper and the LSE Economists." In N. de Marchi, ed., *The Popperian Legacy in Economics.* New York: Cambridge University Press.

Denbigh, Kenneth. 1975. *An Inventive Universe.* New York: Braziller.

Denbigh, K., and Denbigh, J. 1985. *Entropy in Relation to Incomplete Knowledge.* Cambridge, U.K.: Cambridge University Press.

Dennis, Ken. 1977. *Competition in the History of Economic Thought.* New York: Arno.

Dennis, Ken. 1982. "Economic Theory and Mathematical Translation." *Journal of Economic Issues,* Sept. (16):691–712.

Descartes, René. 1972. *Treatise on Man.* Trans. T. Hall. Cambridge, Mass.: Harvard University Press.

Dietz, Ludwig. 1934. *Wirtschaft als Kinetic.* Heidelberg: Lippl.

Dirac, P. 1936. "Does Conservation of Energy Hold in Atomic Processes?" *Nature,* Feb (22):298–9.

Dircks, Henry. 1870. *Perpetual Motion.* London: Spon.

Divisia, Francis. 1925. "L'Indice Monetaire et la Théorie de la Monnaie." *Revue d'Economie Politique* (39):1121–51; (40):49–81.

Dobb, Maurice. 1973. *Theories of Value and Distribution Since Adam Smith.* Cambridge, U.K.: Cambridge University Press.

Dorfman, R., Samuelson, P., and Solow, R. 1958. *Linear Programming and Economic Analysis*. New York: McGraw-Hill.

Douglas, Mary. 1970. *Natural Symbols*. London: Barrie & Jenkins.

Douglas, Mary. 1975. *Implicit Meanings*. London: Routledge & Kegan Paul.

Douglas, Mary. 1986. *How Institutions Think*. Syracuse: Syracuse University Press.

Douglas, Mary, and Isherwood, B. 1979. *The World of Goods*. New York: Basic.

Drake, S., ed. 1960. *On Motion and Mechanics*. Madison: University of Wisconsin Press.

Drazen, Alan. 1980. "Recent Developments in Macroeconomic Disequilibrium Theory." *Econometrica* (48):283–306.

Dupin, Charles. 1827. *Forces Productives et Commerciales de la France*. Paris:

Dupré, John, ed. 1987. *The Latest on the Best*. Cambridge, Mass.: MIT Press.

Dupuit, Jules. 1952. "On the Measure of Utility of Public Works." Trans. Barbach, *International Economic Papers* no. 2.

Durbin, John. 1985. *Modern Algebra*. 2nd ed. New York: Wiley.

Dyson, Freeman. 1971. "Energy in the Universe." *Scientific American* (225):51–9.

Eagly, Robert. 1974. *The Structure of Classical Economic Theory*. Oxford: Oxford University Press.

Eatwell, John. 1975. "Scarce and Produced Commodities." Ph.D. thesis, Harvard University.

Eddington, Sir Arthur. 1930. *The Nature of the Physical World*. London: Macmillan.

Eddington, Sir Arthur. 1935. *New Pathways in Science*. New York: Macmillan.

Edgeworth, Francis Ysidro. 1877. *New and Old Methods of Ethics*. Oxford: John Millar.

Edgeworth, Francis Ysidro. 1881. *Mathematical Psychics*. London: Kegan Paul.

Edgeworth, Francis Ysidro. 1925. *Papers Relating to Political Economy*. 2 vols. London: Macmillan

Ekelund, R., and Hebert, R. 1978. "French Engineers, Welfare Economics, and Public Finance in the 19th Century." *History of Political Economy* (10):636–68.

Elkhana, Yehuda. 1970. "Helmholtz's Kraft: An Illustration of Concepts in Flux." *Historical Studies in Physical Science* (2):263–98.

Elkhana, Yehuda. 1974. *The Discovery of the Conservation of Energy*. London: Hutchinson.

Ellerman, David. 1984. "Arbitrage Theory." *SIAM Review* (26):241–61.

Elliott, J., and Dawber, P. 1979. *Symmetry in Physics*. Oxford: Oxford University Press.

Elster, Jon. 1975. *Leibniz et la Formation de l'Esprit Capitaliste*. Paris: Aubier.

Elzinga, Aant. 1972. *On a Research Program in Early Modern Physics*. Göteborg: Akademiforlaget.

Enke, Steven. 1951. "Equilibrium among Spatially Separated Markets: Solution by Electric Analogue." *Econometrica* (19):40–47.

English, J. 1974. "Economic Theory – New Perspectives." In J. Van Dixhoorn and F. Evans, eds., *Physical Structure in Systems Theory*. New York: Academic.

Enros, Philip. 1979. "The Analytical Society." Ph.D. thesis, History, University of Toronto.

Etner, Franz. 1986. "Les Enseignements Economiques dans les Grandes Ecoles." *Economies et Sociétés* (20):166–74.

Faber, Malte, and Proops, J. 1985. "Interdisciplinary Research Between Economists and Physical Scientists: Retrospect and Prospect." *Kyklos* (38):599–616.

Farjoun, E., and Machover, M. 1983. *Laws of Chaos*. London: NLB Verso.

Feinberg, G., and Goldhaber, M. 1963. "The Conservation Laws of Physics." *Scientific American* (209):36–45.

Feiwel, George, ed. 1982. *Samuelson and Neoclassical Economics*. Boston: Kluwer Nihoff.

Feiwel, George, ed. 1985. *Issues in Contemporary Macroeconomics and Distribution*. Albany: SUNY Press.

Ferguson, C. 1969. *The Neoclassical Theory of Production and Distribution*. Cambridge, U.K.: Cambridge University Press.

Feynman, Richard. 1965. *The Character of Physical Law*. Cambridge, Mass.: MIT Press.

Feynman, Richard. 1985. *Surely You're Joking Mr. Feynman!* New York: Norton.

Fine, Arthur. 1977. "Conservation, the Sum Rule and Confirmation." *Philosophy of Science* (44):95–106.

Fisher, Franklin. 1983. *Disequilibrium Foundations of Equilibrium Economics*. New York: Cambridge University Press.

Fisher, Irving. 1919. *The Nature of Capital and Income*. New York: Macmillan.

Fisher, Irving. 1926. *Mathematical Investigations into the Theory of Value and Prices*. New Haven: Yale University Press.

Fisher, Robert. 1986. *The Logic of Economic Discovery*. New York: New York University Press

Foley, Vernard. 1973. "An Origin of the Tableau Oeconomique." *History of Political Economy* (5):121–50.

Foley, Vernard. 1975. "Reply to Professor McNulty." *History of Political Economy* (7):379–89.

Foley, Vernard. 1976. *The Social Physics of Adam Smith*. West Lafayette: Purdue University Press.

Fontenelle, Bernard de. 1790. *Oeuvres*. Vol. 6, Paris: Bastien.

Forman, Paul. 1971. "Weimar Culture, Casuality and Quantum Theory." *Historical Studies in the Physical Sciences* (3):1–116.

Foucault, Michel. 1973. *The Order of Things*. New York: Vintage.

Foucault, Michel. 1980. *The History of Sexuality*. vol. I. New York: Vintage.

Fox, Robert. 1974. "The Rise and Fall of Laplacean Physics." *Historical Studies in the Physical Sciences* (4):89–136.

Franklin, Allan. 1979. "The Discovery and Nondiscovery of Parity Nonconservation." *Studies in the History and Philosophy of Science* (10):201–57.

424   **Bibliography**

Franksen, O. 1969. "Mathematical Programming in Economics by Physical Analogies," *Simulation* (12):297–14; (13):25–42, 63–87.
Franksen, O. 1974. "Basic Concepts in Engineering and Economics." In J. van Dixhoorn and F. Evans, eds., *Physical Structure in Systems Theory*. New York: Academic.
Fraser, L. 1937. *Economic Thought and Language*. London: A. Black.
Freudenthal, Gideon. 1986. *Atom and Individual in the Age of Newton*. Boston: Reidel.
Friedman, Milton, and Wallis, Alan. 1942. "The Empirical Derivation of Indifference Functions." In O. Lange, F. McIntyre, and T. Yntema, eds., *Studies in Mathematical Economics and Econometrics*. Chicago: Universtiy of Chicago Press.
Frisch, Ragnar. 1926. "Sur un Problème d'Economie Pure." *Norsk Matematisk Forenings Skrifter* (16):1–40.
Frisch, Ragnar. 1932. *New Methods of Measuring Marginal Utility*. Tubingen: Mohr.
Frisch, Ragnar. 1933. "Monopole-Polypole-La Notion de Force dans l'Economie" *Nationalokonomisk Tidsskrift* (71):241–59.
Fuss, M., and McFadden, D., eds. 1978. *Production Economics*. Vol. I. Amsterdam: North Holland.
Gabbey, Alan. 1985. "The Mechanical Philosophy and Its Problems. In J. Pitt, ed., *Change and Progress in Modern Science*. Boston: Reidel.
Galaty, David. 1974. "The Philosophical Basis of Mid-Nineteenth Century German Reductionism." *Journal of the History of Medicine* (29):295–316.
Galison, Peter. 1983. "Re-reading the Past from the End of Physics". In L. Graham, W. Lepenies, and P. Weingart, eds., *Functions and Uses of Disciplinary History*. Boston: Reidel.
Garegnani, P. 1976. "On a Change in the Notion of Equilibrium." In M. Brown et al., eds., *Essays in Modern Capital Theory*. Amsterdam: North Holland.
Garegnani, P. 1984. "Value and Distribution in the Classical Economists and Marx." *Oxford Economic Papers* (36):291–325.
Geddes, Patrick. 1883–4. "Analysis of the Principles of Economics." *Proceedings of the Royal Society of Edinburgh* (12):943–80.
Georgescu-Roegen, Nicholas. 1971. *The Entropy Law and the Economic Process*. Cambridge, Mass.: Harvard University Press.
Georgescu-Roegen, Nicholas. 1976. *Energy and Economic Myths*. London: Pergamon.
Georgescu-Roegen, Nicholas. 1979. "Energy Analysis and Economic Valuation." *Southern Economic Journal* (45):1023–58.
Georgescu-Roegen, Nicholas. 1986. "The Entropy Law and the Economic Process in Retrospect." *Eastern Economic Journal* (12):3–26.
Gibbins, Peter. 1987. *Particles and Paradoxes*. Cambridge, U.K.: Cambridge University Press.
Giedymin, Jerzy. *Science and Convention*. Oxford: Pergamon.
Giffen, R. 1889. *The Growth of Capital*. London: Macmillan.

Giffin, Phillip, and Hutchinson, E. 1984. "A Metaphysical Notion: The Symmetry Between Consumer and Producer Demand." *Journal of Post Keynesian Economics* (7):134–6.

Gilliland, Martha. 1975. "Energy Analysis and Public Policy." *Science* (189):1051–6.

Gillispie, C. S. 1965. "Science and Technology." *New Cambridge Modern History.* Vol. 9, Cambridge, U.K.: Cambridge University Press.

Gilmore, Robert. 1983. "Le Châtelier Reciprocal Relations and the Mechanical Analogue." *American Journal of Physics* (51):733–43.

Gleick, James. 1987. *Chaos.* New York: Viking.

Goldman, Lawrence. 1987. "A Peculiarity of the English?" *Past & Present* (114):133–71.

Goldstein, Herbert. 1950. *Classical Mechanics.* Reading, Mass. Addison-Wesley.

Goldstein, Herman. 1980. *A History of the Calculus of Variations.* New York: Springer Verlag.

Gooding, David. 1980a. "Faraday, Thomson, and the Concept of the Magnetic Field." *British Journal For History of Science* (13):91–120.

Gooding, David. 1980b. "Metaphysics versus Measurement: The Conversion and Conservation of Force in Faraday's Physics." *Annals of Science* (37):1–29.

Gossen, H. H. 1983. *The Laws of Human Relations.* Cambridge, Mass.: MIT Press.

Gouldner, Alvin. 1973. *For Sociology.* New York: Basic.

Gouldner, Alvin, 1980. *The Two Marxisms.* Seabury.

Gower, Barry. 1973. "Speculation in Physics: The History and Practice of Naturphilosophie." *Studies in the History and Philosophy of Science* (3):301–6.

Graham, L., Lepenies, W., and Weingart, P., eds. 1983. *Functions and Uses of Disciplinary Histories.* Boston: Reidel.

Gram, Harvey, and Walsh, Vivien. 1983. "Joan Robinson's Economics in Retrospect." *Journal of Economic Literature* (21):518–50.

Grattan-Guinness, Ivor. 1980. *From the Calculus to Set Theory 1630–1910.* London: Dudsworth.

Grattan-Guinness, Ivor. 1984. "Work for the Workers." *Annals of Science* (41):1–33.

Graves, J. C. 1971. *The Conceptual Foundations of Contemporary Relativity Theory.* Cambridge, Mass.: M.I.T. Press.

Green, D. 1894. "Pain Cost and Opportunity Cost." *Quarterly Journal of Economics* (8):218–29.

Green, H. J. 1971. *Consumer Theory.* Baltimore: Penguin.

Griffin, David, ed. 1986. *Physics and the Ultimate Significance of Time.* Albany: Suny Press.

Griffiths, J. B. 1985. *The Theory of Classical Dynamics.* Cambridge, U.K.: Cambridge University Press.

Grinevald, Jacques. 1976. "La Révolution Carnotienne: Thermodynamique, Economie et Idéologie." *Cahiers Vilfredo Pareto* (36):39–79.

Groenewegen, P. D., ed. 1977. *The Economics of A. R. J. Turgot.* Amsterdam: Martinus Nijhoff, 1977.

Grossmann, Hendryk. 1987. "The Social Foundations of Mechanistic Philosophy and Manufacture." *Science in Context* (1):105–91.

Grubbström, Robert. 1972. "The Missing Analogy?" *Operation Research Quarterly* (22):182–5.

Grubbström, Robert. 1973. *Economic Decisions in Space and Time.* Gothenburg: BAS.

Grubbström, Robert. 1980. "Towards a Theoretical Basis for Energy Economics." Technology Report, Naval Postgraduate School, Monterey, California.

Guth, Alan. 1983. "Speculations on the Origin of the Matter, Energy, and Entropy of the Universe." In A. Guth, K. Huang, and R. Jaffe, eds. *Asymptotic Realms of Physics.* Cambridge, Mass.: M.I.T. Press.

Haas, A. E. 1909. *Die Entwicklungsgeshichte des Satzes von der Erhaltung der Kraft.* Wein: Mohr.

Hacking, Ian. 1975. *The Emergence of Probability.* Cambridge, U.K.: Cambridge University Press.

Hahn, Frank. 1975. "Revival of Political Economy: The Wrong Issues and the Wromg Argument." *Economic Record* (51):360–4.

Hahn, Frank. 1985. "Some Keynesian Reflections on Monetarism." In Fausto Vicarelli, ed., *Keynes' Relevance Today.* Philadelphia: University of Pennsylvania Press.

Halévy, Elie. 1972. *The Growth of Philosophical Radicalism.* London: Faber.

Hamilton, William. 1834. "On a General Method in Dynamics." *Philosophical Transactions of the Royal Society* (II):247–57

Hankins, Thomas. 1980. *Sir William Rowan Hamilton.* Baltimore: Johns Hopkins University Press.

Hannon, Bruce. 1973. "An Energy Standard of Value." *Annals of the American Academy of Political Science* (410):139–53.

Hanson, Norbert. 1963. *The Concept of the Positron.* Cambridge, U.K.: Cambridge University Press.

Harcourt, Geoffrey. 1972. *Some Cambridge Controversies in the Theory of Capital.* Cambridge, U.K.: Cambridge University Press.

Harcourt, Geoffrey. 1982. *The Social Science Imperialists.* London: Routledge & Kegan Paul.

Harcourt, Geoffrey. 1984. "Reflecting on the Development of Economics as a Discipline." *History of Political Economy* (16):489–517.

Harcourt, Geoffrey. 1986. "On the Influence of Piero Sraffa on the Contribution of Joan Robinson to Economic Theory." *Economic Journal Conference Papers* (96):96–108.

Harcourt, Geoffrey, and Laing, N., eds. 1971. *Capital and Growth.* Baltimore: Penguin.

Harding, Sandra, ed. 1976. *Can Theories Be Refuted?* Boston: Reidel.

Harman, P. M. 1982a. *Energy, Force and Matter.* Cambridge, U.K.: Cambridge University Press.

Harman, P. M. 1982b. *Metaphysics and Natural Philosophy.* Sussex: Harvester.

Harman, P., ed. 1985. *Wranglers and Physicists.* Manchester: Manchester University Press.

Hatfield, H. 1922. "Earliest Uses of the English Term Capital." *Quarterly Journal of Economics* (26):547–8.

Hayek, Friedrich. 1979. *The Counterrevolution of Science.* Indianapolis: Liberty Press.

Hegel, G. W. F. 1967. *The Phenomenology of Mind.* New York: Harper & Row.

Hegeland, Hugo. 1954. *The Multiplier Theory.* Lund: Gleerup.

Heidelberger, M. 1981. "Some Patterns of Change in the Baconian Sciences in Early Nineteenth Century Germany." In H. Jahnke and M. Otte, eds., *Epistemological and Social Problems in the Sciences of the Early Nineteenth Century.* Boston: Reidel.

Heimann, P. M. 1974. "Helmholtz and Kant: The Metaphysical Foundations." *Studies in the History and Philosophy of Science* (5):205–38.

Heimann, P. M., and McGuire, J. 1971. "Newtonian Forces and Lockean Powers." *Historical Studies in the Physical Sciences* (3):233–306.

Heimann, P. M. 1977. "Geometry and Nature: Leibniz and John Bernoullis' Theory of Motion." *Centaurus* (21):1–26.

Helm, Georg. 1887. *Die Lehre von der Energie.* Leipzig: Felix.

Helmholtz, Hermann von. 1887. "Rede Uber Die Entdeckungs – Geschicte Des Princips Der Kleisten Actions." In *Geschichte Der Koniglich Preussischen Akademie Der Wissenschaften Zu Berlin.* Vol. 2 (1900). Berlin: Preussischen Akademie, pp. 287–304.

Helmholtz, Hermann von. 1971. *Selected Writings.* Russell Kahl, ed. Middletown, Conn.: Wesleyan University Press.

Helmholtz, Hermann von. 1977. *Epistemological Writings.* Boston: Reidel.

Henderson, James. 1984. "Just Notions of Political Economy – George Pryme, the First Professor of Political Economy at Cambridge." *Research In the History of Economic Thought and Methodology* (2):1–20.

Henderson, John. 1984. "The Political Economy Club." *Research in the History of Economic Thought and Methodology* (2):77–105.

Herford, C. H. 1931. *Philip Henry Wicksteed.* London: Dent.

Hertz, Heinrich. 1956. *The Principles of Mechanics.* New York: Dover.

Hesse, Mary. 1965. *Forces and Fields.* Totawa: Littlefield, Adams.

Hesse, Mary. 1966. *Models and Analogies in Science.* South Bend: Notre Dame University Press.

Hesse, Mary. 1974. *The Structure of Scientific Inference.* Berkeley: University of California Press.

Hesse, Mary. 1980. *Revolution and Reconstruction in the Philosophy of Science.* Bloomington: Indiana University Press.

Hessen, Boris. 1931. "The Social and Economic Roots of Newton's Principia." In N. Bukharin, ed., *Science at the Crossroads.* Reprint 1971. London: Cass.

Hetherington, Noriss. 1983. "Issac Newton's Influence on Adam Smith's Natural Laws in Economics." *Journal of the History of Ideas* (44):497–505.

Hicks, J. R. 1946. *Value and Capital.* 2nd ed. Oxford: Clarendon Press.

Hicks, J. R. 1965. *Capital and Growth*. Oxford: Oxford University Press.

Hicks, J. R. 1970. "A Neo-Austrian Growth Theory." *Economic Journal* (80):257–81.

Hicks, J. R. 1973. *Capital and Time*. Oxford: Oxford University Press.

Hicks, J. R. 1975. "Revival of Political Economy." *Economic Record* (51):360–4.

Hicks, J. R. 1979. *Causality in Economics*. New York: Basic.

Hicks, J. R. and Allen, R. 1934. "A Reconsideration of the Theory of Value." *Economica* (14):52–76, 196–219.

Hiebert, Erwin. 1962. *Historical Roots of the Principle of the Conservation of Energy*. Madison: State Historical Society of Wisconsin.

Hiebert, Erwin. 1971. "The Energetics Controversy and the New Thermodynamics." In D. Roller, ed., *Perspectives in the History of Science and Technology*. Norman: University of Oklahoma Press.

Hirschman, Albert. 1970. *Exit, Voice, and Loyalty*. Cambridge, Mass.: Harvard University Press.

Hirshleifer, Jack. 1977. "Economics from a Biological Viewpoint." *Journal of Law and Economics* (20):1–52.

Hollander, Samuel. 1982. "On the Substantive Identity of the Ricardian and Neoclassical Conceptions of Economic Organization." *Canadian Journal of Economics* (15):4:586–612.

Hollander, Samuel. 1987. *Classical Economics*. Oxford: Blackwell.

[Horner, Francis] 1803. Review of Canard. *Edinburgh Review* (2):431–50.

Howard, M., and King, J. 1985[1975]. *The Political Economy of Marx*. 2nd ed. New York: New York University Press.

Howey, R. S. 1960. *The Rise of the Marginal Utility School*. Lawrence: University of Kansas Press.

Howitt, P. 1973. "Walras and Monetary Theory." *Western Economic Journal* (11):487–99.

Hoy, David. 1986. *Foucault: A Critical Reader*. Oxford: Blackwell.

Huettner, David. 1976. "Net Energy Analysis: An Economic Assessment." *Science* (192):101–4.

Hufbauer, Karl. 1982. *The Formation of the German Chemical Community*. Berkeley: University of California Press.

Hurwicz, Leonid, and Richter, Marcel. 1979. "An Integrability Condition with Applications to Utility Theory and Thermodynamics." *Journal of Mathematical Economics* (6):1–14

Hutchison, Keith. 1976. "Mayer's Hypothesis: A Study of the Early Years of Thermodynamics." *Centaurus* (20):279–304.

Hutchison, Keith. 1981. "W. J. M. Rankine and the Rise of Thermodynamics." *British Journal for History of Science* (14):1–26.

Hutchison, Terrence. 1953. *A Review of Economic Doctrines, 1870–1929*. Oxford: Oxford University Press.

Iberall, Arthur. 1984. "Contributions to a Physical Science for the Study of Civilization." *Journal of Social and Biological Structures* (7):259–83.

Iltis, Carolyn. 1973. "The Decline of Cartesianism in Mechanics." *Isis* (64):356–73.

Immler, Hans. 1985. *Natur in der ökonomischen Theorie.* Opalden: Westdeutscher Verlag.

Ingrao, Bruna, and Israel, Giorgio. 1985. "General Equilibrium Theory: A History of Ineffectual Paradigm Shifts." *Fundamenta Scientiae* (6):1–45, 89–125.

Jackson, Stanley. 1970. "Force and Kindred Notions in 18th Century Neurophysiology and Medical Psychology." *Bulletin of the History of Medicine* (44):397–410, 539–54.

Jaffe, William. 1983. *William Jaffe's Essays on Walras.* Cambridge, U.K.: Cambridge University Press.

Jahnke, H., and Otte, M., eds. 1981. *Epistemological and Social Problems of the Sciences in the Early 19th Century.* Boston: Reidel.

Jaynes, E. T. 1957. "Information Theory and Statistical Mechanisics." *Physical Review* (106):620–30; (108):171–90.

Jaynes, E. T. 1983. "How Should We Use Entropy in Economics?" Unpublished paper, Washington Universtiy, December.

Jaynes, E. T. 1985a. "Some Random Observations." *Synthese* (63):36–50.

Jaynes, E. T. 1985b. "Macroscopic Prediction." Unpublished paper, Washington University, May.

Jenkin, Fleeming. 1887. *Papers Literary and Scientific.* 2 vols. London: Longmans, Green.

Jevons, W. S. 1905a. *The Principles of Science,* 2nd ed. London: Macmillan.

Jevons, W. S. 1905b. *Principles of Economics.* London: Macmillan.

Jevons, W. S. 1970. *The Theory of Political Economy.* R. Black, ed. Baltimore: Penguin.

Jevons, W. S. 1972–1981. *The Papers and Correspondence of W. S. Jevons.* 7 vols, R. Black, ed. London: Macmillan.

Johnson, W. 1913. "The Pure Theory of Utility Curves." *Economic Journal* (23):483–513.

Joule, James. 1884. *The Scientific Papers.* London: Macmillan.

Jungnickel, C., and McCormmach, R. 1986. *Intellectual Mastery of Nature.* 2 vols. Chicago: University of Chicago Press.

Kahl, Russell, ed. 1971. *Selected Writings of Hermann von Helmholtz.* Middletown, Conn.: Wesleyan University Press.

Kant, Immanuel. 1953. *Prolegomena to Any Future Metaphysics That Will Be Able to Present Itself as a Science.* Manchester: University of Manchester Press.

Katzner, Donald. 1970. *Static Demand Theory.* New York: Macmillan.

Katzner, Donald. 1983. *Analysis Without Measurement.* New York: Cambridge University Press.

Kauder, Emil. 1965. *A History of Marginal Utility Theory.* Princeton: Princeton University Press.

Kauffman, George. 1986. *Frederick Soddy (1877–1956)* Boston: Reidel

Kellogg, Oliver. 1929. *Foundations of Potential Theory.* New York: Ungar.

Kelly, Thomas. 1937. *Explanation and Reality in the Philosophy of Emile Meyerson.* Princeton: Princeton University Press.

Kendrick, John. 1970. "The Historical Development of National Income Accounts." *History of Political Economy* (2):284–315.

Kennedy, C. 1968. "Time, Interest and the Production Function." In J. N. Wolfe, ed., *Value, Capital and Growth.* Edinburgh: Edinburgh University Press.

Kern, Stephen. 1983. *The Culture of Time and Space 1880–1918.* London: Weidenfeld and Nicholson.

Keynes, John M. 1951. *Essays in Biography.* New York: Norton.

Keynes, John M. 1964. *The General Theory of Employment, Interest and Money.* New York: Harcourt Brace.

Keynes, John M. 1973–. *The Collected Writings.* Cambridge, U.K.: Cambridge University Press.

Kitcher, Philip. 1985. *Vaulting Ambition.* Cambridge, Mass.: MIT Press.

Klein, Martin. 1970. *Paul Ehrenfest.* Vol. I. Amsterdam: North Holland.

Kline, Morris. 1972. *Mathematical Thought from Ancient to Modern Times.* New York: Oxford University Press.

Kline, Morris. 1980. *Mathematics: The Loss of Certainty.* New York: Oxford University Press.

Knight, Frank. 1925. "Economic Psychology and the Value Problem." *Quarterly Journal of Economics* (33):372–409.

Knight, Frank. 1927. "Review of David Atlins, *The Measurement of Economic Value*" and rejoinder by author. *Journal of Political Economy* (35):552–7.

Knight, Frank. 1956. "Statics and Dynamics." In *On the History and Methodology of Economics.* Chicago: University of Chicago Press.

Knight, Frank. 1965 [1921]. *Risk, Uncertainty and Profit.* New York: Harper & Row.

Knorr-Cetina, Karin, and Mulkay, Michael. 1983. *Science Observed: Perspectives on the Social Study of Science.* London: Sage.

Koenigsburger, Leo. 1965. *Hermann von Helmholtz.* New York: Dover.

Koopmans, Tjalling. 1957. *Three Essays on the State of Economic Science.* New York: McGraw Hill.

Koslow, A. 1967. *The Changeless Order.* New York: Braziller.

Koyré, Alexandre. 1978. *Galileo Studies.* Atlantic Highlands: Humanities Press.

Krantz, David, Luce, R., Suppes, P., and Tversky, A. 1971. *Foundations of Measurement.* Vol. I. New York: Academic.

Krause, Ulrich. 1982. *Money and Abstract Labor.* London: NLB.

Krüger, Lorentz, Daston, Lorraine, and Heidelberger, Michael, eds. 1987. *The Probabilistic Revolution.* Cambridge, Mass.: MIT Press.

Kuhn, Thomas. 1958. "The Caloric Theory of Adiabatic Compression." *Isis* (40):132–40.

Kuhn, Thomas. 1959. "Energy Conservation as an Example of Simultaneous Discovery." In M. Clagett, ed., *Critical Problems in the History of Science.* Madison: University of Wisconsin Press.

Kuhn, Thomas. 1977. *The Essential Tension.* Chicago: University of Chicago Press.

Kula, Witold. 1986. *Measures and Men*. Princeton: Princeton University Press.

Kurz, Heinz. 1985. "Sraffa's Contribution to the Debate in Capital Theory." *Contributions to Political Economy* (4):3–24.

Kurz, Heinz. 1986. "Classical and Early Neoclassical Economists on Joint Production." *Metroeconomica* (39):1–37.

Lagrange, J. L. 1965. *Mécanique Analytique*. Paris: Albert Blanchard.

La Lumia, Joseph. 1966. *The Ways of Reason*. New York: Humanities.

Laibman, David. 1973. "Value and Prices of Production." *Science and Society* (37):404–36.

Lanczos, Cornelius. 1949. *The Variational Principles of Mechanics*. Toronto: University of Toronto Press.

Lanczos, Cornelius. 1970. *Space Through the Ages*. New York: Academic Press.

Landshoff, P., and Metherell, A. 1979. *Simple Quantum Physics*. Cambridge, U.K.: Cambridge University Press.

Latour, Bruno. 1987. *Science in Action*. Cambridge, Mass.: Harvard University Press.

Latsis, Spiro. 1976. *Method and Appraisal in Economics*. Cambridge, U.K.: Cambridge University Press.

Laundhardt, Wilhelm. 1885. *Mathematische Begrundung der Volkswirtschaftslehre*. Leipzig: Englelmann.

Laurent, Hermann. 1870. *Traité de Mécanique Rationelle*. Paris: Gauther-Villars

Laurent, Hermann. 1902. *Petit Traité d' Economie Politique Mathématique*. Paris: Schmid.

Layton, Edwin. 1962. "Veblen and Engineers." *American Quarterly* (14):64–72.

Layton, Edwin. 1971. *The Revolt of the Engineers*. Cleveland: Case Western Reserve University Press.

Lehfeldt, R. 1914. "The Elasticity of the Demand for Wheat." *Economic Journal* (24):212–17.

Leontief, W. 1982. "Letter: Academic Economics." *Science* (217):104–7

Letwin, William. 1963. *The Origins of Scientific Economics*. London: Methuen.

Levhari, David. 1965. "A Nonsubstitution Theorem and Switching of Techniques." *Quarterly Journal of Economics* (74):98–105.

Levine, A. L. 1983. "Marshall's Principles and the Biological Viewpoint." *Manchester School*, (51):276–93.

Levine, David. 1982. *Economic Studies: Contribution to the Critique of Economic Theory*. Boston: Routledge & Kegan Paul.

Levine, David. 1980. "On the Classical Theory of Markets." *Australian Economic Papers* (19):1–15.

Lichnerowicz, M., and Lichnerowicz, A. 1971. "Economie et Thermodynamique: Un Modèle d'échange économique." *Economies et Sociétés* (5):1641–86.

Lindsay, Jack. 1974. *Blast Power and Ballistics*. New York: Barnes & Noble.

Lindsay, Robert. 1927. "Physical Laws and Social Phenomena." *Scientific Monthly* (27):127–32.

Lindsay, Robert Bruce. 1973. *Julius Robert Mayer: Prophet of Energy*. New York: Pergamon.

Lindsay, Robert Bruce, ed. 1975. *Energy: Historical Development of the Concept*. Stroudsburg, Penn.: Dowden, Hutchinson, and Ross.

Lindsay, Robert Bruce, ed. 1976. *Applications of Energy: Nineteenth Century*. Stroudsburg, Penn.: Dowden, Huthchinson, and Ross.

Lindsay, Robert Bruce. 1983. "Social Exemplifications of Physical Principles." In A. van der Merwe, ed., *Old and New Questions in Physics*. New York: Plenum.

Lippi, Marco. 1979. *Value and Naturalism in Marx*. London: NLB.

Lisman, J. 1949a. "Economics and Thermodynamics: A Remark on Davis' Theory of Budgets." *Econometrica* (17):59–62.

Lisman, J. 1949b. *Econometrics, Statistics and Thermodynamics*. The Hague: Netherlands Postal and Telephone Services.

Llobera, Josep. 1981. "The Enlightenment and Adam Smith's Conception of Science." *Knowledge and Society* (3):109–36.

Lloyd, W. F. 1837. *Lectures on Population, Value, Poor Laws and Rent*. London: Roorke & Varty.

Lotka, Alfred. 1924. *Elements of Physical Biology*. New York: Dover.

Lowe, A. 1951. "On the Mechanistic Approach in Economics." *Social Research* (18):403–34.

Lucas, Robert. 1981. *Studies in Business Cycle Theory*. Cambridge, Mass.: MIT Press.

Mach, Ernest. 1911. *History and Root of the Principle of the Conservation of Energy*. Trans. by P. Jourdain. Chicago: Open Court.

Mackenzie, Donald. 1981. *Statistics in Britain*. Edinburgh: Edinburgh University Press.

Magill, M. 1970. *On a General Economic Theory of Motion*. Berlin: Springer-Verlag.

Maloney, John. 1985. *Marshall, Orthodoxy, and the Professionalization of Economics*. Cambridge, U.K.: Cambridge University Press.

Mandelbrot, Benoit. 1977. *Fractals: Form, Chance and Dimension*. San Francisco: Freeman.

Markus, Gyorgy. 1987. "Why Is There No Hermeneutics of the Natural Sciences?" *Science in Context* (1):5–51.

Marsden, J., Pingry, D., and Whinston, A. 1974. "Engineering Foundations of Production Functions." *Journal of Economic Theory* (9);124–40.

Marshall, Alfred. 1898. "Mechanical and Biological Analogies in Economics." Reprinted in A. C. Pigou, ed., *Memorials of Alfred Marshall*. London: Macmillan.

Marshall, Alfred. 1947. *Principles of Economics*. 8th ed. London: Macmillan.

Martinez-Alier, Juan. 1987. *Ecological Economics*. Oxford: Blackwell.

Marx, Karl. 1963. *Theories of Surplus Value*. Vol. I, 1968; Vol. II, 1971; Vol. III. Moscow: Progress Publication.

Marx, Karl. 1973. *Grundrisse*. New York: Vintage.

Marx, Karl. 1976. *Capital.* Vol. I, 1978; Vol. II, 1983; Vol. III. New York: Vintage.

Mathias, Peter. 1959. *The Brewing Industry in England.* Cambridge, U.K.: Cambridge University Press.

Mayer, Joseph. 1941. *Social Science Principles in the Light of Scientific Method.* Durham: Duke University Press.

Mayr, Ernst. 1982. *The Growth of Biological Thought.* Cambridge, Mass.: Harvard University Press.

Mayr, Otto. 1971. "Adam Smith and the Concept of the Feedback System." *Technology and Culture* (12):1–22.

Mayr, Otto. 1986. *Authority, Liberty and Automatic Machinery in Early Nodern Europe.* Baltimore: Johns Hopkins University Press.

McCloskey, Donald. 1983. "The Rhetoric of Economics." *Journal of Economic Literature* (21):2:481–517.

McCloskey, Michael. 1984. "Intuitive Physics." *Scientific American* (248):122–30.

McCormmach, Russel. 1970. "H. A. Lorentz and the Electromagnetic View of Nature," *Isis* (61):459–97.

McCormmach, Russel. 1971. "Editor's Foreword." *Historical Studies in the Physical Sciences* (3):ix–xxiv.

McReynolds, Paul. 1968. "The Motivational Psychology of Jeremy Bentham." *Journal for the History of the Behavioral Sciences* (4):349–63.

Meek, Ronald. 1962. *The Economivs of Physiocracy.* Cambridge, Mass.: Harvard University Press.

Mehra, Jagdish. 1975. *The Solvay Conferences in Physics.* Boston: Reidel.

Mehra, J., and Rechenberg, H. 1982. *The Historical Development of Quantum Theory.* New York: Springer-Verlag.

Mehta, Ghanshyam. 1978. *The Structure of the Keynesian Revolution.* New York: St. Martins.

Menard, Claude. 1978. *La Formation D'une Rationalité Economique: A. A. Cournot.* Paris: Flammarion.

Menard, Claude. 1980. "Three Forms of Resistance to Statistics: Say, Cournot, Walras." *History of Political Economy* (12) 524–41.

Menger, Carl. 1963. *Problems of Economics and Sociology.* Trans. by Nock. Urbana: University of Illinois Press.

Menger, Carl, 1981. *Principles of Economics.* Trans. by Dingwell and Hoselitz. New York: New York University Press.

Mey, Harald. 1972. *Field Theory: A Study of its Applications in the Social Sciences.* London: Routledge & Kegan Paul.

Meyerson, Emile. 1931. *Du Cheminement de la Pensée.* Paris: Félix Alcan.

Meyerson, Emile. 1962. *Identity and Reality.* New York: Dover.

Milgate, Murray. 1979. "On the Origin of the Notion of Intertemporal Equilibrium." *Economica* (46):1–10.

[Mill, James]. 1824. "Review of Men and Things in 1823" by James Boone. *Westminster Review* (1):1–18.

Mill, John Stuart. 1973. *A System of Logic.* Vols. 7 & 8. *Collected Works,* ed. John Robson. Toronto: University of Toronto Press.

Miller, Arthur. 1984. *Imagery in Scientific Thought.* Boston: Birkhauser.

Mini, Piero. 1974. *Economics and Philosophy.* Gainesville: University of Florida Press.

Mirowski, Philip. 1981. "Is There a Mathematical Neoinstitutional Economics?" *Journal of Economic Issues* (15):593–613.

Mirowski, Philip. 1982. "Adam Smith, Empiricism, and the Rate of Profit in Eighteenth Century England." *History of Political Economy* (14):2:178–98.

Mirowski, Philip. 1983. "Review of Nelson and Winter's Evolutionary Theory of Economic Change." *Journal of Economic Issues* (17):757–68.

Mirowski, Philip. 1984a "Macroeconomic Fluctuations and 'Natural' Processes in Early Neoclassical Economics." *Journal of Economic History* (44):345–54.

Mirowski, Philip. 1984b. "The Role of Conservation Principles in 20th Century Economic Theory." *Philosophy of the Social Sciences* (14):4:461–73.

Mirowski, Philip. 1985. *The Birth of the Business Cycle.* New York: Garland Press.

Mirowski, Philip. 1986. "Mathematical Formalism and Economic Explanation." In P. Mirowski, ed. *The Reconstruction of Economic Theory.* Boston: Kluwer-Nijhoff.

Mirowski, Philip. 1988a. *Against Mechanism.* Totawa, N.J.: Rowman and Littlefield.

Mirowski, Philip. 1988b. "Energy and Energetics in Economic Theory." *Journal of Economic Issues.* 22:811–30.

Mirowski, Philip. 1989a. "'Tis a Pity Econometrics Isn't an Empirical Endeavor." *Richerche Economisti* (16):111–29.

Mirowski, Philip. 1989b. "On the 'Substantive Identity' of Classical and Neoclassical Economics." *Cambridge [U.K.] Journal of Economics* (13).

Mirowski, Philip. 1989c. "The Measurement Without Theory Controversy." *Economics et Sociétés: Serie Oeconomia* (23):109–31.

Mirowski, Philip. 1989d. "The Probablistic Counter-revolution: Advent of Stochastic Concepts in Neoclassical Econometrics." *Oxford Economic Papers* (41):217–35.

Mirowski, Philip. Forthcoming. *Who's Afraid of Random Trade?* Princeton: Princeton University Press.

Mirwoski, Philip, and Cook, Pamela. 1990. "Walras' *Economics and Mechanics:* Translation, Commentary, Context." In Warren Samuels, ed., *Economics as Rhetoric.* Norwell: Kluwer.

Monroe, Arthur, ed. 1924. *Early Economic Thought.* Cambridge, Mass.: Harvard University Press.

Moore, Henry. 1914. *Economic Cycles.* New York: Macmillan.

Morishima, Michio. 1973. *Marx's Economics.* Cambridge, U.K.: Cambridge University Press.

Morishima, Michio. 1977. *Walras' Economics.* Cambridge, U.K.: Cambridge University Press.

Morishima, Michio. 1984. "The Good and Bad Uses of Mathematics." In P. Wiles and G. Routh, eds., *Economics in Disarray*. Oxford: Blackwell.

Mourant, John A. 1940. *The Physiocratic Conception of Natural Law*. Ph.D. thesis, Philosophy, University of Chicago.

Moyer, D. 1977. "Energy, Dynamics, Hidden Machinery: Rankine, Thomson and Tait, Maxwell." *Studies in the History and Philosophy of Science* (8):251–68

Mulvey, J., ed. 1981. *The Nature of Matter*. Oxford: Oxford University Press.

Murphy, Roy. 1965. *Adaptive Processes in Economic Systems*. New York: Academic Press.

Myrdal, Gunnar. 1944. *An American Dilemma*. New York: Harper.

Neisser, Hans. 1940. "A Note on Pareto's Theory of Production." *Econometrica* (8):253–262.

Nelson, R., and Winter, S. 1982. *An Evolutionary Theory of Economic Change*. Cambridge, Mass.: Harvard University Press.

Nersessian, Nancy. 1984. *Faraday to Einstein*. Dordrecht: Martinus Nijhoff.

North, Sir Dudley. 1846. *A Discourse Upon Trade*. Edinburgh: A & C Black.

Northrop, F. 1941. "The Impossibility of a Theoretical Science of Economic Dynamics." *Quarterly Journal of Economics* (56):1–17.

Odum, E. 1971. *Fundamentals of Ecology*, Philadelphia: Saunders.

Odum, H., and Odum, E. 1976. *Energy Basis of Man and Nature*. New York: McGraw-Hill.

O'Hear, Anthony. 1980. *Karl Popper*. London: Routledge & Kegan Paul.

Ord-Hume, Arthur. 1977. *Perpetual Motion*. New York: St. Martins.

Oster, G., and Wilson, E. 1978. *Caste and Ecology in the Social Insects*. Princeton: Princeton University Press.

Ostroy, J., and Starr, R. 1974. "Money and the Decentralization of Exchange." *Econometrica* (42):1093–113.

Ostwald, Wilhelm. 1907. "The Modern Theory of Energetics." *Monist* (17):481–515.

Ostwald, Wilhelm. 1909. *Energetische Grundlagen der Kulturwissenschaften*. Leipzig: Duncker.

O'Toole, John (pseud.). 1877. "Some Troubles of John O'Toole Respecting Potential Energy." *Nature*, Sept. 20, 439–41; Sept. 27, 457–9.

Pagels, Heinz. 1982. *The Cosmic Code*. New York: Simon & Schuster.

Pais, Abraham. 1982. *Subtle is the Lord. . . .* New York: Oxford University Press.

Palmer, E. 1966. *The Meaning and Measurement of National Income*. Lincoln: University of Nebraska Press.

Palomba, Giuseppe. 1960. "Entropie, Information et Sintropie des Systèmes Economiques." *Metroeconomica* (12):98–108.

Palomba, Giuseppe. 1968. *A Mathematical Interpretation of the Balance Sheet*. Geneva: Droz.

Papineau, David. 1977. "The Vis Viva Controversy: Do Meanings Matter?" *Studies in the History and Philosophy of Science* (8):111–42.

Pareto, Vilfredo. 1953. "On the Economic Phenomenon." *International Economic Papers* no. 3.

Pareto, Vilfredo. 1971a. "Ophelimity in Nonclosed Cycles." In J. Chipman, L. Hurwicz, M. Richter, and H. Sonnenschein, eds., *Preferences, Utility, and Demand.* New York: Harcourt Brace.

Pareto, Vilfredo. 1971b. *Manual of Political Economy.* Trans. Ann Schwier. New York: Kelly.

Park, James, and Simmons, Ralph. 1983. "The Knots of Quantum Thermodynamics." In A. van der Merwe, ed., *Old and New Questions in Physics.* New York: Plenum.

Parsons, T., and Harrison, B. 1981. "Energy Utilization and Evaluation." *Journal of Social and Biological Structures* (4):1–15.

Pasinetti, Luigi, ed. 1980. *Essasys on Joint Production.* New York: Columbia University Press.

Pasinetti, Luigi. 1981. *Structural Change and Economic Growth.* Cambridge, U.K.: Cambridge University Press.

Pearl, D., and Enos, J. 1975. "Engineering Production Functions and Technical Progress." *Journal of Industrial Economics* (24):55–72.

Pearson, Karl. 1924. *The Life, Letters and Labours of Francis Galton.* Vol. II. Cambridge, U.K.: Cambridge University Press.

Pederssen, P. 1935. "Et Produktionsdynamisk Problem." *Nordisk Tidsskrift For Teknisk Okonomi* (1):28–48

Percival, Ian, and Richards, Derek. 1982. *Introduction to Dynamics.* Cambridge, U.K.: Cambridge University Press.

Persons, Warren. 1919. "Index of Industrial Production." *Review of Economics and Statistics,*

Peston, M., and Corry, B. 1972. *Essays in Honour of Lord Robbins.* London: Weidenfeld & Nicolsen.

Peterfreund, Stuart. 1986. "The Re-emergence of Energy in the Discourse of Literature and Science." *Annals of Scholarship* (4):22–53.

Petty, William. 1899. *The Economic Writings.* 3 vols., ed. C. Hull. Cambridge, U.K.: Cambridge University Press.

Petty, William. 1967. *The Petty Papers.* New York: Kelley.

Pickering, Andrew. 1984. *Constructing Quarks.* Chicago: University of Chicago Press.

Pikler, Andrew, 1950. "Ophelimité et Entropie." *Scientia* (14):257–59

Pikler, Andrew. 1951a. "The Quanta-Kinetic Model of Monetary Theory." *Metroeconomica* (3):70–95.

Pikler, Andrew. 1951b. "Econometrics, Statistics and Thermodynamics." *Metroeconomica* (3):41–3.

Pikler, Andrew. 1951c. "Optimum Allocation in Econometrics and Physics." *Weltwirtschafts Archiv* (6):96–132.

Pikler, Andrew. 1954a. "Utility Theories in Field Physics and Mathematical Economics. *British Journal for the Philosophy of Science* (5):47–58, 303–18.

Pikler, Andrew. 1954b. "The Quanta-Kinetic Model of the Monetary Economy: Three Additional Appendices." *Metroeconomica* (6):72–5.

Pikler, Andrew. 1955. "Utility Theory in Field Physics and Mathematical Economics." *British Journal for the Philosophy of Science* (5):47–58, 303–18.

Planck, Max. 1924. *Das Prinzip der Erhaltung der Energie.* Berlin: Teubner.

Planck, Max. 1949. *Voltträge und Erinnerungen.* 5th ed. Stuttgart:

Plotnik, Morton. 1937. *Werner Sombart and His Type of Economics.* New York: Eco.

Poincaré, H. 1889. *Comptes Rendus Académie des Sciences de Paris.* (108):550.

Poincaré, H. 1952. *Science and Hypothesis.* New York: Dover.

Poinsot, L. 1842. *Eléments de Statique.* 8th ed. Paris: Bachelier.

Poisson, S. D. 1811. *Traité de Méchanique.* Paris: Courcier.

Polanyi, Karl. 1944. *The Great Transformation.* Boston: Beacon Press.

Polanyi, Karl, et al. 1957. *Trade and Market in Early Empires.* Chicago: Regnery.

Polanyi, Karl. 1968. "Aristotle Discovers the Economy." In *Primitive, Archaic and Modern Economies.* Garden City: Anchor.

Popper, Karl. 1957. *The Poverty of Historicism.* London: Routledge.

Popper, Karl. 1965. *Conjectures and Refutations.* London: Harper.

Porter, Theodore. 1981a. "A Statistical Survey of Gases: Maxwell's Social Physics." *Historical Studies in the Physical Sciences* (12):77–114.

Porter, Theodore, 1981b. "The Promotion of Mining and the Advance of Science." *Annals of Science* (38):543–70.

Porter, Theodore. 1985. "The Mathematics of Society: Variation and Error in Quetelet's Statistics." *British Journal for the History of Science* (18):51–69.

Porter, Theodore. 1986. *The Rise of Statistical Thinking.* Princeton: Princeton University Press.

Postan, Tim, and Stewart, Ian. 1978. *Catastrophe Theory and Its Applications.* Boston: Pitman.

Pribram, Karl. 1983. *A History of Economic Reasoning.* Baltimore: Johns Hopkins University Press.

Price, W. H. 1905. "Origins of the Phrase 'Balance of Trade'." *Quarterly Journal of Economics,* Nov:157–67.

Prigogine, Ilya. 1980. *From Being to Becoming.* New York: Freeman.

Prigogine, Ilya, and Stengers, Isabelle. 1984. *Order out of chaos.* New York: Bantam.

Proops, John. 1983. "Organization and Dissipation in Economic Systems." *Journal of Social and Biological Structures* (6):353–66.

Proops, John. 1985. "The Physical Input to Economies." *University of Keele Discussion Paper no. 51.* Keele, U.K.

Pynchon, Thomas. 1984. *Slow Learner.* Boston: Little Brown.

Qadir, A. 1978. "Quantum Economics." *Pakistan Economic and Social Review* (16):117–26

Qadir, A., and Qadir, K. 1981. "Inflation in a Growing Economy." *Pakistan Economic and Social Review* (19):149–56.

Rankine, William. 1834. "On a General Method in Dynamics." *Philosophical Magazine* (5):106–17.

Rankine, William. 1881. *Miscellaneous Scientific Papers*. London: Charles Griffin.

Rauner, Robert. 1961. *Samuel Bailey and the Classical Theory of Value*. London: Bell.

Ravenstein, E. 1885. "The Laws of Migration." *Journal of the Royal Statistical Society* (48):167–235.

Ricardo, David. 1952–73. *Works and Correspondence of David Ricardo*, P. Sraffa and M. Dobb, eds. Cambridge, U.K.: Cambridge University Press.

Richards, R. 1922. "Early History of the Term Capital." *Quarterly Journal of Economics* (26): 329–38.

Ringer, Fritz. 1969. *The Decline of the German Mandarins*. Cambridge, Mass.: Harvard Univ. Press.

Robbins, Lionel. 1928. "The Representative Firm." *Economic Journal* (38):387–404.

Robbins, Lionel. 1952. *An Essay on the Nature and Significance of Economic Science*. 2nd ed. London: Macmillan.

Roberts, P. 1982. "Energy and Value." *Energy Policy* (10):171–180.

Robinson, Joan. 1973. *Economic Heresies*. New York: Basic.

Robinson, Joan. 1980. *Further Contributions to Modern Economics*. Oxford: Blackwell.

Roncaglia, Alessandro. 1978. *Sraffa and the Theory of Prices*. New York: Wiley.

Rorty, Richard. 1986. "Foucault and Epistemology." In Hoy (1986).

Rosen, Joseph. 1983. *A Symmetry Primer for Scientists*. New York: Wiley.

Rosenberg, Nathan. 1982. *Inside the Black Box*. New York: Cambridge University Press.

Runyon, Herbert. 1959. "The Economics of Irving Fisher." Ph.D. thesis, Economics, University of Michigan.

Sahlins, Marshall. 1972. *Stone Age Economics*. Chicago: Aldine.

Sahlins, Marshall. 1976. *Culture and Practical Reason*. Chicago: University of Chicago Press.

Salvadori, N. 1985. "Did Sraffa Assume Constant Returns to Scale?" *Metroeconomica* (37):175–86.

Samuelson, Paul. 1941. "The Stability of Equilibrium." *Econometrica* (9):97–120.

Samuelson, Paul. 1942. "Constancy of the Marginal Utility of Income." In O. Lange, F. McIntyre, and T. Yntema, eds., *Studies in the Mathematical Economics and Econometrics in Memory of Henry Schultz*. Chicago: University of Chicago. Press.

Samuelson, Paul. 1947. *Foundations of Economic Analysis*. Cambridge, Mass.: Harvard University Press.

Samuelson, Paul. 1950. "On the Problem of Integrability in Utility Theory." *Economica* (17):355–85.

Samuelson, Paul. 1952. "Economic Theory and Mathematics – An Appraisal." *American Economic Review* (42):55–66

Samuelson, Paul, ed. 1954. Symposium on Mathematics in Economics. *Review of Economics and Statistics* (36).

Samuelson, Paul. 1972a. *The Collected Scientific Papers*. Vol. 3, ed. R. Merton. Cambridge, Mass.: MIT Press.

Samuelson, Paul. 1972b. "Maximum Principles in Analytical Economics." *American Economic Review* (62):249–62.

Samuelson, Paul. 1977. *The Collected Scientific Papers*. Vol. 4, ed. H. Nagatani and K. Crowley. Cambridge, Mass.: MIT Press.

Samuelson, Paul. 1983a. "Complete Genetic Models for Altruism, Kin Selection and Like-Gene Selection." *Journal of Social and Biological Structures* (6):3–15.

Samuelson, Paul. 1983b. "Rigorous Observational Positivism: Klein's Envelope Aggregation; Thermodynamics and Economic Isomorphisms." In F. Adams and B. Hickman, eds., *Global Econometrics*. Cambridge, Mass.: MIT Press.

Samuelson, Paul. 1985. "Models of Thought in Economics." *American Economic Review* (75):166–72.

Samuelson, Paul. 1986a. "Paul Samuelson." In W. Breit and R. Spencer, eds., *Lives of the Laureates*, Cambridge, Mass.: MIT Press.

Samuelson, Paul. 1986b. *The Collected Scientific Papers*. Vol. 4, ed. K. Crowley. Cambridge, Mass.: MIT Press.

Sarasohn, Lisa. 1985. "Motion and Morality." *Journal of the History of Ideas* (46):363–79.

Sarlet, Willy, and Cantrijn, Frans. 1981. "Generalizations of the Noether Theorem in Classical Mechanics." *SIAM Review* (23):467–94.

Sato, Ryuzo. 1981. *The Theory of Technical Change and Economic Invariance*. New York: Academic.

Sato, Ryuzo. 1985. "The Invariance Principle and Income, Wealth Conservation Laws." *Journal of Econometrics* (30):365–89.

Say, Jean-Baptiste. 1821. *Treatise on Political Economy*. Vol. I, trans. by C. Prinsep. London: Longman.

Say, Jean-Baptiste. 1828. *Cours Complet d'Economie Politique*. 6 vols. Paris: Rapilly.

Schabas, Margaret. 1987. "An Anomaly of Laudan's Pragmatic Model." *Studies in the History and Philosophy of Science* (18):43–52.

Schmidt, B. 1982. "Time as Quantum." In M. Baranzini, ed., *Advances in Economic Theory*. Oxford: Blackwell.

Schmidt, B. 1985. *Monetary Expenditure and Quantum Time*. Dijon: Presses universitaire de Dijon.

Schmidt, Christian. 1976. "Note Sur Les Formes d'Analogies Entre l'Equilibre Thermodynamique et Economique." In *Sadi Counot et L'Essor de la Thermodynamique*. Paris: Editions de CNRS.

Schoemaker, Paul. 1982. "The Expected Utility Model." *Journal of Economic Literature* (20):529–63.

Schoemaker, Paul. 1984. "Optimality Principles in Science." In J. Paelinck and P. Vossen, eds., *The Quest for Optimality*. Aldershot: Gower.

Schultz, Henry. 1929. "Marginal Productivity and the General Pricing Process." *Journal of Political Economy,* (37):505–51.

Schultz, Henry. 1931. "Review of G. C. Evans' Mathematical Introduction to Economics." *Journal of the American Statistical Association* (26):484–91.

Schultz, Henry. 1938. *The Theory and Measurement of Demand.* Chicago: University of Chicago Press.

Schumpeter, Joseph. 1954. *A History of Economic Analysis.* New York: Oxford University Press.

Schuster, John. 1977. *Descartes and the Scientific Revolution.* Ph.D. thesis, Princeton University.

Schurr, S. 1984. "Energy Use, Technological Change and Productive Efficiency." *Annual Review of Energy* (9):409–426.

Scott, H. 1933. *Introduction to Technocracy.* New York: John Day.

Scott, Wilson. 1970. *The Conflict Between Atomism and Conservation Theory.* New York: Elsevier.

Sebba, G. 1953. "The Development of the Concepts of Mechanism and Model in Physical Science and Economic Thought." *American Economic Review* (63):259–68.

Sen, A. 1973. "Behavior and the Concept of Preference." *Economica* (40):241–59.

Shackle, G. L. S. 1967. *Time in Economics.* Amsterdam: North Holland.

Shannon, Claude. 1948. "The Mathematical Theory of Communication." *Bell System Technical Journal.*

Shannon, C., and Weaver, W. 1949. *The Mathematical Theory of Communication.* Urbana: University of Illinois.

Sharpe, Robert. 1971. "Physical and Psychic Energy." *Philosophy of Science* (38):1–12.

Shubik, Martin. 1982. *Game Theory in the Social Sciences.* Cambridge, Mass.: MIT Press.

Shubik, Martin. 1984. *A Game Theoretic Approach to Political Economy.* Cambridge, Mass.: MIT Press.

Sklar, Lawrence. 1974. *Space, Time, and Spacetime.* Berkeley: University of California Press.

Slesser, Malcolm. 1975. "Accounting for Energy." *Nature* (254):170–2.

Smith, Adam. 1869. *Essays of Adam Smith.* London: Murray.

Smith, Adam. 1976. *The Wealth of Nations.* Chicago: University of Chicago Press.

Smith, Adam. 1967. "Essay on the History of Ancient Physics." In *The Early Writings of Adam Smith.* New York: Kelly.

Smith, Crosbie. 1978. "A New Chart for British Natural Philosophy." *History of Science* (16):231–79.

Snelders, H. 1971. "Romanticism and Naturphilosophie in the Inorganic Natural Sciences 1797–1840." *Studies in Romanticism* (10):193–213.

Soddy, Frederick. 1920. *Science and Life.* New York: Dutton.

Soddy, Frederick. 1922. *Cartesian Economics.* London: Hendersons.

Soddy, Frederick. 1961. *Wealth, Virtual Wealth and Debt.* Hawthorne, Calif. Omni.

Sohn-Rethel, Alfred. 1978. *Intellectual and Manual Labour.* London: Macmillan.

Solow, Robert. 1985. "Economic History and Economics." *American Economic Review* (75):328–31.

Solvay, Ernest. 1906. *Note Sur des Formules d'Introduction à l'Energetique.* Paris: Giard and Brière.

Sombart, Werner. 1902. *Der Moderne Kapitalismus.* Leipzig:

Sombart, Werner. 1929. *Die Drie Nationalökonomien,* Munich: Duncker and Humblot.

Sorokin, Pitrim. 1956. *Contemporary Sociological Theories.* New York: Harper & Row.

Souter, R. 1933. *Prolegomena to Relativity Economics.* New York: Columbia University Press.

Spencer, Herbert. 1887. *First Principles.* London: Williams and Norgate.

Spragens, Thomas. 1973. *The Politics of Motion.* Lexington: University of Kentucky Press.

Sraffa, Piero. 1926. "The Laws of Returns Under Competitive Conditions." *Economic Journal* (36):535–50.

Sraffa, Piero. 1960. *Production of Commodities by Views of Commodities.* Cambridge, U.K.: Cambridge University Press.

Stark, Werner. 1944. *The History of Economics in Relation to Its Social Development.* London: Routledge.

Stark, Werner. 1962. *The Fundamental Focus of Social Thought.* New York: Fordham University Press.

Stallo, J. B. 1960. *The Concepts and Theories of Modern Physics.* Cambridge, Mass.: Harvard University Press.

Steedman, Ian. 1977. *Marx After Sraffa.* London: NLB.

Steffens, Henry. 1979. *James Prescott Joule and the Concept of Energy.* New York: Science History Publication.

Stevin, Simon. 1955–67. *The Principal Works of Simon Stevin.* 5 vols., ed. E. Crone et al. Amsterdam: Swets & Zeitlinger.

Stewart, Balfour. 1883. *The Conservation of Energy.* 6th ed. London: Routledge.

Stewart, J. Q. 1950. "The Development of Social Physics." *American Journal of Physics* (18):239–53.

Stigler, George. 1941. *Production and Distribution Theories.* New York: Macmillan.

Stigler, George. 1949. *The Theory of Price.* New York: Macmillan.

Stigler, George. 1950. "The Development of Utility Theory." In E. Hamilton, A. Rees, and H. Johnson, eds., *Landmarks in Political Economy.* Chicago: University of Chicago Press.

Stigler, George. 1988. *Memoirs of an Unregulated Economist.* New York: Basic.

Stiglitz, Joseph. 1974. "The Cambridge – Cambridge Controversy." *Journal of Political Economy* (82):893–903.

Stone, Mel. 1978. "Synthesizing Economics and Physics." *Speculations in Science and Technology* (1):453–63.

Stoneman, William. 1979. *A History of the Economic Analysis of the Great Depression.* New York: Garland.

Studenski, Paul. 1958. *The Income of Nations.* New York: New York University Press.

Stuewer, Roger. 1975. *The Compton Effect.* New York: Science History Publication.

Suranyi-Unger, Theo. 1931. *Economics in the 20th Century.* New York: Norton.

Sussman, Martin. 1972. *Elementary General Thermodynamics.* Reading, Mass.: Addison-Wesley.

Szegö, Giorgio. ed. 1982. *New Quantitative Techniques for Economic Analysis.* New York: Academic Press.

Taylor, Overton. 1929. "Economics and the Idea of Natural Laws." *Quarterly Journal of Economics,* Nov:1–39.

Ter Haar, D. 1961. *Elements of Hamiltonian Dynamics.* Amsterdam: North Holland.

Tew, Brian. 1953. "Keynesian Accountancy." *Yorkshire Bulletin of Economic and Social Research* (8):39–53.

Theobald, D. W. 1966. *The Concept of Energy.* London: Spon.

Thoben, H. 1982. "Mechanistic and Organistic Analogies in Economics Reconsidered." *Kyklos* (35):292–305

Thoma, J. 1977. "Energy, Entropy and Information." Research Memo RM-77-32, Laxenburg: IIASA.

t'Hooft, Gerard. 1980. "Gauge Theories of the Forces Between Elementary Particles." *Scientific American* (242):6; 104–38.

Thweatt, William. 1979. "Early Formulators of Say's Law." *Quarterly Review of Economics and Business* (19):79–96.

Tiles, Mary. 1984. *Bachelard: Science and Objectivity.* Cambridge, U.K.: Cambridge University Press.

Tinbergen, Jan. 1929. *Minimumproblemen in de Natuurkunde en de Ekonomie.* Amsterdam: Paris.

Tintner, Gerhard, and Senqupta, Jati. 1972. *Stochastic Economics.* New York: Academic Press.

Todhunter, Isaac. 1876. *William Whewell.* 2 vols. London: Macmillan.

Tollison, R., and Goff, B. 1986. "Citation Practices in Economics and Physics." *Journal of Institutional and Theoretical Economics* (142):581–7.

Trautman, Andrzej. 1962. "Conservation Laws in General Relativity." In Louis Witten, ed., *Gravitation.* New York: Wiley.

Tryon, Edward. 1973. "Is the Universe a Vacuum Fluctation?" *Nature* (246):396–7.

Tustin, Arnold. 1951–2. "An Engineer's View of the Problem of Economic Stability." *Review of Economic Studies* (19):85.

Tustin, Arnold. 1953. *The Mechanism of Economic Systems.* Cambridge, Mass.: Harvard University Press.

Tversky, A., and Kahnman, D. 1981. "The Framing of Decisions and the Psychology of Choice." *Science* (211):453–8.

van Gool, W., and Bruggink, J., eds. 1985. *Energy and Time in the Economic and Physical Sciences*. Amsterdam: North Holland.

Varian, Hal. 1978. *Microeconomic Analysis*. New York: Norton.

Varian, Hal. 1979. "Catastrophe Theory and the Business Cycle." *Economic Inquiry* (7):14–28.

Vaughn, Karen. 1980. "Does It Matter That Costs Are Subjective?" *Southern Economic Journal* (46):702–15.

Veblen, Thorstein. 1969. *The Place of Science in Modern Civilization*. New York: Viking.

Viner, Jacob. 1925. "The Utility Concept in Value Theory and Its Critics." *Journal of Political Economy* (33):369–87.

Walker, Donald. 1987a. "Walras' Theories of Tatonnement." *Journal of Political Economy* (95):758–74.

Walker, Donald. 1987b. "Edgeworth versus Walras on the Theory of Tatonnement." *Eastern Economic Journal* (13):155–65.

Walras, Leon. 1909. "Economique et Mécanique." *Bulletin de la Société Vaudoise de Sciences Naturelles* (45):313–25.

Walras, Leon. 1965. *Collected Papers and Correspondence*. 3 vols., William Jaffee, ed. Amsterdam: North Holland.

Walras, Leon. 1969. *Elements of Pure Economics*. Trans. William Jaffee. New York: Kelly.

Walsh, J., and Webber, M. 1977. "Information Theory: Some Concepts and Measures." *Environment and Planning* (9):395–417.

Walsh, Vivien, and Gram, Harvey. 1980. *Classical and Neoclassical Theories of General Equilibrium*. New York: Oxford University Press.

Walsh, V., and Gram, H. 1983. "Joan Robinson's Economics in Retrospect," *Journal of Economic Literature* (21):518–50.

Walter, E. V. 1984. "Nature on Trial." In R. Cohen and M. Wartovsky, eds., *Methodology, Metaphysics, and the History of Science*. Boston: Reidel.

Warnotte, Daniel. 1946. *Ernest Solvay et L'Institut de Sociologie*. Brussels: Bruyzant.

Weber, Max. 1909. " 'Energetische' Kulturtheorien." In his *Gesammelte Aufsätze zur Wissenschaftlehre* (1922). Tubingen: Mohr, pp. 376–402.

Weinberg, Steven. 1977. "The Search for Unity: Notes for a History of Quantum Field Theory." *Daedalus* (106):17–35.

Weinberger, Otto. 1931. "Rudolf Auspitz und Richard Lieben: Ein Beitrag Zur Geschichte Der Mathematischen Methode in der Volkswirtschaftlehre." *Zeitschrift Fur Die Gesamte Staatswissenschaft* XCI:457–92.

Weintraub, E. R. 1979. *Microfoundations*. Cambridge, U. K.: Cambridge University Press.

Weintraub, E. R. 1985. *General Equilibrium Analysis: Studies in Appraisal*. New York: Cambridge University Press.

Weisskopf, Walter. 1979. "The Method Is the Ideology." *Journal of Economic Issues* (13):869–84.

Westfall, Richard. 1971. *Force in Newton's Physics.* New York: Science History Publication.

Westfall, Richard. 1980. *Never at Rest: A Biography of Isaac Newton.* Cambridge, U.K.: Cambridge University Press.

Whewell, William. 1830. "Mathematical Exposition of Some Doctrines of Political Economy." *Transactions of the Cambridge Philosophical Society* (3):191–229.

Whewell, William. 1833. "Mathematical Exposition of Some Leading Doctrines in Mr. Ricardo's Principles." *Transactions of the Cambridge Philosophical Society* (4):155–98,

White, Cathy. 1980. "The Single Factor Value Theories of Marxism, Technocracy, and Net Energy Analysis. Unpublished manuscript, University of British Columbia.

White, Lesley. 1943. "Energy and the Evolution of Culture." *American Anthropologist* (45):335–56.

White, Lynn, Jr. 1962. *Medieval Technology and Social Change.* Oxford: Oxford University Press.

White, Michael. 1989. "W. S. Jevons and the Laws of Supply and Demand." *History of Political Economy,* in press.

Wibe, Soren. 1980. "Engineering Production Functions and Technical Progress." In S. Wibe and T. Puu, eds., *The Economics of Technical Progress.* New York: St. Martins.

Wicksteed, Philip. 1913. "Review of S. Chapman's Political Economy." *Economic Journal* (23):72–5.

Wicksteed, Philip. 1950. *The Commonsense of Political Economy.* 2 vols. New York: Kelley.

Wicksell, Knut. 1938. *Lectures on Political Economy.* 2 vols. London: Routledge.

Wicksell, Knut. 1958. *Selected Papers on Economic Theory.* Cambridge, Mass.: Harvard University Press.

Wiener, Norbert. 1964. *God and Golem, Inc.* Cambridge, Mass.: MIT Press.

Wieser, Friedrich von. 1956. *Natural Value.* New York: Kelley & Millman.

Will, Clifford. 1981. *Theory and Experiment in Gravitational Physics.* Cambridge, U.K.: Cambridge University Press.

Wilson, Edwin. 1912. Review of Pareto's Manuale. *Bulletin of the American Math. Soc.* (18):462–74.

Wilson, E. O. 1975. *Sociobiology.* Cambridge, Mass.: Harvard University Press.

Winiarsky, Leon. 1900. "L'Energie Sociale et Ses Mensurations." *Revue Philosophique* Tome XLIX: 113–34; 256–84.

Winiarski, Leon. 1967. *Essais sur la Mechanique Sociale.* Geneva: Droz.

Winter, Sidney. 1982. "An Essay on the Theory of Production. In Saul Hymans, ed., *Economics and the World Around It.* Ann Arbor: University of Michigan Press.

Wise, M. N. 1979. "William Thomson's Mathematical Route to Energy Conservation." *Historical Studies in Physical Sciences* (10):49–83.

Wise, M. N. 1988. "Mediating Machines." *Science in Context* (2):77–113.

Wittgenstein, Ludwig. 1978. *Remarks on the Foundations of Mathematics.* Rev. ed. Cambridge, Mass.: MIT Press.

Wong, Stanley. 1978. *The Foundations of Paul Samuelson's Revealed Preference Theory.* Boston: Routledge & Kegan Paul.

Wright, Crispin. 1980. *Wittgenstein on the Foundations of Mathematics.* Cambridge, Mass.: Harvard University Press.

Youmans, Edward, ed. 1865. *The Correlation and Conservation of Forces.* New York: Appleton.

Young, Robert. 1985. *Darwin's Metaphor.* Cambridge, U.K.: Cambridge University Press.

Yourgrau, Wolfgang, and Mandelstam, Stanley. 1955. *Variational Principles in Dynamics and Quantum Theory.* London: Pitman.

Zahar, E. 1980. "Einstein, Meyerson and the Role of Mathematics in Physical Discovery," *British Journal of Philosophy and Science* (31):1–43.

Zawadzki, W. 1914. *Les Mathématiques Appliquées a l'Economie Politique.* Paris: Marcel Rivière.

Zilsel, E. 1942. "The Sociological Roots of Science." *American Journal of Sociology* (47):544–62.

Zipf, George. 1949. *Human Behavior and the Principle of Least Effort.* Cambridge: Addison-Wesley.

Zoretti, Ludovic. 1906. "La Methode Mathématique et les Sciences Sociales," *Revue du Mois* (2):355–65.

Index

446